LAND REFORM AND DEVELOPMENT IN THE MIDDLE EAST

THE ROYAL INSTITUTE
OF INTERNATIONAL AFFAIRS
London: Chatham House, St James's Square, S.W.1
New York: 345 East 46th Street, New York 17, N.Y.

Toronto *Melbourne*
Wellington *Bombay* *Karachi* *Cape Town*
OXFORD UNIVERSITY PRESS

LAND REFORM AND DEVELOPMENT IN THE MIDDLE EAST

A Study of Egypt, Syria, and Iraq

BY

DOREEN WARRINER

London & New York

ROYAL INSTITUTE
OF INTERNATIONAL AFFAIRS

First published 1957

PRINTED IN GREAT BRITAIN
AT THE BROADWATER PRESS, WELWYN GARDEN CITY
HERTFORDSHIRE

CONTENTS

CONTENTS

TABLES

MAPS

PREFACE

It was my intention to prepare a second edition of *Land and Poverty in the Middle East*, published in 1948 and long out of print. This, after I had visited the region again, seemed impossible.

The poverty is not out of date. But the original research and field work needed to establish its extent today could not be undertaken without much time and a knowledge of Arabic. The statistical material is much fuller than it was, and there is more monographic study, but these investigations do not as a rule get down to the bedrock of the rural standard of living.

Moreover, the perspective has changed. There has been development, far more than seemed possible ten years ago. Then it seemed necessary to justify the belief that poverty was a matter which should concern the Arab countries and the West. Today such justification is no longer needed. It now seems more important to stress the dynamics of change, as they affect the poor, rather than to study underdevelopment as a static condition, the only approach to the region which seemed possible in 1947.

The present study supplements the old, and carries its arguments a step farther by reviewing the results of the agrarian reform measures so far undertaken, and the relation of reform to development in the three countries where these are crucial questions. Except in a few short passages, nothing from the earlier book has been used, but I have taken the opportunity to correct mistakes in it, so far as I could ascertain where they lay. Throughout this book I have tried to emphasize what is uncertain, and hope that this may be useful to other students of the subject.

Thanks to a grant made by the Royal Institute of International Affairs, I was able to visit Syria and Iraq in the spring and winter of 1955, and Egypt early in 1956. An invitation to lecture in Cairo from the National Bank of Egypt enabled me to visit Egypt earlier in 1955.

My time was short. I used it to travel to see the new things in Dujaila, Tahrir, and the Jezira, and the old things changing in Amara and Upper Egypt. The accounts of these places are as full as I could make them in the time; though very incomplete, they may be useful to those who can undertake systematic studies.

During these visits, I had much help from many people, among them old friends, that speciality of the region. I cannot thank all who gave me help and hospitality, but would wish to express my sincere gratitude to those who enabled me to visit estates, villages, slums, and settlements, and whose views I have quoted and used freely. In Iraq, I must thank Mrs Bedia Afnan, Mr Hassan Mohammed Ali, Mr Abdul Jabbar Chelabi, Professor and Mrs Michael Critchley, Mr Haider al-Daif, Mayor of Amara, Professor A. A. Duri, Dr K. G. Fenelon, Mr Mohammed Hadeed, Dr Salih Haider, Mr Abdul al-Jawad of Mosul, Dr Jasim Khalaf, Professor and Mrs James Langley, Dr Salah al-Nahi, Mr Hassan Salman, Dr M. J. Ubousi, and Mr Mohyiddin Yusif. Mr K. Haseeb, at present of the London School of Economics, helped me very much by obtaining and interpreting statistics and documents. To Dr S. M. Salim, recently of University College, London, and now lecturer in anthropology at the Baghdad College of Arts and Sciences, I am greatly indebted for advice and guidance, and for his insight into the life of village communities.

In Syria, I must thank Mr George Faris, director of the Bureau des Documentations Syriennes et Arabes, Dr Jamil Mualla, Director-General of the Ministry of Agriculture, Mr Ahmed el-Kassem, Director of Rural Education, Mr Jacob Hannous of Kamishli, and Dr Amin Sharif. With Paul and Elizabeth Benson Booz, then of the American University of Beirut, I travelled through the Jezira to Mosul and Baghdad, and with Cecil Hourani and Yusif Ibish, also of the American University, I visited the Hauran, learning much from them. Professor Himadeh was, as ever, an invaluable adviser.

In Egypt Mr Sayed Marei, now Minister of State for Agrarian Reform, gave me every assistance. Mr Ali Gritli, Mr Nasmi, Mr Shalaby Sarofim and Dr Amin Niazi in Minia, and Mr Mohammed el-Misidy at Armant, gave me much information about the reform and different views of it. Most of all I am grateful to Mr Nikolai Koestner, who once made a revolutionary land reform in Estonia, and is now director of the Research Department of the National Bank of Egypt.

To the Royal Institute of International Affairs, and particularly to Miss Margaret Cleeve, I am indebted for their help in meeting the expenses of my visits to the region, and for steady encouragement at every stage of the work.

July 1956

all I am grateful to Mr Nikolai Koestner, who once made a revolutionary land reform in Estonia, and is now director of the Research Department of the National Bank of Egypt.

To the Royal Institute of International Affairs, and particularly to Miss Margaret Cleeve, I am indebted for help in meeting the expenses of [illegible] region, and for steady encouragement at every stage of the work.

July 1956

INTRODUCTION: THE MEANING OF LAND REFORM

POVERTY still exists in the Middle Eastern countries. But its setting has changed. In Egypt there has been a political revolution and an agrarian reform. In Syria the prairie provinces have been opened up by mechanized farming. In Iraq, the poorest and most primitive of the three countries, new capital has been used to build the long-needed flood-control and irrigation works on the Tigris and the Euphrates.

These are great changes, each in its way a revolution. They transform the situation of ten years ago, when the economy seemed static and the social structure paralysed. None of them wipe out rural poverty. But agrarian reform, capital, enterprise, and technical change can all contribute towards raising the general standard of living. Because these elements are now present, the abolition of poverty is within the bounds of possibility, as ten years ago it was not.

Each country has undergone a different type of change, with a different dynamic. Syria has deployed its enterprise, and owes the rapid increase in national income over recent years principally to new crops, new machines, and new risk-taking. In Iraq money floods the economic scene, and flows into long-term investment in capital construction. Only in Egypt is the dynamic conscious and purposive, making a direct attack on rural poverty through the redistribution of income.

It is not the purpose of this book to analyse these different mainsprings as if they offered comparable or even rival methods of vanquishing rural poverty. The discussion of the problems of 'underdevelopment'—i.e. of raising the general living standard in poor countries—has advanced beyond the point when any remedy could be advocated in terms of a single 'solution'. Nor is it intended to discuss the merits of political revolution, laisser-faire, or engineers' planning in the abstract. On the contrary, a case for each as the highest priority can be made in the context of the conditions of the country concerned. Egypt,

INTRODUCTION: THE MEANING OF LAND REFORM

POVERTY still exists in the Middle Eastern countries. But its setting has changed. In Egypt there has been a political revolution and an agrarian reform. In Syria the prairie provinces have been opened up by mechanized farming. In Iraq, the poorest and most primitive of the three countries, new capital has been used to build the long needed flood-control and irrigation works on the Tigris and the Euphrates.

These are great changes, each in its way a revolution. They transform the situation of ten years ago, when the economy seemed static and the social structure paralysed. None of them wipe out rural poverty. But agrarian reform, capital, enterprise, and technical change can all contribute towards raising the general standard of living. Because these elements are now present, the abolition of poverty is within the bounds of possibility, as ten years ago it was not.

Each country has undergone a different type of change, with a different dynamic. Syria has deployed its enterprise, and owes the rapid increase in national income over recent years principally to new crops, new machines, and new risk-taking. In Iraq money floods the economic scene, and flows into long-term investment in capital construction. Only in Egypt is the dynamic conscious and purposive, making a direct attack on rural poverty through the redistribution of income.

It is not the purpose of this book to analyse these different mainsprings as if they offered comparable or even rival methods of vanquishing rural poverty. The discussion of the problems of 'underdevelopment'—i.e. of raising the general living standard in poor countries—has advanced beyond the point when any remedy could be advocated in terms of a single 'solution'. Nor is it intended to discuss the merits of political revolution, *laisser-faire*, or engineers' planning in the abstract. On the contrary, a case for each as the highest priority can be made in the context of the conditions of the country concerned. Egypt, already cultivated to capacity, needed agrarian reform most urgently, since redistribution of farm income was the only immediate way of raising the rural standard of living. Syria could not do much to raise rural living standards without raising output per head, and that could be done quickly only by cultivating more land. Without investment on a scale far beyond the rate of internal capital accumulation, Iraq could never have hoped to bring its extraordinarily difficult environment under control.

Now that these first necessities have been met, the priorities change. For Egypt political revolution was the *sine qua non*, and agrarian reform the end of the beginning. With a measure of income redistribution completed, the Government next turned its attention to the task of relieving unemployment and increasing the national income through the construction of the High Dam and through new industrialization. In Syria and Iraq, with increasing national incomes, the question of redistribution of income moves into the foreground, and agrarian reform acquires a new relevance in the changed conditions. A state agricultural policy also becomes more essential; now that the obstacles to expansion of the cultivated area have been removed by mechanization and water control in these two countries, it is time to think of better farming.

The aim of this book is to consider the need for agrarian reform as a means of raising the standard of living, in relation to the economic development of each of these countries. This necessitates a study of the relationships between different sets of conditions: the methods of farming and land use; the distribution of landownership and the legal and customary institutions of land tenure; rural social conditions, and the political forces which work for or against social change. Agrarian reform is not a single-track subject; it represents a point of intersection between economic development and social change, and it can therefore be treated only by taking cross-bearings between these different aspects of the life of each country.

But before turning to the study of the three countries, it seems necessary to relate this main topic to the new international 'climate of opinion' in favour of land reform. In recent years there have been agrarian reforms in many countries, and consequently there has been much discussion, in the United

Nations and elsewhere, of the relation between agrarian reform and the development of underdeveloped countries. There is so much variety in the conditions of 'underdevelopment' that broad general arguments about this relationship easily lose their force. They need more underpinning by investigations into the conditions of different countries. Global talk also tends to confuse issues, though it has its uses, and indeed has had some influence in the Middle Eastern countries which taught the world agriculture at a time when the advanced countries of today were very underdeveloped indeed. By examining the relationship between reform and development in the Middle East region, some light may be thrown on the general relationship, and also on the validity of the new conception of agrarian reform for a part of the world where until recently nothing at all had been done to improve the existing agrarian structure.

One result of the world debate is that there is now some confusion as to what 'land reform' really means. In ordinary usage, the term is generally understood to mean the redistribution of property in land for the benefit of small farmers and agricultural workers. Reforms of this kind may involve actual division of large estates into small holdings, as in Eastern Europe between the wars, or the transfer of ownership of the land from a large property holder to the tenant-cultivators of small holdings, as in many Asian countries. In the first case there is actual division of the land itself, and a change in the scale of farming operations. In the second case there is no change in the scale of farming, since the farm holdings were already small. In both cases the significant change is in the distribution of income; the aim is greater social equality.

In the past, land reforms were purely social in their aims. In Eastern Europe and in Mexico between the wars the peasants got the land only, without the means of working it, in the form of credit, marketing facilities, and technical guidance. Results varied: sometimes production increased, and sometimes it did not.[1]

Now a new conception of reform comes from America, which advocates reform as a comprehensive policy, including not only

[1] Some of these results have been reviewed briefly in my lectures *Land Reform and Economic Development*, published by the National Bank of Egypt, 1955.

'opportunity of ownership', but also a variety of other measures to assist farmers by means of greater security of tenure, better credit systems, better marketing facilities, agricultural advisory services and education, and so on. This conception flowered in the course of the cold war, as an answer to Communism. The United States first made advocacy of land reform part of its official foreign policy in 1950, when it supported a Polish resolution in favour of land reform in the General Assembly of the United Nations, and thereby challenged the Communist claim to leadership in the use of land reform as a political warfare weapon.

America's advocacy of reform is, however, much more than a tactical cold war move and has deeper roots. The ideal of the family farm springs from the anti-feudal tradition, and it embodies, by and large, the aims of land policy in the United States.[1] Family farming is regarded as an end in itself, the necessary base for free enterprise and political democracy. The American conception of reform is not merely a simple belief in the homespun values of family farming. Official statements drive home the need for the 'integrated approach', which means creating a framework in which the family farm can flourish, through the organized provision of credit, co-operative marketing, 'extension', and rural services of all kinds. The policy is, in fact, family farming by the Department of Agriculture out of the New Deal.

The essential difference between this new approach and the older and simpler conception is that reform is now regarded as an agricultural policy as well as a social policy. By contrast with the earlier reforms (and with recent Communist reforms) the aim is to give the farmers help, and so accompany the social change with a policy to increase productivity in agriculture.

As a result of this new conception the definition of 'land reform' is now somewhat confused. In their periodic surveys of progress in land reform, the United Nations reports include not only land redistribution, but also farm tenancy and labour legislation; land settlement; co-operation; farm credit; agricultural education and research; the registration of title;

[1] This does not mean that other types of structure, corporation farming for instance, are not important, or that the policy has always been consistent. American authorities do not claim a high degree of consistency. cf. V. W. Johnson and Raleigh Barlowe, *Land Problems and Policies* (New York, McGraw, 1954), p. 7.

methods of land taxation; and long-term policies for the control of land use. The use of the term 'land reform' to cover this all-inclusive catalogue represents the American conception, in accordance with the official American definition of land reform as 'the improvement of agricultural economic institutions'.[1] But although the American *conception* is a great advance on the older conception, a *definition* with so wide a connotation distorts the perspective. The redistribution of land, or rights in land, means a major social and political change, while the other measures lead to an improvement in the economic position of farmers and in agricultural production, without a change in their social position. In the following study it would seem inappropriate, for example, to say that Syria has carried out a land reform because it has started a system of agricultural education, or that Iraq has had a reform because large areas of state land have been registered in the name of large landowners.

For the sake of clarity and perspective, it is better to keep to the ordinary usage of the term and use 'land reform' to mean redistribution of land or rights in land. The term 'reform of the agrarian structure' may be used to include measures of this kind, together with other institutional reforms which affect the social structure, such as land settlement, the regulation of tenancy conditions, and labour legislation. Legal changes, such as registration of title, may affect the social structure, but are not, in the following chapters, included within the agrarian reform concept, for reasons which will be clear.

This distinction is not merely a matter of terminology. Particularly in regard to the Arab countries, it is important not to blunt the edge of the policy by widening it too much.

That the new emphasis on farm services is of great value, particularly in the countries of the Fertile Crescent, goes without saying. The international agencies have given it some practical effect; their experts in the field—contrary to the impression sometimes conveyed by their official publications—can really get down to the grass roots. In the following chapters several instances are quoted which show how constructive this influence has been. More important even than the new schools and new research institutes is the prestige which

[1] See UN, Dept. of Economic Affairs, *Progress in Land Reform* (New York, 1954), p. 49.

American influence accords to agriculture as a profession.

Yet so far as land reform itself is concerned, there is a certain danger in this wider conception for the Arab countries, and no doubt in other countries with similar land systems. Because the conception of land reform has broadened to include a variety of measures to improve land tenure and agricultural organization, the emphasis shifts from the foundation to the accessories, and the original—and still essential—aim of greater social and economic equality tends to be obscured. The integrated approach sometimes seems to offer everything except the land.

This point has been well made by George Hakim.[1]

As generally used in international discussions, the term 'land reform' has come to refer to a wide gamut of problems of a legal, social, and economic character. This large conception does not give sufficient emphasis to the basic issue of the land tenure system. It was this that was mainly in the minds of those who originally raised the subject of agrarian reform in the United Nations and elsewhere. At the heart of the problem of land reform in underdeveloped countries is the question of who owns the land. This fundamental question has been confused and overshadowed by the attention paid to other factors, such as settlement of legal title to land, agricultural indebtedness, and land taxation, which, though undoubtedly related to the main problem, are not more than manifestations of this, the basic malady of the agrarian structure.[2]

The 'basic malady' in the three Arab countries here considered is the prevalence of institutional monopoly in landownership, linked with a monopolistic supply of capital to agriculture. There is nothing peculiar to Middle Eastern countries in this condition. On the contrary, it is a feature of the land systems of many countries in the three agricultural continents which are now conventionally described as 'underdeveloped'. In the sparsely populated countries of Latin America, landowners' monopoly is an outstanding feature of the latifundia system, in which great estates, worked by semi-serf peons, effectively prevent access to landownership for the farm labourers, keeping wages low and land use extensive. In densely populated Asian countries, large landholdings were generally not centrally managed farms, but were rented in small

[1] Formerly Minister of National Economy, Foreign Affairs, Finance, and Agriculture in Lebanon, now Lebanese Minister in Bonn.

[2] 'Land Tenure Reform', *Middle East Economic Papers*, 1954, Economic Research Institute, American University of Beirut.

holdings, usually through a series of intermediaries, to cultivators who paid high rents and had no security. In such systems, monopoly power is used to exact a high price for the use of land, and a high price for farm credit.

Landlordism in the Arab countries shares these characteristics. The great landholdings of south Iraq resemble the latifundia of Latin America in their broad social and economic effects. Egypt has a mixed system, combining highly organized capitalistic estates with tenancy in small units, on the Asian model. One useful result of the international discussions is that they bring out resemblances in the land systems of countries with very different histories and very different natural conditions.

Where the agrarian structure is a rigid institutional hangover from the past, the need for reform is generally twofold, a social need for a higher income for the cultivator, and an economic need for better farming through more investment and better methods. The general economic argument for reform of the agrarian structure in underdeveloped countries is that the existing land systems accentuate the shortage of capital and prevent investment, because they give rise to incomes which are not used to improve agricultural production or to invest in the land. Large landowners spend conspicuously; or purchase more land; or invest in urban house property (very noticeably in the Arab countries); or lend to impoverished cultivators at high rates of interest.

How far the land systems of Egypt, Syria, and Iraq are or were obstacles to economic development is considered in the following chapters. In all three countries the land system is the cause of social evils, keeping the rural population on a low level of income and status. But as obstacles to development the influence varies, as will be seen.

Obsolete monopolistic land systems can be reformed in various ways: by expropriation and redistribution of large properties; by settlement on new land; by giving tenants special credit facilities to purchase land; by legislation to reduce rents and prevent the eviction of tenants; and by labour legislation. These measures, or a combination of them, may be carried out simultaneously in a general agrarian reform policy, as in Egypt, or one or more of the other measures may be used as alternatives to land reform in the strict sense. The question of whether these other methods are real alternatives to redistribution in Syria and Iraq is considered in Chapters III and IV.

As to the type of agrarian structure which should replace the old, it does not do to be dogmatic, and it is not the object of this study to make recommendations. What can be done depends on what people want, and on what kind of farming is practised. New experiments in these directions are described in the following chapters; they do not provide a general formula. Obviously an elaborate organization suits Egypt, but from the standpoint of what the people want Dujaila,[1] in its own simple way, is just as good.

On this question, it should perhaps be emphasized that there is and can be no ideal standard. Because land reform is internationally discussed in the light of the cold war, the impression is created that there are ideal patterns, and that the choice lies between rival models, the American family farm and the Soviet collective. At the grass-roots level, complete individualism and total collectivism are not realistic alternatives. Most new experiments nowadays aim at some form of group farming organization, as a way of combining the satisfactions of independent farming with the economies of large-scale operation.

Moreover, transplanted into a different context, institutions tend to work differently. The 'integrated approach' to family farming does not necessarily produce family farms. The Italian land reform, for example, is extremely well organized; it is limited to uncultivated land which is reclaimed by the authorities and then settled by selected applicants, who receive ownership after payment of the purchase price in instalments spread over thirty years, during which period they are obliged to farm the land 'co-operatively', i.e. to use machinery and follow a common rotation. Some of the large settlements in the South are in reality, though not in law, extremely well-managed state farms with a degree of collective organization. This is an inevitable result of aiming at efficiency, and does not in the least detract from the social achievements of the reform, even though it does not establish independent farm units. If there are no services supplying credit and advisory experts, and no existing co-operative system, they must be set up specially to serve the new landholders. Where settlement on

[1] See below, pp. 162–9.

reclaimed land is involved, there must be costly large-scale investment as a preliminary. Consequently reforms on the 1950 model tend to be limited in scope, and managerially controlled, quite unlike the chaotic reforms in Mexico and Eastern Europe in the 1920's.

Now land reform has become respectable and fashionable. Efficiency has been won, and something has been lost. The older reforms had one merit: they gave people what they wanted. After a lengthy and expensive international seminar on land reform, 'I am afraid', said an Arab civil servant, 'that they make it all seem too difficult.' In the pomposities of international debate, it would be good if the old authentic note—of Zapata, for instance, or Stambulisky—could sometimes break through, so that it would not seem so difficult as experts like to make it.

Land reform in its initial and crucial stage is emphatically not a question for experts; it cannot be advised into existence, but must be based on an impetus arising within the country. Once that impetus is there, and recognized in a decision to legislate, experts can help in overcoming technical difficulties. The choice of the type of group farming appropriate for the country, as will be seen, is not a simple matter, and the experience of administrators who have themselves carried out reforms can be a useful guide. At this stage the integrated approach is relevant, though it is valid only when the economic sails are filled by a political wind. If there is no real drive for reform, experts can produce expensive little demonstration projects, but they will not be able to achieve any general and genuine improvement in the position of the cultivators.

This is obvious enough, but it needs saying, because there is a slightly morbid confidence in experts in the Arab world, even a belief that lack of experts is an obstacle to reform. Good farming, of course, does need experts and costs money, while bad farming costs the earth. But good laws cost nothing, and need no experts. Fortunately there are in the Arab world today politicians who can speak, and some who can even act, for the fellahin. Even the authentic note can be heard at times. In Egypt the impetus is obviously there; it certainly owes a little to the new 'climate of opinion', and so justifies the talk in the conference rooms in New York and Geneva.

I

THE AGRARIAN REFORM IN EGYPT

THE BACKGROUND

THE present Government of Egypt has ideals but no ideology, as revolutionaries nowadays are expected to have. No single intellectual influence has been predominant. It combines pure nationalists and revolutionaries, held together by Colonel Nasser in a tense union for action. Even at the outset it was not united, except on the issue of land reform.

Class interests do not play much part in its outlook. It is true that the Army Group is of middle-class origin,[1] and that its strong supporters are found in the sons of the farming middle class, well-to-do people with fifty acres in the Delta. Its left-wing adherents describe it as 'our bourgeois revolution'. But though the new régime commands respect from liberal opinion, it also encounters much criticism. Business men and professional people have come to terms, and so has the bureaucracy, without enthusiasm. The society over which the young Government rules is as old and sophisticated at the 'second level' as it was at the top. The bourgeoisie cannot produce an emotional response, even if it acknowledges the need for cutting out the dead wood. The aims of the Egyptian revolution are a long way ahead of middle-class opinion.

Confronted with a Government which seems to fit into no ordinary pattern, Western observers have sought for labels, such as 'Kemalist', which relate it to the past or to modern Europe's political categories. But it is they, and not the Government, who are out of date. The *ad hoc* policy which the Government has followed does not correspond to any dated political 'ism', but it does correspond to the new line of thinking about the economic development of underdeveloped countries, a line to which the United Nations report on *Measures for the Economic*

[1] As H. C. Ayrout points out, this class has produced most of Egypt's eminent men (*Fellahs d'Égypte*, 6th ed. (Cairo, Éditions du Sphynx, 1952), p. 47).

Development of Under-Developed Countries first gave international sanction, and which has since been elaborated.[1] This new line starts from a typical situation, or model, of 'underdevelopment', characterized by over-population, underemployment on the land, a low rate of capital accumulation, and an institutional structure inimical to investment. Egypt, on the whole, fits into this pattern, though its agriculture is too advanced to correspond to the usual projection. The rate of population growth exceeds the rate of increase of agricultural production; it has an enormous rural population surplus; and it cannot absorb this surplus, or check the fall in living standards, without public investment on a very large scale. Consequently the policies which fit Egypt's conditions are the policies recommended by the new line of thought: foreign loans for big multi-purpose investment schemes, industrialization, and institutional reform, in a mixed economy.

The revolution is original in that it takes the economists' recommendations literally, and insists on their implementation, both on the national and the international level. It makes the new line of thought a line of action. The lack of a doctrinaire ideology has been an advantage, in that it has increased international bargaining power. The empirical approach allows quick decision and action, in the course of which ideas have emerged. 'À force d'y forger, on devient forgeron'.

The aim is to meet Egypt's needs: more equal income distribution, more land, and more industry. These needs are axiomatic, the stock in trade of the economics textbook; and they have long been recognized and discussed. But discussion never produced practical remedies. The problem of the rapid rate of population growth has been discussed by economists for the past thirty years; its gravity has never been denied. Projects for fuller utilization of the Nile waters have long been considered; but they remained under consideration. Land reform has long been recognized as a social necessity; but in thirty years of parliamentary government not one measure was passed for the benefit of the fellahin, on whom Egypt's economy

[1] UN, Dept. of Economic Affairs, *Measures for the Economic Development of Under-Developed Countries* (New York, 1951). Other important works on the same topic are Ragnar Nurkse, *Problems of Capital Formation in Underdeveloped Countries* (Oxford, 1953), J. Arthur Lewis, *Theory of Economic Growth* (London, 1955), and Gunnar Myrdal, *An International Economy* (1956).

depends. On two occasions, in 1945 and 1950, bills were introduced for the limitation of the size of holdings, but both were overwhelmingly defeated.[1]

Land reform was the issue on which the Army Group decided to take power openly. At the time of the first coup d'état, in July 1952, the decision to undertake land reform was announced; the main lines of the law had already been prepared. But the law was not immediately put into force, and the Group evidently believed that it could be enacted by politicians of the old style. It is said—and there seems no reason to doubt the assertion—that the Group then had no intention of taking over the Government. But in the interval between the first and second coups d'état, the usual pretexts for delaying action—the need for research and the danger of haste—were well aired, and seemed likely to succeed in preventing the reform law from being enacted. When it became apparent that Ali Mahir, under the pretext of 'studying the experience of other countries', was in reality opposing the introduction of the law, the Army Group evidently decided that the one sure lesson to be learnt from the experience of other countries was the danger of land reform on paper. On 7 September 1952 they decided to take over the Government, and on the following day the Agrarian Reform Law was put into force.

How and why reform became a central issue for the Army Group is not self-evident. For reasons of humanity, land reform was needed, but until the Army Group came to power there was no channel through which the need could be expressed. No political party and no group of intellectuals had ever advocated land reform, though individuals had done so. There had never been a fellahin movement, though in the years since the war there had been outbreaks of violence on some estates. Discontent was smouldering; but there was no groundswell of popular feeling. There was no obvious reason for a group of young officers to concentrate on this question. An officers' movement might be expected to devote itself to the reform of the Army and the strengthening of Egypt's military power; but it would not be expected to make a social-revolu-

[1] Charles Issawi, *Egypt at Mid-Century* (London, RIIA, 1954), p. 135. The 1945 bill proposed a 50-acre maximum, and so was more radical than the present law.

tionary measure a test of its power to enforce its convictions.

The motives behind the reform may be surmised to have been three. One was a sincere desire and determination to carry out reform for humanitarian reasons. The second was a revolutionary aim, to break the power of the old ruling oligarchy, with its roots in the big estates. This was the crucial issue which necessitated a show-down. The third reason was that in 1951–2 land reform was very much in the air internationally. America's advocacy of land reform was said to be a green light, and State Department influence certainly played a part in the preparation of the decree, probably strengthening the revolutionary element in the Group.

As there was no ideology at the start, and no political tradition to appeal to, the decree came out in a curious modern dress, combining the abolition of feudalism with Keynesian economics. The 'abolition of feudalism', the main theme of all official statements, is a more exact description of the reform than at first sight appears. The highly capitalized estates, with their big machinery and heavy expenditure on fertilizers and seed, their qualified managers and accountants, and their wretched tied villages are, in an economic sense, capitalistic in the extreme. Yet socially the term is a clear conception. When an Egyptian economist was asked what he meant by a feudal estate, he replied 'It means that the landowner keeps a private army to defend his house and his person; and that armed men stand guard over the crops'—a definition that could hardly be improved. Whatever the system is called, it ought to be abolished; and the use of the term 'feudal' makes political good sense.

The second aim, as stated in the preamble to the law, was to break the landowners' desire to hold wealth in the form of land, and so induce them to invest in industry. This was a muddled bit of thinking, brought in to satisfy the Minister of Finance, Dr Emery, who had been a member of Ali Mahir's Government, and whose support could be won only if reform seemed likely to stimulate investment. The Minister of Finance believed that this result could be achieved by making the land bonds negotiable, but fortunately this inflationary course has not been followed.

The fact that the law was a measure for the redistribution of income was too crude a truth to be told, and there was no way of expressing it. 'The land for the peasants' was not its meaning. The Mexican watchword of 'restitution' had no historical parallel, and 'bread and books' was too revolutionary also. The 'abolition of feudalism' was the safest approach and, in the political sense, that is what it has accomplished.

So far as its actual provisions are concerned, the redistribution enforced by the law is not apparently a revolutionary measure at all. It affects only about 10 per cent of the land area. It allows landowners to retain 300 acres, which in Egyptian conditions represents an annual net income of £5,000–£6,000 at least. Expropriated owners receive a reasonably high rate of compensation.

Consequently it seems surprising that revolutionary means were needed to carry out so moderate a measure. The shock which the law administered to Egyptian opinion was out of all proportion to the degree of change which it enforced. Violent opposition was expected; it appeared only in the case of Adli Lamlun, the scion of a family whose estates in Upper Egypt had been the scene of disturbances in the past. When the reform was announced Lamlun, with a band of retainers, attacked the prefecture at Maghagha, and was then arrested with some of his supporters, tried, and condemned to penal servitude for life.[1] After this sentence the submission of the landowners was secured, though their hostility is still very great.

The explanation of the paradox is simple. The reform was revolutionary in its political effects. It was a political measure directed against the royal family and a small number of very wealthy landowners. Of the total area to be expropriated, about one-third is the property of the 'Mohammed Ali dynasty', i.e. the King and members of his family. Prince Yusuf Kemal, for instance, held as much as 14,000 acres in one block, in the district of Nag Hamadi, in addition to his lands in other parts of Upper Egypt.

So far as the private landowners were concerned, the greater part of the land now in the course of expropriation was held by fifteen to twenty families, as for example the Badrawi family, with 18,000 acres, and Ahmed Abboud, the millionaire industrialist, who owned large sugar plantations in Upper Egypt. The effect of the reform has been far greater in Upper Egypt

[1] He has since been released.

than in the Delta, because these vast holdings monopolize the narrow valley. It was the expropriation of these very large holdings which was revolutionary, not the taking over of 100 or 200 acres from the landowner with 400 or 500. The intention of the reform was to remove the wealthy families from their dominating position in the life of the country—a position never previously challenged.

What the reform abolished, therefore, was a strong concentration of landed wealth, a citadel that first had to be taken by storm, even if it was later to be bought out in bonds bearing 3 per cent interest. This is the political significance of the reform. In economic terms, its significance is a considerable redistribution of income in favour of the fellahin. The reform is best regarded as a labour policy, in the interests of the tenant-cultivators. The law was intended to achieve a general reform of the agrarian structure, including the redistribution of property (land reform in the strict sense), the reduction of rents, and the raising of agricultural wages. Its primary aim is the redistribution of incomes, not agricultural development.

To see why agrarian reform must aim at raising rural living standards, and cannot aim at increasing employment in agriculture or at increasing agricultural production, it is necessary to look briefly at the economic background, in particular the demographic position.

The Demographic Position

The main feature in this background is the rapid rate of population growth on a small land area already cultivated to capacity, and rigidly limited. The typical conditions of under-development exist in an extreme form: an excessively high density of population; rural underemployment on a large scale; and a rate of population increase which greatly exceeds the rate of increase in agricultural production.

So far as the density of population is concerned, Egypt is among the most densely populated countries in the world.[1] On a cultivated area of 6 million acres it has to support 22 million people, of whom about 8½ million are actively em-

[1] For comparable figures of population densities see UN, Dept. of Economic Affairs, *Land Reform; Defects in Agrarian Structure as Obstacles to Economic Development* (New York, 1951), Appendix.

ployed in agriculture and about 16 million dependent on it. Thus each acre of arable land must support 3½ people, and there is only one-third of an acre per head of agricultural population.

The surplus population on the land is now estimated to be 5 million (including dependants), or 30 per cent of the total agricultural population.[1] Though estimates of surplus population are never exact, because there are no exact methods of measurement, it is certain that the surplus is large and that it is increasing.

The rate of population increase now outstrips the rate of increase of agricultural production. For the past fifty years the race between them has been neck and neck, but now the rate of population increase is certainly well in the lead. The land of Egypt is almost rainless, and cultivation depends on irrigation, so that the extension of the area cultivated depends on the expansion of water-storage capacity for the Nile waters provided by the barrages. Since the 1880's there has been a great expansion of the areas cultivated and cropped, through the construction of new irrigation works. But the increase over the last fifty years has not kept pace with population growth, as the following table shows.

TABLE I

Egypt: Expansion of the Cultivated Area in Relation to Population

Year	*Cultivated area (million acres)*	*Crop area (million acres)*	*Population (millions)*
1897	5·1	6·8	9·7
1907	5·4	7·6	11·2
1917	5·3	7·7	12·8
1927	5·5	8·7	14·2
1937	5·3	8·4	15·9
1947	5·8	9·2	19
1949	5·8	9·3	20

(SOURCE: *The Population Problem in Egypt*, p. 11.)

[1] Egypt, Permanent Council of Public Services, Economic Sub-Committee of the National Population Commission, *The Population Problem in Egypt* (Cairo, 1955), p. 22. (Hereafter referred to as *The Population Problem in Egypt*.)

According to these figures, the population doubled between 1897 and 1947, while the cultivated area increased by 14 per cent and the crop area by 37 per cent. There are no figures showing the increase in agricultural production over the whole period, during which yields per acre rose considerably. Between 1924–8 and 1950 the volume of agricultural production rose by 40 per cent, while population in the same period (1927–50) rose by 43 per cent, so that agricultural production barely kept pace. Charles Issawi holds that the volume of production did just keep pace, because he considers that the census figures exaggerate the rate of growth between 1937 and 1947, because the 1937 census underestimated the population, while the 1947 figure was probably inflated, and should be 18 instead of 19 million. This may well be so; the point is that it was a near thing and that the race is not yet over.[1]

During the 1930's the rate of increase of population was

TABLE 2

Population of Egypt

Year		*Population (000)*	*Average annual increase (per cent)*	*Urban population* as per cent of total*
Census of	1882	6,804	—	19
	1897	9,715	2·9	20
	1907	11,287	1·6	19
	1917	12,751	1·4	21
	1927	14,218	1·1	23
	1937	15,933	1·2	25
	1947	19,022	1·9	31
Mid-year estimate for	1948	19,494	2·2	31
	1949	19,888	2·1	31
	1950	20,393	2·5	31
	1951	20,872	2·3	32
	1952	21,473	2·9	32
	1953†	22,062	2·7	32
	1954†	22,651	2·7	32

* Urban comprises the Governorates of Cairo, Alexandria, Canal, Suez, Damietta, and the provincial capitals and district seats. † Preliminary.

(SOURCE: *Statistical Pocket Year-book, 1954.*)

[1] *Egypt at Mid-Century*, pp. 54–5, 61, and 79–80.

much lower than it had been in the 1890's, as a result of the decline in the birth rate, and the position therefore appeared less serious than it is now. There was, however, some controversy as to the extent by which the birth rate had actually fallen.[1] According to the official figures, the rate of increase during the 1930's was 1·2 per cent. The preceding table gives the official estimates of the rate of population growth for the years 1948–54, and shows that the rate of increase is now 2·7 per cent.

The rate of increase is higher because birth rates have risen slightly, while the death rate has fallen, chiefly as a result of the decrease in the infant mortality rate. The following table shows these changes.

TABLE 3

Egypt: Live Births and Deaths

Year	*Births (000)*	*Crude birth rate per 000*	*Deaths (000)*	*Crude death rate per 000*
1948	833	43	398	20
1949	831	42	411	21
1950	905	44	389	19
1951	934	45	402	19
1952	969	45	381	18

(SOURCE: *Statistical Pocket Year-book, 1954*, p. 14.)

The infant mortality rate has declined, from 165 per thousand in 1937 to 130 per thousand in 1950. This improvement is a result of better health conditions, and is likely to continue.

According to these figures, the population increased between 1937 and 1952 by 34 per cent, while agricultural production in 1952 was only 11 per cent over the pre-war level. During the war crop yields fell sharply owing to the shortage of fertilizers, but have since recovered. The following table shows the increase.

[1] According to A. E. Crouchley ('A Century of Economic Development in Egypt', *L'Égypte Contemporaine*, February–March 1939), the rate of increase during the 1930's was 1·0 per cent against 3·0 per cent during the 1890's. C. V. Kiser, however, holds that there was little evidence of a decline in the birth rate during the 1930's and considers that the true rate of natural increase was 1·25 per cent in 1937, when the true birth and death rates were 44·8 and 32·4 respectively ('Demographic Position in Egypt', in F. W. Notestein, ed., *Demographic Studies of Selected Areas of Rapid Growth*, New York, Millbank Memorial Fund, 1944).

TABLE 4

Index of Agricultural Production in Egypt

(1935–9=100)

1949	109
1950	105
1951	101
1952	111
1953	104
1954	115

(SOURCE: *Statistical Pocket Year-book, 1954*, p. 36.)

Even if the official figures overestimate the rate of population growth, there can be no doubt that it is now faster than the rate of increase of agricultural production. It is therefore quite certain that in the period since the second world war population has outstripped agricultural production.

There has been no new land since the 1930's. Land reclamation was stopped during the war and has only recently been resumed.

The existing land area is used with high efficiency. Agriculturally, Egypt is a pressure-cooker. The Nile valley holds the world's land productivity record; cropping rates are high: as Shakespeare said, the land 'shortly comes to harvest'. On four-fifths of the land (the area perennially irrigated) three crops a year can be harvested, though in fact the average cropping rate is five crops in two years. Yields are high, the cotton yield being the world's highest and the maize yield as high as the United States level, while wheat yields are comparatively low, though they exceed the European average.

The following figures show yields, in comparison with other countries.

TABLE 5

Crop Yields in Egypt and Other Countries

(Average 1948–50: 100 kg. per hectare)

	Cotton	*Maize*	*Wheat*
Egypt	5·5	24·9	18·0
U.S.A.	3·2	24·6	11·1
U.K.	—	—	26·8
Europe	1·5	14·3	14·5

(SOURCE: FAO, *Yearbook of Food and Agricultural Statistics.*)

This achievement is not solely the gift of the Nile, though it is the fertility-renewing Nile flood which has given Egypt its 5,000 years of agricultural continuity. The modern economy of Egypt multiplies the fertilizing effect of the Nile by three, through the system of perennial irrigation. Artificial fertilizers are heavily applied, chiefly in the form of nitrates, and maintain the high yields, which fall off sharply when applications diminish, as happened during the war when imports of nitrates were cut down. Capital, skill, and organizing ability have gone into the standardization and improvement of the varieties of cotton. Through the cotton crop the whole economy—and most of the population—is geared to the world market.

The high level of land productivity is accompanied by a very low productivity of labour. Gross and net output per acre are extremely high, while output per man is extremely low. Estimates of the Egyptian national income show that in 1953 the average gross agricultural output per acre amounted to £63, and the average net output per acre (i.e. gross output less estimated inputs of materials) to £45. Net income per head of active agricultural population amounted to £34. This figure does not, however, indicate the income actually received, as rent is not deducted; after deduction of rent net income per head would amount to only £25.[1] The contrast with Europe may be indicated by comparison with figures for a group of fourteen West European countries, which show average gross and net outputs of £28 and £24 per acre in 1950, and an average net income per head of active agricultural population of £190.[2] The figures are not strictly comparable, since the European figures are calculated in arable equivalent acres, and net output is calculated by deduction of purchased materials only; but the difference does not invalidate the contrast in levels of land and labour productivity. Broadly speaking, Egypt's land produces twice as much per acre as these European countries, while its labour earns only one-seventh as much, although the West European group includes some countries with very low rural standards of living.

Since the population on the land is now increasing faster

[1] Ministry of Finance and National Economy, *National Income of Egypt for 1953, Official Estimate* (Cairo, 1955) and National Bank of Egypt, *Economic Bulletin*, vol. 8, no. 2, 1955.

[2] UN, ECE, and FAO, *Output and Expenses of Agriculture in some European Countries*, First Report (Geneva, 1953), p. 16.

than production, incomes per head are certainly falling. It is therefore essential, if a further fall in the living standard is to be avoided, to increase agricultural production. But because the level of land productivity is already so high, there is not great scope for increasing agricultural production on the present land area. More fertilizers and better seed could raise yields, but the cost would be high. In the view of the Population Commission, the maximum possible increase in output per acre might be 25 per cent above the level of 1947–51.[1] Nor is there any prospect of a *large* increase in the areas cultivated and cropped, without more water. Official schemes provide for the reclamation of an area of 300,000 acres by the end of 1956. But the extent to which supplies can be diverted away without damage to land already cultivated is a controversial issue. The scope for increasing employment on the land is nil. The technical improvements which could be made would not increase the demand for labour, and might even reduce it.

These three conditions, extreme and growing congestion on the land, the limited land area, and the high level of land productivity, mean that the fall in the living standard can be checked only by increasing employment in industry and by greatly extending the area cultivated, which is impossible without a great increase in water-storage capacity.

These needs the Government is meeting by its industrial schemes, by an agricultural development and land reclamation programme, and intends to meet by the construction of the High Dam. The industrial schemes include the construction of two new power stations (one already in operation), the iron and steel plant at Helwan, a synthetic fertilizer plant and an electrical power installation at Aswan, the last two being under construction.[2]

Much larger sums, amounting to £40 million over the three years 1953–5, have been invested in agriculture, chiefly to convert land in Upper Egypt to perennial irrigation, by installing pumps, and for general improvement of irrigation and drainage. The four-year programme for reclaiming 300,000 acres by the end of 1956 includes conversion to perennial

[1] *The Population Problem in Egypt*, p. 20.

[2] For further details see UN, Dept. of Economic and Social Affairs, *Economic Developments in the Middle East, 1954–5* (New York, 1956), pp. 31 and 114–15.

irrigation in some districts of Upper Egypt, chiefly on the estates expropriated under the agrarian reform, and also on estates belonging to private landowners. The programme also includes land reclamation in sections of the Tahrir province, described below, and the reclamation work undertaken by the Egyptian-American Rural Improvement Service (EARIS), an organization jointly financed by Point Four and the Egyptian Government, and advised by American experts. This has completed the reclamation of 25,000 acres in the province of Buhaira, by means of forage crops, using no extra water, and is also active in the Fayyum. The land reclaimed is to be assigned to small farmers for purchase over thirty years.[1]

The High Dam above Aswan comprises the long-term programme for the expansion of the cultivated area, and for industrial expansion. Its object is to make fuller use of the Nile water, much of which is now wasted in the flood season. The scheme is still in the course of preparation, but some current estimates of its size and importance may be given. The reservoir behind the dam is intended to have a capacity of 130,000 million cubic metres, and will therefore be the largest in the world. The 25 per cent increase in water-supplies which this storage capacity would provide could add 1,300,000 acres of new land (in the Tahrir province) to the present area of 6 million acres, and would allow the conversion of 700,000 acres in Upper Egypt to perennial irrigation, and so double the cropped area on this land, which at present only carries one crop per annum. This should permit, according to official calculations, an increase in the total agricultural income of some 50 per cent, when the whole of the reclamation work is completed. In addition to the gain in water-supplies, there will also be a considerable gain from the flood-protection works in connexion with the dam.

The work is intended to be undertaken in two stages, the first ten-year period which will see the construction of the dam, reclamation of part of the additional land area, and partial use of the power capacity. The total power production at the site is estimated at 8,300 million kilowatt hours, of which half could be available at the end of the ten-year period in which the dam should be completed.

[1] See EARIS, *Land Reclamation and Land Settlement* (Cairo, 1955).

The cost of the first stage is estimated at £209 million. This sum includes £68 million for the cost of the construction of the dam itself: the cost of constructing four power stations, flood-protection and navigation facilities, turbine and generator equipment, and the cost of reclaiming 400,000 acres and converting 700,000 acres to perennial irrigation.[1] By the time that the dam is completed, the total population of Egypt will have increased by between 5 and 6 million, so that the prospective increase in areas cultivated and cropped will provide only for the prospective increase in population.[2] Thus even with much fuller utilization of the Nile water, there is no prospect of relieving pressure on the land, so long as Egypt remains a mainly agricultural country. But the dam can none the less provide the way out of the demographic impasse, in that it will greatly increase Egypt's industrial capacity, and could raise the rural living standard through increased employment in industry. The full power potential of the dam will be considerably larger than the total which the Egyptian economy is likely to absorb for a number of years after construction is completed, and for this reason only half the energy available is to be harnessed in the ten-year period.

This vast project is rightly regarded by the Egyptian Government as a matter of life and death for the Egyptian economy. As has already been emphasized, Egypt is a test case for the ability of the international economy and its agencies to deal with the problems of underdevelopment. In January 1956 the International Bank for Reconstruction and Development had reached an agreement in principle with the Egyptian Government on a loan of $200 million, and the United States and the United Kingdom had pledged grants of $75 million towards the cost of the scheme. Had the needs of the Egyptian economy been better understood in the West, and had the Egyptian Government succeeded in convincing these Governments of its good faith, the dangers of going back on these undertakings might have been avoided. At the time of writing, the question of finance is still unsettled, and it can only be hoped that a solution can be reached which will make this great undertaking

[1] For details see UN, *Economic Developments in the Middle East, 1954 to 1955*, pp. 116–17.

[2] *The Population Problem in Egypt*, p. 20. See also Gamal Abdel Nasser, 'The Egyptian Revolution', *Foreign Affairs*, January 1955.

an achievement of international co-operation, and not a cause of international conflict.

In the meantime, the only way in which the standard of living of the fellah can be improved is by redistribution of income from agriculture. Over-population does not diminish the need for reform; on the contrary, it increases the need, though it sets limits as to what can be accomplished. The growing pressure of population allows landowners to take a larger share in the national income by raising rents. As population increases, the inequality of incomes increases also. Land reform was needed, not only because the distribution of property was unequal, but also because it gave the landowners a vested interest in retrogression.

THE LAND SYSTEM

The distribution of property in land before the reform was extremely unequal, as the following table shows. Holdings are here identical with properties, not farms.

TABLE 6

Egypt: Agricultural Land by Size of Holdings, 1952

	Owners		Area		
*Size-group (feddans)**	*(000)*	*(per cent)*	*(000 feddans)*	*(per cent)*	*Average area (feddans)*
1 and under	2,018·1	72·0	778	13·0	0·4
Over 1–under 5	623·8	22·2	1,344	22·5	2·1
„ 5– „ 10	79·3	2·8	526	8·8	6·6
„ 10– „ 20	46·8	1·8	638	10·7	13·6
„ 20– „ 30	13·1	0·5	309	5·0	23·6
„ 30– „ 50	9·2	0·3	344	5·7	37·4
„ 50– „ 100	6·4	0·2	429	7·2	67·3
„ 100– „ 200	3·2	0·1	437	7·3	137·2
„ 200	2·1	0·1	1,177	19·8	550·9
Total	2,802·0	100·0	5,982	100·0	2·1

* 1 feddan = 1·038 acres.

(SOURCE: *Statistical Pocket Year-book, 1953*, p. 33.)

From these figures it appears that of the total agricultural land area of nearly 6 million acres,[1] 2 million or 34·3 per cent

[1] As the difference between the feddan and the acre is small, the acre is used throughout this chapter as the more familiar measure.

was held by proprietors with more than 50 acres; 1·8 million or 30·2 per cent was held by proprietors with between 5 and 50 acres; and 2·1 million or 35·5 per cent by proprietors with less than 5 acres. This was a more equal distribution than exists in Syria and Iraq, because there is in Egypt a fairly large class of medium-sized proprietors, numbering 150,000; this class is far less important in the other two countries. Nor are there the enormous properties of 200,000 acres, or more, which characterize the land systems of Syria and Iraq. It will be remembered, however, that cultivation is highly intensive. With a net income of £40 per acre, the income of a 2,500-acre holding in Egypt corresponds to the income of a 50,000-acre holding in Syria and Iraq, where only half the land is cultivated in each year, and yields are very low.

None the less, by any other standard the distribution of property in Egypt was highly unequal. Of the 2¾ million proprietors, 70 per cent had less than half an acre each, while 2,115 had over 200 acres, with an average of 550 acres each. Within the size-group over 200 acres, 188 proprietors owned holdings over 1,000 acres, with an average holding of 2,600 acres each.[1]

Nor does the distribution of ownership reflect the full extent of inequality. In addition to the 2¾ million proprietors, there is a large section of the farm population, numbering perhaps 1½ million families, which owns no land at all, and lives by share-cropping on small areas of land or by casual labour.

On all properties except the smallest and the largest cultivation by tenants is general. In recent years the proportion of the land leased to tenants has greatly increased. According to estimates made by the Ministry of Agriculture, 60 per cent of the land was rented in 1949 against 17 per cent in 1939.[2] Formerly money rents were general, but it would appear that share-cropping tenancies are now more prevalent.

The increase in tenancy is a result of the growing pressure of population. The change from owner-operation to tenancy in a plantation economy is a retrogressive adjustment, offering em-

[1] According to figures showing distribution in size-groups above 200 acres, published by the National Bank of Egypt, *Economic Bulletin*, vol. 5, no. 3, 1952.

[2] Figures quoted by Mohammed Riad Ghonemy, *Resource Use and Income in Egyptian Agriculture before and after the Land Reform, with particular reference to Economic Development* (North Carolina State College, unpublished D. Phil. thesis, 1953), p. 45.

ployment on increasingly unfavourable terms. As population increases, the price of land rises more than the income derived from it. Official figures published by the Ministry of Agriculture show that the average net income per acre in 1947–8 was £17 5*s*.;[1] and the interest rate was 9–10 per cent. The capitalized value of an acre of land should therefore have been £185, but in fact the average price of land was £430. Rent rises more than the net output, so that the landowner could obtain a higher income per acre by leasing the land than he could by farming it himself. Dr Ghonemy quotes the example of the royal estate at Kafr el-Sheikh, in Fuadia province, with an area of 16,000 acres. The average net revenue per acre owned and operated by the estate was £5 in 1937 and £15 in 1949, while the cash rents per acre for land leased on the same estate were £8 and £36 respectively.[2] According to official figures quoted by Dr Ghonemy, the average net revenue per acre of owner-operated land in Egypt was £16–19 in 1946–7 and 1947–8, while the average cash rent per feddan was £22–3.[3]

A further cause of the increase in tenancy was the rise in cotton prices during the war, which enabled small owners to increase their demand for land.

The largest properties were managed partly as plantation estates, with central management and a large administrative staff, and partly leased to tenants. In the past they were run entirely under central management, with paid labour, but tenancy has increased in recent years. On two large estates visited part of the area had been leased before the reform, although these estates were highly capitalized and there had been a large administrative staff. Some large estates were entirely cultivated by small tenants, as, for example, the former royal estate at Faroukia, described below. But some smaller estates were entirely owner operated, as, for example, a property of 400 acres at Mansura, which employed 100 labourers permanently, paid by the grant of a small allotment of land, and 1,300 labourers seasonally, in gangs hired through contractors.

The distinction between owner-operation and share-cropping tenancy is not sharp, because the practice of share-

[1] The unit is the Egyptian pound, which is worth slightly more than the £ sterling, used for convenience throughout this chapter.

[2] *Resource Use and Income*, pp. 55–6. [3] ibid. p. 57.

cropping is not a contract between landowner and tenant to divide the profits of the farm, but simply a method of reducing the costs of management and labour supervision and of cutting labour costs by reducing wages. When land is rented to a tenant-farmer with some capital, rent is payable in money, and the agreement may be of the nature of a leasehold contract. Share-cropping agreements had no legal status, and were usually not written. They run for a short period, sometimes only for one crop season. On big estates intermediaries were used: a portion of the land would be leased, in return for a fixed share of the crop, to large tenants, who would sub-let to small cultivators.

Different divisions of the gross product were used for different crops. A common arrangement was for the landowner to take all, or all but a small fraction, of the cotton crop, half or more of the wheat crop, leaving the maize and berseem for the cultivator and his buffalo. Blank agreements, with no division of the crop specified in advance, were sometimes made.

Working capital was usually provided by the landowner, in the form of seed and fertilizers for the cotton crop; the fixed capital, including the irrigation channels, is maintained by him. (The upkeep of the main canals is the responsibility of the Department of Irrigation.)

The status of the small tenant-cultivator on a holding of 2 or 3 acres was that of a labourer rather than that of a tenant. Formerly he had no security of tenure, and no incentive and no means to invest, since the landowner undertook this function, and his income barely covered his needs. His position was better than that of the casual labourer only in so far as he was more regularly employed. It is for this reason that the Agrarian Reform Law should be regarded, as has already been emphasized, primarily as a policy for agricultural labour. Although, as will be seen, it has not benefited the casual labourers, and has even caused some reduction in their employment, its most important and effective provisions are those which concern the tenant-cultivators, who form a majority of the farm population, and are landless or own small holdings of less than half an acre. Protection of the tenants by preventing eviction and reducing the rent level therefore means raising the income level and the status of a large section of the working population.

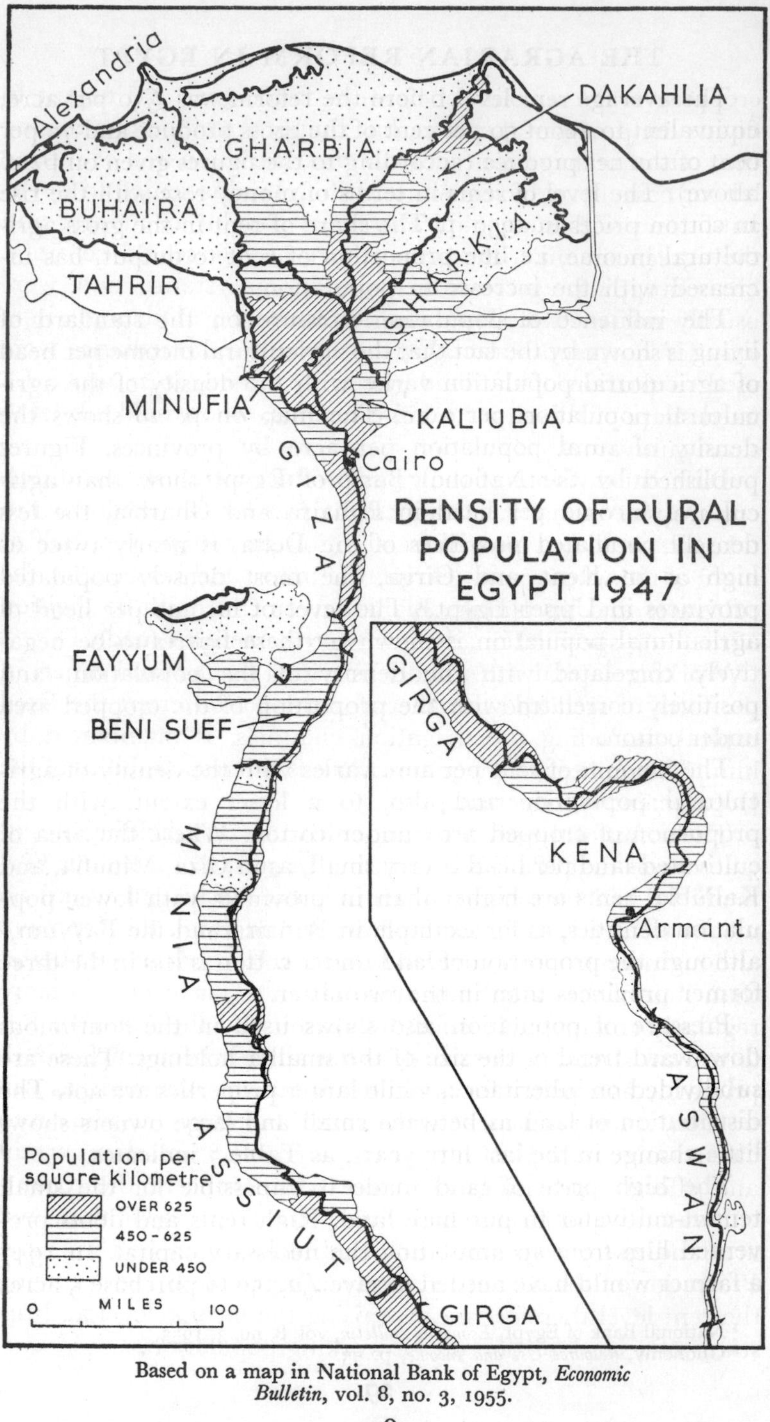

Based on a map in National Bank of Egypt, *Economic Bulletin*, vol. 8, no. 3, 1955.

The average rent level before the reform was £30 per acre, equivalent to about 50 per cent of the gross produce and 75 per cent of the net produce (according to the figures given on p. 26 above). The level of rents in terms of money rose with the rise in cotton prices in 1950–1. The share of rent in the gross agricultural income, i.e. the proportion of rent to output, has increased with the increase in population.

The influence of population pressure on the standard of living is shown by the fact that the agricultural income per head of agricultural population varies with the density of the agricultural population per acre. The map on p. 28 shows the density of rural population per acre by provinces. Figures published by the National Bank of Egypt show that agricultural income per head in Buhaira and Gharbia, the less densely populated provinces of the Delta, is nearly twice as high as in Kena and Girga, the most densely populated provinces in Upper Egypt.[1] The level of income per head of agricultural population is shown by these figures to be negatively correlated with the density of the population, and positively correlated with the proportion of the cropped area under cotton.

The amount of rent per acre varies with the density of agricultural population and also, to a lesser extent, with the proportion of cropped area under cotton. Where the area of cultivated land per head is very small, as in Giza, Minufia, and Kaliubia, rents are higher than in provinces with lower population densities, as for example in Buhaira and the Fayyum,[2] although the proportion of land under cotton is less in the three former provinces than in the two latter.

Pressure of population also shows itself in the continuous downward trend of the size of the smaller holdings. These are subdivided on inheritance, while larger properties are not. The distribution of land as between small and large owners shows little change in the last fifty years, as Table 7 indicates.

The high price of land made it impossible for the small tenant-cultivator to purchase land. High rents and debts prevented him from accumulating the necessary capital. In 1947 a farmer would have needed to save £2,350 to purchase 5 acres

[1] National Bank of Egypt, *Economic Bulletin*, vol. 8, no. 3, 1955.
[2] Ghonemy, *Resource Use and Income*, p. 53.

TABLE 7

Egypt: Agricultural Land by Size of Holdings, 1900–52

Size-group (acres)	*No. of owners (000)*		*Area (000 acres)*		*Average area (acres)*	
	1900	*1952*	*1900*	*1952*	*1900*	*1952*
5 and under	761	2,642	1,113	2,122	1·5	0·8
Over 5–under 10	80	79	560	526	7·0	6·6
,, 10– ,, 20	40	47	551	638	13·8	13·6
,, 20– ,, 30	12	13	301	309	25·1	23·6
,, 30– ,, 50	9	9	345	344	38·3	37·4
,, 50	12	12	2,244	2,043	187·0	174·6
Total	914	2,802	5,114	5,982	5·6	2·1

NOTE: Original table in feddans.

(SOURCE: National Bank of Egypt.)

of land, together with the necessary capital equipment. For labourers with an agricultural wage of 94 millièmes per day (1*s.* 10*d.*) the purchase of land at this price is clearly out of the question.[1]

Consequently the outstanding feature of the land system before the reform was gross inequality, and also growing inequality. The growth of population on the land allowed landowners to use their monopoly power by charging a higher price for the use of land, in the form of ever more extortionate rents, while at the same time it increased inequality through the continuous subdivision of the smaller properties.

Among the landowners two types can be distinguished. One is the very large landowner, generally an absentee and always a lavish consumer, usually in Europe. Of him it has been said 'Il gaspille en une soirée ce qui ferait vivre ses fellahs une année, trouvant très naturels et leur misère et son luxe.'[2] The other is the landowner with 300 or 400 acres, living on his estate or in a provincial town. He may be a professional agriculturist, farming most efficiently, even carrying out scientific experiments with seed varieties, fertilizers, and irrigation dates; or he may leave the management to an agent, and neglect the estate. Among

[1] ibid. p. 61. [2] Ayrout, *Fellahs d'Égypte*, p. 46.

the large estate owners few families did anything to improve the conditions of their workers, and then only by providing some medical service. Nor did the state do anything for the fellahin, except through the provision of health clinics in some villages; in the years after the war these had made considerable progress.

THE AGRARIAN REFORM OF 1952 AND ITS EFFECTS

Any real measure of agrarian reform is bound to be contentious. In Egypt the landowners have never previously experienced any encroachment on their interests, and paid only light taxes on their property. From their standpoint, any reform appears catastrophic. In 1952 it was said that reform was certain to reduce production. In 1954–5, this hope having failed, the commonly voiced criticisms were that the cultivators were no better off, and that labour had been displaced. There were also vague charges of waste and mismanagement on the part of the authorities. Some landowners have found new fields of activity, and are not overtly critical. Others are still hostile, and one even tearfully asserted that the reform was Communism, engineered by the Americans. More disinterested critics think that the peasants have only changed masters, and speak of collective farming. The students of Cairo University, on the other hand, expressed the view that the reform had not done enough, and wanted to go faster and farther than the Government has seen fit to do.

What follows is an attempt to assess, in the light of these criticisms, the results of the law, so far as these could be ascertained in visits to three estates and in conversation with the authorities, with some observers in a position to judge independently, and with a few landowners. One estate was seen on an official visit, the others visited independently of official guidance. Official statements have been checked where possible, since there is a natural tendency on the part of the authorities, in the face of so much criticism, to be over-optimistic. On one important point, the finance of the reform, no information is published, nor were balance sheets available at the estates. On the estates, officials and co-operative society secretaries gave information readily on agricultural questions and on farm incomes, but it was not possible to press inquiries about finance. The information is therefore not complete by any means. On the crucial question, the benefits to the fellahin, there is sufficient evidence to refute the criticism that they are no better off. Nor does the charge of mismanagement appear valid; on the contrary, the reform appears to have been carried through with a high degree of administrative competence. In this respect, it compares well with other countries, even with the highly efficient reform in Italy.

As has been stated, the Agrarian Reform Law had three aims: the redistribution of ownership; the reduction of rent; and the raising of agricultural wages. The provisions of the law, and their results in practice, may be considered under each of these headings.

1. *Expropriation and Redistribution.* The law, in Article 1, laid down that 'no person may own more than 200 acres of land'. Landowners may retain up to 300 acres, if they distribute 50 acres to each of two children. Land in excess of this maximum was to be requisitioned by the Government over a period of five years.

Land under reclamation was exempted from expropriation under Article 2, which allowed companies and private persons to own more than 200 acres of fallow or desert land under reclamation. Land owned by industrial companies is exempted for a period of twenty-five years, and also, under a later amendment, land belonging to agricultural, scientific, and industrial societies in existence before the decree was issued.

Owners of expropriated land receive compensation at the rate of ten times the rental value, assessed at seven times the basic land tax (i.e. at seventy times the basic land tax). Tax assessments were low, amounting to £2–£4 per acre, and the rental value fixed on this basis is therefore much lower than the real rental value. The legal rental value would range from £140 to £280 per acre, whereas land prices before the reform ranged from £400 to £600 per acre. To the sum payable in compensation for the land must be added the value of buildings, installed machinery (chiefly pumps), and trees. Compensation is payable in state bonds, bearing interest at 3 per cent, and redeemable in thirty years. The bonds are not negotiable, but may be used in payment for uncultivated land purchased from the Government for reclamation, or in payment of land tax and death duties.

The requisitioned land was to be distributed among small farmers and farm labourers, in holdings of not less than 2 acres and not more than 5 acres per family. In distributing land preference was to be given to those actually cultivating the land as tenants or labourers. Owners of more than 5 acres are not eligible to receive land. Orchards were to be distributed in lots not exceeding 20 acres among graduates of agricultural institutes, provided that they do not already own more than 10 acres of land.

The new owner was to pay, in instalments over a period of thirty years, the full purchase price of the land, assessed as above, plus interest at 3 per cent and 15 per cent for the costs of administration. Until the purchase price is fully paid, the holding may not be sold or otherwise disposed of. Since the purchase price is based on rental value based on land-tax assessment, the instalment payable annually is much less than the previous rent paid, usually by about 50 per cent.

The distribution of an expropriated estate is not made until its income, the number of persons dependent on it, and their resources outside it as owner and tenant, have been surveyed by the officials of the Higher Committee for Agrarian Reform, the department charged with the execution of the law. Great care is taken to ensure that the land is fairly distributed among all those who are entitled to benefit. The size of holding granted varies between 2 and 3 acres, according to the size of the family. The general rule is that all former tenants receive land, with the exception of those who own more than 5 acres (these are few). Permanent labourers usually receive a holding, but not all casual labourers can do so, since there is not sufficient land. As the new owners do not wish to employ labour, some displacement of labour results. How much is unknown: a figure of 5 per cent of the total number of tenants and labourers previously employed is officially given, and confirmed by observation.[1]

The scale of redistribution is not large. Of Egypt's total agricultural land area of 6 million acres, 1,177,000 acres, or

[1] See Sir Malcolm Darling, 'Land Reform in Italy and Egypt', in *Yearbook of Agricultural Co-operation, 1956* (Oxford, Blackwell).

20 per cent, was held in properties exceeding 200 acres. About half of this total was scheduled for expropriation and redistribution, so that land reform in the strict sense can affect at most only about 10 per cent of Egypt's land. The official figure for land liable to expropriation is 656,736 acres, requisitioned from 1,789 landowners. It is probable, however, that the total actually available for redistribution will be less than the area legally liable to expropriation, because many landowners escaped expropriation through private sales.

Under Article 4 of the law, landowners were permitted to sell land in excess of the legal maximum in lots not exceeding 5 acres, to farmers (not relatives) whose holding did not exceed 5 acres. This provision was included as a compromise, to satisfy the Minister of Finance, who believed in building up a peasant middle class. Very large areas of land were quickly sold, and the price of land fell by 50 per cent. The official figures[1] give 145,000 acres as the total sold privately; but it may well have been more. Landowners evaded the provision obliging them to sell to small farmers, and instead sold to larger farmers, commercial interests, and civil servants.[2] Had this provision continued in force, no land would have been available for distribution. Article 4 was therefore superseded, later in 1952, by a decree which prohibited private sales of land liable to expropriation after 31 October 1952.

The total land available for redistribution is therefore presumably not more than 500,000 acres, perhaps less. Up to the middle of 1955 a total of 320,000 acres had been expropriated, of which 120,000 were the property of the King and other members of the royal family.

The Agrarian Reform Law made no special provision concerning the estates of the royal family, which cover in all 178,000 acres. The law for the confiscation of the property of 'the Mohammed Ali dynasty', however, laid down that these estates should be expropriated in full, leaving no residual holding, and without compensation. Since the Higher Committee

[1] These may be found in the Higher Committee for Agrarian Reform's *Replies to the United Nations Questionnaires relating to Egyptian Agrarian Reform Measures* (Cairo, 1955; hereafter referred to as *Replies to United Nations Questionnaires*).

[2] An official publication of the Higher Committee for Agrarian Reform states that among such sales of land there were some in contravention of the law, which the Higher Committee intend to annul, in order to make the land subject to expropriation (Sayed Marei, *Two Years of Agrarian Reform*, 1954, p. 11).

receives payments of purchase instalments from the farmers in respect of their holdings, but need pay no compensation, the acquisition of these properties greatly facilitates the self-financing of the reform.

Up to the end of 1955, an area of 250,000 acres had been distributed to 69,000 families, comprising 415,000 persons, in holdings averaging $3\frac{1}{2}$ acres.

The recipients of land gain an immediate increase in income. During the first year after the estate is requisitioned, the new landholders pay rent to the state at the fixed rent maximum (i.e. seven times the basic land tax). This is about half the previous rent level. In the following year they receive provisional title to the holding, and thereafter pay the instalments of the purchase price. In addition to the instalment, the farmer also pays the co-operative society, of which he is a member, for seed, fertilizers, machine cultivation, and administrative expenses. The payment is effected by delivery of the whole of the cotton crop. The total sum payable annually works out at about five times the basic tax assessment. In addition, he pays land tax. His total expenses are therefore equal to six times the basic land tax. Assuming that the gross income remains the same, the net income increases by the difference between the previous rent level and the annual payment. Gross income per acre has remained the same, and on the expropriated estates has risen slightly, as a result of heavier use of fertilizers.

An example may illustrate the method by which the income redistribution is carried out. At Faroukia, in the province of Sharkia, an estate of 1,500 acres, formerly the property of King Farouk, has been distributed to 511 former tenants. (A few were excluded by reason of ownership outside the estate.) As tenants, they had formerly paid rent on a share-cropping basis, under which the landowner took all the cotton and half the wheat, leaving the tenant half the wheat for sale, the maize for his own consumption, and the berseem[1] for the buffalo. This was a usual type of arrangement, and comparatively favourable: the landowner provided seed and fertilizer for the cotton crop, and got the labour free.

Under the new law the former tenants received holdings be-

[1] Egyptian clover.

tween 2 and 3 acres, varying with the size of the family, and corresponding roughly to the acreage cultivated before. They deliver the whole of the cotton crop to the co-operative for sale, as they formerly delivered it to the estate manager, and the proceeds of the sale meet the cost of the instalment payment, land tax, the cost of the fertilizers and seed, and administrative expenses. The farmers retain their maize and berseem as before. The chief difference in their position is that the whole income from the wheat crop is their property, instead of half. The gain in money income is equivalent to £20 per holding, or £7 per acre, an increase of 50 per cent on the former net income. Figures for four provinces examined by Sir Malcolm Darling show that an increase of 50 per cent is general.[1]

There is no change in the type of farming or the scale of operation. The estate is still managed as one unit, and sales of the cash crops are handled by the management. Cotton finances the transfer of property, provides the working capital, and covers the costs of administration. In 1954 the proceeds of the sale of the cotton crop through the co-operative amounted to £27,000. This sum covered the annual instalments of the purchase price payable by the farmers (fixed at £12 per acre), land tax (£3 per acre), the cost of seed, fertilizers, and services provided through the co-operative, and the costs of administration. The total annual payment made per acre is £18; on the basis of the land-tax assessment the annual instalment of purchase price should be only £7 (i.e. the tax of £3 × 70 ÷ 30). It is, however, fixed at £12, which must be an arbitrary figure, since for former royal property no compensation is payable. In the absence of published accounts, it cannot be ascertained how much of the £18 paid by the farmer by delivery of the cotton crop is taken up by the costs of operation and working capital and how much is profit.

The requisitioned estates vary considerably in the amount of capital invested per acre, in gross output per acre, in the costs of operation, and in the level of rents charged before the reform. How much of the total income from the sale of the cash crops is to be allotted to new investment in fixed capital, or in additional working capital, and how much is to be distri-

[1] 'Land Reform in Italy and Egypt'.

buted, is a matter for the accountants to decide. In Upper Egypt the large estates were highly capitalized and extremely profitable (as, for example, the 5,000-acre estate at Armant, with a gross income of £235,000 from the sale of the sugar crop). On these estates rents were high and wages low: consequently the gain in the incomes of the new farmers is much greater than on the estates in Lower Egypt, where rents were lower. One estate visited, Bourgaya in Minia province (Upper Egypt), was exceptionally productive, with yields well above the average, and here, according to information given at the estate, farmers' net incomes had risen by nearly 100 per cent, to £39 per acre.

Since there are these local differences, the authorities have worked on the principle of levelling up incomes in Upper Egypt, and so allowing a larger increase in the farmers' net income than in Lower Egypt, where incomes were higher. The object is to guarantee a minimum income of £16 per member of the farmer's family.

Figures have been published by the Higher Committee for Agrarian Reform which show still greater increases in income, ranging between 100 and 200 per cent, on six estates, three in Lower and three in Upper Egypt, where the largest increases are shown.[1] These figures may not be representative of the average, though it is certainly true that redistribution has brought much greater gains in Upper Egypt, because rents were exceedingly high before the reform. On the basis of the figures analysed by Sir Malcolm Darling, and of direct observation, it is safe to conclude that cultivators' incomes have risen by about 50 per cent on estates expropriated in Lower Egypt, and that the income gain is greater in Upper Egypt, and may be as much as 100 per cent.

There can be no doubt that the farmers have gained a considerable increase in income. It is true that they have not become independent owners, and that the co-operatives are managed by state officials, in what is in effect a system of collective farming. Whether this form of organization is essential is considered later. None the less, there is a gain in status as well as in income, for the new farmers have economic security comparable to that of individual ownership.

[1] See *Replies to United Nations Questionnaires*, p. 156.

There can also be no doubt that the new landholders appreciate the change. Inquiries as to whether they are better off would naturally be answered affirmatively when officials are present. But the reply is often so lengthy and emphatic that its sincerity convinces, even though it is unintelligible. Sir Malcolm Darling[1] quotes examples:

> The most enthusiastic of the new owners was the society's secretary. When asked whether he was better off, he touched the ground at his feet, flung his arms upwards to the ceiling and exclaimed—'*that* is the difference between then and now', and still doubting whether we understood the magnitude of the change, he added almost in despair—'I cannot explain to you how much better off we are.'
>
> On another estate, large enough to have 9 societies, members showed the same lively appreciation of the change. 'Before, we had to give up our crops at low valuation: we can now do what we like. We used to mix maize and wheat for our bread; now we eat more wheat, and meat twice a week instead of once. Our extra money we spend on soap, food and clothes, on four shirts instead of two. Ten of us have bought wirelesses at £20 to £25 each, but first of all we buy buffaloes. Twenty of us have recently married; we no longer have to wait four or five years to do this, but we still borrow or sell cattle to do it. Ten per cent have more than one wife, one has just taken a third.' Such was the burden of their talk, summed up in the parting remark, 'We all very happy'. Here the shops had increased from four to nine, and owing to the greater consumption of meat the butchers were killing several times a week instead of once or twice.

2. *The Reduction of Rents*. Article 3 of the law decreed that the rent of agricultural land may not exceed seven times the basic land tax. As has already been explained, this meant that the level fixed was much lower than the previous level of rent. In the case of share-cropping rents, the law decreed that the owners' share shall not exceed one-half, after deduction of all expenses. This provision also meant a large reduction in rent, since before the reform rent on an average represented one-half of the gross produce.

Agricultural land may be let only to a person who intends to farm it himself. Leases of land may not be concluded for less than three years, and must be in writing. In the absence of a written agreement, the rent shall be deemed to be based

[1] 'Land Reform in Italy and Egypt'.

on crop-sharing for a period of three years, during which the owner's share shall be one-half, after deduction of all expenses.

It is always extremely difficult to enforce legislation for the control and reduction of rents, and in a country where the demand for land steadily rises, as it does in Egypt, enforcement would appear impossible. All that can be said with certainty is that rent reduction did take place, and that in January 1955 rents had fallen by about 40 per cent. This fact was attested by many independent authorities, of whom the officials of the Crédit Foncier were the best qualified to hold an impartial opinion. Landowners were loud in criticism of the rent reduction.

Enforcement was possible because the reform alarmed landowners, and also because cotton prices fell. The price of land fell sharply in 1952–3 to about half its previous level, as a result of private sales of land. Without the threat of expropriation, enforcement of the rent reduction would certainly not have been possible. By the end of 1954 land prices were rising again, and possibly as the fear of expropriation recedes rents may rise in contravention of the law.

In the meantime the incomes of farm tenants have risen. An official statement puts the increase at 50 per cent, from an average net income of £19 per acre to £29 per acre. Four million farmers are estimated to benefit, and the aggregate increase in the income of farm tenants is therefore £40 million.[1] These figures possibly exaggerate the extent of the increase, but the numbers affected are presumably correct and an increase certainly took place. This improvement in income and legal status for a very large section of the farm population is by far the most valuable achievement of the reform, greatly exceeding in importance the benefits of redistribution. But it should not be concluded that rent reduction is an easy type of reform, for without the compulsory expropriation of large properties it would not have been effective.

3. *The Raising of Agricultural Wages*. The Agrarian Reform Law provided that the wages of agricultural workers should be fixed annually by an official committee, formed by the Minister

[1] *Replies to United Nations Questionnaires*, p. 8.

of Agriculture, with an official of the Ministry as President, and composed of six members chosen by the Minister, of whom three should represent owners and tenants of land, and three agricultural labourers. Agricultural workers were given the right to form trade unions. A subsequent decree laid down minimum wage rates, 18 piastres (3*s.* 6*d.*) per day for men and 10 piastres (2*s.*) a day for women.

These rates have not generally been enforceable. On expropriated estates, the former tenants become landholders. When estates were operated as a single unit, the majority of the former labourers acquire secure tenant status with a guaranteed minimum income. In neither case is additional employment created, and, as has already been said, there is usually some reduction in employment. In the Liberation province,[1] the minimum wage rates are paid, to about 14,000 labourers employed on land reclamation and building; to this extent wages have risen. The reduction in employment resulting from redistribution has been more than offset by this scheme, and by the land reclamation and industrial construction work undertaken in the last three years.

The Effects on Production and Investment

At the time that the Land Reform decree was issued, its opponents argued that the distribution of the land would certainly reduce production. It was then assumed that the reform would mean division into very small farms in place of the large estates. Since Egyptian agriculture is so highly geared to intensive cropping and high cropping rates, the danger was real. Some of the very large estates—not all—were extremely well farmed and well equipped with capital, which the tenant-cultivators did not possess.

As it is, these forebodings have not been realized, because there has been no transition to small farming. On the three estates visited in 1955 yields were slightly higher than before, as a result of the good harvests and also because more fertilizers were used. This was the case even when yields had previously been exceptionally high, as on the sugar plantations at Armant. Since 1952 yields per acre for all crops have risen and the production of all crops, except cotton, has increased. The area

[1] See below, p. 49.

under cotton has declined as a result of the fall in prices. The overall production results cannot, however, be attributed to the redistribution, which up to the present has affected only a small proportion of the land. But the reduction of rents, which affects a very large proportion of the land, has been accompanied by heavier use of fertilizers, so that the reform has certainly contributed to the increase in production.

The reform is sometimes held responsible for the decline in the quality of cotton since 1952, for the higher grades are not coming forward to the same extent. The true explanation of this decline is that the Government, in fixing cotton-seed prices, mistakenly priced the top grades at a higher level than the low-quality seed. Another supposed effect of the reform, the 'black spot', which concerns Liverpool, is caused by packing cotton in nitrate bags.

The reform was intended to increase investment in industry, by breaking the landowners' desire to hold wealth in the form of land, thus increasing the amount of new investment. It was the original intention to make the land bonds negotiable, to achieve this result. However, as the bonds are not negotiable (except for the purchase of land for reclamation), the payment of compensation cannot cause the landowners to reinvest. Indirectly, the reform probably has caused some transfer of capital into industry, commerce, and building, since the proceeds of the private sales of land were probably reinvested in urban building, possibly also in industry. Prices of land have now risen again, for the demand is insatiable, so that the transfer is not continuing. There may have been a net increase in investment, in so far as 'good Pashas' who have been expropriated now have a finger in many financial pies, and prudence dictates that they should invest more and consume less.

Investment in agriculture and land reclamation has certainly increased. On the large estates which have been expropriated new pumps are being installed, and more fertilizers are used. Some expropriated landowners are active in land reclamation. (One, in Minia, had made a new estate out in the desert, and called it 'Hell'.) British companies are still engaged in land reclamation, and are not affected by the law, since, as has been stated, land under reclamation is exempt from redistribution.

STATE OR CO-OPERATIVE FARMING

The view that reform means collective farming is partially right. Article 4 of the law describes the new landholder as 'the proprietor'. But he does not acquire ownership for thirty years, and in the meantime is not free to sell or sub-let or to farm independently. It was the intention of the law that the functions of the former landowner in distributing seed and fertilizer, and in marketing, should be taken over by a co-operative society, membership of which is obligatory for all grantees of land. The society should carry out these tasks through its Board of Management, composed of eleven members elected by the farmers. The law gave the co-operatives wide powers. They are to provide loans to their members, and to organize the supply of seed, fertilizers, livestock, and agricultural machinery, and the storage and transport of crops—all of which might, of course, be undertaken on behalf of independent farmers by a co-operative society of the ordinary supply and marketing type. But the functions of the co-operative are also to include 'organizing the cultivation and exploitation of the land in the most efficient manner, including seed selection, varieties of crops, pest control and digging of canals and drains.' They are also to sell the principal crops on behalf of the members, 'after deducting the price of the land, government taxes and agricultural and other loans'. They are required to render all agricultural and social services on behalf of their members. Societies are to be officially controlled, and must exercise their duties under the supervision of officials chosen by the Ministry of Social Affairs.

In practice, the management is taken over by the official manager appointed by the Higher Committee. He is highly trained and experienced, sometimes a former estate manager, and has under his control an administrative staff comprising accountants, agronomists, mechanics, store-keepers, and foremen. He is not a member of the Board, but can refer decisions of which he disapproves to the Higher Committee. In practice, disagreement probably does not arise. At Faroukia the members of the Board held a meeting, but the manager had prepared the agenda. They listened impassively while the man from the Ministry explained the arrangements for seed purchase, and approved. The topic of breeding rabbits roused sudden interest, but the manager introduced two girl experts from the Ministry of Agriculture who explained the programme for the distribution of breeding stock, and again the Board acquiesced. They raised points concerning the organization of labour, and it was evident that they were really a Works Council, which can voice grievances and give advice, but does not and cannot control operations.

This is hardly surprising: it could not be expected that the peasants, so long accustomed to acquiescence, could immediately develop the power to manage their own affairs. There are some real co-operative societies in existence, as, for example, the star example of Zafaran; but the newly created ones are artificial. Sir Malcolm Darling believes that a strong educational effort could create a co-operative spirit, for which the Egyptian village is good ground, by reason of its informal mutual-help arrangements, and its family network. In the meantime, the aim of substituting the co-operative society for the landlord is not realized;

> for the time being, the State must take his place, with the infant societies led paternally by the hand until they can learn to walk by themselves. The teacher is therefore all-important, and if not properly taught himself, paternal may never develop into co-operative control, may even harden into bureaucratic.[1]

Sir Malcolm doubts whether co-operative societies of this size—with 1,500 members or more—could function as genuine co-operatives.

Even if the co-operative societies should gain the power to manage their own affairs, they would still be obliged to farm collectively. The way in which the land is laid out obliges all farmers to follow a common rotation. The area of the estate is large—2,000, 5,000, even 10,000 acres. The whole area is divided into blocks, and in each block the land is divided into three or more large fields, each under a single crop. The farmers receive a piece of land in each field, so that their total holding is divided into three. In each harvest season of the year each field is under one crop, and each holding is under three different crops. The pieces composing the holding may be contiguous, stretching crosswise across the lengthwise field division. This was the case at Faroukia, where the field plan resembles that

[1] 'Land Reform in Italy and Egypt'.

used in the new settlements in South Italy—perhaps a result of advice given by Professor Bandini. The general field plan resembles that of the old open-field system in Europe.

The field layout facilitates deep ploughing (otherwise impeded in the Delta by permanent drains) and farming operations in general, as, for example, the co-operative picking of the cotton crop. In Sir Malcolm Darling's view the compulsory rotation is the most productive feature of the reform. There has been no change to small-scale farming. On the contrary, in so far as estates were rented to tenants, as even the largest were in part, the scale of operation is larger. Tractor-cultivation is being introduced, wherever it was not used before, which should allow the cultivator to reduce his working livestock and produce more meat and milk. It used to be said that Egypt is a country of large properties and small farms. So far as the requisitioned land is concerned, the reverse is true, for it is now held by small proprietors and farmed in large units.

Income from the land, however, is distributed in accordance with the output from each holding, and not, as in fully collective farming, in accordance with labour. The cash crops are sold to the co-operative for marketing, and the proceeds are credited to each member, after deduction of the annual instalment of the purchase price, the land tax, and the cost of fertilizers, seed, machine use, and any other services provided by the co-operative. Subsistence and fodder crops are retained by the cultivator. Livestock are owned by the farmers individually, but the estate dairy herds are owned by the co-operative.

On estates of the type so far requisitioned, it would not have been economic to divide the land into independent units. Official control was needed to maintain and add to the fixed capital; on the three estates visited there had been considerable new investment, since the reform, in pumps, wells, and machinery.

Management on estates of this kind is a professional job. There is nothing simple or medieval—as the open-field rotation may suggest—about an Egyptian estate. It combines a variety of complex routines. Lavish use of machinery is combined with lavish use of labour. At Bourgaya, in Minia province, a former private estate of 2,000 acres, previously partly directly farmed and partly leased, and extremely productive, had been divided among 800 families. It used steam ploughing, on the so-called Fowler system, by which two cumbrous 45-h.p. steam engines (fuelled by Diesel oil or cotton stalks) uncoil a cable driving a plough which can cultivate as much as 20 acres a day. The whole area is under perennial irrigation, the fields divided into patches 6 feet square by shallow ridged ditches, which are ploughed over after every harvest and must be re-dug for every crop, so that labour requirements are enormous. Technical methods are as old as history and as new as science can make them. New pumps are being installed, while Archimedes screws are carried swiftly about on donkeys. Camels in the great court-yard load quarter-tons of nitrates; but the vines are fertilized by the manure supplied by 15,000 pairs of pigeons, housed in the fantastic white dovecote. Machine spraying with bulk oil is used in the superb orange grove, still awaiting the 'agricultural graduates', who, according to the law, should farm it co-operatively in units of 10 acres. Orange crates are made at lightning speed from date-palm stalks, held in the craftsman's toes. All this intricacy needs expert supervision. The co-operative board met in an optimistic mood (net income per acre is unusually high) and the Chairman spoke powerfully in favour of the revolution.

The great estates of Upper Egypt are more highly capitalized and mechanized than most estates in Lower Egypt. The low cost of labour is not, as is often believed, the reason for the lack of mechanization, but the permanent drains which in the Delta impede tractor ploughing. In Upper Egypt the drains are not permanent, and although wages are much lower than in the Delta, big estates use more machinery. The sugar-cane plantations in Kena province are very highly capitalized indeed, equipped with railways to move the crop, caterpillar tractors for rooting up the cane, and pump irrigation.

The question of the right form of organization on the plantation estates was difficult. Most of the land is under sugar, which remains in the ground for three years on good land and two years on medium-quality land, and consequently the land cannot be divided into holdings to provide subsistence crops. The Higher Committee at first intended to run these plantations with employed labour. Before the reform these estates were centrally managed as to pump irrigation and heavy machinery, but the land was leased to large tenants who cropped it with gangs of low-paid labourers. The Higher Committee decided that this system was inconsistent with the aim of raising the income of the cultivator, and therefore decided to retain the land in state ownership, leasing it to a large number of share-croppers with secure tenure and a minimum share income.[1]

At Armant, across the Nile twenty miles south of Luxor, an estate of 5,000 acres, formerly the property of Ahmed Abboud, has been reorganized on this basis. Of its total area, 2,250 acres are under sugar-cane, 1,000 under cotton, and the remainder under wheat, vegetables, and berseem. The greater part of the land is under perennial irrigation, supplied by two Diesel pump installations, with five pumps totalling 850 h.p. A new pump is being installed, to convert the basin land to perennial irrigation. The gross income from the sugar-cane alone on this estate amounted to £235,000 per annum. Cane yields average 50 tons to the acre, 20 per cent above the national average.

The estate has now been allotted, under permanent share-cropping agreements, to 1,700 families. The land is divided according to its quality into three areas: the best land, which grows sugar-cane for three years in succession and is then replanted with cane; the second quality, which grows cane for two years followed by one year under another crop before being replanted; and the third quality, not good enough for cane, which grows cotton, wheat, and berseem. Each family receives two pieces of land, a holding of 2–5 acres comprising either one piece of the first quality and one piece of the third, or two pieces of the second quality, so that in any one year half the holding is under cane and half under other crops.

Formerly the land was leased to 100 contractors who employed labour at the wage of £3 per month. The net income now earned by the share-cropping farmers (according to information given at Armant in 1955) is now £6 per month for a holding of 2 acres, £9 for a holding of 3 acres. This corresponds to net income per acre of £36 per annum; gross output per acre for the whole estate averages £100. Costs of management,

[1] It is interesting that a somewhat similar type of organization has been introduced in Puerto Rico on the Proportionate Profit Farms. See UN, Dept. of Economic Affairs, *Progress in Land Reform*, p. 86.

irrigation, machinery, seed, and fertilizers therefore account for £64 per acre.

Harvesting needs more labour than the family can provide, and is carried out in groups of four families working together on each other's holdings, the men cutting and loading the cane on to camels, women stripping the leaves for fodder and loading them on to donkeys. The cane is carried to trucks on the estate railway for transport to the sugar factory and weight is recorded in the tenant's name by a tarbushed overseer. Across the river from Luxor there is a very similar scene in the mortuary chapel of Prince Menna, manager of the royal granaries and director of the cadastral survey, depicted as he checked the output of the harvest fields 3,000 years ago.

The dark side at Armant is seen in the two *esbahs* (the landowners' tied villages) on the borders of the estate. The estate employs five villages, three of which are prosperous, and two very poor. In these villages huts are only six feet high, without windows or doors, and their inhabitants were obviously destitute. Only a few had acquired a holding and the rest lived by casual labour. Earnings were said to be higher, but were evidently still very low. Probably the equalization of incomes results in concentrating employment among the families of the share-croppers, reducing the employment for the labourers. So far no houses have been built for the fellahin, though areas of land have been reserved for the purpose. The contrast between this level of living and the immensely high productivity of the land and its splendid equipment is a grim reminder of the gravity of Egypt's land problem.

The reform in practice is very managerial. The idea of creating a strong small-peasant class, which influenced liberal opinion when the law was passed, has disappeared completely. So far as the very large estates are concerned, it is difficult to see how this course could have been avoided. Up to the middle of 1955, only the very large estates had been taken over. Expropriation of the smaller estates had begun. Presumably the same methods of management will be used here also, though it will be costly to maintain such a large administrative staff on farms of 100–200 acres. On estates where tenancy has been the rule there is no technical reason why farmers should not become independent. Most of Egypt's cotton comes off the small and medium-sized farms, and distribution of seed and fertilizers creates no problems, though doubtless it could be improved. But independence, in a country so densely populated, could only be a short-term condition. Ownership of land does not provide income stability, because of the continuous pressure to subdivide and sub-let which reduces farms to uneconomic sizes, and renders them very weak risk-bearers. The experience of other over-populated countries, for example India, shows that one of the main problems of reform is to make ownership stick. The co-operative form of organization gives greater income stability. What the farmer gains is not economic independence, but a higher income with a guaranteed minimum; he can consume the income gain, since the management looks after investment. Overall financial control has been used to build up a stabilization fund to maintain farm incomes in years of bad harvests or low prices—a wise and very necessary precaution in an economy so dependent on one crop. The lack of independence is the price of greater social and economic security.

In practice, though not in theory, the redistribution of property means that the land is nationalized. Nationalization of the land is nothing new in Egypt's long history; one successful measure, linked with grain stabilization, is described in Genesis, and since then there have been other occasions. The control of Egypt's water is so highly centralized by the Nile itself that to any strong government the step to state ownership of the land seems easy. What is new is the idea of a fair deal for the fellahin, or at any rate a fairer deal. The real change is that the cultivator has a recognized legal status; that, in itself, is an immense change for the better, outweighing any criticism. If the reform can maintain this position, that is the greatest measure of success. The Government has done as much as was practicable, and far more than might have been expected.

It is true that the reform does not benefit the casual labourers, the poorest class. It means a real gain for the majority of the fellahin, either by giving them protection as tenants, or by giving them secure status as co-operative farmers. But it does not benefit the entire farm population. This is inevitable. No reform, even if it went much farther than the present measure, could provide land for all in this congested country, or could increase employment in agriculture. That the reform has not benefited the casual labourers is a result, not of a weakness in reform policy, but of population pressure. The Government can do no more than press on with its plans for more land and more industry.

It might be expected, none the less, that the difference in benefits would create jealousy, as between tenants and new owners, and as between these beneficiaries and the landless. Rent-paying tenants might demand the expropriation of all landowners, and the landless might demand land. On this point, the attitude of the fellahin, no outside observer can venture an opinion. Some authorities think that the situation is unstable, and that there is unrest, while officials of the Higher Committee believe that, so long as redistribution is carried out equitably between the claimants, no new antagonisms are created. Whether that is the case or not, the need for more land and more industry is increased, rather than diminished, by the greater degree of security which the reform provides for the majority of the farm population.

THE LIBERATION PROVINCE

The Liberation (Tahrir) province is a community creation, in the desert west of the Delta and south of Alexandria. Work first began on it eighteen months after the revolution, in December 1953. The area covered by the province is 1,200,000 acres; it is to include twelve districts, each to contain eleven villages. In fifteen years' time, when the additional water from the High Dam is available, there should be 800,000 acres of reclaimed land. At present there are 10,000 acres in process of reclamation, of which 5,000 acres are already under cultivation, water being supplied by pumps from the Rashid branch of the Nile.

'What exists now is only a bridgehead', said Major Mohammed Magdi Hassanein, the manager and moving spirit of the Tahrir province. Its objects are 'to accustom our people to the desert, to make the young intellectuals practically active in reclamation, and to give more work'. 'Humanity is to be the keynote', he said, and referred to the traditions of ancient Egypt as the inspiration. Sport and music are to be the influences in this new liberated life, not technical education, for that the inhabitants will acquire in the course of their work. No foreign experts are to be employed. The women are to participate fully, even to the extent of taking up sport—a revolution indeed. The province thus embodies the hopes of the Government for the new Egypt, an idea which action has created.

The new national spirit is evident in the names of the new settlements. The capital is Nasr, meaning victory, the secret password on the day of the revolution. The four villages which are being completed are named Omar Shahin, after a victim of the Canal fighting, Umm Sabr, after a woman victim, Omar Makram, a popular hero in the time of Mohammed Ali, and Ahmed Arabi, after Arabi Pasha. Each village is to have 230 houses, with 1,500 acres of land, of which 12,000 will be cultivated. So far they are not inhabited; the selected settlers are still being trained.

Land reclamation is not to be the only economic base of the province; it will include new industries. Those which supply the needs of the settlement are already in operation; a machine-repair shop, a furniture factory, and the cement brick works. An ammunition factory is under construction.

Fourteen thousand workers are at present employed in reclamation and construction. They come from Upper Egypt, and also from the adjacent provinces of Minufia and Dakahlia. Workers are paid at the rate of £12 per month,[1] a very high wage by comparison with existing rates, which in Upper Egypt would average only £3 per month. (Its immediate economic effect is a rise in wages for these low-paid workers.)

The land reclamation, the factories, and the building are directed by a large professional staff; it has evidently been possible to attract well-qualified engineers, scientists, and managers. The scheme has found a good architect. Community development schemes are rarely attractive, but the public buildings, the school, and the small mosque are simply and well built in clear pale colours which are in harmony with the desert landscape.

The settlers who are to populate the new villages are selected by Major Gamal Zaki, director of the Social Affairs Department, who 'majored' in the United States in community de-

[1] This official figure was confirmed in private conversations with the workmen.

velopment, and is terrifyingly adept in the jargon of the new subject. Settlers, he said, are selected scientifically on social, medical, and psychological tests. As social qualifications applicants must possess only one wife, no dependants other than children, and no property; they must have been only once married and must have finished their military service. Of 1,100 applicants so far, all had the right social qualifications, but only 382 families were accepted medically, because while most of the men were healthy enough, the women and children fell far short of the standard. Only 180 families survived the psychological tests (on 'special criteria developed by the Psychological Board'). Of these, 132 are now undergoing the six months' training, which includes a three-month probation period. 'We consider both people and land to be under reclamation.' When trained in the central village, they will be moved out to other villages as nuclei for the future settlements.

The training includes primary education, vocational individual training, and combined training as a group. The men's day begins with a pep talk at 5 a.m. followed by a news commentary and breakfast, followed by a full day's work in the fields with a packed lunch, till 5 p.m., followed by rest and dinner at 6 p.m., followed by two hours of social activity. The women do no field work and are excused the social activity; they work at dairy farming and receive instruction in child and house care, cooking, knitting, and sewing; they sing and play volley-ball. The children attend school in the afternoon, and rest collectively, away from their mothers under the supervision of teachers. Each family has an independent house, with water and electricity, a double roof to reduce heat, and a tiny garden.

Women school teachers supervise the women's care of the new houses and report on their standard. The teachers work an eighteen-hour day, with these and other additional duties. Everything is disciplined, standardized, new. The livestock are kept collectively and do not share the new house. Baking is done collectively, the only cooking arrangement in the house being a small oil stove. Even dress is standardized, the boys in blue boiler suits and pale green shirts; the women in short cotton dresses, white socks, and rubber shoes; the teachers in grey.

Still, some care is taken not to force the pace too fast. The doctor, for instance, in giving the women instruction in hygiene, alluded to birth-control, but the men, on returning from the fields, said that he had no right to interfere in such matters, and the subject was not pursued.

The nutritional level is very good, with an average calorie intake of 3,600 per day, including three ounces of animal protein. The impressive visible result is that the children are magnificently healthy, as a result of sufficient food. The babies are splendid, the boys and girls energetic, with no sign of eye diseases. The women, primly tending the model house, seem slightly dazed.

The new settlers will receive ownership of the house and the little garden, but will not receive ownership of land. All farming will be mechanized, in large units, managed co-operatively, in fact collectively, though, said the Director, 'we must keep the word collective out of our vocabulary'. The co-operatives are to be under the management of a council of eleven members, composed of the village mayor and five appointed persons, including the preacher, doctor, school teacher, and five selected representatives of the village. For the first three years they are to be kept under control by giving the mayor a casting vote—'so you may say a dictatorship'. The co-operative members will purchase all equipment jointly, including tractors and livestock, over a period of thirty years, with the exception of the services normally provided by the Government out of taxes, i.e. roads and irrigation.

As to the economic side, it is difficult to form any idea of the prospects. The scheme is financed from the proceeds of the sale of the royal properties (which are alleged to have realized £70 million), so that sufficient funds are available. The cost of reclamation is low, much lower than in European countries. It amounts to £38 per acre for the reclamation of the land alone, £250 per acre if the costs of cement-lined canals, drainage, and housing are included. These figures are compared with £800 per acre in Italy and £4,000 in Holland. No figures were given covering the costs of the entire scheme, but the cost of the factories must be considerable, and there are some items as, for instance, the imported Friesian cattle, which seem extravagant. The reclamation work is expected to be self-financing, as it is calculated that when 250,000 acres have been reclaimed the resulting income will pay for the reclamation of the remainder of the 800,000 acres. Since the output per acre will certainly be high, the economic success of the land reclamation as such seems a reasonable hope.

The crops now grown are chiefly beans and berseem as reclamation crops; but for melons and strawberries Tahrir already has a reputation. It is intended to concentrate on fruit and vegetables, and to centralize marketing so that exports can be directed to the best markets. In recent years there has been a great improvement in the quality of citrus and other fruit in Egypt, but there is still room to improve. Success really depends on whether Egyptians can do with these new crops what they have been able to do with cotton over the last half-century.

The completion of this scheme and the reclamation of the whole area of the province will depend on the additional water which will be provided by the High Dam. But this must take many years to complete. In the meantime the land depends on water which is diverted from existing supplies. The new Liberation Canal is now almost completed, and will serve larger areas. How far existing supplies of water can be utilized without depriving areas which are already under cultivation is a matter of dispute. The supporters of the Tahrir scheme claim that there can be a larger diversion of water, because the present area of the Delta is over-watered. They rightly point out that in the years before the war reclamation was continuous, though it came to a standstill during the war, so that it can be resumed on a larger scale without damage. The construction of the new canal did not, however, pass without protest from neighbouring districts.

The aim of creating a new society as well as new land is ambitious. Many foreign influences have played an acknowledged part in the conception, for community development is a composite product, derived from the experience of many countries. Yugoslavia in the first flush of the Youth Railway also comes to mind: the notice-board photographs of the preacher, for instance, transformed from a pious delicate scholar into a robust 'outgiver' who retains only the long sheikh's coat as a sign of his profession. As in Yugoslavia, among the young teachers there is devotion to an undefined future.

But there is also originality. It is new for Egyptians to find practical inspiration in the fifty centuries of Egyptian history.

It is new to undertake community building with a wider horizon than the rather tedious new insistence on literacy and technology. Egypt has been, and still is, too great in agriculture to find inspiration in better farming as a way of life: but art and sport are missing in its over-professionalized life, and it is wise to emphasize them. The ideal of turning the young intellectuals to practical work is original also, and, if it is realized, Egypt will have solved a major social problem of the whole region.

About all such conscious human conditioning there must remain a faint sense of misgiving. Perhaps there is too much sense of pulling out of the hideous poverty of the old villages and turning away from the accumulated debris of the past. In the other-worldly light of the Alexandria sky, Tahrir seems a little like Akhnaton's City of the Horizon. Yet it must be remembered that more land and more water is the main condition for leverage of the living standard of the country as a whole.

The contrast with Iraq is complete. There money for the dams is available and to spare, and foreign firms are doing the work which will bring the new water-supplies forward. But unless things change, the water and land will be used to grow poor barley crops with half-starved labour; there is no prospect that the resources will be used to serve the people. Egypt, on the other hand, has set its human values first, and gets the men and women and the land ready for the water, while raising funds and the whirlwind by playing Great Power politics. If the pitch seems rather too high, and the expenditure rather too lavish, that is probably the only way in which anything can be achieved in this very old country.

II

SOCIAL STRUCTURE AND TECHNICAL CHANGE IN THE CRESCENT

THE Egyptian revolution had immediate repercussions throughout the Crescent: the 'rose-water revolution' in Lebanon, stormy meetings of fellahin in Aleppo, and riots in Amara. The repercussions continue. The Egyptian reform is so far the only serious attack on rural poverty in the Arab world, and the hopes which it raises outside Egypt are inevitably as important as its achievements inside the country. Socially, the Arab world has one main problem—the low status and low standard of the fellahin.

Economically, however, the position in the Crescent is different. Agrarian reform came first in Egypt because it is more advanced than Syria and Iraq, which are developing rapidly but are not, as Egypt is, in a state of agricultural overdevelopment. The economy of Egypt is fully capitalistic, and on the existing land area cultivation cannot go much further in intensity. The social structure is correspondingly more highly evolved and stratified, with an agrarian hierarchy resembling that of some European countries, present-day Italy for example, or Hungary in the years between the wars. There is a rich landowner class, which has accumulated and invested capital, a farming middle class, small peasant owners, and a large land proletariat.

In Syria and Iraq, by contrast, land areas are expanding, yields are low and variable, and agriculture is extensive, still in part soil mining rather than farming. The social structure is looser and less stratified. Large landowners include merchant money-lenders, old-established *rentiers*, and tribal sheikhs; the investing commercial magnate is a new phenomenon. Peasant farmers exist, but do not form a distinct social stratum, as in Egypt: they are localized in high rainfall districts, as for instance the Kurdish hills and the Jebel Druze, where peasant life recalls Macedonia and Dalmatia. Middle-class farmers can be found in the Jezira, but they too are localized and do not form a separate class. Throughout the Crescent there is much local specialization, in village crafts and domestic industries which still supply the market of the poor.

This variety, the result of a less capitalistic level, and a less integrated national life, means that class antagonisms are less acute. Villages are isolated from each other and from the towns by great distances, often by stretches of uncultivable desert. The relationship between town and country is different. In Egypt the whole economy depends on the cotton crop, through layer upon layer of technical expertise, from the Alexandria cotton broker to the fellah with ten acres who collects the crop from his village and delivers it to the ginnery. In Syria and Iraq the villages are a world apart, a neglected hinterland which supplies food to the cities and gets nothing in return.

Because agriculture is one-sided and unstable, and was until recently primitive, the setting of reform in these countries is a different one. The aim, as in Egypt, is to give a better living standard and a social status to the fellah. But this aim can be realized only through a better system of farming. Grain farming with the horse- or ox-drawn plough is too unproductive and too unstable to provide a sound basis for small ownership. Reform in the Crescent must therefore be an agricultural as well as a social policy, and must be related either to irrigation, which is the only basis for productive farming in small units, or to extensive mechanized farming, in large units.

Today the arch of the Crescent, from Aleppo to Mosul and beyond, has gone over to mechanized farming. The tractor in these countries is not merely a useful technical improvement. It brings a technical revolution which removes old obstacles to the expansion of cultivation. It means the end of the long struggle between the nomad and the cultivator—the crucial conflict which Ibn Khaldun regarded as the meaning of history, as indeed in this region it has been. It completes the disintegration of tribal society, already undermined by motor transport in the inter-war years. The whole cultivable area can now be brought under cultivation. All the conditions which formerly checked the expansion of cultivation are removed.

In the past climate, primitive methods, and political insecurity combined to prevent the extension of cultivation and the improvement of farming. Although cultivation in this region is as old as agriculture itself, most of the land now cultivated has been brought under the plough only in quite recent times.[1] In the early 1950's, agricultural production in the Crescent and Turkey had increased by 50–70 per cent over the pre-war level, and most of this expansion has been achieved by bringing more land under tractor cultivation.

Climatic conditions make the Crescent a region of prairie farming. In the irrigation zone of south Iraq the control of water could enable more intensive farming, by double cropping and better practices to ensure higher yields. But without irrigation, extensive grain cultivation is the only possible type of agriculture in most of the rainfall zone. Except on the coast and in the mountains, rainfall is too low for more intensive land use. The Fertile Crescent is only fertile by comparison with the desert which it surrounds. It is a semi-circle of cultivable land, defined by the 8-inch rainfall line. In the desert steppe belt, between the 4-inch and 8-inch rainfall line, crops can be grown but they are poor and uncertain. The precise position of the rainfall belts on the inner rim of the Crescent is not known: they are indicated, approximately, on the map on p. 85.

Throughout the dry-farming regions, wheat and barley are the main crops; cotton can be grown as a dry crop only in the regions of higher rainfall. For wheat and barley the fallow system, with fallow every second year or even for two years out of three, is the general rotation. Yields vary round the average to a far greater extent than they do in Europe, owing to the irregularity of rainfall. In the Syrian Jezira, for instance, wheat gives a tenfold return in a good year, sevenfold in a normal year, while in a bad year it will only give back the equivalent of the seed.

So long as ploughing depended on the horse or ox, costs were

[1] For the history of settlement for permanent cultivation in Syria see Norman Lewis, 'The Frontier of Settlement in Syria, 1800–1950', in *International Affairs*, January 1955, a most valuable article which is the prelude to a book on the subject. An impression of how recent the change has been can be gained from Gertrude Bell's description, in *The Desert and the Sown* (1907), of her journey from Jerusalem to Amman, Homs, Hama, and Antioch, through regions which were evidently then still mainly nomadic. Dr Salih Haider in *Land Problems of Iraq* (London University Ph.D. thesis, 1942; unpublished) gives figures which show how little land was cultivated in Iraq in the late nineteenth century.

too high in relation to the return. The low yield in the inland plains meant that the cultivator could not cultivate enough land to produce a surplus above his own needs and the needs of his working livestock. The irregularity of rainfall meant that the margin of advantage over nomadic life was narrow and variable, for though grazing offered a poor return, capital could be accumulated in livestock herds, while grain cultivation offered too unsteady a livelihood to allow the normal way of agricultural growth through investment in livestock.

The economic instability of cultivation, and the lack of political security, explain the long survival of communal forms of land use and cultivation. In Syria and Palestine the *musha'a* custom, a periodical reallotment of unequal holdings,[1] was still prevalent in the 1930's, though it was then disappearing. In southern Iraq tribal ownership of land, with customary rights of individual ownership to plots of land within the tribal area, was prevalent in the early years of the present century.

Whether as cause or effect of the difficult natural conditions, the political institutions of the past did not provide a framework for stability or expansion. Communal tenures survived even when the economic basis of communal land use, grazing with intermittent cropping, was giving place to permanent cultivation. In Ottoman times no systematic registration of title was undertaken, and large landholders, either the tribal sheikhs or city merchant money-lenders, profited by the Government's failure to settle title to communal land on the basis of individual ownership. The uncertainty of yields meant that agriculture was permanently short of capital. Many large properties in Syria and in northern Iraq originated through money-lending to impoverished villagers. How little such city landowners interested themselves in agriculture can be seen by the fact that the *musha'a* custom of periodic reallotment often continued in their villages. The city landowner's function was to receive rents and advance loans, not to put money into cultivation. Now their function is changing. Tractor farming transforms the role of the city merchants into that of a technical 'carrier group', and in northern Syria has already transformed the agrarian structure.

[1] It resembled the Russian 'repartitional commune', of which the origin is controversial.

Share-cropping, i.e. the division of the crop between the landowner and the cultivator in a fixed proportion, is still the main form of tenure. It is a customary form, without any contractual legal basis or any legal protection for the cultivator. The proportion taken by the landowner varies in dry farming with the density of population, being high in the neighbourhood of towns, and low on the desert rim. In dry farming the landowner's share is generally pure rent, i.e. is payment for the use of a scarce factor of production, and not payment in respect of productive services. If these are provided, the share taken is higher. For irrigation farming the landowner provides water (for cotton seed is always provided), and the share taken is higher.

The system is, of course, a bad one, in so far as the landowner is a pure rent receiver and does not invest in the land. The cultivators, on a low subsistence margin, have neither the means nor the incentive to invest: they are labourers, rather than tenants, who work for a variable return, and cannot increase it by working harder or farming better.

This system is not peculiar to the countries of the Crescent. It exists through Asia, from Persia to the Philippines, in many local variants, and under different names. There is no generic name to describe what is probably the most widespread form of economic organization in the world. English writers often describe it as 'absentee landlordism', by analogy with nineteenth-century Ireland. But this term is inexact, for it implies that the landowner neglects his functions—the maintenance of soil fertility and fixed capital—by reason of absence. The evil of the system is not absenteeism as such, but the lack of any investing or managerial function. The object of the system is to avoid the costs of management and investment. It has a superficial resemblance to *métayage* in southern Europe, but the resemblance is only superficial, for *métayage* is a method of dividing the profits of the farm on the basis of a contract, whereas the share-cropping relationship in the Fertile Crescent is a simple division of the produce between labour and landownership, with no contract, and with no investment except in the bare necessities of seed and working livestock.

The system exists most generally in over-populated countries, and appears to be symptomatic of a static or retrogressive condition, in which the landowner can obtain a higher return by renting land than by farming it himself. In the Crescent it appears to be a function of landlords' monopoly allied with insecurity. On estates which were formerly tribal property, the practice of share-cropping originated in the sheikh's claim to a portion of the crop as revenue to provide for his political and judicial functions, and continues as rent after these functions cease to be exercised. On estates acquired by city merchants and notables, the share-cropping system originated in payment for debts or protection.

Most of the large properties now in existence in the Crescent appear to be recent in origin, because settlement for permanent cultivation is recent. The land system of the Crescent is often described as feudal, but in the historical sense the description is not accurate. If feudalism is understood to mean tenure in fief, the grant of land in return for military service, then the system cannot properly be so described, for the large properties which now exist did not, in the main, originate in this way. There has been no period of feudal order, and its absence explains much that is puzzling in prevalent social attitudes.

In European countries the pivot of feudal society was the identification of private rights over land and labour with public function. The grant of land in fief, in return for military service, conferred political privilege and function; the right to tax, to administer justice, to exact labour service or produce rents, from the serfs. Politically, it was an instrument for delegating power when the central government was weak—'le désordre érigé en système'. Economically it provided a framework for expansion. 'Nul terre sans seigneur' was a development policy, as well as a crude system of political security and a social hierarchy. In old feudal societies characteristic social attitudes survive the dissolution of the system itself: a sense of political responsibility, or 'noblesse oblige' on the part of the aristocracy; prestige attaching to landownership and strong incentives, on the part of the peasants, to hoard to acquire land.

In the Fertile Crescent these attitudes are lacking. Weulersse has emphasized the paradox, monstrous in Western eyes, of 'peasant populations devoid of peasant atavism, landowners without a feeling for land or respect for it, cultivators who despise cultivation, labourers who hate the plough and villagers who renounce the village to remain true to the tribe.'[1] For the landlord land is a convenient way of holding wealth; for the fellah it is a miserable means of subsistence. Though city patriotism is strong, there is no attachment to a country place among landowners, and no sense of political obligation or social responsibility attaching to landownership, except in so far as tribal loyalties survive. 'Il n'y a pas de noblesse terrienne en Islam, il n'y a pas de "Monsieur de . . ." ', says Weulersse. He considers that the lack of 'sens terrien' makes Arab civilization exceptional, and perhaps unique, because it is a civilization without a basis in land.[2] Other writers take the same view. Ayrout quotes from Ibn Khaldun a saying of Mohammed, that the plough never enters a house without bringing degradation.[3]

If the land is not loved, as it is in Europe, it is doubtless because it is not responsive. Water, the real staff of life, is treasured and fought for and celebrated in literature. There is no need to look for deeper roots for contempt for agriculture than the natural conditions of the desert. The wonderful artifact of Egyptian agriculture proves that this contempt does not hold good when nature favours easier control.

Because natural conditions were adverse for farming and favourable for trade and tribal life, the Fertile Crescent, by contrast with Europe, did not experience a long period of slow growth from tribal society to an urban trading economy through settled agriculture expanding on a land base. The three forms of economic life existed side by side, with agriculture dependent on the town, and threatened by the tribe. The elements from which feudal society evolved in Europe were present in the tribal sheikhs, but Ottoman rule did not rely on them, or attempt to incorporate them into a political system, imposing instead a centralized administration in which military officials were given rights which corresponded to feudal status in Europe. This system was abolished in 1839, and revenue was collected through tax-collectors, usually local notables, or heads of tribes and villages. In 1858 the Ottoman Land Code attempted to replace this system by establishing

[1] Jacques Weulersse, *Paysans de Syrie et du Proche Orient* (Paris, Gallimard, 1946), p. 66.
[2] ibid. pp. 70–1. [3] *Fellahs d'Égypte*, p. 134.

registration of title to land, but without success. Apart from some grants of land made to influential politicians and collaborators, Turkish rule was hostile to large landowners, as rival sources of power. Consequently landownership was based not on military power and political obligation, but on money-lending, tax-collecting, or tribal authority—functions which were not tied in with political responsibility.

Today the landowners of the Crescent are extremely heterogeneous in function and origin. They do not, in any sense, form an aristocracy. There are true aristocrats who hold their properties by the tradition of military power over a community, as, for example, Kemal Jumblatt, a leader of the Druzes in Lebanon, who from the stronghold at Mukhtara has distributed land to his peasants. He now leads the Socialist Party, inspired by the principles of Asian leaders. Centuries divide this last stage of feudal power from the great sheikh landowners of the southern marshes of Iraq, tribal leaders in the process of becoming an aristocracy. The big grain farmers of northern Syria are commercial farmers, speculators and investors, and show more public spirit, as will be seen, than the old-established landowners or the sheikhs. The country-gentleman ethos is lacking, though individuals can generate it for themselves—as for example Hussein Ibish in Syria, and another Kurdish landowner on the Iraq–Syria border—when they undertake real farming.

Yet though the relation between the landowner and the state cannot properly be described as feudal, the relations between the landowner and the cultivators are of a feudal character, since they are determined by a social stratification which is rigid, even though its origin is recent. The extreme case is found in southern Iraq, where the cultivators are serfs entirely dependent on the landowner and subservient to him, and bound to the land in law. In the older regions of Syria, locally and more correctly described as 'seigniorial', a similar though less oppressive relationship exists on large estates.

Reform of the land system therefore involves the abolition of feudal relations, in this sense. But in other respects the social structure is not feudal, and as a label applied to the land systems of the Arab world the term can be grossly misleading, because it obscures the great differences between the countries. Egypt of the Pashas was an Edwardian society, with its sharp contrasts of surfeit and starvation, its luxury and vulgarity. Modern Syria is in a mid-Victorian expansion, with new capitalists and a rising working class. Iraq is a tribal society in the throes of a disembodied industrial revolution. The setting of the land reform problem therefore differs, and the methods of solution will differ also. Egypt's reform is social, Syria's will be political, and Iraq needs reform for reasons which are political, social, and economic.

As a result of the coming of the tractor, the land system itself is now beginning to change. Some of its results are observed in the following chapters: the rise of the merchant-tractorists, the substitution of paid skilled labour for the unskilled share-cropper, the displacement of labour, and the new extension of cultivation. These changes are only now beginning, but they will continue, bringing greater fluidity in social relations.

Because the impetus to reform must come from political forces, and because the serf-seigniorial relationship cannot be altered without political change, it is impossible to forecast the types of reform which will be carried out, or to make proposals, in the abstract, for any specific type of reform.

But whatever kind of reform is undertaken, it must take the technical change into account. There is no need, in countries which have sufficient land in relation to their population, to think in terms of maximum farm sizes in accordance with the area which can be worked by the farm family with draught livestock.[1] For irrigation farming tractors are needed to supplement cultivation by animals,[2] and in dry farming should be the only form of draught power. The tractor can, of course, raise yields, because it can speed work at the best seasons, which in the Crescent is vitally important. But it can very well endanger soil fertility, as in the Jezira it probably does. The remedy is not a return to the horse or the camel or the ox, but better rotations, and other measures to prevent erosion.

Even with better crop rotations, tractor-farming is not likely

[1] As, for example, the International Bank Mission did in recommending that 'Fundamentally the allotment should not be bigger than that which can be managed by the average farm family without outside assistance' (*The Economic Development of Iraq* (Baltimore, Johns Hopkins Press, 1952), p. 269).

[2] See, for example, the recommendations of the Soil Survey report on the Dujaila Settlement, quoted on p. 168 below.

to bring about much improvement in output per acre. Though yields in Syria and Iraq are low, the average wheat yield in Syria is only some 20 per cent lower than the average yield in the United States and Canada, as the following table shows.

TABLE 8

Grain Yields in the Crescent and in Other Countries
1948–50 Average

	100 kg. per hectare		*cwt. per acre*	
	Wheat	*Barley*	*Wheat*	*Barley*
Syria	9·2	9·3	7·3	7·4
Iraq	5·8	7·2	4·0	5·7
United States	11·1	14·0	8·8	11·1
Canada	10·4	12·6	8·2	10·0
United Kingdom	26·8	24·9	21·2	19·7
Europe	14·5	16·6	11·5	13·2

(SOURCE: FAO, *Yearbook of Food and Agricultural Statistics, 1954.*)

The most that could be achieved by better methods in dry farming would probably be an increase of some 10 or 20 per cent above the present level. Nor, of course, will tractor-farming stabilize yields. But the improvement in labour productivity ought to allow some saving in agriculture, to form a reserve against bad years, so that farm incomes could be stabilized, though the variations in output will remain. Tractor-farming is therefore not likely to raise the level of land productivity to any great extent. It does, however, raise the level of labour productivity, and so must play an essential part in any measure of reform which aims at raising the income of the cultivators.

Because reform must be linked with technical change, its methods must necessarily differ from the Egyptian. So far as the size of farm holdings is concerned, the Egyptian reform is not a good model, since tiny holdings of 2–3 acres would not provide a subsistence minimum in the Crescent. It is a good model, however, in so far as the unit of management and operation is large. Egyptian 'co-operative farming' could serve as a model for irrigation settlements, provided that the farm holdings granted are large enough not only to give a good standard for the farm family, but also to allow for a rising standard, and a higher rate of production to satisfy the demands of the growing town population. For dry farming the minimum new holding should be based on the area which a tractor can cultivate. Independent farming in family units should be feasible, provided that tractor repair and maintenance services are organized by the Ministry of Agriculture in local centres. Farm credit will also have to be provided.

The aim of reform in Syria and Iraq should therefore be not a minimum standard, but the best possible standard of living in expanding economies. In its essential aim, better standards and the guaranteed status, the Egyptian reform represents the right starting-point; and in the countries of the Crescent, with their new deployment of enterprise and money, it needs to be worked out in the context of the new farming methods. The realization of the Egyptian aim, in their conditions, could raise the rural living standard well above its wretchedly low level, and so sustain general economic progress. Social reform has had to wait on technical change, for without the tractor the low level of output per man would remain a permanent feature of the agriculture of the Crescent.

A NOTE ON STATE LAND AND THE LEGAL CATEGORIES OF LAND

In the following chapters it will be seen that proposals for reform both in Syria and Iraq concern the distribution of state land to cultivators. It appears necessary, therefore, to give some explanation of the meaning of state land in Moslem law. The conception of state land is confusing to Westerners, who are prone to assume that the state's claim to ownership of the land means a form of public ownership analogous to that which exists in Western countries, in which the state owns the land as a juridical person, and controls its use and disposal. The conception of state ownership in Moslem law is quite different: in theory, the state claims ownership of all land, except in so far as this has been assigned in *mulk* and *waqf* tenure to individuals.

The legal categories of land are based on Moslem sacred law:

le droit coranique, extrêmement riche, complexe et touffu, mais dont la richesse même n'exclut pas un défaut de précision fondamental en ce qui concerne les questions foncières. De là une opposition flagrante avec les principes intransigeants du droit romain, source de nos conceptions juridiques.[1]

Though these categories today have little importance, because they have been superseded by a Western conception of ownership, some explanation of their meaning may be helpful.

Until the 1930's, when the legal basis of ownership was changed by new legislation both in Syria and in Iraq, land law was based on the Ottoman Land Code of 1858. This was an attempt to introduce order into a confused mass of earlier legislation. It recognized five categories of land, as follows.

1. *Mulk land:* land held in absolute freehold ownership. It is governed by the provisions of sacred law and not by those of the civil statute law. Landownership comprises two rights: the *raqaba*, or right of absolute ownership, and the *tasarruf*, or right to the usufruct of land. In *mulk* tenure both rights belong to the individual.

2. *Miri land:* land of which the *raqaba* or absolute ownership belongs to the state, but the usufruct or *tasarruf* to the individual. It is a form of heritable leasehold ownership in which the state leases land to the individual.

3. *Waqf land:* land dedicated to some pious purpose; except in Egypt, it is no longer important.

4. *Matruka land:* land reserved for some public purpose as, for example, village threshing floors; also very small in extent.

5. *Mawat land:* dead or unreclaimed land.

The significance of these categories can be understood by reference to the conception of ownership which existed at the time of the Moslem conquest.[2] The important distinction lay between the first two categories, *mulk* and *miri*. *Mulk* tenure confers absolute ownership; and at the time of the Moslem conquest was confined to land and houses in towns, the only goods which the Moslem conquerors recognized as the property of individuals. All other land was *miri* (from *emiriye*, princely), i.e. belonged to the state as the spoils of war and therefore as the property of the Moslem community. But the rulers did not wish to cultivate this land, and left it in the possession of its effective owners. Thus there arose the conception of two rights of owner-

[1] Weulersse, *Paysans de Syrie et du Proche Orient*, pp. 90–1. [2] ibid. pp. 90–6.

ship over land, the absolute ownership, or *raqaba*, always vested in the state, and the right of usufructuary possession, the *tasarruf*, held by the existing occupiers. The state's right of ownership in practice meant the right to tax the occupiers of land or to exact labour from them; it did not imply any control over the use of land, or any degree of responsibility for its cultivation.

The three other categories are of lesser importance. The third category, *waqf*, is a peculiarity of Moslem law. It is a permanent endowment of land or buildings for religious or pious purposes, such as a mosque, school, or hospital. The endowment is irrevocable and inalienable, and in Ottoman times came under Moslem sacred law. *Waqf* properties were then administered by a special Ministry, which was one of the more important posts in the Empire. The institution was subject to abuse by means of legal subterfuges which diverted the income to private or political ends. A special form of *waqf* allowed individuals to dedicate property to a pious purpose in the future, after their family had died out. This form of permanent entail allowed large proprietors to maintain their property intact against spoliation by the Government and thus helped to promote concentration of ownership in the past. It has now been abolished in Egypt, Syria, and Iraq.

Matruka ('left-over') land was land reserved for public use, and corresponds to the Western conception of public property; it includes roads, rivers, public buildings, market places, or village threshing floors.

Mawat or *mubah* lands were desert or empty lands, the property of the state. Those who brought them into cultivation could acquire *miri* ownership, i.e. the right of usufructuary possession, by proving cultivation over a fixed period.

These minor categories overlap the major categories, *waqf* being a form of *mulk*, while *mawat* land is included within the category *miri*.

How far these legal distinctions had practical influence on the system of tenure is a question that cannot be answered without research. The greater security of urban property in contrast to property in land might be held to explain the strong tendency, still very evident, for landowners to invest in urban house property and to live in towns. But against this view, it appears that even in Ottoman times the distinction between *mulk* and *miri* had ceased to have practical importance, because in the course of time legislation gave security to *miri* landholders, and ownership of the *tasarruf* became equivalent to full ownership in that it conferred right of sale, inheritance, and mortgage.[1] The only conditional feature which remained was the state's right to resume ownership of *miri* land left uncultivated.

While the categories in themselves may not have had much importance, the absence of an effective system for the settlement of title in the late Ottoman period probably did represent an obstacle to settlement for permanent cultivation. There was no legal mould into which the existing communal tenures could dissolve, and consequently tax-collectors, sheikhs, and city merchants could acquire landownership more easily than they might have done had the Ottoman attempt to settle title on the basis of individual ownership been successful.

The Ottoman Land Code of 1858 was intended to introduce a general system of individual ownership; its main purpose was to introduce compulsory registration of title to all *miri* land, as the necessary basis for a reform of the tax system. From 1839, when the military fiefs were abolished, taxes were collected by tax-farmers, whose methods were arbitrary and produced little revenue. The object of the Land Code was to reform the system of taxation by establishing direct contact between the actual cultivators and the state. In order to tax every piece of land, it was necessary to establish its ownership, by means of registration of title, through the *senet tapu*, the grant of title.

At the time that the Code was promulgated, most of the land of the Ottoman Empire was *miri*, and was occupied by customary landholders, without legal title to land. These included settled village communities, practising semi-communal forms of cultivation, tribes exercising customary rights of ownership over large areas, and large landowners who had received grants of land from the Sultan in return for their services. The aim of the Ottoman Government was to grant title directly to the cultivator, and to prevent any intermediary interest in land between the Government and cultivating occupiers of land. Hence the theory that the legal ownership of *miri* land belonged to the state, and that title could be granted only to the usufruct

[1] Weulersse, *Paysans de Syrie et du Proche Orient*, p. 92.

of land, could be used as a weapon in the hands of the Government, serving to establish individual ownership as against the tribal sheikhs, and against the tax-collectors and other intermediaries. The Turks wanted to create a strong central administration over a large number of small cultivators, in order to be able to extract the maximum revenue, and at the same time to weaken all rival sources of power.

The Code was primarily a fiscal and political measure; but it would also have been a measure of land reform, in favour of individual small ownership, if it had been effectively carried out; and it would have introduced a Western idea of ownership, even though the old conception of the two rights was nominally maintained. In fact, the titles which were granted did not correspond to the rights of ownership recognized by custom, nor did they correspond to the areas actually held. Grants generally tended to strengthen the large landowners. The Code explicitly prohibited the recognition of any form of collective ownership, which was general at the time it was promulgated, either in the form of the semi-collective *musha'a* system, or in the form of tribal ownership. Article 8 of the Land Code states that 'The whole land of a village or of a town cannot be granted in its entirety to all of the inhabitants nor to one or two persons chosen from amongst them. Separate pieces are granted to each inhabitant and a title is given to each showing this right of possession.' In actual fact this provision was evaded, owing to the failure of the administration to register land title systematically.

No general registration was ever carried out. (In southern Iraq the Code was not applied even in theory.) The villagers, fearing that the registration was a preliminary to call up for military service, or for taxation purposes, falsified the returns, registering the property either in the name of the head of the tribe, or in the name of a member of the family who could not be liable for military service, or in the name of a city notable. In practice they disregarded the titles which were granted (known as the *senet tapu*) and continued to farm in various semi-tribal ways. Thus complete confusion resulted, since there arose one situation established by law under which certain owners held titles to divided land, and a situation existing in fact, in which the persons cultivating the land had claims recognized by custom or prescriptive right, which were enforceable by law to an uncertain extent.

In the years between the wars, registration of title and survey was carried out on a large part of the cultivated land in Syria and Iraq. This hastened the disintegration of the communal forms of cultivation and communal rights over land, and has given legal security to individual ownership. Since it did not, at the same time, give economic security to the cultivators, it has not affected their position: on the contrary, registration usually consolidated the property of the large landholders.

Today the only important remaining feature of the Moslem conception is that the state still has a formal claim to the possession of unregistered land. The legal status of state land differs in Syria and Iraq, and is considered below in the chapters dealing with each country. It should be noted, however, that the policy of assigning state land to cultivators is in no sense a new policy, and should not be regarded as representing a new direction. In Ottoman times colonization of state lands was carried on in Syria, and under the mandate this policy was continued, though on a small scale. It is only because the procedure of land settlement (i.e. the registration of title) has so generally favoured large landowners at the expense of the cultivators that the assignment of state land to small cultivators now appears to represent a change in the agrarian structure.

III

PRIVATE ENTERPRISE IN SYRIA

THE BACKGROUND

Few underdeveloped countries in the past ten years have made such rapid progress in agriculture and industry as Syria. This point must be emphasized, because it can easily be overlooked. To the outside world, Egypt has a revolution and Iraq has money, but Syria has nothing to show but frequent coups d'état, 'feudal' landowners, and a marked aversion to foreign assistance.[1] It might be concluded that the economic life of the country was stagnant.

A glance at the agricultural production figures should suffice to dispel this impression. As compared with 1934–8, the area cultivated has doubled; grain production has increased by 64 per cent, and cotton production is now eight times its pre-war average. This is a strikingly rapid rate of expansion, even in the Middle East, where the rate of increase in agricultural production has been higher in recent years than in any part of the world except North America and Africa.[2]

The expansion in the cultivated area and in grain production is mainly the result of the cultivation of new land. Since the war the boundaries of cultivation have been pushed out very rapidly in the north along the Turkish frontier in the rainfed cultivation belt which forms the arch of the Fertile Crescent. The zone of new cultivation extends east from the neighbourhood of Aleppo up to the Iraq border, across the provinces of the Euphrates and the Jezira, chiefly in the 8–12 inch rainfall belt, shown on the map on p. 85. These regions now produce two-thirds of the country's grain output and the greater part of the country's exports.

The recent expansion in cotton has taken place in Aleppo

[1] The Government has refused to reach an agreement with Point Four (the US Technical Assistance Administration). It had not, up to the end of 1955, received any loans from the International Bank.

[2] FAO, *State of Food and Agriculture in 1955* (Rome, 1955), p. 76.

and Latakia provinces and also in the Homs–Hama plain, where cotton is grown on land brought under flow irrigation by the canalization of the Orontes. In the newly opened-up provinces of the north cotton is grown on new plantations on the Khabur and the Euphrates.

Cotton is not a new crop in Syria, for in the surroundings of Aleppo it has been cultivated since the eighteenth century. But cultivation on the present scale is new. Large-scale cultivation first began in 1924, and then increased quickly till the depression brought a decline, followed by recovery to the pre-war peak of 40,000 hectares. Expansion began again in response to high world prices in 1949, and reached its post-war peak of 217,000 hectares in 1951. The fall in prices and diseases of the crop led to some contraction.[1] The area under cultivation is

TABLE 9

Area and Production of Main Crops in Syria

Area
*(000 hectares)**

	Average 1934–8	*1950*	*1951*	*1952*	*1953*	*1954*	*Average 1950–4*	*1955*†
Wheat	473	992	1,037	1,167	1,314	1,347	1,171	690
Barley	275	416	344	394	439	543	427	400
Total grain	748	1,408	1,381	1,561	1,753	1,890	1,598	1,090
Cotton	30	78	217	185	128	187	159	249

Production
(000 metric tons)

	Average 1934–8	*1950*	*1951*	*1952*	*1953*	*1954*	*Average 1950–4*	*1955*†
Wheat	459	830	510	900	870	965	815	600
Barley	290	322	155	467	472	635	410	150
Total grain	749	1,152	665	1,367	1,342	1,600	1,225	750
Cotton	5	35	49	45	47	80	51	85

*1 hectare=2·47 acres. † Preliminary estimates.

(SOURCES: FAO, *Yearbook of Food and Agricultural Statistics*, and UN, *Economic Developments in the Middle East, 1945 to 1954*, p. 183.)

[1] UN, *Economic Developments in the Middle East, 1945 to 1954* (New York, 1955), p. 182.

now about 180,000 hectares, and annual production averages 50,000 tons, most of which is exported.

The preceding table shows the increase in areas and production of the main crops.

The total area now utilized for agriculture is 3·9 million hectares (9½ million acres). Three and a half million hectares are used for dry farming, with half the land kept fallow each year, so that the area utilized for agriculture is twice as large as the area sown. About half a million hectares are under irrigation. How much land is still available for a further expansion of irrigation and of dry farming is not known.[1]

Agricultural production has increased more rapidly than population. In the years 1943–53 grain production doubled, while population increased by about 33 per cent, from 2·9 million to 3·9 million.[2] Thus output per head of population has risen. In this respect Syria's economic development has been much more favourable than that of Egypt, where output per head of population has fallen over the last ten years, and also than that of Iraq, where per capita output has increased, but to a lesser extent. The level of output per head in agriculture, measured in the main crops, is now much higher than it is in Egypt and Iraq. An agricultural population of between 1½ and 1¾ million[3] produces 1·3 million tons of grain and 50,000 tons of cotton. In Egypt an agricultural population of about 16 million produces 4½ million tons of grain and 350,000 tons of cotton, while in Iraq an agricultural population of 2½–3 million produces 1½ million tons of grain and 5,000 tons of cotton. In the absence of occupation statistics, no precise comparisons of output per head are possible; but it is clear that Syria's position is more favourable. As compared with Egypt it has twenty times as much arable land per head of agricultural

[1] Various estimates of the potentially cultivable areas have been made, but they are of no value since they do not distinguish clearly between the land which is potentially cultivable by dry farming, and land which must be reclaimed and irrigated before it can be cultivated. Since estimates of this sort are apt to take on a life of their own and become respectable with repeated quotation, it is better to omit them.

[2] The figure of 3·9 million is an estimate quoted by the Minister of Finance in his speech on the budget of 1955.

[3] Rural population was estimated to be 2·1 million in 1943 and 2·9 million in 1953. The agricultural population (i.e. the total number dependent on agriculture) was estimated to be 1·3 million in 1943, and assuming that the agricultural population has increased at the same rate as the rural population, it would number 1·7 million in 1953. It may be less than this, since industrial employment has grown.

population, and as compared with Iraq, it has made a far greater advance in intensive cultivation.

Mechanization has been the chief method of expansion. FAO estimates the number of tractors at 1,454 in 1954 and 2,000 in 1955. In the Jezira province and the northern regions of the Euphrates province almost all the grain crop is cultivated by tractors and harvested by combines, and farming is as fully mechanized as in any country in the world. Mechanization has also advanced in central Syria. Even in conservative Hama, disc-harrows come back into the town at night drawn by John Deeres and Fergusons among the camels and donkeys. Tubular blue neon lights outline advertisements of caterpillar tractors on the road into Aleppo, where the *souk* of the smiths has been turned into a row of machine shops, using electrical power.

The expansion in agriculture, judged by the inertia prevailing ten years ago, is surprising. It completely confutes some current doctrines. It is now fashionable to believe that the economic development of underdeveloped countries needs foreign capital, foreign experts, good public services, long-term planning, agrarian reform, plus, for good measure, a revolution. But Syria has had none of these things, and in the north, where progress has been so fast, every one of these conditions is lacking. Transport is expensive, roads are bad, labour is scarce, credit dear, and land tenure confused and insecure. Revolutions of course Syria has had, but they have been self-destroying seizures of power, without much effect on economic policy, and none on social structure.

Syrian governments have done almost nothing to promote agricultural development. The only important and highly beneficial economic measure was the foundation of the Cotton Bureau, staffed by experts from Egypt and with advice from FAO. This was set up under the Shishakli régime in 1952, when the rapid expansion in cotton had been checked by falling prices, crop diseases, and over-cultivation. The Bureau sells improved seed and controls and selects varieties. Cotton cultivation is now restricted to suitable areas by a system of licensing, and other control measures, such as the destruction of the plants after harvest, are also enforced. These measures were taken when experience showed them to be needed, and not as a matter of policy.

Otherwise, Syrian governments have pursued a policy of *laisser-faire*. No railways have been built since Ottoman times, though the Hejaz Railway, forty years after its destruction, is now being rebuilt. The new northern regions are without roads. Though great progress has been made in education since the mandate ended, little has been done, until very recently, to assist research or education in agriculture.[1] Far from undertaking land reform, the post-mandatory governments did not even continue the system of land registration introduced by the French.

But one essential factor in development Syria has had, the fourth factor of enterprise, so unaccountable and so often forgotten. The merchant class of Syria, and chiefly of Aleppo, famous as traders in other countries, has turned its business acumen back into its own country, and has used its capital to mechanize agriculture. The expansion in cotton has been financed almost entirely from commercial capital.[2] All the new expansion in grain in the province of the Jezira has been financed in the same way, and some mechanization in grain growing in the older settled regions also. The city, which formerly took everything from the village and gave nothing back, not even security, is now putting big money into cultivation. The improvement of the land itself does not get much attention. There is, however, some new investment by private enterprise in long-term improvement of the land in irrigation for cotton cultivation.

This is a great and certainly a healthy change, and one which is long overdue. The Ottoman Empire conspicuously failed to accomplish it. Its institutions were unfavourable to agriculture. How recently the land of Syria has been brought under cultivation, can be seen in the map on p. 76.[3] The struggle between the desert and the sown has been long protracted, and it has not been won for settled cultivation until today. Nomadic

[1] According to the International Bank Mission, in 1953 there was only one trained research agronomist (*Economic Development of Syria*, p. 302).

[2] 'In 1951, it was estimated that some £S200 to £S300 million had been required to finance the planting and moving of the cotton crop, of which all but £S50 million came from outside agriculture' (UN, *Economic Developments in the Middle East, 1945 to 1954*, p. 184).

[3] See Norman Lewis in *International Affairs*, January 1955. A. Granott, *The Land System in Palestine* (London, 1952), pp. 34–7, quotes observations by nineteenth-century travellers on the extent of cultivation.

grazing still continues, but has been pushed back almost entirely on to the uncultivable land.

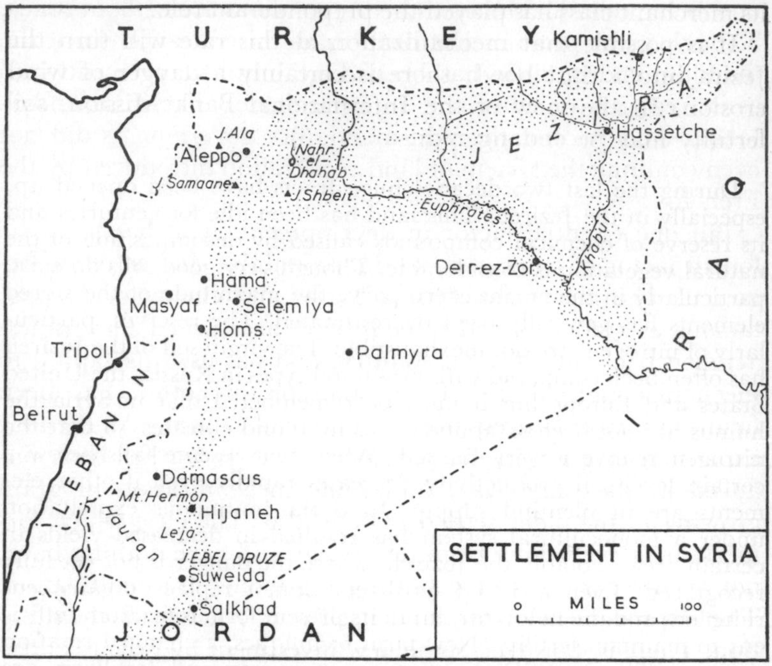

The areas stippled represent territory in which there were few or no permanent inhabitants in 1800, and which is now cultivated and inhabited by a sedentary population. The map is based on one accompanying an article by Norman Lewis, 'The Frontier of Settlement in Syria', in *International Affairs*, January 1955.

In this expansion there are obvious weaknesses—no improvement in soil fertility or in grain yields, a risk of soil erosion, and no stability. Yet it is an essential stage in the development of a country to get all its land cultivated, and not only for economic reasons. Politically this energizing drive was needed to draw together the diverse interests of the different groups and communities and classes of which the country is composed. Europe did not advance much until all its land was cultivated; nor did the United States. In Europe the expansion of the cultivated area was a long process, extending over centuries, and was achieved by the integrating principle of feudal organization. In the United States expansion was rapid, and the process was speculative and wasteful. Different countries have used a different dynamic, and Syria is unusual in that its merchant class has played the preponderant role.

It is possible that mechanization at this rate will turn the Jezira into a dust bowl; there is certainly a danger of wind erosion. In the view of the International Bank Mission, soil fertility may be endangered.

> During the last two decades huge tracts have been opened up, especially in the Jezireh. This land has been idle for centuries and its reserve of chemical compounds caused by decomposition of the natural vegetation is considerable. Though very good soils do exist, particularly in the northeastern parts, the magnitude of the stored elements has generally been overestimated. The reserves, particularly of nitrogen, are not inexhaustible. The virgin soil of the Jezireh has often been compared with virgin soil types in Russia, the United States and Europe but it must be remembered that in Syria the humus has not been so abundant as in humid climates, so that the nitrogen reserve is very limited. When that reserve falls below a certain level soil productivity decreases rapidly even if other elements are in plentiful supply. In Syria continuous exploitation under a monocultural system has resulted in decreased yields in certain areas, notably the Jezireh, where the danger is not yet fully recognized. Even artificial fertilizers cannot replace organic enrichment and the fallow system in its present form is far from sufficient to maintain fertility. New farm techniques, a changed rotation system and increased use of green manuring and fertilizers are urgent needs.[1]

The dry-farming expansion is inevitably precarious and speculative, as is shown by the production figures quoted in Table 9 on p. 72. The spring drought of 1955 brought a harvest failure in the new regions and in most of the country. Banks had to call a moratorium, and the Government had to distribute seed. Great as the achievement of free enterprise has been, it cannot enable Syria to dispense with a policy for soil conservation and agricultural development.

Such a policy must aim at higher crop yields and greater stability, aims which can be attained only by more irrigation. Soil conservation requires afforestation. Research on methods of farming and a system of technical education could also do much. Until very recently the state had done little in any of

[1] *The Economic Development of Syria*, p. 300.

these directions, though the new entrepreneurs have undertaken irrigation and afforestation, and have employed technical experts.

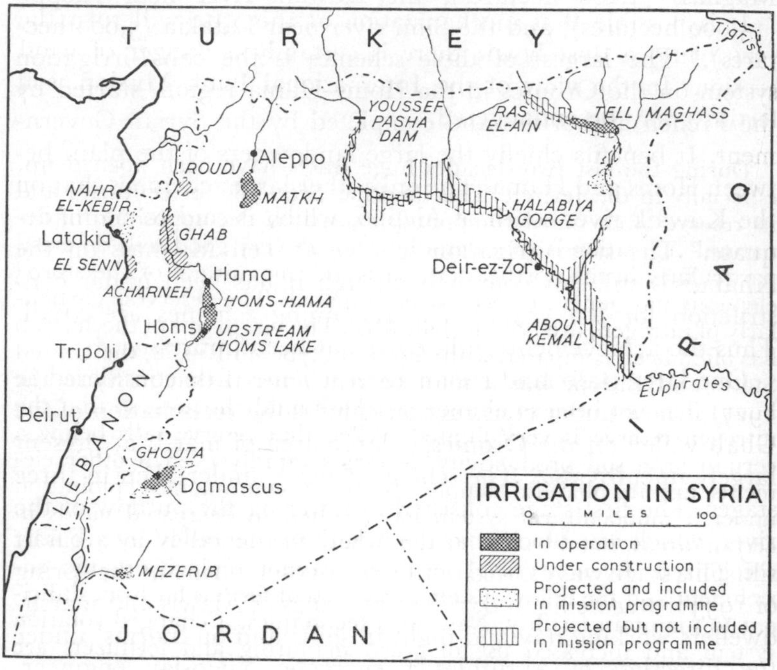

Based on a map in International Bank for Reconstruction and Development, *The Economic Development of Syria.*

The area under irrigation (in 1954 estimated to be 508,958 hectares) could certainly be increased, though the potential expansion cannot be estimated.[1] The location of the irrigated areas is shown on the above map; the areas are very approximate and possibly exaggerate the extent. The greater part of the land now irrigated has been brought under pump or flow irrigation by private enterprise. More than half of the area lies in the provinces of the Jezira and the Euphrates, and is partly new irrigation.[2]

[1] The International Bank Mission considers that the present area might be doubled (ibid. p. 41).

[2] Great uncertainty attaches to any estimates of areas irrigated because the Euphrates irrigation has not been surveyed. But the area irrigated certainly has increased. The Cadastral Survey Office figures give a total of 323,650 hectares irrigated in 1945.

State-operated schemes cover only 48,000 hectares. These are: the Homs–Hama irrigation system (21,600 hectares), the Mezerib in the Hauran (2,200 hectares), the Khabur at Tell Maghass (4,200 hectares), the Kuwaik river near Aleppo (15,000 hectares), and the Sinn river near Latakia (5,000 hectares).[1] The largest of these schemes is the canal-irrigation system on the Orontes in the Homs–Hama region, started by the French authorities and completed by the Syrian Government. It benefits chiefly the large landowners of the plain between Homs and Hama. The only other large scheme is that on the Kuwaik river south of Aleppo, which is said to be inadequate.[2] The state irrigation scheme at Tell Maghass on the Khabur is still not complete, though it has been under construction for ten years.[3] The remaining schemes are small. Thus the achievement to date has not been impressive.[4]

One large state land reclamation scheme (first considered in 1927) is now under construction. This is the reclamation of the Ghab valley on the Orontes, a large area of marsh at present largely uncultivable. The scheme is being undertaken in three stages. The first stage consisted in lowering the outflow of the river, which was blocked at the mouth of the valley by a basalt sill. This stage was carried out by a Yugoslav firm; in the spring of 1955 it was being undertaken by gangs of Alawis and marsh-dwellers working day and night in shifts and on 'norms' under the direction of a ruthlessly energetic Yugoslav engineer, determined to finish the job by the scheduled date, August 1955. The second stage is the construction of canals in the valley itself, now being undertaken by a German firm. When this stage is completed, it is estimated that an area of 26,000 hectares of waterlogged land can be reclaimed. The third stage is to be the construction of two reservoirs, to store water for the irrigation of the valley and also for the Acharneh plain upstream of the valley. It is estimated that a total area of 65,000 hectares will be supplied. In 1955 this section of the work had not been put in hand.

[1] Figures quoted in the Budget Speech by the Minister of Finance, January 1955.

[2] According to the report of the International Bank Mission (*The Economic Development of Syria*, p. 41).

[3] ibid. p. 43.

[4] For details of the seven-year investment programme, see UN, *Economic Developments in the Middle East, 1954–5*, pp. 129–30.

At present the cultivated land in the Ghab valley is held chiefly by large owners. The land which is at present uncultivable is State Domain, i.e. the state has the right of disposal, and consequently the question of the distribution of the new land has to be decided. The Ghab valley scheme is administered by a special Board, which has considered proposals for distributing the new land to small farmers. In 1955 no decision had been reached as to the principles on which the land was to be distributed.

So far as afforestation is concerned, much greater progress has been made. It is, of course, one of Syria's great necessities. As long ago as 1872 Sir Richard Burton, who otherwise rejoiced in the absence of scientific farming in Syria, said that 'It wants only a Brigham Young to order the planting of a round million of trees.'[1] Recently the Government has embarked on an energetic programme for the distribution of saplings through the tree schools (the *pépinières agricoles*). In the three years 1953–5, 3 million saplings were distributed for planting. Private enterprise has a good record here also: one of the big entrepreneurs has planted 1 million poplars in his new plantations.

As a result of the recommendations of the International Bank Mission, funds for forestry, agricultural education and research were greatly increased in the 1955 budget, from £S450,000 to £S800,000.[2]

Agricultural primary schools now number 150. They are directed by Ahmed Kassem, formerly the Director of Agricultural Education in Palestine, where such schools gave a real stimulus to technical improvement through inter-school competition and village rivalry. Until recently there was only one agricultural secondary school, established at Selemiya near Hama in 1910. Four agricultural secondary schools and an agricultural high school have recently been established. The number of experimental stations has been increased; there are now thirteen, of which the oldest is the station at Homs, set up by the French. The two research stations at Homs and Ezra'a in 1955 were directed by young Palestinians. Shortage of staff is a great obstacle.

[1] Richard Burton and F. Tyrwhitt Drake, *Unexplored Syria* (London, 1872), vol. 1, p. 91.

[2] The currency unit is the Syrian pound, which is equivalent to one-tenth of the pound sterling.

It is against this background of expanding agriculture and the beginnings of a state agricultural policy that the problem of land reform must be considered.

So far as the new regions are concerned, it cannot be argued that land reform is a condition of development. In spite of the almost total lack of security of tenure, private enterprise has not been deterred from expansion. In the new regions entrepreneurs, large and small, complain of the lack of security, as they complain of shortage of credit and lack of roads. Yet it is arguable that the easy availability of land at low rents has facilitated expansion, by allowing new farmers to put all their capital into the purchase of seed and machinery.

It is none the less true that the old land system was an obstacle to development. The old *rentier* landowners and poor share-croppers could not have undertaken it. Ten years ago the possibility of development in the Jezira was well known, but seemed to exist only on paper, and at that time it was 'not easy to see where in fact the motive power is to come from'.[1] The motive power has come from outside the old agrarian structure, from the city merchants who are primarily risk-takers, gamblers in grain and investors in irrigation.

In the old settled regions there is a need for reform, as a labour policy to raise earnings. The spectacular expansion in the far north has meant a shift in Syria's economic centre of gravity, away from the old grain-producing regions of the south and centre.[2] But this shift has not drawn much labour away from the old regions into more productive employment in the north. Since grain production is completely mechanized, the demand for labour has not increased in proportion to the increase in production. Some of the old regions, notably the Hauran and the Jebel Druze, feel the competition of the Jezira, and their economic position is weaker. Consequently the expansion of cultivation in the new regions does not raise the rural living standard in the old regions to any noticeable extent, nor does it cause any improvement in the land-tenure system. Cotton cultivation has led to a great improvement in the incomes of the cultivators where they are small owners.

[1] *Land and Poverty in the Middle East* (London, RIIA, 1948), p. 97.
[2] A trend reinforced by the termination of the customs union with Lebanon in 1950, when the use of the port of Latakia was made compulsory.

But the majority of the rural population, the share-croppers and labourers on large estates, have not shared in the economic advance of the country, by reason of their small share in the produce of the land and their low wages.

CHANGES IN THE AGRARIAN STRUCTURE

There are no recent figures available showing the distribution of ownership by size of holding. The Cadastral Survey Office has published figures showing the distribution of ownership in 1951. These figures are presumably based on estimates, since cadastral survey and registration of properties was carried out in the mandatory period only in certain provinces. The figures for these provinces, Damascus, Aleppo, Latakia, Homs, and Hama, may give some indication of the distribution of ownership as it was recorded by the survey, though since the records were not maintained after 1943 the information given is presumably outdated. In other provinces, however, including the newly developed regions, no survey and registration was undertaken, so that the estimates for the provinces of the Jezira, the Euphrates, the Hauran, and the Jebel Druze cannot be based on any accurate record. In the newly developed regions, there is no precise record of areas owned, and there is much variation in areas cultivated. Nor is the area of State Domain land known, except in so far as it was surveyed and registered in the mandatory period in some regions. However, as the figures for the provinces surveyed and registered must bear some relation to existing conditions, and since they indicate regional contrasts which can be confirmed by direct observation, the figures may be quoted.

It will be seen that the figures show the distribution of ownership on a total area of 7·9 million hectares, an area twice as large as the area utilized for agriculture (3·9 million hectares, including fallow). They therefore include uncultivated and uncultivable land, and this ambiguity in the land areas diminishes their value as a guide to the distribution of property.

The figures show a preponderance of small and medium-sized properties in the provinces of the Hauran, Jebel Druze, and Latakia, where there is certainly a larger proportion of small and medium-sized holdings than elsewhere. The importance of large properties in the Aleppo province also corresponds to the results of observation. For the Jezira and Euphrates provinces the figures bear little relation to reality, since the scale of operation and of ownership is certainly very

TABLE 10

Landownership by Size of Holdings in Syria
(hectares)

Province	*Private property*			*State Domain*	*Total area*
	Small (*under 10*)	*Medium* (*10–100*)	*Large* (*over 100*)		
Damascus	178,000	413,345	347,700	24,500	963,545
Aleppo	264,800	732,500	831,848	462,800	2,291,948
Homs	37,500	284,708	157,000	720,000	1,199,208
Hama	8,350	195,200	259,435	269,200	732,185
Latakia	175,000	164,161	207,000	8,000	554,161
Euphrates	74,041	236,300	196,300	2,000	508,641
Jezira	55,600	463,300	277,500	95,600	892,000
Hauran	194,100	188,000	27,000	10,900	420,000
Jebel Druze	110,100	214,900	45,000	—	370,000
Total	1,097,491	2,892,414	2,348,783	1,593,000	7,931,688

(SOURCE: Bureau des Documentations Syriennes et Arabes, *Étude sur l'Agriculture Syrienne* (Damascus, 1955), p. 24.)

large; small and medium properties exist chiefly in the riverain tracts along the Euphrates river.

The most striking feature in Syria's agrarian structure today is the contrast in population densities between the new regions and the old. The newly developed territories are almost empty and short of labour, while in the old settled regions there is some degrce of rural over-population. There is a broad correlation between the distribution of property and the density of the rural population. The under-populated new regions are dominated by large ownership and large-scale operation. The regions with the higher rural population densities are the provinces of the Hauran, the Jebel Druze, Latakia, and Hama, in the first three of which small ownership is important. The province of Hama is an exception to this correlation, since large estates take up most of the good land in the region. The position of the share-croppers is worse in this province than in other parts of the country; and it is not surprising that the agitation for land reform originates here.

Population pressure is, however, a local condition only, and does not affect the country as a whole. Organized settlement in the north, and settlement in the reclaimed lands of the Ghab valley (in the Hama province), would suffice to relieve it. With a better regional distribution of population, more effort to raise the standard of farming, and social legislation, Syria could employ a larger population on the land at a higher standard of living.

A further point of contrast in the agrarian structure of the new regions and the old is that the new farmers employ wage-paid labour, either as skilled workers in tractor and combine work, or as seasonal labour for cotton-picking. In the old regions share-cropping is still predominant. It might be expected that mechanization would have led to substitution of wage labour for share-cropping: but so far as could be ascertained this has not taken place to any great extent, except for cotton-picking.

The contrast in the agrarian structures of the different regions means that the problems of reform differ greatly. Since published information on social and economic change is so meagre, the changes can be reviewed only on the basis of direct observation—necessarily scanty and relying on information obtained from persons who have themselves initiated the changes, or have been affected by them.

The New Regions

The newly-opened-up regions include the eastern part of the province of Aleppo, the northern part of the Euphrates province, and the province of the Jezira. Geographically speaking, the Jezira (meaning 'the island' or 'the peninsula') is the land lying between the Tigris and the Euphrates. Administratively, the province (*mohafazat*) of the Jezira is a smaller region, covering the north-eastern corner of the country. This province has been the centre of most rapid expansion.

These regions lie in the rainfall zone between the Taurus mountains and the Syrian desert, stretching eastwards from Aleppo up to the frontier of Iraq. Within this zone there is a belt of high rainfall, with an annual rainfall of 50–60 centimetres (20–24 inches) running below the mountains; then the rainfall gradually declines and cultivation becomes gradually more risky until the 20-centimetre (8-inch) margin is reached, south of which cultivation is not profitable.

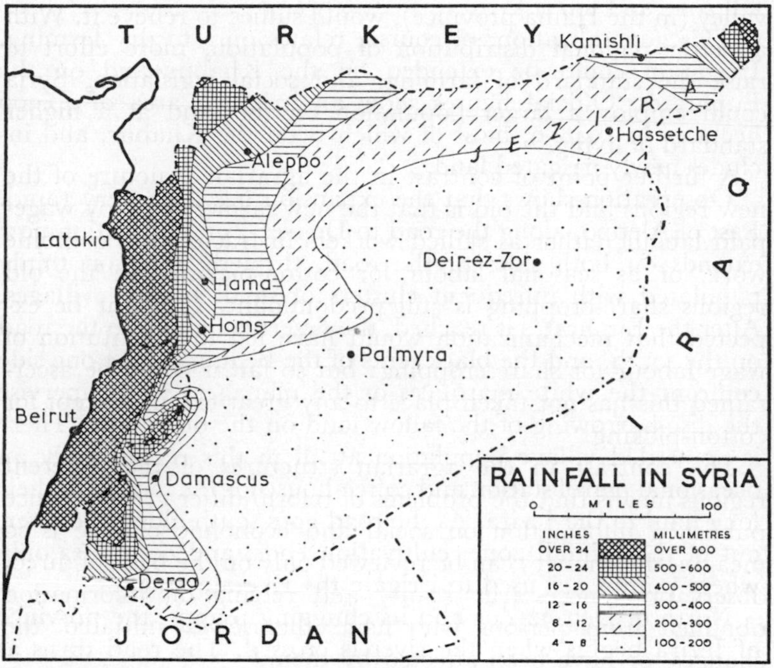

There are no figures to show the rate at which cultivation has been extended, or the extent to which the cultivable land is now cultivated. It seems possible that the limits of expansion for dry farming, in the Jezira province itself, have now been reached.[1] Farmers in Kamishli, who are in the market for land on lease, assert that all the cultivable land is now cultivated. Their contention is borne out by the losses which tractorists incurred in 1951–2 when they pushed cultivation out too far on to the marginal land south of Hassetche, and also by the present tendency on the part of the sheikhs to demand higher

[1] According to the *Statistical Abstract of Syria*, 1950, an area of 444,266 hectares was cultivated (i.e. under crops) in the Jezira in 1948–9. In 1940 an official estimate gave a cropped area of 100,000 hectares. The most rapid expansion took place in 1949–52, but no figures are available for this period.

rents (though rents are still very low by comparison with the more densely settled parts of Syria, amounting to between 10 and 15 per cent of the crop). There is some cultivable land on the Iraqi border, where tribal disputes prevent tractor owners from leasing land, but it is said to be on the border of the rainfall zone and too risky.

This generalization, of course, relates only to dry farming. Irrigation could be extended on the Khabur and on the Euphrates. Official figures show an irrigated area of 40,300 hectares in 1948–9, most of which is on the Khabur, and includes newly irrigated land.

Observation shows that the expansion has been very rapid. East of Aleppo, along the road to Deir-ez-Zor, cultivation now extends on both sides of the road, through a region thinly populated with infrequent clusters of small beehive villages. After the Euphrates is reached, the desert comes up to the road on the south, and the black tents of the Beduin on the one side confront the white marquees of the managers who supervise the disc-harrowing of the fallow land on the other side. There is no settled village population at all in this region, only an occasional petrol station and coffee-house for the lorries on their long haul to the Jezira. As the road goes south along the river, out of the rainfall zone, cultivation ends, and continues only where pumps are used to irrigate the riverain tracts.

North of Deir-ez-Zor and its chugging pumps, the province of Jezira begins when the river is crossed. The road turns at once into a desert track for about 80 miles along the telegraph poles, and then enters the cultivated zone where the road begins again, about 20 miles south of Hassetche. There are still no settled villages, only the new white tents which provide habitation during the harvest and sowing seasons. Police patrols and security officers keep a keen watch for incoming strangers.

Kamishli, the capital of the province, is a mixture of Macedonia and Kansas. The little shops in the *souk* are stuffed with imported tinned food, camel bags and whips, and sequined sandals; the old crafts of rope-making, tanning, and leather work continue beside the smithies repairing big machinery. Ancient Kurdish women in orange and crimson and Beduin in sheepskins sit outside the plate-glass windows of big stores which sell tractors and farm machinery, electrical equipment, refrigerators, washing-machines, baths, and radio sets. There are five or six such shops in a town with a population of some 75,000 (ten years ago it was only 30,000). The town has a new hospital, a new water-supply, and a good new modern hotel with a Lebanese *maître d'hôtel*, Swiss-trained. Its streets are not yet paved.

The little capital is inaccessible. The main line from Baghdad to Aleppo runs through it, carrying some of the region's grain exports, but as the line passes through Turkish territory on the way to Aleppo, traffic is restricted whenever friction arises between Syria and Turkey. Then the road must be used, and the cost of transport is high, for only one road, via Deir-ez-Zor, is open in winter and the journey from Kamishli to Aleppo is 336 miles, most of it on a vile surface, and partly no surface at all. Passengers go by lorry, bus, and car, while the new entrepreneurs use the cheap air service to Aleppo.

The province has changed over from nomadic grazing to highly mechanized grain growing and irrigated cotton cultivation in a short space of time. It is a sparsely populated region; in 1949 its total population as given was 155,643, as compared with 111,300 in 1940. The population is racially mixed, about 50 per cent being Kurdish and 40 per cent Arab. In religion it is predominantly Moslem, with a Christian minority in the towns.

The question arises of whether social and economic change at this pace does not create unrest among the Beduin who are losing their grazing land to cultivation. The region was always unsettled during the mandatory period. The French did not establish their authority there until 1930. They favoured the tribal authorities against the middle-class town population, and so weighted the balance in favour of the nomads against the cultivators. Racial and religious conflicts complicated this situation. There was a demand for autonomy, encouraged by certain of the local French officials,[1] which in 1937 led to a serious revolt of the Kurdish population, supported by the Christians. Though the revolt was put down, unrest continued. It was indeed the main reason why the region could not be developed for cultivation before.

[1] See A. H. Hourani, *Syria and Lebanon* (London, RIIA, 1946), pp. 215-16.

In the last years of the mandate the French authorities, in a last attempt to pacify the region, assigned the ownership of state lands in tribal occupation east of the 'desert line' to the tribal authorities.[1] The tribal sheikhs became the legal owners of very large areas of uncultivated land. These they lease for cultivation to the new tractor farmers, for rents which represent between 10 and 15 per cent of the gross produce; some land has also been sold. As a result the sheikhs have become wealthy, while the tribesmen receive nothing, and lose their rights to graze their herds.

Clearly there is the possibility of social conflict in this situation. The town merchant class is now predominant, and there would seem to be no racial or religious conflicts on the surface. But foreigners are not allowed to enter the Jezira without a special permit, and their entrance and exit are closely watched and strictly controlled. The reason given for this restriction, in Kamishli, was that the Government wishes the social change to proceed as smoothly as possible—which suggests that there is some likelihood of trouble.

Whether or not there is a possibility of unrest among the tribesmen—and there may well be—there was no sign of trouble in 1955. Tribesmen of the Beni Shammar sat sadly in the black tent with green corn on every side, and said that they did not know why they still kept camels.[2] The camels and their attendants have been ousted, and the tribal organization is breaking up. Whether this causes real hardship is difficult to say. Nothing is really known about the effects on the Beduin; the general view was they had moved south across the Iraq frontier into the Sinjar region. The numbers affected are not large, and perhaps there can be an adjustment. The younger generation can find work in the little boom towns, in building and even as tractor and lorry drivers. The Government in 1953 allotted areas of land to tribesmen for individual cultivation, in the district to the east of Hassetche.[3] This measure may suffice to maintain the older generation. It is always

[1] See p. 105 below.

[2] Their sheikh was not with them; he is a member of Parliament, and hostile to the Government, and in favour of Syria's adherence to the Baghdad Pact; the single vote for Nuri Said in Syria's last presidential election may perhaps have been cast by him.

[3] See p. 104 below.

sad to see the end of an old technique, and such an exacting one, the basis of such an ancient way of life. But it has been dying for a long time, and only the romantic will regret this dramatic final stage in the long conflict between the nomad and the cultivator.

The Merchant-Tractorists. Nothing certain is known about the distribution of ownership, except that a large proportion of the land is owned by the tribal sheikhs and cultivated by a new class, the merchant-tractorists. The big farmer entrepreneurs of north Syria are not, for the most part, large landowners, but rent land from the tribal sheikhs, at low rents. When the new entrepreneurs undertake irrigation farming and install pumps, they purchase the land. Predominantly they are pioneer risk-taking capitalists investing in machinery and seed; their capital originated in war-time commercial profits, but they now rely largely on bank credit. Credit is provided by the Agricultural Bank lending at 9 per cent, and by the State Bank lending at 5 per cent. Loans are secured on the machinery, since land cannot be offered as security because it is not the property of the borrower. Shortage of credit is the main grievance of this class. Yet in relation to the risks of Jezira farming these rates are not high. Certainly shortage of credit has not hindered expansion, for losses have been incurred because the new farmers pushed out cultivation to the edge of the rainfed zone where even normal rainfall is insufficient. Natural conditions make cultivation risky, and it is unreasonable to expect the banks to share the risks to a greater extent than they already do. The failure of the 1955 harvest would have made most Jezira farmers bankrupt if the banks had not come to their aid.

Most of these entrepreneurs have learnt what they know of agriculture in the last fifteen years, since they were merchants and traders before with no farming background. Now technical experience has been bought the hard way. When they need experts for cotton they know where to hire them—in Egypt—just as they know where to acquire the capacity to run a repair shop—as agents for foreign machinery firms.

It is noteworthy that most of them are self-made men, with no inherited wealth. The families of the largest operators were Christian emigrants from Turkey after the first world war.

Although there are also Moslem farmer-entrepreneurs, it is the Christian minority which has taken the lead. The whole expansion is an interesting example of how capital has been accumulated and invested outside the ranks of the established landowning class, by people who twenty years ago were neither wealthy nor influential.

Three or four of these entrepreneurs now operate on a large scale—large by the standard of any country, and in little Syria enormous. The whole cropped area of this country, it must be remembered, is only 5 million acres, of which less than half is in the north, including rather less than a million in the Jezira province itself. The areas which the largest operators plant are not known with any certainty, for their farming operations are measured not in acreage but in bags of seed sown—an indication of the uncertainty of the return and the flexibility of their investments. Two, however, operate on at least 100,000 hectares (250,000 acres).

The biggest of these entrepreneurs, commonly known as the King of the Jezira, is Pierre Mamarbachi, an Armenian of Aleppo, who was formerly associated with the family grain-exporting firm, Mamarbachi Brothers, but who now operates independently. He is a small quiet elderly man in a dusty air-conditioned office in Aleppo, who has done big things; the irrigation and cotton plantations on the Khabur, the model village settlement at Tell Manajir on the Euphrates, the planting of a million poplars, and tractor-farming on 100,000 hectares—possibly more. At Kaysouma, forty miles east of Aleppo, he has 6,000 hectares (15,000 acres) under wheat and barley, managed by a qualified agronomist, and employs the labour of four villages, newly sprung up clusters of beehives where before there were only two or three houses. The land which was too stony for cultivation has now been cleared and ploughed to a depth of 40 centimetres and produces $1–1\frac{1}{2}$ tons to the hectare, a high yield for Syria.

Labour shortage is a problem, which he meets by building villages, or moving workers in lorries. He pays his workers cash wages and employs them throughout the year, which is better by far than share-cropping. His vast lands in the Jezira are rented from sheikhs, but his irrigated land has been purchased from the state, and sometimes he pays both the sheikh and the Government, to make sure, since no one can say which really owns some of the land. Local gossip, keenly interested and well informed, said that the drought in the spring of 1955 lost him £2 million, for the millions depend on a few inches of rain. He has experimented with rain-making apparatus, but this was a failure, because there was no cloud.

The second biggest operators are the firm of Asfar and Najjar Brothers, with offices in Damascus, Aleppo, and Kamishli. The firm is a family of five brothers, Syrian Orthodox by religion, who emigrated from Diarbekir some twenty-five years ago. They began to cultivate wheat and barley in the Jezira in 1943, and for five years made no profit, because harvests were bad. The good years from 1948 brought high profits and they are now cultivating 100,000 hectares, round Ras el-Ain and in the district of Kamishli. About half of this land has been purchased, the rest being rented from the sheikhs. They also cultivate 3,000 hectares of irrigated land on the Khabur, supplied by pumps. They are constructing a model settlement at Mabrouka, twenty miles west of Ras el-Ain. On their enormous holding they employ permanently only some 500 workers in all, with 700 additional labourers in the cotton harvest season—an indication of how little employment is given by this type of expansion.

The Najjars have found the shortage of labour a great obstacle, and in order to attract skilled workers as settlers they have introduced an original system offering to finance tractor-farmers with loans of machinery on the basis of a five-year share-cropping contract. Under this scheme they offer to the prospective tenant, or to groups of tenants in partnership, 10,000 dunums[1] (2,500 acres) of land and advance capital to the value of £10,000 in the form of combines and tractors, seed and fuel, wages at the rate of £S150 (£15) per month, and the same allowance for the share-cropping tenant himself. The gross output is divided in the proportion of 40 per cent for the Najjar family and 60 per cent for the tenant. The 5 per cent rent is paid to the sheikh by the Najjars, out of their share, while the tenant, out of his share, must repay 20 per cent of the cost of the machinery. At the end of the five years the machinery should become the property of the tenant, and he should then

[1] 1 Syrian dunum = 0·25 acres.

be offered a lease of the land, paying 5 per cent to the sheikh and 5 per cent to the Najjars. Up to the present seventeen such contracts have been made, with small groups working either as partners or as managers with employed labourers who receive a 2 per cent share of the gross produce in addition to their wages. None of these contracts is yet completed, and the 1955 crop failure will delay the payments.

This scheme is an attempt to adapt the customary practice of share-cropping to mechanized farming. From the point of view of the family the expenditure on labour involved is higher than the cost of labour employed directly, but this is more than compensated by the reduction in the cost of supervision and management. This cost item is high, because during the ploughing season tractors work continuously day and night. From the point of view of the tenants the drawback is the difficulty of repaying fixed sums of money when output is so variable. Although the risks may be too great to make this type of settlement both stable and highly profitable, it is a practical attempt to set up farm units which are suited to the technical conditions in the new regions of the north.

The construction of the Mabrouka Settlement, in which the brothers feel great pride, and the contract scheme have given the family a deserved reputation for public spirit, not less commendable because it is welded to private enterprise. It pleases Syrians to see brothers working together, and there is no friction between the family and its Moslem managers and staff. Elie Najjar, the young manager of the Damascus office, represents Kamishli in Parliament as a member of the Democratic Bloc, and urges on the Government the need for devoting more funds to the construction of roads. The parliamentary representation of growing local needs, as distinct from the preservation of traditional wealth, is a new and healthy element in Syrian politics.

There are a few other large operators in the region, among them Abdul-Masih Asfahan, a Syrian Catholic, and Abdul-Aziz el-Nazla. The other tractor-entrepreneurs are small in comparison, planting from 200 to 1,500 bags. In Kamishli alone there are said to be 600 of these smaller farmers, mostly Christian refugees from Turkey. These are the people who buy refrigerators and washing-machines, while the sheikhs buy their annual Cadillac. The smaller farmers run machine-service garages and petrol-stations.

This new class has played an essential part in developing the country, by its willingness to take risks. It does not, as yet, form a stable class, for it does not invest much in land improvement. The irrigation farming is, of course, a permanent improvement in agriculture; but as yet it is on a small scale, compared with dry farming. The variety of the functions undertaken by these new entrepreneurs provides an interesting contrast to the attitude of the landowners in the older regions.

The Old Regions: The Provinces of Homs and Hama

In the old regions of the country the share-cropping system continues unchanged. The proportion of the produce taken by the landowner varies with the density of the agricultural population, being highest near the towns and lowest on the desert rim. When irrigation water is supplied by the landowner, the proportion taken by the landowner is higher. In central Syria a prevalent share division is 50:50, if the cultivator provides seed, labour, or draught livestock, and the landowner provides only land. If the landowner provides seed, working livestock, and water, as well as land, he takes 75 per cent of the gross produce, and the cultivator takes 25 per cent.

In the Homs–Hama plain region there has been a great improvement in methods of farming, resulting from the irrigation scheme on the Orontes, which has enabled cultivation of cotton. For cotton cultivation landowners generally undertake to supply seed and water, and livestock or tractor work. The proportion of share-croppers working for 25 per cent of the crop has increased: and the proportion of labour employed has increased also. The extent of this change is not known; but local informants estimated that about half the share-croppers in this region work on the 25:75 division. Technical progress has thus reduced the cultivators' share in the gross output of the land, though it may not have reduced their total income, since in the Homs region gross output is certainly higher. In Hama the increase in population in a rather densely settled area, coupled with this change in the customary division, has probably reduced cultivators' incomes.

Conditions of extreme poverty can be seen in the villages on landowners' estates in this region. In the Ghab valley there is a striking contrast between the destitution and disease apparent in the villages on the chief landowner's estate at the bottom of the valley and the prosperity of a peasant village at the head of the valley, Bab el-Takah. In this village the farmers owned holdings of 100, 150, and 200 dunums (25, 37, and 50 acres); they were healthy and well-clothed. Prosperity had come, they said, with the introduction of the cotton crop. To cultivate their lands they jointly hire a tractor from a Hama merchant, giving half the cotton in return for tractor work and seed, an interesting example of enterprise on an informal co-operative basis.

The Hauran and the Jebel Druze. These two regions, among the oldest settled in the country, now have a serious problem of congestion on the land. In the Hauran, a district of black basalt houses and stony fields, the *musha'a* custom of re-allotting land at regular intervals was practised until recently, and may still continue. The villagers live on a narrow subsistence margin. The failure of the 1955 harvest would have been disastrous for them, had the Government not distributed seed. Formerly the surplus labour from these villages went to Haifa to work in the docks; it now goes to Beirut, and to a lesser extent to the Jezira.

Some useful efforts to improve agricultural methods are now beginning. Artesian wells are being dug under the supervision of the FAO Mission. There is a new experimental station at Ezra'a, under the direction of a young Palestinian, working on dates of sowing and on rates of fertilizer application, under the guidance of the FAO Mission. This is the first experimental station for dry farming. There is no tractor ploughing in this region, because the land is too stony and the peasants too poor.

The Jebel Druze villages are also mainly peasant owned, though one of the hereditary ruling families, the Atrash, has large properties. The villages are over-populated, growing figs and olives and grain in tiny terraced fields on the mountainside. The capital, Suweida, has declined in importance and feels the impact of Jezira competition, since it formerly thrived on the grain trade.

The Ghouta of Damascus, intensively cultivated and well irrigated, and also densely populated, has some peasant properties. The greater part of the land is held in medium-sized properties worked by share-croppers, and owned by civil servants and professional and commercial families in Damascus. In recent years they have invested considerably in fruit-trees; some were anxious to emphasize that they were not absentee owners now. A slight improvement in rural living standards has occurred, through the wider opportunities for earning in industry. The only rural welfare services are provided by the health and home training for women carried out in three villages by the Near East Foundation—patient long-term work which every international agency should study. The Foundation has succeeded in training competent young women to teach in their schools and to work with village midwives, that most conservative profession.

In these old regions, with their traditional rural poverty, the economic advance of the country has brought little or no improvement. Their needs are various: in the share-cropping regions the land system does not prevent technical advance, but it does prevent social progress, and reform is certainly needed. In the peasant regions resettlement could relieve the pressure of population. In all regions, rural welfare services and agricultural education are much needed.

Landowners in these old regions reside on their estates to a greater extent than they did in the past. There is great variation in social and economic function among them: some have invested in pump irrigation for cotton, and have shown interest in improving cultivation, while others are absentees with little interest in agriculture. Generally speaking, they are not much interested in long-term improvement. In the Homs–Hama region the big estates have been responsible for the over-cultivation of cotton and excessive use of water, which has lowered the water-table, so that the neighbouring villages are short even of drinking-water.[1]

One landowner, however, has undertaken a large all-round development scheme entirely on his own initiative, combining land reclamation, irrigation, and experimental farming with the settlement of peasant proprietors on reclaimed land. This is the Kurd Hussein Ibish, once world famous as a big-game

[1] In the winter of 1955 the village of Selemiya on the border of the rainfed zone was obliged to fetch its drinking-water from Hama, twenty miles away.

hunter and explorer, who took up farming late in life. During the second world war he bought up at a low price—for he was not a rich man—the poor marshlands of the Wadi Awaj, where malaria and Beduin raids on the springs prevented cultivation. On these lands he has now drained and reclaimed 24,000 hectares, partly for irrigation and partly for dry farming, growing cotton, sugar beet, and water melons. The estate at Hijaneh, about twenty-five miles south of Damascus, extends for many miles parallel to the Jordan road. About 6,000 families are now settled there, partly as owners, partly as labourers. About two-thirds of the land Ibish has allotted to the peasants in ownership, simply because he believes this to be right. All profits are reinvested in the land, since he is not interested in anything but the community he has created, where he is judge and absolute ruler. He prefers Alawis as farmers (they are the best workers) and will take tractor drivers only from Zahle, because this town first introduced tractors into Syria (in 1936).

Not surprisingly, this remarkable man is regarded by Damascus society as an eccentric; his prejudices against electricity, cars, Damascene and Beiruti merchants are more easily intelligible to the English mind. The story is told that when Kuwatli visited Ibish to offer him the premiership he refused, on the ground that it was better to rule in Hijaneh than to be the slave of a parliamentary majority. When the peasants were assembled on this occasion to offer the homage expected by politicians, Ibish introduced the President with the words: 'This is the man who makes you pay taxes'. Counting the world well lost for agriculture, Ibish in character and appearance recalls the English or Scottish landowners of a generation ago, a tall, gaunt old man in tweeds, who would look right in Banbury market or on the Warwickshire County Council.

The old landowner families of the Homs–Hama region are not of this stamp. They use tractors, and have installed canals and pumps to make use of the water provided by the irrigation of the Orontes valley. But they are still *rentiers* in mind and income, who live on the labour of their share-croppers, advancing seed and lending money to the cultivator in return for three-quarters of the gross produce. Their mentality is that of the *grand seigneur*.

One who is called the richest man in Syria expressed the views of his class in a long diatribe against the West. The Americans, he said, wrongly believe that social unrest has social causes, whereas in fact the true explanation of social unrest in Syria is the victory of Zionism. In his opinion the whole country, including the Army, is permeated by Communism, and it is the Americans and the Jews who are to blame. This point of view has an element of truth, since the Socialist Party, which is strongest in this landowner's *seigneurie*, is extremely nationalist as well as socialist.

Yet the landowner's argument seemed to carry less conviction when he went on to speak of the imminent danger that the land in the Ghab valley, now under reclamation and adjoining his estates, would be distributed to small farmers, for this would cause a shortage of labour in the region. The settlement of the Ghab lands would, of course, be beneficial to the fellahin, because it would relieve the pressure of population and cause a rise in wages and share-croppers' incomes on the adjacent estates. Thus the old attitude persists; its power is still an obstacle to reform.

CHANGES IN THE LAW OF LAND TENURE

Legal changes carried out in the mandatory period and in recent years have changed the law of land tenure and introduced a conception of ownership based on the French Civil Code. The Ottoman Land Code has never been explicitly abrogated, and its confusing categories of land are still used, but they now have little importance.

The first important change was the introduction of a general system of land survey and registration of title. In 1923 the French authorities granted a concession to M. Duraffourd, to undertake survey and registration as Director of the Bureau de Cadastre. The Law concerning Immovable Property (No. 3339 of 1930) laid down the principles and procedure. Registration was compulsory and survey was efficient. Up to 1943 an area of 3,544,883 hectares had been surveyed and registered.[1] This area covered most of the cultivated land in the older settled parts of the country. No survey or registration was

[1] M. Duraffourd died in 1940, but his staff continued the work of the Bureau until the termination of the Mandate.

undertaken in the Jebel Druze or the Hauran, for political reasons, or in the Jezira, which was in a constant state of upheaval, and where not much land was cultivated. In the Euphrates province only small areas were registered.

Registration of title conferred absolute rights of ownership on the individual, and was advantageous in that it introduced greater security. It brought no change in the distribution of property, although the French authorities did grant secure title to peasant cultivators. On the whole, however, the benefits of greater security went to the existing large landowners.

Settlement of title was sometimes, though by no means always, accompanied by the consolidation of the strips into which the peasants' holdings were divided. It was generally accompanied by the cessation of the practice of periodic reallotment of holdings (*musha'a*), a practice which continued in most parts of Syria. Occasionally the registration of *musha'a* land areas was carried out by registering each villager's share in the land as a fraction of the total area. This practice was adopted because the Director of the Survey was impressed by the failure of the Ottoman Government to settle land in divided holdings, and believed that the *musha'a* custom had a real basis in the social life of the country, and should continue if the villagers desired it. However, this practice was not generally followed, and for the most part title was registered in divided holdings, so that registration generally involved the establishment of individual ownership of specific areas of land.

The other important change concerned the legal status of State Domain land. In conformity with the Moslem conception of ownership, the state claimed formal ownership of all land (with the exception of *mulk* and *waqf*). But after 1918 state ownership acquired a new meaning, because the State of Syria had come into the possession of large areas of land which had formerly belonged to the Ottoman Crown estates. These lands had been the personal property of the Sultan Abdul Hamid, and had formerly been administered by a special department in Constantinople, the Sanniya, and had earned a large revenue. After the Young Turk revolution of 1908, ownership of these lands passed to the Ottoman State and thence to the ownership of each of the successor states, in accordance with the Treaty of Lausanne.

Under the system of survey and registration, these lands were registered as the property of the state. Since these lands were held by the state as a juridical person, this form of state property corresponded to a Western conception. A special department, the Directorate of State Domain, was set up to administer them. Laws were passed governing their disposal by sale or lease. These lands were for the most part thinly settled and little cultivated, though they included some good land in the Homs region. Colonization was undertaken, but the work was not completed. The leasing of State Domain was an important source of revenue.[1]

There were, therefore, two categories of state land: the land which was registered in the name of the state, and at the disposal of the Directorate of State Domain; and the land over which the state claimed formal possession according to the Moslem conception. This included all occupied land to which title was not registered, and also all unoccupied and uncultivated land. A law was passed in 1926 confirming the Ottoman right of prescriptive ownership, by which persons who brought uncultivated land into cultivation could acquire ownership if they could prove a period of cultivation. For the occupation to be legal, a licence from the state was necessary, and proof of five years' cultivation entitled the occupier to have the land registered in his name. Thus the old Ottoman prescriptive right was given legal status. However, if such land were already registered as State Domain, no prescriptive right of ownership could be acquired over it, though it could be leased or purchased from the Directorate of State Domain.

Special legislation was passed in 1940 and 1941 assigning unregistered state land east of the 'desert line' to the tribal authorities, granting them registered title through a special emergency procedure (under Legislative Decrees No. 132 of 1940 and No. 141 of 1941).[2] This emergency legislation was largely responsible for the present distribution of ownership in the Jezira.

The main results of the legislation carried out by the French authorities were therefore:

[1] In 1946 the revenue from State Domain amounted to £S14,958,000, while revenue from other sources amounted to £S94,746,000 (Nassib Bulos, *Legal Aspects of Land Tenure in Jordan and Syria* (Beirut, UNRWA, 1953)).

[2] See p. 88.

1. The introduction of absolute freehold individual ownership, under the system of survey and registration. This gave greater security to landowners in the regions where it was carried out, and tended to break up the semi-communal forms of tenure.

2. The introduction of a Western conception of ownership for registered state land.

The Moslem conception of state ownership only retained its validity for unregistered land, which might be land in the occupation of individuals, or land uncultivated and unoccupied.

The Syrian Civil Code of 1949 codified the legislation of the mandatory period. It retains the categories of land used in the Ottoman Land Code, with some modifications, as follows:

1. *Mulk:* absolute freehold, in urban areas only.
2. *Miri:* property of which the title is vested in the state and in regard to which a right of possession may be acquired.
3. *Matruka:* subject to easements: property of which the title is vested in the state, but in regard to which the public or a group enjoy a right by usufruct under administrative law (Public State Domain).
4. *Matruka mahmia* (protected): property owned by the state, government authorities or municipalities (Private State Domain).
5. *Mubah* or *mawat* (deserted or dead): uncultivated land of which the title is vested in the state, but which has not been surveyed or registered.

The *waqf* category was not included, as it is treated by the Code as a 'real right', not a special category.[1] During the mandatory period the French authorities permitted and encouraged the sale of the then extensive *waqf* properties to business enterprises, irrigation concessions, and large landowners. The Civil Code prohibited the creation of family *waqfs*, stating that *waqfs* may not be created except for a charitable purpose. The Husni Zaim administration abolished existing family *waqfs*.

The five categories listed in the Code no longer have much practical importance, since the distinction between *mulk* and

[1] Nassib Bulos, *Legal Aspects of Land Tenure in Jordan and Syria.*

miri is no longer valid. In law, owners who receive registered title are still *miri* holders, i.e. nominally tenants of the state, but in practice they own the land absolutely. The important distinction lies between registered land and unregistered land. Registered land may be either the property of individuals, or of the state. Land registered in the name of the state corresponds to the fourth category, Private State Domain. Public State Domain, the third category, includes land used for public purposes, for example public buildings, market places, and roads. The only element of the Ottoman Code remaining in force was the state's right of ownership over all unregistered land, i.e. the land included in the fifth category, as 'dead' or uncultivated.

So far as this last category was concerned, the Code maintained the provisions of the law of 1926, which entitled persons who had brought *mubah* or *mawat* land into cultivation to have the land registered as their property if they could prove five years' cultivation.

The Syrian Constitution of 1950 laid down the principles on which land reform legislation could be based. It declared that maximum limits of ownership were to be defined when title to property was registered. These maxima, however, were not to be retroactive, i.e. did not relate to properties already registered. (Legislation to enforce a general limitation on large ownership would therefore require an amendment of the Constitution.) The Constitution also affirmed that small and medium ownership was to be encouraged, and that State Domain lands were to be distributed to cultivators without land.

However, after the termination of the Mandate, the system of survey and registration introduced by the French authorities was not continued, allegedly for lack of funds, in reality, it must be presumed, because large landowners were able to acquire properties by extending cultivation over unregistered land. The necessary mechanism for carrying out the provisions of the Constitution therefore did not exist.

ATTEMPT AT REFORM

The first and so far the only attempt to carry out the provisions of the Constitution was made under the Shishakli régime in 1952. The Decree for the Distribution of State Lands

(No. 96 of 30 January 1952) was intended to be a radical social reform. It formed part of the 'programme for workers and peasants', announced in January 1952. Its stated object was to put an end to the illegal occupation of state land. The first provision

> declared null and void all possession by feudal lords and other influential persons over unregistered state land, no matter how vast and extensive such land may be, if its area exceeded a limit of 150 hectares per owner in the Jezireh and the Furat [Euphrates] Desert districts and 50 hectares in other parts of Syria.

The decree further declared that only title-deeds to specified areas were to be recognized, and that where landowners held areas of land exceeding the boundaries specified in the title-deeds, these areas were to be ignored, i.e. surrendered. The Directorate of State Domain was authorized, after obtaining the approval of the Council of Ministers, to distribute these lands 'acquired through force and usurpation' to needy peasants in return for small sums payable in instalments. If purchasers failed to cultivate the land, within a period of two years, it would revert to the state.[1]

The law had two defects. First, it was inapplicable, because the area and location of the unregistered state land were unknown. Second, it rested on a confusion as to the legal status of occupiers of unregistered state land. Under the law of 1926, incorporated into the Civil Code, persons who brought unregistered state land into cultivation could acquire registered title by proof of a period of cultivation. However, as the system of registration had been allowed to lapse, there was no legal procedure for establishing ownership, though in practice the right of ownership acquired by cultivation was recognized. Thus the old Ottoman method of acquiring ownership was no longer tied in with the legal system. The tenure held by landowners who had extended cultivation over unregistered state land was not usurped or fraudulent, on the basis of customary law, but neither was it legal, on the basis of the Civil Code. The discontinuance of registration of title broke the link between the old legal system and the new.[2]

[1] *First Statement on Achievements of Syria's Government of the New Regime, during three months in office, December 1951–March 1952*, by General Fawzi Selo [Prime Minister] (Damascus, 1952), pp. 50–1.

[2] Nassib Bulos, *Legal Aspects of Land Tenure in Jordan and Syria.*

When the legal defect was recognized, the decree was repealed, and a new decree (No. 135 of 29 October 1952) replaced it. This law abolished the distinction between registered and unregistered state land, and so abolished the last vestige of the Moslem conception of formal ownership. It declared that all *mawat* lands (i.e. dead lands brought into cultivation) were subject to the administration of State Domain, and thus assimilated the status of these lands to the State Domain proper, which the state owned as a juridical person. The law stipulated that no prescriptive title could be acquired over *mawat* lands, despite the fact that they had not been registered in the Registers of Immovable Property or in those of State Domain.

The Decree did not, however, dispossess squatters completely but validated their title to an area not exceeding 200 hectares per person, and a similar area for every member of the family of the recipient. Any area in excess of this figure reverted automatically to the State.

Article 5 of the Decree states that these lands would be sold or leased in accordance with the regulations made by the Council of Ministers. The idea was to sell or lease these lands for a nominal value to landless peasants. It is estimated that as a result of this decree, some five million dunums of land would be added to the State Domain.[1]

But since the area of State Domain land was still unknown, the decree could not be carried out. It was therefore necessary to resume the survey and registration of land. In 1952 a training centre for land surveyors was set up. The former members of M. Duraffourd's staff were recruited, when available, and survey began again in 1953.

According to the figures issued by the Cadastral Survey Office quoted on p. 83 above, the area comprised in the State Domain is some 1½ million hectares. This figure, however, includes only the registered State Domain, and not the *mawat* lands which were brought under the Directorate of State Domain under Decree No. 135 of 1952. Most of the registered State Domain lies in the provinces of Homs and Hama; the total extent of State Domain land, including the *mawat* land, is unknown. Even the area of registered State Domain is not known precisely, since the registers have not been maintained.

[1] ibid.

So long as the Shishakli régime continued it was intended to proceed with the distribution of land under this decree. In January 1953 a decree was issued governing the conditions for distribution of the state land. Persons already cultivating the land and other applicants were to be allowed to purchase the land at a price equivalent to 25 per cent of its real value, and could acquire up to 50 hectares of non-irrigated land and 10 hectares of irrigated land. In the Jezira and Euphrates provinces they could acquire up to 200 hectares of non-irrigated land, and the same area for every member of the family of the recipient.

The only direct action taken under the law has been the distribution of tribally occupied land to its Beduin occupants in the district of Hassetche in the Jezira. According to information received in Kamishli in April 1955, the tribesmen have secured ownership. It should be borne in mind, however, that in this case the state has not distributed land to new owners, but has confirmed the tribesmen's right to hold individual ownership of land formerly occupied collectively. In practice this means that the state gives the tribesmen the right to take an income from the merchant-tractorists who cultivate the land. The usual practice is for the sheikh to take the rent from the tractorist as his own right, and to distribute small gifts among the tribesmen. The practical result of granting registered title is that the tribesmen share the rent among themselves, a useful measure of social security, which protects them against displacement without preventing mechanized cultivation.

An indirect result of the 1952 legislation has been the resumption of survey and registration of title. Progress has been slow, owing to the shortage of qualified staff and funds. In the 1955 budget funds were increased to 1 million Syrian pounds. In the Jezira province aerial survey is being carried out, but here too progress has been slow, and large sums allocated (£S400,000 in 1954 and £S300,000 in 1955) were not spent. The boundaries shown in the air photographs are to be the basis for claims for title registration.

The possible effect on the legal limitation on size of newly registered holdings cannot be foreseen in the absence of figures for the total area of state land. Most of the dry land farmed in big areas by the new entrepreneurs in the Jezira is the property of the tribal authorities who acquired registered title under the emergency decrees of 1940 and 1941, and would therefore not be affected by the limitation on new ownership. The attempt to enforce a limitation on ownership may of course be ineffective. The 200 hectares maximum, plus 200 for every member of the family, would allow a fairly large unit of 2,000 or 3,000 hectares, since families are elastic. The existence of the limitation may simply mean that the entrepreneur who wishes to purchase land to install pumps will register it in the name of remote and elderly relatives.

In principle, it seems unwise to put any obstacle on the size of properties in the regions of rapid expansion.[1] It may check the entrepreneurs' desire to purchase, and so prevent investment, without benefiting new settlers. If the state were able to undertake a positive policy of encouraging settlement in the new regions (or indeed on state land in the whole of the country), the imposition of a fixed acreage maximum would be reasonable. In present conditions, to impose a purely negative restriction on the size of newly registered holdings may penalize the 'developer' and good employer, while exempting the *rentier* landowners in the old regions, killing the plant where it is growing, while leaving the dead wood intact. The real weakness of the new farming is its failure to maintain soil fertility. But limitation of acreage will not remedy this defect.

If it is the object of government policy to prevent new great inequalities in landownership from arising, the best method would be to retain the state land in public ownership, and lease it to farmers in large units for long periods, so that farm sizes could be adjusted to the needs of closer settlement when leases terminate, and leasehold conditions could enforce better cropping practices.[2] Such a policy would fit in with the legislation of the mandatory period governing State Domain land, and with the 1952 law which brings all state land under the administration of the Directorate of State Domain.

[1] The International Bank Mission felt it necessary to recommend a limitation of size for new holdings, though it sensibly recommended 1,000 hectares as a suitable maximum (*The Economic Development of Syria*, pp. 68 and 202).

[2] For an interesting example of the use of this type of tenure in a developing economy see the Australian policy of crown leasehold, described in UN, Dept. of Economic Affairs, *Progress in Land Reform*, pp. 186–9.

To deal with the problem of inequality in incomes from agriculture without penalizing the developers, the right method would be to reform the system of taxation, with progressive rates according to the size of the property, and allowing rebates for newly installed pumps and tree plantations.

THE POLITICAL PROSPECTS

As the preceding sections have shown, Syria is in the fortunate position of having much land for dry farming and for irrigation in relation to its farm population. There is no need for a general measure for redistribution of ownership. A redistribution policy, on the lines carried out in Egypt, is a necessity in countries which are densely populated and where great inequalities in property allow landowners to exact a monopoly price for the use of land. The object of imposing maximum limits on the size of holdings, in these conditions, is to break up the institutional monopoly by distributing land areas in excess of the legal maximum to small farmers, and thus to secure a wider distribution of income from agriculture.

In Syria, by contrast with Egypt, the differences in the agrarian structures of the different regions make general limitation of the sizes of holdings impracticable. In the Ghouta of Damascus, for example, which is intensively cultivated and irrigated, 100 hectares is a large holding; while in the extensively cultivated Jezira 1,000 hectares is rightly considered a small farm. Nor is general limitation necessary, since over the country as a whole there is no shortage of land, and in the new regions there is no monopoly of landownership. In the north the sheikh landowners cannot exact high rents, because the land is sparsely populated and would not be cultivated by the investing entrepreneurs if rents were not low and competitive. The large incomes of the new merchant-tractorists are not derived from institutional monopoly, but from the profits of risk-taking and investment.

But it is also clear that in the older regions there is a need for reform. In the central regions, large landowners, predominantly of the *rentier* type, hold a monopoly of the good land and use it to take an excessive share of the produce. Technical progress has not benefited the share-cropping villagers. The immediate problem of reform today is the poverty of the peasants in these regions, and also in the southern regions, which are mainly peasant owned but somewhat over-populated. This poverty could be relieved by resettlement, in the northern provinces and in state irrigation schemes, both in the north and in the old regions. Where the landowners' monopoly power is strong, legislation to increase the share-croppers' income could be effective, though it is not likely to achieve a great improvement if no resettlement is undertaken.

Thus Syria needs a reform policy, both for today and for tomorrow. The problem is to combine an immediate policy to relieve rural poverty with a long-term policy to utilize land resources more fully, and to conserve them. The country is developing: there is no need to think in terms of maximum and minimum holdings. Tenure policy can aim at granting holdings that will not only ensure the farmer an adequate living standard, but will also enable him to produce for a growing internal and external market.

Resettlement is the key to both problems.

But large-scale resettlement of population by the state in the dry-farming zones would require heavy investment, both in working capital and public services such as roads. Mechanized farming requires large-scale operation, and the climate is far too risky for small farmers to achieve stability, so that new holdings would have to be large, and organized in group settlements with central services. The mere offer of land, even at a low price, will not attract labour (as is shown by the experiment carried out by the Najjar family, described on p. 91 above). Since the Government cannot even undertake the construction of roads in the Jezira, it is unrealistic to suppose that it could find the capital, or the organizing ability, to undertake settlement in dry farming on these lines. So far as any organized settlement has been undertaken, it is the work of the new entrepreneurs, who have built model villages for their skilled labourers. If it were politically possible to associate the big entrepreneurs with the work of a public settlement authority, their practical abilities might overcome administrative delays and muddles. But the idea that private enterprise should be openly and actively associated with Government is alien to political tradition.

The most that the state can do at present would be to

organize small-farmer settlement in state irrigation schemes, less difficult, because yields per acre are higher and more stable, and intensive cultivation in small units would be easier to organize successfully. The settlement of the state lands under reclamation in the Ghab valley in favour of small farmers would have considerable local importance in weakening the power of the landowners, since the valley lies near the densely populated Hama region, where the conditions of the share-croppers are among the worst in the country.

But agrarian reform in Syria is not so much an abstract necessity in the interests of development as a social necessity which arises from the recent social evolution and economic progress of the country. The demand for reform is now expressed by the Arab Socialist Party (officially the Arab Resurrection Socialist Party). The party can rightly claim to represent the interests of the peasants, since it finds its chief support in the fellahin of the Homs–Hama region, and only to a much lesser extent in the industrial workers of Aleppo and Damascus. Its leader, Akram Hourani, is himself from Hama, a man of the people who has had a stormy career. He first held office in Hinnawi's Government in 1949, and later advised Shishakli in drawing up the programme for workers and peasants (which included the abortive state land law of 1952). Opposition mobilized against him, and before Shishakli's fall, in the autumn of 1952, Hourani was under house arrest in Damascus, from which he eventually escaped to Lebanon, to return in 1954. At the elections in August 1954 the party gained 15 seats, of which 5 represent Hama; 1 seat was gained in Homs in a by-election in November 1955.

The party is generally described by its enemies as Communist, for while it does not subscribe to Communist doctrine, it does represent an uncompromising attitude to Western political influence and its driving force is pan-Arab nationalism. Detached observers regard the party as canalizing a social movement, which in one form or another was bound to appear as the natural outcome of conditions in the Homs–Hama district, and representing demands which the progress of the country should be able to meet. Both these attitudes are right: the party can be regarded as a spontaneous labour movement which may become Communist if its aims cannot be achieved otherwise. Hourani himself makes the impression of an intensely concentrated personality, dynamic and intransigent, and driven by convictions autonomous enough to need no formal dogma. Michel Aflak, another leader, is philosophic and idealistic and an economist. The party procession, celebrating victory in Homs with dancing, singing, and tribal drums, seemed neither socialist nor Communist; but simply Revolt in the Desert, for its flag dates from the first world war.

Whatever its ultimate direction, the party at present represents a well-articulated demand for land reform, at the moment expressed in moderate terms as a demand for improvement in the conditions of share-croppers and farm labourers. The leaders recognize that it is impracticable to attempt reform through limitation of holdings since it would be difficult to enforce different maxima in different parts of the country. In the Jezira, where wages are high, such limitation would be contrary to the interests of labour.

In 1955 the party submitted to Parliament a draft Law for the Protection of the Fellah. This covers both share-croppers and agricultural labourers. For share-croppers it provides that all agreements between landowners and cultivators should be based on a written contract; that eviction of the cultivator should be illegal, except for breach of contract; that all cultivators should be entitled to receive loans from the Agricultural Bank; and that in share-cropping agreements the landowner's share should not exceed one-third of the total crop on irrigated land and one-fourth of the total crop on other land. In the old regions, this would greatly increase the share taken by the fellah, which is generally not more than one-half on dry land and one-quarter on irrigated land. For the agricultural labourers the draft law proposes the extension of the Labour Law of 1946 to cover their conditions, and gives them the right to form trade unions.

Though the changes proposed by the bill are reasonable enough in the conditions of Syria's economy, the bill has no chance of acceptance in the present Parliament. The party's demands and its growing support may none the less encourage the Government to proceed with its own draft law, which proposes special labour legislation for agricultural workers, instead of the more radical proposal for the extension of the labour law, and for the share-croppers proposes an improvement in security by means of written contracts, without the essential point, the limitation of the landowner's share, proposed in the Socialist bill. The survival of the parliamentary system in Syria will depend on whether it can produce a measure of reform which will give the fellah a degree of protection.

Doubtless the best solution for Syria's problem of reform would be both legal and economic action. Settlement on irrigated land would relieve population pressure, and weaken the landlords' monopoly where it is strong. The trade union policy of the Socialist Party could certainly force up farm earnings and improve labour conditions. The policies would reinforce each other, since without some movement to new land the demand for higher earnings will be difficult to meet, while resettlement alone will not compel landowners to provide a higher minimum level.

The prospects for a real improvement for the fellahin in Syria are much greater than they are either in Egypt or in Iraq, despite the fact that nothing has so far been done. There is great scope for improvement in farming, as in Egypt there is not; and there is scope for parliamentary action by a party which represents the fellahin, while in Iraq and Egypt no such representation exists.

Whether the social problem can be solved through the mechanism of parliamentary democracy remains to be seen. Syrian society is no longer static; it is evolving as a result of economic change. The rapid upward and outward expansion resembles that of Western Europe during the nineteenth century; or perhaps the Middle West would be a better comparison. There has been a similar upsurge of private enterprise, and a rapid rate of technical change through the investment of private risk capital. Big profits and big losses have been made. The state has played little part in economic life. This nineteenth-century type of expansion has been accompanied by social changes of a nineteenth-century kind: the rise of new liberal entrepreneurs, the 'carrier group' for expansion; and the emergence of a radical labour movement.

The extent of these changes should not be exaggerated; there is no reason to speak of Westernization or social revolutions. The inhabitants of the Damascus *souk* are recognizably much the same as they were when Isabel Burton visited it nearly a century ago. Tribesmen still camp round Hama, and the Jebel Druze can still get rid of a Government.

None the less, the social changes which accompany economic expansion are perceptible, and the comparison with European social evolution is not misleading. The merchant-tractorists in the north are liberals, objecting to state intervention and to the high level of military expenditure (33 per cent of the ordinary budget), just as Victorian business men objected to these things. In origin, function, and outlook they are quite distinct from the old *rentier* landowners, because they represent the greater part played by capital in the economy of the country, while the rise of the Socialist Party represents the demand of labour for a greater share in the growing national income.

These are the real forces making for reform of the land system, not the old-style politicians or the capable higher civil servants. Syrian Governments still reflect the old established order, old wealth and old power, as they inevitably must while the social changes are still in progress. Institutional reform usually lags behind economic change. To demand that the state should carry out the measures of reform which the economic development of the country requires presupposes a Government detached from the old social structure and exercising functions beyond the needs of the established order. In the meantime individuals have done what governments cannot do. The new entrepreneurs have carried out experiments in settling farmers on the land in the new regions; and one landowner at least has settled farmers in the south—a reflection of the need for reform for the sake of increasing production. At the same time the Socialist Party reflects the need of reform for the sake of social progress. Syria is a fortunate country, not only in having new land and new enterprise, but also in having new men who can realize the social needs of the country.

Syria's nineteenth-century type of development has been accompanied by the emergence of strong 'inner-directed' personalities who break through the crust of tradition in practical ways. The shift to the north has been undertaken by the new entrepreneurs, who undermine the political influence of the old landowners. There is not likely to be a link-up between the liberal Manchester men and the fiery leadership of the labour movement. But the two are not in conflict; for the expansion in production is being carried out on new land by new entrepreneurs who offer higher wages, while the socialist movement springs from the worsening conditions in the old regions, and is directed against the *rentier* landowners.

This nineteenth-century social evolution is taking place in a twentieth-century world. The house is wired for social progress, which might be achieved gradually through the parliamentary system, which Syria for the moment precariously maintains. But the currents which come along the wires are too strong, and may fuse the lights, if they force the landowners to take the side of the West and the socialists to take the side of the East.

IV
MONEY IN IRAQ
THE BACKGROUND

Iraq is underdeveloped in the exact literal sense. Its resources are half-utilized; its population is small and poor; its society is primitive and disintegrating; and its environment is only now being brought under control. These conditions are inter-related. The population is small and poor because in the past it could not master its environment, and the environment remained uncontrollable because capital was lacking—a low-pressure vicious-circle economy, as compared with Egypt's high tensions.

In every way but one, rural poverty, the economic position is the reverse of that of Egypt, where the environment is tightly controlled, resources are skilfully utilized, population densely settled, and society highly evolved. Though Iraq's resources are underdeveloped, its conditions do not correspond with the 'underdevelopment' model now most frequently postulated by economists. Two things are unusual: the adverse natural conditions of the Tigris–Euphrates valley, and the abundance of capital. Few countries have so much to develop, or so much to develop it with.

The conjunction of these unusual conditions makes Iraq's situation extraordinary. 'Money is not the only thing that is needed', says Professor Arthur Lewis, 'but money is the *sine qua non*.' In this country money is truly a *sine qua non*, because without it the environment could never be brought under control. Yet Iraq's experience is fascinating, because it demonstrates what money can and cannot do.

Briefly, the adverse factors in the environment are these. The waters of the Tigris and the Euphrates do not provide a regular natural renewal of the fertility of the soil, as the Nile does. Until 1956 the danger of flood was always present in south Iraq, major floods occurring once in every two or three years on both rivers. The exceptionally severe Tigris floods of 1954 threatened Baghdad itself, and destroyed crops on about one-quarter of the area in the irrigation zone.

Yet at the same time there was a shortage of water, which meant that in most of the irrigation zone only a winter crop could be grown, and there was and still is much underemployment on the land. There are two flood periods, December to March, due to the winter rains, and March till June, when the snow melts in the upper reaches of the rivers; and there could therefore be two crop seasons. But until 1956 there was no storage capacity except in the areas served by the two barrages at Kut and Hindiya, and the water available could not be utilized.

Floods combined with shortage of water are not the only obstacles with which agriculture in south Iraq has to contend. Soil salinity is another.[1] The irrigation zone is a delta of marine origin, and the subsoil is saline. As a result of seepage from the high-level rivers and canals, the water-table is high, and capillary action raises the subsoil water to the surface, where it evaporates, leaving the salt behind. Salinity in high proportion can reduce grain yields and may throw the land out of cultivation. Drainage is the only remedy, and must usually be aided by pumping. Many landowners, however, do not undertake drainage, but simply abandon the ruined land, and shift cultivation to new land by digging new canals.

These obstacles to cultivation have affected the southern half of the country. The methods of farming in this zone are wasteful, and not merely primitive. Elsewhere in the Middle East irrigation is accompanied by an intensification of cultivation, through higher yields, high-value crops, and double cropping. But in south Iraq extensive cultivation is practised on irrigated land, and both land and water are wasted. Long

[1] The pump-irrigated lands escape the danger of salinity because the water-table is low, and in some of the flow-irrigated land there is natural drainage (from the Tigris near Baghdad, and farther south where the Tigris drains into the Euphrates). Rather more than half the irrigated land is supplied by flow, the remainder by pumps and other methods. The Haigh Commission estimated that as much as 60 per cent of the flow-irrigated land in south Iraq is affected by salinity (Iraq Govt., Irrigation Development Commission [the Haigh Commission], *Report on the Control of the Rivers of Iraq and the Utilization of their Waters* (Baghdad, 1951), p. 174).

stretches of poor barley, without apparent limits, alternate with long stretches of camel thorn, derelict salt-encrusted land, and expanses of last year's flood water.

The country is sparsely populated. Seen from the air, the region between Baghdad and Basra appears almost empty. The two great rivers wind through an arid featureless plain, with an occasional cluster of mud huts or a small town in the bend of a river. In the north there are vast agoraphobic landscapes of tractor ploughing, with not a house or a tree to be seen for miles.

The last population census, taken in 1947, gave a total of 4,816,185. In 1955 the total was estimated to be 5 million. Nothing certain is known about the rate of increase, though death rates and birth rates are certainly both high.[1] Of this total, between 2½ and 3 million may be estimated as dependent on agriculture.[2] In the last three years the movement to the towns has accelerated, and the lower figure may be nearer the present total.

In relation to this small population, the cultivated area is large. According to the Agricultural Census of 1952–3, the area utilized for agriculture[3] amounted to 13·7 million acres, of which 6·3 million acres were sown with crops and 6·7 million left fallow, the remainder being in orchards, date gardens, vineyards (300,000 acres), and other uses. Assuming that the agricultural population is 2½ million, the area of agricultural land per head is 5 acres, or 2 hectares, somewhat more than in Syria and twenty times as much as in Egypt.

[1] The fact that birth rates and death rates are both high is shown by the fact that half the population is under 20, as Professor Iversen points out (Carl Iversen, *Monetary Policy in Iraq* (Baghdad, National Bank of Iraq, 1954), p. 69; see also Doris G. Addams, 'Current Population Trends in Iraq', *Middle East Journal*, Spring 1956).

[2] The 1947 census gave a rural population of 3,196,304, representing 66·4 per cent of the total population. This number includes an estimated population of 250,000 in nomadic tribes. The Agricultural Census for 1952–3 gave a total of 1·4 million people working on agricultural holdings. This number does not include non-working members of farm families, pastoral farmers or nomadic tribes (*Report on the Agricultural and Livestock Census of Iraq 1952–3*, vol. 1, p. 18). The total population dependent on agriculture, including the non-working members of farm families, should therefore amount to between 2½ and 3 million.

[3] The use of the term 'cultivated land' in Iraq causes confusion, since it may mean the area under crops, or the area under crops and fallow. For this reason the Agricultural Census Report uses the term 'utilized for agriculture', which includes the areas sown in one year and the area in fallow (ibid. table 4).

In addition to the areas which are cultivated now, there are large areas of cultivable land which could be brought under cultivation if water could be stored for irrigation. Estimates of the potentially cultivable area vary, because they depend on what assumptions are made as to capacity for water-storage. The most recent estimate, which is based on the assumption of large storage capacity provided by ten new dams, gives a figure of 5 million acres of additional land.[1] Figures of this kind have a hypnotic effect on official minds. The tendency to regard the extension of cultivation as the main aim of development derives from the engineer's approach which has dominated most thinking about the future of the country. Yet the immediate need is not to add to the area cultivated, but to get better cultivation on the land already in use, particularly in the irrigation zone.

The productive area of 13½ million acres is divided roughly equally between the irrigation zone of the south, in the alluvial plain between the two rivers, and the rainfed zone of the north, where dry farming predominates (see map on p. 123). In both zones land is cropped on the alternate fallow system, half being sown with wheat and barley each year, the other half remaining fallow. In the north this system is necessary because rainfall is insufficient for continuous cropping. The natural conditions in the northern region resemble those of north Syria; yields are low and fluctuating in the plains, while in the hill districts rainfall is higher and cultivation can be more intensive.

Because physical conditions are so adverse, agriculture has been the missing link in the economic development of the country. Surprising as it may seem, in view of the immense antiquity of agriculture in the land of the two rivers, modern Iraq is virtually a new agricultural country. Perhaps as much as three-quarters of the area at present cultivated has been brought under the plough since 1918, and one-third of it since 1945. In Turkish times very little land was cultivated, and the population was very small.[2] Economic life centred not in the

[1] Knappen-Tippetts-Abbett-McCarthy Engineers, *Report on the Development of the Tigris and Euphrates River Systems* (New York and Baghdad, Iraq Development Board, 1954; mimeo), commonly known as the KTAM Report.

[2] According to Dr Salih Haider, the population of the three vilayets of Baghdad, Basra, and Mosul around 1880 was 1½ million (*Land Problems of Iraq*).

villages or the country, but in the tribe and the town, as units of political and economic security.

Agriculture developed in dependence on these two bases. In the north grain yields were too unstable for the accumulation of capital in agriculture, and landownership became a function of the town merchant, money-lending to the peasants in the surrounding villages. In the south tribal life continued for many centuries, because nomadic grazing was more secure and profitable than cultivation. Both the city merchant and the tribal organization represented adjustments to an environment which they could not control. Both are extremely ancient adjustments, in which the town and tribe existed in mutual dependence—and mutual hostility.

In the inter-war years agricultural production increased, chiefly in the south. The areas under flow irrigation increased with the construction of the barrages at Hindiya and at Kut. In the north shortage of manpower and horse-power kept the area cultivated small.

Since the second world war expansion has continued, shifting to the north with mechanized cultivation. The following table shows the increase in production in recent years, compared with the pre-war average. It also illustrates the instability of agricultural production. The drought of 1955, which affected the northern zone badly, reduced the harvest to half the 1954 level, as it did in Syria.

TABLE 11

Area and Production of Main Crops in Iraq, 1934–8 and 1950–4

Area
(000 hectares)

	Average 1934–8	*1950*	*1951*	*1952*	*1953*	*1954*	*Average 1950–4*	*1955**
Wheat	661	950	927	968	1,197	1,390	1,086	1,485
Barley	743	1,000	863	882	1,096	1,122	992	1,194
Total grain	1,404	1,950	1,790	1,850	2,293	2,512	2,078	2,679
Rice	152	217	189	75	95	119	137	60
Cotton	16	32	44	50	21	56	40	—

TABLE 11—*continued*

Area and Production of Main Crops in Iraq, 1934–8 and 1950–4

Production

(*000 metric tons*)

	Average 1934–8	*1950*	*1951*	*1952*	*1953*	*1954*	*Average 1950–4*	*1955**
Wheat	478	545	488	500	762	1,160	691	483
Barley	575	851	839	700	1,111	1,239	948	768
Total grain	1,053	1,396	1,327	1,200	1,873	2,399	1,639	1,251
Rice	205	241	190	126	163	180	180	98
Cotton	2	8	6	3	2	7	5	8
Dates	260	305	313	111	350	350	285	—

* Preliminary estimates.

(SOURCES: Iraq Govt., *Statistical Abstracts, 1953* and *1954* and FAO, *Yearbook of Food and Agricultural Statistics*.)

Grain production has increased by 56 per cent over the pre-war level, while the area under grain has increased by 50 per cent. The increase in grain production is nearly as great as it is in Syria, and there has been some improvement in yields. Rice, grown in the primitive provinces of Amara and Diwaniya, remains static. Cotton has been a failure: after a little expansion in the 1950–1 boom it has fallen back to an average level of 5,000 tons.

Most of the new increase in grain production has taken place in the north, in the dry-farming zone. In recent years wheat production has doubled in the provinces of Mosul and Kirkuk, which now produce 70 per cent of the country's wheat. Tractor-farming has spread, though less sensationally than in Syria. According to the Report on the Agricultural Census of 1952–3, there were then 2,091 tractors in the country, but probably a large proportion was not in use. Tractor work is most evident in the north, where it is undertaken by the old-established merchant landowners of Mosul, Arbil, and other northern towns, and not, as in Syria, by new entrepreneurs. But many have taken up tractor-cultivation only to abandon it—because they cannot get spare parts and machine service.

Cotton production has been a failure for two reasons: there is no public authority to combat pests and improve varieties, as there is in Syria; and a 25 per cent export tax on cotton kept prices below the world level, in the interest of the cotton industry (chiefly the Iraq Spinning and Weaving Company). This tax was wisely abolished early in 1956. In Syria governments have not done much to help agriculture, but in Iraq they have actually hindered it. There was no Ministry of Agriculture until 1952, when a ministry was established on the recommendation of the International Bank.

Increased production has not touched the poverty of the fellahin. They live on a bare subsistence margin, in windowless mud huts built up out of the earth. Health conditions are appalling. 'It is not exaggerating to state', says Professor Michael Critchley, 'that the average agricultural worker (*fellah*) is a living pathological specimen, as he is probably a victim of ankylostomiasis, ascariasis, malaria, bilharzia, trachoma, bejel, and possibly of tuberculosis also.'[1] The crude death rate is believed by medical authorities to be about 30 per thousand population. 'An overall average of 300 to 350 per thousand for the country as a whole is probably not far wrong for the infant mortality rate.'[2]

For this misery two things are responsible: the low level of production, itself the result of adverse physical conditions and primitive methods; and the land system. The fellah's income is low because the land produces little, and because the landowner takes most of what it produces.

All past thinking about the development of the country has concentrated on the control of the environment. It has been carried out by consulting engineers, and has followed a tradition established early in this century. Iraq has not lacked technical advice.[3] The methods of control have long been known. The first survey of the irrigation potential was made fifty years ago by Sir William Willcocks, then Director of Reservoirs in Egypt, who was invited by the Turkish Government in 1903 to survey the delta of the Euphrates and the Tigris and to recommend the works needed to bring them

[1] A. Michael Critchley, 'The Health of the Industrial Worker in Iraq', reprinted from *British Journal of Industrial Medicine*, vol. 12, 1955, p. 73.

[2] Addams, 'Current Population Trends in Iraq', *Middle East Journal*, Spring 1956.

[3] Contrary to the opinion of the Point Four Mission, which in the spring of 1955 asserted that Iraq had had no technical assistance until they came.

under control. His report, published in 1905,[1] provided the framework for all the surveys which have since been made.[2] Modern Egypt and the irrigation systems of the second millennium B.C. were his guides, and the 'resurrection of Babylonia' his inspiration. Of the schemes which he recommended, only two were carried out, the Hindiya barrage, completed under his supervision in 1913, and the Kut barrage, completed in 1939, the only major work completed between the wars.

Since that time there have been several surveys of particular projects. A general survey was made by the Haigh Commission, which reported in 1951, and followed Willcocks in recommending the two big flood-control schemes, Lake Habbaniya (on which work was interrupted by war in 1913 and again in 1939), and Wadi Tharthar: two new barrages, one on the Euphrates in connexion with the Habbaniya reservoir, and another on the Tigris in connexion with the Wadi Tharthar scheme; and a number of other major irrigation works. In 1952 another general survey was made by the American firm, Knappen, Tippetts, Abbett, and McCarthy, which recommended still more dams, giving financial estimates and estimates of the potential increase in cultivation which could be attained by full utilization of land and water resources.[3] It represents the culmination of the engineer's approach and possibly its *reductio ad absurdum*.

The engineer's approach is two-dimensional, a blue-print in land and water, which money can turn into dams and dykes and drains. Except in so far as they provide labour, the people of Iraq do not enter into it. Because the engineer's approach is proper to the foreign consultant, it has created the belief that water-control is all that development means. When the oil money began to flood the Development Board, the plans for spending it seemed ready-made in the long lists of irrigation projects.

The human resources of the country have never been surveyed. Much more is known about the rivers of Iraq than about its inhabitants. Though the censuses of agriculture and

[1] *The Irrigation of Mesopotamia* (London, Spon, 1911; 2nd ed. 1917). The report was first published in Cairo in 1905.

[2] Even the estimates of cost were of the same order as the actual costs of these schemes today.

[3] KTAM Report.

industry have begun to fill some of the gaps, there has been no long series of investigations into the possibilities of raising living standards comparable to the studies of the land and water potential.

Now that the first big steps towards the control of the environment have been taken, it is time to think in three dimensions. Because the country is not economically or physically unified or integrated, the social structure is extremely heterogeneous. It comprises tribal societies in various stages of disintegration; growing shanty-town agglomerations; many small strange groups unified by craft, religion, and race rather than by economic status; and on the land the sharp class division between the large landowners and the serf fellahin. Between this social complexity and the high-level projects and the big money there is little connexion; the engineer's approach cannot mesh in with the intricacies of real life.

In the past Iraq was poor because its people could not master their environment. Today Iraq is poor because it has more money than it can invest; and the reason why this is so is that the social structure of the country is not adapted to expansion.

Oil Revenues and Development

Since 1951 the revenue accruing to the Government of Iraq from oil royalties has increased rapidly as a result of the increase in oil production. Between 1950 and 1954 oil production rose from 4 million tons per annum to 30 million tons, and oil revenues accruing to the Government increased from £2 million[1] to £67 million. By 1960 the annual revenue from oil is expected to amount to at least £100 million per annum. Revenues have risen more than in proportion to the increase in production, as a result of new agreements reached between the Government and the Iraq Petroleum Company and its associated companies, which gave the Government more favourable terms, in 1952 (retroactive to 1951) at the time of the Persian Oil crisis, and in 1955 (retroactive to 1954) when the Baghdad Pact was agreed.[2]

[1] The currency unit is the Iraqi dinar, equivalent to the pound sterling, here used as the more familiar unit.

[2] For the terms of the agreements, and for statistics of oil production and revenues, see UN, Dept. of Economic and Social Affairs, *Economic Developments in the Middle East, 1945 to 1954*, pp. 97–8.

Under a law of 1952, retroactive to 1951, 70 per cent of these revenues is assigned to the Development Board. The Board was first instituted in 1950 to supervise the spending of the loan granted by the International Bank for the construction of the Wadi Tharthar flood-control scheme, and to prepare 'a general economic and financial plan for the development of the resources of Iraq and the raising of the standard of living of its people.' The members of the Board are nominated by the Council of Ministers for a period of five years; they include an American expert and a British expert on irrigation. Later, in 1953, a Ministry of Development was set up; the Minister represents the Board on the Council of Ministers and provides the link with Parliament.

The Board's annual income now amounts to some £50 million per annum. For the first four years of its operations revenue totalled £104 million. Its income in future is likely to rise to £65 million; over the five years 1956–60 it anticipates a total expenditure of £450 million.

These sums are very large in proportion to the economy. No estimate of the national income is at present available,[1] but the significance of £50 million can be judged from comparison with the total state expenditure, which up to 1950 did not exceed £30 million, and the total value of Iraq's exports, which in 1947–50 averaged £16 million.

Whatever criticisms are made of development policy—and these are inevitably many—it is important to keep a sense of perspective from the past. Ploughing back the oil into water represents an immense step forward. Before 1951 oil revenues were small, and the greater part of the income from oil was drained out of the country, consuming its main capital asset. Now a large proportion of this income is directed towards making good that loss, by investment which can lay the foundation for a more productive agriculture and provide the power for industry, against the day when oil revenues come to an end.

The main result of the Board's expenditure, so far, has been the completion of the two big water-control schemes, the Wadi

[1] An estimate made in a UN publication, *National Incomes Per Capita in Selected Countries* (New York, 1949), gave a total national income of £150 million, presumably guessed from cost-of-living figures. As this estimate took no account of income from oil, it is best disregarded.

Tharthar flood-control scheme on the Tigris, and the Habbaniya flood-control and irrigation scheme on the Euphrates, both inaugurated in April 1956. The Wadi Tharthar scheme includes a new barrage at Samarra, which will provide water for a new power station. The Habbaniya scheme includes the new barrage at Ramadi. These schemes were constructed by foreign firms.[1] In addition to these two schemes now in opera-

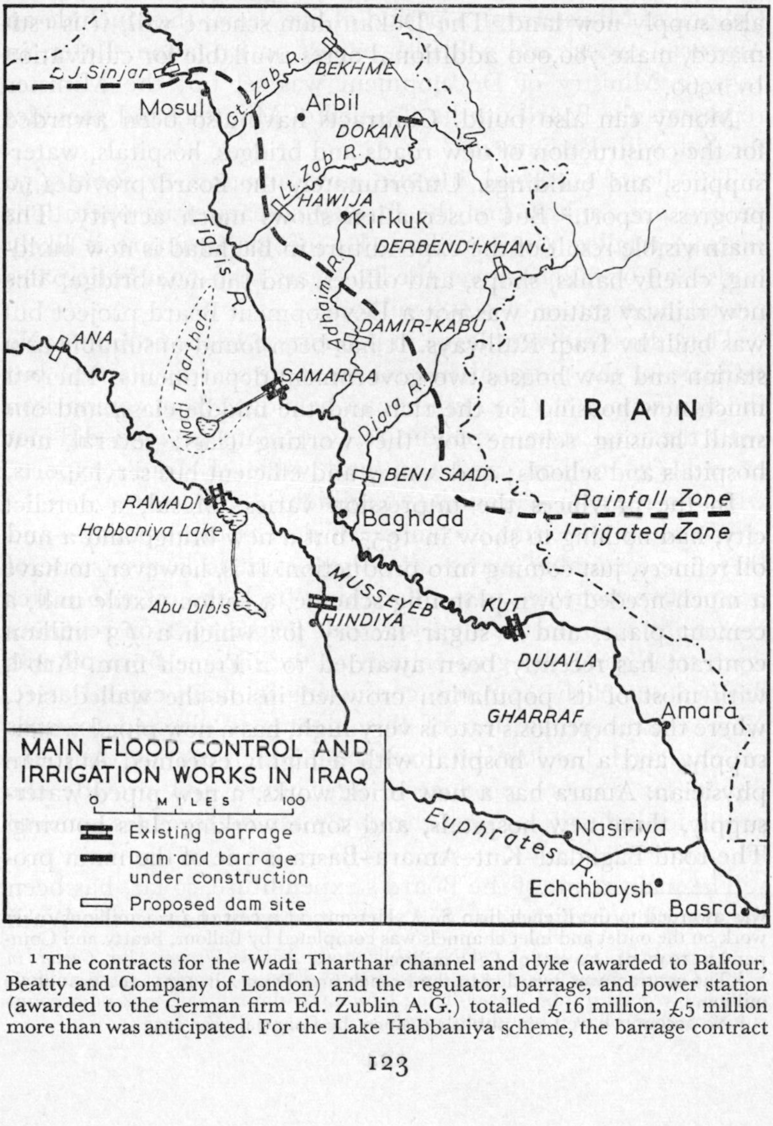

[1] The contracts for the Wadi Tharthar channel and dyke (awarded to Balfour, Beatty and Company of London) and the regulator, barrage, and power station (awarded to the German firm Ed. Zublin A.G.) totalled £16 million, £5 million more than was anticipated. For the Lake Habbaniya scheme, the barrage contract

tion, the Dokan dam and reservoir scheme on the Lesser Zab is in construction, to be completed in 1958.[1] The sites of these works are shown on the map on p. 123.

Thus money can provide flood-control, more water and more land. The two schemes already completed will protect south Iraq from floods. In addition to providing for flood diversion, the Ramadi barrage will supply additional water to land already cultivated and allow double cropping; it can probably also supply new land. The Dokan dam scheme will, it is estimated, make 780,000 additional acres available for cultivation by 1960.

Money can also build. Contracts have also been awarded for the construction of new roads and bridges, hospitals, water-supplies, and buildings. Unfortunately the Board provides no progress report.[2] But observation shows much activity. The main visible result of the expenditure in Baghdad is new building, chiefly banks, shops, and offices, and the new bridge. The new railway station was not a Development Board project but was built by Iraqi Railways. It has been found unsuitable as a station and now houses two government departments. There is much new housing for the rich and the middle class, and one small housing scheme for the working class; several new hospitals and schools; and a new and efficient bus service.

In the provinces the impression varies. Mosul, a derelict city, had nothing to show in 1955 but a new bridge and a new oil refinery, just coming into production. It is, however, to have a much-needed town-planning scheme, a cotton textile mill, a cement plant, and a sugar factory for which a £3 million contract has recently been awarded to a French firm. Arbil, with most of its population crowded inside the walled city, where the tuberculosis rate is very high, has a new piped water-supply, and a new hospital with a highly esteemed Austrian physician. Amara has a new brick works, a new piped water-supply, three new hospitals, and some working-class housing. The road Baghdad–Kut–Amara–Basra is one of the main pro-

was awarded to the French firm S. A. Hersent, at a cost of £1·4 million; other work on the outlet and inlet channels was completed by Balfour, Beatty and Company in 1947–51 at a cost of £2·7 million.

[1] The contract was awarded to the French firm Dumez in 1954, at a cost of £9 million.

[2] No accounts have been published since the financial year 1953–4.

jects of the Board, and on the Amara–Basra section work has begun. The Baghdad–Kut section is impassable after rain, and in 1955 showed nothing new but stranded Cadillacs and Pontiacs. In the Kurdish hills road-building has made progress. Perhaps the best result is the provision of clean drinking-water, from which ninety towns are to benefit.

What money apparently cannot do is increase production. In the preceding section it was shown that agricultural production has increased considerably in recent years; but this increase has been achieved by landowners' private enterprise, chiefly in the north, and cannot be attributed in any degree to development expenditure. Nor, with one or two minor exceptions, has there been any increase in industrial production as a result of the new investment.

Nor can money bring about a general rise in the standard of living, except in so far as clean drinking-water does mean a very real rise for the towns. The effect of development expenditure in Baghdad is to make the contrast between rich and poor more striking. The great increase in imports benefits chiefly the rich, whose consumption of cars, air-conditioning, and luxurious new houses is very conspicuous. The *sarifa* (mud hut) slums are growing fast, without sewage or drinking-water. Very little has been spent on social welfare.

In the larger towns, chiefly Baghdad, Basra, and Kirkuk, the expansion in employment has raised wages. But the supply of unskilled labour is very elastic, because of the low level of earnings on the land. There is much underemployment in the small towns (evidenced by the coffee-house sitters) and in the villages (where men sit round the threshing-floor and the women gather the crops). Consequently the increased demand for labour does not raise wages much, and consumption levels remain low.

Criticism of the results of the expenditure cannot be openly expressed, because the opposition parties have been suppressed and the press controlled since 1954. But there is much dissatisfaction, and a belief that the spending of £100 million ought to show more results. Not all the criticism is justified. There have been no major bungles; in the execution of the projects, technical standards are very high. The big water-control schemes cannot show immediate results, except in so far as they prevent crop destruction. In the provinces there is more improvement than the citizens of Baghdad believe. But it is true that there have been long delays in decision, and it is also true that the money does not percolate downwards. Wealth accumulates and men decay.

Although the failure to undertake economic planning is criticized by economists, the criticism is unrealistic, because when capital is free and no undertaking need show a return, the usual criteria do not apply. To plan means to choose between alternative investments in relation to an anticipated return. Choice is essential, because capital is scarce and must be paid for. But in Iraq capital is not scarce and increases without cost; there is therefore no pressure to select schemes on the basis of their net return. Moreover, investment in irrigation and flood-control does not allow any calculation of the net return in increased productivity. The only calculable effect is the physical possibility of irrigating more land; and so the future development is often envisaged simply as more acres.

When expense is no object, it is much easier to start big schemes than small. 'We like the millions', an Arab ruler told Gerald de Gaury. The same is true of the Development Board. It is said to be easier to get a contract for millions than for thousands. So a £10 million dam can be built while tractors lack spare parts and Dujaila, the pioneer settlement, is undrained. Iraqi planners have yet to learn to do little things.

The result is that too much is invested in the big projects, and not enough in working capital, or in human resources. The country is an economist's cloud-cuckoo land, in a Hayekian gap without a crisis, and building Keynesian pyramids without inflation or multipliers. The crisis is avoided because the big expenditure on deep investment need not show a profit. Inflation is avoided because imports have increased, and because the supply of labour is elastic.

Consequently the result of the expenditure to date resembles, in essentials, the results of planning in the Communist countries of Eastern Europe: concentration on investment in long-term production capacity, at the expense of agriculture and consumer-goods industries. But Iraq is not in the position of a Communist country which must reduce consumption in order to increase productive capacity. It need not concentrate all its capital investment in long-term means of production at the expense of consumption; it can aim at generating an all-round expansion in production, and a rise in its living standard.

At present, the major difficulty is that there is too much of the *sine qua non* in relation to investment opportunities. Where there is so much need for investment in every direction, the choice of priorities might be expected to present great difficulties. The country clearly needs everything: water-control, better farming, clean drinking-water, sewage, drainage, health services, roads, industry, afforestation, education—the list could be prolonged. Yet the problem has not been to decide between different possible uses for the money, but to find uses to which the money could be put. The necessity of choice between alternatives has never arisen, because the annual revenue perpetually exceeds the anticipated and actual expenditure.

The Board has not undertaken any economic planning, though it was set up for this purpose. It has confined itself to financial programming, allocating its total revenues in advance in large sums under different headings. Its main job is to approve proposals put forward by the ministries, obtain the approval of Parliament for specific expenditures, arrange surveys, invite tenders, and then award the contract to a firm, usually foreign. Where the work can be undertaken by an Iraqi authority the Board sanctions the expenditure by the appropriate Ministry or other public authority. It also grants loans to municipal and other public undertakings, for such purposes as drinking-water supply and the Baghdad bus service.

The Board's first expenditure programme, for the six financial years 1951–6, foresaw a total revenue of £155 million[1] over the six years, and allocated this total under six main headings: irrigation, flood-control, and drainage (£53 million); main roads and bridges (£27 million); building (£18 million); land reclamation (£23 million); industrial and mining schemes (£32 million); and administration (£3 million). This was an engineer's programme. The schemes for irrigation, flood-control, and drainage were itemized in detail, listing the Haigh Commission's recommended projects and some others. Road

[1] Iraq Govt., Development Board, *Annual Report, 1953–4* (Baghdad, 1954).

and bridge projects were also listed. The land reclamation and industrial programmes were bulk allocations, with no mention of specific projects.

Unfortunately, no detailed review of the results of this programme is possible. The following table shows the revenue and expenditure of the Development Board for the first four years of the programme.

TABLE 12

Revenue and Expenditure of the Development Board

Provisional figures
(£000)

	1951–2	1952–3	1953–4	1954–5	Total 1951–5
Revenue					
Oil royalties	6,702	22,876	34,823	40,039	104,440
Miscellaneous revenue	765	1,123	454	690	3,032
Total	7,467	23,999	35,277	40,729	107,472
Expenditure					
Administration	100	214	302	277	893
Irrigation	841	2,491	4,795	6,689	14,816
Main roads & bridges	630	1,752	1,917	2,790	7,089
Buildings	788	2,265	2,451	609	6,113
Land reclamation	772	1,035	2,331	1,378	5,518
Industry	—	81	461	2,045	2,587
Total	3,131	7,838	12,257	13,788	37,016
Surplus	4,336	11,161*	23,020	26,941	70,456

* In 1952–3 £5 million were appropriated for the ordinary budget.

(SOURCE: *Quarterly Bulletin of the National Bank of Iraq*, no. 14, April–June 1955.)

From the table it appears that the Board succeeded in spending only one-third of its total revenue during the four-year period. Under each heading, expenditure fell far short of the total allocated. Industry was the weakest section, only half a million pounds being spent during the first three years, against a total anticipated expenditure of £8 million for the period. Even the sum spent on irrigation, far the largest item, fell far short of the anticipated expenditure.

The results are, however, rather less unfavourable than the above figures suggest, as the Board has lent large sums to municipal and local authorities and public undertakings, totalling £6,276,000 in 1952–3 and £14,113,000 in 1953–4;[1] later figures are not available, but further loans have certainly been made. Thus the total direct expenditure does not represent the total investment resulting from the Board's operations. None the less, it is certainly true that the Board has not been able to spend and lend more than two-thirds of its revenue, perhaps less. No figures are available for the year 1955–6. At the end of 1955, however, the Board was reputed to hold a bank deposit of £40 million.

Before the period of this programme had elapsed, a new oil agreement in 1955 (retroactive to 1954) increased the Board's revenues, and in April 1955 a new programme was issued, superseding the six-year programme.[2] It anticipated a total revenue of £300 million over the five years 1955–9, and allotted this sum on much the same lines as in the previous programme, giving irrigation and flood-control £108 million, to include the Derbend-i-Khan dam scheme at a cost of £16 million. To meet the criticisms of the first programme, rather larger allocations were made for housing (£9½ million, including £3 million for working-class housing) and health institutes (£10¾ million).

Revenues again exceed expectations. A year later, in April 1956, another programme was issued,[3] revising the previous programme upwards, and providing for a total expenditure of £500 million over the six financial years 1955–60. Under this programme, irrigation, flood-control, and drainage was scheduled to receive 30 per cent of the total, or £154 million; communications £125 million; buildings £96 million; housing £24 million and summer resorts £2½ million; industry £67 million; agriculture £14 million; and miscellaneous schemes (ancient buildings, drinking-water, and swamp-filling) £10 million.

The provision for housing is four times the amount allocated in the previous programme; the Board intends to start a building programme for 10,000 houses in the main towns, and also

[1] Iraq Development Board, *Annual Report for the Financial Year 1953–4* (Baghdad, 1954).

[2] *Law No. 43 for the year 1955 for the General Programme of the Development Board and the Ministry of Development* (Baghdad, 1955).

[3] *Law No. 54 of 1956, amending the Law of General Programme of the Development Board No. 43 of 1955.*

to construct 'big groups of houses in rural areas'. The building programme includes £5·7 million for hospitals, £8 million for schools and educational institutes, and £2 million for a malaria fighting project. Thus much fuller provision is made for social services. The allocation which seems grossly inadequate is the £14 million for agriculture (including research, livestock improvement, and education)—only 3 per cent of the total, and inadequate both in relation to the irrigation programme, and in relation to the increase in national income which could be achieved.

Engineers' Planning

In his masterly report—rightly described as *A Plan of Action*—Lord Salter describes the Board's policy as engineers' planning.

> Water policy . . . is primarily an engineering problem. . . . It starts naturally with such general surveys as those made by the Haigh Commission and by K.T.A.M. These provide the basis of the decisions as to where the great water structures shall be built. The technical surveys also of course indicate what natural potentialities the land possesses for fruitful cultivation with the aid of irrigation and drainage. What they provide in this respect, however necessary and useful, cannot be decisive in the consideration of policy. It is only a starting point for the real, and difficult, task of planning. A dam site may be wisely decided upon on the basis of an engineer's survey. But much more is needed before a prudent policy can be formed as to what irrigation and drainage, or where and when, should be undertaken. For a survey indicates only what land could be developed if there were the settlers, properly equipped with knowledge and all they need for success, to cultivate it. It may provide an engineer's plan to make enough land cultivable to support a population of 20 millions. But the total population of Iraq is in fact only a little over 5 millions. Neither natural increase, nor any probable and permitted immigration, will even double that number for many years to come. The engineer makes a plan for developing the land. But Iraq's task is to develop a nation. The land exists for man, not man for the land.[1]

Lord Salter urges what in effect is a complete change of policy. First, he recommends that no further big dam schemes should be undertaken, since the works now under construction (together with the Derbend-i-Khan dam already decided upon) 'give as much flood protection as is reasonable, provide as

[1] *The Development of Iraq; a Plan of Action* (London, Caxton, for Iraq Development Board, 1955), p. 49.

much new water as can be used, and as much new land as can be settled.' Drainage should take priority over new irrigation works—a recommendation eminently wise.

Instead of more irrigation works, Lord Salter recommends: (1) much greater investment in human resources, through increased expenditure on health and education; (2) greater investment in agriculture, through an active agricultural policy—for 'little, lamentably little, has been done to increase and improve agriculture'. He emphasizes the need for including animal husbandry in plans to increase agricultural output—again a key point, for in livestock-breeding Iraqis are outstanding.

The 1956 programme meets these recommendations by making larger assignments of funds to housing and the social services, though it does very little for agriculture. But will it be possible to act on Lord Salter's main recommendation—to put the standard of living first? The difficulties of spending the money would disappear if that were made the target. But the Development Board is only a group of civil servants. They cannot be responsible for government policy. Engineers can plan without regard to production and consumption, and this is the only kind of planning that can be undertaken under the present political system and with the existing social structure. At bottom, all the Board's problems are the result of new wine in old bottles.

Consider, for example, the launching of new industries. Superficially, the difficulty is administrative. Industrial projects do not lend themselves to the routine procedure of technical survey, tenders, and contracts. The market must be considered; and how can this be surveyed? The Board has decided on a general survey of the industrial potential for multiple development, to be carried out by I. D. Little, the American consultants; and doubtless a good job will be done. But the real obstacle to industrial expansion is the poverty of the bulk of the population. It is sometimes said that there is a shortage of enterprise: but where there is an expanding market, Iraqis can show themselves as enterprising as others.[1]

Or consider the need for improving methods of agriculture,

[1] The recent expansion in small brick works, along the Shatt el-Arab and the Tigris in Amara, supplying Basra, Kuwait, and Abadan, is an interesting example; so too, is the mat industry in Echchbaysh.

where so little has been done. Agricultural progress needs the big things, and also many little things, gradually welded into a standard of good farming practice.[1] There are great possibilities —in cotton production, in improving seed varieties for grain, and in breeding livestock. No experimental work has been done on dates of sowing or irrigation, or rates of fertilizer application. But how are supplies and knowledge to be channelled into agriculture? There are no co-operative or local associations of farmers. In the Kurdish peasant villages in Arbil small-scale improvements, such as artesian wells, are beginning, because the administration can deal directly with farmers. Elsewhere it cannot. The great landowners constitute the Parliament, and could make an agricultural policy, if they so desired.

Rural housing is to be improved, according to the 1955 plan, but only in the state land settlements, which comprise about 3,500 families. No funds are allocated for rehousing villagers on large estates. Health services are to be improved—but in the towns only.

If the policy of spending mainly on big capital construction continues, the result will be simply a further increase in employment in building. The main social effect of the development expenditure so far has been an increased rate of migration to the towns, to Baghdad, Basra, and Kirkuk (not Mosul). The population of these towns is increasing very fast, mainly from Amara and Kut, the provinces where the fellahin are most oppressed.

At present the movement to the towns seems to come only from the poorest provinces where there is a strong 'push' factor at work, so that it is possible to obtain labour at low wages, and there is not much increase in consumption.[2] This move-

[1] Professor Iversen, considering development policy from the angle of currency stability, suggests that shallow investment should offset deep investment, and could be increased by providing supplies of agricultural equipment, which could lead to small but widespread improvements in the productivity of labour (*Monetary Policy in Iraq*, pp. 150–3).

[2] Professor Iversen considers that the land system, by keeping labour tied (through the landowner's right to forbid his labourers to leave if they are in debt), is a factor restricting the supply of labour (ibid. p. 147). In Amara where the landowners are extremely powerful, they cannot exercise their authority to prevent movement now, because the usual method of punishing the runaway's family is no longer possible when the family has left. Once the movement acquires real momentum, the landowner cannot reclaim his serfs.

ment is not likely to reduce agricultural production, for landowners can invest in tractors and combines. One landowner in Arbil expressed the view that the landowners would be forced to use tractors and combines in spite of the difficulties they have so far experienced with spare parts and repairs, because in a few years' time there would be no labour left on the land at all.

That view may be exaggerated, and yet it is certain that the exodus will go on, because the big capital construction works will continue, and so will urban building. For the fellahin a big rural exodus is the best thing that could happen. But as a long-term policy Iraq cannot abandon cultivation and live entirely on canned food. A country which is undertaking investment in irrigation on a large scale is indirectly investing in agriculture, and must make some provision for the future of the agricultural population. By the time that perennial irrigation allows intensive cultivation, the cultivators may not be there.

This is the setting of the land reform question. It is the land system which is responsible for the great inequality of incomes, the lack of an expanding internal market, the low-wage influx into the slums, and the lack of an agricultural policy. Without land reform, the oil money can do little to raise the standard of living. If land reform were undertaken, the money could be used to equip farmers for better living and better farming. Without it, the big dams will be a succession of Keynesian pyramids, giving employment but not increasing production. The 'resurrection of Babylonia' was an engineer's dream fifty years ago. In the meantime Iraq has acquired what an Iraqi jurist describes as 'the feudalism of Hammurabi'.[1]

From a social standpoint, the serf status of the fellahin is an obvious evil. It is also an economic bottleneck. If Iraq is to develop, it must have a healthy and well-to-do population on the land. Reform is a social and an economic necessity, the key which can unlock the door to a prosperous future.

Reform is also a political necessity, since with the present social structure the development money cannot benefit the people. As Lord Salter points out, the question of who is to

[1] Dr S. A. Nahi, *An Introduction to Feudalism and the Land System in Iraq* (Baghdad, 1955; in Arabic), p. 7.

benefit from the water-control and irrigation projects on which their expenditure has been concentrated is one which directly concerns the Development Board.

The great water schemes, the dams, reservoirs, main irrigation works and main drainage outfalls, etc., are being constructed wholly at the expense of public revenue, derived from the oil royalties, which belong to the whole country not to any one section of it. These water schemes will of course increase the productivity of the land, and therefore its value—to an extent that in time will equal—and indeed ultimately exceed—their cost. It is not unnatural that sections of the community should regard it as unjust that one section, already more privileged than others, should now be further enriched to such an extent at the public expense, and should resent a policy which would have that effect. They may well have an ultimate power which is altogether out of proportion to their present representation in Parliament and their ability to influence legislation by constitutional means. It is this contrast between immediate, and potential, political power that constitutes the danger and the difficulty of the problem.

In these circumstances one tempting course is to outflank the problem instead of attacking it directly. There are large areas of Miri Sirf land, owned by the Government. With the aid of new irrigation and drainage works this land can be made cultivable. Small settlers can be established, without any question of enriching the already rich arising. And in this case, apart from the direct benefit to the new settlers of farming their holdings, either as small owners or as tenants of the State, the existence of such opportunities of new settlement would, perhaps, lead to an improvement of the conditions of work of workers on the great estates. It is along this line, the line of least resistance, that policy has tended to develop.[1]

The line of least resistance evades the real issue. The big water-control schemes will and should benefit the land which is already cultivated. Even if it were politically possible to use all the new irrigation water for small-holder settlements, this policy would not be economic, for, as has already been emphasized, the immediate need is not to extend the area cultivated, but to double-crop the land which now carries only a winter crop. More intensive farming on the land already cultivated would bring a quicker increase in production than the setting up of special settlement schemes.

With the existing tenure system, the new schemes will benefit the landowners, and at no cost. In 1954 a bill was submitted

[1] *The Development of Iraq*, pp. 54–5.

to Parliament which empowered the Government to recover by instalments from private landowners the costs of drainage undertaken under the expenditure programme of the Development Board. The bill was passed by the Chamber of Deputies but rejected by the Senate, where the sheikh landowners predominate. Private landowners pay no tax on their property in land, and income tax is not progressive.[1] The new control of Iraq's water and land will thus serve to increase the incomes of a class which now contributes little to development and which is opposed to social progress.

THE LAND SYSTEM

The Origins of Large Landownership

The extraordinary feature of the land system in Iraq is the size of the estates which dominate the irrigation zone. These great holdings are tribal in origin, and have only recently become private property, as a result of the appropriation of tribal land by the tribal sheikhs in the last thirty years.

Up till the end of the Ottoman period, the basis of landownership was the tribal *dirah*, a large area not limited to land actually tilled, but including also non-cultivated land or submerged marsh land, over which the tribe exercised a customary right of occupation. The tribal system, as it then existed, had no legal basis and no protection from the state. In law, the tribal lands were regarded as state land and the tribal occupants as tenants-at-will.

Under the tribal system cultivation was partly communal, partly individual. The method of farming necessitated some communal organization, since single households could not undertake the clearing of land, the building of dams across channels, and the strengthening of the river banks. The head of the clan, the sirkal, managed these functions on behalf of the tribe, organizing canal clearance and irrigation, allotting the seed, and appointing the dates of sowing, harvesting, and threshing. Within the tribal *dirah* the area cultivated was small, and shifted about as canals silted up and the land was impoverished by salt, and so the area cultivated by each peasant shifted also. Individual prescriptive rights to land were known

[1] Under the income tax law of 1956, however, income from the rent of agricultural land becomes liable to income tax.

(*lazma*, *nagsha*, and other customary forms), but these were restricted to a small class in the tribe, in areas permanently cultivated. For the most part there was no individual ownership, since occupancy of a fixed plot of land for a long period was not usual. The cultivators were mobile; cultivation was not their only occupation, and livestock grazing remained the more important alternative.

The function of the sheikh was political; he maintained the tribal militia and kept the *mudhif* (the guest-house and civic and social centre). Revenues to enable him to carry out these duties were collected by the sirkals from the tribesmen; one-third or one-half of the cultivated land was set aside to provide for the sheikh's income. This income accrued to the office of the sheikh, and not to his person. His right to revenue depended on his political functions.

The tribesmen, under this system, were neither individual owners nor labourers; they were cultivators of land communally owned. Dr Salih Haider has well summarized their status as that of 'agricultural labourers in the cultivated part of the tribal *dirah*, as well as partners in it. The latter aspect of their position is still more definite in the uncultivated part of the tribal *dirah*.'[1]

Since the early years of the twentieth century the tribal system has been breaking up, as a result of settlement for permanent cultivation, the opening of markets, greater political security and technical change. When steamship transport came to the Persian Gulf at the end of the nineteenth century markets for Iraqi grain opened, and the sheikhs found it profitable to take more grain from their cultivators, in order to export. In the 1920's pump irrigation gave them a strong motive for acquiring land as their own property. These economic changes were consolidated by the settlement of title to land carried out from 1933 onwards which is described below. The sheikhs have now become legal owners of the *dirah*, the sirkals have become the managers and agents; and the tribesmen have become share-cropping fellahin, with no rights or status.

The fellahin are in law tied to the land; a law of 1933 provided that no labourer could leave the land if he was in debt to the landowner; and as labourers are usually in debt they are

[1] Salih Haider, *Land Problems of Iraq.*

in effect serfs. If a labourer deserts the estate, the landowner can punish him by destroying his family's hut and driving them out. Though the cultivator is a share-cropper, he is not properly speaking a tenant, since he has no security or freedom of action.

> The land which he cultivates, the crops that he grows, the times of sowing and harvest, all these are decided by the landlord or his agent, who also provides the seed, organizes the marketing and controls the irrigation. The share-cropper therefore differs from the paid labourer only in so far as he does not receive a fixed daily wage; instead his wage is a proportion of the crop and depends therefore mainly on factors beyond his control.[1]

The high level of rents is the main cause of rural poverty, and not the shortage of land. The area cultivated by one family in south Iraq averages 30 donums (20 acres), of which half is cropped and half left fallow. This area should be sufficient to support a family and produce a surplus for sale, even with such an extensive system of farming; but when two-thirds of the produce is taken as rent, it is not sufficient.

The proportion of the crop taken by the landowner varies with the type of cultivation. On flow-irrigated land it is generally three-fifths, and two-thirds if the landowner provides the seed. On pump-irrigated land the landowner takes five-sevenths. In date plantations the share is still higher, as the landowner has made an investment. In the districts where landowners carry on more intensive farming, with a double-cropping system, as in the Gharraf (the region supplied by the Kut barrage), the position of the share-cropper is much better, for though the proportion of the produce taken by the landowner is as high, and sometimes higher, than on single-cropped land, the gross produce is much greater and the cultivator's income is therefore higher also. The condition of the fellahin is worst in the regions where output per acre is low and where the sheikhs are powerful, as in the rice-growing districts of Amara.

The prestige of the sheikhs rests on their former function of leadership in a tribal society which owed the state no allegiance. The foundation of the new kingdom strengthened them, giving them legal ownership of land and representation in Parliament, while it has at the same time weakened them by remov-

[1] H. D. Walston in an unpublished paper on *Land Tenure in the Fertile Crescent*, 1954.

ing the need for tribal wars and tribal rule, through the creation of a national army and a national administration. They thus secured a position of privilege in the state, without obligation to it. Now that their economic function as investors is diminished by the new money, their function is simply to preserve their position in the packed Parliament, and to resist change.

In northern Iraq the land system differs from that of the south. The law of inheritance follows the practice of equal division between heirs, as laid down in the Ottoman Land Code, and this practice tends to break up the larger holdings. In the south tribal custom, reinforced by the *Sharia* law, prescribes inheritance by the eldest son, so that holdings are not subdivided on inheritance, and the large estates are kept intact.

Economic conditions are also different in the north. In the plain regions of the rainfed zone production is highly unstable and there is much variation in yields and between different localities.[1] The large landowners in the Mosul region, predominantly city merchants, have acquired land either by inheritance or by lending to impoverished cultivators, and taking the land when debts cannot be paid. For the most part their wealth has not been accumulated through agriculture: the wool trade, grain-milling, cotton-ginning, and the ownership of urban house property are their main sources of income. New fortunes were made by war profits. The largest fortune in Mosul today has been made in the wool trade.

Even the largest holdings are small by comparison with those in the south. Merchants of Mosul or Arbil say 'I have a few villages', not farms or acres. The largest landowner of Mosul, an enterprising merchant-tractorist, has twenty villages, roughly equivalent to 20,000 donums (12,000 acres), which would not rank as very large in the southern half of the country. The landowners of the Mosul region now undertake more investment than the sheikhs of the south. They have extended the culti-

[1] The *Report on the Agricultural and Livestock Census of Iraq, 1952–3*, vol. 1, p. 52' states that in one part of Kufri district, in the Kirkuk province, 'more than forty villages had no crops at all over a period of two years and as there was no food for the animals, they had to be driven away to other parts', while in other districts crop yields were good, amounting to a sixfold and eightfold return on the seed sown.

vated area greatly in recent years by the use of machinery, and have also introduced pump irrigation for cotton on the Tigris. The more enterprising have rented land from the sheikhs of the Shammar, who have recently acquired title to very large areas of state land in the north.[1] The Chief of the Shammar, Ahmed el-Ajeel, is the largest landowner in the province and extremely wealthy; he undertakes tractor-farming on his own account. The lesser sheikhs are grasping and sit in the offices of the Mosul merchant-tractorists, insisting that they should take a grain crop every year instead of leaving the land fallow to recover its fertility.

Rents taken by the landowners are lower in the north, because population is sparse. On irrigated land where pumps are installed the landowner's share amounts to 50 per cent of the gross produce, while in the south it is between 66 and 75 per cent. On dry land rents are low, ranging from one-quarter to one-eighth of the gross produce, or even, in remote districts, to only one-sixteenth. In the Kurd hill villages, where rainfall is higher, the land is held by peasant owners, and the standard of living is higher than in the plains, most noticeably in regard to housing.

The Distribution of Ownership

There are no published figures showing the distribution of landownership. The Directorate-General of Land Settlement (i.e. the department which settles land title) presumably has in its possession the data for classification of properties by size, since properties are registered in the name of their owner. Unfortunately, and for obvious reasons, this classification is not made.

The Agricultural Census of 1952–3 provides a classification of numbers of agricultural holdings in size-groups. For the purposes of the census, a holding is a unit of management, not a unit of property. It is defined as 'a farm or agricultural estate organized as one unit'. This unit

may therefore be very large, extending perhaps to several hundred thousand mesharas,[2] or very small, perhaps as small as two olks

[1] See below, p. 160.

[2] The Iraqi unit of area is the meshara or donum, equal to 0·25 hectares and 0·62 acres.

(200 square metres). Some individuals farmed more than one holding as defined above, sometimes in different *Liwas*, but on the other hand, some holdings were jointly held by two or more persons.

This explanation reveals the difficulty in defining the holding. It presumably means that the units of property and management are not the same. This is generally true of the largest estates, which are managed in several large units by the landowner's agents.

Although the census figures cannot be used to show the distribution of ownership, they give an indirect indication of the scale of ownership, in that they show a preponderantly large scale of operation. The census figures relate to a total area in holdings of 25½ million donums or mesharas (6·4 million hectares or 15·8 million acres). Unfortunately the census gives only the number of holdings, and not the area, held in each size-group, so that the proportion of the land held in the large estates is not ascertainable. But the census shows that there are some very large holdings, recording 104 with over 20,000 donums (12,000 acres).

TABLE 13

Distribution of Holdings by Size in Iraq

Donums	*Hectares*	*Acres*	*Number*
Under 4	(under 1)	(under 2½)	24,270
4 and under 20	(1–5)	(2½–12)	25,849
20 ,, ,, 100	(5–25)	(12–60)	41,905
100 ,, ,, 600	(25–150)	(60–360)	27,555
600 ,, ,, 1,000	(150–250)	(360–600)	1,847
1,000 ,, ,, 2,000	(250–500)	(600–1,200)	1,702
2,000 ,, ,, 5,000	(500–1,250)	(1,200–3,000)	1,221
5,000 ,, ,, 10,000	(1,250–2,500)	(3,000–6,000)	424
10,000 ,, ,, 20,000	(2,500–5,000)	(6,000–12,000)	168
20,000 and over	(5,000 and over)	(12,000 and over)	104
		Total	125,045

(SOURCE: *Report on the Agricultural and Livestock Census of Iraq, 1952–3*, vol. 1, table 2, p. 16.)

The census indicates the difference in agrarian structure between north and south by showing that the average holding is large in the southern provinces of Amara, Kut, Muntafik,

Diwaniya, and Baghdad, and smaller in the northern provinces, with the exception of Kirkuk.

TABLE 14

Average Size of Holding by Provinces in Iraq

(*in donums* (*acres*))

South Iraq			*North Iraq*		
Amara	6,884	(4,128)	Kirkuk	462	(276)
Kut	1,087	(648)	Arbil	131	(78)
Muntafik	709	(426)	Mosul	128	(76)
Diala	255	(150)	Sulaimaniya	61	(36)
Diwaniya	441	(264)			
Baghdad	407	(240)			
Dulaim	296	(174)			
Kerbela	260	(156)			
Hilla	119	(72)			
Basra	25	(15)			

(SOURCE: ibid. p. 16.)

In the southern provinces, the average is low only in Basra, where date cultivation is carried on in small holdings. In Hilla and Kerbela large holdings predominate, but the average is reduced by the large numbers of small holdings on the Euphrates. Amara, Kut, and Muntafik are provinces with an extreme concentration of ownership, Amara and Muntafik being the provinces where tribal authority is strongest. In the northern provinces the average holding is smaller, and in Mosul and Kirkuk the distribution round the average is close.

The census results do not show the existence of the very large properties exceeding 50,000 donums. Figures compiled from the data in the possession of the Directorate of Land Settlement by Jafar Khayyat,[1] covering privately owned land (i.e. excluding State Domain) in six provinces (Baghdad, Kut, Hilla, Dulaim, Kirkuk, and Arbil) and relating to a total area of 14·3 million donums, show that in these provinces there are thirteen properties between 50,000 and 100,000 donums (30,000 and 60,000 acres) and twenty-one properties between 100,000 and 200,000 donums (60,000 and 120,000 acres).

Two landowners are commonly reputed to own properties

[1] *The Iraqi Village: a Study in its Condition and Reform* (Beirut, 1950; in Arabic).

exceeding 1 million donums. These are the Emir Rabia, commonly called the Second King of Iraq, who owns great areas in Kut province, and has introduced tractors and pumps and carries on intensive farming. The other is Mohan el-Khair Allah, in Muntafik province, who does not introduce modern methods. Five or six others are credited with properties of about half a million donums. These include Naif and Muhsin el-Harian (in Hilla), Abdul-Razzak and his relative Abdul-Abbas el-Mirjan (also in Hilla), and Ballasim and Abdullah el-Hussain (in Kut). In Amara the greater part of the cultivated land of the province is the property of four large owners. These enormous holdings are not highly capitalized and efficiently managed commercial enterprises, like the large estates in Egypt, but cover great expanses of poorly cultivated land and land which has gone out of cultivation, or is uncultivated or uncultivable. Landowners reckon their possessions in pumps or fellahin rather than in donums. As a source of wealth they depend partly on investment in pumps or machinery, partly on the exploitation of the cultivators; they are units of political power.

SETTLEMENT OF TITLE

In determining the present distribution of ownership, the settlement of title to land[1] has been a decisive influence. Registration of title in Iraq is not, as it is in many countries, simply a technical operation conferring greater security and ease of transfer on owners who already hold title-deeds establishing ownership. As in the other countries of the Fertile Crescent, and in any country where communal tenures are breaking up, land registration in Iraq confers legal rights on a customary tenure holder, and thus creates new rights of individual ownership. Usually, though not invariably, these new rights are created at the expense of other customary holders. In Iraq settlement of title has in practice been a process of expropriating occupying cultivators and impropriating the tribal authorities as large landowners. This wholesale alienation of tribal land is a quite recent change, carried out within the last twenty years.

[1] The procedure of granting registered title to land is properly described as land settlement, but to avoid confusion with resettlement on new land, it is here called settlement of title.

It will be recalled that in Ottoman times there had been no general registration. In the northern parts of Iraq, then the vilayet of Mosul, grants of registered title were made round the towns. In remote places the *aghas* or *mukhtars* (village headmen and tax collectors) usually succeeded—contrary to the provisions of the Land Code—in registering the land of the village as their property. Where small owners received the *senet tapu*,[1] they were often defrauded of their title by city notables or forced to sell the land to pay debts. In theory, however, registration was carried out in this part of the country, on the small land area cultivated at that time.

In the south the tribal authorities violently opposed registration, and the provisions of the Land Code, which enforced registration, were not carried out, even in theory. The attempt to enforce registration of title to individual holdings led to conflict, even to actual fighting, between sheikhs and tribesmen, and was therefore abandoned. Two decrees, in 1880 and 1892, abrogated the provisions of the Code enforcing registration in the vilayets of Basra and Baghdad. The land remained in the nominal ownership of the state (i.e. as *miri*, with the state retaining both the *raqaba* and the *tasarruf*,[2] while the tribesmen were regarded as tenants-at-will). Revenue was collected by tribute or taxation, the amount taken varying with the relative strength of the tribe and the Government.[3]

In one province of the south grants of *tapu* title were made, and these have produced a permanent state of confusion. The Governor of the Muntafik province, the head of the Sadun family and sheikh of the powerful Muntafik confederation of tribes, purchased *tapu* ownership of the whole province from the Ottoman Government. These titles have never been recognized, and the title-holders have never been able to collect the revenue from the occupying owners. Recently a new law has been passed to attempt to settle these sixty-year-old claims.[4]

When the new State of Iraq came into existence, the state was in law the largest landowner. This ownership was a legal

[1] See above, p. 68. [2] See above, p. 67.

[3] Dr Salih Haider gives an interesting example. The chief of the Muntafiq Confederation, virtually independent and ruling vast areas in the late nineteenth century, paid an annual tribute of 70 horses, valued at £7,000, but in Basra, where the revenue officials were more powerful, agricultural produce was subject to high rates of taxation (*Land Problems of Iraq*).

[4] See below, pp. 155–6.

fiction, for the state had no effective rights over the land, except the uncertain power to tax. Only a fraction of the cultivated land was held, somewhat uncertainly, on *tapu* tenure, while the rest was held on no legal tenure at all.

In addition to the state's nominal claim to ownership of all land, the new State of Iraq became the owner of the former Ottoman Crown Estates, the personal property of the Sultan Abdul-Hamid II. These estates had been acquired between 1883 and 1909 by purchase, gift, and reversion of land. They were extensive and included some of the most fertile land in the Tigris and Euphrates valleys.[1] They were administered by a special department, the Dairat-al-Sanniya, under the direct control of the Sultan. After the deposition of the Sultan in 1909 the Sanniya administration was abolished. Much of the land then went out of cultivation, and the canals silted up. Under the Treaty of Lausanne, the lands of the Ottoman Crown became the property of the states succeeding the Ottoman Empire. In Syria a special department, the Directorate of State Domain, was formed to administer these lands,[2] but in Iraq no such department was set up; the lands fell into the possession of private landowners, and in law were on the same footing as other *miri* land.

In the new state, where the large landowners were powerful, strong pressure to introduce a system of land registration came from the sheikh landholders who were installing pump irrigation on the banks of the two rivers. Whereas in the past the tribal authorities had resisted the central Government in its efforts to register land in individual holdings in the names of the cultivators, they now demanded settlement of title as a means of ousting the tribesmen, whose prescriptive rights to graze and cultivate prevented the pump-owner from securing the land supplied by the pump as his own property. It was now the wealthy who wished to use the state against the cultivators,

[1] For information about the Sanniya Estates I am indebted to Miss Albertine Juwaideh, now working on this subject at Oxford. The estates were well managed, improving both irrigation and agriculture. The position of the cultivators was better than that of the ordinary tribesmen, in so far as the officials prevented exactions by the sheikhs. Though the level of share-rent was high, the cultivators were better off by reason of the larger output and interest-free advances of seed. According to Dr Salih Haider (*Land Problems of Iraq*, p. 422), the contribution of the Sanniya Estates to agricultural and social progress in Iraq was considerable, and far exceeded the value of the irrigation works undertaken by the Government.

[2] See above, pp. 98–9.

not the state which aimed at securing the rights of the cultivators against the wealthy.

The conflict between the rival claims of development for the land and security for the cultivators created a difficult problem. Tribal organization was bound to disintegrate, under the pressure of political and economic changes, and could not have been preserved. To attempt to stabilize the customary rights of the tribesmen would have prevented investment. But to meet the full claims of the pump-owners meant ignoring the customary rights of the cultivators and depriving them entirely of security and status. Only a very strong government could have succeeded in reconciling these rival claims. The mandatory Government did not even attempt to do so. Some uncoordinated and spasmodic attempts to settle title were made between 1919 and 1930, including an abortive attempt to settle the Muntafik claims, and the introduction of triennial revenue assessments in Amara. But there was no general policy. In 1929 Sir Ernest Dowson was requested by the Iraq Government to investigate the problem of settlement of title and to make recommendations for its solution.

Dowson's report[1] is a classical exposition with sound recommendations which in essentials was ineffective. In retrospect it is easy to see why it was so. Its first main recommendation was that no attempt should be made to introduce a general settlement of title in freehold ownership, but that grants should be made, after survey, in ten-year leasehold tenancies. In a country with such great agricultural potentialities it was important for the state to retain its right of ownership so that it could resume control of the land at a later stage in the development of the country.

The second main recommendation was that settlement of the rival claims should be made on the principle of 'beneficial occupational use'. To give due weight to the prescriptive claims, Dowson recommended that settlement should be preceded by local investigations of claims in the community itself, and that special land courts should be set up to hear appeals from, or cases referred to by, the settlement authorities.

It was here that Dowson's past experience was not a good

[1] Sir Ernest Dowson, *An Inquiry into Land Tenure and Related Questions* (Letchworth, for Iraq Govt., 1932).

guide. As an Indian Civil Servant, he approached the problem of settlement in Iraq as if it could be handled by administrators who were independent of the large landowners. 'Painstaking, experienced and impartial' officers, he believed, would be able to arrive at satisfactory settlements by reconciling the claims of the actual occupiers. To settle title meant deciding between the rival claims of the sheikhs, sirkals, and cultivating tribesmen on the basis of confirming the previous rights. If, that is to say, the sheikh had a claim to one-fifth of the produce from each of a hundred cultivators, he should receive a holding of land equivalent to one-fifth of the total, and each cultivator should receive a holding equivalent to four-fifths of the land he cultivated. The settlement officers were not impartial, and generally acceded to the claim of the sheikh to the whole of the tribal land. As Dowson observed 'Personal influence . . . is commonly the decisive factor at any moment in any particular land dispute: and anyone may find the most convincing claims set aside.'[1]

Where personal influence was so strong, and the authority of the Government so weak, 'beneficial occupational use' was too elastic a principle to be satisfactory. It would have been better to have proposed the allotment of a specific area of land to every adult male cultivator whose right to participate was recognized. This course was suggested to Dowson as the only practicable one, in view of the difficulty of investigating and settling the rival prescriptive claims, but he rejected it on the grounds that 'it savours of a new allotment of land rather than of a recognition of a claim based upon previous use'.[2]

Wisdom after the event is easy. Dowson could not have foreseen that the principle he recommended allowed too much discretion. But because so much nonsense is now talked about evolutionary reform, it is worth recalling that twenty-five years ago, when the land system was still fluid, it would have been possible to grant title to land to a broad section of the fellahin, and so to constitute a class of small farmers, on the basis of rights which custom then recognized.

In the event, both Dowson's main recommendations were set aside. From 1933 onwards land settlement was carried out, under the supervision of British officials, on a systematic basis.

[1] ibid. p. 27. [2] ibid. p. 53.

Tribal land was alienated, in what are in effect freehold tenures, to the sheikh landholders. This result has not been universal. The principle of subdividing land in proportion to the income received by the sheikh, leaving a portion to him and to the cultivators, has been practised in some parts of the country, as for example on the Middle Euphrates, where the water-wheel owners form a settled peasant class. The effective principle has been that the size of the plot varied inversely with the power of the Government. Where it was powerful, the tribesmen gained a useful share of the total, and where it was not, the land was assigned in enormous holdings to the tribal sheikhs as their individual property.

Registration of title was carried out under the Land Settlement Law of 1932, which gave the Government the right to settle title to land and established the procedure of registration. During the 1930's settlement was carried out chiefly on the pump-irrigated lands. The Law for the Sale of Miri Sirf Land of 1940 greatly accelerated the process of assigning tribal land to large landowners, especially in the flow-irrigated regions.[1]

The Forms of Tenure

The two main forms of tenure for private landowners in Iraq are *tapu* and *lazma*. Large areas are retained in state ownership as *miri sirf*. Small areas are held in the old categories of *mulk*, *waqf*, and *matruka*.

The three main forms were established by the Land Settlement Law of 1932. It laid down that all land not found to be *mulk*, *matruka*, or *waqf*, should be classified as *miri*, either granted in *tapu*, or in *lazma*, or retained in state ownership as *miri sirf* (from *emiriye sirfa*, absolute state property). According to the law, both *tapu* and *lazma* are included in the *miri* category, and according to the conceptions of Moslem law are conditional tenures, because the state grants the *tasarruf* or right of usufruct, and retains the *raqaba*, or right of absolute ownership. They should properly be described as *miri tapu* and *miri lazma*, though in ordinary usage they are not so described. In practice, both grant what in English law would be considered absolute ownership, since they confer rights of disposal and

[1] Hassan Mohammed Ali, 'Miri Sirf Land Development in Iraq', *International Social Science Bulletin*, vol. 5, no. 4, 1953.

inheritance which are subject only to minor or nominal restrictions.

Tapu corresponded to the old Ottoman tenure, while *lazma* was a new form of tenure instituted in 1932 by the Law of Granting Land on *Lazma* Tenure. *Lazma* had been one of the chief forms of customary tenure recognized in Ottoman times, and the law gave it legal status. The object of instituting the new form was to confer individual ownership while preserving tribal solidarity. The law decreed that *lazma* tenure could be granted by the settlement authorities to any person who had enjoyed the usufruct of land, if he could prove that the land had been cultivated (according to local usage, i.e. allowing for fallow) over a period of fifteen years preceding the date of settlement. Land so granted was heritable and transferable, and could be mortgaged. The transfer of *lazma* land was to be subject to the approval of the Tapu Department of the Ministry of Justice, and permission might be refused if the transfer was likely to cause a breach of the peace, or reduce the holding to an uneconomic size. The object of making transfer subject to official sanction was to prevent the sale of land outside the tribe, and so safeguard tribesmen against the alienation of their land. However, the institution of this new form of tenure has not had this effect. *Lazma* was used chiefly by the pump-owners to acquire ownership of land on which they had installed pumps, and the prescriptive rights of the tribesmen were usually disregarded.

There is now no practical distinction between *tapu* and *lazma* tenure, except as regards the formal requirement of official approval for transfer of *lazma* land. Before 1939 owners of *tapu* and *lazma* land had to pay taxes on their land and water, and *lazma* owners paid at higher rates. In 1939 these payments were abolished, in return for amortization of their capitalized value over a period of ten years, so that this distinction has now been abolished.

The remainder of the land to which title has not been settled remains in the formal ownership of the state—as *miri sirf*. This category includes land actually in the possession of sheikhs or other landowners who in fact enjoy undisturbed rights of possession. These occupiers pay a light tax on their holding. The *miri sirf* lands also include all uncultivated lands which are not registered. In regard to these lands the state's power of disposal is important, because it gives the Government the right to grant title to land which will become cultivable through the new irrigation works. Special legislation (described in the next section) was passed in 1945 and 1951 giving the Government the right to confer ownership on small farmers.

Figures published by the Agricultural Census show that the land in holdings was distributed in 1952–3 between the different forms of tenure as follows.

TABLE 15

Types of Land Tenure in Agricultural Holdings in Iraq

	(000 donums)	*(000 acres)*	*(per cent)*
Tapu	10,109	6,065	39·6
Lazma	6,713	4,028	26·3
Other tenures	1,012	607	4·0
Rented lands	7,702	4,621	30·1
Total	25,536	15,321	100·0

(SOURCE: *Report on the Agricultural and Livestock Census of Iraq, 1952–3*, vol. 1, table 3, p. 17.)

This classification is, however, confused. Presumably 'rented land' refers to *miri sirf* tenure, i.e. land rented from the Government. Much of the land classified as 'rented' is in Amara, where 97 per cent of the land in holdings is returned under this heading, and where the land is in law *miri sirf*.

Figures published by the Directorate-General of Land Settlement relate to a larger area and include uncultivated land, as follows:

TABLE 16

Land Title in Iraq: Area Settled by 1953

Type of tenure	*000 donums*	*000 acres*
Tapu	10,922	6,553
Lazma	10,295	6,177
Miri sirf	39,256	23,553
Other tenures	4,030	2,418
Total	64,503	38,701

(SOURCE: Govt. of Iraq, *Statistical Abstract, 1953*, table 133, p. 98.)

The areas settled in *tapu* and *lazma* tenures, according to these figures, are larger than the areas in agricultural holdings recorded under these tenures, from which it might be inferred that landowners have acquired title for land not yet cultivated, and staked their claims on land which development projects will make cultivable.

It is worth noting that the greater part of the land now held in *tapu* and *lazma* tenure has been settled in the years 1943–53. In 1953 21 million donums were held in these tenures, as compared with 9 million donums in 1943. From 1945 onwards successive Iraqi Governments have stated that their aim is to encourage small ownership by distributing state land to cultivators. During the same period settlement of title has proceeded steadily in the opposite direction.

Though most of the cultivated land has now been settled, the problem of settlement is still acute in the provinces of Amara and Muntafik. In Amara attempts to enforce registration under special legislation have led to a serious social conflict.

The Amara Laws. In Amara, a remote and primitive province in the marshes of the Tigris, the land is still in the formal possession of the state (i.e. is *miri sirf*) and in the actual possession of the sheikhs, whose status in law is that of tenants of the state, in that they pay tax to the Government in respect of the tribal land which they occupy. Their holdings are exceedingly large. According to the Agricultural Census, 'large holdings of 20,000 mesharas [12,000 acres] or more were found in each of the administrative sub-divisions of the Liwa, and among the 29 holdings in this size group, seven holdings were over 50,000 mesharas [30,000 acres].'[1] Three sheikhs and the family of a fourth are believed to hold most of the cultivated land.

The economy is no longer nomadic, though livestock grazing is as important as cultivation. The large numbers of sheep (half a million), goats, camels, horses, cows, and buffaloes show that the transition to permanent cultivation is still in process. Of the total area in holdings of 3·2 million donums (2 million acres), less than one-third is sown with crops, the rest being fallow, uncultivated, and in part uncultivable.[2] Agriculture is partly

[1] *Report on the Agricultural and Livestock Census of Iraq, 1952–3*, vol. 1, p. 35.
[2] ibid. p. 36.

anchored to the river banks by pumps, and partly shifts within the cultivable land area. Wheat, barley, and rice are the main crops, irrigated by pump and flow. In the north of the province there is rainfed land, some of which has recently been converted by a large landholder to pump irrigation.

The social structure is still tribal. One of the three big landholders, for example, the Senator Mohammed el-Araiby, has 6,000 'people' (i.e. fellahin—tribesmen), a family of 200, and 4 wives. Smaller landholders have between 1,500 and 2,000 people and 2 or 3 wives. The social pattern repeats itself at intervals in every reed-hut settlement along the banks of the water-courses. The sheikh welcomes the guest on the mud bank in front of his guest-house, a large two-roomed brick building furnished with carpets from Kashan and Tabriz, embossed plush armchairs, and Coca Cola posters. Near the guest-house is the *mudhif*, the tribesmen's social centre, a conventional arched reed building, with carpets or reed mats and the beaked coffee-pots in the fire on the floor. The women have a house apart, though the rich sheikhs keep their wives in 'palaces' in Baghdad or Amara town. The sheikh's income is held in big round reed baskets, 10 feet across and 4 feet high, which hold rice or grain, carefully packed with mud and watched by his retainers. A lesser sheikh may have 30 such mounds, representing about 50 tons, awaiting shipment by motor launch. The crops are grown by the cultivators, who must deliver two-thirds or even three-quarters of the produce to the sheikh. Wealth may be shown in the furniture of the house and in the sheikh's dress. The wealth of Mohammed el-Araiby is shown in the possession of bedding for 3,000 people, last used on the occasion of the King's visit.

On the surface, Amara seems an idyllic patriarchal world, with its formal manners and its ancient crafts and skills. The great sheikh is a royal figure, in gold and brown *arba'a*; his tribesmen rise as he passes. The groom displays a white Arab mare and the *Abeed* (negroes, formerly slaves) serve coffee. Hospitality is a duty, magnificently performed. The lesser sheikhs are simple rustic persons, who enjoy boar hunting and keep jesters. The fellahin fish from pitch-lined high-prowed canoes among the palm trees.

But there is great poverty. Its main cause is the extortionate share of the crop taken by the sheikhs, and also the low level of output per head, resulting from low yields and the small area of land cultivated. Bilharzia and other parasitic diseases are general, and so is trachoma. Amara town has a leprosy hospital. New schools are being started, but many children cannot attend because they must work. Some sheikhs oppose education, though there is one, a lesser sheikh at Kalat Salih, who has built a school for his people.

This apparently stable society is now being undermined very rapidly from without. The tribal structure has long been disintegrating as a result of the impact of the central Government, which involves the transfer of judicial powers to the courts. Emigration from the province has been in progress since the 1920's and is now much accelerated. The land system was the chief reason why tribesmen migrated in the past, and this 'push' factor has been reinforced by the Amara Law of 1952.

Unrest first appeared openly in 1952 after the enactment of the Amara Law. This laid down a special procedure for settlement of title in the province. The usual procedure in the past, as has already been explained, was to grant the whole tribal area to the sheikh, without regard to the rights of the cultivators. The Amara Law aimed at preventing this result, for it contained provisions which gave the fellah the right to receive a fixed area as his property. But the law was formulated in such a way that the sheikh and his family could claim the whole of the cultivated land. Thus the benefits to the peasants were illusory, and the law created a legal basis for claims which it could not satisfy. After the second coup d'état in Egypt and the announcement of the Egyptian land reform there were riots in Amara town, which were put down by the police with some loss of life.

Though the law was not carried out, its provisions must be explained, since its consequences have been important.

The Law for Granting Lazma Rights in Miri Sirf Land in Amara Liwa (No. 42 of 1952) laid down the principles on which the right of ownership in *lazma* might be acquired by different classes of occupiers. It distinguished three classes of claimants:

1. The primary *multazim*.

2. The secondary *multazim*.
3. The fellah.

The primary *multazim* means the tax-collector in direct contact with the Government, i.e. the sheikh, who may be regarded either as a collector of taxes on behalf of the Government, or as a tenant of the state paying rent. The secondary *multazim* is the sheikh's agent or sirkal, the head of the clan, who collects taxes and rents on behalf of the sheikh.

The law provided that the primary *multazim* could claim half the area of the holding in respect of which he has paid taxes, and in addition 200 donums (120 acres). The secondary *multazim* could claim one-quarter of the area which he leased from the primary *multazim*, provided that this area did not exceed 150 donums (90 acres). The fellahin could claim 15 donums (9 acres) per family.

The law allowed the sheikh and his family to secure most of the land, because it provided that a secondary *multazim* who was a close relative of the sheikh might be regarded as a primary *multazim*, so that the sheikh could nominate members of his family as his lessees or agents, entitled to a half-share in any part of the holding which the sheikh decided. After the sheikh's own share of half the total holding had been deducted and the members of his family had taken half shares in the remainder, there was little left for the cultivators. Further, since the area of the holding contained both cultivated and uncultivated land, the sheikh and his family might claim the whole cultivated area as their property, leaving only the uncultivated and uncultivable to the fellahin.

When efforts were made to carry out the law, the cultivators exercised their right of appeal against the decisions of the settlement officers. The sheikhs retaliated by destroying their houses and turning out their families. The law gave an impetus to the rural exodus which is now proceeding at the rate of ten lorry loads a day for Baghdad. This movement has already weakened the authority of the sheikhs and reduced their incomes. One of the most hated and extortionate, who formerly had 4,000 people, now has only 1,500. Some smaller sheikhs cannot pay their taxes. The fellahin are beginning to mock their masters and think them arbitrary and despotic. A tribesman from Amara, now a house watchman in Baghdad, told his former landowner (now a professor) that he and his four sons could now earn £50 per month between them, and that they could sleep without being kicked awake by the *mamur* to go an errand—an attitude which the ex-landowner fully approved, because he too had found social relations insupportable.

As a result of the unrest in the province, an emergency decree was issued in 1954 which cancelled the law of 1952 and laid down new principles. These principles were embodied in a new law, passed in April 1955, the Law for the Distribution of State Lands in Amara Liwa (No. 53 of 1955). This made two improvements. It provided, first, that the holding for division should include only the cultivated land, including the areas under fallow, and second, that this area should be divided into two equal halves, each half having a river front, canals, and drainage equivalent to the other half. One-half was to be granted to the primary and secondary *multazims*, i.e. the sheikh and his agents, the other half to the fellah household, in units of 7–20 donums (4–12 acres) of flow-irrigated land for rice cultivation and corresponding areas for other types of land. The household receiving land may not sell, bestow, or mortgage the property until a period of ten years after the grant of title. The uncultivated land can be distributed by the settlement officer. The parts suitable for cultivation are to be granted to the fellahin in holdings equivalent to 7–20 donums of flow-irrigated rice land.

At the end of 1955 the survey preparatory to redistribution was being carried out by the settlement officers. One consequence was that the son of the chief sheikh of the province had been thrown into prison, because he claimed more land than his father would allow. Whether in fact the law will be carried out, and whether the fellahin will be satisfied, remains to be seen. 'The police are working day and night', said the *mutasarrif*, in December 1955, 'that is why everything is quiet.'

The Muntafik Law. The Muntafik province lies in the marshes of the Euphrates. Very large landholdings predominate[1]

[1] The *Report of the Agricultural and Livestock Census* for 1952–3 (p. 57) shows that there are 12 holdings exceeding 20,000 donums (12,000 acres), and 26 between 10,000 and 20,000 donums (6,000–12,000 acres).

which are in the possession of sheikh landholders. About half the land in holdings is registered in *tapu* tenure, the remainder in *lazma.*

Concerning these *tapu* lands, there is a sixty-year-old conflict between the actual occupiers of the land (sheikhs, sirkals, and tribesmen), and the Sadun family, which claims legal ownership under *tapu* title granted in Ottoman times. During the nineteenth century this family secured the leadership of the three tribes which formed the Muntafik Confederation, and as sheikhs held all the lands tribally occupied, which in law were state land. The head of the Sadun family, then Governor of the province, purchased *tapu* title to these lands from the Ottoman Government, registering the land in the name of the family and its connexions. The family then increased their pressure on the tribesmen cultivators, demanding a fixed rent irrespective of the actual yield, instead of the proportion which they had claimed as sheikhs. The sub-sheikhs and tribesmen revolted and refused to pay, driving the Sadun landowners off their land.[1] Some of the land has since been resold by the Sadun family to townspeople in Baghdad and Basra. The Sadun family and these other owners still claim legal ownership, but have never been able to collect their rents.

During the British occupation the British authorities reached a temporary solution, which recognized the rights of the landowners; they collected the dues as a percentage (7·5 per cent) of the produce, on behalf of the owners, and paid them into the treasury, to be paid to the landowners when a final settlement of their claims could be reached. An attempt at settlement was made in 1929, by a law 'for the settlement of disputes concerning Muntafik land', which led only to an expensive commission of investigation, and reached no settlement. The land has never been surveyed and investigation alone can reveal nothing, since the areas to which the *tapu* claims relate were never defined.

Twenty years later, in 1952, another law was passed, the Law for the Settlement of the Disputes concerning State Land held by Tapu in Muntafik Province. The holders of *tapu* title, under this law, were to be compensated by the Government in

[1] S. M. Salim, *Economic and Political Organization of Echchbaysh* (University of London unpublished Ph.D. thesis, 1955).

cash or in state land, and the actual occupants were to receive rights of possession, after they had paid half the compensation due to the *tapu* holders. At present local committees are bogged down by administrative delays in land valuation.

This question has little importance from the social standpoint, since it is chiefly the occupying sheikh landholders who are affected by the Sadun claims. A law which offers compensation for antiquated claims to undefined areas of land is simply an illustration of the dead hand in legislation.

Tenancy Legislation. It is unrealistic to suppose, with the existing political system, that any real improvement in the position of the share-croppers can be made by legislation to control rents. A law for this purpose was in fact passed in 1952, the Law Determining the Share of the Cultivator in the Produce of the Land. This law provides that landowners may not take more than 50 per cent of the produce. It also prohibits the landowner from making special levies on his cultivators, a practice followed by landowners who wish to raise money for some special purpose (to buy a car, for example, or to educate a son abroad). In the northern parts of the country local officials consider that this latter provision has had some effect. The provision prohibiting the landowner from taking more than 50 per cent of the crop has had little effect, because the share customarily taken in these parts of the country is usually less than 50 per cent.

In the irrigated zone, where the share taken by the landowner and his agents amounts to two-thirds, the general view was that the law is not enforced. According to the President of the Miri Sirf Land Development Committee,

> this law does not improve the miserable conditions of the peasants, since the application of the law is greatly doubted, and even if applied, the peasant's share of the crop is far from being enough to cover the cost of a reasonable living.[1]

Even in countries where the landowners as a class are less powerful than they are in Iraq, the enforcement of rent regulations for share-croppers is difficult. In south Iraq, where the landowning class has complete domination over the serfs, such regulation seems obviously out of the question.

[1] Hassan Mohammed Ali, *Land Reclamation and Settlement in Iraq* (Baghdad, 1955).

Without an expropriation of the very large landholdings, no legislation can succeed, for the problem of reform is a problem of political power. Iraq needs serf emancipation. Some have believed, or pretended to believe, that evolutionary reform is possible by settling farmers on state land to be developed under the new irrigation schemes. Some reference has already been made above to the 'line of least resistance' policy.[1] The Development Board naturally follows this line, and speaks confidently of the land that will be available for small-holder settlement in the future.[2] But experience so far is not encouraging, as may be seen from the results of the state lands settlement legislation.

THE SETTLEMENT OF STATE LANDS

No legislation which would infringe on the property rights of the large landowners can secure parliamentary approval. The Parliament is composed of the landowners, who secure election by means of their dominance over the cultivators; and this dominance is unquestioned by any internal political force.

> It may be [says Lord Salter] that some among the great landowners will accept or welcome some changes on the principle of 'reform that you may preserve'. In the meantime, however, successive Governments have usually felt that new legislation on land tenancy must be kept within the bounds of what will not be actively resisted by landowners.[3]

These bounds are narrow.

At first sight it appears puzzling that any measures at all, however limited and ineffective, should have been enacted by Iraqi Parliaments, for even when political parties were permitted to exist, the small and disunited opposition groups did not influence policy. The explanation is that the landowners are not the only force on which Iraqi Governments can rely; they depend also on the Army, the Palace and, to some extent, on British support, and are therefore to some degree independent of the landowners. The Prime Minister can therefore arrange, if the stability of the Government seems to require

[1] See above, p. 134.

[2] According to the *Annual Report* of the Development Board for 1953–4 (p. 17), the Dokan dam scheme will provide water for 1·3 million donums (780,000 acres) for small farmer settlement.

[3] *The Development of Iraq*, p. 54.

it, for any particular measure to be passed, by techniques which involve a present to the landowners, in the form of state land, or otherwise. Foreign pressures may be effective, up to a point. If an international mission recommends settlement of farmers on state land, as the International Bank did at a time when a loan was wanted, landowners will be fixed and a law can be passed, and even a little action will be taken. If there is fear of 'Communism' among the fellahin, as there was after the Egyptian revolution, a law can be passed to reduce rents and prohibit unusual extortions, though when the danger recedes it need not be enforced. Serious local unrest, as the example of Amara shows, can get a bad law improved, and perhaps enforced. The old Turkish statecraft requires a semblance of beneficent intentions, though it is unable—and unwilling—to undertake any serious measure of reform. Among the bureaucracy the beneficent intentions are genuine; what has been achieved is the work of enlightened civil servants.

Since large areas of land are still held in the possession of the state as *miri sirf*, and as much of this land can be made cultivable by the new irrigation schemes, there would appear to be great scope for the settlement of small farmers without the necessity of a conflict with the large landowners. To the enlightened civil servants, the distribution of state land seems to provide a way round the political structure of the country. Colonization has even been advocated as an indirect and evolutionary way towards a general improvement in the position of the fellahin; it should, according to this argument, cause a shortage of labour on the land and so induce landowners to offer their cultivators better conditions.[1]

To this indirect approach the main objection is that over the past ten years very little has been done. Two laws governing the distribution of state land passed in 1945 and 1951 have had meagre results for the fellahin, while the large landowners have continued to benefit greatly from the assignment of state land under the process of registration of title.

The Miri Sirf Lands Development Law of 1945 (now known as the Dujaila law) laid down the principles for distribution

[1] Norman Burns in 'The Dujailah Land Settlement', *Middle East Journal*, Summer 1951, quotes a statement to this effect by Darwish el-Haidari, now Director of Agriculture in the Development Board.

of the state lands to be opened up by the new Dujaila canal. This law secured the approval of Parliament because the sheikh landowners in the neighbourhood of the canal expected to get the newly watered state lands for themselves. In fact they were able to secure nearly half the new land as their registered property, and permanent water rights, in return for a single payment of £1 5*s.* per donum, a nominal sum, as the price of their consent to the settlement scheme.[1]

The law laid down the conditions on which ownership might be acquired by small proprietors on the Dujaila lands. Farmers are entitled to acquire ownership of holdings of 100 donums (62 acres) after ten years of occupancy and cultivation, free of rent and other charges, provided that they fulfil the conditions of a contract signed when the holding is allotted to them. When *tapu* title to land has been granted, after ten years, the owner is bound not to sell the land for another ten years, nor may he lease the holding. The qualifications for applicants were local origin and farming experience. A proportion of the holdings was to be allotted to graduates of agricultural schools, retired officials, and ex-service men.

The results of this settlement scheme are described in the following section. It has not been technically successful, nor has the law been carried out in detail, but socially, it is a success. That there is a great demand for ownership was shown by the fact that 50,000 applications for holdings were received by the authorities.

The Miri Sirf Lands Development Law of 1951 was intended to govern the distribution of holdings on all state land which has been or would be developed or reclaimed. It fixed maximum areas of holdings for different regions and different types of farming: 500 donums (300 acres) on high pump-irrigated land, 400 donums (240 acres) on rainfed land, 200 donums (120 acres) for low pump areas, and 20 donums (12 acres) on mountainous land (i.e. land with high rainfall). The lands were to be reclaimed in large areas under the management of an official Committee, which, with the assistance of engineers and other experts, was to direct and finance reclamation and irrigation, employ labour and maintain cultivation for two years, after which time the land was to be entrusted to the

[1] Burns, 'The Dujailah Land Settlement'.

Government (for control of irrigation) and divided into small holdings. Otherwise the law followed the same lines as the Dujaila law: settlers were to be selected by the Committee, from among the local inhabitants, who should have priority. Land could also be assigned to graduates of agricultural schools and recognized religious schools. Holdings were to be distributed free of charge and recipients were prohibited from sub-letting.

The official returns of the Directorate-General of Miri Sirf lands give the following figures for land distributed under this law.

TABLE 17

Distribution of State Land in Iraq in 1952–4

Place and Province	*Areas distributed (donums)*	*No. of holdings*	*No. of persons living on these lands*
Dujaila (Kut)	143,080	1,478	7,390
Shahrazoor (Sulaimaniya)	32,990	497	2,485
Sinjar (Mosul)	1,794,560	6,863	34,315
Hawija (Kirkuk)	45,700	351	1,755
Latafiya (Baghdad)	23,250	465	2,325
Garma	30,000	300	1,500
The Barrage (Kut)	5,200	65	325
Musseyeb River	10,500	175	875
Makhmur (Kirkuk)	13,340	188	940
Lands in other districts	27,960	384	1,920
Total	2,126,580	10,766	53,830

(SOURCE: Iraq Govt., *Statistical Abstract, 1954*, table 110.)

If this total had in fact been distributed to small farmers, the distribution of state land would represent a large and beneficial change in the agrarian structure. However, the figures are misleading. The greater part of the total is accounted for by the 1,800,000 donums, listed as distributed in 6,863 holdings in the Sinjar region of Mosul province. According to information given by the Mosul Chamber of Agriculture, large areas of the best state land in this region have been granted in registered title to the sheikh of the Shammar, Ahmed el-Ajeel, now the largest landowner in the province, and to his sub-sheikhs. This area includes the lands now farmed by Ahmed el-Ajeel on his own account, and also the lands leased by lesser sheikhs to the merchant-tractorists of Mosul. If this information is correct, the main outcome of the 1951 law has simply been a continuation of the usual practice of assigning tribal land to tribal chieftains.

There is, however, an area of about 1 million donums north and south of the Sinjar mountain, which has been surveyed, and found mostly too dry for cultivation and too risky for small farmers. Some settlement is to be undertaken on the better land; and 935 applicants have been selected.[1]

The area which actually has been distributed to small farmers, in settlement schemes which come under the Miri Sirf Land Development Committee, according to a report by Hassan Mohammed Ali, the Committee's President, amounts to only 232,960 donums (140,000 acres), distributed to 3,434 settlers.[2] There are six schemes, Dujaila, Shahrazoor, Hawija, Makhmur, Latafiya, and the Sinjar Scheme in Mosul, in operation, and one, the Greater Musseyeb, which is being reclaimed for settlement in the near future. Of these, only the Dujaila scheme is important in size, accounting for about half the total area and settlers. The remaining schemes are small and, except for the Latafiya scheme, are rather unfavourably situated.

That a few little schemes of this kind can be hailed as a step towards evolutionary reform shows how completely the original conception of settlement of title has been forgotten. Twenty-five years ago Dowson regarded the registration of title as a means of confirming the prescriptive rights of the cultivators; the problem, as he saw it, was simply to establish a procedure to ascertain their rights. In 1951 new legislation was needed to give the state the right to assign title to small cultivators on state land. The prescriptive rights of the cultivators have been so regularly overriden that the right to settle on state land is now a privilege. In the space of a generation the landowners' power of possession has become the right of exclusion.

The settlements are, of course, directly beneficial to the farmers who obtain holdings. But the numbers who benefit are too small to affect the position of cultivators in general.

[1] Hassan Mohammed Ali, *Land Reclamation and Settlement in Iraq*, p. 175.
[2] ibid. p. 75.

Even if this type of settlement were to be carried out on a much larger scale, it would not be able to bring about an improvement in the conditions of cultivators on privately owned estates by causing a shortage of labour, because there is so much underemployment on the land. The rural exodus to the towns reduces the numbers of cultivators on private estates to a far greater extent than settlement schemes even on a bigger scale could do, yet there is so far no sign that it causes landowners to improve the conditions of the fellahin, nor is it likely that landowners will make any efforts in this direction, since tractors can be substituted for labour.

The view that the settlement of farmers on state land can be a step in the direction of evolutionary reform is therefore untenable. It would be a step in the right direction, if there were a direction. But the prospect of achieving any general improvement in this way is an illusion, fostered to please the Americans, and which unfortunately deceives Iraqis also. The present political position is as unfavourable to reform as it has ever been, although economic conditions make reform imperative.

Although so little has been achieved in the direction of general reform, the results of the Dujaila scheme have been useful, in themselves and for the lesson which they teach.

THE DUJAILA SCHEME

The Dujaila settlement is the largest and oldest of these schemes, having been started in 1946 as an example and experiment. It lies about 25 miles south-east of Kut, and extends over an expanse of flat and treeless land, about 25 miles long and 15 miles across. Communications inside the settlement are difficult, and the farmers on donkeys and horses are more mobile than experts and officials in cars on the choppy dirt roads which connect the different tracts.

The settlement depends on the Dujaila canal, which receives water from the Tigris upstream of the Kut barrage, completed in 1939. The main canal is 30 miles long, and serves a total area of 400,000 donums (240,000 acres).[1] This area was all State Domain (*miri sirf*) land before. Rather more than half of it, 250,000 donums (150,000 acres), was assigned to the settle-

[1] This figure is quoted by Hassan Mohamed Ali in *Social Science Bulletin*, vol. 5, no. 4, 1953.

ment, and the remainder to private landowners, the neighbouring sheikhs. The greater part of the total area is irrigable by flow, and the flow-irrigated land is divided into thirteen separate tracts, each served by a lateral canal. Of these tracts, eight belong to the settlement, and five to the neighbouring sheikhs. These private estates adjoin the settlement on all sides.

The area granted to small holders in the settlement in April 1955 was said to be 180,000 donums (108,000 acres), with 1,800 families on holdings of 100 donums each. This figure is only a rough guess, and does not indicate exactly the area of cultivated land. Between the eight tracts which are cultivated, there are stretches of uncultivated land, some of which has already gone out of cultivation, so that the area of land actually cultivated cannot be estimated exactly.

It proved impossible to ascertain the total cost of the settlement scheme itself. A figure of £600,000 is quoted, but this includes the cost of construction of the main canal and lateral canals for the private land as well as for the settlement. Apart from the heavy expenditure on irrigation, it would appear that not much has been spent on the scheme. There are a few administrative buildings and schools but no machinery or other equipment. School building was partly financed out of the funds of the now defunct co-operative. The farmers build their own mud huts. Each farmer receives an initial credit of £100, repayable in instalments over five years. But apart from this, they receive no equipment. As the settlers pay no rent, none of the cost is recoverable.

The conditions under which settlers were to be granted land were laid down in the first Miri Sirf law of 1945, i.e. the right of ownership of holdings of 100 donums (60 acres) after ten years of occupancy and cultivation, free of rent and other charges, if the conditions of a contract signed when the holding is allotted to them are fulfilled. The contract obliges the farmer to build a house, storage for crops, and small feeder canals, and to buy trees, seed, and livestock. It also obliges him to follow a fixed crop rotation, including cotton and other intensive crops, but this provision has not been enforced.

The law also laid down the qualifications for applicants, such as local origin and farming experience: it provided that a proportion of the holdings should be allotted to graduates of agricultural schools, ex-policemen, and ex-soldiers. This clause is frequently criticized, because it is said to favour absentee ownership. The ex-soldiers and policemen—agricultural graduates apparently did not apply—prefer to live in Kut and other towns and rent the land to cultivators. How far sub-letting is practised, and on what terms, could not be ascertained; but it is said to be a fairly general practice.

Thus the scheme has not been enforced as the law originally intended, for there is little change in methods of farming; and ownership by the cultivator is not general. The farmers enjoy a remarkable degree of independence. The area of land assigned to them—100 donums or 60 acres of which half is cropped—is about twice as large as that usually cultivated by share-croppers on private estates. The owners pay no rent or instalment of purchase price, whereas on private land the cultivator is obliged to pay at least half and more usually two-thirds of produce as share-rent.

In Baghdad, however, rumour says that the scheme is a failure. Certainly there is no attempt on the part of the authorities to conceal the mistakes or defects in the scheme. On the contrary, they tend to exaggerate them. In the course of a visit to Dujaila in the company of the President of the Development Board, the President of the Miri Sirf Land Development Committee, and other members of the Development Board, there was prolonged and lively controversy about the scheme, chiefly in relation to the frustrating experiences of a Unesco team, which had striven for three years to conduct fundamental education on the borders of the settlement. The controversy, however, turned chiefly on the nature of fundamental education and the need for it, rather than on the organization of the scheme itself. As to these main defects, there is little disagreement.

The real cause of the possible failure of the scheme—for it is not by any means a failure yet—is the lack of drainage. The results of this are apparent even to the inexpert eye. As the rough track from Kut enters the settlement, it passes through land heavily encrusted with salt, either abandoned or cultivated only in patches carrying very poor crops. This first impression is misleading, for these sections are by far the worst. One tract out of the eight has been abandoned almost entirely, and two others are badly affected by salinity, but on the remainder, where cultivation has begun more recently, salt has not yet appeared to the same extent, though it must appear 'with mathematical precision', as an FAO expert put it, as cultivation continues. The destruction of the fertility of the soil has already necessitated moving about 300 farmers to other land. Crop yields have fallen from 400 kg. per donum (12½ cwt per acre) in the past years to 250 kg. per donum (7½ cwt per acre). Even this low yield is good for Iraq.

The danger of salinity could have been foreseen, since it has long been known that permanent irrigation without drainage is not possible in most of south Iraq,[1] or indeed in any arid region where natural drainage is not adequate. Salinity is not by any means a problem peculiar to the Dujaila lands. (Salt-encrusted land can be seen all along the road from Baghdad to Kut.) On private lands it is countered simply by abandoning the land, but in a settlement intended for permanent cultivation this course cannot be followed. Every visiting expert since 1950—and there have been many—has recommended drainage. Cost was an obstacle before 1951, but now that the Development Board has a large unspent balance there can be no reason for further delay. Not until 1954 did the Board allocate funds for drainage, and then only for one of the eight tracts, where work began in 1955. A sum of £40,000 was granted to drain this one tract of 25,000 donums (15,000 acres); if this sum is sufficient, the cost of reclamation is about £3 per acre, which is not high in comparison with cost of reclaiming waste land in European countries.

Much else has gone wrong at Dujaila, so much else that it is difficult to decide where responsibility lies. There is, for example, no co-operative or marketing organization of any kind, though this is much needed, because the settlement is remote and communications poor. A co-operative society was started in 1950, to which farmers were obliged to belong, and to subscribe £1 5*s*. towards its capital. The society made a good start, undertaking marketing and purchase of farm equipment and providing credit and machine service. It owned 10 tractors, 5 ploughs, 2 lorries, and a flour mill. It broke down quickly,

[1] The Haigh Commission's report in 1951 was emphatic (see above, p. 114). So too was the *Iraq Irrigation Handbook* of 1943, and so was Willcocks, in 1905.

owing to mismanagement, and two members brought an action against the society, which was declared bankrupt (though unnecessarily, since its assets exceeded its liabilities). A little official help might have avoided this failure.

There is no organization to enforce a better system of crop rotation, and not much experiment in new crops. Most of the land is too heavy for cotton, and no cotton is grown. The cotton ginnery which was built to handle the crop now stands idle. Some advance has been made in vegetable cultivation, and trees have been planted. There is a small nursery for trees and seedlings managed by a skilled gardener. Demonstration plots are well managed, under the direction of an FAO expert. Experiments have shown that Egyptian clover (berseem) can increase the yields of the grain crops. Swiss chard is found to give good results even on poor soil. Thus a beginning has been made, though rather late in the day. A date-palm avenue round the central buildings on one of the tracts relieves the aridity of the scene.

Some schools exist, situated in different tracts, but not all children attend school because the distances are so great. There is a health clinic which gives inoculations against bilharzia, which affects most of the inhabitants, and treatment for trachoma, also widespread. But there is no doctor in the settlement, and none nearer than Kut.

One successful venture is a small textile factory, weaving and spinning cheap woollen fabrics. This has been started by Mr Chitra, an Indian expert in rural industries, working for the UN Technical Assistance Board, who has started similar factories in two other settlements. He enjoys official support and can get his plans approved and executed more easily than other foreign experts, who display a natural professional jealousy. There was some argument among members of the Development Board authorities as to the need for industries of this kind in rural settlements. But since agricultural work is highly seasonal, and likely to remain so, a factory giving off-time employment seems needed. In view of the isolation of the settlement, it would be useful if it could become, as Mr Chitra hopes, the nucleus for a community development. Such factories are the more needed, in view of the difficulty which the Development Board has experienced in starting industries.

The weaknesses in organization result from a lack of co-ordination between local needs and the central authorities. The original conception was sound, but there has obviously been no sustained interest at the top level. Several different Ministries—Agriculture, Irrigation, Education, Health—are responsible for different activities, and neglect them, since there is no organization at the settlement itself to co-ordinate their spheres or to urge action on the authorities.

The defects in administration, however, are unimportant compared with the deterioration of the land itself, which will, unless action is taken, render the scheme a failure. To ascertain how much land could be saved by reclamation, a soil survey was undertaken in 1953–5 by the Department of Agriculture, under the direction of Mr Burnell West, an American soil technologist employed by FAO.

The survey reported that agricultural production could be maintained at a satisfactory level only where artificial drainage could be supplied. The salinity derived from two main sources, the receding Persian Gulf, and the salt left in the soil by past ages of irrigation.[1] 'A thorough drainage investigation must be made of the entire project. . . Otherwise the salinity will increase and the land will be forced out of production in a relatively few years.'[2] Some of the salty land could be reclaimed by leaching, a long process of washing out the soil, but other land is too impermeable to be reclaimed, and must be abandoned. The report recommended summer cropping on the reclaimed land, with rice and barley to prevent the salt rising, and advised against the alternate fallow system.[3]

The soil survey report also recommended better farming practices, as follows:

1. A crop-rotation system, to include the use of legume crops to be ploughed under as green manure, and the cultivation of fodder crops, such as clover and lucerne, to enable numbers of livestock to be increased.

[1] The report makes an interesting comment which means that the usual view of Iraq's past history needs revision: 'No evidence has been found that the early irrigators supplied any artificial drainage. There is no doubt that the ancients were forced to abandon a large part of the land covered by this project because of excessive salinity' (*Report of the Soil Survey, Dujaila Project*, by Burnell G. West, FAO mission, published by the Ministry of Agriculture, Government of Iraq, 1955, p. 5).

[2] ibid. p. 14. [3] ibid. pp. 13–16.

2. The use of heavier draught animals or tractors for deep tillage, needed every few years, and for weed control.
3. Experiments to establish the rates of application of water.
4. Weed control, through irrigation before cultivation, to allow weeds to germinate before the land is ploughed.
5. The use of animal manure, and the cultivation of a wood lot or sesbania as a substitute for dung fuel.[1]

These are grass-root recommendations, not the usual arm-chair planning; they begin from what is now done, and suggest practicable improvements. The recommendations would apply to agriculture throughout south Iraq, and ought to be the basis of a general agricultural policy. The most noteworthy is the recommendation to increase the number of livestock by better feeding, for this is the only branch in which farmers at Dujaila, and elsewhere, are really proficient.

Energetic action and expenditure are therefore needed. Dujaila is a test case for the administration. Burnell West, asked whether the project could be saved, said 'I would not give much for the future of the country if it cannot be.'

As an experiment, Dujaila can be regarded as a success. It has taught an essential lesson, that land must be drained before settlement. On the new state land settlements drainage is to be undertaken before the land is settled.

As an example, it is also a success, because it shows that settlement can bring direct benefits to the settlers. In spite of the fall in yields, farmers are doing well, and are far better off than they would be as share-croppers on private estates, where they would cultivate half the area, pay two-thirds of the produce as rent, and have no social services at all. In the first years, when yields were high, some farmers are said to have earned £600 a year, and the average income was £300. Now, with the fall in yields, it is lower, but even so the farm families have enough to eat and a surplus to spend. Those who make money use it to buy a new English rifle, or an extra wife—habits which officials find reprehensible, the equivalent of keeping coal in the bath. But the pattern of life is still tribal, and these are advances in well-being as it is understood by those concerned.

[1] ibid. pp. 17–25.

This improvement in well-being is, after all, the object of the settlements. The American conception of land reform as an 'integrated programme', involving the provision of fully equipped services, tends to give the impression that reform is an elaborate technical procedure, only to be undertaken with everything laid on. Measured by this ideal, the scheme falls short. But in essentials, it is good enough. There is an atmosphere of rather desolate freedom in spite of—indeed because of—the poor organization.

Dujaila shows that land reform is worth doing, even if it is not done with administrative efficiency, simply because redistribution of land can bring immediate improvements in the living standard. Reform need not wait on better farming: the agriculture of south Iraq is so primitive that there is no risk that a decline in production could follow a division of the big estates. There is no need to aim at perfection in equipping the farmers, or in the organization of services. If Iraq has to wait for land reform until the Government can provide schools, experts, health services, and co-operatives, it will wait too long. These good things can come, and will come, once ownership has been redistributed. What is wrong with Dujaila can be put right, but what is wrong with the big estates cannot be remedied except through a general measure of reform, including the redistribution of ownership.

Other Settlement Schemes

On the remaining *miri sirf* land settlement schemes (described in *Land Reclamation and Settlement in Iraq*, by Hassan Mohammed Ali), the Point Four Mission exercises advisory functions, under its agreement with the Iraqi Government. Members of the Mission have surveyed physical and economic conditions, carried out demonstration projects, and prepared cropping plans. They have also recommended the introduction of supervised credit, a system of granting loans to farmers under the supervision of technical advisers who ensure that the loan is spent in furtherance of a plan to improve the farm, drawn up in consultation between the farmers and the supervisor.[1]

[1] The system is operated in the United States by the Farmers Home Administration, for farmers who cannot cover their credit needs through the ordinary channels

The most promising scheme appears to be the settlement at Latafiya, which has better conditions than the rest, in that it has fairly good soil (adjacent to the British-owned Latafiya Estates) and is situated only thirty miles from Baghdad, and so could supply the growing demand for fruit and vegetables. It has sufficient water, but requires drainage, as Dujaila does, and so far has only a drainage demonstration project. Fifteen thousand acres have been settled in 30-acre holdings. Forty per cent of the settlers are ex-officials and ex-service men, who generally sub-let their holdings. The rest are tribesmen from the vicinity. Great efforts have been made by the American advisers to improve cropping practices by demonstration, chiefly by the introduction of alfalfa (lucerne). Although the average annual net income per farm (according to a sample inquiry) amounts to £133, a high proportion of the farmers are indebted, mostly to their former landlords. Supervised credit has been introduced, chiefly to buy livestock, and horses and cattle have been distributed. This settlement, though it clearly has weaknesses, appears to have the makings of success, chiefly because it is near Baghdad and so gets more attention from the authorities.

The Hawija scheme, near Kirkuk, is a small settlement included in a much larger area which can be brought under cultivation by more irrigation. Lack of livestock is the chief drawback, and efforts to set up credit co-operatives, under the guidance of an FAO co-operative expert, have so far failed. The adjacent Makhmur scheme is also small, part of the area to be irrigated when the Dokan dam scheme is completed. Both these settlements have fruit-tree nurseries.

The Shahrazoor project, near Halabja in the Kurdish hills, appears to have been least successful. It relies on canal irrigation, natural springs, and rainfall, but though water-supplies are potentially adequate, the canal does not at present supply sufficient water. Two successive years of harvest failure in 1953 and 1954, the result of pest damage, brought the majority of the farmers heavily into debt to merchants. An attempt was made to introduce supervised credit, but although the request for funds was approved by the Agricultural Bank, few settlers

and also in connexion with loans for farm purchase. See UN, *Progress in Land Reform*, p. 214.

took the loans, 'the rest having refused to follow the program recommended by the Committee economist, and preferring to use the loans as they see fit'.[1]

A survey of about 1 million donums of state land round Mount Sinjar in the Jezira on the Syrian border reveals conditions resembling those on the marginal lands in the Jezira in Syria. Crop failures occur every four or five years, yields are very low, and livestock insufficient. Much of the land is altogether unsuitable for cultivation, and even on the better land, which retains most of the moisture, rainfall is inadequate for steady yields. Some of the better land is already settled, and tractor-ploughing is used by the sheikh landowners. On the poorer land a number of villages have been settled by Beduin in the course of the last six years (possibly including the tribesmen who have lost grazing land in Syria, cf. p. 88). 'Some of these villages were in a very badly pauperised condition, and the people in one village were on the edge of starvation.'[2] As a result of crop failure, they had insufficient seed to plant for the 1953 harvest, which would have given them a good return. 'They acknowledged that one difficulty . . . had been that they did not know how to farm.'[3]

The survey recommended settlement on the better land, in units of 150 or 200 donums according to the type of land, with access to public grazing land, and estimated the livestock needed to establish a family. The Miri Sirf Land Development Committee approved these recommendations, and 935 settlers have been granted land in village sites provided with artesian wells to provide drinking-water.

The picture which emerges from the report is on the whole a gloomy one: heavy debt, and a shortage of credit and no effective way of overcoming it as yet; too little livestock, as a result, and consequently a tendency to buy too much food off the farm; bad health and poor organization. Yet in spite of all these disadvantages, it is said, no doubt truly, that the settlers at Latafiya and Hawija are better off than farmers on private estates. The settlements have been established only recently, and with the help of the expert advisers and some determination on the part of the authorities, these defects can probably

[1] Hassan Mohammed Ali, *Land Settlement and Reclamation in Iraq*, p. 121.
[2] ibid. p. 170. [3] ibid. p. 163.

be overcome in time. It is, however, obvious that a better selection of sites and land would make success more certain and allow model settlements to come into existence instead of these struggling small groups.

What is useful and good in these settlements is that they do provide an experimental field. They can ascertain by experience the crops that can be successfully grown and marketed, and the system of credit (supervised or co-operative) that is most practicable. The function of the Point Four advisers is obviously valuable, because it can keep the needs of the settlers before the authorities, and can thus prevent failure of the schemes. In the Sinjar region the expert survey evidently averted a failure in selecting poor land. If this experience is digested, it should enable the authorities to ascertain the type of farming, size of farm unit, and the equipment and organization suited to the different regions, and so to evolve a pattern which could be the aim of a general reform policy.

THE SOCIAL VACUUM

The real obstacle to reform in Iraq is not a shortage of experts, or money, or administrative inefficiency. Nor is it, in reality, the 'feudal' landowners. The town middle class represents the public opinion of the country in that it is conscious of the need for change; it provides the official class, criticizes development policy, and it is growing very fast. It cannot, however, link up with the fellahin and provide the political force which would recast the social structure of the country. There is no social or political force which can challenge the power of the sheikhs. The educated townspeople do not, at present, constitute this force, though their number, their intelligence, and their importance in administration, should qualify them to become it. That the sheikhs of Amara should rule over the civil servants of Baghdad and the merchants of Mosul seems incongruous to the outsider. The townsman himself shares this attitude, regarding the sheikhs with a mildly amused contempt which he is careful not to show in their presence.

Why, then, do the townspeople not play a greater part in the political life of the country? They are not simply leftish intellectuals who aspire to lead the 'mob', as some Middle East experts believe. To lead the growing and rather menacing hordes of slum dwellers is just what they cannot do, and just what ought to be done. On the surface, the reason is that the urban middle class is politically powerless, because the opposition parties are suppressed; but this formal suppression can hardly have been decisive. The real reason lies deeper, in the political nexus which rules the country, and which is extremely difficult to define.

The question of who rules Iraq finds different answers within the country. Some say that three statues, King Feisal, General Maude, and Sadun (i.e. the landowners), are the real Government. Simple people believe that the British rule Iraq by remote control, while the more sophisticated think that it is the Prime Minister who rules the British. There is truth in both views. It would be idle to pretend that IPC is not a political power. On the principle of no taxation without representation, a company which produces at least half the national income must exert some influence. But the conventions of independence must be maintained, in particular the façade of parliamentary sovereignty, to show that Britain does not intervene.

The sheikhs, of course, have power and prestige outside this façade, of which they are the other main support. They are, however, a ruling class only *pro forma*. The real work of administration is carried out by the civil servants, who are opposed to the surviving sheikh tradition. Government policy is never initiated by the sheikhs, but by the Prime Minister, supported on the twofold base of British influence and the large landowners. How any given decision is reached and why the 'Pack of Cards'[1] is from time to time reshuffled remains a mystery. It is a miracle that, in this situation, the Development Board should have been able to reach any decisions at all.

What is wrong is not that the money is misused. Such allegations of corruption as are made reveal very small-scale inducements. On the contrary, as has been shown, Iraq needs the money desperately, and from the technical standpoint it has been well spent. Yet in the atmosphere of Baghdad there is a feeling of corruption, because the Government's only reliable supporters within the country are the privileged class who support it on condition that their wealth and privileges are un-

[1] See Desmond Stewart and John Haylock, *New Babylon* (London, Collins, 1956).

touched. 'The whole position', as Kipling wrote of Egypt in 1913, 'is essentially false'.

The strength of the political nexus rests on tradition, and it may not be a necessity, but it is too powerful to be challenged by the Iraqi middle class alone. Urban society is very old and tradition-bound. It is also extremely urbanized in its outlook: prone to despise the fellahin as backward, and knowing little and caring less about their condition. Among effendis distaste for the land is universal. Even for the rich landowner there is no country life. The tribesman's contempt for manual work is shared by the middle class.

Yet this middle class is not negligible. It is, as far as it can be, extremely constructive. Individual civil servants are hard and devoted workers who draft legislation which does not get into the statute book, or undertake systematic social investigations in their spare time. Among the provincial governors (the *mutassarifs*) and the city mayors there is strong public spirit and high competence. Free to some extent from the dead hand of the central Government, these men are in direct touch with the needs of the people of their provinces and cities. They have begun to compete with each other in showing what can be done with the funds assigned to them by the ordinary budget, and now that the 1955 expenditure programme of the Development Board will put bigger funds at their disposal, they may find ways, as one of them has already done, of mobilizing the coffee-house sitters for community development. But no common opinion unites these sincere people, who should be the leaders in a new society, for they are all ultimately dependent on the Government.

The root of the trouble is simply that there is no new economic class to rival the power of the landowners. The outstanding feature of Iraq's economic revolution is that it is disembodied. The ample funds for investment have arisen without any change in the economy or the society. The oil industry is a one-sided 'developer' because it does not, like other mining industries, require an expansion of the transport and power systems: it uses its own transport and power and requires little in the way of public services. It does not employ large numbers of workers, and so does not have much direct effect on the general level of incomes. IPC is a giant, but its impact is almost entirely financial. An industry which is practically extra-territorial provides funds for investment.

Since these funds do not arise from local enterprise and savings, and since the direct impact of oil on the economy is so slight, there is no new class of business men, no liberal Manchester, to challenge the power of the old aristocracy. There are some new industrialists, it is true, but they are few, and apart from one or two large undertakings the new firms are mostly small. It will be long before there are enough of them to change the balance of political power. For many years past efforts have been made to stimulate new industry, through tax and tariff concessions, but so far without much success, because the market is limited by the poverty of the mass of the population. If there were a strong impetus to develop on capitalistic lines, the prospects of political change through fuller representation of the townspeople would be far greater.

As it is, this half-tribal half-urban society faces the task of constructing the physical framework for development and also the social structure for expansion. This task far exceeds the powers of Iraqi society as it is at present constituted. It is not simply a question of a shortage of 'experts', as is often believed, but of much more serious deficiencies.

As the Baghdad civil servants themselves say, there is a social vacuum, a gap between the economic potential and the social structure. It is inaccurate to speak of conflict between the old and the new society, for the old society is collapsing, and if the new society is represented by the urban agglomeration of Baghdad, then it is taking the imprint of the West like wax—the superficial imprint, without the things that the Western world believes to be its best. There is no stable social structure, only familiar incongruities: the sheikhs in Cadillacs, the tribesmen in buses, the *souks* using electric power, and the new bank buildings in the unpaved and undrained streets. It is inaccurate also to say that Iraq is in a state of transition; whatever is happening, it is change without direction or purpose. Hence the economic problem of where to start: hence the difficulty of spending the money.

But change there is, though it is difficult to pin down by any conventional approach. The typical formal history of the country describes the stages by which a segment of the Ottoman Empire became an independent state and duly acquired a proper Constitution and the correct forms of parliamentary government. Little of reality is revealed by this approach, for the documents do not show how the institutions work. The typical economic report is no better: it surveys a statistical desert, filled with unreliable estimates, and recommends more irrigation, flood-control, transport, afforestation and education, and so on. But these approaches overlook the men who are to do these jobs, and the social life of Iraq slips down between the cracks. The social vacuum can be felt, though it cannot be analysed. The outside observer, unsure of any generalization about it, can only take sights from various angles.

First, there is the phenomenon of the foreign experts. They are clearly a symptom of something lacking. Foreign advisers are nothing new in Iraq; but before the war they were fewer, and far more influential. Now their numbers have multiplied till they infest the Development Board and the Ministries. They advise the Government on broad lines of economic policy, as have, for instance, the International Bank Mission,[1] Professor Iversen,[2] and Lord Salter.[3]

Other authorities advise on town planning, forestry, drainage: they are transient, leaving with the swallows, and each is ignorant of the advice of his predecessors. The representatives of foreign firms with contracts, surveying, studying, and actually constructing, are in a different category, since they are employed by their own firms and paid to do a definite job in a definite time; their position is easier, and their work harder. They are obviously indispensable and must continue to play a part, a technical part, for a long time to come, for they meet a real need.

The most interesting are the experts who advise on moral and social questions, the new missionaries whose essential function is to infuse an element of uplift. Some are office-bound, but others, to their credit, are mobile over long distances and visit remote areas. They carry on their campaigns in the Ministries with spirit, and as individualists. The Point Four men advise on the *miri sirf* settlements. At the Latafiya settlement they can

[1] *The Economic Development of Iraq* (Baltimore, Johns Hopkins Press, 1952).
[2] *Monetary Policy in Iraq.* [3] *The Development of Iraq.*

be found inculcating the virtues of homespun self-help, urging on the baffled manager the need for ensuring that only those cultivators who can pay may be allowed to have the tractor; and insisting that if any farmer wishes to hire the tractor to work land which the experts consider unsuitable he is to be allowed to do so, in order to learn by experience. At Dujaila in 1955 Unesco officials were propagating the principles of fundamental education to the inhabitants of the saline tracts.[1] Up in the north an FAO expert strove to instil the spirit of agricultural co-operation, as it has worked in Nigeria. Mexican girls teach hygiene as in Mexican social centres. Between the settlements darts the UN Technical Assistance expert, not frustrated at all, busily engaged in setting up rural industries on the lines that have worked well in India. The whole civilized world seems to be contributing its mite; but the thought arises that this sort of impetus ought not to come from outside, and that so long as it does it is bound to be frustrated.

All these efforts are in themselves admirable, and should not be decried. But all strive to instil social values which have been proved in other settings, and often the values conflict. They cannot possibly 'take', because the experts themselves are not a permanent or responsible element in the community, and they are not, of course, co-ordinated in any way. Though the old society is crumbling at the edges, it still preserves some of its solidarity, and whatever social obligation is felt is based on the tribe or the clan. The Point Four experts are trying to teach the value of individualist self-help to people whose whole social outlook is opposed to it. The co-operative experts try to teach the value of co-operation in the economic sphere, through conscious organized methods, to people who co-operate unconsciously with great ease. Probably it is impossible for foreign advisers to work with the old society at all, because it is breaking up, and presumably their only direct influence is on the civil servants with whom they come into contact, and who are as frustrated and disunited as themselves.

Insight into the nature of the old society is difficult to gain. It lies not far below the surface, and glimpses of it can be seen even in the most urbanized circles. The important families of Baghdad still retain their tribal surnames and boast of their

[1] The Unesco Mission has since left Dujaila, in despair.

tribal ancestry. In law-suits townspeople often claim the protection of the tribal regulations which impose lesser penalties. At a cocktail party a young society girl may explain the difficulty which one of her friends had to get the blue tattoo marks removed from her nose; and it emerges that the rich families of Mosul, until quite recently, used to give their one-year-olds into the care of the Beduin for four or five years, to avert the vengeance which may come on those who love their children too much. These are the superficial signs of a world still tied to its tribal origins, but they do not show how far its values are still dominant.

There is, however, one study of Iraqi society at the village level which vividly reveals the existence of the social vacuum, Dr Salim's study of Echchbaysh.[1] The community studied, a population of 11,000 living in 1,600 small islands in the great permanent marsh of the Hor el-Hammar,[2] has undergone rapid economic change over the past thirty years, for agriculture has declined with the shrinkage of the cultivated area caused by flooding, and the people have therefore turned over to mat-making as a main occupation, producing, at the rate of a million a year, the reed mats which are used as a roofing and building material for huts and houses throughout Iraq. It has also undergone a political change (because its sheikh was deposed and the sheikhdom abolished by the Iraq authorities in 1924, when the sheikh's *mudhif* was bombed by the RAF and the sheikh exiled). Yet though it is a commercialized market economy, without traditional rule, the social structure of tribal life, and the social values associated with it, are still strong and intact.

Two quite distinct class divisions exist side by side. One is a social gradation, corresponding to the old tribal society, in which the religious men (Sayyids), the sirkals (the chiefs of the nine clans which compose the community), the *mukhtars* (lineage headmen), and the *Ajaweed* (the council of 'good people' or elders of the clan) constitute the class ruling over the ordinary tribesmen, the *Abeed* (negroes, formerly slaves), and the *Subba* (a non-Moslem group of craftsmen, excluded from clan membership). The sirkals, in consultation with the headmen and elders, administer the tribal code, by which rights and

[1] *Economic and Political Organization of Echchbaysh.* [2] See map, p. 123.

obligations are still enforced on a clan basis. In the *mudhif* etiquette is elaborate and rigid, recognizing the gradations of rank in a complex archaic society.

Side by side with this order, in which heredity determines rank, there exists a new class division on the basis of economic function, which has arisen in the transition from cultivation to mat-weaving. There are now two broad groups on the basis of income level, those who enjoy a comfortable living standard—with brick houses and furniture—which includes the 'rich men', landholders and shopkeepers, and those who live on a low standard, the artisans, employees, and mat-weavers and cultivators. The 'rich men', whose incomes range upwards from £1,000 per annum, are money-lenders, dealers in the mat trade, and owners of motor launches. Their origins are various, four having sprung from the class of 'religious men' and one from the former chiefly clan.

But the new rich have acquired no prestige, and social standing is still in accordance with the hereditary classes, not in accordance with wealth. The rich men and shopkeepers are collectively described as 'Ahl es-Soug', which means literally 'the people of the market', but in fact means 'those who have departed from tribal traditions to acquire wealth'. Prestige in society depends on membership of the *Ajaweed*, and qualifications for membership are character, numerous kinsmen, and knowledge of the tribal law. Wealth confers no standing of any kind.

The men with high reputations in the tribe, the *Ajaweed*, are mostly mat-weavers and cultivators having only the lowest standard of living and frequently in debt, but they are far more influential in the society than any of the rich men. Of the wealthy men, only those whose families belonged to the religious men or the chiefly clan enjoy high social standing, and only because of their ancestry and in spite of their wealth.

'A penniless Sayid, in fact, enjoys very much higher prestige than a rich Sayid.'[1] The prevailing social values are those of a warrior society, 'in which the two dominant themes are courage and generosity. . . . Meanness is the nadir of vice. To be mean implies a want of confidence in one's own ability to gain more plunder.' Dr Salim provides ample evidence for his view

[1] Salim, *Economic and Political Organization of Echchbaysh*, pp. 549 and 589.

that 'Nothing could be more contemptible than thrift, bargaining, or the slightest appearance of attaching value to one's material possessions.'[1] 'What is the use of money to a man if he loses his dignity?' is the view of the guest-house, or 'Money and commerce are the greatest evils which have befallen the people of Echchbaysh.' Social standing and economic status no longer correspond.

Tribal tradition is not only strong in maintaining these attitudes to wealth; it also prevents the people from taking up occupations which would greatly improve their standard of living, such as vegetable growing, dairy production, and fishing. These are by tradition the occupations of the weaker clans and therefore despised. There is no communal enterprise; necessary small dams and drains to save the land from flooding are not undertaken.

On the whole, this community has gained greatly from the political change which brought them directly under the control of the central Government in that conditions are more peaceful, there is less extortion of high rents, and schools and dispensaries have been started. What is most significant from the standpoint of development is that the people, though they have been able to make their needs known to the authorities, are unable to get any action. Two small projects, the dredging out of a short length of the Haffar canal and the construction of a regulator at Gurmat Hassan, would enable thousands of acres to be cultivated and also improve communications. These projects are simple and not expensive, and the leaders of the community have requested the local authorities to have them undertaken, and have also attempted to undertake the work themselves.[2] Even local funds are not lacking; the municipality has an uninvested surplus capital of £10,000 which could be used for constructing houses needed by teachers and other officers, to build bridges, or reclaim land.

This is the social vacuum at the village level. The village is still a community, but it has no power of development on com-

[1] ibid. p. 569.

[2] 'Because of their extreme simplicity, the people of Echchbaysh and other inhabitants of the district cannot find any explanation for the failure to put it into effect, despite repeated appeals to the Government, other than that the Government, for some reason known only to itself, is deliberately neglecting the project' (ibid. p. 301). The Gurmat Hassan regulator is now under construction.

munity lines. The poor livelihood, the insecurity of the floods, and the exactions of the money-lenders drive people out to seek work outside as seasonal labourers. Echchbaysh is a microcosm for the whole country; its values are those of the tribe, and its economy is dependent on the 'people of the market', while its real needs are neglected.

Baghdad in the chaos of 'development'—one need not call it progress—reveals the vacuum in urban life. At the last census in 1947 Baghdad's population was 364,000; now it may be twice as large. Sixteen thousand cars a day, canary and crimson and iridescent purple, pass down the seedy two-mile length of Rashid Street. The plate-glass of the car dealers and air conditioners and the Bata and Orosdi-Beck stores throws the surrounding squalor into higher relief. Shops are bulk-breaking booths stuffed with imports of canned food, Penguins, razor blades, just unpacked from their crates. Cinemas show the most violent films obtainable, including one banned by the film censorship in England; but the bookshops operate under a censorship which bans *War and Peace* and *A Tale of Two Cities*. New roads cut through old slums, leaving their inhabitants living in the rubble on either side. The only public amenity is the bus service, clean and efficient in exotic London red double and single-deckers.

Nightmare new slums are growing. Most of the families come in clans from Amara. Tribes from the marshes bring their buffaloes to live with them. One such new slum is at Sheikh Omar, outside the Bund (the dyke round the city) adjoining the sewage dumps. Here some 40,000 people are living in mud huts, rebuilt after being destroyed in the 1954 floods. With the traditional gentle manners they welcome the guest into the filth. There is much trachoma and dysentery, but no bilharzia or malaria, because the water is too polluted for snails and mosquitoes. The infant mortality rate is 250. A woman has a 50:50 chance of raising a child to the age of ten. There are no social services of any kind; the dispensary which existed before the floods was not put back again. There would be no drinking-water if Professor Michael Critchley, of the Baghdad College of Medicine, had not succeeded in persuading the authorities to put in pipes and taps. Earnings of the poorest average 100 fils (2*s.*) a day. On the adjacent dumps dogs with rabies dig in the sewage, and the slum-dwellers pack it for re-sale as garden manure.

Opposite the royal palace is a slum enclosed behind a high wall, where families are earning as much as £2 per week, but pay £1 10*s*. per month for the tiny patch of land on which they build their huts, divided by a warren of narrow alleys. There children die more frequently in their second year, when they begin to crawl in the dust. The higher standard of living is shown in the possession of a wooden bed, a clothes chest, and highly coloured pictures of Queen Elizabeth and General Neguib.

These are the places where the experts do not go. Professor Critchley, revered by the dwellers in the *sarifa*, brings his students, and would like to invite the King to visit his people. It needs no expert advice to see that what Baghdad needs is more housing for the working class and a sewage system. Iraq is in the early throes of its urban revolution, and as yet it has no Chadwick among its civil servants and no Shaftesbury among its aristocracy.

The older generation consciously feels the gap between the old and the new. Superficially criticism focuses on the use of the new money, the failure to use it to meet social needs. But there are deeper issues at stake. An explicit view was put forward by the assistant *mutasarrif* of Mosul. In the past, he said, the rich commanded respect, for they paid the tithe for beneficent purposes as enjoined by religion, and did not antagonize the poor by demonstrating their wealth. Now the whole balance of society was destroyed, and the poor felt envy and spite towards the rich. This cancer in social life could be cut out, he thought, not by going back in time, but by finding a new balance. Mosul feels the strain most, because its labour and capital are draining away to Baghdad and it has lost the position it held in Ottoman times. But all who think seriously about the future of the country share this feeling that the new life has lost standards and solidarity.

The young reject the old outright, but feel the strain of the divided mind no less. The young bureaucrat just back from California with a degree in economics has apparently learnt nothing but contempt for his fellow countrymen, and particularly for those who struggle on as teachers or 'trainees' with the international agencies on the settlements. Behind a smart-alec manner he hides a wretched conviction that 'nothing will be done by this Government'.

The social vacuum is not peculiar to Iraq. But it is more evident there than elsewhere, because of the money. In Syria internal capital and enterprise are playing a leading part in development, and foreign experts are employed on technical work only. In Egypt the Government itself takes the lead, and is some way ahead of opinion. But in Iraq the social obstacles to development are stronger, and the economic potential greater. How the gap will be filled cannot be foreseen. Perhaps the 2,000 Iraqi students now in Britain and America may help to fill it. Perhaps the Development Board, if its scope of action can be made independent of Parliament, will acquire greater courage, and mobilize opinion behind it. Or perhaps, as the more frustrated foreign experts are inclined to say, 'something will crack'.

CONCLUSION

THE DYNAMICS OF CHANGE

It is the international aspects of the social and economic changes proceeding in the Middle East that chiefly interest Westerners. They ask whether land reform and development will weaken or strengthen the influence of Communism; improve the chances of agreement between Israel and the Arab States; find room for the Palestine refugees; and promote stability in the region.

Though this study is concerned with the effect of these changes on the position of the fellahin, and not with their international aspects, such questions as these inevitably do arise, and it therefore seems necessary to explain why there is so little that can usefully be said about them. Many elements are involved in what is called the Middle East crisis, and attempts to find definite answers to questions of this kind usually lead to over-simplification. Perhaps the only thing that can certainly be said is that no long-term social change or process of development is likely to contribute towards the solution of any immediate political conflict.

Consider, for example, the belief that land reform will check the influence of Communism. In the countries surveyed, Communism is a term which has ceased to have a precise meaning. Examples have been quoted to show that it is currently used to describe the views of opposition parties, or elements in the governments; it may refer also to any uncompromising attitude to Western political influence; or to real social unrest (as in Amara and Mosul). How far Communist doctrine or activity is involved in this unrest is of course anybody's guess. Clearly land reform can weaken the influence of Communism in so far as it arises from such unrest, because reform both meets the needs of the fellahin and fills the social vacuum by giving the bureaucracy a social function. It has already been emphasized that the international consensus of opinion in favour of reform is a valuable influence, because it means that the Western Powers are less committed to the support of the big landowners; but this influence can only serve to make the struggle for reform a little easier for those who are concerned with the welfare of their own people—and who will probably be described as Communists by their political opponents.

Certainly greater social equality, and a more stable economy, would provide a social structure more resistant to Soviet influence, more resistant, indeed, to any external influence. But this long-term certainty has no bearing on the present situation.

Or consider the question of reform as it affects relations between Israel and the Arab States. It used to be believed that when the Arab States ceased to be feudal, they would become more 'progressive' and so less hostile to Zionism—a view which now seems strangely old-fashioned. Today the rising middle class, the Egyptian revolutionary leadership, and the Arab socialist party hold stronger nationalist views than the big landowners, who are more concerned with maintaining their own position against these forces than with hostility to Israel. For the poverty of Jordan, most directly affected by the Arab-Israeli conflict, land reform is not a remedy, and its hopes of economic development depend on the possibility of the Jordan valley scheme, which requires a political agreement before it can be undertaken.

It might well be that the strengthening of the Arab social structure which is implied in a land reform policy could eventually create more favourable conditions, but again, this hopeful speculation does not lessen existing tensions.

Or consider the question of the future of the Palestine refugees. The first conclusion which many people in Britain are inclined to draw from an account of the actual and potential development of the Arab countries is that they could absorb the refugees. Egypt clearly cannot, but since Syria and Iraq have small populations and plenty of land, it appears obvious—to those who have not seen the villages—that these countries could find room for more labour, and so offer a way out of the tragic situation in the Jordan valley.

Political considerations altogether apart, the belief that the availability of land in itself represents 'absorptive capacity', i.e. creates employment, is the old bad economics, for it ignores the social structure and the type of farming. The economic obstacle to the absorption of the refugees into agricultural employment is the low standard of living in the villages. No one who has seen an Iraqi village, or a Syrian village on the estate of a big landowner, would believe that there could be opportunities of settling the refugees in such conditions. The Jordan camps are wretched, because their inhabitants have lost homes and land, but their health conditions are better than those of the poor villages in Syria and most villages in Iraq.

With land settlement and more intensive farming, both Syria and Iraq could employ more people at higher standards of living. Yet to argue that these countries should undertake land reform in order to absorb the refugees is to vitiate the real case for it. It represents an attempt to shift the responsibility for the solution of an urgent problem, and is an example of the alibi approach which pervades so much thinking about the region and within it—shifting the responsibility on to somebody else, and shelving the problem when that somebody else has been identified.

These brief references to the Power conflicts suggest, not that the question of land reform is irrelevant, but that its relevance is distorted if it is regarded as a solution for them. It is a way of raising the standard of living and of improving agricultural production, and rather a slow way. It is not likely to pluck irons out of the fire for the West, or to settle issues in the cold war. Power in the region will ultimately belong to those who take the responsibility for rural poverty, and break with the alibi approach, as the Government of Egypt does, but power is a by-product and not the object of reform.

So far as any general conclusion can be drawn from the preceding survey of the three countries, it is simply that the picture of the Arab world as static and medieval is no longer true. Each country is in a state of rapid economic and social change. It is true that Egypt, Syria, and Iraq do not constitute the whole of the Arab world, but they represent its most important components, and they determine, in some degree, what happens in the rest of it. The 'feudal potentate' no longer dominates the social scene. Even though there has been no land reform in Syria and Iraq, the balance of social power is changing. The position of the large landowners is undermined, though not overthrown, by the impact of money and enterprise.

This is one aspect of the general shifting of power positions in the region. Alibi thinking is prevalent, because the changing balance of power gives rise to disparities in the economic and political position of each of the participants. Britain's 'special position', i.e. political dominance, has gone, but British opinion is still largely conditioned by the attitudes appropriate to the time when Britain was the arbitrator between Jews and Arabs, and main owner of the oilfields. The United States, on the other hand, now has immense capital investment in the region, but is as yet unwilling to consider whether this does not imply some responsibility for its development. The Arab States have greater economic power than their political structure enables them to use. Soviet policy can play on these unbalances more easily than Communist doctrine can influence opinion.

In this situation, it is obviously impossible to forecast the possible effects on the Western Power position of the changes that have been described. They constitute new elements which alter the framework within which solutions must be found, without providing any formula for solution, or clearing the problems away.

But must the conclusion remain so indefinite? Do these changes simply increase instability? They are all, in one way or another, steps towards the abolition of poverty, the great need of the region. The possibility of ending poverty does exist. Is it possible that the Western desire for stability could be reconciled with the fulfilment of the region's need? To answer this question, it is necessary to take the theme of the three dynamics a little farther, to see how their operation is likely to affect the region as a whole.

To illustrate the relationship between economic development and social change, the preceding studies have suggested some historical comparisons—the mid-Victorian expansion, the Edwardian surfeit, and the industrial revolution. These comparisons are useful because they remind us that new things can happen, and happen as a process of evolution, in any society, without being a mere reflex of foreign influence. Too often the Arab world is pictured as a more or less inanimate body subject to shock treatment from Zionism or Communism, and reacting by nationalism or xenophobia. This habit of applying labels is a crude attempt to pin down a complex reality into an intelligible pattern; behind it lies the false assumption that these societies have no power of change within themselves. Historical comparisons can correct this tendency to think in terms of physical impact and reaction, and help us to realize that they are living organisms.

Yet the Arab countries do not live in time pockets of the past. They exist in our own time, and in their own place. In a period when the demand for oil is inexhaustible, the Middle East possesses 66 per cent of the world's total proved reserves.[1] No historical parallel will serve to illustrate the paradox of a barren and primitive region which has as high a rate of industrial development as that of the most advanced countries.

The extraordinarily rapid expansion of the oil industry in the last ten years is the result of an enormous investment of foreign capital.[2] American private capital has been invested in the Middle East on a larger scale than anywhere else in the Old World, and it is one of the few regions in which new British capital is invested to an increasing extent. Now that the oil companies aim at expanding production to the maximum before atomic energy becomes a competitor, the rate of expansion is likely to be even higher.[3] Atomic power is not likely to be a significant source of energy for the next ten years, and it may be as much as twenty or twenty-five years before it supplants oil in its main uses.

The West's need for oil gives the Arab oil-producing countries great economic power, which their own economy cannot use, partly by reason of the social structure, and partly because their territories are too small, or too barren, to absorb such investment. In Iraq, through the policy of engineer's planning, oil revenues are used constructively, and even there, as has been shown, money does not do all it might because in-

[1] UN, Dept. of Economic and Social Affairs, *Economic Developments in the Middle East, 1954 to 1955*.

[2] Cumulative gross investment in properties, plant, and equipment, before depreciation, in the oil industry of the Middle East region increased from \$1 thousand million in 1945 to \$2·2 thousand million in 1954 (ibid.).

[3] P. H. Frankel, 'Has the World Enough Oil?', *Listener*, 12 July 1956.

vestment comes up against the barriers of the social structure. In Kuwait there is also considerable investment, but revenues far exceed opportunities in the sheikhdom, and a large proportion is invested under British guidance in British securities. In Saudi Arabia much of the revenue is wasted in conspicuous consumption, or used for political propaganda and bribery. So long as this situation continues, the region must be unstable, both internally and externally. The money dynamic alone is not sufficient to raise the standard of living, though oil revenues are and will be sufficient for the long-term investments which are needed throughout the Arab world.

The dynamic of private enterprise, though it has done much, also cannot alone provide the basis for stability and higher standards. Natural conditions are too adverse. By reason of the desert environment, the only stable basis for agriculture is more irrigation. For this a strong and enterprising policy on the part of the state is essential; without it, the countries of the Arab world must remain poor and unstable.

The revolutionary dynamic comes from Egypt, the advanced agricultural country which has no oil, and no money for the big development schemes which it so urgently needs. To British opinion—or at any rate to that small section of it which takes a sustained interest in Arab affairs—this dynamic appears to be a disturbing factor, stirring up upheavals from Aden to Algeria and from Jordan to Bahrein. Yet the ideals of the Egyptian revolution—the national function of the professional middle class, the new status for the fellahin—fill the social vacuum and meet the needs of the region better than any imported ideology. To bring the Arab world together by giving its social structure greater strength and coherence is certainly an essential condition of development, and also of stability.

None of the three dynamics in isolation from the rest can open the way to the abolition of poverty. Only if they were linked together would the way be open. When the revolutionary drive can use the money originating from oil production and transport to invest in the big schemes needed, and in the human resources, the problem of raising the general standard of living will be soluble. The question is not whether the Arab world will 'go Communist'. It is whether the great reservoir of wealth can be used to mop up the great reservoir of poverty—

of the fellahin, the tribesmen, and the refugees. If the Arab world is to face this problem, and to survive at a higher living standard, after the demand for oil has ceased, the pace of change must be fast, for it must get its economy and its political and social structure on to a new basis within the lifetime of a single generation.

'Death', said the traffic signs on the Aley road in 1944, 'is so permanent'. Happily for the Arab world, that sort of permanency need not threaten it. The Western Powers have to recognize that stability is not identical with the permanency of the existing structure. Towards the abolition of poverty, British policy contributes, and is immeasurably more far-sighted than it was ten years ago in its wise insistence that the oil money should be invested in productive capacity; but British policy is still inclined to aim exclusively at shoring up traditional positions. American policy begins to contribute greatly through its emphasis on agrarian reform and agricultural development; but it cannot co-ordinate this long-term thinking with the tremendous impact of American private investment in the region.

No doubt there are some who will suggest that the solution for all these problems can be found by handing them over to the United Nations. That too is alibi thinking, unless both Britain and America are prepared to learn something from each other's contribution to the real needs of the Middle East.

BIBLIOGRAPHY

Addams, Doris G. 'Current Population Trends in Iraq', *Middle East Journal*, Spring 1956.

Ayrout, H. C. *Fellahs d'Égypte*. 6th ed. Cairo, Éditions du Sphynx, 1952.

Bulos, Nassib. *Legal Aspects of Land Tenure in Jordan and Syria*. Beirut, UNRWA, 1953.

Burns, Norman. 'The Dujailah Land Settlement', *Middle East Journal*, Summer 1951.

Critchley, A. Michael. 'The Health of the Industrial Worker in Iraq', reprinted from *British Journal of Industrial Medicine*, vol. 12, 1955.

Egypt, Higher Committee for Agrarian Reform. *Replies to the United Nations Questionnaires relating to Egyptian Agrarian Reform Measures*. Cairo, 1955.

—— Permanent Council of Public Services, Economics Sub-Committee of the National Population Commission. *The Population Problem in Egypt*. Cairo, 1955.

Egyptian-American Rural Improvement Service. *Land Reclamation and Resettlement*. March 1955 (pamphlet).

Darling, Sir Malcolm. 'Land Reform in Italy and Egypt', *Year Book of Agricultural Co-operation*, 1956.

Dowson, Sir Ernest. *An Inquiry into Land Tenure and Related Questions; Proposals for the Initiation of Reform*. Letchworth, for Iraq Government, 1932.

Ghonemy, Mohamed Riad. *Resource Use and Income in Egyptian Agriculture before and after Land Reform, with particular reference to Economic Development*. N. Carolina State College, unpublished D. Phil. thesis, 1953.

Haider, Salih. *Land Problems of Iraq*. London University unpublished Ph.D. thesis, 1942.

Hakim, George. 'Land Tenure Reform', *Middle East Economic Papers*, 1954 (published by the Economic Research Institute, American University of Beirut).

Hassan, Mohammed Ali. 'Miri Sirf Land Development in Iraq', *International Social Science Bulletin*, vol. 5, no. 4, 1953.

—— *Land Reclamation and Settlement in Iraq*. Baghdad, 1955.

International Bank for Reconstruction and Development. *The Economic Development of Iraq*. Baltimore, Johns Hopkins Press, 1952.

—— *The Economic Development of Syria*. Baltimore, Johns Hopkins Press, 1955.

Iraq, Directorate-General of Agriculture, Soils and Agricultural Chemistry. *Report of the Soil Survey and Soil Classification, Dujaila Project, August 1955*, by Burnell West, Soil Technologist, Food and Agriculture Organization. Baghdad, 1955.

—— Irrigation Development Commission (President F. F. Haigh). *Report on the Control of the Rivers of Iraq and the Utilization of their Waters*. Baghdad, 1951.

—— Principal Bureau of Statistics. *Report on the Agricultural and Livestock Census of Iraq*, 1952–3. Vol. 1. Baghdad, 1954.

Iversen, Carl. *Monetary Policy in Iraq*. Baghdad, National Bank of Iraq, 1954.

Khayyat, Jafar. *The Iraqi Village; a Study in its Condition and Reform*. Beirut, 1950 (in Arabic).

Knappen-Tippetts-Abbett-McCarthy Engineers. *Report on the Development of the Tigris and Euphrates River Systems*. New York and Baghdad, Iraq Development Board, 1954; mimeo.

Lewis, Norman. 'The Frontier of Settlement in Syria, 1800–1950', *International Affairs*, January 1955.

Marei, Sayed. *Two Years of Agrarian Reform*. Cairo, Higher Committee for Agrarian Reform, 1954.

Nahi, S. A. *An Introduction to Feudalism and the Land System in Iraq*. Baghdad, 1955 (in Arabic).

Salim, S. M. *Economic and Political Organization of Echchbaysh, a Marsh Village Community in South Iraq*. University of London unpublished Ph.D. thesis, 1955.

Salter, J. A., 1st Baron. *The Development of Iraq; a Plan of Action*. London, Caxton, for Iraq Development Board, 1955.

Stewart, Desmond and John Haylock. *New Babylon*. London, Collins, 1956.

UN, Dept. of Economic and Social Affairs. *Economic Developments in the Middle East, 1945 to 1954*. New York, 1955. (Supplement to World Economic Report, 1943–4.)

—— —— *1954 to 1955*. New York, 1956.

—— Dept. of Economic Affairs. *Progress in Land Reform; Analysis of Replies by Governments to a United Nations Questionnaire*. New York, 1954.

Walston, H. D. *Land Tenure in the Fertile Crescent*. Unpublished, 1954.

Warriner, Doreen. *Land and Poverty in the Middle East*. London, RIIA, 1948.

Weulersse, Jacques. *Paysans de Syrie et du Proche Orient*. Paris, Gallimard, 1946. (*Le Paysan et la Terre*.)

INDEX

INDEX

Thin
10.V.57

ENGLISH ECONOMIC HISTORY

SELECT DOCUMENTS

COMPILED AND EDITED BY

A. E. BLAND, B.A., P. A. BROWN, M.A.,
AND R. H. TAWNEY, B.A.

LONDON
G. BELL AND SONS, LTD.
1930

First published October, 1914.
Reprinted 1915, 1919, 1920, 1921, 1925, 1930.

INTRODUCTION

THE object of this book is to supply teachers and students of English Economic History with a selection of documents which may serve as illustrations of their subject. It should be read in conjunction with some work containing a broad survey of English economic development, such as, to mention the latest and best example, Professor W. J. Ashley's "The Economic Organization of England."[1] The number of historical "source books" has been multiplied so rapidly in recent years that we ought, perhaps, to apologise for adding one to their number. We ventured to do so because in the course of our work as teachers of Economic History in the University Tutorial Classes organised by the Workers' Educational Association, we found it difficult to refer our students to any single book containing the principal documents with which they ought to be acquainted. That Economic History cannot be studied apart from Constitutional and Political History is a commonplace to which we subscribe; and we are not so incautious as to be tempted into a discussion of what exactly Economic History means. It is sufficient for our purpose that a subject which is called by that name is being increasingly studied by University students, and that while the principal documents of English Constitutional History are available in the works of Stubbs, Prothero, Gardiner and Grant Robertson, there is no book, as far as we know—except Professor Pollard's "The Reign of Henry VII. from Contemporary Sources"—which illustrates English economic development in a similar way. We are far from comparing our own minnow with these Tritons. But it may perhaps do some service till more competent authors take the field It is hardly necessary for us to apologise for translating our documents into English, and for modernizing

[1] Messrs. Longman Green & Co.

the spelling throughout. We are likely not to be alone in thinking that it would be a pity if a passing acquaintance with the materials of mediæval economic history were confined to those who can read Latin and Norman-French.

A word of explanation as to the selection and arrangement of our extracts may perhaps be excused. Our object was not to produce a work of original research, but to help students of economic history to see it more intelligently by seeing it through the eyes of contemporaries. Hence, though a considerable number of our documents are published here for the first time, we have not consciously followed the lure of the unprinted, and have chosen our extracts not because they were new, but because they seemed to illustrate some important aspect of our subject. For the same reason we have not confined ourselves entirely to "documents" in the strict acceptation of that term, but have included selections from such works as Roger of Hoveden, The Libel of English Policy, The Commonweal of this Realm of England, Hakluyt's Voyages, and the Tours of Defoe and Arthur Young, when they seemed to throw light upon points which could not easily be illustrated otherwise. The arrangement of our selections caused us some trouble. It is, perhaps, hardly necessary to urge that a document must be studied with reference to its chronological setting; and the simplest plan, no doubt, would have been to print them in strict chronological order. We felt, however, that the work of all but the more expert readers would be lightened if we grouped them under definite, even if somewhat arbitrary, headings of period and subject, and added short bibliographies of the principal authorities. This seemed to involve the writing of short introductory notes to explain the contents of each section, which we have accordingly done. But no one need read them. No one but students beginning the subject will. If an excuse is needed for stopping with the year 1846, we must plead that to end earlier would have been to omit documents of the first importance for the study of modern economic history, and that to continue further would have caused our book to be even more overburdened than it is at present.

That the attempt to produce in one volume a satisfactory selection of documents to illustrate English Economic History from the Norman Conquest to the Repeal of the Corn Laws can hardly be successful, that we have neglected some subjects —taxation, colonization, and foreign trade—and paid excessive attention to others—social conditions, economic policy, and administration—that every reader will look for a particular document and fail to find it, of all this we are sadly conscious. We are conscious also of a more serious, because less obvious, defect. Partly through a pardonable reaction against the influence of economic theorists, partly because of the very nature of the agencies by which historical documents are compiled and preserved, the natural bias of economic historians is to lay a perhaps excessive stress on those aspects of economic development which come under the eyes of the State and are involved in its activity, and to neglect the humbler but often more significant movements which spring from below, to over-emphasize organisation and to under-estimate the initiative of individuals. If a reader of these selections exclaims on putting them down, "How much that is important is omitted!" we can only confess ourselves in mercy and express the hope that they may soon be superseded.

It remains for us to thank those who have helped us with suggestions and criticisms, or by permitting us to reprint extracts from documents already published. We have to acknowledge the kind permission to reprint documents given to us by the Clarendon Press, the Cambridge University Press, the London School of Economics, the Department of Economics of Harvard University, The Royal Historical Society, The Early English Text Society, the Co-operative Union, Ltd., the Controller of H.M. Stationery Office, the Corporation of Norwich, the Corporation of Nottingham, Messrs. Kegan Paul, Trench and Trübner, Messrs. Duncker & Humblot, Dr. G. von Schanz, Professor G. Unwin, Professor F. J. C. Hearnshaw, The Rev. Canon Morris, Miss M. D. Harris, Mr. and Mrs. J. L. Hammond and Mr. F. W. Galton. Among those who have assisted us with suggestions or in other ways we must mention Mr. Hubert Hall, Mr. M. S. Giuseppi, Mr. S.

C. Ratcliff, all of the Public Record Office, The Ven. Archdeacon Cunningham, Mr. W. H. Stevenson, of St. John's College, Oxford, Mr. A. Ballard, Miss Putnam, Mr. R. V. Lennard, of Wadham College, Oxford, Mr. K. Bell, of All Souls' College, Oxford, Mr. H. Clay, Mr. F. W. Kolthammer, Miss O. J. Dunlop, Miss H. M. Stocks, and Mr. and Mrs. J. L. Hammond. For reading our proofs, or part of them, we are indebted to Mr. E. Barker, of New College, Oxford, Mr. C. G. Crump and Mr. C. H. Jenkinson, of the Public Record Office, Dr. Knowles, of the London School of Economics, and Professor G. Unwin, of the University of Manchester.

We desire especially to express our gratitude to Mr. A. L. Smith, of Balliol College, Oxford, to whose encouragement it was largely due that this book was undertaken, and to Professor Unwin, who has not only read through the whole of it in proof, but by his advice and inspiration has laid us under an obligation that we cannot easily acknowledge.

A. E. B.
P. A. B.
R. H. T.

CONTENTS

PART I: 1000-1485

SECTION I

THE EARLY ENGLISH MANOR AND BOROUGH

SECTION II

THE FEUDAL STRUCTURE

SECTION III

THE JEWS

SECTION IV

THE MANOR

SECTION V

TOWNS AND GILDS

SECTION VI

THE REGULATION OF TRADE, INDUSTRY, AND COMMERCE

SECTION VII

TAXATION, CUSTOMS AND CURRENCY

PART II: 1485-1660

SECTION I

RURAL CONDITIONS

SECTION II

TOWNS AND GILDS

SECTION III

THE REGULATION OF INDUSTRY BY THE STATE

SECTION IV

THE RELIEF OF THE POOR AND THE REGULATION OF PRICES

SECTION V

THE ENCOURAGEMENT OF INDUSTRY AND COMMERMERCE

PART III: 1660-1846

SECTION I

INDUSTRIAL ORGANISATION AND SOCIAL CONDITIONS

SECTION II

AGRICULTURE AND ENCLOSURE

SECTION III

GOVERNMENT REGULATION OF WAGES, CONDITIONS OF EMPLOYMENT, AND PUBLIC HEALTH

SECTION IV

COMBINATIONS OF WORKMEN

SECTION V

THE RELIEF OF THE POOR

SECTION VI

FINANCE AND FOREIGN TRADE

PART I: 1000-1485

SECTION I

THE EARLY ENGLISH MANOR AND BOROUGH

1. Rights and Duties of All Persons [*Rectitudines singularum personarum*], *c.* 1000—2. The form of the Domesday Inquest, 1086—3. The borough of Dover, 1086—4. The borough of Norwich, 1086—5. The borough of Wallingford, 1086—6. The customs of Berkshire, 1086—7. Land of the Church of Worcester, 1086—8. The manor of Rockland, 1086—9. The manor of Halesowen, 1086—10. The manor of Havering, 1086.

The task of reconstructing the economic life of Saxon England is not easy, and while the document translated below (No. 1) vividly analyses the obligations and rights of the various classes of tenants and officers on Saxon estates of the eleventh century, it raises many difficulties and is probably only true for the more settled parts of the country. It affords, however, clear proof of a high agricultural and social development; and though the exact significance of specific terms, and the status of different classes, may remain obscure, a comparison of the *Rectitudines* and the *Gerefa* [1] with later extents and custumals, and with Domesday Book itself, establishes the essential continuity of English economic life and customs, notwithstanding the shock of the Norman Conquest.

The further study of Domesday Book will undoubtedly yield valuable results supplementing the information derived from Saxon documents. While it is primarily a supreme example of the defining spirit and centralising energy of the conquering race, it is also a permanent record of England before and at the time of the Norman invasion. Especially,

[1] *See* Cunningham, *Growth of English Industry and Commerce*, i., 570-576.

perhaps, is this apparent in the detailed descriptions of the boroughs, which at once set forth Saxon customs and illustrate the effects of the Conquest. The extracts given below are intended to show in brief, first, the methods both of the commissioners who conducted the survey, and of the officials who reduced the information to a common form; [1] second, the fiscal preoccupation of the government; third, the origin and character of the early borough, especially manifest in the case of Wallingford (No. 5), and fourth, the different classes of tenants, free and unfree. Of particular interest are the following features: the manner of levying the feudal army (No. 6), the evidence of the looser organisation of the Eastern Counties, and the greater degree of freedom prevailing among tenants in the Danelaw (Nos. 4 and 8), the ample franchises that might be enjoyed by a great Saxon prelate (No. 7), the salt-pans of Worcestershire (No. 9), and the gildhall of the burgesses of Dover (No. 3).

AUTHORITIES

The more accessible writers dealing with the subject of this section are:—Kemble, *The Saxons in England*; Maine, *Village Communities in the East and West*; Seebohm, *The English Village Community*; Vinogradoff, *Villeinage in England, The Growth of the Manor*, and, *English Society in the Eleventh Century*; Andrews, *The Old English Manor*; Maitland, *Domesday Book and Beyond*; Pollock and Maitland, *History of English Law*; Ballard, *The Domesday Boroughs*, and, *The Domesday Inquest*; Round, *Domesday Studies*, and, *The Domesday Manor* (Eng. Hist. Rev. xv.); Stubbs, *Constitutional History*, and, *Lectures on Mediæval History*; Ellis, *Introduction to Domesday Book*; Gomme, *The Village Community*; de Coulanges, *Origin of Property in Land*; Freeman, *The History of the Norman Conquest of England;* Petit Dutaillis. *Studies Supplementary to Stubbs' Constitutional History.*

Almost the whole of Domesday Book has now been translated and is printed county by county in the Victoria County History series.

[1] *cf. Dialogus de Scaccario*: "Finally, that nothing might be thought lacking, he brought the whole of his far-seeing measures to completion by despatching from his side his wisest men in circuit throughout the realm. The latter made a careful survey of the whole land, in woods and pastures and meadows and arable lands also, which was reduced to a common phraseology and compiled into a book, that every man might be content with his own right and not encroach with impunity on that of another."

For a general survey of the Saxon period the student should refer to Cunningham, *Growth of English Industry and Commerce, Mediæval Times*, pp. 28–133.

1. Rights and Duties of all Persons [*Rectitudines Singularum Personarum. Cambridge, Corpus Christi*, 383], *c.* 1000.

The Thegn's Law.—The thegn's law is that he be worthy of his book-right,[1] and that he do three things for his land, fyrdfare,[2] burhbote [3] and bridge-work. Also from many lands a greater land-service arises at the king's command, such as the deer-hedge at the king's abode and provision of warships (*scorp to fyrdscipe*)[4] and sea-ward and head-ward [5] and fyrd-ward, almsfee and churchscot, and many other diverse things.

The Geneat's Service.—Geneat-service is diverse according to the custom of the estate. On some he must pay land-gafol [6] and grass-swine [7] yearly, and ride and carry and lead loads, work, and feast the lord, and reap and mow and cut the deer-hedge and maintain it, build and hedge the burh,[8] bring strange wayfarers to the tun, pay churchscot and almsfee, keep head-ward and horse-ward, go errands far and near whithersoever he be told.

The Cotter's Service.—The cotter's service is according to the custom of the estate. On some he must work for his lord each Monday throughout the year and for three days each week in harvest. On some he works through the whole harvest every day and reaps an acre of oats for a day's work, and he shall have his sheaf which the reeve or lord's servant will give him.[9] He ought not to pay land-gafol. It befits him to have 5 acres; more, if it be the custom of the estate;

[1] The right conferred by his book or charter.

[2] Military service.

[3] Repair of the king's castles or boroughs.

[4] Reading with Leo *fyrdscipe* for *frithscipe*. For the difficult word "*scorp*" *cf.* Pat. 9 John m. 3. *Rex omnibus scurmannis et marinellis et mercatoribus Anglie per mare itinerantibus. Sciatis nos misisse Alanum . . . et alios fideles nostros scurimannos . . . ad omnes naves quas invenerint per mare arrestandas.*

[5] Guard of the king's person.

[6] Rent or tribute. Gafol is sometimes a tax payable to the king, and sometimes a rent or dues payable to the lord.

[7] Payment for pasturing swine.

[8] The lord's house.

[9] This clause appears only in the Latin version.

and if it be less, it is too little, because his work shall be oft required; he shall pay his hearth-penny on Holy Thursday, as all free men should; and he shall defend his lord's inland,[1] if he be required, from sea-ward and the king's deer-hedge and from such things as befit his degree; and he shall pay his churchscot at Martinmas.

The Gebur's Services.—The gebur's services are diverse, in some places heavy, in others moderate; on some estates he must work two days at week-work at such work as is bidden him every week throughout the year, and in harvest three days at week-work, and from Candlemas [2] to Easter three. If he do carrying, he need not work while his horse is out. He must pay on Michaelmas [3] Day 10 gafol-pence, and on Martinmas [4] Day 23 sesters of barley and two henfowls, at Easter a young sheep or two pence; and from Martinmas to Easter he must lie at the lord's fold as often as his turn comes; and from the time of the first ploughing to Martinmas he must plough an acre every week and himself fetch the seed in the lord's barn; also 3 acres at boonwork and 2 for grass-earth [5]; if he need more grass, he shall earn it as he shall be allowed; for his gafol-earth he shall plough 3 acres [6] and sow it from his own barn; and he shall pay his hearthpenny; two and two they shall feed a hunting-hound; and every gebur shall pay 6 loaves to the lord's swineherd when he drives his herd to mast. On the same lands where the above customs hold good, it belongs to the gebur that he be given for his land-stock [7] 2 oxen and 1 cow and 6 sheep and 7 acres sown on his yardland; wherefore after that year he shall do all the customs that befit him; and he shall be given tools for his work and vessels for his house. When death befals him, his lord shall take back the things which he leaves.

This land-law holds good on some lands, but, as I have said before, in some places it is heavier, in others lighter, for all land-customs are not alike. On some lands the gebur must pay honey-gafol, on some meat-gafol, on some ale-gafol. Let him who keeps the shire take heed that he knows what are the ancient uses of the land and what the custom of the people.

[1] *i.e.*, Acquit his lord's inland or demesne.
[2] February 2. [3] September 29. [4] November 11. [5] Pasture-land.
[6] *i.e.*, He must plough 3 acres as his rent (gafol). [7] Outfit.

Of those who keep the Bees.—It belongs to the bee-churl, if he keep the gafol-hives, that he give as is customary on the estate. Among us it is customary that he give 5 sesters of honey for gafol; on some estates more gafol is wont to be rendered. Also he must be oft ready for many works at the lord's will, besides boon-ploughing and bedrips [1] and meadow-mowing; and if he be well landed [2], he must have a horse that he may lend it to the lord for carrying or drive it himself whithersoever he be told; and many things a man so placed must do; I cannot now tell all. When death befals him, the lord shall have back the things which he leaves, save what is free.

Of the Swineherd.—It belongs to the gafol-paying swineherd that he give of his slaughter according to the custom of the estate. On many estates the custom is that he give every year 15 swine for sticking, 10 old and 5 young, and have himself what he breeds beyond that. To many estates a heavier swine-service belongs. Let the swineherd take heed also that after sticking he prepare and singe well his slaughtered swine; then is he right worthy of the entrails, and, as I said before of the bee-keeper, he must be oft ready for any work, and have a horse for his lord's need. The unfree swineherd and the unfree bee-keeper, after death, shall be worthy of one same law.

Of the Serf-Swineherd.—To the serf swineherd who keeps the inherd [3] belong a sucking-pig from the sty and the entrails when he has prepared bacon, and further the customs which befit the unfree.

Of Men's Board.—To a bondservant (*esne*) belong for board 12 pounds of good corn and 2 sheep-carcases and a good meat-cow, and wood, according to the custom of the estate.

Of Women's Board.—To unfree women belong 8 pounds of corn for food, one sheep or 3*d*. for winter fare, one sester of beans for Lent fare, in summer whey or 1*d*.

To all serfs belong a mid-Winter feast and an Easter feast, a ploughacre [4] and a harvest handful,[5] besides their needful dues.

[1] Reaping at the lord's command.

[2] If he have good land, good, that is, either in quality or quantity or both.

[3] The lord's herd.

[4] An acre for ploughing.

[5] A sheaf from each acre in harvest.

Of Followers.[1]—It belongs to the follower that in 12 months he earn two acres, the one sown and the other unsown; he shall sow them himself, and his board and provision of shoes and gloves belong to him; if he may earn more, it shall be to his own behoof.

Of the Sower.—It belongs to the sower that he have a basketful of every kind of seed when he have well sown each sowing throughout the year.

Of the Ox-herd.—The ox-herd may pasture 2 oxen or more with the lord's herd in the common pastures by witness of his ealdorman[2]; and thereby may earn shoes and gloves for himself; and his meat-cow may go with the lord's oxen.

Of the Cow-herd.—It belongs to the cow-herd that he have an old cow's milk for seven days after she has newly calved, and the beestings[3] for fourteen nights; and his meat-cow shall go with the lord's cow.

Of Sheep-herds.—The sheep-herd's right is that he have 12 nights' manure at mid-Winter and 1 lamb of the year's increase, and the fleece of 1 bellwether and the milk of his flock for seven nights after the equinox and a bowlful of whey or buttermilk all the summer.

Of the Goat-herd.—To the goat-herd belongs his herd's milk after Martinmas Day and before that his share of whey and one kid of the year's increase, if he have well cared for his herd.

Of the Cheese-maker.—To the cheese-maker belong 100 cheeses, and that she make butter of the wring-whey[4] for the lord's table; and she shall have for herself all the buttermilk save the herd's share.

Of the Barn-keeper.—To the barn-keeper belong the corn-droppings in harvest at the barn-door, if his ealdorman give it him and he faithfully earn it.

Of the Beadle.—It belongs to the beadle that for his office he be freeer from work than another man, for that he must be oft ready; also to him belongs a strip of land for his toil.

Of the Woodward.—To the woodward belongs every windfall-tree.

Of the Hayward.—To the hayward it belongs that his toil

[1] A free but landless retainer. [2] The reeve (gerefa).
[3] The first milk of a milch-cow after calving.
[4] The residue after the last pressing of the cheese.

be rewarded with land at the ends of the fields that lie by the pasture meadow; for he may expect that if he first neglects this, to his charge will be laid damage to the crops; and if a strip of land be allowed to him, this shall be by folk-right next the pasture meadow, for that if out of sloth he neglect his lord, his own land shall not be well defended, if it be found so; but if he defend well all that he shall hold, then shall he be right worthy of a good reward.

Land-laws are diverse, as I said before, nor do we fix for all places these customs that we have before spoken of, but we shew forth what is accustomed there where it is known to us; if we learn aught better, that will we gladly cherish and keep, according to the customs of the place where we shall then dwell; for gladly should he learn the law among the people, who wishes not himself to lose honour in the country. Folk-customs are many; in some places there belong to the people winter-feast, Easter-feast, boon-feast for harvest, a drinking feast for ploughing, rick-meat,[1] mowing reward, a wainstick at wood-loading, a stack-cup [2] at corn-loading, and many things that I cannot number. But this is a reminder for men, yea, all that I have set forth above.[3]

2. THE FORM OF THE DOMESDAY INQUEST [*Inquisitio Eliensis, Domesday Book, Additamenta, p.* 497], 1086.

Here below is written the inquest of the lands, in what manner the King's barons enquire, to wit, by the oath of the sheriff of the shire, and of all the barons and their Frenchmen and of the whole hundred, of the priest, the reeve, six villeins of each town. Then how the manor is named; who held it in the time of King Edward; who holds it now; how many hides; how many ploughs on the demesne, and how many of the men; how many villeins; how many cotters; how many serfs; how many freemen; how many socmen; how much wood; how much meadow; how many pastures; how many mills; how many fishponds; how much has been added or taken away; how much it was worth altogether; and how much now; how much each freeman or socman there had or has. All this for three periods; to wit, in the time of King

[1] A feast on the completion of the hayrick.
[2] Probably a feast at the completion of corn-stacking.
[3] The best printed text is in Liebermann, *Die Gesetze der Angelsachsen*, I., 444.

Edward; and when King William granted it; and as it is now; and if more can be had therefrom than is had.

3. THE BOROUGH OF DOVER [*Domesday Book, I*, 1], 1086.

Dover in the time of King Edward rendered 18*l*., of which money King Edward had two parts and Earl Godwin the third. On the contrary the canons of St. Martin had another moiety.[1] The burgesses gave twenty ships to the King once a year for fifteen days and in each ship were twenty-one men. This they did for that he had fully granted to them sac and soc.[2] When the King's messengers came there, they gave for the passage of a horse 3*d*. in winter and 2*d*. in summer. The burgesses, however, found a pilot and one other assistant, and if need were for more, it was hired from the messenger's own money.

From the feast of St. Michael [3] to the feast of St. Andrew [4] the King's truce (that is, peace) was in the town. If any man broke it, the King's reeve received therefor common amends.

Whosoever, dwelling in the town continually, rendered custom to the King, was quit of toll throughout all England.

All these customs were there when King William came to England.

Upon his very first coming to England the town was burned, and therefore the value thereof could not be computed, how much it was worth when the Bishop of Bayeux received it. Now it is valued at 40*l*., and yet the reeve renders therefrom 54*l*., that is, to the King 24*l*. of pence which are twenty in the ounce (*ora*) [5] and to the Earl 30*l*. by tale.

In Dover there are 29 messuages, from which the King has lost the custom. Of these Robert of Romney has two, Ralph de Curbespine three, William son of Tedald one, William son of Oger one, William son of Tedold and Robert Niger six, William son of Goisfrid three, in which was the gildhall of the burgesses, Hugh de Montfort one house, Durand one, Ranulf de Columbels one, Wadard six, the son of Modbert one. And all these of these houses avow the Bishop of Bayeux as their protector, donor and grantor.

[1] There was clearly a difference of opinion.
[2] Rights and profits of jurisdiction.
[3] September 29. [4] November 30.
[5] *cf*. Fleta ii. 12: "*Viginti denarii faciunt unciam.*"

Of the messuage which Ranulf de Columbels holds, which belonged to an exile (that is, an outlaw), they agree that half the land is the King's, and Ranulf himself has both. Humphrey the Bandylegged (*Loripes*) holds one messuage wherefrom half the forfeiture was the King's. Roger de Ostreham made a house over the King's water and has held hitherto the King's custom. And the house was not there in the time of King Edward.

At the entry of the port of Dover there is a mill which by great disturbance of the sea shatters almost all ships, and does the greatest damage to the King and the men; and it was not there in the time of King Edward. Touching this the nephew of Herbert says that the Bishop of Bayeux granted to his uncle Herbert son of Ivo that it should be made.

4. The Borough of Norwich [*Domesday Book, II*, 116], 1086.

In Norwich there were in the time of King Edward 1320 burgesses. Of whom one was so much the King's own (*dominicus*) that he could not withdraw nor do homage without his licence; whose name was Edstan. He had 18 acres of land and 12 of meadow and 2 churches in the borough and a sixth part of a third; and to one church pertained a messuage in the borough and 6 acres of meadow. This borough Roger Bigot holds of the King's gift. And of 1238 burgesses the King and the Earl had soc and sac[1] and custom; and over 50 Stigand had soc and sac and commendation[2]; and over 32 Harold had soc and sac and commendation; of whom one was so much his own (*dominicus*) that he could not withdraw nor do homage without his licence. In all they all had 80 acres of land and 20 acres and a half of meadow; and of these one was a woman, Stigand's sister, with 32 acres of land; and between them all they had half a mill and the fourth part of a mill, and still have; and in addition they had 12 acres and a half of meadow which Wihenoc took from them; now Rainald son of Ivo has the same; and in addition 2 acres of meadow which belonged to the church of All Saints; these also Wihenoc took, and now Rainald has them. There is also in the borough a church of St. Martin which Stigand held

[1] *i.e.*, Rights of jurisdiction. [2] *i.e.*, Feudal lordship.

in the time of King Edward, and 12 acres of land ; William de Noiers has it now as part of the fee of Stigand. Stigand also held a church of St. Michael, to which belong 112 acres of land and 6 of meadow and 1 plough. This Bishop William holds, but not of the bishopric. And the burgesses held 15 churches to which belonged in almoin 181 acres of land and meadow. And in the time of King Edward 12 burgesses held the church of Holy Trinity ; now the bishop holds it of the gift of King William. The King and the Earl had 180 acres of land. The Abbot has a moiety of the church of St. Lawrence and one house of St. Edmund. This was all in the time of King Edward. Now there are in the borough 665 English burgesses and they render the customs ; and 480 bordiers who owing to poverty render no custom. And on that land which Stigand held in the time of King Edward there dwell now 39 burgesses of those above ; and on the same land there are 9 messuages empty. And on that land of which Harold had the soke there are 15 burgesses and 17 empty messuages which are in the occupation of the castle. And in the borough are 190 empty messuages in that part which was in the soke of the King and Earl, and 81 in the occupation of the castle. In the borough are further 50 houses from which the King has not his custom. . . . And in the borough the burgesses hold 43 chapels. And the whole of this town rendered in the time of King Edward 20*l.* to the King and to the Earl 10*l.* and besides this 21*s.* 4*d.* for allowances and 6 quarts of honey and 1 bear and 6 dogs for bear-[baiting]. And now 70*l.* king's weight and 100*s.* by tale as gersum to the Queen and 1 goshawk and 20*l.* blanch to the Earl and 20*s.* by tale as gersum to Godric. . . . Of the burgesses who dwelt in Norwich 22 have gone away and dwell in Beccles, a town of the abbot of St. Edmund, and 6 in Humbleyard hundred, and have left the borough, and in King's Thorpe 1, and on the land of Roger Bigot 1, and under W. de Noies 1, and Richard de Sent Cler 1. Those fleeing and the others remaining are altogether ruined, partly owing to the forfeitures of Earl Ralph, partly owing to a fire, partly owing to the King's geld, partly through Waleram.

In this borough if the bishop wishes he can have one moneyer. . . .

Land of the Burgesses.—In the hundred of Humbleyard

always 80 acres and 14 bordiers and 1 plough and 3 acres of meadow; and they are worth 13*s.* 4*d.*

The French of Norwich.—In the new borough are 36 burgesses and 6 Englishmen and of yearly custom each one rendered 1*d.* besides forfeitures; of all this the King had two parts and the Earl the third. Now there are 41 French burgesses on the demesne of the King and the Earl, and Roger Bigot has 50, and Ralph de Bella Fago 14, and Hermer 8, and Robert the crossbowman 5, and Fulcher, the abbot's man, 1, and Isac 1, and Ralph Visus Lupi 1, and in the Earl's bakehouse Robert Blund has 3, and Wimer has 1 ruined messuage.

All this land of the burgesses was on the demesne of Earl Ralph and he granted it to the King in common to make the borough between himself and the King, as the sheriff testifies. And all those lands as well of the knights as of the burgesses render to the King his custom. There is also in the new borough a church which Earl Ralph made, and he gave it to his chaplains. Now a priest of the sheriff, by name Wala, holds it of the King's gift, and it is worth 60*s.* And so long as Robert Blund held the county, he had therefrom each year 1 ounce of gold.

5. The Borough of Wallingford [*Domesday Book, I,* 56], 1086.

In the borough of Wallingford King Edward had 8 virgates of land, and in these there were 276 haws[1] rendering 11*l.* of rent (*gablo*), and those who dwelt there did service for the King with horses or by water as far as Blewbury, Reading, Sutton, Bensington, and to those doing this service the reeve gave hire or corrody not from the king's revenue (*censu*) but from his own.

Now there are in the borough all customs as there were before. But of the haws there are thirteen less; for the castle eight have been destroyed, and the moneyer has one quit so long as he makes money. Saulf of Oxford has one, the son of Alsi of Farringdon one, which the King gave him, as he says. Humphrey Visdelew has one, for which he claims the King to warranty. Nigel holds one of Henry by inheritance from Soarding, but the burgesses testify that the

[1] *i.e.*, Houses.

latter never had it. From these thirteen the King has no custom; and further William de Warenne has one haw from which the King has no custom. Moreover there are 22 messuages of Frenchmen rendering 6*s*. 5*d*.

King Edward had 15 acres in which housecarles dwelt. Miles Crispin holds them, they know not how. One of these belongs to[1] (*jacet in*) Wittenham, a manor of Walter Giffard.

Bishop Walchelin has 27 haws rendering 25*s*. and they are valued in Brightwell, his manor.

The abbot of Abingdon has 2 acres on which are 7 messuages rendering 4*s*., and they pertain to Oxford.

Miles has 20 messuages rendering 12*s*. 10*d*., and they belong to (*jacent in*) Newnham, and also one acre on which there are 6 haws rendering 18*d*. In Hazeley he has 6 messuages rendering 44*d*. In Stoke one messuage rendering 12*d*. In Chalgrove one messuage rendering 4*d*. In Sutton one acre on which there are 6 messuages rendering 12*d*., and in Bray one acre and 11 messuages rendering 3*s*. there. All this land pertains to Oxfordshire; nevertheless it is in Wallingford. . . .

Alwold and Godric have the rent (*gablum*) of their houses and bloodwite if blood is shed there, if the man should be received within them before he be claimed by the King's reeve, except on Saturday owing to the market, because then the King has the forfeiture; and they have the fine for adultery and theft in their houses; but other forfeitures are the King's.

In the time of King Edward the borough was worth 30*l*. and afterwards 40*l*.; now 60*l*. And yet it renders of farm 80*l*. by tale. What pertains to Adbrei is worth 7*s*. and the land of Miles Moli 24*s*. What the abbot of Abingdon has is worth 8*s*. What Roger de Laci has, 7*s*. What Rainald has, 4*s*.

The underwritten thegns of Oxfordshire had land in Wallingford.

Archbishop Lanfranc, 4 houses pertaining to Newington rendering 6*s*. Bishop Remigius, one house pertaining to Dorchester rendering 12*d*. The abbot of St. Alban one house rendering 4*s*. Abbot R. one house in Ewelme rendering 3*s*.

Earl Hugh, one house in Pyrton rendering 3*s*.

Walter Giffard, 3 houses in Caversham rendering 2*s*.

Roger de Olgi, 2 houses in Watlington rendering 2*s*. and one house in Perie rendering 2*s*.

[1] Or, "is valued in."

Ilbert de Lacy and Roger son of Seifrid and Orgar, 3 houses rendering 4*s.*

Hugh de Bolebec 3 houses in Crem rendering 3*s.*

Hugh Grando de Scoca, one house rendering 12*d.*

Drogo, in Shirburne and in Weston, 3 houses rendering 4*s.*

Robert Armenteres, in Ewelme, one house rendering 12*d.*

Wazo, one house in Ewelme rendering 3*s.*

6. Customs of Berkshire [*Domesday Book, I*, 56], 1086.

When geld was given in the time of King Edward in common throughout the whole of Berkshire, a hide gave 3½*d.* before Christmas and as much at Whitsuntide. If the King sent an army anywhere, from 5 hides went one knight only, and for his food or wages 4*s.* were given to him from each hide for two months. This money, however, was not sent to the King, but was given to the knights. If anyone summoned for military service went not, he forfeited to the King the whole of his land. And if anyone stayed behind and promised to send another in his place, and yet he who was to be sent stayed behind, his lord was quit for 50*s.* A thegn or knight of the King's own (*dominicus*) left to the King at death for relief all his arms and one horse with a saddle and one without a saddle. And if he had hounds or hawks, they were presented to the King, that he might receive them if he would. If anyone killed a man having the King's peace, he forfeited to the King both his body and all his substance. He who broke into a city by night made amends in 100*s.* to the King, not to the sheriff. He who was warned to beat the woods for hunting and went not, made amends to the King in 50*s.*

7. Land of the Church of Worcester [*Domesday Book, I*, 172 *b*], 1086.

The church of St. Mary of Worcester has a hundred which is called Oswaldslaw, in which lie 300 hides, wherefrom the bishop of that church, by a constitution of ancient times, has all the profits of the sokes and all the customs belonging thereto for his own board and for the king's service and his own, so that no sheriff can have any plaint there, neither in any plea nor in any cause whatsoever. This the whole county testifies. These aforesaid 300 hides were of the demesne itself of the church, and if anything thereof had been in any wise demised or granted to any man soever, to serve the bishop therewith, he who held the land granted to him could not retain for himself any custom at all therefrom, save through the bishop, nor could he retain the land save until the completed term which they had determined between themselves, nor could he go anywhither with that land.

8. The Manor of Rockland, co. Norfolk [*Domesday Book*, *II*, 164, 164 *b*], 1086.

In Rockland Simon holds 3 carucates of land which one freeman, Brode, held in the time of King Edward. Then as now 2 villeins and 12 bordiers.[1] Then 4 serfs, now 1, and 8 acres of meadow; then as now 2 ploughs on the demesne and 1 plough among the men. Wood for 6 swine. Then 4 rounceys,[2] now none. Then 8 beasts, now 5. Then 30 swine, now 15. Then 100 sheep, and now likewise. And in the same [town] the same Simon holds 6 freemen and a half, whom the same Brode had in commendation only; 70 acres of land and 4 acres of meadow; then as now 1 plough and a half. Of these 6 freemen and a half the soke was in the King's [manor of] Buckenham in the time of King Edward, and afterwards, until William de Warenne had it. Then and always they were worth 3*l.* 10*s.*

After this there were added to this land 9 freemen and a half, 1 carucate of land, 54 acres, this is in demesne; then as now 9 bordiers and 8 acres of meadow; then as now 6 ploughs, and 2 half mills. The whole of this is [reckoned] for one manor of Lewes and is worth 3*l.* 11*s.* Of four and a half of the 9 freemen the soke and commendation was in the King's [manor of] Buckenham in the time of King Edward, and afterwards, until William de Warenne had it, and the whole was delivered in the time of Earl Ralph. The whole is 1 league in length and a half in breadth, and [pays] 15*d.* of geld.

9. The Manor of Halesowen, co. Worcester [*Domesday Book*, *I*, 176], 1086.

Earl Roger holds of the King one manor, Halesowen. There are 10 hides there. On the demesne there are 4 ploughs

[1] Cotters. [2] Horses.

and 36 villeins and 18 bordiers, 4 "radmans" and a church with 2 priests. Among them all they have 41½ ploughs. There are there 8 serfs and 2 bondwomen. Of this land Roger Venator holds of the Earl one hide and a half, and there he has one plough and 6 villeins, and 5 bordiers with 5 ploughs. It is worth 25*s.* In the time of King Edward this manor was worth 24*l.* Now 15*l.* Olwin held and had in Droitwich a saltpan worth 4*s.* and in Worcester a house worth 12*d.*

The same Earl holds Salwarpe, and Urso of him. Elwin Cilt held it. There are 5 hides there. On the demesne there is one plough and 6 villeins, and 5 bordiers with 7 ploughs There are there 3 serfs and 3 bondwomen and a mill worth 10*s.* and 5 saltpans worth 60*s.* Half a league of wood and a park there. In the time of King Edward it was worth 100*s.* Now 6*l.* There can be two ploughs more there.

10. THE MANOR OF HAVERING, CO. ESSEX [*Domesday Book, II*, 2 *b*], 1086.

Hundred of Bintree.—Harold held Havering in the time of King Edward for one manor and for 10 hides. Then 41 villeins, now 40. Then as now 41 bordiers and 6 serfs and 2 ploughs on the demesne. Then 41 ploughs among the men, now 40. Wood for 500 swine, 100 acres of meadow; now one mill, two rounceys and 10 beasts and 160 swine and 269 sheep. To this manor belonged 4 freemen with 4 hides in the time of King Edward, rendering custom. Now Robert son of Corbutio holds 3 hides, and Hugh de Monte Forti the fourth hide, and they have not rendered custom since they have had them. And further the same Robert holds 4 hides and a half which one freeman held at this manor in the time of King Edward; the freeman held also a soke of 30 acres, rendering custom; and now John son of Galeram holds it. And this manor in the time of King Edward was worth 36*l.*, now 40*l.* And Peter the sheriff received therefrom 80*l.* of rent and 10*l.* of gersom.[1] To this manor pertain 20 acres lying in Lochetun, which Harold's reeve held in the time of King Edward; now the King's reeve holds the same, and they are worth 40*d.*

[1] *i.e.*, Fine.

SECTION II

THE FEUDAL STRUCTURE

1. Frankalmoin, *temp.* Hen. II.—2. Knight Service, 1308—3. Grand Serjeanty, 1319—4. Petty Serjeanty, 1329—5. An action on the feudal incidents due from land held by petty serjeanty, 1239-40—6. Free socage, 1342—7. Commutation of a serjeanty for knight service, 1254—8. Commutation of service for rent, 1269—9. Subinfeudation, 1278—10. Licence for the widow of a tenant in chief to marry, 1316—11. Marriage of a widow without licence, 1338—12. Alienation of land by a tenant in chief without licence, 1273—13. Wardship and marriage, 1179-80—14. Grant of an heir's marriage, 1320—15. Wardship, 1337—16. Collection of a carucage, 1198—17. An acquittance of the collectors of scutage of a sum of 10*l.* levied by them and repaid, 1319—18. Payment of fines in lieu of knight service, 1303—19. The assessment of a tallage, 1314—20. A writ *Precipe*, *c.* 1200—21. Articles of enquiry touching rights and liberties and the state of the realm, 1274—22. Wreck of sea, 1337.

THE general characteristics of feudalism as a system by which the administrative, legislative and judicial functions of the state had their basis in the tenure of land, are well known. In the following documents an attempt has been made to illustrate the development of English feudalism under the direction of a strong central government, which succeeded in controlling the centrifugal force of feudal institutions and in establishing a national administration dependent on the crown and antagonistic to local franchise. By the end of the thirteenth century the crown was firmly entrenched behind well developed courts of permanent officials, having at the same time retained its control of local affairs by preventing the office of sheriff from becoming hereditary; in the sphere of justice, the central courts of King's Bench and Common

Pleas, supplemented by the itinerant Justices of Assize and by the energy of the Chancellor in devising new remedies and new legal actions, were slowly but surely undermining the manorial justice of the greater tenants, a process well understood by the framers of *Magna Carta*; while the creation of Parliament brought into being an institution destined to rival and ultimately to supersede the exclusive claims of the lords, the feudal council, to advise and control the crown. While therefore the worst tendencies of feudalism were neutralised, the sovereign's hold on the land was tightened, and feudal obligations were reduced to a rigid system which persisted until the Civil War of the seventeenth century. The administration of this branch of royal rights, facilitated by the existence of Domesday Book and the rapid development of the Exchequer, was locally in the hands of the sheriffs for a century and a half after the Conquest; but the growth of business, due to the increase of population and the subdivision of the original knights' fees, necessitated the creation of a separate official. Already in the time of Richard I., there appears "the keeper of the king's escheats," and early in the reign of Henry III. the sheriffs are relieved by the two escheators, one on each side of the Trent, who answer directly at the Exchequer, although it is not until the year 17 Edward II. (1323-4) that their accounts are transferred from the Pipe Roll to a separate enrolment.

The office of escheator passed through a period of experimental fluctuation during the first half of the fourteenth century; Edward I. in 1275 temporarily abolished the original two escheatries, dividing the realm into three stewardships with the sheriffs as escheators in each county; Edward II. in 1323 divided the country into ten escheatries,[1] a plan readopted by Edward III. in 1340; between 1332 and 1340 there were five escheators, between 1341 and 1357 the office was held by the sheriffs, though separate patents were issued, while

[1] Besides these ten, the palatinate county of Chester had its own escheator, and the Mayor of London exercised the office in London. Minor escheatries were carved out from time to time.

from 1357 onwards the office suffered no change of importance until the Tudor period, when the Court of Wards was established (32 Henry VIII.) and the feodary appears. The functions of the escheator were to take into the king's hand and administer the lands of all tenants in chief and of others whose lands by death, escheat or forfeiture, fell to the crown, to deliver seisin to the heirs, after taking security for the payment of relief, to make partitions of lands among heiresses, to assign dowers to the widows of tenants, and in general to watch over the interests of the crown in all matters of feudal obligation.

The documents given below show the machinery in operation. Instances are given of the different tenures[1] (Nos. 1 to 6), while the uncertainty prevailing in the twelfth century as to the incidents due from land held by serjeanty is illustrated in No. 5. The gradual substitution of a money economy for a feudal economy, which finds expression in scutage (No. 17) and otherwise (No. 18), encouraged an elasticity of tenure which made a change from serjeanty to knight service (No. 7) and from personal service to a rent (No. 8) convenient equally to lord and tenant. The degree to which subinfeudation had commonly proceeded in the thirteenth century is shown in No. 9, and the burden of the feudal incidents is exemplified in Nos. 10 to 15. The ordinary revenues of the Crown from feudal incidents and aids, rents, the profits of justice, and escheats, were never sufficient to meet emergencies, just as the feudal army was inadequate for a protracted campaign, and hence the Crown was forced to resort on the one hand to a universal land-tax (No. 16) or a limited exaction from the crown demesnes (No. 19), and on the other to a tax on the feudal unit, the knight's fee (No. 17); the provisions for the collection of a carucage illustrate the royal determination to exact the uttermost farthing, while the assessment of a scutage was conducted on the modern principle of extracting the money first and settling the liability afterwards. No. 20 is a rare surviving instance of an original writ *Precipe* issued

[1] Unfree tenure is illustrated below in section III., The Manor.

before *Magna Carta,* and shows precisely the method of the royal procedure in attracting legal causes to the King's jurisdiction out of the hands of the lord. The section concludes with the important articles of enquiry initiated by Edward I., which led to the compilation of the Hundred Rolls and the proceedings *quo warranto*, and also set out in detail the King's conception of his sovereignty and of the royal origin of all feudal franchises and liberties (No. 21); while the last document (No. 22) furnishes a curious instance of one of the minor royal rights.

AUTHORITIES

The principal modern writers dealing with the subject of this section are:—Pollock & Maitland, *History of English Law*; Maitland, *Lectures on Constitutional History*; Stubbs, *Constitutional History*; Hazlitt, *Tenures of land and customs of manors*; Round, *Feudal England*; Round, *The King's Serjeants and Officers of State*; Baldwin, *Scutage and Knight Service in England*; McKechnie, *Magna Carta*; Freeman, *Norman Conquest;* Hatschek, *Englische Verfassungsgeschichte*; Digby, *History of the Law of Real Property.*

Documentary authorities:—The principal original sources are, *The Red Book of the Exchequer* (Hall, Rolls Series); *The Hundred Rolls* (Record Commission), *Placita de quo Warranto* (Record Commission); *Placitorum Abbreviatio* (Record Commission); *Testa de Nevill* (Record Commission),[1] *Inquisitions Post Mortem* (Record Office Calendars), *Feudal Aids* (Record Office Calendars).

1. FRANKALMOIN [*Ancient Deeds*, B. 4249]. *temp.* Henry II.

To all sons of Holy Mother Church, present and to come, Roger son of Elyas of Helpstone, greeting. Know ye that I have given and granted and by my present charter confirmed to God and the church of St. Michael of Stamford and the nuns serving God there, for the souls of my father and my mother and for the salvation of my soul and the souls of my ancestors and successors, in free and pure and perpetual alms, 2 acres of land, less 1 rood, in the fields of Helpstone, to wit, 3 roods of land on Peselond between the land of Payn the knight and between the land of Robert Blund, and ½ acre between the land of William Peri and between the land of William son of Ede, and 2 roods between the land of Sir Roger de Torpel, lying on both sides. I have given, moreover, to

[1] A new edition is in course of preparation.

God and the church of St. Michael and the nuns serving God there, in free and pure and perpetual alms ½*d.* of rent which John son of Richard of Barnack used to render to me on the day of St. Peter's Chains [1] for a house and for a rood of land in Helpstone. And the aforesaid land and ½*d.* of rent I, Roger, and my heirs will warrant to the aforesaid nuns against all men and against all women. Witnesses:—Payn of Helpstone, Roger his son, Geoffrey of Lohoum, Geoffrey of Norbury, Walter of Helpstone, Robert son of Simon, Geoffrey son of John, Geoffrey son of Herlewin, Walter of Tickencote, Richard Pec.

2. Knight Service [*Inquisitions post mortem, Edward II*, 2, 19], 1308.

Somerset.—Inquisition made before the escheator of the lord the King at Somerton on 29 January in the first year of the reign of King Edward [II], of the lands and tenements that were of Hugh Poyntz in the county of Somerset on the day on which he died, how much, to wit, he held of the lord the King in chief and how much of others and by what service, and how much those lands and tenements are worth yearly in all issues, and who is his next heir and of what age, by the oath of Matthew de Esse [2] . . . Who say by their oath that the aforesaid Hugh Poyntz held in his demesne as of fee in the county aforesaid on the day on which he died the manor of Curry Mallet, with the appurtenances, of the lord the King in chief for a moiety of the barony of Curry Mallet by the service of one knight's fee; in which manor is a capital messuage which is worth 4*s.* a year with the fruit and herbage of the garden; and there are there 280 acres of arable land which are worth 4*l.* 13*s.* 4*d.* a year at 4*d.* an acre; and there are there 60 acres of meadow which are worth 4*l.* 10*s.* a year at 18*d.* an acre; and there is there a park the pasture whereof is worth 6*s.* 8*d.* a year and not more owing to the sustenance of deer; and the pleas and perquisites of the court there are worth 4*s.* a year; And there are there 12 free tenants in fee, who render yearly at the feasts of Michaelmas and Easter by equal portions 74*s.* 8*d.* for all service; and there are there 16 customary tenants, each of whom holds ½ virgate of land

[1] August 1. [2] And eleven others named.

in villeinage, rendering yearly at the said terms by equal portions 4*s*., and the works of each are worth from the feast of the Nativity of St. John the Baptist[1] to the feast of Michaelmas 2*s*. a year; and there are there 28 customary tenants, each of whom holds 1 fardel[2] of land in villeinage, rendering yearly at the said terms by equal portions 2*s*., and the works of each for the same time are worth 12*d*. Sum of the extent:—22*l*. 12*s*. 8*d*.

Further, the aforesaid jurors say that Nicholas Poyntz, son of the aforesaid Hugh Poyntz, is next heir of the same Hugh and of the age of 30 years and more. In witness whereof the same jurors have set their seals to this inquisition.

The aforesaid Hugh de Poyntz held no other lands or tenements in my bailiwick on the day on which he died, except the lands and tenements in these inquisitions.[3]

3. Grand Serjeanty [*Inquisitions ad quod damnum*, 135, 10], 1319.

Norfolk.—Inquisition made at Bishop's Lynn before the escheator of the lord the King on 30 March in the 12th year of the reign of King Edward, son of King Edward, by Robert de Causton.[4] . . . Which jurors say upon their oath that it is not to the damage or prejudice of the lord the King or of others if the lord the King grant to Thomas de Hauvill that he may grant to the venerable father John, bishop of Norwich, a custom called lastage[5] which he has and receives in the port of Bishop's Lynn in the county of Norfolk, to receive and hold to him and his successors, bishops of that place, for ever. Asked of whom that custom is holden in chief, they say, Of the lord the King in chief. Asked also by what service, they say that Thomas de Hauvill holds the manors of Dunton and Rainham and the custom called lastage in the ports of Bishop's Lynn and Great Yarmouth, in the county aforesaid, and Boston, in the county of Lincoln, by grand serjeanty, to wit, by the service of keeping a falcon of the lord the King yearly.[6]

[1] June 24. [2] A quarter of a virgate.
[3] A second inquisition is appended.
[4] And eleven others named. [5] Here a toll of ships' ladings.
[6] The service of grand serjeanty was usuall⁻ more onerous.

Asked how much that custom is worth yearly in the port of Lynn, they say that the aforesaid custom in the aforesaid port of Lynn is worth 16*s.* according to the true value in all issues yearly. In witness whereof the aforesaid jurors have set their seals to this inquisition at Lynn the day and year abovesaid.

4. Petty Serjeanty [*Fine Roll, 3 Edward III, m.* 5], 1329.

The King to his beloved and faithful, Simon de Bereford, his escheator on this side Trent, greeting. Because we have learned by an inquisition which we caused to be made by you that Nicholaa, who was the wife of Nicholas de Mortesthorp, deceased (*defuncta*), held on the day on which she died the manor of Kingston Russell with the appurtenances for the term of her life of the gift of William Russel, and that that manor is held of us in chief by the service of counting our chessmen (*narrandi familiam scaccarii nostri*) in our chamber, and of putting them in a box when we have finished our game; and that the aforesaid Nicholaa held on the day aforesaid the manor of Allington with the appurtenances for the term of her life of Theobald Russel by knight service; and that the aforesaid Theobald, son of the aforesaid William, is William's next heir of the manors aforesaid and of full age: We have taken Theobald's homage for the manor which is thus held of us and have given it back to him. And therefore we command you, that after you have taken security from the aforesaid Theobald for rendering to us a reasonable relief at our Exchequer, you cause the same Theobald to have full seisin of the manor aforesaid with the appurtenances and of the other lands and tenements which the same Nicholaa so held for the term of her life of the inheritance aforesaid in your bailiwick on the day on which she died, and which on account of her death have been taken into our hand, saving the right of every man. Witness the King at Gloucester, 26 September. By writ of privy seal.

5. An Action on the Feudal Incidents due from Lands held by Petty Serjeanty [*Bracton's Note-Book, III,* 290. *No.* 1280], 1239-40.

Jollan de Nevill was summoned to shew wherefore without licence of the lord the King he gave in marriage William, son and heir of Randolf son of Robert, who ought to be in the wardship of the lord the King because Randolf held his land of the King by the service of serjeanty, etc. And Jollan comes and says that the aforesaid William held no such land of the lord the King in chief save by the following service, to wit, that he ought to be verger (*portare unam uirgam*) before the justices in eyre at Lincoln, wherefore it seems to him that no wardship pertains thereof to the lord the King, and he says that at another time he was impleaded by Earl Richard [1] touching that wardship on account of certain land which the same Randolf held of the same Earl, and in such wise that an inquisition was made whereby it was proved that the same Earl had no right in that wardship, and also he says that another inquisition was made between the lord the King and him, Jollan, whereby it was proved that the wardship pertained to Jollan, and the inquisition was delivered to the Chancellor, and he puts himself on that inquisition, and thereof he says that after the wardship remained to him by that inquisition he sold the wardship and marriage forthwith to the Chancellor at Lincoln for 20 marks. And therefore let the inquisition be viewed etc.[2]

6. Free Socage [*Fine Roll*, 16 *Edward III*, *m*. 15], 1342.

The King to his beloved and trusty, Richard de Monte Caniso, his escheator in the counties of Essex, Hertford and Middlesex, greeting. Because we have learned by an inquisition which we caused to be made by you that a tenement with the appurtenances in the parish of St. Clement Danes without the bar of the New Temple, London, which was of Thomas de Crauford, barber, deceased, and which is worth by the year in all issues 6*s*. 8*d*. according to the true value of the same, is holden of us in chief in free socage by the service of 18*d*. a year to be rendered therefrom to us at our Exchequer for all services, and that the wardship of the land and heir of the

[1] Earl of Cornwall, the king's brother.

[2] For the uncertainty prevailing as to the burdens of this tenure in the thirteenth century, *cf*. Bracton, *f*. 35*b*. "Since such services are not done for the king's army or the defence of the country, no marriage or wardship is due therefrom to the chief lord, any more than from socage." But the gloss of this dictum quotes an instance of a justice upholding the claim of a chief lord to the wardship and marriage of the heir of a tenant by petty serjeanty.

same Thomas does not pertain to us, because the wardship of such tenements holden of us in form aforesaid ought to pertain to the next friends of the same heirs to whom the aforesaid tenements cannot come by hereditary right, and that John, son of the said Thomas, is next heir of the same Thomas and of the age of fourteen years : We have taken the fealty of the same John due to us from the tenement aforesaid. And therefore we command you that after you have received from the aforesaid John security for rendering to us his reasonable relief at our Exchequer, you deliver to the same John the tenement aforesaid with the appurtenances, which was taken into our hand by reason of the death of the aforesaid Thomas; saving the right of any man. Witness the King at Woodstock, 18 June.

7. Commutation of a Serjeanty for Knight Service [*Inquisitions ad quod damnum*, 1, 30], 1254.

This is the inquisition made by the oath of James de Northon[1] . . . in the presence of the keepers of the pleas of the crown,[2] what damage it would be to the lord the King to grant to his beloved and trusty Adam de Gurdun that for the service which his father used to do to the same lord the King, to wit, of finding a serjeant for the lord the King for 40 days in his army and expedition, for the land which the same Adam and his mother hold of the lord the King by serjeanty in Tisted and Selborne in the county of Southampton, hereafter he do to the lord the King the service of half a knight's fee : Who say that it is not to the damage of the lord the King to grant to Adam de Gurdun that for the service which his father used to do to the lord the King . . . he do hereafter the service of half a knight's fee. In witness whereof they have set their seals to this inquisition.

8. Commutation of Service for Rent [*Inquisitions ad quod damnum*, 2, 40], 1269.

Inquisition made before the sheriff on All Souls Day[3] in the 53rd year of the reign of King Henry son of King John, what and what sort of customs and services are due to the lord the King from two virgates of land with the appurtenances

[1] And eleven others named. [2] The coroners. [3] November 2.

which Adam de Ardern holds of the aforesaid lord the King in Colverdon and Walesworth, within the manor of the aforesaid lord the King of Barton without Gloucester, and how much those customs and services are worth yearly in money, if they were converted into money, and whether it would be to the damage of the aforesaid lord the King or to the injury of the manor aforesaid, if the lord the King should grant to the aforesaid Adam that for the customs and services aforesaid he should render to the aforesaid lord the King the value of the same yearly in money; and if it should be to the damage of the lord the King aforesaid or to the injury of the same manor, to what damage and what injury; by the oath of the below written persons, to wit, Philip de Hatherle[1] . . . Who say upon their oath that the aforesaid Adam holds of the aforesaid lord the King within the manor aforesaid in Colverdon a virgate of land with the appurtenances and renders 10*s.* a year to the lord the King, and another virgate of land with the appurtenances in Walesworth and renders 20*s.* to the same lord the King, and for the aforesaid two virgates of land he owes suit to the court of the lord the King at the Barton aforesaid, and it is worth 2*s.* a year, and he shall carry writs within the county and shall have no answering of the aforesaid writs, and it is worth 2*s.* a year, and he ought to be tallaged for the two virgates of land aforesaid, when tallage is imposed, at the will of the lord the King. And if the aforesaid lord the King should grant to the aforesaid Adam to hold the aforesaid land for the aforesaid service,[2] it would not be to the damage of the lord the King nor to the injury of the manor aforesaid.

9. Subinfeudation [*Rotuli Hundredorum, II*, 350], 1278.

Township of Thornborough.—The abbot of Biddlesdon holds 6 hides of land and a virgate in Thornborough, to wit, of John de Hastings one hide of land, and John himself holds of Sir John son of Alan, and Sir John himself holds of the lord the King in chief.

Again, the said abbot holds a half hide of land and a virgate of Alice daughter of Robert de Hastings, and she holds of Sir John son of Alan, and he holds of the King in chief, and the said abbot renders to the said Alice 30*s.* a year.

[1] And twelve others named.

[2] *i.e.*, for the money-payments specified above.

Again, the same abbot holds of Hugh de Dunster 2½ hides of land and a virgate, and renders for the said land to the nuns of St. Margaret of Ivinghoe 40*s.* a year, and maintains the chapel of Butlecote for the aforesaid land. And Hugh held of John de Bello Campo a hide and a virgate of land, rendering to John de Bello Campo 4*d.* a year, and John himself holds of Sir John son of Alan, and he holds of the lord the King in chief.

Again the same abbot holds of the gift of Roger Foliot a half hide and a virgate, and Roger himself held of Reynold de Fraxino, and Reynold held of John son of Alan, and he of the lord the King in chief.

Again, the same abbot holds of the gift of William de Fraxino and his ancestors a hide of land, and they held of John son of Alan, and he of the lord the King in chief.

And it is to be known that all the aforesaid land used to render foreign service,[1] except the land which the said abbot has of the gift of John de Hastings and Alice daughter of Robert de Hastings, but John son of Alan and his heirs will acquit the said abbot towards the lord the King and all other men, to wit, of the ward of Northampton, of scutage, of a reasonable aid to make the king's son a knight and to marry his daughter, for ever, and of all services pertaining to them.[2]

10. Licence for the Widow of a Tenant in Chief to Marry [*Fine Roll*, 10 *Edward II*, *m.* 19], 1316.

The King to all to whom etc. greeting. Know ye that by a fine of 100*s.* which our beloved John de la Haye has made with us for Joan, who was the wife of Simon Darches, deceased, who held of us in chief as of the honour of Wallingford, we have given licence to the same Joan that she may marry

[1] *i.e.*, service due to the King, a permanent burden upon the land. *See* Bracton, *f.* 36. "Item sunt quedam servitia que dicuntur forinseca . . . quia pertinent ad dominum regem . . . et ideo forinsecum dici potest quia fit et capitur foris sive extra servitium quod fit domino capitali."

[2] The process of subinfeudation was brought to an end by the Statute of *Quia Emptores*, 1290. "Our lord the king . . . has . . . enacted that henceforth it be lawful for any freeman to sell his land or tenement or any part thereof at his pleasure, so always that he who is enfeoffed thereof hold that land or tenement of the same chief lord, and by the same services and customs, whereby the enfeoffor formerly held them."

whomsoever she will, provided that he be in our allegiance. In witness whereof etc. Witness the King at Westminster, 11 July.

11. MARRIAGE OF A WIDOW WITHOUT LICENCE [*Fine Roll*, 12 *Edward III*, *m.* 26], 1338.

The King to his beloved and trusty, William Trussel, his escheator on this side Trent, greeting. Whereas Millicent, who was the wife of Hugh de Plescy, deceased, who held of us in chief, who (*que*) lately in our Chancery took a corporal oath that she would not marry without our licence, has now married Richard de Stonley without having obtained our licence hereon: We, refusing to pass over such a contempt unpunished, and wishing to take measures for our indemnity in this behalf, command you that without delay you take into our hand all the lands and tenements which the aforesaid Richard and Millicent hold in Millicent's dower of the inheritance of the aforesaid Hugh in your bailiwick; so that you answer to us at our Exchequer for the issues forthcoming thence, until we deem fit to order otherwise thereon. Witness the King at the Tower of London, 6 May. By the King.

12. ALIENATION OF LAND BY A TENANT IN CHIEF WITHOUT LICENCE [*Fine Roll*, 1 *Edward I*, *m.* 7], 1273.

Order is made to the sheriff of Hereford that without delay he take into the King's hand the manor of Dilwyn, which Edmund, our[1] brother, holds of the King in chief, and which he has now alienated to John Giffard without the King's licence; and that he keep it safely until the King make other order thereon, so that he answer to the King at the King's Exchequer for the issues arising therefrom. Given as above [at St. Martin le Grand, London, 5 October]. By the King's council.

13. WARDSHIP AND MARRIAGE [*Pipe Roll*, 26 *Henry II*, *Rot.* 5, *m.* 2*d.*], 1179–80.

Otto de Tilli renders account of 400*l.* to have the wardship of the land of his grandson; and let his daughter be given [in

[1] *i.e.*, the King's brother. The enrolling clerk confuses the first person of the original writ with the third person of the enrolment formula.

marriage] at the King's will. In the treasury are 100*l.* And he owes 300*l.*

Adam son of Norman and William son of Hugh de Leelai render account of 200 marks for marrying the daughter of Adam with the son of William, with the King's good will. In the treasury are 50 marks. And they owe 100*l.*

14. GRANT OF AN HEIR'S MARRIAGE [*Fine Roll*, 13 *Edward II*, *m.* 3], 1320.

The King to all to whom etc., greeting. Know ye that by a fine of 6*l.* which our beloved clerk, Adam de Lymbergh, has made with us, we have granted to him the marriage of John, son and heir of Joan de Chodewell, deceased, late one of the sisters and heirs of Philip le Brode, deceased, who held of us in chief, which John is under age and in our wardship; to hold without disparagement.[1] In witness whereof etc. Witness the King at Odiham, 26 March. By the council.

And command is given to Richard de Rodeney, the King's escheator on this side Trent, that he deliver to the same Adam the body of the heir aforesaid, to be married in the form aforesaid. Witness as above.

15. WARDSHIP [*Fine Roll*, 11 *Edward III*, *m.* 18], 1337.

The King to his beloved and trusty, William Trussel, his escheator on this side Trent, greeting. We command you, straitly enjoining, that forthwith, on view of these presents, you cause the body of the heir of Roger de Huntyngfeld, deceased, who held of us in chief, wheresoever and in whosesoever hands it be found in your bailiwick, to be seized into our hand and to be sent to us without delay, wheresoever we shall be in England, to be delivered to us or to him whom we shall depute as guardian of the said heir: and that you in no wise neglect this, as you will save yourself harmless against us. Witness the King at the Tower of London, 2 September.

By le ter of the secret seal.

[1] *i.e.*, The heir is not to be married below his rank. *cf. Magna Carta*, 6. "Heirs shall be married without disparagement, so that before a marriage be contracted, the near kindred of the heir shall be informed thereof."

16. THE COLLECTION OF A CARUCAGE [*Roger of Hoveden, Rolls Series*, iv. 46], 1198.

In the same year Richard, King of England, took an aid of 5*s*. from every carucate of land or hide of the whole of England, for the collection whereof the same King sent throughout every county of England a clerk and a knight, who, together with the sheriff of the county to which they were sent, and with lawful knights elected hereto, after taking oath faithfully to execute the King's business, summoned before them the stewards of the barons of that county and from every town the lord or bailiff of that town and the reeve with four lawful men of the town, whether freemen or unfree (*rusticis*), and two of the more lawful knights of the hundred, who swore that they would faithfully and without deceit say how many ploughlands (*carucarum wannagia*) there were in every town, to wit, how many in demesne, how many in villeinage, how many in alms granted to men of religion, which the grantors or their heirs are bound to warrant or acquit, or wherefrom men of religion ought to do service; and by command of the King they put on each ploughland first 2*s*. and afterwards 3*s*.; and all these things were reduced to writing; and the clerk had thereof one roll, and the knight a second roll, the sheriff a third roll, the steward of the barons a fourth roll of his lord's land. This money was received by the hands of two lawful knights of each hundred and by the hand of the bailiff of the hundred; and they answered therefor to the sheriff, and the sheriff answered therefor by the aforesaid rolls at the Exchequer before the bishops, abbots and barons appointed hereto. And for the punishment of any jurors who should conceal aught in this business contrary to their oath, it was decreed that any unfree man convicted of perjury should give to his lord his best plough-ox, and moreover should answer from his own property, to the use of the lord the King, for as much money as he should be declared to have concealed by his perjury; and if a freeman should be convicted, he should be at the King's mercy, and moreover should refund from his own property, to the use of the lord the King, as much as should be concealed by him, like the unfree man. It was also decreed that every baron together with the sheriff should make distraints upon his men; and if through default of the barons distraints were not made, that which should remain to be rendered by their men should be taken from the demesne of the barons, and the barons themselves should have recourse to their men for the same. And the free fees of parish churches were excepted from this tallage. And all escheats of barons, which were in the hand of the lord the King, paid their share. Serjeanties, however, of the lord the King, which were not of knights' fees, were excepted ; nevertheless a list was made of them and of the number of carucates of land and the value of the lands and the names of the serjeants, and all those serjeants were summoned to be at London on the octave of the Close of Pentecost, to hear and execute the command of the lord the King. And those who were elected and appointed to execute this business of the King decreed, by the valuation of lawful men, 100 acres of land to each ploughland.

17. An Acquittance of the Collectors of Scutage of a sum of 10*l.* levied by them and repaid [*Chancery Miscellanea*, 1, 18, 9], 1319.

To all Christ's faithful to whom the present letters shall come, John de Twynem, receiver of the money of the lord John of Brittany, earl of Richmond, in the barony of Hastings, greeting in the Lord. Know ye that, whereas John Fillol and William de Northo were appointed[1] to collect and levy in the counties of Surrey and Sussex the scutage of the lord the King of the armies of Scotland of the twenty-eighth, thirty-first and thirty-fourth years of the reign of King Edward, father of King Edward that now is, and afterwards by command of the lord the King were appointed[2] to pay to the said lord John of Brittany, earl of Richmond, the scutage of the tenants of the barony aforesaid of the aforesaid thirty-first and thirty-fourth years, I have received of the aforesaid John Fillol and William de Northo by the hands of the said John to the use of the said lord John of Brittany, earl of Richmond, 10*l.* for the scutage of five knights' fees in Wartling, Cowden and Socknersh, of the aforesaid thirty-fourth year ; of which 10*l.* I will acquit the aforesaid John and William, their heirs and executors, and save them harmless, against the said earl and others whom-

[1] *Fine Roll*, 8 *Edward II.*, *m.* 19.
[2] *Scutage Roll*, 8–11 *Edward II.*, *mm.* 2, 1.

soever. In witness whereof I have set my seal to these presents. Given at Lympne, 12 September, at the beginning of the thirteenth year of the reign of the King abovesaid.[1]

18. Payment of Fines in Lieu of Knight Service [*Patent Roll*, 31 *Edward I*, *m.* 12*d*], 1303.

The King to the sheriff of York, greeting. Though we lately commanded you that you should cause to be summoned archbishops, bishops, abbots, priors and other ecclesiastical persons, and also widows and other women of your bailiwick, who hold of us in chief by knight service or by serjeanty, or hold of the guardianships of archbishoprics and bishoprics or other guardianships or wardships in our hand, that they should have at our side on the feast of Whitsunday next coming at Berwick-upon-Tweed their whole service due to us, well furnished with horses and arms, and ready to march with us and with others our faithful against the Scots, our enemies; wishing, however, on this occasion graciously to spare the labours of the same prelates, religious persons, women and others, who are unskilled in or even unfit for arms, we command you, straitly enjoining, that forthwith on sight of these presents, in full county-court and none the less in market towns and elsewhere throughout the whole of your bailiwick where you shall deem most expedient, you cause it to be publicly proclaimed that the same prelates, religious persons, women and others insufficient or unfit for arms, who owe us their service and are willing to make fine with us for the same service, come before our treasurer and barons of the Exchequer on the morrow of the Ascension of the Lord next coming, or sooner, if they can, at York, or then send some one thither on their behalf, to make fine with us for their service aforesaid, and to pay the same fine to us on the same morrow, to wit, 20*l.* for a knight's fee and otherwise in proportion to their knight service or serjeanty due to us in this behalf; or else that they be at our side on the aforesaid feast of Whitsunday with horses and arms, and the whole of their service, as they are bound; and that you have this writ at our said Exchequer on the morrow abovesaid. Witness the King at Laneham, 16 April.

[1] Scutage was imposed on all tenants of knights' fees, but might be reclaimed by the lord if he did the service due.

19. The Assessment of a Tallage [*Patent Roll*, 8 *Edward II*, p. 1, *m.* 14, *schedule*], 1314.

The King to his beloved and faithful, Hervey de Stanton, Henry le Scrop, John de Merkingfeld and Ralph de Stokes, greeting. Whereas in the sixth year of our reign we caused our cities, boroughs and demesnes throughout England to be tallaged, and certain our lieges to be appointed in the counties of our realm to assess our tallage in our cities, boroughs and demesnes, separately by heads or in common, as they should deem the more expedient for our advantage, and that tallage for certain causes yet remains to be assessed in our city of London: We appoint you to assess that tallage in the city aforesaid and the suburb of the same separately by heads or in common, as you shall deem the more expedient for our advantage. And therefore we command you that without delay you go to the city aforesaid and the suburb of the same to assess the said tallage according to the means of the tenants of the same city and suburb, to wit, from their moveables a fifteenth and from their rents a tenth, so that that tallage be assessed as soon as possible, and the rich be not spared nor the poor burdened overmuch in this behalf; and that after that tallage be assessed in the form aforesaid, you deliver estreats thereof under your seals without delay to our sheriffs of London separately for that tallage to be levied without delay and paid to us at our Exchequer; and that you apply such diligence upon the expedition of the premises that we may deservedly commend you thereupon, in no wise omitting to appear at the Exchequer aforesaid as soon as you conveniently can to certify our treasurer and barons of the Exchequer aforesaid of that which you shall have done in the premises; for we have commanded our sheriffs of the city aforesaid that when they be forewarned by you, three or two of you, they cause to come before you, three or two of you, all those of the city and suburb aforesaid whom they shall deem necessary for the said tallage, and that they be aiding and attending to you hereon, as you shall enjoin upon them on our behalf. In witness whereof, etc. Witness the King at Spalding, 24 October, in the eighth year.

20. A Writ *Precipe* [*Chancery Files*], *c.* 1200.

G. Fitz Peter,[1] earl of Essex, to the sheriff of York, greeting. Command (*precipe*) Ralph de Nevill justly and without delay to render to Robert, son of Richard de Haverford, Fivelay and Moseton and Sloxton with the appurtenances which the same Robert claims to be his right and inheritance, and whereof he complains that Ralph unjustly deforces him; and if he refuse and Robert give us security to prosecute his claim, summon the same Ralph by good summoners to be before us at Westminster on the quinzaine of Michaelmas to show wherefore he does it not; and have there the summoners and this writ. Witness H. Bard at Shoreham, 21 June.[2]

21. Articles of Enquiry touching Rights and Liberties and the State of the Realm, 2 Edward I.[3] [*Patent Roll*, 2 *Edward I.*, *m.* 6], 1274.

How many and what demesne manors the King has in his hand in every county, as well, to wit, of ancient demesnes of the crown, as of escheats and purchases.

Also what manors used to be in the hands of Kings, the King's predecessors, and who hold them now and by what warrant and from what time, and by whom and in what manner they were alienated.

Also touching fees of the lord the King, and his tenants who now hold them of him in chief, and how many fees each of them holds, and what fees used to be holden of the King in chief and are now holden by a mesne lord, and by what mesne, and from what time they have been alienated, and how and by whom.

Also touching the lands of tenants of the ancient demesne of the crown, as well free sokemen as bond, whether [holden] by bailiffs or by the same tenants, and by what bailiffs and by what tenants, and by whom they have been alienated, how and at what time.

In like manner let enquiry be made touching the farms of

[1] Geoffrey Fitz Peter, justiciar of England, 1198–1213.

[2] It was to writs of this nature that the barons objected. *Cf. Magna Carta*, 34. "The writ called *Precipe* shall not hereafter be issued to any one touching any tenement, whereby a freeman may lose his court." It illustrates the method by which the King stole from the barons the administration of justice.

[3] Printed in Fœdera, I., ii., 517.

hundreds, wapentakes and ridings, cities, boroughs and other rents whatsoever, and from what time [they have been alienated].

Also how many hundreds, wapentakes and ridings are now in the hand of the lord the King, and how many and what are in the hands of others, and from what time and by what warrant, and how much each hundred is worth yearly.

Touching ancient suits, customs, services and other things withdrawn from the lord the King and his ancestors, who have withdrawn them and from what time, and who have appropriated to themselves such suits, customs and other things pertaining to the lord the King and accustomed, and from what time and by what warrant.

Also what other persons claim from the King to have the return and estreats of writs, and who hold pleas of replevin,[1] and who claim to have wreck of sea,[2] by what warrant, and other royal liberties, as gallows, assizes of bread and ale, and other things that pertain to the crown, and from what time.

Also touching those who have liberties granted to them by Kings of England and have used them otherwise than they ought to have done, how, from what time, and in what manner.

Again, touching liberties granted which hinder common justice and subvert royal power, and by whom they were granted, and from what time.

Further, who have newly appropriated to themselves free chaces or warrens without warrant, and likewise who have had such chaces and warrens from of old by grant of the King, and have exceeded the bounds and metes thereof, and from what time.

Also what lords or their stewards or bailiffs whosoever or also the ministers of the lord the King have not suffered execution of the commands of the lord the King to be made, or also have contemned to do them or in any wise hindered them from being done, from the time of the constitutions made at Marlborough in the 52nd year of the reign of the lord King Henry, father of the King that now is.

[1] The recovery of goods equivalent in value to goods wrongfully seized by way of distraint.

[2] For a curious instance of this liberty, *see* No. 22.

Again, touching all purprestures[1] whatsoever made upon the King or the royal dignity, by whom they have been made, how, and from what time.

Touching knights' fees of every fee soever, and land or tenements given or sold to religious or others to the prejudice of the King, and by whom, and from what time.

Touching sheriffs taking gifts for consenting to conceal felonies done in their bailiwicks, or who have been negligent in attaching such felons by any favour, as well within liberties as without; and in like manner touching clerks and other bailiffs of sheriffs, touching coroners and their clerks and bailiffs whomsoever, who have so done in the time of the lord King Henry after the battle of Evesham, and in the time of the lord the King that now is.

Touching sheriffs and bailiffs whomsoever taking gifts for removing recognitors from assizes and juries, and from what time.

Again, touching sheriffs and bailiffs whomsoever who have amerced for default those who were summoned to inquisitions made by command of the lord the King, when by the same summons sufficient persons came to make such inquisitions, and how much and from whom they have taken for the cause aforesaid, and at what time.

Again, touching sheriffs who have delivered to bailiffs, extortionate and burdensome to the people beyond measure, hundreds, wapentakes or ridings at high farms, that so they might raise their farms; and who were those bailiffs and on whom such damages were inflicted, and at what time.

Again, when sheriffs ought not to make their tourn save twice a year, who have made their tourn more often in a year, and from what time.

Again, when fines for redisseisin or for purprestures made by land or water, for hiding of treasure and for other such things, pertain to the lord the King, and sheriffs ought to attach the same, who have taken such fines, and from whom and how much.

Again, who by the power of their office have troubled any maliciously and hereby extorted lands, rent or other payments, and from what time.

Who have received command of the lord the King to pay

[1] Encroachments.

his debts and have received from the creditors any portion for paying them the residue, and nevertheless have caused the whole to be allowed them in the Exchequer or elsewhere, and from what time.

Who have received the King's debts or part of his debts and have not acquitted the debtors, as well in the time of the lord King Henry as in the time of the lord the King that now is.

Who have summoned any to be made knights and have received bribes from them to have respite, and how much and at what time. And if any great men or others without the King's command have distrained any to take up arms, and at what time.

Again, if any sheriffs or bailiffs of any liberty soever have not made summons in due manner according to the form of the writ of the lord the King, or have otherwise fraudulently or insufficiently executed the royal commands through prayer, price or favour, and at what time.

Again, touching those who have had approvers[1] imprisoned and have caused them to appeal[2] loyal and innocent persons for the sake of gain, and sometimes have hindered them from appealing guilty persons, and from what time.

Again, who have had felons imprisoned and permitted them for money to depart and escape from prison free and unpunished, and who have extorted money for dismissing prisoners by plevin,[3] when they have been replevied, and from what time.

Again, who have received any gifts or bribes for exercising or not exercising or executing their offices, or have executed the same or exceeded the limits of the King's command otherwise than pertained to their office, and at what time.

And let all these things be enquired of, as well in the case of sheriffs, coroners, their clerks and bailiffs whomsoever, as in the case of lords and bailiffs of liberties whatsoever.

Again, what sheriffs or keepers of castles or manors of the lord the King, for any [works], or also what surveyors of such works wheresoever made by the King's command, have accounted for a greater sum in the same than they have reasonably spent and hereupon have procured false allowances to be made to them. And likewise who have retained or moved

[1] A criminal who turns King's evidence.
[2] To bring an action for treason or felony. [3] Surety or pledge.

away to their own use stone, timber or other things bought or purveyed for such works, and what and how much damage the lord the King has had thence, and at what time.

Touching escheators and subescheators, during the lord the King's seisin, doing waste or destruction in woods, parks, fishponds, warrens within the wardships committed to them by the lord the King, how much, and in the case of whom, and in what manner and at what time.

Again, touching the same, if by reason of such seisin they have unjustly taken goods of deceased persons or of heirs into the hand of the lord the King, until they were redeemed by the same, and what, and how much they have so taken for such redemption and what they have retained thereof to their own use, and at what time.

Again, touching the same, who have taken gifts from any for executing or not executing their office, how much and from whom and at what time.

Again, touching the same, who have insufficiently extended [1] the lands of any man for favour to him or another to whom the wardship of those lands should be given, sold or granted, to the deception of the lord the King, and where and in what manner, and if they have taken anything therefor, and how much, and at what time.[2]

22. Wreck of Sea [*Fine Roll*, 10 *Edward III*, *m.* 1], 1337.

The King to the sheriff of Kent, greeting. Because we have been given to understand that a great mass of a whale lately cast ashore by the coast of the river Thames between Greenwich and Northfleet in your county, which should pertain to us as our wreck, and whereof a great part has been carried away by certain evil-doers in contempt of us, remains still in your keeping, to be delivered to us or others at our command, as is fitting: We order you, straitly enjoining on you, that you cause all of the whale aforesaid, which is thus in your keeping, to be entirely delivered without any delay to our beloved and

[1] Surveyed.

[2] The results of this enquiry were embodied in the Hundred Rolls and served as a basis for the *Placita de quo warranto*; these records are as important for the thirteenth century as is Domesday Book for the eleventh.

trusty Nicholas de la Beche, constable of our Tower of London, to be kept to our use, as has been more fully enjoined on him by us ; and that you in no wise neglect so to do ; for we have commanded the same Nicholas to receive from you that mass, to be kept in the form aforesaid. Witness the King at Westminster 14 January. By the King himself.

trusty Nicholas de la Beche, constable of our Tower of London, to be kept to our use, as has been more fully enjoined on him by us; and that you in no wise neglect so to do, for we have commanded the same Nicholas to receive them from you there, to be kept in the form aforesaid. Witness the King at Westminster, 15 January. By the King himself.

SECTION III

THE JEWS

1. Charter of liberties to the Jews, 1201—2. Ordinances of 1253—3. Expulsion of a Jew, 1253—4. Punishment for non-residence in a Jewry, 1270—5. Grant of a Jew, 1271—6. Ordinances of 1271—7. Removal of Jewish communities from certain towns to others, 1275—8. Disposition of debts due to Jews after their expulsion, 1290.

The documents in the following section illustrate the anomalous position of the Jews in England, the nature of the royal protection, which accorded them a security due to them as the king's personal property (No. 1), the restrictions put upon their religious and social life (No. 2) and upon their possession of land (No. 6), the summary treatment dealt out to them if they failed to fulfil their function (No. 3), or dwelt outside the narrow range of a Jewry-town (No. 4), the arbitrary manner in which they were transferred from person to person, or uprooted from one town and transplanted (Nos. 5 and 7), and the manner of their expulsion (No. 8).

Their function in the state was twofold, to supply the crown at any moment with ready money, and to act as a channel for the conveyance to the king of the property of his subjects. The degree of their usefulness must be gauged by the provisions of their charter (No. 1). It is reasonable to suppose that their expulsion was only determined on when the crown had drained their resources, or when, as was the case, there were other supplies available from a class of financiers less obnoxious to the racial and religious prejudices of the age. The place of the Jews was immediately occupied by the merchants of Lucca, and later by the Friscobaldi, the Bardi and Peruzzi and other wealthy societies of Italian merchant-bankers.

AUTHORITIES

The principal modern writers dealing with the subject in this section are:—Jacobs, *The Jews in Angevin England*; Jacobs, *London Jewry* (Anglo-Jewish Exhibition Papers); Gross, *Exchequer of the Jews* (Anglo-Jewish Exhibition Papers); Rigg, *Select Pleas of the Exchequer of the Jews* (Selden Society); Rye, *Persecution of the Jews in England* (Anglo-Jewish Exhibition Papers); Abrahams, *The Expulsion of the Jews from England.*

1. Charter of Liberties to the Jews [1] [*Charter Roll*, 2 *John*, *m.* 5.], 1201.

John by the grace of God, etc. Know ye that we have granted to all Jews of England and Normandy that they may freely and honourably reside in our land, and hold of us all things that they held of King Henry, our father's grandfather, and all things that they now hold reasonably in their lands and fees and pawns and purchases, and that they may have all their liberties and customs as well and peaceably and honourably as they had them in the time of the aforesaid King Henry, our father's grandfather.

And if a plaint shall have arisen between Christian and Jew, he who shall have appealed the other shall have witnesses for the deraignment of his plaint, to wit, a lawful Christian and a lawful Jew. And if the Jew shall have a writ touching his plaint, his writ shall be his witness; and if a Christian shall have a plaint against a Jew, it shall be judged by the Jew's peers.

And when a Jew be dead, his body shall not be detained above ground, but his heir shall have his money and his debts; so that he be not disturbed thereon, if he have an heir who will answer for him and do right touching his debts and his forfeit.

And it shall be lawful for Jews without hindrance to receive and buy all things which shall be brought to them, except those which are of the Church and except cloth stained with blood. And if a Jew be appealed by any man without witness, he shall be quit of that appeal by his bare oath upon his Book. And in like manner he shall be quit of an appeal touching those things which pertain to our crown, by his bare oath upon his Roll.

And if there shall be dispute between Christian and Jew

[1] Printed in Selden Society Publications, Vol. 15, p. 1.

touching the loan of any money, the Jew shall prove his principal and the Christian the interest.

And it shall be lawful for the Jew peaceably to sell his pawn after it shall be certain that he has held it for a whole year and a day.

And Jews shall not enter into a plea save before us or before those who guard our castles, in whose bailiwicks Jews dwell.

And wherever there be Jews, it shall be lawful for them to go whithersoever they will with all their chattels, as our own goods, and it shall be unlawful for any to retain them or to forbid them this freedom.

And we order that they be quit throughout all England and Normandy of all customs and tolls and prisage of wine, as our own chattel. And we command and order you that you guard and defend and maintain them.

And we forbid any man to implead them touching these things aforesaid against this charter, on pain of forfeiture to us, as the charter of King Henry, our father, reasonably testifies. Witnesses; Geoffrey Fitz Peter, Earl of Essex; William Marshal, Earl of Pembroke; Henry de Bohun, Earl of Hereford; Robert de Turnham; William Briwere; etc. Dated by the hand of Simon, Archdeacon of Wells, at Marlborough, on the 10th day of April in the second year of our reign.

2. ORDINANCES OF 1253[1] [*Close Roll*, 37 *Henry III*, *m.* 18].

The King has provided and decreed, etc., that no Jew dwell in England unless he do the King service, and that as soon as a Jew shall be born, whether male or female, in some way he shall serve the King. And that there be no communities of the Jews in England save in those places wherein such communities were in the time of the lord King John, the King's father. And that in their synagogues the Jews, one and all, worship in subdued tones according to their rite, so that Christians hear it not. And that all Jews answer to the rector of the parish in which they dwell for all parochial dues belonging to their houses. And that no Christian nurse hereafter suckle or nourish the male child of any Jew, and that no Christian man or woman serve any Jew or Jewess, nor eat with them, nor dwell in their house. And that no Jew or

[1] Printed in Selden Society Publications, Vol. 15, p. xlviii

Jewess eat or buy meat in Lent. And that no Jew disparage the Christian faith, nor publicly dispute touching the same. And that no Jew have secret intercourse with any Christian woman, nor any Christian man with a Jewess. And that every Jew wear on his breast a conspicuous badge. And that no Jew enter any church or any chapel save in passing through, nor stay therein to the dishonour of Christ. And that no Jew in any wise hinder another Jew willing to be converted to the Christian faith. And that no Jew be received in any town without the special licence of the King, save in those towns wherein Jews have been wont to dwell.[1]

And the justices appointed to the guardianship of the Jews are commanded to cause these provisions to be carried into effect and straitly kept on pain of forfeiture of the goods of the Jews aforesaid. Witness the King at Westminster on the 31st day of January. By the King and Council.

3. Expulsion of a Jew[2] [*Jews' Plea Rolls*, 6, *m.* 8], 1253.

The King, etc., to the sheriff of Kent, etc. Know that we caused to be assessed before us upon Salle, a Jew, a tallage to be rendered on Wednesday next before Whitsunday in the thirty-seventh year, and because the same Jew rendered not his tallage on the said day, and on the same day received a command on our behalf before the justices [appointed to the guardianship of the Jews] that within three days after the aforesaid Wednesday he should make his way to the port of Dover to go forth there with his wife and never to return, saving to the King his lands [rents and tenements and chattels]: We command you that by oath of twelve [good and lawful men] you make diligent enquiry what lands [rents and tenements and chattels] he had on the said day, and who [holds or hold the same] and how much they are worth, saving the service, etc., and how much they are worth for sale; and that you enquire also by oath, etc., what chattels he had in all chirographs outside the chest, and what they are worth, and to whose hands they have come, and that you cause proclamation to be made that none of Salle's debtors hereafter render a

[1] See below, No. 6.
[2] Printed in Selden Society Publications, Vol. 15, p. 29.

penny to him,—let the proclamation be made in every hundred, city, etc.,—and that you take into our hand all the lands, rents and tenements and chattels aforesaid, and keep them safely until [we make other order thereon]; and let the inquisition come on the morrow of Holy Trinity.

4. Punishment for Non-residence in a Jewry[1] [*Jews' Plea Rolls*, 6, *m.* 7*d.*], 1270.

Devon. Because Jacob of Norwich, a Jew, dwells at Honiton without the King's licence, where there is no community of Jews, the sheriff is ordered to take into the King's hand all goods and chattels of Jacob, and to keep them safely until [the King make other order thereon], and to have his body before [the justices appointed to the guardianship of the Jews] on the octave of Holy Trinity, to answer, etc.; and to certify [the Treasurer and Barons of the Exchequer] what goods [and chattels] of the said Jacob he has taken, on the same day, etc.

5. Grant of a Jew[2] [*Jews' Plea Rolls*, 6, *m.* 10], 1271.

Henry, etc., to all, etc., greeting. Whereas we have given and granted to Edmund, our dearest son, Aaron, son of Vives, a Jew of London, with all his goods and chattels and other things which may pertain to us touching the aforesaid Jew; We, at the instance of our aforesaid son, willing to show more abundant grace to the aforesaid Aaron, grant that in all pleas moved or to be moved for or against him, there be associated with the justices appointed to the guardianship of the Jews, on behalf of and by the choice of our son, an assessor to hear and determine those pleas according to the Law and Custom of Jewry. We have granted also to the same Jew that by licence of our aforesaid son he may give and sell his debts to whomsoever he will, and that any man soever may buy them, notwithstanding the Provision made of late that no Jew may sell his debts to any Christians, and that no Christian may buy the same, without our will and licence. In witness where-

[1] Printed in Selden Society Publications, Vol. 15, p. 61.
[2] Printed in Selden Society Publications, Vol. 15, p. 62.

of, etc. Witness myself at Westminster on the —— day of January in the 55th year of our reign.

6. Ordinances of 1271[1] [*Patent Roll*, 55 *Henry III*, *m.* 10*d.*].

The King to his beloved and trusty men, his Mayor and Sheriffs of London, and to all his bailiffs and trusty men to whom [these present letters shall come], greeting. Know ye that to the honour of God and the Church Universal, and for the amendment and profit of our land and the relief of Christians from the damages and burdens which they have borne on account of the freeholds which the Jews of our realm claim to have in lands, tenements, fees, rents and other holdings; and that prejudice may not grow hereafter to us or the commonalty of our realm or to the realm itself: We have provided by the counsel of the prelates, magnates and chiefs who are of our council, and also have ordained and decreed for us and our heirs that no Jew have a freehold in manors, lands, tenements, fees, rents and holdings whatsoever by charter, gift, feoffment, confirmation or any other obligation, or in any other wise; so however that they may dwell hereafter in their houses in which they themselves dwell in cities, boroughs or other towns, and may have them as they have been wont to have them in times past; and also that they may lawfully let to Jews only and not to Christians other their houses, which they have to let; so, however, that it be not lawful for our Jews of London to buy or in any other wise purchase[2] more houses than they now have in our city of London, whereby the parish churches of the same city or the rectors of the same may incur loss. Nevertheless the same Jews of London shall be able to repair their ancient houses and buildings formerly demolished and destroyed, and restore them at their will to their former condition. We have also provided and decreed by the same our council that touching their houses aforesaid to be dwelt in or let, as is aforesaid, no Jew plead or be able to plead by our original writs of Chancery but only before our justices appointed to the guardianship of the Jews by the writs of Jewry hitherto used and accustomed. Touching lands and holdings, however, whereof Jews were

[1] Printed in Selden Society Publications, Vol. 15, p. 1.
[2] *i.e.*, Acquire.

enfeoffed before the present Statute, which also they now hold, we will that such infeudations and gifts be totally annulled, and that the lands and tenements remain to the Christians who demised the same to them; so, however, that the Christians satisfy the Jews of the money or chattel specified in their charters and chirographs,[1] which the Jews gave to the Christians for such gift or infeudation, without interest; with this condition added, that if those Christians cannot satisfy them thereof forthwith, it be lawful for the Jews aforesaid to demise those tenements to other Christians, until their chattels can be levied therefrom without interest by reasonable extent, according to the true value of the same, saving, however, to the Christians their lodging, so that the Jew receive therefrom his money or chattel by the hands of Christians and not of Jews, as is aforesaid. And if it happen that any Jew hereafter receive feoffment from any Christian of any fee or tenement against the present Statute, the Jew shall altogether lose the said tenement or fee, and the same shall be taken into our hand and kept safely, and those Christians or their heirs shall have again that land or tenement from our hand; so, however, that they then pay to us the whole sum of money which they received from the Jews for such feoffment; or if their means are not sufficient therefor, then they shall render to us and our heirs at our Exchequer yearly the true value of those tenements or fees, by true and reasonable extent of the same, until we be fully satisfied of such money or chattel.

Moreover touching nurses of young children, bakers, brewers, and cooks employed by Jews, because Jews and Christians are diverse in faith, we have provided and decreed that no Christian man or woman presume to minister to them in the aforesaid services.

And because Jews have long been wont to receive by the hands of Christians certain rents of lands and tenements of Christians as in perpetuity, which rents were also called fees, we will and have decreed that the Statute made of late by us thereon remain in full force, and be not impaired in any wise by the present Statute.

And therefore we command, straitly enjoining on you, that you cause the Provision, Ordinance and Statute aforesaid to be publicly proclaimed throughout your whole bailiwick, and

[1] Indented bonds.

to be straitly kept and observed. In witness whereof, etc. Witness the King at Westminster, July 25.

In the same manner order is made to the several sheriffs throughout England.

7. Removal of Jewish Communities from certain Towns to Others [1] [*Jews' Plea Rolls*, 18, *m.* 6], 1275.

By writ of the lord the King directed to the justices in these words:—Whereas by our letters patent we have granted to our dearest mother, Eleanor, Queen of England, that no Jew shall dwell or stay in any towns which she holds in dower by assignment of the lord King Henry, our father, and of ourself, within our realm, so long as the same towns be in her hand; and for this cause we have provided that the Jews of Marlborough be transferred to our town of Devizes, the Jews of Gloucester to our town of Bristol, the Jews of Worcester to our town of Hereford, and the Jews of Cambridge to our city of Norwich, with their Chirograph Chests, and with all their goods, and that henceforth they dwell and stay in the aforesaid towns and city among the rest of our Jews there: We command you that you cause the aforesaid Jews of Marlborough, Gloucester, Worcester and Cambridge to be removed from those towns, without doing any damage to them in respect of their persons or their goods, and to transfer themselves to the places aforesaid with their Chirograph Chests, as safely to our use as you shall think it may be done. Witness myself at Clarendon on the 16th day of January in the third year of our reign.

The sheriffs of the counties aforesaid, and the constables, are ordered to cause the aforesaid Jews to be transferred to the places aforesaid.

8. Disposition of Debts due to Jews after their Expulsion [2] [*Close Roll*, 18 *Edward I*, *m.* 1], 1290.

Edward etc. to the Treasurer and Barons of the Exchequer, greeting. Whereas formerly in our Parliament at Westminster on the quinzaine of St. Michael in the third year of our reign, to the honour of God and the profit of the people

[1] Printed in Selden Society Publications, Vol. 15, p. 85.
[2] Printed in Selden Society Publications, Vol. 15, p. xl.

of our realm, we ordained and decreed that no Jew thenceforth should lend anything at usury to any Christian on lands, rents or other things, but that they should live by their commerce and labour; and the same Jews, afterwards maliciously deliberating among themselves, contriving a worse sort of usury which they called courtesy (*curialitatem*), have depressed our people aforesaid on all sides under colour thereof, the last offence doubling the first; whereby, for their crimes and to the honour of the Crucified, we have caused those Jews to go forth from our realm as traitors: We, wishing to swerve not from our former choice, but rather to follow it, do make totally null and void all manner of penalties and usuries and every sort thereof, which could be demanded by actions by reason of the Jewry from any Christians of our realm for any times whatsoever; wishing that nothing be in any wise demanded from the Christians aforesaid by reason of the debts aforesaid, save only the principal sums which they received from the Jews aforesaid; the amount of which debts we will that the Christians aforesaid verify before you by the oath of three good and lawful men by whom the truth of the matter may the better be known, and thereafter pay the same to us at terms convenient to them to be fixed by you. And therefore we command you that you cause our said grace so piously granted to be read in the aforesaid Exchequer, and to be enrolled on the rolls of the same Exchequer, and to be straitly kept, according to the form above noted. Witness myself at King's Clipstone on the 5th day of November in the eighteenth year of our reign.

SECTION IV

THE MANOR

1. Extent of the manor of Havering, 1306-7—2. Extracts from the Court Rolls of the manor of Bradford, 1349-58—3. Deed illustrating the distribution of strips, 1397—4. Regulation of the common fields of Wimeswould, *c.* 1425—5. Lease of a manor to the tenants, 1279—6. Grant of a manor to the customary tenants at fee farm, *ante* 1272—7. Lease of manorial holdings, 1339—8. An agreement between lord and tenants, 1386—9. Complaints against a reeve, 1278—10. An eviction from copyhold land, *temp.* Hen. IV.-Hen. VI.—11. Statute of Merton, 1235-6—12. An enclosure allowed, 1236-7—13. An enclosure disallowed, 1236-7—14. A villein on ancient demesne dismissed to his lord's court, 1224—15. Claim to be on ancient demesne defeated, 1237-8—16. The little writ of right, 1390—17. Villeinage established, 1225—18. Freedom and freehold established, 1236-7—19. A villein pleads villeinage on one occasion and denies it on another, 1220—20. An assize allowed to a villein, 1225—21. A freeman holding in villeinage, 1228—22. Land held by charter recovered from the lord, 1227—23. The manumission of a villein, 1334—24. Grant of a bondman, 1358—25. Imprisonment of a gentleman claimed as a bondman, 1447—26. Claim to a villein, *temp.* Hen. IV.-Hen. VI. —27. The effect of the Black Death, 1350—28. Accounts of the iron-works of South Frith before and after the Black Death, 1345-50.—29. The Peasants' Revolt, 1381.

The attempt to find an inclusive definition of the manor, true alike for every century and for all parts of the country, involves a risk of divorcing the institution from its historical associations, and of depriving it of its social and economic significance. The typical manor exists only in theory, actual manors being continuously modified by the inevitable changes due to the growth of population and commercial expansion. Such modifications of economic structure proceeded with great rapidity between the Conquest and the beginning of the fourteenth century. A comparison of the neat simplicity of the royal manor of Havering in Domesday Book (Section I., No. 10) with its highly complex organisation in the time of Edward I. (below, No. 1), reveals an extraordinary development; the 10 hides, 40 villeins and 40 ploughs of the one are represented by the 40 virgates of the other, but the elaborate hierarchy of tenants in the later survey throws into strange relief the primitive customary nucleus and gives it the appearance already of an archaic survival. It is reasonable to assume that the generation which immediately followed the Conquest witnessed a crystallisation of custom, which preserved untouched for centuries the lord's demesne and the common fields; while on the other hand the colonisation of the waste by progressive enclosures slowly altered the social balance, emphasising the disabilities of the villein class and widening the gulf between lord and customary tenant. The economic position of the customary tenants was becoming worse by the operation of natural laws, for not only was the subdivision of the virgates reaching its limits, but common rights were being continuously diminished by enclosure. Large numbers of the Havering virgaters in 1307 were occupying quite small holdings, while the purprestures, or encroachments on the waste, were becoming formidable. These considerations suggest that early manorial history can best be studied by investigations into the extent of enclosure in the twelfth and thirteenth centuries, and that concentration on the unprogressive nucleus of the manor, on villeinage and customary tenure, may well blind the student to the greater economic significance of the developments outside the common fields. It thus appears probable that the visitation of the Black Death will fall into place as an incident rather than an epoch.

The documents given below attempt to illustrate manorial history in both its praedial and its personal aspects. The essential features of the manor, in its legal aspect, namely, the customary court, customary tenure, and customary services, are shown in the Extent (No. 1) and the extracts from a Court Roll (No. 2), while the common-field system and the distribution of strips appear in Nos. 3 and 4. The commutation of service for rent (Nos. 1, 8, 9) and the transition from customary to leasehold tenure (Nos. 7, 10) show natural forces at work undermining the traditional economy; while the leasing of customary holdings (No. 7) or of a whole manor to all the tenants in common (No. 5) or to a farmer (No. 10), the grant of manors to the tenants at fee farm in perpetuity (No. 6), and the enclosure of waste (Nos. 1, 11, 12, 13), illustrate the wide range of variety possible in the actual management of the agricultural unit. There appears to be little doubt that the villeins suffered a considerable depression as the result of the Norman Conquest; their refusal, however, to acquiesce permanently in the changed conditions is clear from their continued efforts to rise out of their disabilities and to improve their social and economic status, a movement which begins by the attempts of individuals to climb in the scale by flight (No. 2), by claims to be on the king's ancient demesne (Nos. 14, 15), and by the bringing of actions before the justices of assize, a procedure open only to freemen (Nos. 17–22), and gathers force in the fourteenth century until it culminates in the "great fellowship" which organised a self-conscious class revolt throughout the country (No. 29). No. 16 is an instance of the little writ of right, one of the privileges of the favoured tenants on ancient demesne. Manumission was always a possible method of achieving freedom (No. 23), and it may be that the grant of a bondman (No. 24) was a stage in the process of emancipation. Manumission became common at a time when the demand for English wool was encouraging pasture at the sacrifice of tillage, but even in the fifteenth century men might suffer atrocious ignominy through the imputation of villeinage (Nos. 25, 26). The dislocation caused by the Black Death is dramatically illustrated in the Court-Roll (No. 2), the letter from the abbot of Selby (No. 27), and the accounts of the South Frith ironworks in the year before and the year after the first visitation (No. 28); it is to be noted, in the latter document, that for the years 1347–8 and 1348–9 there are no accounts extant at all.

AUTHORITIES

The principal modern writers dealing with the subject in this section are:—Pollock and Maitland, *History of English Law*; Vinogradoff, *Villeinage in England*; Ashley, *The Character of Villein Tenure* (English Historical Review, VIII.); Rogers, *History of Agriculture and Prices*; Rogers, *Six Centuries of Work and Wages*; Maitland, *History of a Cambridgeshire Manor*; Bateson, *Mediæval England*; Vinogradoff, *Oxford Studies in Social and Legal History, II.*; Hone, *The Manor and Manorial Records*; Elton, *Custom and Tenant Right*; Gasquet, *The Great Pestilence*; Little, *The Black Death in Lancashire* (English Historical Review, V.); Oman, *The Great Revolt*; Powell, *The Rising in East Anglia in* 1381.

Documentary authorities:—Durham Halmote Rolls (Surtees Society); Custumals of Battle Abbey (Camden Society); Boldon Book Survey of Possessions of the See of Durham (Surtees Society); Select Pleas in Manorial Courts (Maitland, Selden Society); The Court Baron (Maitland & Baildon, Selden Society); Cartulary of Ramsey Abbey (Rolls Series); Inquisition of Manors of Glastonbury Abbey (Roxburgh Club); Manchester Court Leet Records (Harland, Chetham Society). A large number of manorial records are edited among the publications of the Society of Antiquaries and County Record and Archæological Societies.

Literary authorities:—Robert Grosseteste, *Epistolæ* (Rolls Series); Walter of Henley, *Husbandry* (Lamond); *Piers Plowman*; Chaucer, *Canterbury Tales.*

1. Extent of the Manor of Havering [*Rentals and Surveys, Roll* 189], 1306–7.

The Manor of Havering extended by the order of the King before . . . . and Richard le Rus in the thirty-fifth year of the reign by Richard of the Elms (*de Ulmis*)[1] . . .

Who say on their oath that the King has there in demesne 223½ acres of arable land, whereof the acre is worth 6*d.* a year.

Sum, 111*s.* 9*d.*

Further, 38 acres of arable land, which Adam de Rumford holds, which are of the demesne and were arrented by William Brito and his fellows, as is found below.

Further, 5 acres of arable land, which Walter le Blake holds, and they are of the demesne and were arrented by the same as below, etc.

[1] And 28 others named.

Further, 15 acres of meadow, whereof each is worth 16*d.* a year. Sum, 20*s.*

Further, 4 acres of meadow, which Baldwin le Blund holds, which are of the demesne and were arrented by the same as below, etc.

Further, 23 acres of several pasture, whereof each is worth 14¼*d.* a year. Sum, 27*s.* 3¾*d.*

Further, they say that the King can have in the common pasture, to wit, in the woods, heaths and marshes, his oxen and cows, sheep, horses and swine and other his beasts at his will, and so that all the tenants of the same manor may have their beasts and all their cattle in the aforesaid common when they will. And if the King have no beasts in the common, he shall take nothing therefor.

Further, they say that the King has a plot of land in his park enclosed with hedge and dyke, which is called the King's garden ; but it is not tilled ; therefore there is no profit.

Further, they say that the King has there his park enclosed round with a paling, and as well the men of the same manor as others of the neighbourhood outside the manor ought to renew and repair that paling as often as need be,[1] according as is found below ; and in that park no cattle nor any beasts ought to enter except by licence of the King's bailiff. And if any cattle or any beasts enter the same park without licence of the bailiff, they are forfeit and must be ransomed at the will of the bailiff, if they are foreign, and if they are of the manor, then they are to be ransomed for 1*d.* for each foot, if it please the bailiff to take so much.

Further, they say that the King has in the same manor three foreign woods pertaining to the aforesaid manor, which the King's bailiffs of the same manor have always had in keeping, together with the aforesaid manor, and they have had attachments and all other esplees[2] of the same woods, to complete the farm of the same manor, to wit, Westwode, Haraldeswode and Crocleph. And in those three woods all the tenants of the same manor ought to have common of herbage for all their

[1] *cf. above, Rectitudines, p. 5, under Geneat's Service,* "he must . . . cut the deer-hedge and maintain it."

[2] Produce or profits.

beasts and all their cattle throughout the whole year, except between the feast of Michaelmas and the feast of Martinmas,[1] and then also there may enter into the same woods the horses of the aforesaid tenants, as also throughout the whole year, and the swine of the same tenants for pannage,[2] and no other beasts. And if sheep or oxen be found in the aforesaid woods, or geese, except when driven to the water or the market or elsewhere, so that they make no stay in the same, whosesoever they be, they ought to be imparked and kept until they shall have satisfied the King's bailiff for that trespass. And if within the aforesaid time any foreign beast, which does not belong to any tenant of the manor, be found in the aforesaid woods, the King's bailiff can ransom it, to wit, for 40*d*. for each ox or cow, or 1*d*. for each foot of each beast, or otherwise, as he shall please, within 40*d*. And if any foreign cart shall pass through the aforesaid woods within the aforesaid time, it shall give to the King's bailiff 1*d*. of custom. And if any foreigner shall drive his beasts through the aforesaid woods within the aforesaid time, he shall give to the King's bailiff 1*d*. of custom. And these customs are called "leph" within the aforesaid time.

Further, they say that the King's bailiff ought to have all the wood thrown down by the wind and all windfall wood in the aforesaid three woods within the aforesaid time, to complete the farm of the manor.

And the pannage of the whole manor and the aforesaid customs called "leph" and the wood and windfall wood within the aforesaid time are extended in the profit of the manor at 100*s*.

Further, they say that no men of the foreign neighbourhood ought to have common in the aforesaid woods at any time of the year, nor ought their beasts or cattle to enter the aforesaid woods except by licence of the bailiff. And if they enter, they ought to be imparked and kept until they shall satisfy the bailiff for that trespass.

Further, they say that every customary cart which carries wood or charcoal or any other thing of custom for sale and passes through any of the aforesaid woods shall give to the bailiff 4*d*. of custom.

[1] November 11. [2] Food for swine.

Names of the tenants holding virgate lands, and rents of the same virgates and customs which pertain to them.

3½ Virgates. John de Walda holds 3½ virgates with their homages appurtenant and renders 76*s*. a year at the two terms, without customs. Sum, 76*s*.

Virgate. Maurice Algar holds ½ virgate with its homages appurtenant and renders 9*s*. a year at the two terms.

William the Smith holds two parts of half a virgate with its homages appurtenant and renders 6*s*. a year at the two terms.

Richard Maneland holds a third part of half a virgate with its homages and renders 3*s*. a year at the two terms. *Sum*, 18*s*.

Virgate. Richard de Dovere holds one virgate with its homage appurtenant and renders 30*s*. a year at the two terms; which virgate was of Hamo Peverel. Sum, 30*s*.

Virgate. Nicholas de la Hulle holds a fourth part of a virgate with homages and renders 5*s*. a year.

Walter de la Hulle holds a fourth part of a virgate with homages and renders 4*s*. 2*d*. a year at the two terms.

Richard son of Thomas de Bruera holds a fourth part of a virgate with homages and renders 30*d*. a year at the two terms.

William Annore holds a fourth part of a virgate with homages and renders 6*s*. a year at the two terms.[1] Sum, 17*s*. 8*d*.

. . . . . .

Virgate. William Emeline holds a third part of a fourth part of a virgate and renders 20*d*. a year at the two terms.

William Snelling holds a third part of a fourth part of a virgate and renders 20*d*. a year at the two terms.

John Dasel holds a third part of a fourth part of a virgate and renders 20*d*. a year at the two terms.

William Trilling holds two parts of half a virgate and renders 10*s*. a year at the two terms.

[1] Thirty-one virgates follow in like detail.

William Don holds a third part of half a virgate with homage at the Faucur and renders 5*s.* a year at the two terms.

Simon Pecoc holds a third part of a fourth part of a virgate and renders 2*s.* 6*d.* a year at the two terms.

Isabel Pecoc holds a third part of a fourth part of a virgate and renders 2*s.* 6*d.* a year at the two terms.

Richard the Fuller holds a third part of a fourth part of a virgate and renders 2*s.* 6*d.* a year at the two terms. Sum, 27*s.* 6*d.*

Half a Virgate. Henry de la Bruer holds a fourth part of a virgate and renders 7*s.* 6*d.* a year at the two terms.

Simon Pecoc holds an eighth part of a virgate and renders 3*s.* 9*d.* at the two terms.

Isabel Pecoc holds an eighth part of a virgate and renders 3*s.* 9*d.* a year at the two terms. Sum, 15*s.*

Sum total of rent of 39 virgates a year: 46*l.* 9*s.* 5½*d.*

Virgate. Further, John de Walda holds a virgate of land which was arrented first to the use of the King in the presence of William Brito and his fellows, approvers, and renders therefor 30*s.* a year of rent of assize.

And thus there are in all in the aforesaid manor 40 virgates of land which render yearly in rent of assize:

Sum, 47*l.* 19*s.* 5½*d.*

Further, from works of the aforesaid 40 virgates 14*l.* yearly.

And be it known that each virgate ought to do all the works underwritten, and the works of each virgate are worth by themselves 7*s.* a year.

Virgate works.—Further, it is acknowledged by the aforesaid jurors that each virgate in the aforesaid manor owes all the customs underwritten, and so in proportion half a virgate and other parts according to the portion and quantity of land, as the virgate is divided, to wit, to plough 4 acres a year in the winter season, and the ploughing of each acre is worth 4*d.* Further, it ought to harrow those 4 acres, and the harrowing of each acre is worth ½*d.* Further it ought to thresh and winnow 1 quarter of rye for seed, and that threshing and winnowing is worth 2*d.* Further it ought to reap, bind and cock 4 acres, and this custom is worth 3*d.* for each acre, to wit, of rye. Further it ought to plough 4 acres in the summer season, and the ploughing of each acre is worth 3*d.* Further it ought to harrow those 4 acres, and the harrowing of each acre is worth ½*d.* Further it ought to thresh and winnow 1½ quarters of oats, and the threshing and winnowing is worth 1½*d.* Further it ought to reap, bind and cock 4 acres of oats, and that custom is worth 2½*d.* for each acre. Further it ought to find two men for one day to hoe until noon, and that custom is worth 2*d.* Further it ought to find two men for one day to hoe in the summer season until noon, and that custom is worth 2*d.* Further it ought to carry the corn from the field of the lord the King to the grange with one waggon for one day until noon, and that carrying is worth 3½*d.* Further it ought to find four men to lift the hay in the meadow of the lord the King for one day, and that custom is worth 2*d.* Further it ought to carry a waggonload of hay, and each carrying is worth 3*d.* Further it ought to manure with manure of the lord the King 4 selions[1] 40 perches in length in the next field ploughed for fallow, and that manuring is worth 4*d.* And it ought to do all these customs beforewritten at its own cost.

Sum of the aforesaid works, 6*s.* 2*d.* And of lawful increment for each virgate, 10*d.* a year. And thus the sum of the works of each virgate is 7*s.* a year.

Further, each virgate ought to enclose 6 perches of the paling of the park of the lord the King in the same manor with timber given by livery of the foresters and parkers. Further, all the tenants in the said manor ought to pay pannage for all the swine which they have between the feast of St. Michael[2] and the feast of St. Martin,[3] except those whom the King's charter protects, wheresoever they be within the manor, to wit, they owe a tenth part of the value of each pig which is worth more than 5*d.*, whether there be acorns (*pesona*) or not; so nevertheless that for a pig worth more than 20*d.* the tenant shall give only 2*d.* Further all the tenants and sub-tenants throughout the bounds ought to guard the prisoners of the lord the King by night, except the cotmen, who ought to guard the said prisoners by day; and the prisoners ought to be imprisoned at the houses of the cotmen by night and day from house to house until their term be finished.

[1] Strips. [2] September 29. [3] November 11.

Names of the tenants of the forelands and rents of the same forelanders—

Foreland.

The relict of William Arnold holds 1 foreland and renders yearly	2*s.*
Richard of the Elms holds 1 foreland and renders yearly	4*s.*
John the Smith	3*s.*
John of the Oak of the burnt wood ..	18*d.*
Richard de la Strate	9*d.*
Arnewic May	12*d.*
Gilbert de la Berewe	3*s.* 4*d.*
William le Hettere holds 1 foreland and renders yearly 1*d.* and a ploughshare worth 6*d.*	7*d.*
John de Bollond	5*s.*
William Goldstan	2*s.*
Adam de Rumford	12*d.*
John de Haketon	2*s.*
Richard of the Elms	6*d.*
Nicholas de Wybrugge	4*s.* 4*d.*
Roger son of Elias holds 1 foreland which Gerald le Petit held and renders yearly ..	3*s.* 6*d.*
Andrew de la Lake	22*d.*
The heirs of William son of Guy	10*d.*

Sum. Sum of the rents of the aforesaid forelanders yearly, 37*s.* 2*d.*

Names of the tenants assigned to serve the King's table.

Of the Table of the King. Simon Weyland holds the swineherd's land, and renders ½ mark a year, because there are no swine.

Virgate. The heir of William the Weaver holds the shepherd's land, and renders 12*s.* a year, because there are no animals.

John le Messager holds one ploughman's land, and renders 12*s.* a year, because there is no plough.

Adam le Wardur holds another ploughman's land, and renders 12*s.* a year, because there is no plough.

William Anore holds the smith's land, and renders 5*s.* a year, because there is no plough.

Reckoned as a virgate for the works of the paling.

Sum of rents of the aforesaid lands of the King's table, 47*s.* 8*d.*

King's Messenger. Geoffrey son of Peter holds 6 acres of land, for which land he ought to carry the writs of the lord the King, when they come in the manor of the lord the King, wheresoever the bailiff shall wish within the county, at his own cost, and receiving 1½*d.* for going a reasonable day's journey out of the county and nothing for the return journey.

Names of the cotters and rents of assize of their tenements and the customs of the same.

Cotters. Geoffrey Scurel holds one cotland and renders

Virgate. yearly 5*s.* and for works 49*d.*

Peter le Abbot and his partners hold one cotland and render yearly 4*s.* and for works 49*d.*

William son of Savary holds one cotland and renders yearly 4*s.* and for works 49*d.*

Juliana relict of Edmund and her partners hold one cotland and render yearly 5*s.* and for works 49*d.*

Richard del Ho holds one cotland and renders yearly 3*s.* and for works 49*d.*

William de Ros and Adam Pays hold one cotland and render yearly 5*s.* and for works 49*d.*

William de Uphavering the younger holds one cotland and renders yearly 5*s.* and for works 49*d.*

Reckoned as a virgate for the works of the paling.

Sums. Sum of rents of assize of the aforesaid cotters yearly, 31*s.*

Sum of the same works yearly, 28*s.* 7*d.*

Sum of both, that is, rents of assize and the same works yearly, 59*s.* 7*d.*

Lands occupied over[1] the King and arrented by William Brito and his fellows.

Richard Hageman holds 16 acres of land of new purpresture[2] and renders yearly half a mark.[3]

. . . . . .

[1] In feudal law seisin *or* possession is conceived of as concrete rather than abstract. Any encroachment on the waste, therefore, is regarded as the imposition of a new seisin upon the old seisin, as an occupation over the lord, who in this case is the King.

[2] Encroachment. [3] A hundred more similar entries follow.

Sum. Sum, 102*s.* 11½*d.*

Richard Segar holds two dayworks with a house of the same [*i.e.* of new purpresture] and renders yearly 8*d.*

The same holds 1½ acres of old purpresture and renders yearly 6*d.*[1]

. . . . . .

Sum. Sum, 10*l.* 1*s.* 6*d.*

Edmund Prest holds 5 acres and renders yearly 10*d.*[2]

. . . . . .

The prior of Hornchurch holds 66 acres and 2 dayworks of land and 1 rood of meadow of encroachment and renders yearly half a mark.

Richard de Dovere holds the watercourse from Romford bridge to the park of Havering, and for the watercourse from the end of the fishpond of the abbot of Waltham between Havering and Weald to the mete and bound of the limits of Havering as far as the watercourse extends, and renders yearly 12*d.*

Richard de Dovere holds 85 acres of demesne in several places and renders yearly 20*s.*

Sum. Sum, 117*s.* 7*d.*

Sum total of all lands occupied over the King, 21*l.* 2*s.* 0½*d.*

Subtenants. Names of all subtenants in the town of Havering who have chattels to the value of 40*d.* of whom it is acknowledged by the aforesaid jurors that each such tenant ought to reap, bind and cock one acre of oats of the demesne of the lord the King in autumn, and to find one man to mow in the King's meadow for one day at his own cost. And every of them, according as they join in a plough for ploughing their own land, shall plough for the lord the King each year for one day at the summer ploughing and for another day at the winter ploughing.[3]

. . . . . .

Sum. Sum of the rents of the aforesaid sub-tenants without ploughing, 4*l.* 6*s.*

[1] A hundred and two more similar entries follow.

[2] Thirty-nine more similar entries follow.

[3] 174 names follow.

The King is in seisin of the wardship of the lands and heirs of all the tenants of the same manor, and can hold them when he deems it to his advantage, and then he shall have no heriot. And if he deem it not to be expedient for him to hold the wardship of the lands and heirs in his own hand, he can demise the same, and then he shall have a heriot and relief.

Further, they say that all the tenants of the same manor can marry their sons and daughters without licence of the King or of his bailiffs, except the cotmen.

Further, they say that the King can tallage all the tenants of the same manor, except those who hold by charters of Kings at their will, according to their means, when he tallage other his demesne manors.

Further, they say that the pleas of court can be worth 40*s.* a year.

Further, they say that heriots and reliefs and other perquisites can be worth in common years 53*s.* 4*d.*

Further, they say that view of frankpledge can be worth in common years 6*s.* 8*d.*

Sum. Sum total of all sums of the same manor, 112*l.* 10*s.* 11¾*d.*, except free tenants and the ploughing of subtenants and customary carts.

2. Extracts from the Court Rolls of the Manor of Bradford, co. York [*Court Rolls*, 129, 1957], 1349–1358.

Court of Bradford holden on Saturday, the eve of St. Lucy the Virgin, 23 Edward III.[1]

[m.20.] Henry son of William the Clerk of Bradford, executor of the will of the said William, was summoned to answer Richard de Wilseden, chaplain, touching a plea wherefore he renders not to him 7*s.* 10*d.*, which he owes him, because the aforesaid William, his father, whose executor he is, was bound to him, and which he ought to have paid him at Michaelmas last past, and which the same Henry still detains

Damages. from him, to the heavy damage of the said Richard

[1] December 12, 1349, the year of the Black Death. The monotonous death roll is noteworthy.

of 2*s*. etc. And the aforesaid Henry, being present in court, cannot deny that he owes him the said money. It is therefore awarded that the same Richard recover against him the aforesaid 7*s*. 10*d*., together with his aforesaid damages. And the aforesaid Henry is in mercy for the unjust detention, etc. **Mercy, 2*d*.**

. . . . . .

Amice, daughter and heir of Roger de Oulesnape, came here into Court and took a cottage and 4 acres of poor bondage land in the town of Stanbury after the death of the aforesaid Roger, to hold to her and her heirs according to the custom of the manor by the services, etc., saving the right, etc. And she gives to the lord 2*s*. of fine for entry. Pledge, Roger son of Jurdan. **Entry, 2*s*.**

William Couper, who held a cottage and 4 acres of bondage land there, is dead; and hereupon came Roger, his son and heir, and took those tenements, to hold to him and his heirs according to the custom of the manor by the services, etc., saving the right, etc. And he gives to the lord 2*s*. of fine for entry. Pledge, Thomas de Kyghley. **Entry, 2*s*.**

Robert son of Roger son of Richard, who held a toft and 8 acres of bondage land there, is dead. And hereupon came John, his brother and heir, and took those tenements, to hold to him and his heirs according to the custom of the manor by the services, etc., saving the right, etc. And he gives to the lord 3*s*. of fine for entry. Pledge, Roger son of Jurdan. **Entry, 3*s*.**

Jordan de Stanbury, who held a messuage and ½ bovate of bondage land there, is dead. And hereupon came John, his son and heir, and took those tenements, to hold to him and his heirs by the services etc., saving the right, etc. And he gives to the lord 5*s*. of fine for entry. Pledges, John son of Roger and Roger son of Jurdan. **Entry, 5*s*.**

John de Oldefeld, who held a messuage and ½ bovate of bondage land there, is dead. And Alice, his daughter and heir, is of the age of half a year.

And hereupon came John Swerd and took those tenements, to hold for a term of ten years next following fully complete, by the services, etc. And he gives to the lord 2*s*. of fine. Pledge, Adam de Oldefeld.

Fine, 2*s*.

Adam Dykson came here into Court and took a messuage and ½ bovate of very poor land, which was of Adam atte Yate, to hold according to the custom of the manor, by the services, etc., saving the right, etc. And he gives to the lord 2*s*. of fine for entry. Pledge, John de Helwyk.

Entry, 2*s*.

Roger Dikson, who held half a messuage and ½ bovate of land, is dead. And hereupon came Robert de Oldefeld, next friend of William, son and heir of the aforesaid Roger, and took those tenements to the use of the said William, to hold to him and his heirs, according to the custom of the manor by the services, etc. And he gives to the lord 5*s*. of fine in the name of the said William. Pledge, John Swerd.

Entry, 5*s*.

John Barne of Manningham, who held a messuage and a bovate of bondage land there, is dead. And hereupon came Margery his wife and took those tenements, to hold according to the custom of the manor for the term of her life by the services, etc. And she gives to the lord 2*s*. of fine. Pledge, John atte Yate.

Fine, 2*s*.

Margaret and Agnes, daughters and heirs of Hugh Browne, Alice, Joan and Juliana, daughters and heirs of John Kyng, Juliana, who was the wife of Hugh Kyng of Thornton, Robert son of John Bollyng and Elizabeth his wife, Alice, who was the wife of William le Clerk of Clayton, Alice, daughter and heir of Robert de Manyngham, and Thomas her husband, William, son and heir of Ellen Coke, and John (dead), son and heir of John de Wyndhill, came here into Court and did their fealties, and they have a day at the next Court to acknowledge their tenements and services, etc. and also to show their deeds etc.

Fealties. Respite of acknowledgment of services.

Agnes Chapman came here into Court and took a small house in Bradford called the Smythhouse, to hold at the will of the lord by the services. And

Fine, 12*d.* (*sic.*) she gives to the lord 18*d.* of fine to have such estate, etc.

William Barne, who held 2 messuages and 2 bovates of bondage land in Manningham, is dead. And hereupon came Hugh, his brother and heir, and took the aforesaid tenements, to hold to him and his heirs according to the custom of the manor by the services, etc., saving the right, etc. And Entry, 8*s.* he gives to the lord 8*s.* of fine for entry. Pledges, Thomas de Chellowe and John his son.

Richard Gilleson, who held there in the same manner 2 messuages and 2 bovates of land, is dead. And hereupon came John, his son and heir, and took those tenements, to hold to him and his heirs according to the custom of the manor by the services, etc., saving the right, etc. And he gives to the lord 10*s.* Entry, 10*s.* of fine for entry. Pledges, Hugh Barne and the whole homage, etc.

John son of Richard Gillesson came here into Court and rendered into the hands of the lord 2 messuages and 2 bovates of very poor land there to the use of Thomas de Chellowe for ever. Which tenements were afterwards granted to the same Thomas, to hold to him and his heirs according to the custom of the manor by the services, etc., saving the right, etc. Entry, 10*s.* And the same Thomas gives the lord 10*s.* of fine for entry. Pledges, Hugh Barne and John Gilleson.

William Wilkynson, who held there in like manner a messuage and a bovate of land, is dead, and Alice his daughter and heir is of the age of half a year. And hereupon came John Magson, her next friend, to whom, etc.[1] and took the wardship of the aforesaid land and heir until her full age, etc., by the services, Fine, 2*s.* etc. And he gives to the lord 2*s.* of fine for entry. Pledges Hugh Barne and Thomas de Chellowe.

Thomas Neucomen, who held a messuage and a bovate of bondage land in Bradford, is dead. And hereupon came Margery, daughter and heir of the

[1] *Sc.* the inheritance cannot descend.

same Thomas, and took the aforesaid tenements, to hold to her and her heirs according to the custom of the manor by the services, etc., saving the right, etc. And the fine for entry is put in respite until the next court.

Fine respited.

Distraint.

William Tompsey of Bradford, the lord's bondman, who held a messuage and a bovate of bondage land in Bradford, is a runaway, because [he holds] other tenements in Moreton by York by hereditary descent. Therefore he is distrained to dwell on the tenement here. Let the tenements at Moreton be seized into the lord's hand, etc.

Tenements to be seized.

William Clerk of Clayton, who held a messuage and 2 bovates of land in Clayton by knight service, is dead. Let William, his son and heir, of the age of two years, together with the tenements aforesaid, be seized into the hands of the lord the Earl. And hereupon comes Alice, who was the wife of the same William Clerk, and says that she was jointly enfeoffed of the aforesaid tenements with the aforesaid William, her husband, and craves a day at the next Court to show her charters thereof, and has it. William, the son and heir, is committed to the wardship of the aforesaid Alice to be kept safely without a wife. Pledges, William son of Adam of Horton and Roger del Holyns.

Respite.

Fine, 10s.

Whereas before these times a stall was taken from the lord's waste in the market place of Bradford to be holden by the services of 6*d*. a year, and hereupon one Adam Notebroun, receiver of the money of the lord the Earl [took it], to hold in the said form, etc., and afterwards the same Adam alienated that stall to one Hugh son of Thomas in fee for [20*s*.], on account whereof the stall was seized into the lord's hand according to the form of the statute; and hereupon the same Hugh comes here and says that he took the stall for 20*s*. and paid only 10*s*. thereof to the same Adam, etc., and craves that he [may pay the said 10*s*.] and hold the stall in the form in which [it was held] after it was taken; which is granted to him by the steward. Pledge for payment of the aforesaid 10*s*. . . . . And order is made to levy from the aforesaid Adam another 10*s*. to the use of the lord, unless he may have better grace by the counsel of the lord, etc.

Order to levy.

Inquisition of office.

It is presented by William de Berecroft . . . that Thomas son of Thomas (12*d*), Ralph atte Tounhend (8*d*.), William . . . (12*d*.), and William son of John (6*d*.) exercise the trades of tanner and shoemaker. Therefore they are in mercy. And it is ordered that they be attached to abjure, etc.

Mercy, 10*d*.

Further, they present that Hugh son of Thomas exercises the trade of butcher together with the trades of shoemaker and tanner. Therefore it is ordered that he be attached to abjure those two trades, etc.

Mercy, 12*d*.

Further, that Alice Geldoghter and Adam Notebroun are bakers and sell bad bread contrary to the assize. Therefore they are [in mercy].

. . . . . .

Sum of this tourn, with waifs and strays, 24*s*. 1*d*.

. . . . . .

Court of Bradford holden on Thursday next before the feast of St. Gregory the Pope, 24 Edward III.

. . . . . .

Acknowledgment of service.

Thomas le Harpour and Alice his wife, daughter and heir of Robert de Manynghame, come here into Court and acknowledge that they hold of the lord a messuage and a cottage and 8 acres of land by knight service by homage and fealty and suit of court every three weeks, rendering therefrom yearly 2*s*. at the usual terms; and they give to the lord 4*s*. for relief.

. . . . . .

Fine, ½ mark.

William Iveson came into Court and made fine with the lord by ½ mark for licence to exercise the trades of tanner and shoemaker until Michaelmas next. Pledge, William son of Hugh the Bailiff.

. . . . . .

[m. 31.] Court holden at Bradford the day and year aforesaid.[1]

Leyrwite. Agnes Chilyonge of Manningham, the lord's bondwoman, came here in Court and made fine of 12*d.* with the lord for her leyrwite[2]; pledge, William Walker; and the fine is not more because she is very poor and has nothing.

[m. 32.] Court holden at Bradford on Friday next before the feast of the Nativity of St. John the Baptist, 28 Edward III.[3]

Fine, 20s. John Abbot, William son of Henry de Allerton, John Dughti, Robert de Oldfeld, and Adam de Oldfeld, who mainprised[4] for the aforesaid John Abbot to keep the peace towards all persons and specially towards Roger Fairegh, under a penalty of 10*l.* to be paid to the lord Duke, now, because the aforesaid John Abbot beat and evilly entreated the aforesaid Roger Faiergh, on account whereof the aforesaid penalty of 10*l.* ought to be levied from the aforesaid John Abbot and his mainpernors,[5] because the express cause for which the aforesaid penalty should be rightly levied is now come to pass; nevertheless, the aforesaid lord Duke, mindful that they are all his bondmen, and regarding their poverty, has granted of his special grace that the aforesaid John Abbot and his mainpernors may make fine of 20*s.* for the aforesaid 10*l.* forfeited, to be paid at Michaelmas next; and each of them is the others' pledge.

Merchet. Roger son of Roger de Manynghame has made fine of ½ mark for the merchet of Cecily his wife, the lord's bondwoman; pledge, Thomas de Manynghame.

Merchet. Thomas Gabriell has made fine of ½ mark in like

[1] Monday before May 1, 1354.
[2] Fine on giving birth to an illegitimate child.
[3] Friday before June 24, 1354.
[4] *i.e.* Became sureties.
[5] *i.e.* Sureties.

manner for the merchet[1] of Maud his wife, the lord's bondwoman ; pledge, Thomas de Tiresale.

Fine, 6d. Thomas de Tiresale has made fine of 6*d.* with the lord for licence to have John son of Roger Childyong, the lord's bondman, in his service until Michaelmas next, so that he then render the aforesaid John to the lord's bailiffs, etc.

Chevage. Agnes daughter of Adam atte Yate, the lord's bondwoman, has made fine for her chevage[2], for licence to dwell wheresoever she will, to wit, 6*d.* to be paid yearly at Michaelmas and Easter in equal portions ; pledge, Robert atte Yate.

Distrain. It is presented by Roger Judson, Thomas son of Roger, Thomas Gabriel, Adam del Oldfeld, Robert de Oldfeld, and John atte Yate, that Cecily de la More,[3] the lord's bondwoman, has been violated by John Judson ; therefore let her be distrained to make fine therefor with the lord.

Distrain. Further, it is presented that Isabel daughter of William Childyong, the lord's bondwoman, has married one William Cisson, a free man, without licence. And Alice daughter of John Gepson, the lord's bondwoman, has married one William del Hale, a free man, at Beston, without licence ; therefore let them be distrained to make fine with the lord for their merchet, etc.

Inquest. Let inquest be made touching the sons and daughters of William del Munkes, who dwell at Darthington and are the lord Duke's bondmen and bondwomen of Bradford, etc.

Arrest. Further, it is presented that Alice daughter of William Childyong, the lord's bondwoman, dwells at York ; therefore let her be taken, etc.

Sum of this Court :—35*s.* 3*d.*	Merchets, 13*s.* 4*d.*
Thereof further for chevage, 6*d.*	Perquisites, 21*s.* 11*d*

[1] *i.e.* Fine upon marriage.

[2] *i.e.*, head-money, a fine paid yearly by bond-tenants dwelling away from the manor.

[3] *Interlined above* Cecily *is* Roger Judson.

[m. 45 *d.*] Court holden at Bradford on Wednesday, 12 December, 32 Edward III [1358].

Day given under a penalty. Again Anabel del Knoll has a day, as above,[1] to rebuild a house on a plot of land which she holds of the lord at will, and under the same penalty as in the Court preceding.

Arrest bondmen. It is ordered, as many times before, to take William son of Richard Gilleson, Roger son of William del Mersh, dwelling with John de Bradlay, Thomas son of John atte Yate, William son of William Childyong (in Pontefract), Alice daughter of John atte Yate (in Selby), Alice daughter of William Childyong (in Methelay), and William son of William Childyong, the lord's bondmen and bondwomen of his lordship here, etc., who have withdrawn without licence, and to bring them back hither until [they make fine for their chevage].

. . . . .

[m. 46.] Roger son of Roger makes plaint of Alice de Bollyng [in a plea] of trespass, pledge to prosecute, William Walker, to wit, that she has not made an enclosure which she is bound to make between his holdings and her own holdings in Mikelington, so that for lack of enclosure there divers cattle entered and fed off his corn, to wit, his rye and oats and grass, to his damages of 10*s.* And the aforesaid Alice defends and says that the aforesaid Roger, and not she, is bound to make an enclosure there, and hereon she puts herself upon the country. But the jurors hereupon elected, tried and sworn, say on their oath that the aforesaid Roger is bound to make the aforesaid enclosure between the aforesaid holdings. And therefore it is awarded that the aforesaid Roger be in **Mercy, 4*d*.** mercy for his false claim, and that the said Alice go **Without a day.** without a day.

Mercy, 2*s*. It is presented by the parker that William Walker (6*d.*) with 11 beasts, Roger de Manyngham (4*d.*)

[1] Anabel has persistently refused to rebuild the house during the last six years; she discharges her obligation two years later [m. 50].

with 3 beasts, John de Gilles (2*d.*), Thomas Staywal (2*d.*) with one beast, Roger Megson (2*d.*) with one beast, Denis Walker (2*d.*), Richard Wright (4*d.*) with 2 beasts and William Coke (2*d.*) with a horse, have fed off the grass of the lord's wood in Bradford-bank; therefore they are in mercy.

Again it is presented that William Notbroun (6*d.*) and Adam Notbroun (6*d.*) with their cattle have broken down the hedge around the lord's wood, and with the said cattle have fed off the grass of the lord's **Mercy, 12*d*.** wood; therefore they are in mercy.

Again it is presented that Richard Milner of Idel **Mercy, 10*d*.** (6*d.*), Richard Baillif (2*d.*) and William Smyth of Caleshill (2*d.*) have carried millstones over the lord's soil here without licence; therefore they are in mercy.

Again it is presented by John de Denholm, John Judson, Adam Dikson, Robert del More, Thomas de Chellowe, Hugh Barn, Robert atte Yate, John atte Yate, Richard Curtays, John Rous, Roger Johanson and John de Gilles, that William Tomse, the lord's bondman, dwelling in Moreton by York, Roger de Stanbiri, the lord's bondman, dwelling in Wirkley, and John Bonde, dwelling in Sighelesden, and John son of Roger son of William del Mersh, dwelling with John de Bradlay, the lord's bondmen here, have withdrawn without licence; and hereupon order was made to take them all, so that they be [here] until, etc. And the aforesaid William Tomse and Roger de Stanbiri were taken and were brought before the steward at Pontefract on Saturday next after the feast of the Circumcision of the Lord. And the aforesaid **Fine, 26*s*. 8*d*.** William Tomse there made fine of 26*s*. 8*d*. before the said steward, to wit, in order to have his goods at the steward's will,[1] to be paid at the feasts of St. Peter's Chains and St. Michael next by equal portions. And **Chevage, 2*s*.** also the aforesaid William made fine for chevage, to wit, a fine of 2*s*. to be paid yearly at the feasts of

[1] *i.e.* In order to retain his own possessions during the steward's good pleasure. In law a bondman's goods belong to his lord.

Whitsunday and St. Martin in Winter by equal portions; and William Cooke of Brotherton became his pledge as well for his yearly chevage as for his other fine for his said goods. And Roger de Stanbiri likewise on the same day was brought before the aforesaid steward at Pontefract and made fine of

Fine, 20*s*.

20*s*. to have his goods at the steward's will, to be paid at the terms of Easter and Michaelmas next; and also

Chevage, 12*d*.

the aforesaid Roger made fine of 12*d*. for his chevage, to be paid yearly at the terms aforesaid; and Thomas Dantrif became his pledge as well for his yearly chevage as for his fine aforesaid. And it was granted to the same William and Roger that they may stay outside the lordship here in the places where they were staying before, and that too at the lord's will, for their chevages aforesaid, to be paid yearly, as is aforesaid.

Take bondmen.

And order is made to take all the other bondmen named above, because they come not, and to bring them back hither to their nests until, etc.[1]

. . . . . .

Sum of this Court:—51*s*. 9*d*., the whole perquisite. Further from chevage as above:—3*s*. a year to be paid at the terms as above.

[1] *cf*. Bracton, *De Legibus Anglie*, *ff*. 6 *b*. *and* 7. "Serfs are under the power of their lords, nor is the lord's power loosed so long as they abide in villeinage, waking and sleeping, whether they hold land or not. Moreover, if they are not abiding in villeinage, but wandering abroad through the country, going and returning, they are always under the power of the lords, so long as they return; and when they have lost the habit of returning, they begin to be runaways, after the likeness of tame stags. Moreover, if when they are abroad as merchants or wage-earners they pay chevage at fixed times . . and so long as they pay chevage, they are said to be under the power of the lords, and the lord's power is not loosed. And when they cease to pay they begin to be fugitives . . . and ought to be pursued forthwith." And *ibid*. *f*. 26. "It was said in the King's court before the justices of the Bench at Westminster by John de Metingham and his fellows, justices there, that if a bondman born and bred shall be a runaway . . . and shall have returned and be found on the bond estate where he was born, and be taken there by his true lord or his ministers as a bird in its nest, and this be proved, if such a man venture to deny it in the King's court, he shall be a serf for ever."

3. Deed illustrating the Distribution of Strips
[*Ancient Deeds*, B 4397], 1397.

To all Christ's faithful to whom the present writing shall come, Morgan Gogh, greeting in the Lord. Know ye that I have demised, granted and by this my present writing indented confirmed to John Druwere a cottage with a curtilage situate in Modbury between the cottage of John Janekyns on the east side and the tenement of Thomas Cobbe on the west side, and three acres, one rood of arable land lying in the fields of Modbury, whereof one acre lies in Brokeryg between the lord's land on either side, one acre in Totecombe between the lord's land and the land of Thomas Cobbe, three roods in Brokeryg between the lord's land and the land of William Cockes, a half acre there between the land of Thomas Cobbe and the land of Ralph Smale, and a half acre of meadow lies in Sturtilmede between the meadow of Gilbert Scolemaystre on either side, with pasture for one plough-beast and two draught-beasts in common; which land, meadow and pasture John Pipere lately held for term of his life; to have and to hold all the aforesaid cottage with the curtilage, land, meadow, and pasture, to the aforesaid John for term of his life, of me and my heirs or my assigns freely, quietly, well and in peace, rendering therefor yearly to the aforesaid Morgan and his heirs or his assigns 3*s.* 4*d.* sterling at the four principal terms of the year by equal portions for all services, saving the royal service, and doing suit to my court yearly upon reasonable summons. . . . Nor shall it be lawful for the aforesaid John to demise to any man the said cottage, with the curtilage, land, meadow and pasture, as well in parcels as in whole, during his life, under penalty of loss of the aforesaid cottage with all its appurtenances. . . . In witness whereof the parties aforesaid have interchangeably set their seals to these indentures. These witnesses :—Richard Pokeswell, Thomas Wodham, Robert Grey, John Hunte, John Iryssh and many others. Given at Modbury on Thursday next after Michaelmas, 21 Richard II.

4. Regulation of the Common Fields of Wimeswould
[*Hist. MSS. Com.*, *Middleton MSS.*, *p.* 106], *c.* 1425.

For neat [*i.e.* cattle] pasture we ordain Orrow and Breches, Woldsyke and Wylougbybroke, for to be broken[1] on Crowche-

[1] *i.e.* Thrown open for grazing.

messeday [14 September]; and whoso break this, every man shall pay for each beast that may be taken in any other several pasture a penny to the church; therefor to go a seven nightday [*i.e.*, to endure for a week].

Also, for the neat pasture, after that be eaten, all the wheat-field, to wit, Hardacre field namely, save Strete headlands, where they may not go for destroying of corn; this for to endure another sevennightday under the pain before said.

Also, on Holy Thursday eve we ordain the commons of the Peasfield for horses to be broken, and no other beasts to come therein. For if there be any man that have any horse that is feeble and may not do his work for fault of meat, and this may reasonably be known, let him relieve of his own, so that he save his neighbour from harm, for if any man may . . . which beasts 'lose' in corn or in grass, he shall for each beast pay a penny to the church, and make amends to his neighbour.

Also, on Whitsun eve every man [shall] break his several pasture as he likes, and no man tie his horse on other . . . his own for to be several till Lammas, each man to eat his own, under the pain beforesaid.

Furthermore, if any man . . . plough-oxen for to be relieved on his several grass, let him tie them in his best manner or hold them in, as other men do their horses . . . on no other man's grass going to or fro abroad, as they will pay for each beast a penny to the church and make [amends] . . . to him that has the harm.

Also, if any man tie his horse or reach on any headlands or by brookside into any man's corn, he shall make amends to him that has the harm, and for each foot that is within the corn pay a penny to the church.

Also if any man shall be taken at night time destroying other corn or grass, he shall be punished as the law will, and pay 4*d.* to the church.

Also, all manner of men that have any pease in the field when codding time comes, let them cod in their own lands and in no other man's lands. And other men or women that have no peas of their own growing, let them gather them twice in the week on Wednesday and on Friday, reasonably going in the land-furrows and gathering with their hands and with no sickles, once before noon and no more, for if any man or woman other that has any peas of his own and goes into any other, for each time [he shall] pay a penny to the church and lose his cods, and they that have none and go oftener than it is before said, with sickle or without, shall lose the vessel they gather them in and the cods, and a penny to the church.

Also, no man with common herd nor with shed herd [shall] come on the wold after grass be mown till it be made and led away, but on his own, and then let them go all together in God's name; and if they do, each man pay for his quantity of his beasts a certain to the church, that is for to say, a penny for each beast.

Also, if there be any man that throws in any sheaves on any land for to tie on his horses, he shall make a large amends to them that have the harm, and for each foot pay a penny to the church, but on his own. Furthermore, if any man tie his horse in any stubble and it be mown in reasonable time [he] shall pay the aforesaid pain.

Also, if any man may be taken at nighttime in the field with cart or with bearing of any other carriage in unreasonable time between bell and bell [he shall] pay 40*d.* to the church, save as thus, if any man in peas harvest, he and his servants, in furthering of his work and saving of his corn, bind at morning or till it be moonshine, all other works at nighttime except, save this.

Also, all manner labourers that dwell in the town and have commons among us shall work harvest work and other works for their hire reasonable as custom is, and not to go to other towns but if they have no work or else no man speak to them, so that they may be excused, for if they do, they shall be chastised as the law will.

Also, no man or woman that works harvest work bear home no sheaves of no man's, but if [*i.e.* unless] they be given them well and truly, for if it may be wist, for each sheaf that they bear home without leave [they] shall pay a penny to the church.

Also, no man or woman glean no manner of corn that is able to work for his meat and twopence a day at the least to help to save his neighbour's corn; nor no other gleaners, that may not work, glean in no manner of wise among no sheaves, for if they do, they shall lose the corn and a penny to the church for each burden.

Also, neither common herd nor shed herd come in the wheat

cornfield till the corn be led away, nor in the peas cornfield in the same wise till the peas be led away, and the common herd and shed herd may go together as they should do, on pain of each beast a penny to the church.

Also, that no man take away his beasts from the common herd from Michaelmas tide to Yule to go in the wheatfield to 'lose' the wheat, for if any man may take any beast therein, they shall pay for each beast a penny to the church as often as they may be taken destroying the corn, and the herd [shall pay] his hire.

Also, if our hayward pen a flock of neat of the country, he shall take six pence, for a flock of sheep four pence, and for each horse a penny.

And that our wold be laid in several at Candlemas, for if any herd let his beasts come thereon after, [he shall] pay for each time four pence to the church.

Also, whosoever has any meadows within the corns, my lord or any man else, let make them to 'dele' them out and take a profit of them on God's behalf, and whoso trespass, let make amends.[1]

5. Lease of a Manor to the Tenants [*Cart. Rams.* II, 244], 1279.

To all Christ's faithful who shall see or hear the present writing, William, by the grace of God Abbot of Ramsey, greeting in the Lord.

Know ye that we have demised at farm to our men of Hemingford our manor of Hemingford from Michaelmas in the eighth year of the reign of King Edward, son of King Henry, at the beginning of the ninth, until the end of seven years next following, for 40*l.* sterling to be paid to us therefrom yearly at the four terms, to wit, at Michaelmas 10*l.*, on St. Andrew's Day[2] 10*l.*, at the Annunciation[3] 10*l.* and at Midsummer 10*l.*

Our aforesaid men shall hold the aforesaid manor with all its appurtenances, except the gift of the church when it fall vacant, and our fishery, and the mill, which we have kept in our hand.

[1] This document is defective, and at the best its bucolic English is hard to interpret. [2] November 30. [3] March 25.

Also they shall have all profits of the town except our tallages, sheriff's aid, hundred aid, "wardpenys," and scutage of the lord the King, and except the issues of causes which cannot be determined without us or our bailiffs, of the issue whereof they shall have a moiety, and except view of frankpledge[1] and the Maunde acre and the acres of the reeve of Ramsey.

And be it known that if any customary tenant die without heir of his body, we will demise his land and his messuage to whomsoever we will and keep in our hand the gersum[2] arising thence.

Also no customary tenant shall make fine for relieving or marrying his daughters without our presence, but their gersums shall be made before us in the presence of the reeves or any of the farmers, who shall have and collect the said money towards their farm.

Nor may the said farmers demise house or land to any stranger or one of another's homage, without our special licence.

For we will that such gersums beyond the fixed farm be entirely paid to us.

Moreover the said farmers have received the following stock :—

The corn grange full of corn on either side the door by the door posts and by the beams beyond the door, and so sloping to the roof of the granary.

They have received also the oat barn full of oats by the east door post.

The breadth of the grange was 28 feet within, the length 39 feet, and the east end of the grange is round ; the height in the middle is 19 feet ; and at the side from the door to the curve of the round end the length of the wall is 30 feet, the height $5\frac{1}{2}$ feet.

They have received also a heap of barley 36 feet in length, 11 feet in breadth, 11 feet in height, and 18 feet in breadth in the middle.

[1] In law every man was forced to be in frankpledge, that is, to be one of a group, each member of which was responsible for the others' good behaviour. The 'view' was a half yearly survey of such groups, at which offences were presented and punished.

[2] Fine.

Moreover they shall be quit of a serjeant[1] in autumn every year except in the last year, in which they shall have a serjeant, by whose view, according to the custom of the abbey, the stock shall be made up.

They shall also be quit of our yearly lodging due, except that as often as we shall come there they shall find for us salt, straw and hay without an account.

And at the end of the seven years they shall render to us the aforesaid manor with the stock with which they received it.

Also they shall give back the land well ploughed twice.

And be it known that the fruits which were then in the barn ought to be counted for the first year, because they were of our stock.

In witness of which demise of the land and the manor we have caused our seal to be set to this present writing.[2]

6. Grant of a Manor by a Lord to the Customary Tenants at Fee Farm [*Patent Roll*, 6 *Edward III*, *p.* 2, *m.* 27], *ante* 1272.

The King to all to whom, etc., greeting. We have inspected a writing which Richard, sometime earl of Cornwall, made to his customary tenants of his manor of Corsham in these words:—

To all to whom the present writing shall come, Richard, earl of Cornwall, greeting. Know all of you that we have demised and granted and by our present writing confirmed for us and our heirs to all our customary tenants of our manor of Corsham all our manor of Corsham, with the rents, demesnes, meadows, feedings and pastures to the said manor pertaining, saving to us a third part of the meadow of Myntemede, which third part the said customary tenants shall mow, carry and cock at their own costs, saving also to us the site of our fish-pond, our parks, our warren, pleas, perquisites and all escheats which can escheat to us or our successors; to have and to hold to the said customary tenants and their successors of us and of our heirs for ever, for 110 marks to us and our heirs or assigns yearly to be paid to our bailiff in the said manor at two terms of the year, to wit, on the octave of Easter 55 marks and on the octave of Michaelmas 55 marks, for all services and demands

[1] *i.e.* Free from the inspection and audit of the lord's officer.

[2] This document is of great interest as an instance of an early stock-and-land lease.

to us or to our heirs or assigns belonging, saving to us all the things aforenamed. And we will that our said customary tenants for ever be quit of tallage and view of frankpledge and all other customs and services to us or to our heirs pertaining. Our aforesaid customary tenants, however, have granted for them and their successors that, if they keep not this covenant according to the form of the present writing, all their tenements which they hold of us shall revert to us and our heirs without any contradiction, if it be through them that the form of this writing be not kept. We will also and we grant that if any of our said customary tenants of our said manor of Corsham be rebellious, contravening the form of this writing, our bailiff for the time being shall have power to distrain him by lands and chattels to observe more fully all the things abovesaid according to the tenour of this writing. And in witness thereof we have caused our seal to be set to this writing. These witnesses :—Sir Richard de Turry, Sir Sampson de la Bokxe, Sir Henry Crok, Sir Philip de Eya, Walter Galun, then bailiff, Martin de Hortham, Sir Gilbert, then prior of Corsham, Richard de Cumberwell, Ralph, then vicar of Corsham, and others.[1]

And we, ratifying and approving the demise, grant and confirmation aforesaid, grant and confirm them for us and our heirs, as far as in us lies, to the aforesaid customary tenants and their successors, as the writing aforesaid reasonably testifies, and as they now hold the manor aforesaid with the appurtenances, and they and their ancestors and predecessors have held that manor hitherto, and have reasonably used and enjoyed the liberties aforesaid, saving to us a third part of the said meadow of Myntemede and the site of the fishpond, the parks, warren, pleas, perquisites and all escheats abovesaid, as is aforesaid. In witness whereof, etc. Witness the King at Woodstock, 1 July. By a fine of 5 marks. Wilts.

7. Lease of Manorial Holdings [*Fine Roll*, 10 *Edward III*, *m.* 7], 1332.

The King to all to whom, etc., greeting. We have inspected a writing which John late earl of Cornwall, our brother, now deceased, made in these words :

[1] The date of the original deed must be earlier than 1272, in which year the earl died.

John, son of the illustrious King of England, earl of Cornwall, to all and singular who shall see or hear the present writing indented, greeting in the Lord. Know ye that, having regard to the no small decrease and decay of rents and farms pertaining to our manor of Kirton in Lindsey in times past, for that tenants of escheated tenements in the same manor, having no estate of the same tenements save from year to year or at least at the will of the lords, our predecessors there, have made no outlay or the least which they could on the maintenance of the buildings on the same tenements; and wishing to raise again the aforesaid rents and farms as much as we can for our advantage; we have granted for us and our heirs and by our present writing have demised to John of Westminster and Emma his wife and Thomas, son of the same John and Emma, those two parts of all those tenements with the appurtenances in the town of Kirton aforesaid which the same John before the making of this writing held of us during our pleasure, as of an escheat formerly in our hand of the tenements which were sometime of Thomas of Bromholm; to have and to hold to the same John and Emma his wife and Thomas, son of the same John and Emma, and each of them that lives the longer, for their whole life, of us and our heirs, rendering therefrom yearly to us and our heirs 100*s.* sterling at the feasts of Easter and Michaelmas by equal portions; and we, the aforesaid earl, and our heirs will warrant the aforesaid two parts of the tenements aforesaid with their appurtenances to the aforesaid John and Emma his wife and Thomas, son of the same John and Emma, for their whole life, as is aforesaid, against all people for the aforesaid rent. In witness whereof we have thought fit to set our seal to this writing. These witnesses:—Sirs John de Haustede, Thomas de Westone and William de Cusancia, knights, Sir William de Cusancia, rector of the church of Wakefield, our treasurer, and William de Munden, our clerk and secretary, and others. Given at York on Tuesday next after the feast of All Saints in the 6th year of the reign of King Edward the Third after the Conquest, our dearest brother.

And we, ratifying and approving the demise aforesaid, grant and confirm it for us and our heirs, as much as in us lies, as the writing aforesaid reasonably testifies, willing and granting for us and our heirs that the same John, Emma and Thomas have and hold the tenements aforesaid with the appurtenances for the whole life of each of them by the aforesaid service of rendering to us and our heirs yearly the said 100*s*. according to the tenour of the writing of the same earl abovesaid. In witness whereof etc. Witness the King at Leicester, 1 October.

By the King himself.

8. An Agreement Between Lord and Tenants [*Duchy of Lancaster*, *Misc. Bks.*, 5, *f.* 103], 1386.

Warkington.—At the view of frankpledge holden there on 20 October, 10 Richard II., it was granted to all the lord's tenants in the presence of John Mulso, Nicholas Lovet, Edmund Bifeld, Stephen Walker of Keteryng and others there present, that if it pleased the lord they might hold certain bond lands and tenements at a certain rent and service, as follows, during a term of six years next after the date abovewritten, the term beginning at Michaelmas last past; to wit, that each tenant of a messuage and a virgate of bond land shall render to the lord 18*s*. yearly at four terms, to wit, at the feasts of St. Edmund the King and Martyr,[1] Palm Sunday, the Nativity of St. John the Baptist,[2] and Michaelmas, by equal portions, and shall do two ploughings a year at what times of the year he shall be forewarned by the bailiff of the manor for the time being, and shall work in "le Keormede" as he used before, save that the lord shall find him food and drink for the ancient customs, that is, for half a sheep and for each scythe ½d., and so he shall reap in Autumn for two days, to wit, one day with two men and another day with one man, at the lord's dinner[3]; he shall give 4*d*. for a colt if he sell it, he shall pay heriot if he die within the term, and he shall make fine for marrying his daughters and for his sons attending school, and for "leyrewite" as he used before.[4]

9. Complaints Against a Reeve [*Court Rolls*, 179, 4, *m*. 1*d*.], 1278.[5]

Elton.—St. Clement's Day.[6] Michael the Reeve complains of Richer son of Jocelin and Richard the Reeve and his wife that when he was in the churchyard of Elton on the Sunday

[1] November 20. [2] June 24. [3] *i.e.* The lord providing dinner.
[4] The lord here is the Abbot of Bury St. Edmunds.
[5] Printed in Selden Society Publications, II., 95. [6] November 23.

next before the feast of All Saints[1] in this year, there came the aforesaid Richer, Richard and his wife and insulted him with vile words before the whole parish, charging him with having collected his own hay by the labour services due to the lord the Abbot [of Ramsey], and with having reaped his own corn in autumn by the boon-works done by the Abbot's customary tenants, and with having ploughed his land in Everesholmfeld with ploughs "booned" from the town, and with having released to the customary tenants their works and carryings on condition that they demised and leased their lands to him at a low price, and with having taken gifts from the rich tenants that they should not become tenants at a money rent, and with having put the poor tenants at a money rent.[2] And the aforesaid Richard and Richer are present and deny, etc. and ask for an enquiry by twelve jurors. Who come and say that the said Michael is guilty of none of the charges. Therefore the said Richard and Richer shall satisfy him, and for the trespass shall be in mercy; Richard's fine, 2*s.*, pledge William son of James; Richer's fine, 12*d.*, pledge, Jocelin. And the damages are taxed at 10*s.* to be received from Richard the Reeve, which sum Michael has released except 2*s.*

10. An Eviction from Copyhold Land [*Chancery Proceedings, Early*, 16, 376], *temp.* Henry IV-Henry VI.

To the most reverend father in God, the Archbishop of Canterbury, Chancellor of England.

Beseecheth lowly your poor bedefolks, Elizabeth Baroun, Harry Baroun and Richard Baroun, which be the King's tenants, that whereas the said Elizabeth was possessed and seised of a messuage and 4 acres of land in the town of Great Hormead in the shire of Hertford, and the said messuage and land held to her and to her heirs at the will of my lord of Oxford as of his manor of Hormead in the same shire by copy of court roll after the custom of the said manor, there hath one Harry Edmond, farmer of the said manor, without cause reasonable and contrary to the custom of the said manor, entered in the said messuage and land and put out the said Elizabeth, and

[1] November 1.
[2] The commutation of services for rent was not always popular.

certain goods and chattels of the said Elizabeth, Harry and Richard, to the value of 40 marks in the said house being, seized, and it withholdeth, and over that the said Harry Edmond with his adherents daily lie in wait to beat and slay the said Harry and Richard, your beseechers, so that they dare not well abide in their houses neither go about their husbandry, to their uttermost destruction and undoing for ever, without succour of your gracious lordship: Please your good grace to consider the premises and that your said beseechers have no remedy at the Common Law, to grant a writ directed to the said Harry Edmond, commanding him to appear before you at a certain day upon a certain pain by you to be limited, to be examined of the premises, and thereupon to do that good faith and conscience require, and that for the love of God and in way of charity.

This is the answer of Harry Edmond to the bill of Elizabeth Baron, Harry Baron and Richard Baron, in the Chancery.

First, whereas it is surmised by the said Elizabeth that she was possessed and seised of a messuage and four acres of land in the town of Great Hormead in the shire of Hertford, and the said messuage and land held to her and to her heirs at the will of my lord of Oxford as of his manor of Hormead in the same shire by copy of court roll after the custom of the said manor, and that the said Harry Edmond, farmer of the same manor, without cause reasonable and contrary to the custom of the said manor, entered into the said messuage and land and put out the said Elizabeth: The said Harry saith that the said messuage and land be holden of my said lord of Oxford bondly at the will of my said lord as of his said manor by the services of three shillings and halfpenny of yearly rent and by a certain service called the common fine, as it falleth more or less after the entries and . . . . of the tenants of the said manor by the custom of the said manor, by cause whereof the said Harry with one Thomas Denys, under-steward of the court of the said manor, by the commandment of my said lord of Oxford entered into the said messuage and land, after which entry my said lord let the said messuage and land to the said Harry for term of years, by virtue of which lease he [entered] the said messuage and land, as lawful is for him, which matter the said

Harry is ready to prove as this Court will [award], and prayeth as for that to be dismissed out of this Court.

[And as for t]he seizing and withholding of certain goods and chattels of the said Elizabeth, Harry Baron and Richard, to the value of [40 marks, as is sur]mised by the said bill, the said Harry Edmond saith that the seizing and withholding of the said goods and chattels is a matter determinable at the Common Law, and not in this Court of the Chancery. Wherefore as for that he prayeth to be dismissed out of this Court.

And as for the declaration of the said Harry as for the said goods and chattels, the said Harry saith that he never seized nor withheld the said goods and chattels neither no parcel thereof, as it is surmised by the said bill, which matter the said Harry Edmond is ready to prove as the Court will award, if the Court rule him thereto.

And as for the lying in await surmised by the said bill the said Harry Edmond saith that the said lying in await is matter determinable by the Common Law and not in this Court of the Chancery, wherefore as for that matter he prayeth to be dismissed out of this Court of the Chancery. But, for the declaration of the said Harry Edmond in that matter, the said Harry Edmond saith that he never lay in await neither to beat nor to slay the said Harry Baron nor the said Richard, as they surmise by their said bill, which matter the said Harry Edmond is ready to prove as this Court will award, if the said Court will rule him thereto.[1]

11. Statute of Merton, c. 4 [*Statutes of the Realm, Vol. I, p.* 2], 1235–6.

Also, because many great men of England, who have enfeoffed their knights and freeholders of small tenements in their great manors, have complained that they cannot make their profit of the residue of their manors, as of wastes, woods, and pastures, though the same feoffees have sufficient pasture, as much as belongs to their tenements: it is thus provided and

[1] This case illustrates first, the protection coming to be given by Chancery to villein or customary tenure, and second, the growing desire of lords to substitute leasehold for copyhold, a process which began at least as early as the beginning of the fourteenth century; see No. 7 above, and Part II., Section I.; *cf.* also Savine, in E.H.R. xvii., 296.

granted, that when any persons so enfeoffed bring an assize of novel disseisin touching their common of pasture, and it is acknowledged before the justices that they have as much pasture as suffices for their tenements, and that they have free entry and issue from their tenements into their pasture, then they shall be content therewith ; and they of whom they had complained shall go quit of the profit which they have made of the lands, wastes, woods, and pastures ; and if they allege that they have not sufficient pasture, or sufficient entry and issue as belongs to their tenements, then the truth shall be inquired by assize ; and if it be acknowledged by the assize that their entry or issue is in any way hindered by the same [deforcers] or that they have not sufficient pasture and sufficient entry and issue, as is aforesaid, then shall they recover their seisin by view of the jurors : so that by their discretion and oath, the plaintiffs shall have sufficient pasture and sufficient entry and issue in form aforesaid, and the disseisors shall be in the mercy of the lord the King, and shall yield damages, as they ought to have rendered before this provision. And if it be acknowledged by the assize that the plaintiffs have sufficient pasture with free and sufficient entry and issue, as is aforesaid, then the others may make their profit lawfully of the residue, and go quit of that assize.

12. An Enclosure Allowed [*Bracton's Note-Book*, III, 212, *No.* 1198], 1236–7.

The assize comes to recognise if Elias of Leyburn unjustly etc. disseised Wymar of Leyburn of common of his pasture pertaining to his free tenement in the same town of Leyburn after, etc.[1]

And Elias comes and says that an assize ought not to be made thereof because that pasture belonged to five lords, and a covenant was made between the lords that each should make his profit of his part, and by this covenant he caused his part to be tilled, and thereof he put himself on a jury.

The jurors say that the wood was at one time common, in such wise that there were five sharers who had the wood common, and afterwards by their consent a partition was made between them that each should have his part in severalty, and

[1] *sc.* The King's last return from Brittany.

it was granted that each might assart[1] his part and grow corn, saving however to each of them common of herbage after the corn was carried, and most of them assarted their part, but the wood whereof complaint is made was not then assarted, and because he to whom the wood pertains has now assarted a part, the said Wymar has brought a writ of *novel disseisin*. But because it is acknowledged that the wood was thus partitioned among the sharers, it is decided that the aforesaid Elias has not disseised him, and so Elias is dismissed *sine die* and Wymar is in mercy. And it shall be lawful for each sharer to assart his wood, saving to each of them common of his pasture after the corn and hay is carried.

13. An Enclosure Disallowed [*Bracton's Note-Book*, III, 211, *No.* 1196], 1236–7

The assize comes to recognise if Robert de Fislake unjustly etc. raised a dyke in Woodhouse to the injury of the free tenement of Adam de Bladewrthe in the same town after etc.[2] Whereon Adam complains that Robert caused to be enclosed a meadow lying near his land, in which he ought to have common of herbage after hay-carrying, and that it ought to lie to pasture every third year with the fallow, wherefore he says that the dyke is to his injury and puts himself on a jury thereof. And Robert does the like.

The jurors say that the aforesaid Adam always used to have common in that meadow and in the land of Robert by that meadow after the corn and hay were carried, and when the land lay fallow, then in both meadow and fallow, and Robert caused the meadow to be enclosed so that Adam can have no entry to that pasture. And so it is awarded that the dyke be thrown down, and the meadow made as it should be, so that the aforesaid Adam have entry and issue, and that Robert be in mercy, etc.

14. A Villein on Ancient Demesne Dismissed to his Lord's Court [*Bracton's Note-Book*, III, 65. *No.* 1030], 1224.

The assize comes to recognise if Bartholomew son of Eustace unjustly and without a judgment disseised William son of

[1] Bring into cultivation. [2] *sc.* The king's last return from Brittany.

Henry of his free tenement in Pilton after the last, etc. And Bartholomew comes and says that the assize ought not to be made thereof because the said William held the tenement only in villeinage, and is his villein, and does for him all customs such as ploughings and others, and says further that he cannot marry his daughter save by his lord's licence etc.

And William son of Henry comes and says that he is a free man and that he holds his tenement freely and that at another time he impleaded in the court of the lord the King as a free man touching the aforesaid tenement, to wit, touching the services and the like, and thereof he brings the rolls of Sir Martin de Patteshull to warrant and likewise a writ which the same Martin wrote with his own hand, which also was sent to the sheriff of Rutland for the same plea, and the sheriff's clerk has shown him the writ, etc. A day is given to hear his judgment on such a day, etc.

On the day the court records at Westminster that the same William in the time of King John was convicted at Bedford of owing villein customs from that tenement, such as ploughing, reaping and many others at his own food, and of being unable to marry his daughter or sister without licence of his lord. And so it is decided that the assize of *novel disseisin* does not lie because the tenement is not free, and so William is in mercy. And if he will, let him plead in the manor by writ of right.

15. Claim to be on Ancient Demesne defeated (*Bracton's Note-Book*, III, 250, *No.* 1237], 1237–8.

The men of the Prior and convent of St. Swithin of Crondall, Hurstbourne and Whitchurch, complained to the lord the King that whereas they had been granted to the same Prior and convent and their church in pure and perpetual alms by the ancestors of the lord the King, the Prior and convent demanded of them other customs and services than they used to do in the times in which they were in the hands of the aforesaid predecessors, etc.

And Oliver the Steward and Horder come and say that they demand no other services than the men used and ought to do, and that the lands were never in the hands of the ancestors of the lord the King, because two hundred years before the conquest of England they were given to the Prior and Convent of

St. Swithin and by others than Kings, to wit, earls and others, etc., and then they owed and used to do whatever was commanded them. But in process of time, when the priory was well nigh destroyed by one Abbot Robert,[1] bishop Richard came and for the profit of the Prior and convent disposed of their lands and manors in such wise that he caused an inventory to be made of the holdings and of the names of the tenants and their services, as well tenants in villeinage as in frank fee, and so that he demanded no other services than they did then and were then set forth in the inventory. Afterwards however when the lands were in the hand of farmers at one time and at one time in the hand of the aforesaid villeins for forty years,[2] the farmers remitted to them certain services and customs for money. And when the lands were in the hand of the aforesaid villeins they detained and withheld the rent to the sum of 60*s.* and more, and also a great amount of corn, and withheld a great amount of the lands contrary to the aforesaid enrolment made by the aforesaid bishop Richard. And because the aforesaid men acknowledge that they are villeins, as is aforesaid, and because they cannot deny these things, they are told to do to the Prior and convent the services and customs which they used to do. And the lord the King will not meddle with them since they were never in the hand of him or his ancestors, etc.

16. The Little Writ of Right [*Court Rolls*, 172, 27], 1390.

Richard by the grace of God King of England and France and Lord of Ireland to the bailiffs of Anne, Queen of England, our beloved Consort, of Havering atte Bower, greeting. We command you that without delay and according to the custom of the manor of Havering atte Bower you do (*teneatis*) full right to John de Lancastre of Hatfield Broadoak touching 40*s.* of rent with the appurtenances in Havering atte Bower, of which John Organ, citizen and mercer of London, and Margery his wife deforce him; that we may hear no further complaint thereof for default of right. Witness myself at Westminster the 30th day of January in the thirteenth year of our reign.

[1] 1174–1188. [2] For a similar lease to tenants see No. 5.

17. Villeinage Established [*Bracton's Note-Book*, III, 119, *No.* 1103], 1225.

A jury comes by consent of the parties [to recognise] whether William son of Henry and his ancestors held two parts of a bovate of land with the appurtenances in Pilton in villeinage of the ancestors of Bartholomew son of Eustace, doing these underwritten customs, to wit, 3*s.* 4*d.* a year of farm, and at Christmas 4 hens, and at the summons of Bartholomew, between Christmas and the Purification, one feast, and whether in Lent he ought to plough for one day at his own food, and to harrow for one day at his own food, and on Easter day to give 20 eggs, and in summer to plough for one day at the dinner of Bartholomew,[1] to reap for one day at the food of Bartholomew, to wit, twice a day, and for one day to carry his hay at the food of the same Bartholomew, and in autumn to do boon-work for Bartholomew, with his whole household except his wife, and for Bartholomew's loveboon to find a man at his own food, and in winter to plough for one day at Bartholomew's dinner, and whether, if he wish to marry his daughter or his sister, he shall make fine with Bartholomew as best he may; or whether William or his ancestors have held the land freely, rendering 3*s.* 4*d.* a year and doing foreign service for all service, etc.

The jurors say that the same William and his ancestors used and ought to do all the aforesaid customs which Bartholomew demands, to wit, from 1 bovate of land with the appurtenances, except that on Christmas day when he renders hens he ought to eat with Bartholomew on the same day, and furthermore that they never saw him sell a daughter or sister or give merchet or marry, but have seen that Bartholomew sold to Ralph Cayllard John, brother of William by the same father and mother, for 40*s.*, and the same Ralph did with him his will.

And so it is awarded that William is convicted of villeinage, and if he will do the aforesaid customs, let him hold the bovate of land by the same customs, but if not, let Bartholomew do his will with the land and with William as with his villein, and let him be delivered to him.

[1] *i.e.* Bartholomew providing dinner.

18. Freedom and Freehold Established [*Bracton's Note-Book*, III, 224, *No.* 1210], 1236–7.

The assize comes to recognise if Thomas de Sumerdeby and many others disseised Roger Gladewine of his free tenement in Spitelgate after etc.,[1] whereof he complains that they disseised him of 2½ acres and a toft.

And Thomas and the others come and say that the same Roger is a villein and the tenement whereof view is made is villeinage, and thereof they put themselves on a jury. And Roger says that he is a free man and the tenement is free, and that his ancestors were free men and held freely, and thereof he puts himself on a jury.

The jurors say that the aforesaid Roger holds his tenement in the same town by 2*s.* a year and by two works in autumn at his lord's food, and he shall give two hens at Christmas and eat with his lord. And questioned if he or any of his ancestors had given merchet for marrying his daughter, they say, No. Questioned if he had ever been tallaged, they say, No. And the aforesaid Thomas, questioned if others of his fee do other villein services, he says that others do all manner of villein services. And because he does no service save the aforesaid money payment and the services named, nor gives merchet for a daughter, nor is tallaged, therefore it is awarded that he held freely and that he recover his seisin, and Thomas and the others are in mercy.

19. A Villein Pleads Villeinage on one Occasion and Denies it on Another [*Bracton's Note-Book*, III, 364, *No.* 1411], 1220.

Hamelin son of Ralph was attached to answer Hugh de Gundevill wherefore he brought an assize of *novel disseisin* against the aforesaid Hugh, his lord, touching a tenement in Pinpre, inasmuch as he is a villein and acknowledged himself to be the villein of the aforesaid Hugh's father in the time of the lord King John, etc. before the justices in eyre at Sherborne, as the same Hugh says, and thereon shows that Simon de Patteshull, Eustace de Faucumberge and others their fellows were then justices. And that Thomas acknowledged himself

[1] *sc.* The King's last return from Brittany.

to be his father's villein, as is aforesaid, he puts himself on the record of the court and on the rolls, etc.

And Hamelin comes and denies that he is a villein or ever acknowledged himself to be a villein in the court of the lord the King, as Hugh says, and thereof puts himself in like manner on the record of the court. But he will speak the truth. He says that at that time, to wit, in the eyre of the justices, he held certain land in villeinage which he had bought, and then acknowledged that the land was villeinage, and specifically denies that he ever acknowledged himself to be a villein. The rolls of the eyre are searched, and there it is recorded that one Osbert Crede brought an assize of *mort d'ancestor* in respect of the death of Henry his brother against Hamelin touching a carucate of land with the appurtenances in Pinpre, in such wise that Hamelin answered against the assize that it ought not to proceed because he could not gain or lose that land, because he was the villein of Hugh de Gundevill, father of the aforesaid Hugh. And this was found in many rolls, and when Hamelin should have had his judgment, he absented himself and withdrew without licence, whereupon the sheriff was ordered to have his body on such a day, etc., to hear his judgment thereof, etc. And on that day he came not, and the sheriff reported that he had withdrawn himself and could not be found, wherefore the sheriff was ordered to take the whole of Hamelin's land into the hand of the lord the King, and to keep it safely, etc., because Hamelin withdrew himself and would not stand to right touching Hugh's complaint of him, and to certify the justices of what he should do thereof on such a day etc. On that day Hamelin came not and the sheriff reported that he had taken his land into the hand of the lord the King.

And because the court records that Hamelin acknowledged himself to be a villein, and Hugh afterwards by the aforesaid assize of *novel disseisin* lost his land, it is decided that Hugh recover seisin of that land whereon the assize was taken, and that he have Hamelin as his villein convicted, and that the assize of *novel disseisin* which was taken thereof be held void, and that Hugh be quit of the mercy wherein he was put for that disseisin. And the sheriff is ordered to make diligent enquiry who were the jurors of that assize and to have them on such a day, etc., to hear the judgment on them for the oath which they made thereof. And if Hamelin held any tenement of Hugh, let Hugh do therewith as with his own, etc.

20. An Assize Allowed to a Villein [*Bracton's Note-Book*, III, 527, *No.* 1681], 1225.

The justices in eyre in the county of Essex were ordered to take a grand assize between Thomas of Woodford, claimant, and John de la Hille, tenant, of a virgate and a half of land with the appurtenances in Woodford. And the said John and Thomas came before the justices at Chelmsford and offered themselves, and the bailiff of the Abbot of Waltham came and said both claimant and tenant were villeins, and the tenement was the Abbot's villeinage and therefore the assize thereof ought not to proceed. He was questioned by the tenant whether the latter was a villein or not, and he said Yes, asserting that the said tenement was the Abbot's villeinage.

And Thomas comes [and says] that this ought not to hurt him, because when he impleaded the aforesaid John in the court of the lord Abbot by writ of the lord the King, no mention was made by the Abbot nor by John that the tenement was villeinage nor that John was a villein, but because the Abbot failed to do him right in his court, Thomas went to the county court and complained in the county court that the lord Abbot had failed to do him right in his court, and the Abbot, summoned hereon, came not, and the suit proceeded so far in the county court that the tenant asked and obtained view of the land. Afterwards he put himself on a grand assize as to which of the two had greater right in the aforesaid land without any challenge of villeinage being made on the part of the Abbot or of John. And this he sought to be allowed him.

And the Abbot's bailiff comes and denies the whole, as the court of the lord the King should award. And he said that unknown to the Abbot and without his court failing to do Thomas right, the suit was taken away to the county court, and this he asked to be allowed him. And owing to the doubt a day was given to the parties at Westminster, etc. And because the Abbot permitted John to be impleaded in his court first and in the county court afterwards until he put himself on a grand assize, the Abbot not having lodged the claim which he should have made, it is awarded that the assize proceed.

21. A Freeman Holding in Villeinage [*Bracton's Note-Book*, II, 233, *No.* 281], 1228.

William de Bissopestun, William de Ludington and Geoffrey de Cherlescote, knights, whom the lord the King appointed as justices to take an assize of *novel disseisin* which Thomas son of Adam arraigned against Ralph, Prior of Stiffleppe, and many others, of a tenement in Aldrestun, [were summoned] to make a record of that assize before the justices at Westminster, and to certify the same justices how far the process in the same assize was carried, and the same Thomas was summoned to hear that record. And William and Geoffrey come and record that the assize came to recognise before them if the aforesaid Prior and Thomas son of Payn and Gilbert son of Henry [and] Osmar le Bracur unjustly and without a judgment and after the last, etc., disseised the aforesaid Thomas son of Adam of his free tenement in Aldredestun. And the Prior came before them, and, being asked if he wished to say anything against the assize, said that the assize ought not to be made thereof, because the same tenement was his villeinage, and the same Thomas was his villein and owed villein customs as did all others of the aforesaid manor, such as ploughings and reapings, and he could not marry his daughter as a freeman could.

And Thomas acknowledged that he owed certain customs at the Prior's food, and that he owed him a rent and a fixed fine for his daughter, and said that he was a free man and held freely of the Prior, and thereof put himself on a jury. And hereon a jury was taken and the jurors said that they (the aforesaid Prior and others) disseised him of his free tenement, and after the term,[1] and the damage was taxed and estimated at two marks.

And the Prior says that in part their record is correct, but they say too little, because the jurors said that Thomas ought to give 12*d.* for marrying his daughter, and owed many other customs; and he and his fellows sought respite that they might have the opinion of Sir Robert de Lexinton whether this was a free tenement from which they know what the tenant ought to do and what not; and they could have no respite.

And the justices deny all this, and say that the jurors said

[1] *i.e.* And after the king's last return from Brittany

nothing of the 12*d*.[1] And so it was awarded that the justices made a right judgment, and so they are quit thereof; and let the Prior be in mercy, and proceed further against Thomas if he will.[2]

22. Land Held by Charter Recovered from the Lord [*Bracton's Note-Book*, III, 622, *No*. 1814], 1227.

The assize comes to recognise if William de Sufford and Reynold de Sufford unjustly etc. disseised William the Tailor of his free tenement in Lodenes after the last, etc. And William comes and grants the assize, and Reynold comes not, and it is not known who he is, etc.

The jurors say that the father of the aforesaid William the Tailor was a villein of Roger, father of the aforesaid William de Sufford, and he held of him in villeinage all his life, and after his death Roger came and gave to William the Tailor a messuage and an acre and a rood of land to hold freely for a mark which William the Tailor gave to him, so that he should hold the land for 8*d*. a year and for foreign service, and so William the Tailor held the land and messuage the whole of Roger's life, and after his decease William the Tailor came to the aforesaid William de Sufford and to his mother and gave them 5*s*. to hold the land as he held it before, and so held it until William de Sufford unjustly disseised him. And so it is awarded that William the Tailor recover his seisin, etc.[3]

23. The Manumission of a Villein [*Ancient Deeds*, A 10279], 1334.

Be it manifest to all by these presents that we, brother Robert, Abbot of Stoneleigh, and the convent of the same place, have granted for us and our successors that Geoffrey son of the late

[1] 2*d*. in the text.

[2] On this case Bracton's comment runs: "Note the exception opposed that the complainant was a villein because he did villein services and customs, but fixed, and knew well what and how much. Answer, that though he did villein customs, he was free as to his body. And he did fixed customs and services, a thing which a villein holding villeinage cannot do."

[3] On this case Bracton's comment runs: "Note that a villein's son recovered by assize of novel disseisin land which his father held in villeinage, because the villein's lord gave it to the son by charter, even without manumission."

William Austyn of Wottonhull be free of his body with all his brood and his chattels hereafter for ever; so that neither we nor our successors shall be able to demand or claim anything in him or his brood or his chattels, but by these presents we are wholly excluded. In witness whereof we have put our seal to these presents. Given at Stonle on Monday next after the feast of the Purification of the Blessed Virgin Mary[1] in the eighth year of the reign of King Edward the third after the conquest.

24. Grant of a Bondman [*Duchy of Lancaster*, *Misc. Bks.*, 8, *f.* 81 *d.*], 1358.

To all who shall see or hear this writing, Geoffrey, by divine permission Abbot of Selby, and the Convent of the same place, greeting in the Lord. Know ye that we, with the unanimous consent of our chapter, have given, granted and by this our present charter confirmed to John de Petreburgh John son of William de Stormesworth, our bondman, with all his brood and all his chattels, so that the aforesaid John with all his brood and all his chattels, as is aforesaid, remain henceforth for ever, in respect of us and our successors, free, at large, and quit of all bond of serfdom, so that neither we nor our successors nor any man in our name shall be able henceforth to demand, claim or have any right or claim or any action in the aforesaid John, his brood or his chattels, by reason of serfdom, villeinage or bondage. In witness whereof our common seal is appended to these presents. Given at Selby in our chapter-house on the 10th day of the month of June, A.D. 1358.

25. Imprisonment of a Gentleman Claimed as a Bondman [*Patent Roll*, 25 *Henry VI*, *p.* 2, *m.* 9], 1447.

The King to all to whom, etc., greeting. Know ye that whereas Humphrey, late duke of Gloucester, lately seised of the manor of Bowcombe in the Isle of Wight in the county of Southampton in his demesne as of fee or at least fee tail, lately, upon undue information given to him, claiming one John Whithorne of the county of Wiltshire, gentleman, to be his bondman belonging to him as it were to the manor aforesaid, caused the same John to be taken by his ministers and ser-

[1] Monday after February 2.

vants, and all the lands and tenements of the same John, to wit, 60 messuages, 6 tofts, one dovecote, 600 acres of land, 30 acres of meadow, 6 acres of pasture and 6*s*. 8*d*. of rent with the appurtenances in the city of Salisbury, Fisherton Anger, Middle Winterslow and West Winterslow, Woodmanton, Burchalk, Bulbridge, Ugford St. James, Wilton, Foulston, Barford St. Martin, Fonthill Gifford, Sharnton, Ashton Gifford, Babeton, Deptford, Wily, Alderbury and Avon, in the said county of Wilts, to be seized into his hands, and certain goods and chattels of the same John being at Wilton in the said county of Wilts likewise to be taken into his hands, and the same John to be brought to the same late duke's castle of Pembroke in Wales, where the same late duke imprisoned the same John and detained him there in prisons so dire, in a dungeon so obscure and dark, in such great hunger, misery of life, deprivation of food and clothes, and imposition on the same John of imprisonment, duress and divers other hardships and miseries, putting aside and abandoning all pity, for seven years and more, that the same John by occasion thereof has totally lost the sight of his eyes, miserably incurring bodily blindness for the term of his life and other incurable infirmities, as we have learned ; which messuages, tofts, dovecote, land, meadow, pasture and rent, by and after the death of the aforesaid late duke, have descended to us as kinsman and heir of the same late duke : And now we, being credibly informed upon the truth of the matter in this behalf, have learned from trustworthy testimony that the aforesaid John has always been and is a freeman and of free condition, never infected with the taint of villeinage, and that all the premises, done and brought upon him so enormously and opprobriously as well in his person as in his tenements and goods and chattels aforesaid, as is aforesaid, were done and perpetrated unduly and unjustly of great malice and insatiable avarice against all conscience : We, duly weighing all and singular the premises, and wishing due reformation of such and so great damages, oppressions, injuries and grievances, to be made and had, as far as in us lies, of our especial grace and of our certain knowledge and mere motion and in true execution and due completion of justice, by the tenour of these presents have deemed fit to remove and in fact by these presents we have removed our hands from the messuages, tofts, dovecote, land, meadow, pasture and rent aforesaid, with the appurtenances and with knights' fees, advowsons of churches and other ecclesiastical benefices whatsoever, franchises, liberties and all other things pertaining or belonging to the same, and by these presents have restored the same John to and into those messuages . . . and by these presents we give and grant the same . . . with all and all manner of issues . . . from the time of the death of the said late duke forthcoming or received, to have and hold those messuages . . . to him, his heirs and assigns, of the chief lords of that fee by the services therefrom due and accustomed for ever, as freely, well, entirely, peaceably and quietly as the same John had held or occupied the messuages . . . before the seisin aforesaid made by the aforesaid late duke or his servants or ministers. . . . In witness whereof, etc., Witness the King at Westminster, 16 July.

By the King himself and of the date aforesaid by authority of Parliament.

26. Claim to a Villein [*Early Chancery Proceedings*, 16, 436], *temp.* Henry IV–Henry VI.

To the most reverend father in God, the archbishop of Canterbury, and chancellor of England.

Beseecheth meekly your poor bedeman, John Bishop, that where he late was in his house at Hamble-en-le-Rice in the county of Southampton the 12th day of March last past in God's peace and the King's, there came John Wayte, Richard Newport and John Newport with thirteen other persons in their company arrayed in manner of war, and in full riotous wise in forcible manner there and then entered the house of your said beseecher about midnight, and him lying in his bed took, seized and imprisoned, and his purse with 25*s.* of money therein and the keys of his coffers from him took and the same coffers opened and 28*l.* of his money, 2 standing cups of silver gilt, 7 flat pieces of silver, 2 masers, 6 girdles and a baselard harnessed with silver, of the goods and chattels of William Poleyn of the value of 40*l.* there being in the keeping of your said beseecher, and 5 pieces of kerseys and the stuff of household of your said beseecher to the value of 30*l.* there found, took and bare away, and him from thence the same night to Sydyngworth led and in horrible strait prison kept by the space of two days, and from thence him carried to a place called Spereshot's place in the same [town] and him there in full strait grievous prison in stocks kept still by the space of five days and other full great wrongs to him did against the peace of the King our sovereign lord to the utter destruction of the body of your said beseecher, which is not of power to sue his remedy by the common law, and importable loss of his goods but if more sooner remedy be had for him in this behalf. Please it your gracious lordship to grant several writs to be directed to the said John Wayte, Richard Newport and John Newport, commanding them to appear before you at a certain day by you to be limited to be examined of these premises and to do and receive what good faith and conscience will in this behalf, and that they moreover by your discretion be compelled to find sufficient surety to keep the King's peace against your said beseecher and against all the King's liege people, at the reverence of God and in the way of charity.

Pledges to prosecute { William Poleyn. John Grene.

This is the answer of John Wayte to a bill put against him by John Bishop before the King in his Chancery.

The said John Wayte saith by protestation that the said John Bishop is his villein regardant to his manor of Lee in the county of Southampton, and he and his ancestors and all those whose estate John Wayte hath in the same manor have been seised of the said John Bishop and of his ancestors as villeins regardant to the said manor from the time that no mind is, and saving to the said John Wayte and his heirs all manner advantage to seize and claim the same John Bishop and his heirs and their blood, all their lands and tenements, goods and chattels, and all manner other advantage and objections of bondage of and against the said John Bishop and his blood hereafter, by protestation that the said John Wayte is not guilty of no matter contained in the said bill like as by the same bill it is supposed for plea, saith, inasmuch as all the matters of complaint contained in the said bill be matters determinable by the common law of this land in other courts of our sovereign lord the King, and not in this court, asketh judgment and prayeth to be dismissed out of this court after the form of the Statute.

This is the replication of John Bishop unto the answer of John Wayte.

The said John Bishop saith that he is a free man born and of free condition and not bondman of the said John Wayte, and that all the ancestors of the same John Bishop from the time that no mind is have been free men and of free condition, born within the parish of Corfe in the county of Dorset and not within the manor of Lee in the county of Southampton, as by divers true inquisitions hereof taken before certain commissioners by virtue of the king's commission to them directed it plainly appeareth, which commissions and inquisitions remaineth in this place of record; and he saith moreover that the said John Wayte wrongfully by great force hath taken from him his goods and chattels and him grievously imprisoned in the manner and form declared in his bill, and him put to such cost, loss of his good, let of his labour and business, and other great troubles and vexations, that he is so poor and brought to so great misery that he is not of power to sue against the said John Wayte for remedy of the said wrongs by course of the common law of this land. Wherefore, inasmuch as he withsaith not the matter contained in the said bill of complaint of the said John Bishop, he prayeth that the said John Wayte may be compelled by the rule and discretion of this court to restore him of his said goods and to give him sufficient damages and amends for the said trespass to him done.

27. The Effect of the Black Death [*Duchy of Lancaster, Misc. Bks.* 8, *f.* 57*d.*], 1350.

Proxy for Parliament.—To his most excellent Prince and Lord, the most reverend Lord Edward, by the grace of God illustrious King of England and France and Lord of Ireland, his most humble chaplain, Geoffrey, Abbot of the Monastery of Selby, in the diocese of York, submission and reverence, with the bond of instant prayer to God. Since we are occupied beyond our strength in supporting the charges incumbent on our monastery, as well because our discreeter and stronger brethren, on whom rested the governance of our house, have gone the way of all flesh through the pestilence, as because our house both in decay of rents and in lack of corn and other victuals is suffering undue disaster, and also being hindered by other unavoidable obstacles, we are unable to be present in person in the instant Parliament to be held on the octave of the Purification of the Blessed Virgin Mary next coming, we make and appoint by these presents our beloved in Christ Sir Thomas de Brayton, clerk, and Hilary de Useflete, and each of them singly, our true and lawful proctors to appear for us in your said Parliament on the said day and place with the continuation and prorogation of the days following; giving and granting to the same and to each of them special command in our name to treat with you and with the rest of the prelates, magnates and chiefs of the said realm, being in the same Parliament, on the arduous and urgent affairs touching you and the estate and good governance of your realm of England and other your lands and lordships, which shall be there treated in common, and to consent to the measures which by God's favour shall be ordained then and there by the common council, and also to do and further all and singular other measures which we could have done in the said Parliament, if we had been present there in person; intending to ratify and approve whatsoever our said proctors or any one of them shall deem fit to be done in the premises in our name. In witness whereof our seal is affixed to these presents. Dated, etc.

28. Accounts of the Iron-works of South Frith before and after the Black Death [*Ministers' Accounts*, 891, 8 *and* 9], 1345–6 and 1349–50.

The account of Thomas Judde, receiver of South Frith, from Michaelmas, 19 Edward III, to the morrow of Michaelmas following, 20 Edward III.

. . . .

Sale of Wood.—[He answers] also for 188*l.* 4*s.* 6*d.* for wood sold in South Frith by Sir Andrew de Bures, Walter Colpeper, and William Lengleys, in the month of April, as appears in the particulars; and for 18*l.* 7*s.* for wood sold there by the same in the month of August, as appears by the particulars; and for 6*l.* 7*s.* 5*d.* for wood blown down by the wind, sold during the time covered by this account, as appears by the particulars indented. Sum:—212*l.* 18*s.* 11*d.*

. . . .

Defect of rent.—In defect of rent of 40 acres of land sometime of Hugh Champion in South Frith, because they are in the hand of the lady and lie waste for lack of a tenant, 13*s.* 4*d.* a year ; in defect of rent of Thomas Springget for a smithy which lies waste and is not worked, 12*d.* a year ; in defect of rent of a house sometime of Walter le Smyth, because it is pulled down, and it is testified that he has nothing on the lady's fee, 12*d.* a year. Sum :—15*s.* 4*d.*

. . . .

The account of Thomas Judde, receiver of South Frith, from Michaelmas, 23 Edward III, to the morrow of Michaelmas following, 24 Edward III, for the whole year.

. . . .

Sale of wood.—He answers for 17*l.* 14*d.* received for wood thrown down by the wind, as appears by the particulars indented between Walter Colpepyr and the said receiver.

Sum :—17*l.* 14*d.*

. . . .

Defect of rent.—He accounts in defect of rent of 40 acres sometime of Hugh Campyon, because they are in the hands of the lady and lie waste in the said wood for lack of a tenant, 13*s.* 4*d.* a year ; further, in defect of rent of Thomas Springet for a smithy in the hand of the lady, as above, 12*d.* ; further, in defect of rent of the house of Walter le Smyth, as above, 12*d.* ; further, in defect of rent of Richard atte Ware, as above, 5*s.* 7*d.* for 8 acres 3 roods of land at Bukesworthbrom with other parcels of land there ; further, in defect of rent of Thomas Harry for 3 roods of land, as above, 4½*d.* ; further in defect of rent of William Huchon for 6 acres of land, as above, 3*s.* ; further, in defect of rent of Richard Sampson for 19 acres 1 rood of land, as above, 12*s.* 10*d.* ; further, in defect of rent of Thomas Harry for two smithies, as above, 2*s.* ; further, in defect of rent of Robert le Hore for a house, as above, 7*d.* ; further, in defect of rent of Richard Gambon for a house, as above, 12*d.* ; further, in defect of rent of John Coppynger for a house, as above, 12*d.* ; further, in defect of rent of Richard Sampson for 3 acres of land, as above, 18*d.* ; further, in defect of rent of William atte Sandhelle for 20 acres of land, as above, 13*s.* 4*d.* ; further, in defect of rent of Richard Sewale for 20 acres of land, as above, 13*s.* 4*d.* ; further, in defect of rent of

William Crowle and Simon de Herst for 36 acres 3 roods of land, as above, 18*s*. 4½*d*.; further, in defect of rent of Robert Smale, John Watte, Jordan Odam and William Mowyn, for 23 acres 3 roods of land, as above, 15*s*. 11*d*.; further, in defect of rent of Walter Colpeper for 22 acres 3 roods of land, as above, 5*s*. 8¼*d*.; further, in defect of rent of Walter Mody for 18 acres of land, as above, 9*s*.

Sum of the ancient defect, 15*s*. 4*d*.

New defect through the pestilence this second year.

Sum:—119*s*. 3¼*d*. Whereof 103*s*. 11¼*d*. is of new defect by reason of the pestilence.

. . . .

29. The Peasants' Revolt [*Assize Roll*, 103, *mm*. 10 & 10*d*.], 1381.

Pleas in the Isle of Ely before the justices appointed in the county of Cambridge to punish and chastise insurgents and their misdeeds, on Thursday next before the feast of St. Margaret the Virgin,[1] 5 Richard II.

Inquisition taken there on the said Thursday by the oath of John Baker[2] . . . who say on their oath that Richard de Leycestre of Ely on Saturday next after the feast of Corpus Christi in the 4th year of the Lord the King that now is, of his own will made insurrection, gathering to himself John Buk of Ely and many other evildoers unknown, and went through the whole town of Ely, commanding that all men, of whatsoever estate, should make insurrection and go with him to destroy divers traitors whom he would name to them on behalf of the lord King Richard and the faithful commons; and hereupon he made divers proclamations seditiously and to the prejudice of the lord the King, whereby the people of the same town of Ely and other townships of the isle aforesaid were greatly disturbed and injured. Further they say that the same Richard [de Leycestre] on Sunday following commanded John Shethere of Ely, Elias Glovere, John Dassh, skinner, John Tylneye, wright, and John Redere of Ely, Thomas Litstere of Ely, Richard Swonn of Ely and John Milnere of Ely and many others of the commons there assembled, that they should go with him to the monastery of

[1] July 20. [2] And eleven others.

Ely to stand with him, while he, in the pulpit of the same monastery, should declare to them and all others the matters to be performed on behalf of King Richard and the commons against traitors and other disloyal men, and this under pain of the burning of their houses and the taking off of their heads; and so the same Richard [de Leycestre] was a notorious leader and assembler feloniously, and committed all the aforesaid acts to the prejudice of the crown of the lord the King. Further they say that the same Richard on Monday next following at Ely, as principal leader and insurgent, with the aforesaid men above named and many others unknown of his fellowship, feloniously broke the prison of the lord Bishop of Ely at Ely and feloniously led away divers felons there imprisoned.

And that the same Richard on the said Monday at Ely feloniously adjudged to death Edmund de Walsyngham, one of the justices of the peace of the lord the King in the county of Cambridge, whereby the said Edmund was then feloniously beheaded and his head set on the pillory there, the same being a pernicious example. And that the same Richard was the principal commander and leader in all the felonies, seditions and other misdeeds committed within the isle at the time aforesaid, etc.

And hereupon the aforesaid Richard was taken by the justices aforesaid and afterwards brought before them and charged and diligently examined touching all the felonies and seditions aforesaid, article by article, in what manner he would acquit himself thereof; and he made no answer thereto but proffered a protection of the lord the King granted to him for the security of his person and his possessions to endure for one year according to the form and effect used in the Chancery of the lord the King; and he says that he does not intend to be annoyed or disquieted touching any presentments made against him by the justices, by virtue of the protection aforesaid, etc. And the aforesaid Richard was asked if he would make any other answer to the premises under the peril incumbent, in that the protection aforesaid is insufficient to acquit him of the premises or of any article of the same. And hereupon the same Richard made no further denial of any of the premises presented against him, but said, "I cannot make further answer, and I hold myself convicted." And because it is clear and plain enough to the aforesaid justices that the same Richard is guilty of all the felonies and seditions aforesaid, as has been found before the same justices in lawful manner, therefore by the discretion of the said justices he was drawn and hanged the same day and year, etc., and [it was adjudged] that his lands and tenements, goods and chattels, should be forfeit to the lord the King, as law requires. And order was made to Ralph atte Wyk, escheator of the lord the King, that he should make due execution thereof forthwith for the lord the King, etc. And it is to be known that it was found before the aforesaid justices that the same Richard has a shop in "le Bocherie" in Ely, which is worth yearly beyond reprises 10*s.*, and chattels to the value of 40 marks, which the same Ralph seized forthwith, etc.

Further the aforesaid jurors say that John Buk of Ely was a fellow of the aforesaid Richard Leycestre all the time of the insurrection and tumult at Ely in the accomplishing of all the felonies, treasons and misdeeds, whereof the said Richard was indicted. And specially that the same John, of his malice, at the time when Edmund de Walsyngham was adjudged to death, feloniously came to him and feloniously snatched a purse of Edmund attached to his tunic containing 42½*d.*, and violently assaulted the said Edmund, dragging him to the place of his beheading, and carried away the said money except 12*d.* thereof which he gave to John Deye of Willingham, who there feloniously beheaded Edmund, for his labour. And hereupon the aforesaid John Buk was taken and brought forthwith before the aforesaid justices and charged touching the premises article by article, in what manner he will make answer thereto or acquit himself. And he says that as to all the matters touching Edmund de Walsyngham whereof he is charged, he came with many others to see the end of the said Edmund and to hear the cause of his death, and not otherwise, and this by the command of divers of the said commons. And he was asked further by whose command he came there and snatched the purse with the money aforesaid from the said Edmund in the form aforesaid, and he said that he believes it was by command of the devil. And he confessed further how and in what manner he dealt with the aforesaid purse with the money aforesaid, as was found above. And to all other presentments made against him he made no further answer. And because it is clear and plain enough, as well by his own acknowledgment as by lawful finding otherwise, that the same John is guilty of all the felonies and treasons aforesaid, therefore by the discretion of the said justices he was drawn and hanged, etc.; and [it was adjudged] that his lands and tenements, goods and chattels, should be forfeit to the lord the King, as law requires. And order was made to Ralph atte Wyk, escheator of the lord the King, that he should make due execution thereof forthwith for the lord the King, etc., because it was found before the aforesaid justices that he has goods and chattels to the value of 20*l.*, which the same Ralph seized forthwith and made further execution, etc.

. . . .

[m. 10*d.*] *Ely.*—Adam Clymme was taken as an insurgent traitorously against his allegiance, and because on Saturday next after the feast of Corpus Christi in the 4th year of the reign of King Richard the second after the Conquest, he traitorously with others made insurrection at Ely, feloniously broke and entered the close of Thomas Somenour and there took and carried away divers rolls, estreats of the green wax of the lord the King and the Bishop of Ely, and other muniments touching the Court of the lord the King, and forthwith caused them to be burned there to the prejudice of the crown of the lord the King.

Further that the same Adam on Sunday and Monday next following caused to be proclaimed there that no man of law or other officer in the execution of duty should escape without beheading.

Further that the same Adam the day and year aforesaid at the time of the insurrection was always wandering armed with arms displayed, bearing a standard, to assemble insurgents, commanding that no man of whatsoever condition he were, free or bond, should obey his lord to do any services or customs, under pain of beheading, otherwise than he should declare to them on behalf of the Great Fellowship. And so he traitorously took upon him royal power. And he came, brought by the sheriff, and was charged before the aforesaid justices touching the premises, in what manner he would acquit himself thereof. And he says that he is not guilty of the premises imputed to him or of any of the premises, and hereof puts himself on the country, etc. And forthwith a jury is made thereon for the lord the King by twelve [good and lawful men] etc., who being chosen hereto, tried and sworn, say on their oath that the aforesaid Adam is guilty of all the articles. By the discretion of the justices the same Adam is drawn and hanged, etc. And it was found there that the same Adam has in the town aforesaid chattels to the value of 32*s.*, which Ralph atte Wyk, escheator of the lord the King, seized forthwith and made further execution for the lord the King, etc.

. . . .

Cambridge.—John Shirle of the county of Nottingham was taken because it was found that he was a vagabond in divers counties the whole time of the disturbance, insurrection and tumult, carrying lies and worthless talk from district to district whereby the peace of the lord the King could be speedily broken and the people disquieted and disturbed; and among other dangerous words, to wit, after the proclamation of the peace of the lord the King made the day and year aforesaid, the assigns[1] of the lord the King being in the town and sitting, he said in a tavern in Bridge Street, Cambridge, where many were assembled to listen to his news and worthless talk, that the stewards of the lord the King, the justices and many other officers and ministers of the King were more worthy to be drawn and hanged and to suffer other lawful pains and torments, than John Balle, chaplain, a traitor and felon lawfully convicted; for he said that he was condemned to death falsely, unjustly and for envy by the said ministers with the King's assent, because he was a true and good man, prophesying things useful to the commons of the realm and telling of wrongs and oppressions done to the people by the King and the ministers aforesaid; and his death shall not go unpunished but within a short space he would well reward both the King and his officers and ministers aforesaid; which sayings and threats redound to the prejudice of the crown of the lord the King and the contempt and manifest disquiet of the people. And hereupon the aforesaid John Shirle was brought forthwith by the sheriff before the aforesaid assigns in Cambridge castle, and was charged touching the premises and diligently examined

[1] *i.e.* The justices assigned.

as well touching his conversation as touching his tarrying and his estate, and the same being acknowledged by him before the aforesaid assigns, his evil behaviour and condition is plainly manifest and clear. And hereupon trustworthy witnesses at that time in his presence, when the aforesaid lies, evil words, threats and worthless talk were spoken by him, were asked for, and they being sworn to speak the truth in this behalf, testify that all the aforesaid words imputed to him were truly spoken by him; and he, again examined, did not deny the premises imputed to him. Therefore by the discretion of the said assigns he was hanged; and order was made to the escheator to enquire diligently of his lands and tenements, goods and chattels, and to make due execution thereof for the lord the King.

SECTION V

TOWNS AND GILDS

1. Payments made to the crown by gilds in the twelfth century, 1179–80—2. Charter of liberties to the borough of Tewkesbury, 1314 — 3. Charter of liberties to the borough of Gloucester, 1227—4. Dispute between towns touching the payment of toll, 1222—5. Dispute with a lord touching a gild merchant, 1223–4—6. The affiliation of boroughs, 1227—7. Bondman received in a borough, 1237–8—8. An inter-municipal agreement in respect of toll, 1239—9. Enforcement of charter granting freedom from toll, 1416—10. Licence for an alien to be of the gild merchant of London, 1252—11. Dispute between a gild merchant and an abbot, 1304—12. Complaints of the men of Leicester against the lord, 1322—13. Grant of pavage to the lord of a town, 1328—14. Misappropriation of the tolls levied for pavage, 1336—15. Ordinances of the White Tawyers of London, 1346—16. Dispute between Masters and Journeymen, 1396—17. Ordinances of the Dyers of Bristol, 1407—18. Incorporation of the Haberdashers of London, 1448—19. Indenture of Apprenticeship, 1459—20. A runaway apprentice, *c.* 1425—21. Incorporation of a gild for religious and charitable uses, 1447.

THE origin and early development of towns, the emergence of gild merchant and craft gild, the mutual relationship of the two types of gild, and the part played by each in the evolution of municipal self-government, present problems to which there is no simple solution. The undoubtedly military object of many of the Saxon boroughs fails to explain their economic development; while the possession of a market did not lead of necessity to self-government. Often, indeed, there is little economic difference between a large manor and a small town; the towns pursued agriculture, and the manors engaged in industry. None the less the early borough, with its court co-ordinate with the hundred court, its special peace, and its market, stands out at the time of the Conquest as a distinct variety of *communitas*, and easily became a centre of specialised industry and privileged association. Constitutional and economic growth proceed side by side; a measure of liberty encourages commercial progress, and the profits of trade purchase a larger measure of liberty.

In this section an attempt has been made to illustrate the gradual expansion of the economic life of the town from the twelfth century onwards. The twelfth and thirteenth centuries witnessed a great and growing activity; craft gilds and gilds merchant were arising everywhere, and whether licensed or unlicensed, were paying considerable sums to the crown for privileges bought or usurped (No. 1). The more important boroughs were securing charters from their lords (Nos. 2 and 3), while smaller towns were struggling to win economic freedom, that is to say, local monopoly, against serious obstacles (No. 5). The fate of a town depended much on the lord; the king's boroughs were more favoured than those of an earl or lesser baron, while the latter fared better than towns in the hands of a prelate (Nos. 11 and 12). The exaction of tolls and the claim to exemption from tolls, which prove the existence of considerable intermunicipal trade, were a common cause of litigation. The grant of incompatible privileges to rival communities was a source of profit to the mediæval monarchy; the crown secured payment in hand for the charters, and reaped the benefit of the inevitable dispute that followed (Nos. 4 and 8). The growth of intercourse is further shown by that curious feature of early borough development, the affiliation of distinct groups of towns (No. 6). Nos. 7 and 10 illustrate the coveted privileges of the freedom of a city or borough, and No. 9 the machinery by which a citizen protected himself if his liberty were infringed in another town. The character of tolls imposed by a town for municipal purposes and the possibility of corrupt collectors are shown in Nos. 13 and 14. The specialisation of industry is naturally followed by a differentiation of function, a process which develops normally in the fourteenth century and attains a certain rigidity in the fifteenth. Crafts begin to close their ranks, to lay down elaborate rules of membership, of the conduct of business and the methods of manufacture, to secure incorporation, and to strengthen their hands by establishing disciplinary precedents in relation to the journeymen and apprentices. The competition of the unskilled outsider is suppressed and apprenticeship insisted on (Nos. 15 and 17), the journeyman is restrained (No. 16), and the crafts establish a wide control over the conditions of labour (No. 18). No. 19 is a characteristic indenture of apprenticeship; No. 20 illustrates the tendency to invoke the central authority, which grows in force during the fifteenth century and culminates in the direct control exercised by the Chancellor over gild ordinances in the sixteenth century; while No. 21 is an example of the social religious gild, which was one of the mediæval methods of anticipating the poor law.

AUTHORITIES

The principal modern writers dealing with the subject of this section are:—Madox, *Firma Burgi*; Maitland, *Township and Burgh*; Merewether & Stephens, *History of the Boroughs*; Ballard, *British Borough Charters*; Bateson, *Borough Customs* (Selden Society); Gross, *The Gild Merchant*; Gross, *The Affiliation of Boroughs* (Antiquary, XII.); Drinkwater, *Merchant Gild of Shrewsbury* (Salop Archæol. Transactions, N.S. II.); Unwin, *The Gilds and Companies of London*; Unwin, *Industrial Organisation in the sixteenth and seventeenth centuries*; Green, *Town Life in the Fifteenth Century*; Toulmin Smith, *English Gilds* (Early English Text Society); Davies, *History of Southampton*; Hibbert, *Influence and Development of English Gilds*; Hudson, *Leet Jurisdiction in the City of Norwich*; Leonard, *Early History of English Poor Law Relief*; Denton, *England in the Fifteenth Century*.

For contemporary records the student may be referred to the following:—Riley, *Memorials of London and London Life*; Riley, *Liber Albus*; Sharpe, *Calendars of Letter Books*; Stevenson, *Records of the Borough of Nottingham*; Bateson, *Records of the Borough of Leicester*; *Court Leet of the City of Norwich* (Selden Society); Bickley, *The Little Red Book of Bristol*; *Rotuli Cartarum* (Record Commission); and the *Calendars of Patent, Close and Charter Rolls* (Record Office Publications).

1. Payments Made to the Crown by Gilds in the Twelfth Century [*Pipe Roll*, 26 *Henry II*], 1179-80.

The weavers of Oxford render account of 6*l.* for their gild. They have delivered it into the treasury. And they are quit.

The corvesers of Oxford render account of 15*s.* for an ounce of gold for their gild. They have delivered it into the treasury. And they are quit.

The weavers of Huntingdon render account of 40*s.* for their gild. They have delivered it into the treasury. And they are quit.

The weavers of Lincoln render account of 6*l.* for their gild. They have delivered it into the treasury. And they are quit.

The weavers of York render account of 10*l.* for their gild. They have delivered it into the treasury. And they are quit

The same sheriff [of York] renders account of 2 marks from the gild of glovers and curriers. In the treasury is 1 mark. And they owe 1 mark.

The same sheriff renders account of 20*s.* from the gild of saddlers for [customs which they exact unjustly]. In the treasury is 10*s.* And it owes 10*s.*

The same sheriff renders account . . . of 1 mark from the gild of hosiers by way of mercy. . . And he is quit.

The citizens of Exeter render account of 40*l.* for the fine of a plea touching gilds. In the treasury are 20*l.* And they owe 20*l.*

The same sheriff [of Devon] renders account . . . of 1 mark from the borough of Barnstaple for a gild without warrant. . . . And he is quit.

The burgesses of Bodmin render account of 100*s.* for their false statement and for their gild without warrant. In the treasury are 50*s.* And they owe 50*s.*

The same sheriff [of Cornwall] renders account . . . of 3 marks from the burgesses of Launceston for their gild without warrant . . . And he is quit.

The same sheriff [of Dorset and Somerset] renders account of 6 marks from the borough of Wareham for a gild without warrant. In the treasury are 3 marks. And it owes 3 marks.

The same sheriff renders account . . . of 3 marks from the borough of Dorchester for a gild without warrant. And of 2 marks from the borough of Bridport for the same. . . .
And he is quit.

The same sheriff renders account . . . of 20*s.* from Axbridge for a gild without warrant. And of ½ mark from Langport for the same . . . And he is quit.

The burgesses of Ilchester [render account of] 20*s.* for a gild without warrant.

The weavers of Winchester render account of 2 marks of gold for their gild. In the treasury are 12*l.* for 2 marks of gold. And they are quit.

The fullers of Winchester render account of 6*l.* for their gild. They have delivered it into the treasury.
And they are quit.

The weavers of Nottingham render account of 40*s.* for their gild. They have delivered it into the treasury.
And they are quit.

The weavers of London render account of 12*l.* for their gild. They have delivered it into the treasury.
And they are quit.

Amercements of Adulterine Gilds in the City of London.

The gild whereof Goscelin is alderman owes 30 marks.

The gild of pepperers whereof Edward is alderman owes 16 marks.

The gild of St. Lazarus whereof Ralph le Barre is alderman owes 25 marks.

The gild of goldsmiths whereof Ralph Flael is alderman owes 45 marks.

The gild of Bridge whereof Ailwin Finke is alderman owes 15 marks.

The gild of Bridge whereof Robert de Bosco is alderman owes 10 marks.

The gild of Haliwell whereof Henry son of Godric is alderman owes 20*s.*

The gild of Bridge whereof Walter the Cooper is alderman owes 1 mark.

The gild of strangers (*pelegrinorum*) whereof Warner le Turnur is alderman owes 40*s.*

The gild of butchers whereof William Lafeite is alderman owes 1 mark.

The gild of clothworkers whereof John Maurus is alderman owes 1 mark.

The gild whereof Odo the Watchman is alderman owes 1 mark.

The gild of Bridge whereof Thomas the Cook is alderman owes 1 mark.

The gild whereof Robert Rochefolet is alderman owes 1 mark.

The gild whereof Hugh Leo is alderman owes ½ mark.

The gild whereof William de Haverhill is alderman owes 10 marks.

The gild whereof Thedric Feltrarius is alderman owes 2 marks.

The gild of Bridge whereof Peter son of Alan was alderman owes 15 marks.

The gild whereof John the White is alderman owes 1 mark.

2. Charter of Liberties to the Borough of Tewkesbury [*Charter Roll*, 11 *Edward III*, *m.* 10, *No.* 21], 1314.

Gilbert de Clare, earl of Gloucester and Hertford, to all whom the present letters shall come, greeting. Whereas William and Robert, sometime earls of Gloucester and Hertford,[1] our progenitors, of famous memory, formerly granted and confirmed in turn for them and their heirs by their charters to their burgesses of Tewkesbury and their heirs and successors the liberties below written:

First, that the burgesses of the borough aforesaid should have and hold their burgages in the borough aforesaid by free service, to wit, each of them holding one burgage should have and hold it by the service of 12*d.* a year to be rendered to the same earls, and if holding more should have and hold each of them by the service of 12*d.* a year together with the service of doing suit to the court of the same earls of the borough aforesaid from three weeks to three weeks, for all service, so that after the decease of any of the burgesses aforesaid, his heir or heirs should enter the burgage or burgages aforesaid, of what age soever he or they should be, to hold the same quit of relief or heriot.

[1] *temp.* William I.—Stephen. Note that the privileges here confirmed date from the first century after the Conquest.

And to the same burgesses, each of them, that they might sell, pledge or loan to other burgesses their burgage or burgages aforesaid which they had in the same borough by purchase, at their will, without any ransom to be made, so that those burgesses to whom such burgages were sold, pledged or loaned, should show the charters or writings which they had thereof before the steward of the aforesaid earls in the court of the borough.

And if any of them should hold half a burgage, he should hold it with the same liberty with which tenants of a whole burgage should hold and have the same, according to the quantity of his burgage.

And that no burgess of the borough aforesaid should by reason of a burgage or half a burgage be in any wise tallaged or make ransom of blood or be disturbed by reason of the sale of his horse, ox or other his chattels whatsoever, but each of them should employ his merchandise without challenge.

And to the same burgesses, that they might make their wills and lawfully in their wills bequeath at their pleasure their chattels and burgages which they should hold by purchase.

And if it should happen that any of them were impoverished whereby he must sell his burgage, he should first seek from his next hereditary successor before his neighbours three times his necessaries in food and clothing for the poverty of his estate, and if he should refuse to do it for him, it should be lawful for him to sell his burgage at his will for ever without challenge.

And to the same burgesses, that they might make bread for sale in their own oven or that of another, and ale for sale in their own brewhouse or that of another, save that they should keep the royal assize.

And that they might make ovens, drying-houses, hand mills without hindrance of the earls aforesaid or their bailiffs whomsoever.

And that none of them should come without the borough aforesaid by any summons to the hundred of the same earls of the honour of Gloucester in the county aforesaid by reason of their burgages aforesaid.

And if a foreigner, who should not be a burgess nor the son of a burgess, should buy a burgage or half a burgage in the same borough, he should come to the court of the borough aforesaid next following and make his fine for entry and do fealty.

And that all burgesses who should hold a burgage or half a burgage and should sell bread and ale should come once at the Lawday yearly at the Hockday and there be amerced for breach of the assize, if they ought to be amerced, by the presentment of twelve men; so that each burgess should answer for his household (*manupastu*), sons and tenants, unless they should have been attached for any trespass to answer at the day aforesaid.

And to the same burgesses, that they should be quit of toll and of custom within the lordship of the aforesaid earls in the honour of Gloucester and elsewhere in England, according as they used of old; so that no foreigner should buy corn in the borough aforesaid nor put or keep any in a granary beyond eight days, to wit, between the Gules of August[1] and the feast of All Saints[2]; but if he did and were convicted thereof, he should be amerced at the will of the aforesaid earls or their bailiffs; nor after the feast of All Saints or [before] the Gules of August should he buy corn to put and keep in a granary, nor carry any by water without licence of the aforesaid earls or the bailiffs of the borough aforesaid, and he should pay customs.

And that no foreigner should be received by the steward, clerk or any other on behalf of the same earls to be within the liberty aforesaid, unless it were testified by lawful men of the borough aforesaid, that he were good and trusty.

And if any burgess should be out of the borough at the time of summons of the court aforesaid and could not reasonably be forewarned, he should not be amerced for default.

And if any foreigner should be received within the liberty of the borough aforesaid, he should find mainpernors[3] that he would bear himself in good manner and faithfully to the aforesaid earls and their bailiffs, and would be tractable to the commonalty of the borough aforesaid.

And that they, the burgesses, should be bailiffs and catchpolls[4] of that borough as often as they should be elected hereto, at the will of the aforesaid earls, their stewards and bailiffs, and by election of the commonalty of the borough aforesaid from year to year.

[1] August 1. [2] November 1. [3] *i.e.* Sureties. [4] Constables.

And that the burgesses aforesaid should have common pasture for their beasts in the common pasture of the borough aforesaid, according to their burgages which they have in the same borough, as they have been accustomed hitherto.

We, ratifying and approving the gifts and grants aforesaid, grant and confirm them for us and our heirs for ever. These witnesses:—Sirs Bartholomew de Badlesmere, Roger Tyrel, Gilbert of St. Ouen, Giles de Bello Campo, John de Harecourt, Robert de Burs, John Tyrel, knights, Master Richard de Clare, John de Chelmersford, clerks, and others. Given at Rothwell in the county of Northampton, 26 April, 1314, in the seventh year of the reign of King Edward, son of King Edward.[1]

3. Charter of Liberties to the Borough of Gloucester [*Charter Roll*, 11 *Henry III*, *p.* 1, *m.* 10, No. 88], 1227.

Henry, King, etc., greeting. Know ye that we have granted and by this our charter confirmed to our burgesses of Gloucester the whole borough of Gloucester with the appurtenances, to hold of us and our heirs for ever at fee farm, rendering yearly 55*l.* sterling, as they were wont to render the same, and 10*l.* by tale of increment of farm, at our Exchequer at the term of Easter and at the term of Michaelmas. We have granted also to our burgesses of Gloucester of the merchants' gild that none of them plead without the walls of the borough of Gloucester touching any plea save pleas of foreign tenures, except our moneyers and ministers. We have granted also to them that none of them suffer trial by battle and that touching pleas pertaining to our crown they may deraign[2] according to the ancient custom of the borough. This also we have granted to them that all burgesses of Gloucester of the merchants' gild be quit of toll and lastage[3] and pontage[4] and stallage[5] within fairs and without and throughout seaports of all our lands on this side the sea and beyond the sea, saving in all things the

[1] Extracted from the charter of confirmation of Edward III.
[2] Plead *or* bring evidence.
[3] A toll on the load exacted at fairs and markets, and on the lading of a ship.
[4] Bridge toll.
[5] Tolls for the erection of stalls or booths.

liberties of the city of London, and that none be judged touching a money penalty save according to the ancient law of the borough which they had in the time of our ancestors, and that they justly have all their lands and tenements and sureties and debts, whosoever owe them, and that right be done them according to the custom of the borough touching their lands and tenures which are within the borough, and that pleas touching all their debts by loans which they have made at Gloucester, and touching sureties made there, be held at Gloucester. And if any man in the whole of our land take toll or custom from the men of Gloucester of the merchants' gild, after he have failed to do right, the sheriff of Gloucester or the provost of Gloucester shall take distress thereon at Gloucester, saving in all things the liberties of the city of London. Furthermore for the repair of the borough we have granted to them that they be all quit of "gyeresyeve"[1] and of "scotale,"[2] if our sheriff or any other bailiff exact "scotale." We have granted to them these aforesaid customs and all other liberties and free customs which they had in the times of our ancestors, when they had them well and freely. And if any customs were unjustly levied in the time of war, they shall be annulled. And whosoever shall come to the borough of Gloucester with his wares, of whatsoever place they be, whether strangers or others, shall come, stay and depart in our safe peace, rendering right customs. And let no man disturb them touching this our charter. And we forbid that any man commit wrong or damage or molestation against them thereon on pain of forfeiture of 10*l.* to us. Wherefore we will, etc. that the aforesaid burgesses and their heirs have and hold all these things aforesaid in inheritance of us and our heirs well and in peace, freely, quietly and honourably, as is above written. We will also and grant that the same our burgesses of Gloucester elect by the common counsel of the borough two of the more lawful and discreet burgesses of Gloucester and present them to our chief justice at Westminster, which two or one of them shall well and faithfully keep the provostship of the borough and shall not be removed so long as they be of good behaviour in their bailiwick, save by the common counsel of the borough. We will also that in the same borough of Gloucester by the

[1] A compulsory annual customary gift.
[2] Compulsory purchase of ale.

common counsel of the burgesses be elected four of the more lawful and discreet men of the borough to keep the pleas of the crown and other things which pertain to us and our crown in the same borough, and to see that the provosts of that borough justly and lawfully treat as well poor as rich, as the charter[1] of the lord King John, our father, which they have thereon, reasonably testifies. We have granted also to the same burgesses of Gloucester that none of our sheriffs intermeddle with them in aught touching any plea or plaint or occasion or any other thing pertaining to the aforesaid borough, saving to us and our heirs for ever pleas of our crown, which ought to be attached by the same our burgesses until the coming of our justices, as is aforesaid. We have granted also to the same that if any bondman of any man stay in the aforesaid borough and maintain himself therein and be in the merchants' gild and hanse and lot and scot with the same our burgesses for a year and a day without claim, thenceforth he shall not be reclaimed by his lord, but shall abide freely in the same borough. These witnesses:—W. Archbishop of York, W. Bishop of Carlisle, H. de Burgo, etc., W. Earl Warenne, Osbert Giffard, Ralph son of Nicholas, Richard de Argentem, our stewards, Henry de Capella, John de Bassingeburn and others. Dated by the hand [of the venerable father Ralph bishop of Chichester, our Chancellor], at Westminster on the sixth day of April in the eleventh year, etc.

4. Dispute Touching the Payment of Toll in a Borough [*Bracton's Note-Book, II*, 121, No. 145], 1222.

The bailiffs of the city of Lincoln were summoned to answer the burgesses of Beverley wherefore they permit them not to have their liberties which they have by a charter of the lord King John, which liberties they have used hitherto, etc.; whereon the burgesses say that while they came through the middle of the town of Lincoln on their way to the fair of St. Ives, the bailiffs took their pledges and their cloths contrary to their liberty, and that they are injured and suffer damage to the value of 60 marks, and thereof they produce their suit etc. and proffer their charter,[2] which testifies that the King gave to God and St. John and the men of Beverley that they should

[1] Charter Roll, 1 John, m. 2. [2] 1 John (1200). *Rot. Cart. p.* 53.

be free and quit of toll, pontage, passage, pesage, lastage, stallage and wreck and all other such customs, which pertain to the lord the King himself, throughout all the king's land, saving the liberties of London, etc.; wherefore they say that by that charter they always had quittance of the aforesaid customs until the last fair of St. Ives.

And the mayor of Lincoln and Robert son of Eudo, bailiffs of Lincoln, come and deny force and tort, but acknowledge indeed that they took toll from the complainants within their town, and this they could well do, because they have charters of King Henry, grandfather of the lord the King, and of King Richard, by which those kings granted to them all the liberties and free customs which they had of the ancestors of those kings, to wit, King Edward and King William and King Henry the grandfather, throughout the whole land of England, and all the liberties which the citizens of London have, saving to the same citizens of London their liberties; and thereof they put forward their charters[1] which witness the same; wherefore they say that by those charters they have always had the liberty of taking toll in their town and always hitherto were in seisin of that liberty, and they crave judgment if by the charter of the lord King John they ought to lose their liberty granted to them by his ancestors.

And the burgesses of Beverley say that after the charter of the lord King John they never gave toll, nay rather, they were always quit thereof by that charter, and this they offer to prove, etc. or to make defence that they never gave toll; and being asked if before that charter they gave toll, they say, Yes, and crave judgment hereon and offer to the lord the King two palfreys for an inquisition if after the charter of King John they were always quit of the aforesaid toll, and they are received, and so a jury was made by eight lawful citizens of Lincoln and further by eight lawful men of the vicinage of Lincoln, and let it come on such a day to recognise if those burgesses, when they brought wares through the town of Lincoln, were quit of toll in that town from the first year of the coronation of King John.[2]

[1] 1 John (1200). *Rot. Cart.*, *pp.* 5, 56.

[2] See note to No. 8.

5. Dispute With a Lord Touching a Gild Merchant [*Curia Regis Rolls, Mich.* 8 *Henry III*, *m.* 6], 1223–4.

Buckingham.—Alan Basset was summoned to answer the burgesses of Wycombe wherefore he permits them not to have their gild merchant with its appurtenances, as they were wont to have it in the time of the lord King John, when he had that manor in his hand; whereof the burgesses say that in the time when the lord King John had that manor in his hand, and when the lord the King gave it to the same Alan, they had a gild merchant and a liberty which the same Alan has taken away from them, wherefore they are much injured, for by that gild merchant they had this liberty, that no merchant within their town could sell cloths at retail, neither linens nor woollens, unless he were in the gild merchant or by licence of the bailiffs of the burgesses who were in the gild merchant, and furthermore in the same manner could not sell fells or wood or broom[1] or such merchandise, unless he were in the gild or by licence, as aforesaid; and the same Alan contravened this liberty and granted to all merchants and others that they might sell cloths at retail and fells and such wares as they please, and takes 3*d.* toll; and they used to give for the farm of the lord the King half a mark yearly to have that liberty; and because he has taken away that liberty from them, they are injured and suffer damage to the value of 40 marks, and thereof they produce suit, and if this suffices not, they offer to prove that they had such seisin by the evidence of witnesses (*per vivam vocem*), if they ought, or by the body of a man,[2] or by the country,[3] and they offer 20 marks to have an inquisition thereon.

And Alan comes and defends force and tort and says that he has taken no liberties from them, but will speak the truth; the lord King John gave him that manor with all its appurtenances for his homage and service for 20*l.* a year and for the service of one knight, so that never afterwards did they have a gild merchant, although they often sued for it and murmured among themselves, so that he often asked of them their warrant, if they had any, and they show him none; and the town is amended in that merchants and others can sell their merchandise; and so they ought to have no gild.

1 Genista tinctoria (dyer's greenweed); "*genetein*" in MS.
2 *i.e.* Trial by battle. 3 *i.e.* Trial by jury.

And the burgesses say that his statement is contrary to right, because after his time, when he had that manor, they had that liberty, both before his time and after, and they offer as before 20 marks to have an inquisition thereon. Touching their warrant they say that they had a charter of King Henry, grandfather ot tne iord the King, and it was deposited in the church of Wycombe, and there in the time of war was burned in the church, and thereof they put themselves on a jury.

And Alan defends that they had no charter thereof nor any warrant, nor ever had seisin of that gild in his time, nor can he admit nor will he admit any inquisition without the lord the King; but indeed it may be true that when they had the manor of the King at farm, then they did what they pleased.

A day is given to them on the morrow of Martinmas to hear their judgment, and the burgesses put in their place William son of Harvey and Robert le Taillur.[1]

6. The Affiliation of Boroughs [*Charter Roll*, 11 *Henry III*, *p.* 1, *m.* 13, *No.* 117], 1227.

The King to all, etc., greeting. Know ye that we have granted and by our present charter confirmed to our burgesses of Bedford all their liberties and customs and laws and quittances, which they had in the time of the lord King Henry, our grandfather, specially their gild merchant with all their liberties and customs in lands and islands, in pastures and all other their appurtenances, so that no one who is not in that gild do any trafficking with them in city or borough or town or soke. Moreover we have granted and confirmed to them that they be quit of toll and pontage and stallage and lastage and passage, and of assarts and every other custom throughout the whole of England and Normandy by land and water and by the seashore, "bilande and bistrande," and have all other customs throughout the whole of England and their liberties and laws which they have in common with our citizens of Oxford,[2] and do their trafficking in common with them within London and without and in all other places. And if they have any doubt or contention touching any judgment which they ought

[1] The case was again adjourned and the judgment has not been found.

[2] Oxford was also affiliated to London by charter of 13 Henry III. [Charter Roll, 13 Henry III., p. 1, m. 12.]

to make, they shall send their messengers to Oxford, and what the citizens of Oxford shall adjudge hereon, that they shall hold firm and fixed and certain without doubt, and do the same. And we forbid that they plead without the borough of Bedford in aught whereof they are charged, but of whatsoever they be impleaded, they shall deraign themselves according to the laws and customs of our citizens of Oxford, and this at Bedford and not elsewhere; because they and the citizens of Oxford are of one and the same custom and law and liberty. Wherefore we will and straitly command that our aforesaid burgesses of Bedford have and hold their aforesaid liberties and laws and customs and tenures well and in peace, freely and quietly, fully and honourably, with soc and sac and tol and theam and infangenethef,[1] and with all other their liberties and free customs and quittances, as well and entirely as ever they had them in the time of King Henry, our grandfather, and as fully and freely and entirely as our citizens of Oxford have those liberties and as the charter of King Richard, our uncle, which they have thereof, reasonably testifies. Witnesses as above. Given [at Westminster on 24 March in the 11th year of our reign].

7. Bondman Received in a Borough [*Bracton's Notebook, III*, 243, No. 1228], 1237-8.

Order was made to the bailiffs of Andover that at the first coming of the lord the King to Clarendon they shew cause to the lord the King, wherefore they have detained from Everard le Tyeis William of Amesbury, his bondman and fugitive, inasmuch as he claims him at the time and hours, as he says, etc.

And Adam de Marisco and other bailiffs of Andover come and say that the aforesaid William was at one time dwelling at Wilton and was a travelling merchant and married a woman in the town of Andover, and within the year in which he married the same Everard came and sought him as his bondman and fugitive, but they refused to deliver him to him and dared not without the lord the King's command.

Afterwards the same Everard comes, and remits and quit-claims to the lord the King and his heirs the aforesaid William with his whole brood, etc.

[1] *i.e.* General rights of jurisdiction.

8. An Intermunicipal Agreement in Respect of Toll [*Charter Roll*, 23 *Henry III*, *m.* 3], 1239.

The King to archbishops, etc. greeting. Know ye that whereas a dispute was raised in our Court before us between our good men of Marlborough, complainants, and our good men of Southampton, deforciants, of toll which the aforesaid men of Southampton took from our men of Marlborough against their liberties which they have by charter of King John, our father, and by our charter, as they asserted ; at length by our licence it is covenanted between them on this wise, that all our men of Marlborough, who are in the gild merchant of Marlborough and will establish the same, be quit for ever of all custom and all manner of toll in the town of Southampton and in all the appurtenances thereof, whereof the men of Southampton within their liberty can acquit the said men of Marlborough, notwithstanding that the charter of the same men of Southampton is prior to the charters of the aforesaid men of Marlborough ;[1] and in like manner that the men of Southampton be quit of all custom and toll in the town of Marlborough. We, therefore, willing that the aforesaid covenant be firm and stable for ever, grant and confirm it for us and our heirs. Witnesses :—Richard, count of Poitou and earl of Cornwall, our brother, etc., as above [17 June, Westminster].

9. Enforcement of Charter Granting Freedom from Toll Throughout the Realm [*Chancery Files*], 1416.

Henry by the grace of God King of England and France and Lord of Ireland to John Kerde of Ware Toller, greeting. Whereas among the rest of the liberties and quittances granted to our beloved citizens of our city of London by charters of our progenitors, sometime Kings of England, which we have confirmed by our charter with the clause " *licet*,"[2] it is granted to the same that they and their successors, citizens of the same city, be quit for ever of pavage, pontage, murage,[3] toll and

[1] The legal rule evolved in the thirteenth century for cases where the crown granted to one town freedom from toll, and to another town the right to exact toll, was that priority of grant prevailed ; *cf.* Bracton *f.* 56*b*. By grants of incompatible charters the crown obtained fees from two sets of petitioners, and also costs from the subsequent litigation.

[2] Charter Roll, 2 Henry V., p. 2, No. 11. The clause " *licet* " is a provision for the preservation of liberties in spite of non-user.

[3] *i.e.* Tolls for the repair of streets, bridges, and walls.

lastage[1] throughout the whole of our realm and the whole of our land and power, as is more fully contained in the charters and confirmation aforesaid: We command you, as we have commanded before, that you permit Thomas Sabarn, citizen of the city aforesaid, as it is said, to be quit of such pavage, pontage, murage, toll and lastage, according to the tenour of the charters and confirmation aforesaid, not molesting or aggrieving him in aught contrary to the tenour of the same, or that you signify to us the cause wherefore you have not obeyed our command before directed to you thereon. Witness myself at Westminster, 25 March in the 4th year of our reign.

Sotheworth.

[*Endorsed.*] The answer of John Kerde withinwritten. I certify to you that I have permitted and will hereafter permit Thomas Sabarn withinwritten to be quit of pavage, pontage, murage, toll and lastage, as is commanded me by this writ, and have not molested or aggrieved him on the same accounts, and will not molest or aggrieve him hereafter.

10. Licence for an Alien to be of the Gild Merchant of London [*Charter Roll*, 37 *Henry III*, *m*. 21], 1252.

The King to archbishops, etc., greeting. Know ye that we have granted and by this our charter confirmed to Deutayutus Willelmi, merchant of Florence, that he and his heirs for ever may have this liberty, to wit, that in any tallage to be assessed on the community of our city of London by our command they be not tallaged at more than one mark of silver, and that they, with their own household, may buy, sell and traffic without unlawful gain as freely and quietly throughout the whole of our power as any of our citizens of London; and that the same Deutayutus and his heirs be in the gild merchant of the same city and have all other liberties and free customs, as well within the said city as without, which the same citizens have or shall have or obtain hereafter. Wherefore we will and straitly command for us and our heirs that the aforesaid Deutayutus and his heirs have all the liberties, free customs and quittances aforesaid for ever, as is aforesaid. These witnesses:—Geoffrey de Lezinan, our brother, Peter de

[1] *i.e.* A toll on cargoes and on wares entering a market or fair.

Sabaudia, John de Grey, John de Lessinton, Peter Chaceporc, archdeacon of Wells, Master W. de Kilkenny, archdeacon of Coventry, Artald de Sancto Romano, Robert de Muscegros, Robert Wallerand, Stephen Bauzan, Robert le Norreys, Ralph de Bakepuz, Imbert Pugeys and others. Given by our hand at Windsor, 3 November.[1]

11. Dispute Between the Merchant Gild and the Abbot of Bury St. Edmunds [*B.M. Add. MSS.* 17391, *ff.* 61–65], 1304.

Pleas at the town of St. Edmund before William de Bereford, W. Howard and W. de Carleton, appointed justices of the lord the King, on Tuesday next after the feast of St. Lucy the Virgin[2] in the thirty-third year of the reign of King Edward son of King Henry.

Nicholas Fouk and others by conspiracy premeditated among them at the town aforesaid and by oath taken among them, making unlawful assemblies of their own authority on Monday next after the feast of the Nativity of the Blessed Virgin Mary in the thirtieth year of the lord the King that now is,[3] ordained and decreed that none should remain among them in the said town having chattels worth 20*s.* who would not pay them 2*s.* 1*d.*, which payment they call among themselves hansing-silver, which money they took on that pretext respectively from Reynold del Blackhouse and Robert the Carpenter, men dwelling in the town aforesaid, and also beyond this 12*d.* of gersom from each of the said Reynold and Robert. And likewise . . . they decreed among themselves that every man of the same town having chattels to the value of 10 marks should pay them 46*s.* 8*d.*, which by that authority they took from Robert Scot, a man dwelling in the aforesaid town. And also the same day and year they decreed among themselves that no man should stay in the aforesaid town be-

[1] In the thirteenth century aliens were commonly burgesses of English towns (for an instance see below, Section VI, No. 30), and Englishmen were members of foreign communities. In 1326 the Mayor and commonalty of London deprived such aliens of the freedom of the city (Riley Memorials, 151). This document furnishes the sole extant reference to a gild merchant in London. See, however, Crump, in E. H. R., xviii. 315.

[2] Tuesday after December 13.

[3] Monday after September 8, 1302.

yond a year and a day without being distrained to take oath to maintain their aforesaid assemblies and ordinances. . . .

The aforesaid Nicholas Fouk and others readily acknowledge that the Abbot is lord of the whole town aforesaid, and ought to appoint his bailiffs to hold his court in the same town. But as for the conspiracy aforesaid, etc., they make stout defence that they are not guilty of the aforesaid conspiracy, etc. And as for the Abbot's charge against them that they have made unlawful assemblies in the aforesaid town, decreeing and ordaining that every man dwelling in the same town having chattels to the value of 20*s.*, etc. as above, they say that the aforesaid Abbot makes plaint unjustly, for they say that they have an alderman and a gild merchant in the aforesaid town and are free burgesses, etc., rendering judgments by their alderman of pleas pleaded in the court of the same abbot before his bailiffs in the town aforesaid. And that without any trespasses or unlawful assemblies they meet at their Gildhall in the same town, as often as need be, to treat of the common profit and advantage of the men and burgesses of the aforesaid town, as is quite lawful for them. And that they and their ancestors and predecessors, burgesses, etc., have used such a custom from time whereof no memory is, to wit, of taking 2*s.* 1*d.* from every man dwelling in the aforesaid town, being in the tithing of the Abbot of the place aforesaid, having chattels to the value of 20*s.*, that he may trade among them and enjoy their market customs in the same town, and likewise of receiving 46*s.* 8*d.* from every man of the town aforesaid having chattels to the value of 10 marks to keep[1] their gild merchant. And that there is the following custom among them beyond this, to wit, that twelve burgesses of the aforesaid town have been accustomed to elect four men of the same town yearly to keep their gild merchant, each of whom shall have chattels to the value of 10 marks. Which four men so elected have been accustomed to be forewarned by two burgesses of the gild aforesaid, who are called *les Dyes*, to keep their gild aforesaid; and the same men so elected have been accustomed to find pledges before the alderman and burgesses in the Gildhall aforesaid to keep the gild aforesaid, or that each of them would pay 46*s.* 8*d.*, who should refuse to keep that gild. And for the doing hereof the alderman and burgesses in

[1] *i.e.* To uphold.

K

the town aforesaid have been accustomed to distrain every man in the same town having chattels to the value of 10 marks, wishing to trade among them and to enjoy their market customs. And thus then each of the aforesaid four men so elected should enjoy burgess-ship among them and their custom hereafter, and the burgesses of the aforesaid town in form aforesaid have been used to receive 2*s.* 1*d.*, etc. And this they are ready to verify, whereof they crave judgment, etc. . . .

The jurors say, etc. that. . . . the Abbot must answer whether the aforesaid Nicholas Fouke and others have a gild merchant in the aforesaid town or not, etc. The abbot says that they have not a gild merchant nor cognisances of pleas pertaining to a gild merchant, nor a commonalty nor a common seal nor a mayor; but they hold a gild at the feast of the Nativity of St. John the Baptist in a certain place to feast and drink together, there holding their unlawful assemblies and taking from every man dwelling in the said town the aforesaid 2*s.* 1*d.*and also 46*s.* 8*d.*, levying such money from the men aforesaid, that the payers thereof may be of their fellowship, by distraints made upon them; and he does not deny that the ancestors of the aforesaid Nicholas and others have been long accustomed to receive such extortions of 2*s.* 1*d.* and 46*s.* 8*d.*, but against the Law Merchant and against the will of the aforesaid payers and against the peace, etc., and beyond the amount of a third part of their goods; and by such extortions and ransoms they claim to make burgesses within his liberty and lordship, which there pertains to the Abbot himself and to no other to be done, etc.

A day is given. . . . It is awarded that the aforesaid Abbot [recover] his damages of 199*l.* 13*s.* 4*d.* against the aforesaid Nicholas and others. . . . And let the same Nicholas and others be committed to gaol, etc. Afterwards the aforesaid Nicholas and others came and made fine, etc. And let certain others in the dispute be imprisoned for a month owing to their poverty, etc. And the aforesaid Nicholas and others came before the justices and satisfied the lord Abbot, etc.; therefore let them be delivered from prison, etc.

12. Complaints of the Men of Leicester against the Lord [*Inquisitions Miscellaneous*, 87, *No.* 46], 1322.

Inquisition taken at Leicester on Saturday next after the feast of St. Barnabas the Apostle[1] in the 15th year of the reign of King Edward, son of King Edward, before Roger Beler, guardian of the castles, lands and tenements of Thomas, late earl of Lancaster,[2] and other enemies and rebels of the lord the King in the County of Leicester, in the hand of the lord the King by their forfeiture, by the oath of William le Palmere of Leicester.[3] . . .

Who say on their oath that in the time of Edmund, late earl of Leicester, uncle of the lord the King that now is, while he had the lordship of the town aforesaid, the men of the same town who were in the gild of the same town gave nothing for the retailing or sale of cloth or other merchandise, but in the time of Thomas, late earl of Leicester, by distraints of farmers[4] and extortions they were compelled to make heavy fines yearly.

Further, in the time of the aforesaid Edmund, the fullers dwelling in the same town gave nothing to any man for exercising that craft, but in the time of Thomas they were compelled to pay 40*s*. a year, so that the aforesaid farmers would not permit other fullers to come into the same town, whereby none remains in the same town save one only, and he is poor.

Further, in the time of Edmund, the butchers of the same town used to give nothing to any man for exercising their trade, but in the time of Thomas they were compelled to give 10*s*. a year to the farmers.

Further, in the time of Edmund, for four days at Christmas no court of pleas of the Portmanmoot used to be holden, but in the time of Thomas by extortions and distraints the farmers [4] used to compel those who owed to others any debt, upon plaint made against them, to pay their debts within the aforesaid four days, or to imprison their bodies until they should have paid.

In the time of Edmund vendors of oatmeal sold their meal, giving nothing to any man except toll; in the time of

[1] June 11.

[2] The necessities of Earl Thomas, leader of the opposition to Edward II., had evidently reacted upon his tenants.

[3] And 23 others named.

[4] The lord's lessees, responsible for the farm of the town.

Thomas they were not permitted to sell the aforesaid meal except by great measures, and then the beadles of the farmers of the same town took by extortion from the buyers a great quantity for measuring it, and to have that profit the said beadles gave to the farmers 40*s*. a year.

Further, in the time of Edmund, the farmers of the demesne lands of the same Edmund used to have the dung found in the four high roads and not elsewhere in the lanes; in the time of Thomas, by force and might they collected and took the dung in all the lanes, against the will of the burgesses.

Further, in the time of Edmund, from payers of toll the farmers used to take nothing by way of a double toll, and that by view of any of the jurors of the same town; in the time of Thomas the farmers took from payers of toll the heaviest ransoms at their will, exceeding the value of the thing whereon the toll was so paid, and often more than the true value.

Further, in the time of Edmund, the porters of the castle of the town of Leicester meddled not in the town of Leicester with the making of any attachments, except with a bailiff of the same town; in the time of Thomas, by force and might they made attachments and other executions without any bailiff of the town, and wrought great wrongs in the said town, whereby the burgesses suffered great grievances.

In the time of Edmund, if any burgess were impleaded in the court of the castle, the mayor and bailiffs of the same town used to claim their court and freely have it at the Portmanmoot; in the time of Thomas the farmers refused to admit their claims or to grant their court, but compelled burgesses to answer there by various and heavy distraints.

Further, in the time of Edmund, buyers of wool used to hire carts to carry their wool at their will; in the time of Thomas they were compelled to give to the farmers 1*d*. on each sack and could hire carts only at the will of the said farmers.

Further, in the time of Edmund, the foresters of "le Fruth" used not to make attachments in the town of Leicester nor meddle there for any trespasses of dry wood committed; in the time of Thomas, by extortion, force and might, they made attachments both upon those who bought at their doors from poor women carrying dry sticks on their heads, and upon others, and caused the buyers to be amerced at the court of "le Hethilegh."

In the time of Edmund, the brewers of the same town used to be amerced once a year according to the measure of their guilt and at the rate of 6*d.* or 12*d.* at most; in the time of Thomas, the farmers levied from the same by extortions and heavy ransoms at their will from one half a mark and from another 10*s.*, which they call farms of "Cannemol."

Further, in the time of Edmund, the weavers of the same town used to give nothing to any man for exercising their trade; in the time of Thomas the said farmers took by extortion from every weaver 40*d.* for permission to work in broad cloth.

Further, in the time of Edmund the vendors of salt herrings and fish could sell such their merchandise by themselves and their servants (*servos*) with their own hands, giving nothing of their own except toll; in the time of Thomas they were not permitted to sell their merchandise, but the ministers of the farmers deputed hereto sold the same and took great sums of money by extortion.

Further, in the time of Edmund, retailers of cloth selling in their windows used not to be amerced except by view of jurors of the same town and once a year at 12*d.*; in the time of Thomas they were compelled by heavy extortions to make fines at his will.

In witness whereof the jurors have set their seals to this inquisition.

13. Grant of Pavage to the Lord of a Town [*Patent Roll, 2 Edward III, p. 1, m. 5*], 1328.

The King to the venerable father in Christ H. by the same grace bishop of Lincoln, greeting. Know ye that we have granted to you, in aid of paving your town of Newark, that from the day of the making of these presents to the end of three years completed next following you take in the same town, by those whom you shall think fit to depute hereto and for whom you will be answerable, the underwritten customs on things for sale coming to the same town, to wit, on each quarter of corn for sale ¼*d.*, on each horse and mare for sale ½*d.*, on each hide of horse and mare, ox and cow, fresh, salted and tanned, for sale, ¼*d.*, on each cart carrying meat, salted or fresh, for sale, 1½*d.*, on 5 bacons for sale ½*d.*, on each salmon, fresh or salt, for sale, ¼*d.*, on each 100 mackerel for sale ½*d.*, on each lamprey for sale ½*d.*, on 10 sheep, goats or swine for sale 1*d.*, on 10 fleeces for sale ½*d.*, on each 100 woolfells of sheep, goats, stags, hinds, bucks and does for sale 1*d.*, on each 100 fells of lambs, kids, hares, rabbits, foxes, cats and squirrels ½*d.*, on each cart-load of sea-fish for sale 2*d.*, on each horse-load of sea-fish for sale ½*d.*, on each truss of cloths brought by cart 3*d.*, on each horse-load of cloth for sale or other diverse and minute things for sale coming to the same town ½*d.*, on each cart-load of iron for sale 1*d.*, on each 100 of steel for sale ¼*d.*, on each cart-load of tin for sale ½*d.*, on each quarter of woad 2*d.*, on each tun of wine for sale 2*d.*, on each sack of wool for sale 2*d.*, on each horse-load of wool 1*d.*, on each horse-load of apples, pears or nuts for sale ¼*d.*, on each 100 of linen web and canvas for sale ½*d.*, on each 100 of linen for sale ¼*d.*, on each new cart for sale ¼*d.*, on each cart laden with timber for sale ½*d.*, on each 1000 laths 1½*d.*, on each 100 stockfish and Aberdeen fish ½*d.*, on each cart laden with hay or grass for sale ¼*d.*, on each cart carrying rushes for sale 1*d.*, on each cart-load of heath for sale ½*d.*, on each truss of chalons[1] for sale ½*d.*, on each horse-load of glass (*verro*) ½*d.*, on each horse-load of garlic for sale ½*d.*, on each 1000 herrings for sale ¼*d.*, on each 100 boards for sale 1*d.*, on each cart-load of faggots for sale ¼*d.*, on each quarter of salt for sale ¼*d.*, on each dozen horse-loads of coals for sale ½*d.*, on each cart-load of coals for sale ½*d.*, on each cart-load of brushwood for sale ½*d.*, on each horse-load of brushwood for sale by the week ¼*d.*, on each 1000 nails for house gables (*ad cumilum domus*) for sale ¼*d.*, on each 100 horse shoes for horses and clout-nails for carts ½*d.*, on 2000 of all manner of nails for sale except nails for carts and house gables ¼*d.*, on each truss of every kind of ware for sale coming to the same town and exceeding the value of 2*s.*, ¼*d.* And therefore we command you that you take the customs aforesaid until the end of the said three years in the form aforesaid, and that after the term of the said three years be complete the said customs wholly cease and be annulled. In witness whereof, etc., to endure for the aforesaid three years. Witness the King at Northampton, 8 May.

By the King himself.

[1] Coverlets made at Chalons-sur-Marne.

14. Misappropriation of the Tolls Levied for Pavage [*Fine Roll*, 10 *Edward III*, *m.* 22], 1336.

The King to his beloved and faithful John de Mounteny, Nicholas de Beaulu, Robert Scuffyn, and William de Merston, greeting. Know ye that whereas on the 8th day of May in the second year of our reign by our letters patent we granted unto the venerable father Henry, bishop of Lincoln, that he should have in the town of Newark pavage for the term of three years next following, and afterwards, wishing to do further grace to the same bishop in this behalf, we granted unto him that from the end of the term aforesaid he should take in the town aforesaid such pavage until the end of four years then next following, the collection of which pavage amounts to no small sum, as it is said; and we have received a petition shown before us and our council, containing that the collectors of the pavage aforesaid in the time aforesaid have detained by them the money which they have collected from that pavage by virtue of the grants aforesaid, and still detain the same, converting it to other uses than to the repair and amendment of that town, as would be fitting, to the deception of us and contrary to the form of the grants aforesaid: We, wishing to apply a remedy in this behalf, as well for us as for the safety of the town aforesaid in times to come, as we are bound, have appointed you, three and two of you, to survey all works, if any have been done by the collectors aforesaid from such money levied and collected during the time of the grants aforesaid in the same town, and to enquire, if need be, of the names of the collectors aforesaid, and to cause those collectors to come before you, three or two of you, and to hear and determine finally the account of all the same collectors of all their receipts from the time aforesaid for such cause, and to distrain the same collectors to apply without delay in such repair all money levied on account of the premises and not applied in the repair aforesaid, and to appoint and depute certain fit collectors of the pavage aforesaid in the town aforesaid of the same town, to collect and levy the money there and to apply the same in the repair and amendment of the pavage aforesaid in times to come, as you shall deem best to be done according to your discretions for our advantage and the safety of the town aforesaid. And therefore we command you that at certain days which you, three or two of you, shall provide herefor, you hear and determine the account aforesaid, and do and accomplish all and singular the premises in the form aforesaid ; for we have commanded our sheriff of Nottingham that at certain days which you, three or two of you, shall cause him to know, he cause to come before you, three or two of you, the collectors aforesaid, and as many and such good and lawful men of his bailiwick by whom the truth of the matter in the premises may the better be known and enquired of. In witness whereof, etc. Witness the King at Walsingham, 15 February. By petition of the Council.

15. ORDINANCES OF THE WHITE TAWYERS OF LONDON [*Guildhall Letter-Book F, f.* 126], 1346.

In honour of God, of Our Lady, and of all Saints, and for the nurture of tranquillity and peace among the good folks the Megucers, called "*Whittawyers*," the folks of the same trade have, by assent of Richard Lacer, Mayor, and of the Aldermen, ordained the points under-written.

In the first place, they have ordained that they will find a wax candle, to burn before Our Lady in the Church of All Hallows near London Wall. Also, that each person of the said trade shall put in the box such sum as he shall think fit, in aid of maintaining the said candle.

Also, if by chance any one of the said trade shall fall into poverty, whether through old age, or because he cannot labour or work, and have nothing with which to help himself ; he shall have every week from the said box 7*d.* for his support if he be a man of good repute. And after his decease, if he have a wife, a woman of good repute, she shall have weekly for her support 7*d.* from the said box, so long as she shall behave herself well, and keep single.

And that no stranger shall work in the said trade, or keep house [for the same] in the city, if he be not an apprentice, or a man admitted to the franchise of the said city.

And that no one shall take the serving man of another to work with him, during his term, unless it be with the permission of his master.

And if any one of the said trade shall have work in his house that he cannot complete, or if for want of assistance such work shall be in danger of being lost, those of the said trade shall aid him, that so the said work be not lost.

And if any one of the said trade shall depart this life, and have not wherewithal to be buried, he shall be buried at the expense of their common box ; and when any one of the said trade shall die, all those of the said trade shall go to the Vigil, and make offering on the morrow.

And if any serving-man shall conduct himself in any other manner than properly towards his master, and act rebelliously towards him, no one of the said trade shall set him to work, until he shall have made amends before the Mayor and Aldermen ; and before them such misprision shall be redressed.

And that no one of the said trade shall behave himself the more thoughtlessly, in the way of speaking or acting amiss, by reason of the points aforesaid ; and if any one shall do to the contrary thereof, he shall not follow the said trade until he shall have reasonably made amends.

And if any one of the said trade shall do to the contrary of any point of the Ordinances aforesaid, and be convicted thereof by good men of the said trade, he shall pay to the Chamber of the Guildhall of London, the first time 2*s*., the second time 40*d*., the third time half a mark, and the fourth time 10*s*., and shall forswear the trade.

Also, that the good folks of the same trade shall once in the year be assembled in a certain place, convenient thereto, there to choose two men of the most loyal and befitting of the said trade, to be overseers of work and all other things touching the trade, for that year, which persons shall be presented to the Mayor and Aldermen for the time being, and sworn before them diligently to enquire and make search, and loyally to present to the said Mayor and Aldermen such defaults as they shall find touching the said trade without sparing any one for friendship or for hatred, or in any other manner. And if any one of the said trade shall be found rebellious against the said overseers, so as not to let them properly make their search and assay, as they ought to do ; or if he shall absent himself from the meeting aforesaid, without reasonable cause, after due warning by the said overseers, he shall pay to the Chamber, upon the first default, 40*d*. ; and on the second like default, half a mark ; and on the third, one mark ; and on the fourth, 20*s*. and shall forswear the trade for ever.

Also, that if the overseers shall be found lax and negligent about their duty, or partial to any person, for gift or for friendship, maintaining him, or voluntarily permitting him [to continue] in his default, and shall not present him to the Mayor and Aldermen, as before stated, they are to incur the penalty aforesaid.

Also, that each year, at such assemblies of the good folks of the said trade, there shall be chosen overseers, as before stated. And if it shall be found that through laxity or negligence of the said governors such assemblies are not held, each of the said overseers is to incur the said penalty.

Also, that all skins falsely and deceitfully wrought in their trade, which the said overseers shall find on sale in the hands of any person, citizen or foreigner, within the franchise, shall be forfeited to the said Chamber, and the worker thereof amerced in manner aforesaid.

Also, that no one who has not been an apprentice, and has not finished his term of apprenticeship in the said trade shall be made free of the same trade; unless it be attested by the overseers for the time being or by four persons of the said trade, that such person is able, and sufficiently skilled to be made free of the same.

Also, that no one of the said trade shall induce the servant of another to work with him in the same trade, until he has made a proper fine with his first master, at the discretion of the said overseers, or of four reputable men of the said trade. And if any one shall do to the contrary thereof, or receive the serving workman of another to work with him during his term, without leave of the trade, he is to incur the said penalty.

Also, that no one shall take for working in the said trade more than they were wont heretofore, on the pain aforesaid, that is to say, for the *dyker*[1] of *Scottes stagges*, half a mark; the *dyker of Yrysshe*, half a mark; the *dyker of Spanysshe stagges* 10*s.*; for the hundred of *gotesfelles*, 20*s.*; the hundred of *rolether*, 16*s.*; for the hundred skins of *hyndescalves*, 8*s.*; and for the hundred of *kiddefelles*, 8*s.*[2]

16. Dispute Between the Master Saddlers of London and Their Journeymen [*Guildhall, Letter-Book H, f.* 309], 1396.

Whereas there had arisen no small dissension and strife between the masters of the trade of Saddlers of London, and

[1] A package of ten. [2] Printed in Riley, Memorials, 232.

the serving-men, called *yomen*, in that trade; because that the serving-men aforesaid against the consent, and without leave of their masters, were wont to array themselves all in a new and like suit once in the year, and often times held divers meetings, at Stratford and elsewhere without the liberty of the said city, as well as in divers places within the city; whereby many inconveniences and perils ensued to the trade aforesaid; and also, very many losses might happen thereto in future times, unless some quick and speedy remedy should by the rulers of the said city be found for the same; therefore the masters of the said trade on the 10th day of the month of July, in the 20th year, etc., made grievous complaint thereon to the excellent men, William More, Mayor, and the Aldermen of the City aforesaid, urgently entreating that, for the reasons before mentioned, they would deign to send for Gilbert Dustone, William Gylowe, John Clay, John Hiltone, William Berigge, and Nicholas Mason, the then governors of the serving-men aforesaid; to appear before them on the 12th day of July then next ensuing.

And thereupon, on the same 10th day of July, precept was given to John Parker, serjeant of the Chamber, to give notice to the same persons to be here on the said 12th day of July, etc. Which Governors of the serving-men appeared, and, being interrogated as to the matters aforesaid, they said that time out of mind the serving-men of the said trade had had a certain Fraternity among themselves, and had been wont to array themselves all in like suit once in the year, and, after meeting together at Stratford, on the Feast of the Assumption of the Blessed Virgin Mary[1] to come from thence to the Church of St. Vedast, in London, there to hear Mass on the same day, in honour of the said glorious Virgin.

But the said masters of the trade asserted to the contrary of all this, and said that the fraternity, and the being so arrayed in like suit among the serving-men, dated from only thirteen years back, and even then had been discontinued of late years; and that under a certain feigned colour of sanctity, many of the serving-men in the trade had influenced the journey-men among them and had formed covins thereon, with the object of raising their wages greatly in excess; to such an extent, namely, that whereas a master in the said

[1] August 15.

trade could before have had a serving-man or journey-man for 40 shillings or 5 marks yearly, and his board, now such a man would not agree with his master for less than 10 or 12 marks or even 10 pounds, yearly; to the great deterioration of the trade.[1]

And further, that the serving-men aforesaid according to an ordinance made among themselves, would oftentimes cause the journey-men of the said masters to be summoned by a beadle, thereunto appointed, to attend at Vigils of the dead, who were members of the said Fraternity, and at making offering for them on the morrow, under a certain penalty to be levied; whereby the said masters were very greatly aggrieved, and were injured through such absenting of themselves by the journey-men, so leaving their labours and duties against their wish.

For amending and allaying the which grievances and dissensions, the Mayor and Aldermen commanded that six of the said serving-men should attend in the name of the whole of the alleged Fraternity, and communicate with six or eight of the master saddlers aforesaid, etc., both parties to be here, before the said Mayor and Aldermen on the 19th day of July then next ensuing to make report to the Court as to such agreement between them as aforesaid. And further, the Mayor and Aldermen strictly forbade the said serving-men in any manner to hold any meeting thereafter at Stratford aforesaid, or elsewhere without the liberty of the said city on pain of forfeiture of all that unto our Lord the King and to the said city they might forfeit.

On which 19th day of July, came here as well the masters aforesaid as the governors of the serving-men; and presented to the Mayor and Aldermen a certain petition, in these words: "Gilbert Dustone, William Gylowe, John Clay, John Hiltone, William Berigge, and Nicholas Mason, do speak on behalf of all their Fraternity and do beg of the Wardens of the Saddlers that they may have and use all the points which heretofore they have used."

Which petition having been read and heard, and divers reasons by the said masters unto the Mayor and Aldermen shown, it was determined that the serving-men in the trade aforesaid should in future be under the governance and rule

[1] For further evidence of combinations, see below, No. 32.

of the masters of such trade; the same as the serving-men in other trades in the same city are wont, and of right are bound to be; and that in future they should have no fraternity, meetings, or covins, or other unlawful things under a penalty, etc. And that the said masters must properly treat and govern their serving-men in the trade in such manner as the serving-men in like trades in the city have been wont to be properly treated and governed. And that if any serving-men should in future wish to make complaint to the Mayor and Aldermen, for the time being, as to any grievance unduly inflicted upon him by the masters aforesaid, such Mayor and Aldermen would give to him his due and speedy meed of justice as to the same.[1]

17. Ordinances of the Dyers of Bristol [*Patent Roll, 13 Henry IV, p. 2, m.* 31], 1407.

These are the petition, ordinances and articles, which are granted and confirmed to the masters, burgesses of the craft of dyeing of the town of Bristol . . . by the assent and advice of the whole Common Council . . . holden in the Gildhall of Bristol . . . the 8th year of the reign of King Henry the Fourth after the Conquest, to endure for ever, as well for the honour of the town of Bristol as for the profit and amendment of the said craft; the tenour of which petition and ordinances follows hereafter:

To the honourable and discreet Sirs, the Mayor, Sheriff and Bailiffs of the town of Bristol, and to all the honourable folk of the Common Council, the said masters make supplication: Whereas certain persons of the said town of divers crafts, not cunning in the craft of dyeing, who were never apprentices nor masters of the said craft, take upon them divers charges and bargains to dye cloths and wools of many folk of the same town and the country round, which cloths and wools have been divers times ill dressed and worked through their ignorance and lack of knowledge, to the great damage of the owners and scandal of the whole craft aforesaid and of the drapery of the same town; whereupon, most wise Sirs, please it your special grace to grant to the said suppliants the ordinances underwritten, to put out and bring to nought all deceits and damages

[1] Printed in Riley, Memorials, 542.

which could hereafter befal within the craft aforesaid, and this for God and as a work of charity.

First, be it ordained and assented that each year two masters of the said craft be elected by the common assent of all the masters of the same craft in the town of Bristol, and their names presented to the Mayor of Bristol in full court of the Gildhall of the same town, and there to be sworn on the Holy Gospels within the quinzaine of Michaelmas at the latest to survey well and lawfully all manner of defects which shall be made henceforward as well in dyed cloths as in wools put in woad within the franchise of Bristol. And if any damage is done to any person through defect of dyeing by any man or woman of the said craft, that then he shall pay sufficient amends to the parties damaged according to the discretion of the said two masters and of four other indifferent persons elected by the Mayor and his Council, as the trespass demands. And if it so be that any man or woman will not abide by the ordinance and award of the said two masters and other indifferent persons elected by the Mayor as before is said, that then the Mayor and his council for the time being shall cause them to be compelled to pay and satisfy the said persons so damaged of all that is adjudged by them. And in case that the said two masters after their oath made be negligent in executing their office touching their said mistery, that they be punished and amerced according to the advice of the Mayor and of the court aforesaid to the use of the chamber and to the common profit as is aforesaid.

Further, that no servant or apprentice of the said mistery be henceforth admitted to the liberties of Bristol to be a burgess sworn to exercise the said mistery until it be testified to the court before the Mayor of Bristol by the said two masters that they are able and well learned in the said craft of dyeing, to save and keep the goods of the good folk who are wont to be served for their money in the exercise of the mistery aforesaid. And if any master of the said mistery make any such servant or apprentice, if he be not able and well learned in the said craft, as before is said, he shall incur the penalty of 20*s.* for each time, to wit, to the use and profit of the commonalty, as before is said, 13*s.* 4*d.*, and to the masters for their light, 6*s.* 8*d.*, without any pardon, provided always that the Mayor of the town of Bristol have his power and jurisdiction to accept and make burgesses of each person presented to him, as has been used and accustomed before these times, these ordinances notwithstanding.

Further, forasmuch as often before these times divers folk, as well those who have not been apprentices, servants or masters of the said mistery, as other folk who are of other misteries, not cunning nor having knowledge in the aforesaid art of dyeing, have taken upon them to dye cloths and wools put in woad, as well of good folk of the town as of the country round, which, by reason of ill management and through lack of knowledge of the said folk, are greatly impaired of their colours and many other defects to the great loss and damage of the owners of the said cloths and great scandal of the town and shame of the whole craft aforesaid, whereby the masters and apprentices of the said craft of dyeing go vagrant for lack of work, because the said folk of other crafts have been occupied in their said craft, to their great mischief and undoing, therefore it is ordained and assented that henceforward no manner of man of the same craft nor any other mistery do dye any cloth or wool, unless it be presented by the said masters that he be good and able and sufficiently learned in the said craft, upon pain of paying to the Mayor and Bailiffs of the chamber for the use and common profit, as before is said, at the first default 6*s.* 8*d.*, at the second default 13*s.* 4*d.*, at the third default 20*s.*, and for each default after the said three defaults 20*s.*, without any pardon, so that the said masters have for their labour the third part arising from the said defaults for their light, provided always that all the burgesses of this town may make their profit for dyeing in their houses their own cloths, as has been used before these times, these ordinances notwithstanding.

And after the view of the said petition and ordinances aforesaid by the Mayor and Common Council, it was assented that all the masters of the said mistery of dyeing dwelling within the franchise of Bristol should come before the Mayor to hear their said ordinances and whether they would assent thereto and grant them or not. And by command of the . . . Mayor, Ralph Dyer . . . and many others of the mistery aforesaid came in their own persons, to whom all the said ordinances were published and declared, and every of them in the presence of the Mayor aforesaid granted and assented to all the ordinances and pains aforesaid, praying of their common assent that the ordinances and pains aforesaid be ratified, confirmed and enrolled of record in the papers of the Gildhall of Bristol, and be put in due execution for ever, saving always to the jurisdiction of the Mayor and Common Council of the town of Bristol that if any ordinance or any new addition hereafter touching the mistery aforesaid which may be profitable as well for the town as for the aforesaid mistery, that then by the advice and ordinance of the Mayor of Bristol for the time being and the Council of the town and also of the masters of the said mistery, they shall be corrected and amended according to good faith and reason and put in due execution, the ordinances aforesaid notwithstanding. Provided also that the dyers abovesaid be bound by these ordinances to make the assay of woad and to work wools and cloths as well in woad as in madder of the goods of all merchants and burgesses of Bristol, taking for their labour reasonably as has been accustomed and used before these times. In witness whereof, at the special prayer and request of the said masters to keep and maintain their ordinances aforesaid, we have put hereto the seal of the office of the Mayoralty of the town of Bristol. Given in the Gildhall of the same town 17 March, 8 Henry IV.[1]

18. Incorporation of the Fraternity of the Haberdashers of London [*Patent Roll*, 26 *Henry VI*, *p.* 2, *m.* 23], 1448.

The King to all to whom, etc., greeting. Know ye that of our especial grace and the inspiration of charity, and for the especial devotion which we bear and have towards the Blessed Virgin Catherine, we have granted and given licence for us and our heirs, as much as in us lies, to our beloved lieges, the men of the mistery of Haberdashers within our city of London, that they may begin, unite, found, create, erect and establish a gild or fraternity in honour of the same Virgin of men of the mistery aforesaid and others, and have and hold that gild or fraternity so begun, united, founded, created, erected and established, and enjoy and exercise the same to them and their successors for all future times to endure; and that they and their successors may increase and augment the same gild

[1] From the confirmation of 13 Henry IV. Printed in *The Red Book of Bristol*, ii. p. 81.

or fraternity and hold the gild or fraternity aforesaid of the said mistery of Haberdashers and any persons whom they will receive within the fraternity aforesaid, and may elect and make four wardens from themselves as often as they shall please or need shall be for the governance, custody and rule of the said fraternity for ever, as shall best please them ; and that the said wardens and their successors each year may make a livery of vesture of one suit among the brethren and sisters of the same fraternity, and their meetings and gatherings in places of our city aforesaid, and there in honest manner hold and keep their feast of food and drink at the feast of St. Catherine the Virgin, and make ordinances among themselves as often as they shall please and as they shall deem most necessary and opportune, and ordain and rule their mistery and correct and amend defects of their servants by view of the Mayor of the city aforesaid for the time being or of any person whom he shall depute hereto in his place, as they shall deem fit to be done for the greater utility of the commonalty of our people ; and that none within the liberty of the city aforesaid keep a shop or house of that mistery, unless he be of the liberty of that city, nor any be admitted to the liberty of the said city in the same mistery, unless he be presented by the aforesaid wardens or their successors and by four other good and lawful men of the same mistery, and it be testified to the Mayor of our said city for the time being that he is good, faithful and fit for the same. And further of our more abundant grace and at the supplication of our said lieges, the men of the mistery aforesaid, we will and grant for us and our heirs, as much as in us lies, that the same wardens and their successors be perpetual and capable and the said fraternity be by itself a solid and perpetual and corporate fraternity, and that that fraternity be hereafter named the fraternity of St. Catherine the Virgin of Haberdashers in the city of London, and the said wardens and their successors [the wardens] of the fraternity of St Catherine the Virgin of Haberdashers in the city of London, and we incorporate the said wardens and their successors and the fraternity aforesaid to endure for ever, and we make them as it were one body and declare, accept and approve them for one body and hold them for one body. We have granted also for us and our heirs, as far as in us lies, to the aforesaid wardens, that they and their successors, by the name of the wardens of the fraternity of St. Catherine the Virgin of Haberdashers in the city of London, may acquire to them and their successors in fee and perpetuity lands, tenements, rents, annuities and other possessions as well of those which are held of us in free burgage as others, provided that by inquisitions to be taken thereon in due form and returned into the Chancery of us and our heirs it be found that it can be done without damage or prejudice to us or our heirs or others whomsoever, and that they may have a common seal and be impleaded and implead others by the name of the wardens of the fraternity of St. Catherine the Virgin of Haberdashers in the city of London for ever before any judges in any courts, and that they may have and hold to them and their successors all lands and tenements, rents, annuities and other possessions whatsoever acquired by the aforesaid wardens and their successors, and enjoy the same for ever without obstacle, impeachment or hindrance of us or our heirs, our justices, escheators, sheriffs or other bailiffs or ministers of us or our heirs whomsoever, the Statute published touching lands and tenements not to be put in Mortmain, or any other Statute or ordinance made to the contrary, notwithstanding. And further of our more abundant grace we have granted for us and our heirs to our aforesaid lieges and wardens and their successors aforesaid for ever that the same wardens and their successors, wardens of the fraternity aforesaid for the time being, have and make full search as well in and of the mistery of Haberdashers and of every thing touching it, as of all goods and things in any wise belonging to or incumbent on the craft of Haberdashers aforesaid brought or hereafter to be brought by any alien or any aliens from parts remote into our realm of England, when they or any of them shall bring the same to the same our city or the suburbs thereof or within three miles distant round about the said city, and also of each such alien and of such misteries and things which they, our privileged lieges, use or have used before these times, and may present all defects in that behalf found by them as well upon our said lieges as upon aliens, according to their discretions, to the Mayor of our city aforesaid for the time being or his deputy in this behalf, if need be, and correct and reform the same by his survey. And further we will and by these our letters we grant to our aforesaid lieges, the men of the mistery aforesaid, that no officer, minister, artificer, merchant or any other whosoever hereafter search or presume to search in any wise any our privileged liege employing the craft aforesaid nor his goods of haberdashery, save only the four wardens of the craft aforesaid for the time being ; so that it be not to the prejudice of the Mayor of our city of London. In witness, etc. Witness the King at Westminster the 3rd day of June. By the King himself and of the said date, etc.

19. Indenture of Apprenticeship [*Ancient Deeds*, A 10022], 1459.

This indenture made between John Gibbs of Penzance in the county of Cornwall of the one part and John Goffe, Spaniard, of the other part, witnesses that the aforesaid John Goffe has put himself to the aforesaid John Gibbs to learn the craft of fishing, and to stay with him as apprentice and to serve from the feast of Philip and James[1] next to come after the date of these presents until the end of eight years then next ensuing and fully complete ; throughout which term the aforesaid John Goffe shall well and faithfully serve the aforesaid John Gibbs and Agnes his wife as his masters and lords, shall keep their secrets, shall everywhere willingly do their lawful and honourable commands, shall do his masters no injury nor see injury done to them by others, but prevent the same as far as he can, shall not waste his master's goods nor lend them to any man without his special command. And the aforesaid John Gibbs and Agnes his wife shall teach, train and inform or cause the aforesaid John Goffe, their apprentice, to be informed in the craft of fishing in the best way they know, chastising him duly and finding for the same John, their apprentice, food, clothing linen and woollen, and shoes, sufficiently, as befits such an apprentice to be found, during the term aforesaid. And at the end of the term aforesaid the aforesaid John Goffe shall have of the aforesaid John Gibbs and Agnes his wife 20*s*. sterling without any fraud. In witness whereof the parties aforesaid have interchangeably set their seals to the parts of this indenture. These witnesses :—Richard Bascawen, Robert Martyn and Robert Cosyn and many others. Given at Penzance, 1 April in the 37th year of

[1] May 1.

the reign of King Henry the Sixth after the Conquest of England.

20. A Runaway Apprentice [*Early Chancery Proceedings, File* 6, *No.* 7], *c.* 1425 (?).

To the most reverend father in God and his most gracious lord, the bishop of Winchester, chancellor of England.

Beseecheth meekly William Beverley of London that whereas William Batyngham has been arrested and detained in prison in Salisbury at the suit of the said beseecher, for that he was his apprentice and departed from his service here in London, and has been the whole time since . . . wandering in divers towns, as in Winchester, Bristol and elsewhere, so that the said beseecher could not find him until now of late suddenly, and so it is that upon the matter abovesaid his said suit cannot be determined in Salisbury, for that the retaining and departing did not take place within the said town: Please it your most gracious discretion to grant to the said beseecher a writ directed to the mayor, bailiffs and keeper of the gaol there and to each of them to have the body of the said William Batyngham with such a clause "by whatsoever name he be known," before you at a certain day to be limited by you, considering that he has no other remedy, and that for God and in work of charity.[1]

21. Incorporation of a Gild for Religious and Charitable Uses [*Patent Roll*, 25 *Henry VI*, *p.* 2, *m.* 5], 1447.

The King to all to whom, etc., greeting. Know ye that of our especial grace and out of reverence for the Holy Trinity we have granted and given licence for us and our heirs, as much as in us lies, to Ralph, lord of Cromwell, and Thomas Thurland that they and one of them, to the praise and honour of the Holy Trinity, may begin, found, erect, unite, create and establish a fraternity or gild perpetual in the church of St. Mary of Nottingham of an alderman and two wardens and brethren and sisters of the parishioners of the same church and others who of their devotion shall wish to be of the same

[1] This case illustrates the growing habit of appealing to the Chancellor's equitable jurisdiction, a characteristic feature of fifteenth century administrative and legal history.

fraternity or gild, to endure for perpetual times to come; and that the said alderman and wardens and brethren and sisters of the fraternity or gild aforesaid, when it shall be thus begun, founded, erected, united, created and established, and their successors, be in fact and name one body and one perpetual commonalty, and have perpetual succession and a common seal to serve for the affairs of that fraternity or gild, and be persons able and capable in law to purchase to them and their successors in fee and perpetuity lands and tenements, rents and other possessions whatsoever of persons whomsoever; and that the same alderman and wardens and brethren and sisters and their successors for ever, by the name of the alderman and wardens and brethren and sisters of the fraternity or gild of the Holy Trinity of Nottingham, may plead and be impleaded before any judges soever in any courts and actions whatsoever. And further we will and by these presents we grant that the same alderman and wardens and brethren and sisters and their successors may augment the same fraternity or gild when it shall be thus begun, founded, erected, united, created and established, and receive new brethren and sisters into the same fraternity or gild, as often and when it shall seem to them hereafter necessary and opportune; and also once a year elect and make from themselves and their successors an alderman and two wardens to support the charges of the business touching and concerning the said fraternity or gild, and to rule and govern the same fraternity or gild. And further, of our more abundant grace we have granted and given licence for us and our heirs, as far as in us lies, to the aforesaid alderman and wardens and brethren and sisters and their successors, that, when the same fraternity or gild shall be thus begun, founded, erected, united, created and established, or their successors, for the maintenance of two chaplains to celebrate divine service for the good estate of us and Margaret our consort while we shall live and for our soul when we shall have departed this life and the souls of all our progenitors deceased, and for the good estate of the brethren and sisters of the same fraternity or gild, while they shall live, and for their souls when they shall have departed this life, and the souls of all the faithful departed, in the church aforesaid, according to the ordinance of the aforesaid Ralph, lord of Cromwell, and Thomas, or one of them, or their executors or assigns, to be made in this behalf, and for the relief of the poor and feeble brethren and sisters of the said fraternity or gild, they may purchase lands and tenements, rents and services, which are held of us in chief or burgage or by any other service soever or of others by any service soever, to the value of 20 marks a year beyond reprises, from any person or any persons soever willing to give or grant the same to them, without fine or fee to be taken or paid therefor to the use of us or our heirs, to have and to hold to the same alderman and wardens and brethren and sisters of the fraternity or gild abovesaid and their successors for the maintenance of the said two chaplains and for the relief of the poor and feeble aforesaid, as is said above, for ever; the Statute published touching lands and tenements not to be put in Mortmain, or any other statute or ordinance published or made to the contrary, notwithstanding; provided that it be found by inquisitions duly to be taken thereon and lawfully returned into the Chancery of us and our heirs, that it can be done without damage or prejudice to us or our heirs or others whomsoever. In witness whereof, etc. Witness the King at Bury St. Edmunds, 20 February.

By writ of privy seal, and of the date aforesaid by authority of Parliament, and for 20 marks paid in the hanaper.

SECTION VI

THE REGULATION OF TRADE, INDUSTRY AND COMMERCE

1. Assize of Measures, 1197—2. Grant to the lord of a manor of the assize of bread and ale and other liberties, 1307—3. An offence against the assize of bread, 1316—4. Inquisition touching a proposed market and fair, 1252—5. Grant of a fair at St. Ives to the abbot of Ramsey, 1202—6. Grant of a market at St. Ives to the abbot of Ramsey, 1293—7. Proceedings in the court at the fair of St. Ives, 1288—8. The Statute of Winchester, 1285—9. The recovery of debt on a recognisance, 1293—10. Procedure at a fair pursuant to the Statute for Merchants, 1287—11. The aulnage of cloth, 1291—12. The Ordinance of Labourers, 1349—13. Presentments made before the Justices of Labourers, 1351—14. Excessive prices charged by craftsmen, 1354—15. Fines levied for excessive wages, 1351—16. Writ to enforce payment of excess of wages to the collectors of a subsidy, 1350—17. Application of fines for excessive wages to a subsidy, 1351-2—18. Labour legislation; the Statute of 12 Richard II., 1388—19. Labour legislation; a Bill in Parliament, 23 Henry VI., 1444-5—20. Organisation of the Staple, 1313—21. Arguments for the establishment of home staple towns, 1319—22. Ordinances of the Staple, 1326—23. The election of the mayor and constables of a Staple town, 1358—24. Royal letters patent over-ruled by the custom of the Staple, 1436—25. Prohibition of export of materials for making cloth, 1326—26. Commercial policy, *temp.* Edw. IV.—27. The perils of foreign travel, 1315—28. Grant of letters of marque and reprisals, 1447—29. Grant of liberties to the merchants of Douay, 1260—30. Aliens at a fair, 1270—31. Confirmation of liberties to the merchants of Almain, 1280—32. Alien weavers in London, 1362—33. The hosting of aliens, 1442—34. An offence against Stat. 18 Henry VI. for the hosting of aliens, 1440—35. Imprisonment of an alien craftsman, *c.* 1440—36. Petition against usury, 1376—37. Action upon usury, *c.* 1480.

THE documents in this section are suggestive rather than comprehensive. No attempt has been made to illustrate the industrial and commercial development of England as a whole; but its more important aspects are indicated, and the machinery of administration outlined. Down to the end of the thirteenth century industry is of local rather than of national importance, and is regulated by custom rather than by law; while there was undoubtedly considerable intercourse between town and town, the conduct of trade, the oversight of conditions of labour, and the settlement of disputes were matters for the townsmen themselves to deal with in accordance with chartered rights or intermunicipal covenants. For example, the unpaid debt of an individual burgess was exacted by the *communitas burgensium* to which the injured creditor belonged, from any member of the *communitas burgensium* to which the defaulting debtor belonged, by the method of forcible seizure of goods. Although, therefore, the state attempted to secure uniformity of weights and measures and of cloth, and to maintain the quality and cheapness of the necessaries of life in the interests of traders and consumers alike, none the less the assizes of weights and measures and of cloth (No. 1), of bread and ale (Nos. 2 and 3) and of wine, came to be regarded, as might be expected in a feudal age, as franchises to be purchased by the lord of a manor, or enforced by the elected officers of a town. The regulation of trade and industry shares the characteristic features of its environment.

The same is true of early commercial intercourse with foreign communities. The right to hold a fair is a liberty granted by the crown to a lord, and for centuries the great fairs were the chief international marts (Nos. 4–7, 30). The freedom which alien merchants enjoyed under a clause of *Magna Carta* was extended by charters granting privileges similar in detail to those procured by English towns (Nos. 29–31), and it is not until the reign of Edward I. that a serious attempt is made to nationalise regulation (Nos. 8–11). Thereafter conflicts arise not only between the central legislature and the local chartered body or privileged lord (No. 11), but between a growing self-conscious merchant class and the alien communities which had hitherto controlled the export and import trade of the country (Nos. 21, 22). The State assumes new responsibilities, and Parliament attempts to standardise old and enforce new regulations for the nation at large (Nos. 12, 18, 19, 25). The Statute emerges over against the Charter on the one hand and the Ordinance on the other. The difficulties of Parliament are twofold; it has to fight, first, against old concessions which would be upheld by the Courts (No. 11), and second, against the uncertain operation of the royal prerogative (No. 34). It has often been urged that the mediæval statute was little more than the expression of an ideal, and that administrative machinery was insufficient for its adequate execution. The truth is rather that Parliament was one of several competing regulative institutions, and that notwithstanding the most punctilious and inquisitorial administrative methods, its measures were neutralised by existing privileges and by fresh exemptions extracted from a chronically bankrupt and insincere monarchy. That the administration was not of itself ineffective is clear from the enforcement of the Statutes of Labourers in the fourteenth century (Nos. 12–17) and of the Statute of 18 Henry VI restricting the freedom of aliens in the fifteenth century (Nos. 33, 34). The Crown was always preoccupied with the state of the revenue; statutes are enforced or overridden, according as their operation will benefit or deplete the Exchequer. It was the experience of centuries that gave point to queen Elizabeth's affection for the prerogative. None the less great strides were made in the fourteenth and fifteenth centuries towards the end largely achieved in the Tudor period. The Elizabethan legislation sums up and rounds off the work of the previous two hundred years. The regulation of wages and of the conditions of labour (Nos. 12–19), the protection of industry, commerce and shipping, making national trade an important factor in international diplomacy (Nos. 20, 22, 25, 27, 28), the emergence of a native mercantile class eager to win the export trade for their own country by means of the staple (Nos. 20–24), the jealousy of the alien, growing in intensity throughout the fourteenth and fifteenth centuries (Nos. 21, 33, 34, 35), the development of a home cloth manufacture competing with the best foreign products (Nos. 22, 25, 32), and the provision of remedies against the mediæval bugbear of usury (Nos. 36, 37), all assist in the gradual ripening of a national economy, the fruits of which were gathered first in the Tudor era.

AUTHORITIES

The principal modern writers dealing with the subject of this section are:—Rogers, *History of Agriculture and Prices*; Rogers, *Six Centuries of Work and Wages*; Cunningham, *Growth of English Industry and Commerce*; Ashley, *Economic History*; Ashley, *James van Artevelde*; Cunningham, *Alien Immigrants*; Putnam, *The Enforcement of the Statutes of Labourers*; Schanz, *Englische Handelspolitik gegen Ende des Mittelalters*; Varenbergh, *Relations diplomatiques entre le Comté de Flandre et l'Angleterre*; Ochenkowski, *England's Wirthschaftliche Entwickelung im Ausgange des Mittelalters*; Höhlbaum, *Hansisches Urkundenbuch.* See also the *English and American Historical Reviews.*

Contemporary authorities:—Thomas Aquinas, *De Usuris*; Political Poems and Songs (Wright, Rolls Series); Parliament Rolls (Record Commission); Calendars of Patent, Close and Fine Rolls (Record Office Publications).

1. Assize of Measures [*Roger of Hoveden, Rolls Series*, IV, 33], 1197.

It is established that all measures of the whole of England be of the same amount, as well of corn as of vegetables and of like things, to wit, one good horse load; and that this measure be level as well in cities and boroughs as without. Also the measure of wine and ale and of all liquids shall be of the same amount according to the diversity of liquids. Weights and measures also, great and small, shall be of the same amount in the whole realm, according to the diversity of wares. Measures also of corn and liquids, wine and ale, shall have marks put thereon,[1] lest by guile they can be falsified.

It is established that woollen cloths, wherever they be made, be made of the same width, to wit, of two ells within the lists,[2] and of the same good quality in the middle and at the sides.

[1] "*Inclaventur in eis claves.*" [2] The selvages.

Also the ell shall be the same in the whole realm and of the same length, and the ell shall be of iron.

It is forbidden to all merchants throughout the whole of the realm that any merchant set in front of his shop red or black cloths or shields or any other thing, whereby the buyers' eyes are often deceived in the choice of good cloth.

It is also forbidden that any dye for sale, save black only, be made anywhere in the realm, except in cities or chief boroughs.

It is also established that in every city or borough four or six lawful men of the same town, according to the size of the town, together with the sheriff,[1] or with the reeves of the city or borough, if the same be not in the hand of the sheriff, be assigned to keep the assize in this form: that they see and be sure that all things are sold and bought by the same measure, and that all measures are of the same size according to the diversity of wares. And if they find any who shall be confessed or convicted of having sold by other than the established measure, his body shall be taken and sent to prison, and all his chattels shall be seized into the hand of the lord the King, nor shall he be delivered save by the lord the King or his chief justice. Touching the keepers themselves it is established that if they perform this keeping so negligently that they be convicted by others than themselves before the justices of the lord the King of transgressing any written assize either of measures or of the width of cloths, the keepers shall remain at the mercy of the lord the King touching their chattels.

It is commanded also that after the feast of the Purification of St. Mary no man in any county sell anything save by the ordained measure, which shall be [everywhere] of the same size; nor after the fair of mid-Lent at Stamford sell any cloth of smaller width than two ells within the lists.

2. Grant to the Lord of a Manor of the Assize of Bread and Ale and other Liberties [*Inquisitions ad quod damnum*, 63, 16], 1307.

Nottingham.—Inquisition taken at Nottingham before William de Chelardeston, sheriff of Nottingham, on Sunday, a fortnight after Easter in the 35th year of the reign of King

[1] Reading *simul cum vicecomite* for *similiter in vicecomitatu.*

Edward, whether the lord the King, without doing prejudice or injury to any man, can grant to his beloved and trusty Peter Pycot that he and his heirs may have for ever in his manor of Ratcliffe upon Soar, in the county of Nottingham, view of frankpledge of his men and tenants of the same manor and whatever pertains to such view, and amends of the assize of bread and ale broken by the same men and tenants, and a pillory and a tumbrel and "infangenethef"[1] and gallows for the execution of judgment, for a fixed rent thereof according to the true value of the same liberties, to be rendered each year by the hands of the sheriff of that county for the time being to the lord the King and his heirs at their Exchequer, or not, and if prejudice or injury should be done to any man by the grant aforesaid, then to whom and in what manner and how, and how much the liberties aforesaid to be possessed in the same manor can be worth yearly according to the true value of the same, by the oath of Robert Pouterel of Thrumpton.[2] . . . Who say upon their oath that the lord the King, without doing prejudice or injury to any man, can grant to the aforesaid Peter Pycot that he and his heirs may have for ever in his manor of Ratcliffe upon Soar view of frankpledge.[3] . . . They say further that all the liberties aforesaid in the said manor are worth 2*s*. a year according to the true value thereof. In witness whereof the aforesaid jurors have set their seals to this inquisition. Given at Nottingham the day and year abovesaid.

3. An Offence Against the Assize of Bread [*Guildhall, Letter-Book* D, *f*. 189], 1316.[4]

On the Saturday next before the Feast of the Invention of the Holy Cross,[5] in the 9th year of the reign of King Edward, son of King Edward, Richard de Lughteburghe was attached to make answer as to a certain false wastel[6] loaf of his. And the same Richard said that he was not a baker, and that he did not have that wastel bread baked; but that, as a regrator, he bought it of a certain baker who lives in Southwark.

[1] The right to take and judge thieves within the manorial precincts.
[2] And eleven others named.
[3] And the other liberties specified above. For an explanation of view of frankpledge, see note to Section IV., No. 5 above.
[4] Printed in Riley, Memorials, 119.
[5] May 1.
[6] Medium quality.

And upon this he was charged by the Mayor and Aldermen with being in partnership with the baker aforesaid, in baking such bread, and sharing with him in the gain thereby, or loss, if such should happen: whereupon, being asked how he would acquit himself thereof, he said that he was not the partner of the said baker, nor had he any share with him; and he put himself upon the country as to the same. Therefore the country was summoned for the Tuesday next ensuing, and he was delivered into the custody of the sheriffs, etc.

On which day the said Richard came, and the jury came by John de Estwode and others in the panel named. Which jurors said upon their oath, that the aforesaid Richard is a partner of the said baker for gain in baking the bread aforesaid. Therefore it was adjudged that he should have the punishment of the hurdle. And he was so punished now for the first time, because his loaf was wanting to the amount of 2*s.* 9*d.* in the proper weight of half a mark for the halfpenny wastel loaf.

Also Alan de Lyndeseye, baker, was sentenced to the pillory, because he had been convicted of baking *pain demaign* that was found to be of bad dough within, and good dough without. And because such falsity redounds much to the deception of the people who buy such bread, he was committed for punishment, etc.

4. Inquisition Touching a Proposed Market and Fair [*Inquisitions ad quod damnum*, 1, 21], 1252.

Henry by the grace of God King of England, Lord of Ireland, Duke of Normandy and Aquitaine and Count of Anjou, to his mayor and bailiffs of Bristol, greeting. We command you that by the oath of good and lawful men of your town, by whom the truth of the matter may the better be known, you make diligent enquiry if it would be to the nuisance of the town aforesaid if we should grant to our beloved abbot of Pershore that he have a market at his manor of Hawksbury on Monday and a fair there at the feast of St. Matthew in Autumn[1]; and if it be to your nuisance, to what extent; and that without delay you send to us the inquisition made thereon under your seal and the seals of those by whom it shall be made, and this writ. Witness myself at Westminster, 26 February in the 36th year of our reign.

[1] September 21.

Inquisition made by command of the lord the King by the mayor and bailiffs of Bristol, if it would be to the nuisance of the town of Bristol if there were a market on Monday at the manor of Hawksbury which E. abbot of Pershore holds, and if there were a fair there at the feast of St. Matthew in Autumn, by William de Feria, clerk,[1] . . . Who say by their oath that it would not be to the nuisance of the town of Bristol in any wise if there were a market on the aforesaid Monday at the said manor of Hawksbury, and a fair there on the aforesaid feast of St. Matthew in Autumn.[2]

5. Grant of a Fair at St. Ives to the Abbey of Ramsey [*Cart. Rams.*, *f.* 191 *b.*], 1202.

John by the grace of God King of England, etc., greeting. Know ye that we, for our salvation and for the souls of our ancestors and successors, have granted and by our present charter have confirmed to God and the church of St. Mary and St. Benedict of Ramsey, and to the abbot and monks there serving God, a fair at St. Ives, to begin on the fourth day before the feast of St. Laurence and to endure for eight days[3]; to have and to hold for ever, so nevertheless that it be not to the nuisance of neighbouring fairs.

Wherefore we will and straitly command that the aforesaid abbot and monks have and hold the aforesaid fair well and in peace, freely and quietly, entirely, fully and honourably, with all liberties and free customs to such fair pertaining. Witnesses :—Robert earl of Leicester, William earl of Arundel, and others.

Given by the hand of Simon, archdeacon of Wells, at Harcourt on the seventh day of June in the fourth year of our reign.

6. Grant of a Market at St. Ives to the Abbey of Ramsey [*Cart. Rams.*, *f.* 191 *b.*], 1293.

Edward by the grace of God King of England, lord of Ireland and Duke of Aquitaine, to archbishops, bishops, abbots,

[1] And eleven others named.

[2] The abbot is granted the market and a fair on the eve, day and morrow of the Decollation of St. John the Baptist (August 28–30) by charter dated November 24, 1252 [*Charter Roll*, 37 *Henry III*, *m.* 19].

[3] August 6–13.

priors, earls, barons, justices, sheriffs, reeves, ministers and all his bailiffs and faithful, greeting. Know ye that we have granted and by this our charter confirmed to our beloved in Christ, the abbot and convent of Ramsey, that they and their successors for ever have a market every week on Monday at their manor of St. Ives in the county of Huntingdon, unless that market be to the nuisance of neighbouring markets. Wherefore we will and straitly command, for us and our heirs, that the aforesaid abbot and convent and their successors for ever have the aforesaid market at their manor aforesaid with all the liberties and free customs to such market pertaining, unless that market be to the nuisance of neighbouring markets, as is aforesaid. These witnesses:—the venerable fathers John, of Winchester, Anthony, of Durham, William, of Ely, bishops, William de Valencia, our uncle, Roger le Bygod, earl of Norfolk and marshal of England, John de Warenna, earl of Surrey, Henry de Lascy, earl of Lincoln, William de Bello Campo, earl of Warwick, Robert de Tybetot, Gilbert de Thornton, John de Metingham, Robert de Hertford, Robert Malet, and others. Given by our hand at Westminster on the fourteenth day of May in the twenty-first year of our reign.

7. Proceedings in the Court at the Fair of St. Ives [*Court Roll*, 178, 93, *m.* 1*d.*], 1288.[1]

Court on Saturday [24 April, 1288].

John son of John of Eltisley makes plaint of Roger the Barber that he has unjustly broken a covenant with him, because, whereas the same John was in the town of Ramsey on Monday next after the Epiphany of the Lord last past, a year ago, in the house of Thomas Buk, the said Roger came there and undertook to cure his head of baldness for 9*d.*, which he paid in hand. On Tuesday the aforesaid Roger put him in plaster, and on Wednesday likewise, and afterwards withdrew from the town, so that from that day to this he would have nothing to do with the matter, to John's damage of ½ mark; and he produces suit. The aforesaid Roger, being present, denied [tort and force] and put himself on his law,

[1] Printed in Selden Society Publications, Vol. 23, p. 35.

and in finding pledges of his law withdrew from the bar without licence. Therefore the aforesaid John craved judgment on him as on a man convicted. Wherefore it is awarded that the said Roger satisfy him of the 9*d.* principal, and of his damages, which are pardoned him; and that for the trespass he be in mercy, 6*d.* Pledge,——

8. THE STATUTE OF WINCHESTER, *cc.* 4, 5 [*Statute Roll*, 1, *m.* 41], 1285.

And for the greater security of the country the King has commanded that in the great towns, which are enclosed, the gates be shut from sunset until sunrise; and that no man lodge in the suburbs, or in any foreign part of the town save only in the daytime, nor yet in the daytime, if the host will not answer for him; and that the bailiffs of towns every week, or at the least every fortnight, make enquiry as to all persons lodging in the suburbs, and in foreign parts of the towns; and if they find any who receives or lodges in any manner persons who may be suspected of being against the peace, the bailiffs shall do right therein. And it is commanded that from henceforth watches be kept, as has been used in times past, that is to say, from the day of the Ascension to the day of St. Michael, in every city by six men at every gate; in every borough by twelve men; in every town by six men or four, according to the number of the inhabitants who dwell [in the town], and that they keep watch continually all night, from sunset to sunrise. And if any stranger pass by them, he shall be arrested until morning; and if no suspicion be found, he shall go quit; and if they find cause of suspicion, he shall be delivered to the sheriff forthwith, and he shall receive him without danger, and keep him safely, until he be delivered in due manner. And if they will not suffer themselves to be arrested, hue and cry shall be levied against them, and those who keep watch shall follow with all the town, with the towns near, with hue and cry from town to town, until they be taken and delivered to the sheriff, as before is said; and for the arrest of such strangers none shall be called in question.

And further, it is commanded, that highways from one market town to another be enlarged, where there are woods, hedges, or ditches, so that there be neither ditches, underwood, nor bushes wherein a man may lurk to do hurt, near the road, within two hundred feet on the one side, and two hundred feet on the other side, provided that this statute extend not to oaks, or to great woods, so as it be clear underneath. And if by default of the lord who will not abate the ditch, underwood, or bushes in the manner aforesaid, any robberies be done, that the lord be answerable therefor; and if murder be done, that the lord make fine at the King's pleasure. And if the lord be not able to clear away the underwood, that the country aid him in doing it. And the King wills, that in his demesne lands and woods, within his forest and without, the roads be enlarged as aforesaid.

And if, perchance, a park be near the highway, it is requisite that the lord of the park diminish his park, so that there be a space of two hundred feet from the highway, as before said, or that he make such a wall, ditch, or hedge, that evil doers will not be able to pass or return, to do evil.

9. The Recovery of Debt on a Recognisance [*Chancery Files*, 415], 1293.

To the reverend and discreet and their dearest lord, J. de Langton, chancellor of the illustrious King of England, Robert le Venur, guardian of the city of Lincoln, and Adam son of Martin of the same city, clerk, deputed to receive recognisances of debts, greeting. With all reverence and honour we make known to your reverend discretion by these presents that Simon le Sage of Scarborough and William Kempe of the same town, of the county of York, and each of them for the whole sum, acknowledged before us that they owe to William le Noyr of Lincoln 28*s.* sterling to be paid to him or his attorney at the feast of St. Michael in the twenty-first year of the reign of King Edward, according to the form of the statute of the said lord the King published at Westminster. And because the aforesaid Simon and William have not kept the term of their payment at all, we beseech your reverend discretion humbly and devoutly, that you will order a writ to be sent to the sheriff of York to compel the same Simon and William to pay the said money according to the form of the statute aforesaid. May your reverend discretion prosper long and well. Given at Lincoln on Friday next after the feast of St. Martin in the year aforesaid.[1]

10. PROCEDURE AT A FAIR PURSUANT TO THE STATUTE FOR MERCHANTS [*Court Rolls*, 178, 96, *m.* 4], 1287.[2]

Pleas in the Fair of St. Ives, 15 Edward I, in the first year of John, lord Abbot, before William of Stow.

At the command of the lord the King, according to the tenour of the letter attached to the present roll, the community of London with the other communities at the fair of St. Ives was summoned to hear the order of the lord the King according to the new form of this statute touching merchants frequenting English fairs, and before them the aforesaid letter was read. And afterwards by the community of the citizens of London there were elected two of the more discreet and trusty men of the same city, to wit, Richard Poyntel and William of Paris, to whom in full court was delivered one of the two seals sent to the keepers of the fair, enclosed under the

[1] This procedure was first authorised by the Statute of Acton Burnel (1283), the main provisions of which run as follows:

"Forasmuch as merchants, who before these times have lent their goods to divers folk, are fallen into poverty, because there was no speedy law provided whereby they could readily recover their debts at the day fixed for payment, and for that reason many merchants have ceased to come to this land with their merchandise to the damage of the merchants and of the whole realm: the King, by himself and his council . . . has ordained and established that the merchant who will be sure of his debt cause his debtor to come before the mayor . . . and . . . to acknowledge the debt and the day of payment, and that the recognisance be enrolled. . . . And if the debtor pay not at the day fixed for him . . . the mayor . . . shall forthwith cause the moveables of the debtor to be sold to the amount of the debt . . . and the money to be paid without delay to the creditors. . . . And if the debtor have no moveables in the power of the mayor from which the debt can be levied, but have the same elsewhere in the realm, then the mayor shall send to the Chancellor . . . the recognisance made before him . . . and the Chancellor shall send a writ to the sheriff in whose bailiwick the debtor shall have moveables, and the sheriff shall cause satisfaction to be made to the creditor. . . . And if the debtor have no moveables wherefrom the debt can be levied, then his body shall be taken, wheresoever he be found, and kept in prison until he have made satisfaction, or his friends for him."

Two years later (1285) the Statute for Merchants strengthened the creditor's security by providing that imprisonment should immediately follow non-payment of the debt.

[2] Printed in Selden Society Publications, Vol. 23, p. 19.

seal of the lord the King and opened in the presence of the said merchants; and the other seal was delivered in the same court to one Henry of Leicester, clerk and attorney of Sir John de Bauquell, to whom the lord the King committed the merchants' seal, as appears in the letter attached to the present roll:—

Edward by the grace of God King of England, lord of Ireland and duke of Aquitaine, to the keepers of the fair of St. Ives, greeting. Whereas our beloved clerk, John de Bauquell, citizen of London,—to whom we have committed the merchants' seal to be kept, and the office thereof, according to the form of the statute provided hereon by our council, to be executed by him or others fit herefor, whom he shall be pleased to depute hereto, in fairs within our realm during our pleasure,—has deputed Henry of Leicester, clerk, under him in our presence to execute the aforesaid office in his place in the fairs aforesaid: We command you to admit hereto for this turn the aforesaid Henry in place of the aforesaid John: We command you also, that by assent of the community of merchants coming to the same fair you cause to be chosen two lawful merchants of the city of London, who, after taking oath, shall receive recognisances according to the form of our aforesaid statute, after the aforesaid seal, which we are sending to you in a box under our seal, has been opened in their presence, and one piece thereof delivered to the same merchants and the other piece to the aforesaid clerk. Witness Edmund, earl of Cornwall, our kinsman, at Westminster on 22 April in the fifteenth year of our reign.[1]

11. The Aulnage of Cloth [*Court Roll*, 178, 97, *m. 2d.*], 1291.[2]

Court on Monday [14 May, 1291].

Hamo of Bury St. Edmunds brought a letter patent of

[1] The clause of the Statute (1285) relating to fairs runs as follows: "And a seal shall be provided to serve for fairs, and the same seal shall be sent to each fair under the seal of the King by a clerk sworn; and by the keeper of the fair and by the community of the merchants there shall be elected two lawful merchants of the city of London, who shall take oath, and the seal shall be opened before them, and the one piece shall be delivered to the aforesaid merchants, and the other shall remain with the clerk, and before them or one of the merchants, if both cannot be present, the recognisances shall be made."

[2] St. Ives fair court. Printed in Selden Society Publications, Vol. 23, p. 42. This incident illustrates the difficulties of the central administration in dealing with local franchises.

Sir Roger de Lisle, clerk of the Great Wardrobe, attached to this roll, ordering that he be admitted by the keepers of the fair of St. Ives to measure woollen cloths made in England, linen and canvas. And because the charter of the lord the King touching the fair orders that no bailiff or minister of the lord the King in any wise interfere with the fair aforesaid or its appurtenances, whereby the Abbot and Convent of Ramsey and their bailiffs should be prevented from having administration of all things pertaining to that fair as well within the town as without for ever, answer was made to the same Hamo by the steward that he would in no wise admit him to execute such office, which would be to the disherison and prejudice of the church of Ramsey and contrary to the liberty specified in the fair-charter, unless Hamo would come into the court and yield up his letter patent into the hands of the steward. To which court he came and of his free will delivered up the aforesaid letter and afterwards craved special grace; and at the instance of the merchants, his letter patent having been abandoned and annulled, he is admitted for the present.

12. THE ORDINANCE OF LABOURERS [*Close Roll*, 23 *Edward III*, *p.* 1, *m.* 8*d.*], 1349.[1]

The King to the sheriff of Kent, greeting. Because a great part of the people and specially of the workmen and servants has now died in this plague, some, seeing the necessity of lords and the scarcity of servants, will not serve unless they receive excessive wages, and others preferring to beg in idleness rather than to seek their livelihood by labour: we, weighing the grave disadvantages which might arise from the dearth specially of tillers and workmen, have had deliberation and treaty hereon with the prelates and nobles and other learned men in session with us, by whose unanimous counsel we have thought fit to ordain that every man and woman of our realm of England, of whatsoever condition, free or servile, able-bodied and under the age of sixty years, not living by trade nor exercising a certain craft, nor having of his own whereof he shall be able to live, or land of his own, in the tilling whereof he shall be able to occupy himself, and not serving another man, shall be bound to serve him who shall require him, if he be required to serve in a suitable service, regard being

[1] Printed in Putnam *op. cit.*, *p.* 8*, Appendix.

had to his rank, and shall receive only the wages, liveries, hire or salaries which used to be offered in the places where he should serve in the twentieth year of our reign of England, or in the five or six common years last preceding; provided that lords be preferred to others in the bondmen or tenants of their lands so to be retained in their service; so however that such lords so retain as many as shall be necessary and not more; and if such a man or woman, so required to serve, refuse so to do, the same being proved by two trusty men before the sheriff, bailiff, lord, or constable of the town where this shall come to pass, he shall be taken forthwith by them or any of them and sent to the nearest gaol, there to stay in strait keeping until he find security to serve in the form aforesaid.

And if a reaper, mower or other workman or servant, of whatsoever rank or condition he be, retained in the service of any man, withdraw from the said service without reasonable cause or licence before the end of the term agreed upon, he shall undergo the penalty of imprisonment, and none, under the same penalty, shall presume to receive or retain such an one in his service.

Furthermore no man shall pay or promise to pay to any man more wages, liveries, hire or salaries than is accustomed, as is aforesaid, nor shall any man in any wise demand or receive the same, under penalty of the double of that which shall be so paid, promised, demanded or received, to go to him who shall feel himself aggrieved hereby; and if none such will prosecute, it shall go to any one of the people who shall prosecute; and such prosecution shall be made in the court of the lord of the place where such a case shall befal; and if the lords of towns or manors shall presume in any wise to contravene our present ordinance, by themselves or their ministers, then prosecution shall be made against them in the form aforesaid in counties, wapentakes and ridings, or other such courts of ours, at a penalty of threefold of that so paid or promised by them or their ministers; and if by chance any one shall have covenanted with any man so to serve for a greater salary before the present ordinance, the latter shall in no wise be bound by reason of the said covenant to pay to such a man more than has been customary at other times; nay, rather, he shall not presume to pay more under the penalty aforesaid.

Moreover saddlers, skinners, tawyers, shoemakers, tailors,

smiths, carpenters, masons, tilers, boatmen, carters and other artificers and workmen whosoever shall not take for their labour and craft more than used to be paid to such in the twentieth year and other common years preceding in the places in which they chance to be employed, as is aforesaid; and if any shall receive more, he shall be committed to the nearest gaol in the manner aforesaid.

Moreover butchers, fishermen, hostlers, brewers, bakers, poulterers and all other sellers of victuals whatsoever shall be bound to sell such victuals for a reasonable price, regard being had to the price at which such victuals are sold in the neighbouring places; so that such sellers have a moderate profit and not excessive, as shall be reasonably required by the distance of the places wherefrom such victuals are carried; and if any man sell such victuals otherwise and be convicted thereof in the form aforesaid, he shall pay the double of that which he shall receive to him that suffered loss, or, for lack of such, to him who will prosecute in this behalf; and the mayor and bailiffs of cities and boroughs, market and other towns, and ports and places by the sea, shall have power to enquire of all and singular who in any wise transgress against this ordinance, at the penalty aforesaid to be levied to the use of those at whose suit such transgressors shall be convicted: and in case the same mayor and bailiffs shall neglect to execute the premises and shall be convicted hereof before the justices appointed by us, then the same mayor and bailiffs shall be compelled by the same justices to pay to such as suffered loss, or, for lack of him, to any other prosecuting, threefold the value of the thing so sold, and none the less shall incur grievous punishment at our hands.

And because many sturdy beggars, so long as they can live by begging for alms, refuse to labour, living in idleness and sin and sometimes by thefts and other crimes, no man, under the aforesaid penalty of imprisonment, shall presume under colour of pity or alms to give anything to such as shall be able profitably to labour, or to cherish them in their sloth, that so they may be compelled to labour for the necessaries of life.

We order you, straitly enjoining upon you, that you cause all and singular the premises to be publicly proclaimed and kept in the cities, boroughs and market towns, seaports and other places in your bailiwick where you deem expedient, as well within liberties as without, and due execution to be made thereof, as is aforesaid; and that in no wise you omit this, as you love us and the common utility of our realm and will save yourself harmless. Witness the King at Westminster, the eighteenth day of June. By the King himself and the whole council.

The like writs are directed to the several sheriffs throughout England.

The King to the venerable father in Christ, W. by the same grace bishop of Winchester, greeting. Because a great part of the people, etc., as above, as far as "to labour for the necessaries of life," and then thus: and therefore we request you that you cause the premises to be proclaimed in the several churches and other places of your diocese where you shall deem expedient; commanding rectors, vicars of such churches, ministers and other your subjects that by salutary warnings they beseech and persuade their parishioners to labour and to keep the ordinances aforesaid, as instant necessity demands; and that you constrain the wage-earning chaplains of your said diocese, who, as is said, refuse in like manner to serve without excessive salary, and compel them, under penalty of suspension and interdict, to serve for the accustomed salary, as is expedient; and that you in no wise omit this as you love us and the common utility of our said realm. Witness as above.

By the King himself and the whole council.

The like letters of request are directed to the several bishops of England and to the guardian of the archbishopric of Canterbury, the see being vacant, under the same date.

13. Presentments made before the Justices of Labourers[1]

[*Assize Roll*, 267, *mm*. 1, 8], 1351.

Hundred of Chelmsford.

The twelve [jurors] present that Arnulph le Hierde of Maldon, late servant of John Dodebroke from Michaelmas, 24 Edward III, until Michaelmas next following, 25 Edward III, for one year and for a quarter of a year next following and for the whole of that time, the said Arnulph took a quarter of wheat for twelve weeks and 5*s*. a year for his stipend. Further, he took from the feast of St. Peter's Chains until Christmas in the same time 10*s*. beyond that which he took above; and hereupon the said Arnulph withdrew from his service

[1] Printed in Putnam, *op. cit.*, *p*. 169*, Appendix.

before the end of the term, to the damage of the said John of 40*s.*, against the Statute, etc. . . .

Trespass.—Further, they present that Robert Grys of Danbury, potter, makes brass pots and sells them at threefold the price which he used [to take], against the Statute, etc., in oppression of the people.

Trespass.—Further, they say that John Sextayn the younger, tailor, John Banestrat, tailor, Roger atte Tye of Great Baddow, take salaries for their labours from divers folk against the Statute, etc., and this threefold that which they used to take.

Trespass.—Further, they say that William Denk, servant of Geoffrey le Smyth, took from the said Geoffrey 20*s.* a year, and is at his table, and was sworn before John de Sutton and his fellows to serve according to the Statute, etc., where he should not take but 8*s.*, etc. . . .

Trespass.—Further, they present that Richard Smyth of Great Baddow commonly takes for his work double that which he used to take, against the Statute.

Trespass.—Further, they present that John Plukkerose, William Smyth of Danbury and William Molt, shoemakers, of Great Baddow, make shoes and sell them at almost double the price which they used [to take], against the Statute, etc., in oppression of the people.

Trespass.—Further, they say that Alan son of Sayer Banstrat of Great Baddow, sawyer, will not serve unless he take for his salary as much as two others take, against the Statute, etc., in oppression of the people. . . .

Grand Inquisition.

Trespass.—Further, they present that John Galion, vicar of Nazeing, will not minister to any the sacrament of marriage unless he have from each man 5*s.* or 6*s.*, and in this manner by extortion the said John has taken from John Wakerild 4*s.* 10*d.*, from William Gurteber 5*s.*, from John Mabely 9*s.*, and from many others to the sum of 20*s.*, in oppression of the people by tort and against the peace. . . .

Trespass.—Further, they present that John Hindercle took for stipend from the rector of Parndon for the time of August this year 10*s.* against the Statute.

Further, they present that John Hindercle, William Pourche, are butchers and forestallers of victuals, against the Statute.

14. Excessive Prices Charged by Craftsmen [*King's Bench, Ancient Indictments*, 38, *m.* 22*d.*] 1354.

Further they [the jurors] say that dyers, drapers and tanners are dwelling in the town of Ware, where they were not wont to be, but within the borough of Hertford, to the grave damage of the lord the King and the lady Queen Isabel, lady of the same town of Hertford, and of the whole commonalty of the town of Hertford aforesaid, and against the liberty of the aforesaid Queen, and that the same dyers and tanners use their craft in too excessive wise, to wit, the aforesaid dyers take for a cloth sometimes half a mark, sometimes 40*d.* and sometimes more, where they were wont to take for a cloth 6*d.* only, and the aforesaid tanners buy oxhides and divers other hides at a low price and refuse to sell them unless they gain on the sale fourfold, to the greatest oppression and damage of the whole people.

15. Fines Levied for Excessive Wages, 25 Edward III [*Exch. K.R. Estreats*, 11, 2], 1351.

Layer de la Hay.

From Simon Meller for his excess	40*d.*
From Robert Throstle for the same	6*d.*
From Thomas Poggill for the same	12*d.*
From Roger Bollok for the same	12*d.*
From Geoffrey Edmund for the same	6*d.*
From Richard Tailliour for the same	2*s.*
From Alice Smyth for the same	6*d.*
From John Smart for the same	12*d.*
From Margaret Everard for the same	12*d.*
From Alice Gerlond for the same	12*d.*
From Alice Weper for the same	6*d.*
From Agnes Heyward for the same	12*d.*
From John Crawe for the same	6*d.*
From Christina Bostis for the same	6*d.*
From Richard Cook for the same	12*d.*
From Edmund atte Well for the same	6*d.*
From Walter Bilet for the same..	6*d.*
From Geoffrey Sloman for the same	6*d.*

Sum, 16*s.* 10*d.* Proved

16. Writ to Enforce Payment of Excess of Wages to the Collectors of a Subsidy [*Close Roll*, 24 *Edward III*, *p.* 1, *m.* 6*d.*], 1350.

The King to his beloved and trusty Walter de Mauny and his fellows, our justices appointed to hear and determine divers trespasses and certain other things contained in our commission made to you, in the county of Northampton, greeting. Whereas lately it was ordained by us and our council that servants, as well men as women, should be bound to serve and should receive only the salaries and wages which used to be offered in the places where they ought to serve in the twentieth year of our reign over England or the five or six common years next preceding, and that all and singular such servants, workmen and artificers . . . taking more . . . be assessed at the whole additional sum which they shall receive . . . and the whole additional sum so received be levied and collected from every of them to our use in relief of the singular towns to which the said artificers, servants and workmen belong, and in aid of payment of the sums at which the same towns or the men thereof are assessed for the tenth and fifteenth now current . . .: you, nevertheless, . . . attempt to cause such excesses of wages, liveries, hires and salaries . . . with the fines made before you . . . to be enrolled on your rolls and levied to our use, against the intent of that agreement, as by complaint of the people it has been given us to understand: We . . . command you to compel all and singular artificers, servants and workmen, as well men as women, of whatsoever condition they be, convicted or hereafter to be convicted before you of such excessive salaries, liveries, hires or stipends whatsoever received by them in the aforesaid county, as well by imprisonment of their bodies as in other lawful manner which shall seem good to you in this behalf, to pay without delay that which they have so received in excess to the subtaxers and subcollectors of the singular towns to which the same artificers, servants and workmen belong, in aid of payment of the tenth and fifteenth aforesaid, according to the agreement abovesaid. Provided that the fines made or to be made therefor, and other things belonging to us therefrom, be converted to our use, as is just. Witness the King at Westminster, 12 June.

By the council.

17. Application of Fines for Excessive Wages to the Subsidy of a Fifteenth [*Subsidy Roll*, 107, 41.], 1351–2.

Hundred of Winstree.

From the town of East Mersea, 46*s.* 4¾*d.*, from fines of workmen of the same town.

From the towns of West Mersea and Fingringhoe, 4*l.* 8*s.* 11¾*d.*, from fines of workmen of the same town (*sic*).

From the towns of Peldon and Abberton, 44*s.* 7½*d.*, from fines of workmen of the same town (*sic*).

From the towns of Wigborough, Great and Little, 62*s.* 2*d.*, whereof the fifteenth is 12*d.*, the fines of workmen 61*s.* 2*d.*

From the town of Layer de la Hay, 32*s.* 9¾*d.*, whereof the fifteenth is 2*s.* 9¾*d.*, the fines of workmen 30*s.*

From the town of Layer Breton with Salcott, Virley, 46*s.* 6*d.* whereof the fifteenth is 16*s.* 6*d.*, the fines of workmen 30*s.*

From the town of Layer Marney, 28*s.* 7¼*d.*, whereof the fifteenth is 18*s.* 7¼*d.*, the fines of workmen 10*s.*; whereof, of the fifteenth, the goods of Robert de Marny[1] in the same town [contribute] 10*s.*

From the town of Langenhoe, 40*s.* 1*d.*, from the excess of fines of workmen of the same towns (*sic*).

Sum of this hundred, 19*l.* 10*s.* 2*d.*, whereof from the fifteenth [arises] 38*s.* 11*d.*, from fines of workmen 17*l.* 11*s.* 3*d.*[2]

18. Labour Legislation; the Statute of 12 Richard II. [*Statute Roll*, 2, *mm.* 13, 12], 1388.[3]

c. 3. Further it is agreed and assented that all the Statutes of artificers, labourers, servants and victuallers made as well in the time of our lord the King that now is as in the time of his noble grandfather, whom God assoil, not repealed, be straitly holden and kept and duly executed, and that the said artificers,

[1] His lands were for the time being in the King's hand as an escheat.

[2] Note that in half the towns in this hundred the inhabitants' share of the subsidy is wholly covered by the fines. The ordinance and statute were enforced in Essex more severely than elsewhere.

[3] This Statute is perhaps the most important of all the enactments relating to labourers between the Black Death and the reign of Elizabeth. It distinguishes between the impotent poor and the able-bodied vagabond, and, besides establishing Quarter Sessions, and fixing maximum wages, is the basis of all subsequent Vagrancy and Poor Law legislation. For printed text see Statutes of the Realm, Vol. II., 56–59.

labourers, servants and victuallers be duly judged by the justices of the peace as well at the suit of the King as of the party, according as the said Statutes require; and that the mayors, bailiffs, and stewards of lords and constables of towns duly do their offices touching such artificers, servants, labourers, and victuallers, and that stocks be in every town for the punishment of the same servants and labourers, as is ordained in the Statutes aforesaid. And furthermore it is ordained and assented that no servant or labourer, be it man or woman, depart at the end of his term out of the hundred, rape or wapentake where he is dwelling, to serve or dwell elsewhere, or by colour of going afar on pilgrimage, unless he carry a letter patent containing the cause of his going and the time of his return, if he ought to return, under the King's seal that shall be assigned hereto and delivered into the keeping of some good man of the hundred or hundreds, rape or wapentake, city and borough, who shall keep the same according to the discretion of the justices of the peace, and lawfully make such letters when need be, and in no other wise on his oath, and that around the said seal be written the name of the county and across the said seal the name of the said hundred, rape, wapentake, city or borough; and if any servant or labourer be found in a city, borough or elsewhere, coming from any place, wandering without such letter, he shall be taken forthwith by the said mayors, bailiffs, stewards or constables and put in the stocks and kept until he have found surety to return to his service or to serve or labour in the town from which he comes, until he have such letter for departing with reasonable cause; and be it remembered that a servant or labourer may freely depart from his service at the end of his term and serve elsewhere, so that he be in certainty with whom, and have such letter as above; but it is not the intent of this ordinance that servants who ride or go on the business of their lords or masters be comprehended within this ordinance during the time of the same business; and if any carry such letter which can be found to be forged or false, he shall go to prison for forty days for the falsity, and further until he have found surety to return and serve and labour as aforesaid. And that none receive a servant or labourer going forth from their hundreds, rape, wapentake, city or borough, without letter testimonial or with a letter, for more than one night, unless it be by reason of illness or other reasonable cause, or unless he will and can serve and labour there by the same testimony, on a penalty to be limited by the justices of the peace; and that as well artificers and craftsmen as servants and apprentices, who are not of great account and of whose craft or mistery men have no great need in time of harvest, be forced to serve in harvest at cutting, gathering and bringing in the corn; and that this statute be duly executed by mayors, bailiffs, stewards and constables of towns on a penalty to be limited and adjudged by the said justices of the peace in their sessions, and that none take above 1*d.* for making, sealing and delivering the said letter.

c. 4. And furthermore, because servants and labourers will not and for long time have not been willing to serve and labour without outrageous and excessive hire and much greater than has been given to such servants and labourers in any time past, so that for dearth of the said labourers and servants, husbandmen and tenants of land cannot pay their rents or hardly live on their lands,[1] to the exceeding great damage and loss as well of the lords as of the whole commons; and also because the wages of the said labourers and servants have not been put in certainty before these times; it is agreed and assented that the bailiff for husbandry take 13*s.* 4*d.* a year and his clothing once a year at most, the master hind 10*s.*, the carter 10*s.*, the shepherd 10*s.*, the oxherd 6*s.* 8*d.*, the cowherd 6*s.* 8*d.*, the swineherd 6*s.*, the woman labourer 6*s.*, the dairymaid 6*s.*, the ploughman 7*s.* at most, and every other labourer and servant according to his degree, and less in the country where less is wont to be given, without clothing, bounty (*curtoisie*) or other reward by covenant.[2] And that no servant of artificers or victuallers within cities, boroughs or other towns take more than the labourers and servants above named according to their estate, without clothing, bounty or other reward by covenant, as is said above. And if any give or take by covenant more than is specified above, at the first time that they shall be attainted thereof they shall pay, as well the givers as the takers, the value of the excess

[1] It is the small man, as well as the great lord, who is injured by the wage-labourers' demands.
[2] Compare the wages here allowed with those set out below, No. 19.

so given or taken, and at the second time of their attainder, double the value of such excess, and at the third time treble the value of such excess; and if the taker so attainted have nothing wherewith to pay the said excess, he shall go to prison for forty days.

c. 5. Further it is ordained and assented that he or she who is employed in labouring at the plough and cart or other labour or service of husbandry until they be of the age of 12 years shall remain thenceforward at that labour without being put to a mistery or craft; and if any covenant or bond of apprentice be made henceforth to the contrary it shall be holden for nought.

c. 6. Further, it is agreed and assented that no servant of husbandry or labourer or servant of an artificer or victualler carry henceforward baslard, dagger or sword, on pain of forfeiture of the same, except in time of war for defence of the realm, and then by survey of the arrayers for the time being, or when travelling through the country with their masters or on a message of their masters; but such servants and labourers shall have bows and arrows and use them on Sundays and feast days, and entirely forsake games of ball as well hand as foot and the other games called quoits, dice, casting the stone, skittles and other such unsuitable games; and that the sheriffs, mayors, bailiffs and constables have power to arrest and do arrest all the contraveners hereof and the baslards, daggers and swords aforesaid, and to seize and keep the said baslards, daggers and swords until the session of the justices of the peace, and present them before the said justices in their sessions together with the names of those who carried them. And it is not the King's intent that prejudice be done to the franchises of lords touching the forfeitures due to them.

c. 7. Further, it is agreed and assented that touching every man who goes begging and is able to serve or labour, it be done with him as with him who departs out of hundreds and other places aforesaid without a letter testimonial, as is said above, excepting people of religion and hermits approved, having letters testimonial of the ordinaries. And that beggars unable to serve remain in the cities and towns where they are dwelling at the time of the proclamation of this Statute;

and that if the people of the said cities or towns will not or cannot suffice to find them, the said beggars withdraw to the other towns within the hundred, rape or wapentake, or to the towns where they were born, within forty days after the said proclamation be made, and dwell there continually for their lives. And that with all those who go on pilgrimage as beggars and are able to labour it be done as with the said servants and labourers, if they have not letters testimonial of their pilgrimage under the seals aforesaid. And that the clerks of the Universities who go begging thus have letters testimonial of their chancellor on the same penalty.

c. 8. Further, it is ordained and assented that those who feign themselves to be men that have travelled out of the realm and have been there imprisoned carry letters testimonial of the captains where they have dwelt, or of the mayors and bailiffs where they make their landing, and that the same mayors and bailiffs enquire of such folk where they have dwelt and with whom and in what place is their dwelling in England; and that the same mayors and bailiffs make them a letter patent under the seal of their office testifying the day of their landing and where they have been, as they have said; and that the said mayors and bailiffs make them swear to keep their right way to their country, unless they have a letter patent under the King's great seal to do otherwise. And that if any such travelled man be found without such letter, it be done with him as with the servants and labourers aforesaid; and this ordinance shall be applied to travelled men who go begging through the country after their landing.

c. 9. Further it is ordained and assented that the aforesaid ordinances of servants and labourers, beggars and vagrants, hold good and be executed as well in cities and boroughs as in other towns and places within the realm, as well within franchise as without. And that the sheriffs, mayors and bailiffs and keepers of gaols shall be bound and charged to receive the said servants, labourers, beggars and vagrants, and to detain them in prison in the form aforesaid, without letting them to mainprise or bail and without taking fee or aught else from them by themselves or by others, as long as they be thus in prison or at their entry in or issue from the same prison, on pain of paying 100*s*. to the King.

c. 10. Further, it is ordained and assented that in every commission of the justices of the peace there be assigned only six justices beside the justices of assize, and that the said six justices hold their sessions in every quarter of the year at least, and this for three days if need be, on pain of being punished according to the advice of the King's council at the suit of every man who will make plaint, and enquire diligently, among other things touching their offices, if the said mayors, bailiffs, stewards and constables and also gaolers have duly made execution of the said ordinances and statutes of servants and labourers, beggars and vagrants, and punish those who are punishable by the said penalty of 100*s.* on the same penalty, and punish at their discretion those who are found in fault who are not punishable by the said penalty; and that every of the said justices take for his wages 4*s.* a day for the time of their said sessions, and their clerk 2*s.* a day, from the fines and amercements arising and forthcoming from the same sessions, by the hands of the sheriffs; and that the lords of franchises be contributors to the said wages according to the proportion of their part of the fines and amercements aforesaid; and that no steward of a lord be assigned in any of the said commissions, and that no association be made to the said justices of the peace[1] after their first commission. And it is not the intent of this statute that the justices of the one Bench and of the other and the serjeants at law, in case they be named in the said commissions, be bound by force of this statute to hold the said sessions four times a year as are the other commissioners, who are continually dwelling in the country, but that they do it when they can well attend hereto.

19. Labour Legislation; a Bill in Parliament, 23 Henry VI [*Rot. Parl.* 23 *Henry VI*, *m.* 4, *No.* 19], 1444–5.

Prayen the Commons of this present Parliament that where the common people of this realm is greatly annoyed because of sudden departing of servants of husbandry from their masters at the end of their terms without due warning made unto their said masters, where if such warning were had they might be purveyed of other servants against the end of their term, and also because that justices of peace many times by favour,

[1] *i.e.* No additions made to the commission.

prayer or commandment, set so little and so easy fines upon such as be convict before them, that many dread not the execution of the law but greatly are emboldened to offend :

That it like the King our Sovereign Lord to ordain by authority of this present Parliament that every servant of husbandry purposing to depart from his master at the end of his term, at the middle of his term or else before make covenant with another man to serve him for the next year, if he be in such case as the law will compel him to serve, the same covenant to be made in the presence of the constables of the towns where such servants at that time be in service ; and that the said servant and he that shall so make covenant with him, in presence of the said constables, at the middle of the said term or before, warn the master of the said servant of the said covenant so newly made, so that the same master may purvey him another servant against the end of his term ; and if any covenant with any such servant be made in other wise, or that such warning in manner and form abovesaid be not had, the same covenant be void, and the said servant be compelled to serve his former master still for the next year, but if[1] any lawful and reasonable cause being of later time shall require the contrary ; also that the salaries and wages of servants, labourers and artificers, exceed not the assessing that followeth, that is to say, the salary of a bailiff of husbandry by year 23*s.* 4*d.* and clothing price of 5*s.* with meat and drink ; of a chief hind, a carter, a chief shepherd, 20*s.* and clothing price of 4*s.* with meat and drink ; a common servant of husbandry 15*s.* and clothing price of 40*d.* ; a woman servant 10*s.* and clothing price of 4*s.* with meat and drink ; a child within age of 14 years 6*s.* and clothing price of 3*s.* with meat and drink ; the same form be observed of salaries of servants with hostlers, victuallers and artificers in cities, boroughs, and elsewhere being, and such as less deserve, less to take, and also in places where less is used to be given, less to be given hereafter. And that from the feast of Easter unto Michaelmas the wages of any freemason or master carpenter exceed not by the day 4*d.* with meat and drink, and without meat and drink 5½*d.* ; a master tiler or slater, rough mason and mean carpenter and other artificers concerning building, by the day 3*d.* with meat and drink, and without meat and drink 4½*d.* ; and every other labourer by the

[1] *i.e.* Unless.

day 2*d.* with meat and drink, and without meat and drink 3½*d.* And from the feast of Michaelmas unto Easter a freemason and a master carpenter by the day 3*d.* with meat and drink, and without meat and drink 4½*d.*; tiler, mean carpenter, rough mason and other artificers aforesaid, by the day 2½*d.* with meat and drink, and without meat and drink 4*d.*; and every other workman and labourer by the day 1½*d.* with meat and drink, and without meat and drink 3*d.*; and who that less deserves, to take less; provided that the said assessing extend not to labourers in time of harvest about harvest labour, in which the wages of a mower exceed not by the day 4*d.* with meat and drink, and without meat and drink 6*d.*; a man reaper or carter 3*d.* by the day with meat and drink, and without meat and drink 5*d.*; a woman labourer and other labourers in harvest by the day 2½*d.* with meat and drink, and without meat and drink 4½*d.*; and such as are worth less, less to take, and in places where less is used to be taken, less be taken hereafter; and that no artificer, workman or labourer take anything for any holiday nor for no workday, except after the rate of the time of the day in which he labours; and if any person refuse to serve or labour according to the premises, that every justice of the peace in their shires have power at every time to call them to examination thereof, and such as they find defective to commit to prison, there to abide till they have found surety sufficient to serve and labour in form by law required; and if any servant, artificer, workman or labourer, do contrary to the premises or deny his service, occupation or labour, by reason of no giving wages or salaries contrary to this statute, that he lose to the party that will sue in this part 20*s.*; and that the givers of excessive salaries or wages run in the same pain. . . .

Further, that the justices of peace assess no fine upon any that shall be convict before them of things done against any Statute of Labourers or Artificers or by that cause shall put him in the King's grace, beneath 3*s.* 4*d.* . . .[1]

20. Organisation of the Staple[2] [*Patent Roll*, 6 *Edward II*, *p.* 2, *m.* 5], 1313.

The King to all to whom, etc., greeting. Know ye that

[1] This bill became a Statute (*Stat.* 23 *Henry VI. c.* 12).

[2] This document, afterwards referred to as the Staplers' charter (*cf*

whereas before these times divers damages and grievances in many ways have befallen the merchants of our realm, not without damage to our progenitors, sometime Kings of England, and to us, because merchants, as well denizen as alien, buying wools and woolfells within the realm aforesaid and our power, have gone at their pleasure with the same wools and fells, to sell them, to divers places within the lands of Brabant, Flanders and Artois: We, wishing to prevent such damages and grievances and to provide as well as we may for the advantage of us and our merchants of the realm aforesaid, do will and by our council ordain, to endure for ever, that merchants denizen and alien, buying such wools and fells within the realm and power aforesaid and wishing to take the same to the aforesaid lands to sell there, shall take those wools and fells or cause them to be taken to a fixed staple to be ordained and assigned within any of the same lands by the mayor and community of the said merchants of our realm, and to be changed as and when they shall deem expedient, and not to other places in those lands in any wise: granting to the said mayor and merchants of our realm aforesaid, for us and our heirs, that the mayor and council of the same merchants for the time being may impose upon all merchants, denizen and alien, who shall contravene the said ordinance and shall be reasonably convicted thereof by the aforesaid mayor and council of the said merchants, certain money penalties for those offences, and that such money penalties, whereof we or our ministers shall be informed by the aforesaid mayor, shall be levied to our use from the goods and wares of merchants so offending, wheresoever they shall be found within the realm and power aforesaid, by our ministers, according to the information aforesaid and the assessment thereof to be made by the mayor himself, saving always to the said mayor and merchants that of themselves they may reasonably chastise and punish offending merchants, if their goods and wares chance to be found in the staple aforesaid outside our realm and power aforesaid, without interference or hindrance on the part of us or our heirs or our ministers whomsoever,

Patent Roll, 13 *Edward* II, *m.* 19 *d*), contains the earliest reference in the English records to an organised body of wool merchants with a mayor and council; it is clear from the last words of the ordinance that both Staple and Staplers were older than the royal interest in them.

as they have hitherto been wont to do. In witness whereof etc. Witness the King at Canterbury, 20 May.

By the King himself.

21. ARGUMENTS FOR THE ESTABLISHMENT OF HOME STAPLE TOWNS [*Exch. K. R. Accounts*, 457, 32.], 1319.

London. Whereas our lord the King by his writ has signified to us that in particular in his Parliament last holden at York debate was raised touching the establishment of certain places within his realm whereat sales and purchases of wools should be made and not elsewhere; which business (which should turn to the profit of our said lord and of the people of his realm) and also the fixing of the places most convenient herefor, through certain disturbances,[1] remained undetermined; and signified also that divers moneys counterfeiting the coin of our said lord are brought by foreign people into his realm to the subversion of his money and to the prejudice of our said lord; whereon our lord the King wishes to have our advice and counsel; we do him to wit that in full treaty and discussion with divers merchants, citizens and burgesses of the realm, we have agreed, if it please our lord the King, that there be two places established for the said sales and purchases, namely, one on this side Trent, and another beyond, which places should fulfil the conditions below-written, that is to say, the places should be strong, well situated and secure for the repair of foreign merchants and the safety of their persons and their goods, and there should be ready access for all manner of merchandise, an exchange good, easy and prompt, and a good and convenient haven in the same places; and that the law and usages and franchises, which merchants repairing to the Staple in these times have had and used, they should use and enjoy henceforth at the places where they shall be, without being drawn into another law or another custom; and that the foreigners who shall come to the said places go not further in the realm nor send privily or openly by any manner of people to make any purchase of wools elsewhere than at the places established; and hereby the towns of our said lord which are now decayed and impoverished will be restored and enriched. If it be established in the form above

[1] The struggle with Thomas, earl of Lancaster.

written, it will befal to the great profit of our lord the King and of all his realm ; principally, by the security of the persons and goods of merchants and other people of the realm, whom in these times death, robberies and other damages without number have in large measure befallen ; and also by the increase of the profit of the change of our lord through the plate and bullion which shall be brought there ; and also by the drawing of all manner of merchants and their merchandise that shall come there ; moreover, owing to the great treasure of the goods of England that is and remains in the power of aliens, tort, trespass, robberies, and homicide cannot be readily redressed nor rightly punished in our parts on this side the sea for fear of the persons and goods which the aliens have in their power[1], whereby they are enriched and emboldened to maintain the mortal enemies of the King, and comfort them with people, arms and victuals ; and by the ordinance aforesaid the merchants and the people of our said lord, to whom he can resort when need be, will be enriched, and the enemies of the King impoverished and all alien merchants in his subjection, and other profits without number will arise, which we cannot by any means fully show forth. With regard to money, if it please our lord, let it not be suffered to be brought from the parts beyond the sea, save only gold, plate and bullion ; and to do away with the counterfeit money current among the good, wheresoever it be found, let it be pierced and sent to the change.[2]

22. Ordinances of the Staple [*Patent Roll*, 19 *Edward II*, *p.* 2, *m.* 8], 1326.

Edward, etc., to the mayor of our city of London, greeting. We command you, straitly enjoining, that the things below

[1] *i.e.*, through fear of malicious reprisals abroad ; it is urged apparently that by the establishment of staples at home English merchants will stay in the realm and enjoy the profits of commerce without undertaking the risks. The policy of exclusive home staples was thrice attempted without success, in 1326, 1332 and 1353.

[2] Endorsed is a list of counties whose representatives agree to the foregoing advice, namely, Middlesex, Essex, Hertford, Buckingham, Bedford, Oxford, Berks, Gloucester, Hereford, Worcester, Salop, Stafford, Chester and Warwick, together with London and Stamford.

The arguments presented above were the outcome of a conference between the council, and representatives of cities and boroughs and of the merchants throughout the realm. See Eng. Hist. Rev., Jan. 1914.

written, ordained by us and our council for the common profit and relief of the people of all our realm and power, you cause to be proclaimed and published and straitly kept and observed in our city aforesaid and everywhere in your bailiwick.

First, that the staple of the merchants and the merchandise of England, Ireland and Wales, namely, of wools, hides, woolfells and tin, be holden in the same lands and nowhere else, and that too in the places below written, that is to say, at Newcastle upon Tyne, York, Lincoln, Norwich, London, Winchester, Exeter, and Bristol, for England, Dublin, Drogheda and Cork, for Ireland, Shrewsbury, Carmarthen and Cardiff, for Wales. And for the tin of Cornwall, at Lostwithiel and Truro. And for the tin of Devonshire, at Ashburton, and not elsewhere in England, Ireland or Wales.

And that all alien people there and not elsewhere in England, Ireland or Wales, may freely buy and seek wools, hides and fells and other merchandise, and tin in Ashburton, Lostwithiel and Truro, and not elsewhere, and when they have bought their merchandise at the said places and in the form abovesaid and paid their customs, and have thereon letters sealed with the seal of the cocket[1], they may carry the said wools, hides, fells, tin and other merchandise into what land soever they will, if it be not into a land that is at war or enmity with us or our realm. And that the merchant strangers be warned hereof.

And that no alien by himself or another privily or openly may buy elsewhere wools or other merchandise abovesaid except at the said places, upon forfeiture of the wools or other merchandise abovesaid which he shall have so bought.

And that the merchants of England, Ireland and Wales, who wish to carry wools, hides, fells or tin out of the staples to be sold elsewhere, may not carry them from the staples out of our power until they have remained fifteen days at any of the staples to sell them, and then they may go with the said merchandise whither they will, without making or holding a staple anywhere out of the said lands or within the said lands elsewhere than at the places abovesaid.

And that all people of England, Ireland and Wales, may sell and buy wools and all other merchandise anywhere that they will in the said lands, so that the sale be not made to aliens

[1] The seal used by the customers.

except at the staple. And that wools, hides, fells and tin be nowhere carried out of the said lands by aliens or denizens except from the staples aforesaid.

And that the merchants of our power make not among themselves any conspiracy or compact to lessen the price of wools or other merchandise abovesaid, or to delay merchant strangers in the purchase or sale of their merchandise, and that those who shall do so and can be attainted hereof be heavily punished according to the ordinance of us and of our good council. And that every man be admitted on our behalf who will sue to attaint and punish such, and that such suit be made before our Chief Justices or others whom we will assign hereto and not elsewhere. And that the merchants and the people of Gascony and of the duchy of Aquitaine, who now are or for the time shall be of the fealty and obedience of us or of our son and heir[1], be holden as denizens and not as aliens in all these affairs.

And that all merchants, native and strangers, be subject to the law merchant in all things that touch trafficking at the places of the staples.

And that no man or woman of a borough or city, nor the commons of the people outside a borough or city in England, Ireland or Wales, after Christmas next coming, use cloth of their own buying that shall be bought after the said feast of Christmas, unless it be cloth made in England, Ireland or Wales, upon heavy forfeiture and punishment, as we by our good council will ordain hereon. And be it known that by the commons in this case shall be understood all people except the King and Queen, earls and barons, knights and ladies and their children born in wedlock, archbishops and bishops and other persons and people of Holy Church, and seculars, who can spend yearly from their rents 40*l.* sterling, and this so long as it please us by our good council further to extend this ordinance and prohibition.

And that every man and woman of England, Ireland and Wales, may make cloths as long and as short as they shall please.

And that people may have the greater will to work upon the making of cloth in England, Ireland and Wales, we will

[1] Prince Edward was created duke of Aquitaine on September 10, 1325. *Pat.* 19 *Edward II, p.* 1, *m.* 25.

that all people know that we shall grant suitable franchises to fullers, weavers, dyers and other clothworkers who live mainly by this craft, when such franchises be asked of us.

And that it be granted to the wool-merchants that they have a mayor of the staples abovesaid.

And that all merchant strangers may have the greater will to come into our power and may the more safely stay and return, we take them, their persons and goods, into our protection. And we forbid, upon heavy forfeiture, that anyone do them wrong or injury in person or goods, while they be coming, staying or returning, so that if anyone do them injury contrary to this protection and prohibition, those of the town to which the evildoers shall belong shall be bound to answer for the damages or for the persons of the evildoers, and that the mayor or bailiffs of the town where the shipping is take surety for which they will answer at their peril from the sailors of the same shipping every time that they shall go out of the havens, that they will not do evil or misbehave towards any man contrary to these articles.

In witness whereof we have caused these our letters to be sealed with our seal. Given at Kenilworth, 1 May.

23. The Election of the Mayor and Constables of a Staple Town [*Chancery Files*, 582], 1358.

To the reverend father in Christ William by divine permission bishop of Winchester and Chancellor of the illustrious lord the King of England and France, his humble mayor and constables and the whole community of merchants of the staple of the lord the King at Westminster, greeting with all reverence and honour. Let your reverend lordship deign to know that on the feast of the Translation of St. Thomas the Martyr[1] in the 32nd year of the reign of the aforesaid lord the King of England after the Conquest, all the merchants, as well alien as denizen, who frequent the said staple, being assembled for the election of a mayor and constables of the same staple for the coming year, as custom is, beginning at the feast of St. Peter's Chains[2] next coming, with unanimous assent and consent we elected Adam Fraunceys to be mayor, and John Pyel and John Tornegeld to be constables of the staple

[1] July 7. [2] August 1.

aforesaid for the coming year. May your lordship fare well through time to come. Given in the said staple of Westminster the last day of July in the 32nd year of the reign of King Edward the Third after the Conquest of England[1].

24. ROYAL LETTERS PATENT OVERRULED BY THE CUSTOM OF THE STAPLE [*Early Chancery Proceedings*, 11, 289], *c.* 1436.

To the reverend father in God the Bishop of Bath, Chancellor of England.

Meekly beseecheth your servant, Hugh Dyke, that whereas our lord the King on the second day of December in the fourteenth year of his reign, considering the great kindness which the said Hugh, William Estfield and Hammond Sutton did to him, and specially for that they then granted to lend to our said lord the King the sum of 8,000 marks, and our said lord the King wishing graciously to favour the same William, Hammond and Hugh in this behalf, by his letters patent, by the advice and assent of his council in his Parliament, granted and gave license to the same William, Hammond and Hugh, that in the sale of their wools at the town of Calais they should be preferred before all other merchants there to the value of the sum aforesaid, and that they and every of them, or others in their name whom the said William, Hammond and Hugh would name hereto, might freely sell their wools aforesaid to the value aforesaid within your said town to what person soever and in what manner soever they should wish, before the other merchants aforesaid, and retain by them the sums forthcoming thence without any restriction or partition to be made thereof in the Staple of Calais among the merchants of the same, any statute or ordinance made to the contrary notwithstanding, as is more fully contained in the said letters; and although one Thomas Ketyll, servant to the said Hugh, at the commandment and will of his master, sold a sarpler of wool to a stranger for the sum of 12*l.* 5*s.*, to have and enjoy to him without any restriction or partition to be made thereof, as parcel of the sum aforesaid, nevertheless Thomas Thurland of Calais, because the said Thomas Ketyll would not deliver the said sum of 12*l.* 5*s.* to put the same in partition in the Staple, put him in prison and detained him for a long time

[1] Ratified by the Crown on July 16 (*Pat. Supp.*, 22 *m.* 12).

contrary to the tenour of the letters aforesaid to the prejudice of our lord the King and the great damage and loss of the said Hugh and Thomas Ketyll. Wherefore please it your benign grace to grant a writ of *subpœna* directed to the said Thomas Thurland to appear before you in the Chancery of our lord the King upon pain of 30*l.* to answer as well our lord the King as the said Hugh and Thomas Ketyll touching the premises, and to do right to the parties, by way of charity.

25. PROHIBITION OF EXPORT OF MATERIALS FOR MAKING CLOTH [*Guildhall, Letter-Book E, f.* 167],[1] 1326.

Edward by the grace of God, King of England, etc., to our well-beloved Hamon de Chigewelle, Mayor of our city of London, greeting. We have read the letters that you have sent us, in the which you have signified unto us that Flemings, Brabanters and other aliens have been suddenly buying throughout our land all the teasels that they can find ; and also are buying butter, madder, woad, fullers' earth, and all other things which pertain to the working of cloth, in order that they may disturb the staple and the common profit of our realm ; and further, that you have stopped twenty tuns that were shipped and ready for going beyond sea, at the suit of good folks of our said city ; upon your doing the which we do congratulate you, and do command and charge you, that you cause the said tuns well and safely to be kept ; and if any such things come into our said city from henceforth, to be sent beyond sea by merchants aliens or denizens, cause them also to be stopped and safely kept, until you shall have had other mandate from us thereon ; and you are not to allow any such things to pass through your bailiwick, by reason whereof the profit of our staple may be disturbed. We have also commanded our Chancellor, that by writs under our Great Seal he shall cause it everywhere to be forbidden that any such things shall pass from henceforth out of our realm, in any way whatsoever. Given under our Privy Seal at Saltwood the 21st day of May, in the 19th year of our reign.

[1] Printed in Riley, Memorials, 149.

26. Commercial Policy [*Political Songs and Poems, Rolls Series*, II, 282], *temp.* Edward IV.

For there is no realm in no manner degree
But they have need to our English commodity;
And the cause thereof I will to you express,
The which is sooth as the gospel of the mass.

. . . . . .

Meat, drink and cloth, to every man's sustenance
They belong all three, without variance.
For whoso lacketh any of these three things,
Be they popes or emperors, or so royal kings,

It may not stand with them in any prosperity;
For whoso lacketh any of these, he suffereth adversity;
Whiles this is sooth by your wits discern
Of all the realms in the world this beareth the lantern.

For of every of these three by God's ordinance,
We have sufficiently unto our sustenance,
And with the surplusage of one of these three things
We might rule and govern all Christian kings.

For the merchants come our wools for to buy
Or else the cloth that is made thereof surely,
Out of divers lands far beyond the sea,
To have this merchandise into their country.

. . . .

Therefore let not our wool be sold for nought,
Neither our cloth, for they must be sought;
And in especial restrain straitly the wool,
That the commons of this land may work at the full.

And if any wool be sold of this land,
Let it be of the worst both to free and bond,
And none other in [no] manner wise,
For many divers causes, as I can devise.

If the wool be coarse, the cloth is mickle the worse,
Yet into little they put out of purse
As much for carding, spinning and weaving,
Fulling, roving, dyeing and shearing;

And yet when such cloth is all ywrought,
To the maker it availeth little or nought,
The price is simple, the cost is never the less,
They that worketh such wool in wit be like an ass.

. . . .

For and ye knew the sorrow and heaviness
Of the poor people living in distress,
How they be oppressed in all manner of thing,
In giving them too much weight into the spinning.

For nine pounds, I ween, they shall take twelve,
This is very truth, as I know myself;
Their wages be bated, their weight is increased,
Thus the spinners' and carders' avails be all ceased.

27. THE PERILS OF FOREIGN TRAVEL [*Court Roll*, 178, 104, *m.* 3*d.*],[1] 1315.

The King sent his writ to the bailiffs of the abbot of Ramsey of the fair of St. Ives in these words:—Edward by the grace of God King of England, Lord of Ireland and Duke of Aquitaine, to the bailiffs of the abbot of Ramsey of the fair of St. Ives, greeting. Whereas, on the frequent complaint of our beloved cousin, Alice countess Marshal, representing to us that lately by our licence she caused a ship about to sail to the parts beyond seas to be laden with jewels of gold and silver and other her goods and chattels to the value of 2000*l.*, to be taken thence to the said parts to await her coming there; and that John Crabbe, master of a ship of The Mew, Miles of Utenham, Christian Trilling, Crabekyn, nephew of John Crabbe, John Labay and John Winter, together with certain other evildoers of the parts of Flanders, met the aforesaid ship so laden on its way towards the said parts on the sea between Boulogne and Whitsand, and in hostile manner took and carried away the same ship so laden with cloths, jewels and other goods aforesaid, and still detain the same jewels and goods of the aforesaid countess, to her no small damage and loss: we many times requested Robert, count of Flanders by our special letters to hear the plaint of the aforesaid countess on the premises, to be set forth to the same count

[1] Printed in Selden Society Publications, Vol. 23, p. 93.

by her or her proctor or attorney in this behalf, and thereupon to cause full justice to be done to her touching the said cloths, jewels and other goods so carried off; whereupon the same count afterwards wrote back to us, saying that he had caused certain of the aforesaid evildoers to be punished, and was ready to hand over the others whom he might secure to due punishment, as reason should permit. But, because the aforesaid count delayed to show justice to the said countess touching the restitution of the cloths, jewels and goods aforesaid according to the form of our aforesaid requests, we afterwards thought fit to require him divers times by our special letters to cause due restitution or suitable satisfaction, as right should require, to be made to the same countess for the cloths, jewels, goods and chattels aforesaid. And though the count has received our letters aforesaid and has been many times requested with great diligence on behalf of the same countess by her attorneys or proctors to cause full justice to be done to her in the premises, nevertheless he has neglected to do anything therein at such our requests, although a great part of the same goods had come into his hands, but has altogether failed to show her justice, as the mayor and aldermen of our city of London have made known to us by their letters patent sealed with their common seal.

We, refusing to refrain longer from causing the aforesaid countess to be provided with a remedy agreeable to right touching the recovery of her goods aforesaid, command you that you cause to be arrested without delay all goods and wares of the men and merchants of the power and lordship of the said count of Flanders, except the goods and wares of the burgesses and merchants of Ypres, which shall happen to be found within your bailiwick, to the value of 200*l.* in part satisfaction of the said 2000*l.*, and to be kept under such arrest safely and without detraction or diminution, until you shall have other orders from us thereon; and that you make known to us plainly and openly under your seals what goods and of what sort you cause to be arrested on that account, and whose they are, and also the value thereof, returning to us this writ. For we have commanded the mayor and sheriffs of London to cause to be arrested without delay and to be kept under such arrest, until full satisfaction be made to the aforesaid countess of her said goods so carried off, the goods and wares of the men and merchants of the power of the said count within their bailiwick to the value of 1000*l.*; and the bailiffs of the town of Great Yarmouth to cause the arrest of goods to the value of 300*l.*; and the bailiffs of the town of Ipswich to cause the arrest of goods to the value of 300*l.*; and the bailiffs of the town of Lynn to cause the arrest of goods to the value of the 200*l.* residue. Witness myself at Westminster on the 24th day of April in the eighth year of our reign.

To which writ answer was made that no goods or chattels of the power and lordship of Robert, count of Flanders, were found in the fair of St. Ives after this writ was delivered to us. Therefore nothing at present has been done therein.

28. Grant of Letters of Marque and Reprisals [*Patent Roll*, 26 *Henry* VI, *p.* 1, *m.* 27.], 1447.

The King to all to whom, etc., greeting. John Hampshire and Henry May, gentlemen, have shown to us that, whereas they, with twenty nine persons, merchants and mariners, our lieges, in the month of December in the twenty second year of our reign, in a ship called *Clement* of Hamble, came out of our duchy of Normandy sailing to our realm of England, there came upon them thirty mariners of Brittany and took and carried away the goods and merchandise of the aforesaid John and Henry and other our lieges aforesaid to the value of 1336 marks, and their bonds, indentures and bills making mention of debts to the sum of 700 marks, and beyond this likewise took and carried away the whole tackling of the ship aforesaid and all their victuals found in the same ship, and inhumanly stripped the same John and Henry to their shirts and certain of our other said lieges as well of their shirts as of their other garments, and abandoned and left the said John and Henry and our other lieges abovesaid in the ship aforesaid, bereft and spoiled of all manner of tackling necessary and requisite for the safe conduct of the same ship, in the midst of the sea, in which ship the same John and Henry and the rest of our lieges aforesaid, labouring in tempest and various storms of the sea for three days and three nights together, and despairing of their life in regard to all human aid, and putting all hope and trust of their salvation wholly in God and the glorious Virgin Mary, at length, after the days and nights aforesaid were past, they arrived in port, at least a place of safety, by God's help; and although at the instance of the aforesaid John and Henry we have oft fitly requested our cousin the duke of Brittany by letters of our privy seal that he would cause the same John and Henry to be provided with due and just restitution to be had in this behalf, yet the same John and Henry, using all diligence with due and speedy suit made to the same our cousin in this behalf for three years and more, have not yet obtained and cannot in any wise obtain any restitution thereof, to the gravest expense and no small damage and burden to the same John and Henry; wherefore they have humbly and instantly made supplication to us that we would graciously deign to provide for relief to be made to them in this behalf: We, considering that justice is and has been against all conscience denied or at least delayed to the same John and Henry diligently suing for their right, and willing to make provision that justice or at least the execution of justice perish not in this behalf, as far as in us lies, by the inspiration of piety, therefore, graciously inclining to the supplication of the same John and Henry most benignly made to us in this behalf, have granted to the same John and Henry marque and reprisal, so that they, by themselves or their factors, attorneys or servants having or to have sufficient power from them, and, if the same John and Henry perchance die in the meantime, by their heirs and executors, may take and arrest the bodies, ships, vessels, goods, wares and merchandise of any subjects soever of the aforesaid duke, wheresoever they may be found within our realms, lordships, lands, powers and territories, as well on this side as beyond the sea, by land, sea or water, within liberties and without, to the value of the said 2036 marks, and lawfully and with impunity detain the same until full satisfaction shall have been made to them of that sum and of the whole and entire tackling of the ship aforesaid and of the victuals aforesaid or of the true value of the same, and of the damages, costs, outlays and expenses which they have reasonably sustained and will sustain on our behalf, and, for default of such satisfaction, that they may give, sell, alienate them and dispose and order thereof as with their own goods, as it shall seem to them best to be done, without hindrance, disturbance, vexation or annoyance at the hands of us or our heirs or the officers or ministers of us or our heirs whomsoever. And we give to all and singular our admirals, captains, castellans and their lieutenants and deputies, sheriffs, mayors, bailiffs, constables, searchers, wardens of seaports and other maritime places, masters and mariners of ships and other places whatsoever, and other our officers, ministers, lieges and subjects whomsoever, as well on this side as beyond the sea, by land, sea or water, wheresoever they be stablished, that they be intendant, counselling, aiding and respondent in the premises to the same John and Henry or their factors, attorneys, deputies or servants having or to have sufficient power from the same John and Henry, and, if they die as is aforesaid, then to their heirs or executors, as often as and when they be duly requested by the same John and Henry or either of them or the others aforesaid or any of them on our behalf. In witness, etc. Witness the King at Westminster, 26 September. By writ of privy seal and of the date, etc.[1]

29. Grant of Liberties to the Merchants of Douai [*Charter Roll*, 45 *Henry* III, *m*. 4, *No*. 32.], 1260.

The King to archbishops, etc. Know ye that we have granted and by this our charter have confirmed for us and our heirs to our beloved burgesses and merchants of Douai that for ever throughout the whole of our land and power they have this liberty, to wit, that they or their goods, found in any place soever in our power, shall not be arrested for any debt for which they are not sureties or principal debtors, unless by chance such debtors be of their commune and power, having goods wherefrom they can make satisfaction for their debts in whole or in part, and unless the burgesses of Douai, by whom that town is governed, fail in justice to those who are of our land and power, and this can be reasonably ascertained; and that the said burgesses and merchants for ever be quit of murages on all their goods, possessions and merchandise throughout our whole realm; and that the burgesses and merchants aforesaid shall not lose their chattels and goods found in their hands or deposited elsewhere by their servants, so far as they can sufficiently prove them to be their own, for the trespass or forfeiture of their servants; and also

[1] For an earlier measure for the protection of shipping, see below, Section VII., No. 2.

if the said burgesses and merchants or any of them die within our land and power testate or intestate, we or our heirs will not cause their goods to be confiscated so that their heirs should not entirely have them, so far as the same be proved to be the chattels of the said deceased, provided that sufficient knowledge or proof be had touching the said heirs; and that they with their merchandise may safely come into our land and power and stay there, paying the due and right customs; so also that if at any time there be war between the King of the French or others and us or our heirs, they be forewarned to depart from our realm with their goods within forty days. Wherefore we will and straitly command, for us and our heirs, that the aforesaid burgesses and merchants and their heirs for ever have all the liberties aforewritten throughout the whole of our land and power. And we forbid, upon our forfeiture of 10*l.*, that any man presume to molest or annoy them in aught unjustly contrary to this liberty and our grant. These witnesses:—the venerable father H. bishop of London, Richard de Clare, earl of Gloucester and Hertford, Humphrey de Bohun, earl of Hereford and Essex, Hugh le Bygod, Philip Basset, Hugh le Despenser, our justiciar of England, James de Alditheleg, Roger de Mortuo Mari, John Maunsell, treasurer of York, Robert Walerand, and others. Given by our hand at Westminster, 24 November in the 45th year of our reign.[1]

The burgesses and merchants of Douai give the King 100 marks for this charter, which sum should be allowed in the 90*l.* in which the King is bound to them, whereof there is the King's writ of *liberate* at the King's Exchequer; and the writ should be searched for and the 100 marks noted therein.

30. Aliens at a Fair [*Court Rolls*, 178, 93, *m.* 3], 1270.

Court of Wednesday [14 May, 1270].

Gottschalk of Almain, burgess of Lynn, makes plaint of the communities of Ghent, Poperingen, Douai, Ypres and Lisle, as men of the countess of Flanders, to wit, that whereas the same Gottschalk caused 14 sacks of wool worth 140 marks to be brought from the realm of England to Bruges in Flanders, to trade with it there, and lodged the wool at the house of one Henry Thurold on Sunday next after Ash Wednesday in the forty-ninth year of the reign of King Henry, the bailiffs of

[1] Charters of this character were granted at this period to almost every town of importance in England.

the said countess came and arrested the said wool against the peace of the realm and still detain it. Wherefore the same Gottschalk, for the unjust detention of the wool aforesaid, made petition to the lord the King at Kenilworth and elsewhere until now; whereupon the lord the King many times directed his letters to the same countess, asking her to satisfy the same Gottschalk of the aforesaid wool or the price thereof, and she has hitherto neglected to do anything for the same Gottschalk, to his damage of 200 marks; and he produces suit. The aforesaid communities, being present, do not deny the accustomed words of the court[1] or the detention of the aforesaid wool or the damage of the aforesaid Gottschalk, but craved licence to consult forthwith on the matter and withdrew. And afterwards they came, making no defence against the charge of the said Gottschalk, but the men of Ypres presented a charter of certain liberties granted to them by the King's Court, stating that they should not be distrained for any debt unless they were the sureties or principal debtors. For the men of Lisle there came one Alard of Leeuw and showed a charter of the lord the King for himself only, stating that he should not be distrained unless he were a principal debtor or surety. Another man named Peter Blarie of Lisle says that he has no charter. The men also of the communities of Ghent and Douai[2] craved respite until Saturday to show their charters, which they say that they have from the King's Court, and that day was granted to them. The aforesaid Gottschalk, however, craved judgment for the default of the aforesaid merchants; and a day is given to the parties, to wit, to-morrow. . . .

Be it remembered that Gottschalk of Almain, burgess of Lynn, gives to the lord a seventh part of all which he may recover against the communities of Ypres, Ghent, Douai, Poperingen and Lisle, to wit, of the 120 marks which he seeks for 14 sacks of wool detained to his damage of 200 marks.

31. Confirmation of Liberties to the Merchants of Almain [*Patent Roll*, 9 *Edward* I, *m*. 1], 1280.

The King to all to whom, etc., greeting. Whereas the lord King Henry, our father, of famous memory, lately granted by

[1] *i.e.* "Tort and force." [2] See No. 29 for the charter of Douai.

his letters patent,[1] which we have inspected, at the instance of Richard, King of the Romans, our uncle, of good memory, to the merchants of the realm of Almain who have a house in the city of London commonly called the Gildhall of the Teutons, that he would maintain and protect them, all and singular, throughout the whole of his realm in all the same liberties and free customs which they have used and enjoyed in the times of him and his progenitors, and would not draw them nor in any wise permit them to be drawn out of such liberties and free customs, as is more fully contained in the letters aforesaid made thereon to the aforesaid merchants: We, wishing that favour to be continued to the same merchants, wish them to be maintained and protected in all the same liberties and free customs which they have used and enjoyed in the times of us and our progenitors, and we will not draw them or in any wise permit them to be drawn out of such liberties and free customs. In witness whereof, etc. Witness the King at Westminster, 18 November.

32. Alien Weavers in London [*Guildhall, Letter-Book* G, *f.* 93],[2] 1362.

Unto the most honourable Lords, and rightful, the Mayor and Aldermen of the City of London, humbly pray the Weavers alien working in the same City, that the points and Ordinances underwritten may be granted and allowed to them, for the common profit of the land and of the City and for the saving of their said trade.

In the first place, that three good folks of the weavers alien may be ordained and sworn to keep and rule their trade, and the points underwritten.

Also, that if any alien shall come to the said city to work in the said trade, and to make his profit, he shall do nothing in the same before he shall have presented himself to the Masters alien of the said trade, and by the said Masters have been examined if he knows his trade or not; and thereupon, let orders be given by the said Masters what he shall take by the day for his work.

[1] June 15, 1260. *Fœdera I.*, i. 398.
[2] Printed in Riley, Memorials, p. 306

Also that no one of the said trade of weavers alien shall be so daring as to work at the trade by night.

Also, that no one in the said trade shall work at the trade on Saturdays; or on the Eve of Double Feasts after None rung in the parish where he resides.

Also, if any workman has served his alien master by the day or by the week, and the said master will not pay the workman for his work, according as they shall have agreed, the good folks who shall be ordained and sworn to keep and rule their said trade, shall have power to forbid the said master to be so daring as to work at the said trade, until he shall have paid his workman what he is bound to pay him. And if he shall do the contrary, and be convicted thereof, let him pay to the Chamber the penalty that is underwritten.

Also, whereas heretofore, if any dispute occurred between a master alien in the said trade and his workman, such workman was wont to go to all the workmen within the City in the said trade, and by covin and conspiracy between them made, they would give orders that no one of them should work or submit to serve until the said master and his workman should have agreed; by reason whereof the masters of the said trade were in great trouble, and the people left unserved; it is ordered that, from henceforth if any dispute shall occur between any master alien and his workman in the said trade, the same dispute shall be rectified by the Wardens of the trade. And if any workman who shall have offended, or have misbehaved towards his master alien will not submit to be adjudged before the said Wardens, let such workman be arrested by a serjeant of the Chamber at the suit of the said Wardens, and brought before the Mayor and Aldermen; and before them let him be punished, at their discretion.

Also, if any alien of the said trade shall be found doing mischief in the way of larceny, to the value of 12 pence; the first time, let him make amends to him against whom he shall have so offended, at the discretion of the Masters alien of the said trade. And if he shall be found guilty thereof a second time, let him be brought before the Mayor and Aldermen, and before them be punished according to his deserts.

Also if any alien of the said trade shall be found guilty in any point aforesaid, let him be amerced, the first time, in 40 pence, to the use of the Chamber; half a mark, the second time; 20 shillings the third time; and the fourth time, let him forswear the trade in the said city, and every time, let him also pay 12 pence to the Wardens for their trouble.

John le Grutteret and Peter Vanthebrok, Flemings, and John Elias, Brabanter, were chosen on the 23rd day of February in the 36th year and sworn to keep and oversee the Articles aforesaid, and the alien men of the same trade.

33. THE HOSTING OF ALIENS [*Exch. K. R. Accounts*, 128, 31, *m.* 15], 1442.

This is the view of William Chervyle, surveyor and host ordained and deputed by Robert Clopton, late mayor of the city of London, upon John Mantell, captain of a carrack coming to Sandwich, and James Ryche, scrivan[1] of the said carrack, and James Douhonour, merchants, coming from Sandwich with the said carrack, to survey as well their merchandise found in their keeping and also coming afterwards, as the employment of the same, to wit, the said John Mantell and James Ryche between the 18th day of January, and James Dohonour between the 25th day of January in the 20th year of the reign of our sovereign lord King Henry the Sixth, until the feast of Michaelmas next following.

The merchandise coming and found in the said carrack of the said John Mantell and James Ryche and James Dohonour—

First, 14 butts of sweet wine.
Further, 30 barrels of the same sweet wine.
Further, 144 butts of sweet wine.
Further, 10 butts of currant raisins.

The merchandise sold by the said John Mantell, James Ryche and James Douhonour:—

First, sold in the month of February to the prior of Canterbury, 1 butt for	4*l.* 6*s.* 8*d*
Further, to John Brokley, 2 butts for ..	8*l.* 6*s.* 8*d.*
Further, to Andrew Tye, 2 butts for	8*l.*
Further, to John Style, 4 butts for	14*l.*
Further, to Davy Selly, 3 butts for	12*l.*
Further, to Richard Tremayne, 2 butts for ..	8*l.*
Further, to John Chyppenham, 30 barrels for	16*l.*

[1] The scrivan (*i.e.*, writer) had charge of the merchandise on board.

Further, sold in the month of March to Simon Eyre, 101 butts for	305*l.*
Further, to John Style, 20 butts for	75*l.*
Further, to John Style, 10 butts for	40*l.*
Further, to Davy Selly, 4 butts for	16*l.*
Further, to Thomas Greye, 3 butts for ..	11*l.* 10*s.*
Further, to John atte Wode, 2 butts for ..	7*l.*
Further, to John Bale, 4 butts for	16*l.*
Further, to Harry Purchase, 3 butts of currant raisins for	29*l.*
Further, to John Gybbe, 3 butts for	29*l.*
Further, to Nicholas Wyfold, 3 butts for ..	31*l.*
Further, to John Pecok, 1 butt [for]	9*l.* 10*s.*
Sum of the said sales..	639*l.* 13*s.* 4*d.*

The purchases made by the said John Mantell and James Ryche and James Dohonour for the employment of the merchandise aforesaid :—

First, bought of Simon Eyre, 200 cloths "westrons" for	305*l.*
Further, of John Brokley, 40 yards of murrey in grain	18*l.*
Further, of Henry Kempe, 5 cloths "Northamptons"	40*l.*
Further, of Philip Malpas, 60 cloths "westrons" ..	90*l.*
Further, of John Bale, 60 pieces of Suffolk "streyts" for	38*l.*
Further, of William Dyllowe, 10 cloths "Northamptons"	60*l.*
Further, of John Andreu, 8 cloths "Ludlowes" ..	16*l.*
Further, of Thomas Grey, 1101 quarters of pewter for	15*l.*
Further, of William ——, 40 cloths "westrons" ..	60*l.*
Further, of John at Wode, 20 cloths "westrons" for	32*l.*
Further, of John Style, 80 Suffolk "streyts" for ..	46*l.*
Sum of the purchases aforesaid	745*l.*[1]

34. An Offence against Stat. 18 Henry VI. for the Hosting of Aliens [*Exch. K. R. Accounts*, 128, 31, *m.* 28], 1440.

I, Stephen Stychemerssh, citizen of the city of London, certify your reverences, the venerable and discreet barons of the Exchequer of the most excellent prince, our lord the King, and all whose interest it is, that on the fifth day of the month of April in the 18th year of the reign of King Henry the Sixth, there were assigned to me, the aforesaid Stephen, by Robert

[1] This survey was made pursuant to Stat. 18 Henry VI. The result of the transaction would have delighted the "mercantile" theorist.

Large, then mayor of the city aforesaid, Surlio Spyngell, Baptista Spyngell, Teras Spyngell, John Bryan, Raphael and Jeronimus, their clerks, merchant strangers, to be under me, the aforesaid Stephen, as their host, to survey all and singular merchandise brought and hereafter to be brought by the aforesaid Surlio, Baptista, Teras, John, Raphael and Jeronimus into the city aforesaid and the suburbs of the same; and upon the assignment aforesaid so made by the aforesaid late mayor, I, the aforesaid Stephen Stychemerssh, went to the aforesaid Surlio, Baptista, Teras, John, Raphael and Jeronimus on the eighth day of April in the said 18th year in the parish of St. Peter in the ward of Bread Street, requiring them to be under my survey and governance according to the form of a Statute [published in the Parliament] holden at Westminster in the said 18th year; which Surlio Spyngell, Baptista Spyngell, Teras Spyngell, John Bryan, Raphael and Jeronimus, though often required by me and after the corporal pain of imprisonment had been inflicted by the aforesaid late mayor and other warnings put upon them, have altogether neglected and contemned and still neglect and contemn to obey or observe the aforesaid statute or ordinance, alleging for themselves certain letters patent [1] of the lord the king under his great seal to them and other merchants of Genoa of a licence granted to them by the said lord the King not to be under any such host, so that touching their merchandise brought from the said fifth day of the month of April or touching the sales of the same merchandise nothing at present has been done by me, nor could I have any knowledge thereof, contrary to the form of the statute or ordinance aforesaid.[2]

35. Imprisonment of an Alien Craftsman [*Early Chancery Proceedings*, 11, 455], c. 1440.

To the right reverend father in God, the bishop of Bath and Wells, Chancellor of England.

Meekly beseecheth your good and gracious lordship your

[1] Patent Roll, 18 Henry VI., p. 3, m. 22 (1440).

[2] This document illustrates the difficulty of the legislature in its attempts at national regulation. A mediæval statute was not a dead letter, but competed perforce with local liberty and royal prerogative. The crown at once collected fines for breaches of a statute and fees for exemption from its operation.

continual orator, Henry Wakyngknyght, goldsmith, tenderly to consider that whereas he, by the Mayor's commandment of London, caused by the subtle suggestion of the Wardens of the Craft of Goldsmiths of London, now late is imprisoned within the Counter in Bread Street, no cause laid against him but only that he is a stranger born, occupying his craft in London, so utterly intending to keep him still in prison for ever to his utter destruction and undoing—howbeit your said orator occupieth not his said craft openly in shops but privily, in no derogation of any franchise or custom of the goldsmiths of London—without your gracious lordship to him be shewed in this behalf. Wherefore please it your said gracious lordship, the premises considered, and also the holy time of Easter now coming, to grant unto your said orator a *corpus cum causa* directed to the Mayor and Sheriffs of London, commanding them by the same to bring up the body of the said Henry with the cause of his arrest before your lordship into the King's Chancery at a certain day by your lordship to be limited, there to answer in the premises as reason and conscience shall require, for the love of God and in way of charity.

[*Endorsed.*] Before the lord the King in his Chancery on Monday next, to wit, 23 March.

36. Petition against Usury [*Parliament Roll*, 50 *Edward* III, *No.* 158], 1376.

Further, the commons of the land pray that whereas the horrible vice of usury is so spread abroad and used throughout the land that the virtue of charity, without which none can be saved, is wellnigh wholly perished, whereby, as is known too well, a great number of good men have been undone and brought to great poverty: Please it, to the honour of God, to establish in this present Parliament that the ordinance [1] made in the city of London for a remedy of the same, well considered and corrected by your wise council and likewise by the bishop of the same city, be speedily put into execution, without doing favour to any, against every person, of whatsoever condition he be, who shall be hereafter attainted as principal or receiver or broker of such false bargains. And that all the Mayors and Bailiffs of cities and boroughs through-

[1] Ordinance dated 1363. *See* Cunningham, *Growth of English Industry and Commerce, Mediæval Times*, p. 361 *n.*

out the realm have the same power to punish all those who shall be attainted of this falsity within their bailiwicks according to the form of the articles comprehended in the same ordinance. And that the same ordinance be kept throughout all the realm, within franchises and without.

Answer.—Let the law of old used run herein

37. Action upon Usury [*Early Chancery Proceedings*, 64, 291],[1] *c.* 1480.

To the right reverend father in God, the Bishop of Lincoln and Chancellor of England.

Right humbly beseecheth unto your lordship your Orator William Elryngton of Durham, mercer, that whereas he now 4 years past and more had for a stock of one Richard Elryngton the sum of 30*l.*, wherefore your said Orator was by his obligation bounden unto the said Richard in 40*l.* and odd silver; which sum of 30*l.* your said Orator should have to be employed in merchandise, during the space of 7 years, yielding yearly unto the said Richard, for the loan thereof 4*l.* of lawful money of England, and at the 7 years' end to yield whole unto the said Richard the said sum of 30*l.*; whereupon your said Suppliant occupied the said sum by the space of 2 years, and paid yearly unto the said Richard 4*l.*; and after that your said Orator, remembering in his conscience that that bargain was not godly nor profitable, intended and proffered the said Richard his said sum of 30*l.* again, which to do he refused, but would that your said Orator should perform his bargain. Nevertheless, the said Richard was afterward caused, and in manner compelled, by spiritual men to take again the said 30*l.*, whereupon before sufficient record the said Richard faithfully promised that the said obligation of 40*l.* and covenants should be cancelled and delivered unto your said Orator, as reason is. Now it is so that the said Richard oweth and is indebted by his obligation in a great sum of money to one John Saumpill, which is now Mayor of Newcastle, wherefore now late the said Richard, by the mean of the said mayor, caused an action of debt upon the said obligation of 40*l.* to be affirmed before the mayor and sheriff of the said Town of Newcastle, and there by the space almost of 12 months

[1] Printed in Abram's *Social England*, 215.

hath sued your said Orator, to his great cost, and this against all truth and conscience, by the mighty favour of the said mayor, by cause he would the rather attain unto his duty, purposeth now by subtle means, to cast and condemn wrongfully your said Orator in the said sum of 40*l.*, to his great hurt and undoing, without your special lordship be unto him shewed in this behalf, wherefore please it your said lordship to consider the premise, thereupon to grant a *certiorari*, direct unto the Mayor and Sheriff of the said Town. to bring up before you the cause, that it may be there examined and ruled as conscience requireth, for the love of God and in way of charity.

SECTION VII

TAXATION CUSTOMS AND CURRENCY[1]

1. Form of the taxation of a fifteenth and tenth, 1336—2. Disposition of a subsidy of tonnage and poundage, 1382—3. The king's prise of wines, 1320—4. The custom on wool, 1275—5. The custom on wine, 1302—6. The custom on general imports, 1303—7. Administration of the search, 1303—8. Provision for the currency and the search, 1335—9. Opinions on the state of English money, 1381-2.

THE following documents illustrate in the first place the sources of royal revenue other than (*a*) the direct rents accruing to the King as a great landlord, (*b*) the payments due to him as feudal overlord, and (*c*) the profits of justice and administration, Nos. 1 and 2 representing the ordinary forms of Parliamentary grants, and Nos. 3 to 6 the prerogative right of the Crown to payments for the privilege of commercial intercourse by way of prise or custom; and in the second place the continuous efforts of mediæval governments to secure a good and easy currency (Nos. 7 to 9), a problem which they failed to solve either by the direct method of forbidding the export and controlling the import of money, or by the indirect method of insisting on the exchange of goods for goods by alien merchants frequenting the realm.

AUTHORITIES

The principal modern writers dealing with the subject of this section are :—Dowell, *History of Taxation and Taxes in England*; Stubbs, *Constitutional History*; Hall, *Customs Revenue*; Shaw, *History of Currency*; Crump & Hughes, *English Currency* (Economic Journal, V.).

Contemporary authorities :—Wolowski, *Traité de Nicholas Oresme.*

[1] For feudal taxation see Section II.

1. Form of the Taxation of a Fifteenth and Tenth [*Fine Roll*, 10 *Edward* III, *m.* 13], 1336.

This is the form which the assessors and taxers of the fifteenth, granted to our lord the King in his Parliament holden at Westminster on the Monday next after Sunday in mid-Lent last past, in the tenth year of his reign, by the earls, barons, freemen and the commonalties of all the counties of the realm, and also of the tenth there granted to our said lord the King in all the cities, boroughs and the ancient demesnes of the King, of the same realm, from all their goods which they had on the day of the said grant, ought to observe, and thereby to assess, tax, collect and levy the same fifteenth and tenth in the counties of Northumberland, Cumberland and Westmoreland, to wit, that the chief taxers without delay cause to come before them from each city, borough and other town of the counties, within franchise and without, the more lawful and wealthier men of the same places in such number that therefrom the chief taxers may sufficiently choose four or six of each town, or more if need be, at their discretion, by whom the said taxation and that which pertains thereto to be done may best be done and accomplished; and when they shall have chosen such, then they shall cause them to swear on the Holy Gospels, to wit, those of each town by themselves, that those so sworn will lawfully and fully enquire what goods each man of the same towns had on the said day within house and without, wheresoever they be, without any favour, upon heavy forfeiture, and will lawfully tax all those goods, wheresoever they have come from then till now by sale or otherwise, according to the true value, save the things below excepted in this form, and will cause them to be listed and put on a roll indented quite fully as speedily as they can, and to be delivered to the chief taxers one part under their seals, and retain by themselves the other part under the seals of the chief taxers, and when the chief taxers shall have in such wise received the indentures of those who shall be sworn to tax in cities boroughs and other towns, the same chief taxers shall lawfully and minutely examine such indentures, and if they discover that there is any defect they shall forthwith amend it, so that nothing be concealed, neither for gift nor for reward of a person taxed less than reason requires; and the King wills that the chief taxers go from hundred to hundred and from town to town, where need shall be, to survey and enquire that the subtaxers in the same towns have fully taxed and valued the goods of every man, and if they find anything concealed, amend it forthwith and cause the Treasurer and Barons of the Exchequer to know the names of those who shall have so trespassed, and the manner of their misdeed; and the taxation of the goods of the subtaxers of the towns shall be made by the chief taxers and by other good men whom they choose so to do, so that their goods be well and lawfully taxed in the same manner as those of others. The taxation of the goods of the chief taxers and of their clerks shall be reserved to the Treasurer and Barons of the Exchequer. And the chief taxers, as soon as they shall have received the presentment of the subtaxers shall cause the fifteenth and tenth to be levied to the use of the King without delay and without doing favour to any man, in the form which is enjoined upon them by the commission. And they shall cause to be made two rolls of the said taxation agreeing in all points, and retain the one by them to levy the taxation and have the other at the Exchequer at the feast of St. Peter's Chains next coming, on which day they shall make their first payment. And be it known that in this taxation of the goods of the commonalty of all the counties there shall be excepted armour, mounts, jewels and robes for knights and gentlemen and their wives, and their vessels of gold and silver and brass, and in cities and boroughs shall be excepted a robe for the man and another for his wife and a bed for both, a ring and a buckle of gold or silver, and a girdle of silk, which they use every day, and also a bowl of silver or of mazer from which they drink. And the goods of lepers, where they are governed by a superior who is a leper, shall not be taxed or taken, and if the lepers be governed by a sound master, their goods shall be taxed like those of others. And be it remembered that from people of counties out of cities, boroughs and the king's demesnes whose goods in all exceed not the value of 10*s.*, nothing shall be demanded or levied; and from the goods of people of cities, boroughs and the king's demesnes, which exceed not the value of 6*s.* in all, nothing shall be demanded or levied.

2. The Disposition of a Subsidy of Tonnage and Poundage [*K. R. Customs Accounts*, 159, 4], 1382.

This indenture made between Thomas Beaupyne of Bristol and John Polymond of Hampton appointed in Parliament to make order for the safe keeping of the sea by means of the subsidy of 6*d.* in the pound and 2*s.* on the tun [of wine] on the coasts of the west, granted in the said Parliament for the same cause, of the one part, and William Bast of the other part, witnesseth that the said William has received from the said Thomas and John 180*l.* of the said subsidy to find a ship and a barge of 180 men to serve our lord the King on the sea for a quarter of a year, the said quarter beginning on Michaelmas Day next or within fifteen days after, as he shall deem best to be done, by the testimony of the mayor of Dartmouth or the admiral's lieutenant in those parts, taking from the commencement of the said voyage 20*s.* for each man for the said quarter, together with all the profit that he may seize from enemies in the mean time without impeachment, according to the form ordained and agreed upon in the said Parliament, to be on the sea for the preservation of English shipping according to their power, without making for the land of England unless it be through tempest of the sea or other reasonable cause during the said quarter; for the good and lawful performance of which voyage in the manner abovesaid the said William hereby binds himself, his heirs and executors, and all his goods and chattels, moveable and immoveable, to our said lord the King to perform the said voyage as is abovesaid; and the survey of the number of the said men, according to the form of this indenture, shall be made and witnessed by the admiral in those parts or his lieutenant. In witness whereof to these indentures the parties aforesaid have interchangeably put their seals. Written at Exeter, 24 August in the sixth year of the reign of King Richard the Second after the Conquest.

3. The King's Prise of Wines [*Fine Roll*, 13 *Edward* II, *m.* 3], 1320.

The King to his beloved clerk, Roger de Northburgh, keeper of his wardrobe, greeting. Whereas we lately confirmed certain ordinances made of late by the prelates and chiefs of our realm, and commanded the same to be observed in all and singular their articles, and in those ordinances it is contained that all gifts and grants made by us to our loss and to the diminution of our crown after 16 March in the third year of our reign, on which day we made our commission to the aforesaid prelates and chiefs touching the making of the said ordinances, . . . be wholly revoked, and afterwards we granted to Stephen de Abindon, our butler, our right prise of wines, to wit, from each ship coming to our realm laden with wines one tun of wine before the mast and one tun of wine behind the mast, at our will, he paying to the merchants from whom he should receive those wines in our name 20*s.* for each piece and 20*s.* to us for each piece in our wardrobe; which grant was made after the said 16 March, and is known to redound to our damage: We, wishing the said ordinances to be duly put into execution in this behalf, command you that you fully charge Stephen, in his account of the things pertaining to his office of butler to be rendered before you, with the wines of our right prise aforesaid for the whole time in which the same Stephen was our butler, notwithstanding our grant aforesaid and our commands afterwards following hereon. Witness the King at Odiham, 23 May.[1]

By the council.

4. The Custom on Wool [*Fine Roll, 3 Edward I, m.* 24], 1275.

For the new custom which is granted by all the great men of the realm and at the prayer of the communities of the merchants of all England, it is provided that in every county in the largest town where there is a port two of the more lawful and able men be elected, who shall have one piece of a seal in keeping, and one man who shall be assigned by the King shall have another piece; and they shall be sworn that they will lawfully receive and answer for the King's money, that is to say, on each sack of wool ½ mark, and on each 300 fells which make a sack ½ mark, and on each last[2] of hides 1 mark, that shall go out of the realm, as well in Ireland and Wales as in England, within franchise and without.

[1] The prise of wines was the royal right, limited at least from the time of Edward I., of purchasing 2 tuns of wine from every ship at the rate of 20*s.* a tun, whatever the market price might be; 60*s.* a tun was a normal price in the 14th century (*see K. R. Accounts,* 77. 21). The value of this grant to Stephen is obvious.

[2] 12 dozen.

Furthermore in every port whence ships can sail there shall be two good men sworn that they will not suffer wools, fells or hides to leave without letters patent sealed with the seal which shall be at the chief port in the same county; and if there is any man who goes otherwise therewith out of the realm, he shall lose all the chattels which he has and his body shall be at the King's will. And forasmuch as this business cannot be performed immediately, it is provided that the King send his letters to every sheriff throughout all the realm, and cause it to be proclaimed and forbidden through all the counties that any man, upon forfeiture of his body and of all his chattels, cause wools, fells or hides to be taken out of the land before the feast of Trinity this year, and thereafter by letters patent sealed with the seals as is aforesaid, and not otherwise, upon the aforesaid forfeitures. And the King has granted of his grace that all lordships, through the ports whereof wools or hides shall pass, shall have the forfeitures when they are incurred, each in its port, saving to the King ½ mark on each sack of wool and fells, and 1 mark on each last of hides.[1]

5. THE CUSTOM ON WINE [*Charter Roll*, 30 *Edward I*, *m.* 2], 1302

The King to Archbishops, etc., greeting. Touching the prosperous estate of the merchants of our duchy aforesaid [Aquitaine] a special care weighs upon us, in what wise under our lordship the immunity of tranquillity and full security may be secured to the same merchants for times to come; so, therefore, that their desires may be the more abundantly increased to the service of us and our realm, we, favourably inclining to their petitions, for the fuller assurance of their estate, have deemed fit to ordain and to grant to the same merchants for us and our heirs for ever in the form that follows:

First, that all merchant vintners of the duchy aforesaid, safely and securely, under our defence and protection, may come into our said realm of England and everywhere within our power with wines and other merchandise whatsoever and that within the same our realm and power, in cities,

[1] This and the two following documents fix the normal rates of customs on exported and imported goods for the mediæval period. The custom on wools, woolfells and hides, came to be known as the great or ancient custom.

boroughs and market-towns, they may traffic in gross[1] as well with denizens or inhabitants of the same realm as with aliens, strangers or friends (*privatis*), and that they may take or carry whither they will, as well within our realm and power aforesaid as also without, their merchandise which they shall happen to bring into the same our realm and power or to buy or otherwise acquire within the same our realm and power, and to do their will therewith, paying the customs which they shall owe, except only wines, which it shall not be lawful for them in any wise to take out of the same our realm and power without our will.

Further, that the said merchant vintners of the said duchy may lodge at their will in the cities and towns aforesaid, and stay with their goods at the pleasure of those to whom the inns or houses belong.

Further, that every contract entered upon by the same vintners with any persons, whencesoever they be, touching all manner of merchandise, be valid and stable, so that neither of the merchants may disown that contract or withdraw from the same, after God's penny[2] shall have been given and received between the contractors. And if by chance a dispute arise on such a contract, proof shall be made thereof according to the uses and customs of the fairs and towns where the said contract shall happen to be made and entered upon.

Further, we remit and quit to the said merchants of the said duchy that ancient prise of two tuns of wine which we used to take from every ship laden with wines touching within our realm or power, one, to wit, before the mast, and the other behind, promising further and granting to the same merchants for us and our heirs for ever that we will in no wise hereafter against the will of the same merchants make or suffer to be made the aforesaid prise or any other of wines or other their wares by us or another or others for any necessity or chance, without payment to be made forthwith according to the price at which the said merchants will sell wines and other wares to others, or other satisfaction wherewith they shall count themselves content, so that a valuation or estimation be not put upon their wines or other wares by us or our ministers.

Further, that on each tun of wine gauged, as the seller of the wine shall be bound to supply that which it lacks from the

[1] *i.e.* Wholesale. [2] Earnest money.

gauge, so he shall be satisfied by the buyer of that which is over the gauge according to the price at which the tun of wine shall be sold.

Further, that as soon as ships with new wines touch within our realm and power, old wines, wheresoever they be found in towns or other places to which the said ships shall come, shall be viewed and proved, if they be whole and also uncorrupt, and of those who shall view the said wines, one moiety shall be of merchant vintners of the duchy aforesaid, and the other of good men of the town where this shall be done, and they shall be sworn to do the premises faithfully and without fraud, and they shall do the accustomed justice with corrupt wines.

Further, whereas it was of old time accustomed and used that the buyer and seller should pay 1*d.* for each tun for gauge, each of them, to wit, ½*d.*, let it be so done hereafter and observed for a custom.

Further, we will that all bailiffs and ministers of fairs, cities, boroughs and market-towns, do speedy justice to the vintners aforesaid who complain before them of wrongs, molestations done to them, debts and any other pleas, from day to day without delay according to the Law Merchant, and if by chance default be found in any of the bailiffs or ministers aforesaid, whereby the same vintners or any of them shall sustain the inconveniences of delay, although the vintner recover his damages against the party in principal, nevertheless the bailiff or other minister shall be punished by us as his guilt demands, and that punishment we grant by favour to the merchant vintners aforesaid to hasten justice for them.

Further, that in all sorts of pleas, saving the case of a crime for which the penalty of death is inflicted, where a merchant vintner of the duchy aforesaid shall be impleaded or shall implead another, of whatsoever condition he who is impleaded shall be, stranger or native, in fairs, cities, or boroughs where there shall be a sufficient number of merchant vintners of the duchy aforesaid, and inquest should be made, one moiety of the inquest shall be of such merchant vintners of the duchy aforesaid, and the other moiety of other good and lawful men of that place where that plea shall happen to be, and if it shall happen that a sufficient number of merchant vintners of the duchy aforesaid be not found, there shall be put on the inquest those who shall be found there sufficient of themselves, and the residue shall be of other good and sufficient men of the places in which that plea shall be.

Further, that no other exaction or charge of prest shall be in any wise put upon the wines of the said merchants.

Further, we have deemed fit to ordain, and we will that ordinance for us and our heirs for ever to be straitly observed, that for any liberty soever which we or our heirs shall grant hereafter, the aforesaid merchant vintners shall not lose the above written liberties or any of them; willing that those liberties extend only to the said merchant vintners of our duchy aforesaid. But for the abovesaid liberties and free customs the merchant vintners aforesaid have granted to us that on each tun of wine which they shall bring or cause to be brought within our realm or power, and whereon they shall be bound to pay freight to mariners, they shall pay by name of custom to us and our heirs, beyond the ancient customs due and paid in money whether to us or to others, 2*s.* within forty days after the same wines be put ashore out of the ships. And we will that the aforesaid merchant vintners, in respect of wines whereon they shall have paid to us the aforesaid custom of 2*s.* in one place of our realm or elsewhere within our power, shall be entirely free and quit of payment of the aforesaid custom of 2*s.* in all other places of our said realm and power; provided that for other merchandise whatsoever which they shall happen to employ within our realm and power they be held to pay to us the same customs which the rest of the merchants shall pay to us for such merchandise. These witnesses:—the venerable father, W. bishop of Coventry and Lichfield, John de Warenna, earl of Surrey, Roger le Bygod, earl of Norfolk and marshal of England, John de Britannia, Hugh le Despenser, William de Brewosa, Walter de Bello Campo, steward of our household, Roger le Brabazon, John de Merk and others. Given by the King's hand at Westminster, 13 August.

6. The Custom on General Imports [*Charter Roll*, 2 *Edward III*, *m.* 11, *No.* 37], 1303.[1]

Edward by the grace of God King of England, Lord of

[1] From the confirmation by Edward III, see *Fœdera*, II. ii, 747; the charter is not among the enrolments of Edward I. These customs were known as the petty custom, and this charter as the *Carta Mercatoria.*

Ireland and Duke of Aquitaine, to archbishops, bishops, abbots, priors, earls, barons, justices, sheriffs, reeves, ministers, and all his bailiffs and faithful, greeting. Touching the good estate of all merchants of the underwritten realms, lands and provinces, to wit, Almain, France, Spain, Portugal, Navarre, Lombardy, Tuscany, Provence, Catalonia, our duchy of Aquitaine, Toulouse, Quercy, Flanders, Brabant, and all other foreign lands and places, by whatsoever name they be known, coming to our realm of England and staying there, an especial anxiety weighs upon us, in what wise under our lordship a means of tranquillity and full security may be devised for the same merchants for times to come: in order therefore that their desires may be rendered apter to the service of us and our realm, we, favourably inclining to their petitions, for the fuller assurance of their estate, have deemed fit to ordain and to grant to the said merchants for us and our heirs for ever as follows: First, to wit, that all merchants of the said realms and lands, safely and securely, under our defence and protection, may come into our said realm of England and everywhere else within our power with their merchandise whatsoever free and quit of murage, pontage and pavage,[1] and that within the same our realm and power in cities, boroughs and market-towns they may traffic in gross only[2] as well with denizens or inhabitants of the same our realm and power aforesaid as with aliens, strangers or friends (*privatis*), so nevertheless that the wares which are commonly called mercery and spices may be sold at retail as before was wont to be done, and that all the aforesaid merchants may cause their merchandise, which they chance to bring to our aforesaid realm and power or to buy or otherwise acquire within the same our realm and power, to be taken or carried whither they will as well within our realm and power aforesaid as without, except to lands of manifest and notorious enemies of our realm, paying the customs which they shall owe, wines only excepted, which it shall not be lawful for them in any wise to take away from the same our realm or power after they shall have been brought within the same our realm or power, without our will and special license.

Further, that the aforesaid merchants may lodge at their will in the cities, boroughs and town aforesaid, and stay with

[1] Tolls for the repair of walls, bridges and streets.
[2] *i.e.* Wholesale.

their goods at the pleasure of those to whom the inns or houses belong.

Further, that every contract entered upon by those merchants with any persons soever, whencesoever they be, touching any sort of merchandise, shall be valid and stable, so that neither of the merchants can withdraw or retire from that contract after God's penny shall have been given and received between the principal contracting persons; and if by chance a dispute arise on such a contract, proof or inquisition shall be made thereof according to the uses and customs of the fairs and towns where the said contract shall happen to be made and entered upon.

Further, we promise to the aforesaid merchants for us and our heirs for ever, granting that we will in no wise make or suffer to be made henceforth any prise or arrest or delay on account of prise of their wares, merchandise or other goods by us or another or others for any necessity or case against the will of the same merchants, save upon immediate payment of the price for which the merchants can sell such wares to others, or upon satisfaction otherwise made to them, so that they hold themselves contented; and that no valuation or estimation be set by us or our ministers on their wares, merchandise or goods.

Further, we will that all bailiffs and ministers of fairs, cities, boroughs and market-towns do speedy justice to the merchants aforesaid who complain before them from day to day without delay according to the Law Merchant touching all and singular plaints which can be determined by the same law; and if by chance default be found in any of the bailiffs or ministers aforesaid whereby the same merchants or any of them shall sustain the inconveniences of delay, although the merchant recover his damages in principal against the party, nevertheless the bailiff or other minister shall be punished in respect of us as the guilt demands, and that punishment we have granted by way of favour to the merchants aforesaid to hasten justice for them.

Further, that in all sorts of pleas, saving the case of crime for which the penalty of death shall be inflicted, where a merchant shall be impleaded or shall implead another, of whatsoever condition he who is impleaded shall be, stranger or native, in fairs, cities, or boroughs, where there shall be a sufficient number of merchants of the aforesaid lands, and inquest should be made, one moiety of the inquest shall be of the same merchants, and the other moiety of other good and lawful men of that place where that plea shall happen to be, and if a sufficient number of merchants of the said lands be not found, there shall be put on the inquest those who shall be found there fit, and the residue shall be of other men good and fit of the places in which that plea shall be.

Further, we will, ordain and decree that in each market-town and fair of our realm aforesaid and elsewhere within our power our weight be set in a certain place, and before weighing the scales shall be seen to be empty in the presence of buyer and seller, and that the arms be level, and that then the weigher weigh level, and when he have put the scales on a level, forthwith move his hands away, so that it remain level; and that throughout our whole realm and power there be one weight and one measure, and that they be marked with the mark of our standard, and that each man may have scales of a quarter and less, where it shall not be against the lord of the place or a liberty granted by us or our ancestors, or against the custom of towns or fairs hitherto observed.

Further, we will and grant that a certain loyal and discreet man resident in London be assigned as justice for the said merchants, before whom they may specially plead and speedily recover their debts, if the sheriffs and mayors do not full and speedy justice for them from day to day, and that a commission be made thereon granted out of the present charter to the merchants aforesaid, to wit, of the things which shall be tried between merchants and merchants according to the Law Merchant.

Further, we ordain and decree, and for us and our heirs for ever we will that that ordinance and decree be straitly observed, that for each liberty which we or our heirs shall hereafter grant, the aforesaid merchants shall not lose the above written liberties or any of them. But for the obtaining of the aforesaid liberties and free customs and the remission of our prises to them, the said merchants, all and singular, for them and all others of their parts, have granted to us with one heart and mind that on each tun of wine which they shall bring or cause to be brought within our realm or power, whereon they shall be bound to pay freight to the mariners, they shall pay to us and our heirs by name of custom 2*s.* beyond the ancient customs due and accustomed to be paid in money to us or others within forty days after the said wines be put ashore out of the ships; further, on each sack of wool which the said merchants or others in their name shall buy and take or cause to be bought and taken from our realm, they shall pay 40*d.* of increment beyond the ancient custom of half a mark which had before been paid; and for a last of hides to be carried out of our realm and power half a mark above that which before was paid of ancient custom; and likewise on 300 woolfells to be taken out of our realm and power 40*d.* beyond the fixed sum which had before been given of ancient custom; further, 2*s.* on each scarlet and cloth dyed in grain; further, 18*d.* on each cloth wherein part of the grain is intermixed; further, 12*d.* on each other cloth without grain; further, 12*d.* on each quintal of wax.

And whereas some of the aforesaid merchants deal in other merchandise as avoir-du-pois and other fine goods, such as cloths of Tars, silk, cendals and other diverse wares, and horses also and other animals, corn and other goods and merchandise which cannot easily be put at a fixed custom, the same merchants have granted to give us and our heirs on each pound of silver of the estimation or value of such goods and merchandise, by what name soever they be known, 3*d.* in the pound at the entry of those goods and merchandise into our realm and power aforesaid within fifteen days after such goods and merchandise shall have been brought into our realm and power and there unladen or sold; and likewise 3*d.* on each pound of silver at the export of any such goods and merchandise bought in our realm and power aforesaid, beyond the ancient customs before given to us or others; and touching the value and estimation of such goods and merchandise whereon 3*d.* on each pound of silver, as is aforesaid, are to be paid, credit shall be given to them by the letters which they shall show from their lords or fellows, and if they have no letters, it shall stand in this behalf by the oaths of the merchants, if they be present, or of their yeomen in the absence of the same merchants. It shall be lawful, moreover, for the fellows of the fellowship of the merchants aforesaid to sell wools within our realm and power aforesaid to other their fellows, and likewise to buy from the same without payment of custom, so, nevertheless, that the said wools come not to such hands that we be defrauded of the custom due to us.

And furthermore it is to be known that after the said merchants shall have once paid in the form aforesaid in one place within our realm and power the custom above granted to us for their merchandise, and have their warrant thereof, they shall be free and quit in all other places within our realm and power aforesaid of payment of such custom for the same merchandise or wares by the same warrant, whether such merchandise remain within our realm and power or be carried without, except wines which shall in no wise be taken out of our realm and power aforesaid without our will and license, as is aforesaid. And we will, and for us and our heirs we grant that no exaction, prise or prest or any other charge be in any wise imposed on the persons of the merchants aforesaid, their merchandise or goods, against the form expressed and granted above. These witnesses:—the venerable fathers, Robert, archbishop of Canterbury, primate of all England, Walter, bishop of Coventry and Lichfield, Henry de Lacy, earl of Lincoln, Humphrey de Bohun, earl of Hereford and Essex and constable of England, Aymer de Valencia, Geoffrey de Geynvill, Hugh le Despenser, Walter de Bello Campo, steward of our household, Robert de Bures and others. Given by our hand at Windsor, 1 February in the 31st year of our reign.

7. Administration of the Search for Money Exported [*Chancery Miscellanea*, 60, 5, 153], 1303.

To the most excellent lord, the lord prince Edward, by the grace of God King of England, Lord of Ireland, Duke of Aquitaine, his humble and devoted mayor and bailiffs of the town of Southampton, obedience, reverence and honour. We have received your command in these words:

Edward, by the grace of God, King of England, Lord of Ireland and Duke of Aquitaine, to his mayor and bailiffs of Southampton, greeting. Because we have learnt by an inquisition which we lately caused to be made by our beloved and trusty Robert de Glamorgan and John de la Lee, that Pelegrin de Castello, our merchant of Bayonne, wished to take the 24*l.*—which you, believing that he wished to carry the same to parts beyond the sea against our prohibition that no man should carry any money or silver in bullion out of our realm, arrested on that account in a ship in our port of Southampton,—to the parts of Devon and Cornwall to buy there lead and tin and other merchandise, and not to parts beyond the sea against the prohibition aforesaid, as you charged against him: We command you, as we have before commanded, that, if the aforesaid 24*l.* have been arrested for the cause aforesaid and no other, then you cause the same to be delivered without delay to the aforesaid Pelegrin, or that you signify to us the cause wherefor you have refused or were unable to execute our command before directed to you thereon.

Wherefore we signify to you that the searchers of the town of Southampton aforesaid, by your writ of the wardrobe sealed with your privy seal directed to the said searchers on 7 January commanding the said 24*l.* to be brought to Odiham and delivered there into your said wardrobe [paid and delivered the same], of which payment and delivery of the said 24*l.* so made the aforesaid searchers have a due acquittance of receipt. And by the tenour of these presents we signify that for no other cause were the aforesaid 24*l.* arrested, save only in the form aforesaid. In witness whereof we transmit to you these our letters sealed with our seal. Given at Southampton, 9 March.

Wherefore the same Pelegrin sues for a writ of the lord the King to be directed to the keeper of the wardrobe of the lord the King, for satisfaction to be made to him according to the form of the return of the writ.

8. Provisions for the Currency [*Fine Roll, 9 Edward III. m.* 10], 1335.

The King to the sheriff of York, greeting. Forasmuch as we have heard that many folk beyond the sea strive to counterfeit our good money, the sterling of England, with worse money, and to send this bad money into our realm, to the deception of us and the damage and oppression of our people if a remedy be not set thereto; we, willing to prevent such damages and oppressions, and to provide a suitable remedy hereon and that our said good money may be multiplied within our realm and the lands of our power, to the profit of us and our subjects, by assent of the prelates, earls and barons of our said realm assembled in our Parliament holden at York on the morrow of the Ascension last past, have ordained and established the things that ensue in the manner underwritten :—

First, it is provided that no man of religion or other henceforth carry the sterling out of the realm of England, nor silver in plate, nor vessels of gold or silver, on pain of forfeiture of the money, plate or vessel that he shall carry, without special licence from us.

Further, that no false money nor counterfeit sterling be brought into the realm or elsewhere in our power, on pain of forfeiture of the money; so always that all folk of what realms or power soever they be, may safely bring to the exchanges for bullion and not elsewhere silver in plate, vessels of silver and all manner of moneys of silver, of what value soever they be, save false money and counterfeit sterling, and there receive good and suitable exchange.

And that no sterling halfpenny or farthing be molten to make a vessel or other thing by goldsmiths or others on pain of forfeiture of the money so molten, and that the goldsmith or other who shall have so molten it, be put in prison and there stay until he shall have rendered to us the moiety of that which he shall have so molten, notwithstanding charter or franchise granted or used to the contrary.

And that all manner of black money now commonly current in our realm and power be utterly excluded, so that none be current after the month next after proclamation be made, on pain of forfeiture of the same money.

And that every man who will sue for us against such as shall commit fraud against this ordinance be admitted hereto and have the fourth penny of that which shall be so deraigned at his suit to our profit.

And that the mayor or bailiffs in every port where merchants and ships are take oath of the merchants and masters of ships going and returning that they will commit no fraud against this ordinance in any point.

And that there be a table of exchange at Dover and elsewhere where and when it shall seem good to us and our council to make exchanges. And that the wardens of the said tables make exchanges by testimony of the controllers whom we will appoint there.

And that no pilgrim pass out of our realm to the parts beyond the sea except at Dover, on pain of imprisonment for a year. And that good ward and strict be made in all places on the seacoast in ports and elsewhere where there is any manner of landing, by good and lawful men sworn, who in our name shall cause diligent search to be made that none, of what condition or estate soever he be, take sterling money, silver in plate, or vessel of gold or silver out of our realm without our licence, nor bring into the said realm or power false money or counterfeit sterling, as is aforesaid, on the pains and forfeitures aforesaid. And the money, vessel or plate so forfeited shall be delivered at our exchanges by indenture, whereof the one part remaining with the searchers shall be delivered at the Exchequer, and by the same indentures the warden of the exchanges shall be charged with that which he shall have received.

And that the searchers have of our gift for all their work the fourth penny of as much as they find so forfeited. And if the searchers make release or show favour to any and be attainted hereof they shall be liable to forfeiture of as much as they shall have in goods; and that the hostlers in every port where there is passage shall be sworn to make search upon their guests in like manner as the searchers shall do, and shall have the fourth penny of that which they find forfeit to us, as the said searchers shall have. And it is our intention that the said searchers have power to search the hostels and to inform themselves of the doings of hostlers; and that the hostlers, in case they be found deceitful against the said articles, shall be punished and incur the forfeiture aforesaid.

Wherefore we command you, straitly enjoining, that forthwith upon sight of these letters you cause all the articles and points aforesaid to be cried and published in cities and boroughs, market towns, ports and all other places within your bailiwick, as well within franchise as without, where you shall see fit so to do; and that in all other places within your bailiwick where need shall be, except the places where such wardens and searchers shall be deputed by us, you cause such searchers and wardens to be established and sworn to keep and observe this our ordinance in the form aforesaid, on the pains contained in this form; and that you certify the Treasurer and Barons of our Exchequer without delay of the names of those who shall be hereafter assigned by you as searchers and wardens. Given under our great seal at York, 6th June in the 9th year of our reign.

In like manner command is given to the several sheriffs throughout England. . . .

The oath of the searchers.—You shall swear that you will well and lawfully make search of all the things contained in your commission whereof search ought to be made according to the commission, and that you will lawfully perform all the other things contained in the same, and that you will lawfully charge yourself with that which you shall find forfeited to the King and will make a lawful indenture thereof and render a lawful account, and that you will spare none for love or for favour, to have private gain, whereby the King may be a loser. So help you God and his saints.

9. Opinions of Officers of the Mint on the State of English Money [*Rot. Parl., III.*, 126–7], 1381–2.

To our lord the King and to all the lords and commons of his realm, make known, as they have often done before these times without being heard, the officers over the moneys of the Tower of London, how for lack of good ordinance no gold or silver comes into England, but of that which is in England a great part has been and from day to day is carried out of the land, and that which remains in England by fault of the deceit of clippers and otherwise is become right feeble, and from day to day such damage increases. Wherefore please it you to take good counsel and remedy hereon, otherwise we, the said officers, warn you, and before God and before you we will be excused, that if you do not apply a speedy remedy thereto in short time to come, where you think to have 5*s*. you will not have 4*s*.

Richard Leicester.—First, as to this that no gold or silver comes into England, but that which is in England is carried beyond the sea, I maintain that it is because the land spends too much in merchandise, as in grocery, mercery and peltry, or wines, red, white and sweet, and also in exchanges made to the Court of Rome in divers ways. Wherefore the remedy seems to me to be that each merchant bringing merchandise into England take out of the commodities of the land as much as his merchandise aforesaid shall amount to ; and that none carry gold or silver beyond the sea, as it is ordained by statute. And let a good ordinance be made hereof, as well by search as otherwise. And so meseems that the money that is in England will remain, and great quantity of money and bullion will come from the parts beyond the sea.

As to this, that the gold is right feeble because of clipping, there seems to me no other remedy than that gold be generally weighed by those who shall take it; and hereon let proclamation be made, and this will be a smaller loss than to change the money, as may be more fully declared.

As to this, that there is a great lack of halfpence and farthings, the Master is bound by his indenture to make halfpence according to the quantity of his work of silver. Let the Warden of the Mint be charged to survey that the Master of the Mint do in all points that which appertains to his office.

As to this, that the gold agrees not with the silver, it cannot be amended unless the money be changed. And to change the money in any manner seems to me universal damage to the lords, commons and all the realm, as may be more fully declared.

As to this, that new money is made in Flanders and in Scotland, let proclamation be made that all manner of moneys, as well of Flanders, Scotland and all other countries beyond the sea whatsoever, be forbidden from having any currency in England, and that none take them in payment except to bring them for bullion to the coinage of our lord the King.

Further, it will be altogether for the better and a very great profit to all the commons, that of the gold money now current, which is so clipped and otherwise impaired, that of this money, when it shall come to the Tower and to the coinage, henceforth our lord the King take for his seigneurage, and the Master for the work for him and his other officers, nothing more than 10*d.* in the pound.

Further there will be an increase of the money and profit to the whole realm if of all other bullion the King take only 12*d.* for his seigneurage and the Master of the Mint 12*d.* for his work.

Lincoln, Goldsmith.—To the noble lords of the Council of our lord the King, touching the charge which you have given me, please you to take note of this answer.

Touching the first article, that gold and silver is taken out of the realm, the first remedy against this is that no clerk or purveyor be suffered to take any silver or gold or to make any exchange to be taken to the Court of Rome, and no merchant be suffered to pay any money but only merchandise for merchandise; and also that the money of the Noble, at the same weight that it now is, be put at a greater value.

And touching the second article, the remedy is that all the money be of one weight, so that the money that is not of the weight ordained be bought according to the value.

And touching the third article, the remedy is that halfpence and farthings be made in great plenty.

And touching the fourth article, the remedy is that there be one weight and one measure throughout the realm and that no subtle weight be suffered.

And touching the fifth article, the remedy is contained above in the first article.

Richard Aylesbury.—As to this, that no gold or silver comes into England, but that which is in England is carried beyond the sea, we maintain that if the merchandise which goes out of England be well and rightly governed, the money that is in England will remain and great plenty of money will come from beyond the sea, that is to say, let not more strange merchandise come within the realm than to the value of the denizen merchandise which passes out of the realm.

Further he says that it were good if the Pope's Collector were English and the Pope's money were sent to him in merchandise and not in money, and that the passages of pilgrims and clerks be utterly forbidden, upon pain, etc.

And as to this, that the gold is too feeble because of clipping, there seems to us no other remedy than that the gold be generally weighed by those who shall take it, and hereon let proclamation be made.

As to this, that the gold agrees not with the silver, it cannot be amended unless the money be changed, and to this we dare not assent for the common damage that might befall.

As to this, that new money is made in Flanders and in Scotland, let proclamation be made that all manner of money of Scotland be forbidden. Let other moneys also that come from beyond the sea have no currency in England, and let none take them in payment except at the value to bring for bullion and to the coinage of our lord the King. And let none take gold or silver out of the realm beyond the sea, as it is ordained by Statute, and hereof let good ordinance be made as well by search as otherwise.

And further he says, if it please by way of information, that [it would be well] if the pound of gold that is now made in the Tower to the sum of 45 nobles (which pound, because the money thereof is so clipped and otherwise impaired, is worth at present, taking one with another, 41½ nobles), were made into 48 nobles, the noble to be current at the present value; and let the King and the Master and other officers of the Mint take 20*d*. in each pound for the seigneurage and work and every other thing.

PART II: 1485-1660

SECTION I

RURAL CONDITIONS

1. Villeinage in the Reign of Elizabeth, 1561—2. Customs of the Manor of High Furness, 1576—3. Petition in Chancery for Restoration to a Copyhold, c. 1550—4. Petition in Chancery for Protection against Breach of Manorial Customs, 1568—5. Lease of the Manor of Ablode to a Farmer, 1516—6. Lease of the Manor of South Newton to a Farmer, 1568—7. The Agrarian Programme of the Pilgrimage of Grace, 1536—8. The Demands of the Rebels led by Ket, 1549—9. Petition to Court of Requests from Tenants Ruined by Transference of a Monastic Estate to lay hands, 1553—10. Petition to Court of Requests to stay Proceedings against Tenants pending the hearing of their Case by the Council of the North, 1576—11. Petition from Freeholders of Wootton Basset for Restoration of Rights of Common, *temp.* Charles I.—12. Petition to Crown of Copyholders of North Wheatley, 1629—13. An Act Avoiding Pulling Down of Towns, 1515—14. The Commission of Inquiry Touching Enclosures, 1517—15. An Act Concerning Farms and Sheep, 1533-4—16. Intervention of Privy Council under Somerset to Protect Tenants, 1549—17. An Act for the Maintenance of Husbandry and Tillage, 1597-8—18. Speech in House of Commons on Enclosures, 1597—19. Speeches in House of Commons on Enclosures, 1601—20. Return to Privy Council of Enclosers furnished by Justices of Lincolnshire, 1637—21. Complaint of Laud's Action on the Commission for Depopulation, 1641.

The agrarian changes which attracted attention from the latter part of the fifteenth century to the accession of Elizabeth, and again, to a less degree, at intervals between 1558 and 1660, are a watershed in economic history, separating mediæval from modern England as decisively as did, in other departments of national life, the Reformation and the Tudor monarchy. For the controversial questions surrounding their causes and consequences we must refer the student to the list of books given below. All that can be attempted here is to notice the special points upon which the following documents throw light.

In arranging the documents in this section it seemed best not to group them in strict chronological order, but to place together those relating to similar aspects of the subject. Documents 1 to 6 illustrate the status and tenure of different classes of landholders. By the beginning of the sixteenth century personal villeinage has almost disappeared; only one document therefore (No. 1) is given to it. Nor has it seemed necessary to print documents referring specially to the freeholders who, compared with other classes of tenants, were little affected by the agrarian changes. On the other hand, the position of the customary tenants, and of the lessees who farmed manorial demesnes, raises important questions. Documents 2 to 4 illustrate manorial customs and the way in which cases between lords and copyholders turned upon them (Nos 3 and 4). Without entering into controversial questions with regard to copyhold tenure one may say (*a*) that it is customary or villein tenure to which the courts from the beginning of the fifteenth century, first the court of Chancery—before which both these cases come—and then the Common Law courts, have given protection, (*b*) that what the Courts do is to enforce manorial customs, which vary from place to place. It is, therefore, essential for a tenant who wants, *e.g.*, to be protected against eviction (No. 3), or against loss of profitable rights (No. 4) to show that the lord is committing a breach of the custom. Hence the dispute (No. 3) as to whether the land at issue is customary land or part of the lord's demesnes. If it is the former the tenants are likely to be protected by the Courts: if it is the latter, they are not. The position of the capitalist farmer, who played so large a part in the rural economy of the sixteenth century, is illustrated by documents 5 and 6. No. 5 is specially interesting as showing how the earlier practice of dividing up the demesne lands among numerous small tenants was replaced by that of leasing them in a block to one large farmer. Documents 7 to 12 illustrate certain points which have already been mentioned, *e.g.*, the importance of manorial customs (Nos. 8, 10 and 12). But their peculiar interest consists in the light which they throw on the grievances of the peasants. They suffer from enclosing (Nos. 7, 8, 10, 11), from excessive fines (Nos. 8, 9, 10, 12), and from rack renting (Nos. 8, 9, 12). They are gravely prejudiced by the land speculation following the dissolution of the monasteries (No. 9). They are too poor and too easily intimidated to get redress even when they have a good case (Nos. 10, 11, 12). The justices who ought to administer the acts against depopulation depopulate themselves (No. 8). The peasants' main resource is the Crown and its Prerogative Courts (Nos. 8, 9, 10, 12). Surely the government will protect men who make good soldiers and pay taxes (No. 12)! Occasionally, however, they have some hope of Parliament, *e.g.*, in 1536, when the royal officials are in bad odour in the North (No. 7), and under Charles I (No. 11). The exact date of this last document is uncertain. May it not be 1640–1, when the Long Parliament was going to restore all good customs?

Documents 13 to 21 illustrate the policy of the government towards the agrarian problem. The government tried to stop depopulation partly for financial and military reasons, partly through a genuine dislike of economic oppression. Its main instruments were four, namely:—(*a*) Statutes (Nos. 13, 15, 17, 18, and 19). Between 1489 and 1597 11 Acts were passed which had as their object the prevention of depopulation, viz., 4 Hen. VII, c. 19, 6 Hen. VIII, c. 5, 7 Hen. VIII, c. 1, 25 Hen. VIII, c. 13, 27 Hen. VIII, c. 22, 5 and 6 Ed. VI, c. 5, 2 and 3 Phil. and Mary, c. 2, 5 Eliz. c. 2, 31 Eliz. c. 7, 39 Eliz. c. 1, 39 Eliz. c. 2, All these were repealed by 21 James I, c. 25, except the last. which was repealed by the Statute Law Revision Act of 1863. (For a summary of these Acts see Slater, *The English Peasantry and of the Enclosure Common Fields, App. D.*) (*b*) Royal Commissions. The first (No. 14) was appointed in 1517: 6 others followed, in 1548, 1566, 1607, 1632, 1635, and 1636 (No. 21). (*c*) Intervention by the Privy Council

(Nos. 16 and 20). (*d*) The Prerogative Courts; viz., the Court of Requests (Nos. 9 and 10), the Court of Star Chamber (No. 21), the Council of the North (No. 10), and the Council of Wales (Acts of the Privy Council, New Series, Vol. XXX, pp. 36–7). How far their intervention was successful is an open question, for a discussion of which reference must be made to the books mentioned below.

AUTHORITIES

The more accessible of the modern writers dealing with agrarian conditions from 1485–1660 are :—Cunningham, *English Industry and Commerce, Early and Middle Ages*, and *ibid., Modern Times*, Part I; Ashley, *Economic History*, Vol. I, Part II; Nasse, *The Land Community of the Middle Ages*; Gonner, *Common Land and Inclosure*; Page, *The End of Villeinage in England*; Hasbach, *The English Agricultural Labourer*; Prothero, *Pioneers and Progress of English Agriculture*, and *A History of English Farming*; Johnson, *The Disappearance of the Small Landowner*; Tawney, *The Agrarian Problem in the Sixteenth Century*; Russell, *Ket's Rebellion in Norfolk*; Leadam, *The Domesday of Inclosures*, and in Trans. R.H.S. New Series, Vol. VI; Gay, in Trans. R.H.S., New Series, Vols. XIV and XVIII, and in *The Quarterly Journal of Economics*, Vol. XVIII; Leonard, Trans. R.H.S., New Series, Vol. XIX; Savine in *The Quarterly Journal of Economics*, Vol. XIX. A useful summary of the principle Statutes against Depopulation is given by Slater, *The English Peasantry and the Enclosure of the Common Fields*, App. D.

Full bibliographies of this subject are given in *Two Select Bibliographies of Mediæval Historical Study*, by Margaret E. Moore, and in *A Classified List of Printed Original Materials for English Manorial and Agrarian History*, by Francis G. Davenport. The following list of sources does not pretend to be exhaustive.

(1) Documents relating to agrarian history are printed in the following works :—Northumberland County History; Baigent, Crondal Records; Surveys of Lands belonging to William, first Earl of Pembroke (Roxburghe Club); Topographer and Genealogist, Vol. I, Surveys of Manors Belonging to the Duke of Devonshire; Chetham Society, Survey of the Manor of Rochdale (ed. by Fishwick); Davenport, History of a Norfolk Manor; Scrope, History of the Manor and Barony of Castle Combe; Strype, Ecclesiastical Memorials; Selden Society, Select Cases in the Court of Star Chamber and Select Cases in the Court of Requests (both edited by

Leadam); Leadam, The Domesday of Enclosures; Tawney, The Agrarian Problem in the Sixteenth Century, App. I; Cunningham English Industry and Commerce, Modern Times, Vol. I, App. B.

(2) The principal contemporary literary authorities are as follows:—J. Rossus (Rous), Historia regum Angliæ (about 1470, edited by T. Hearne); More, Utopia (1516); Starkey, A Dialogue between Cardinal Pole and Thomas Lupset (about 1537, Early English Text Society, England in the Reign of King Henry VIII); Forest, The Pleasant Poesy of Princely Practice (1548, *ibid.*); Fitzherbert, Surveying (1539), and Book of Husbandry (1534); Select Works of Crowley (Early English Text Society); Lever's Sermons (Arber's Reprints); The Common Weal of this Realm of England (about 1549, edited by E. M. Lamond); Certain causes Gathered Together wherein is shewed the Decay of England only by the great Multitude of Sheep (Early English Text Society); Tusser, Five Hundred Points of Good Husbandry (1572); Stubbes, Anatomy of the Abuses in England (1583); Harrison, The Description of Britain (1587, most accessible in Furnivall's Elizabethan England); Trigge, The Humble Petition of Two Sisters (1604); Norden, The Surveyor's Dialogue (1607); Standish, The Common's Complaint (1612), and New Directions of Experience to the Common's Complaint (1613); Bacon, The History of King Henry VII (1622); Powell, Depopulation Arraigned (1636); Fuller, The Holy and Profane State (1642); Halhead, Enclosure Thrown Open, or Depopulation Depopulated (1650); Moore, The Crying Sin of England in not Caring for the Poor (1653); and A Scripture Word Against Enclosure (1656); Pseudonismus, Considerations Concerning Common Fields and Enclosures (1653); Lee, A Vindication of a Regulated Enclosure (1656).

1. Villeinage in the Reign of Elizabeth [*Tingey. Selected Records of Norwich, Vol. VI, p.* 180], 1561.

Robert Ringwood brought in a certain indenture wherein Lewis Lowth was bound to him to serve as a prentice for seven years, and Mr. John Holdiche came before the Mayor and other Justices and declared that the said Lewis is a bondman to my Lord of Norfolk's grace, and further that he was brought up in husbandry until he was xx years old. Whereupon he was discharged of his service.[1]

[1] The above case is remarkable as illustrating (*a*) the survival of villeinage as a working reality into the reign of Elizabeth; (*b*) the use of Statute law (growing since the first Statute of Labourers) to supplement the (legally) almost extinct jurisdiction of lord over villein.

2. Customs of the Manor of High Furness [*R.O. Duchy of Lancaster; Special Commissions; No.* 398], 1576.

[*Presentment of customs of the manor.*]

For the Queen

3. That the jury ought to present at the court after every tenant's death or alienation, and who is his heir, and which tenant hath aliened, and to whom, and what, and who ought to be admitted tenant to the same, which presentment and admittance ought to be made in open court and be entered by the steward . . . in this form.

Ad hanc curiam juratores presentant quod C.D. tenens customarius hujus manerii, seisitus in dominico suo ut de feodo secundum consuetudinem manerii unius messuagii etc, post ultimam curiam alienavit tenementa predicta cuidam H.F. habenda et tenenda eidem H.F. et heredibus suis secundum consuetudinem manerii, per quod predictus H.F. per consuetudinem manerii debet solvere dominae Reginae pro ingressu suo inde habendo 20*s*.

4. No person shall hereafter sell his customary tenement or any part of it, before he first be admitted tenant or come to court, and require to be admitted . . . offering his fine for the same.

The purchaser of any tenement shall publish the sale at the next court after the purchase, and cause it to be entered on the rolls, that her Majesty may be duly answered of the fines, forfeitures and duties as well of the seller as the purchaser [penalty 20*s*.]. Any purchaser not so coming to the second court after the purchase shall forfeit 40*s*., and the lands purchased shall be seized by the steward.

5. As heretofore dividing and portioning of tenements hath caused great decay chiefly of the service due to her Highness for horses, and of her woods, and has been the cause of making a great number of poor people in the lordship, it is now ordered that no one shall divide his tenement or tenements among his children, but that the least part shall be of the ancient yearly rent to her Highness of 6*s*. 8*d*., and that before every such division there shall be several houses and ousettes for every part of such tenement.

Provided always that it be lawful for any one, who has bought any tenement or farmhold under the yearly rent of

6*s.* 8*d.* having houses and ousette upon it, which has been used as a dwelling house, [to leave it] to which of his children he thinks best.

And no person holding any part of any tenement shall bargain or put it away to any person except that person who is tenant of the residue of the tenement, if he will buy it at a reasonable price. If not, the tenant may sell it to any other customary tenant of the manor.

10. Every customary tenant and occupier shall uphold his houses according to our custom, forfeiting 6*s.* 8*d.* *toties quoties.*

11. No person shall fell timber without delivery of the bailiff, who shall deliver necessary timber to every tenant or occupier according to our custom.

12. No tenant or occupier shall sell underwood, etc., nor cut down any other man's wood in the lordship. Penalty 3*s.* 4*d.*, half to her Highness, half to the party grieved. Every tenant so grieved may have his action for damages in the court of the lordship.

13. No tenant is to stop any common way nor turn aside a beck. Penalty 6*s.* 8*d.*

For the tenants.

1. Any tenant, lawfully seised of a messuage or tenement in fee to him and his heirs according to the custom of the manor, might and may lawfully give or sell the same by writing, and that the steward or his deputy ought to be made privy to it at or before next court under penalty of 20*s.*

The tenant may without the privity of the steward give his tenement in writing by his last will to which of his sons he thinks best, or any other person. If any customary tenant die seised of an estate of inheritance without a will or devise, then his eldest son or next cousin ought to have the tenement, as his next heir, according to the custom of the manor.

2. If any customary tenant die seised of a customary tenement, having no sons but a daughter or daughters, then the eldest daughter being unpreferred in marriage shall have the tenement as his next heir, . . . and she shall pay to her younger sister, if she have but one sister, 20 years' ancient rent, as is answered to her Majesty; and if she have more than one sister, she shall pay 40 years' ancient rent to be equally divided among them.

3. The widow of any customary tenant having any estate of inheritance ought to have her widowright, viz., one-third of the same, as long as she is unmarried and chaste, according to our custom.

4. For the avoiding of great trouble in the agreements with younger brothers, it is now ordered that the oldest son shall pay to his brothers in the form following:—

If there is but 1 brother, 12 years' ancient rent.

If there are 2 brothers, 16 years' ancient rent, to be equally divided.

If there be 3 or more, 20 years' ancient rent, to be equally divided.

Provided that any father being a tenant may make a will dividing the money among his sons as he think best, provided he exceed not these sums and rates.

5. Whereas great inconvenience has grown by certain persons that at the marriages of sons or daughters have promised their tenements to the same son or daughter and their heirs according to the custom of the manor, and afterwards put the tenement away to another person, it is ordered, that whatever tenements a tenant shall promise to his son or daughter being his sole heir apparent at the time of his or her marriage, the same ought to come to them according to the same covenant, which ought to be showed at the next court.

6. If a tenant has a child, not his heir, an idiot or impotent, and die without disposition of his tenement, the same child shall be sustained out of the said tenement by direction of the steward or his deputy and 4 men sworn in court.

7. Finally be it agreed that no bye-law shall be any way prejudicial to her Majesty.

3. Petition in Chancery for Restoration to a Copyhold [*Record Commission. Chancery Proceedings, Ed. VI*], c. 1550.

Richard Cullyer and John Cullyer *v.* Thomas Knyvett, esquire.

To quiet Plaintiff in possession of certain land holden of the manor of Cromwell in Wymondham by copy of court roll, according to the custom of the said manor.

To the right honorable Sir Richard Rich, knight, lord Rich and lord Chancellor of England.

In most humble wise sheweth and complaineth unto your

lordship your daily orators, Richard Cullyer of Wymondham in the county of Norfolk, yeoman, and John Cullyer his son, that where one Edmund Mychell was seised in his demesne as of fee of and in twenty acres of land lying in Wymondham aforesaid, holden of the manor of Cromwell, in Wymondham aforesaid, by copy of court roll at will of the lord of the said manor, according to the custom of the said manor, which twenty acres of land have used to be demised and demittable by copy of court roll for term of life, lives, or in fee, to be holden at will of the lord of the said manor by copy of court roll, according to the custom of the said manor time out of remembrance of man; and the said Edmund Mychell, so being seised of the said twenty acres, for a sum of money to him paid by the said Richard Cullyer, the father, did surrender the said twenty acres according to the custom of the said manor, by the name of twenty acres of bond land enclosed in a close called Reading, in Brawyck, in Wymondham aforesaid, into the hands of the lords of the said manor by the hands of William Smythe, in the presence of Geoffry Symondes and John Love, being then copyholders of the said manor, to the use of your said orators, their heirs and assigns: By force whereof your said orators, after that they had paid the accustomable fine due for the same to the lords of the said manor, were admitted tenants thereof, to hold the same, to them and their heirs, at will of the lord of the said manor by copy of court roll, according to the custom of the said manor, and from the time of the said surrender which was made, as is aforesaid, thirty years past; and continued seised of the said twenty acres in their demesne as of fee, as tenants at will, by copy of court roll, according to the custom of the said manor; and have received and taken the profits thereof, doing and paying the rents, customs and services of the same to the lords of the same manor, according to the custom of the said manor; and at their great travail, costs, and charges have stubbed, drained, and dyked the premises, whereby they have improved the said twenty acres and made it much better than it was at the time that the same was surrendered to them as is aforesaid: And now so it is, right honorable lord, that the moiety of the said manor is descended to one Thomas Knyvett esquire, as son and heir to Sir Edmund Knyvett, knight, deceased, who, of a covetous mind, contrary to the mind and without the assent of one

John Flowrdew, gentleman, who is tenant in common with him of the said manor land, of late claimed ten acres of the said twenty acres to be the demesnes of the said manor, and have prohibited your said orators to occupy the same ten acres; and because your said orators doth not leave the occupation thereof, the said Thomas Knyvett hath divers times disturbed the possession of your orators in the premises by taking of divers distresses, and now of late have taken and distrained in the said close four steers and one bull of the value of five pounds, of the goods and chattels of the said John Cullyer, one of your said orators; which the said Thomas did impound and withhold from your said orators until deliverance was made to him thereof by virtue of the King's majesty's writ of *replevin*; which writ of *replevin* is removed into the King's court of his common pleas at Westminster, by a writ of *recordere facias* [*sic*], where the said suit doth yet depend undetermined; and forasmuch as your said beseechers have no better estate in the premises but as copyholders according to the custom of the said manor, and that the court rolls of the said manor, whereby your beseechers should prove the said twenty acres to be an ancient copyhold land, do remain in the possession of the said Thomas Knyvett, and for that also that your orators be poor men and the said Thomas Knyvett a gentleman of great worship, your said poor orators be most like to lose their said land, and to be clearly without remedy in the premises, unless your lordship's favour be to them shewed in that behalf: In consideration whereof, it may please your lordship to grant the King's most gracious writ of *subpœna*, to be directed to the said Thomas Knyvett, commanding him by virtue thereof personally to appear before your lordship in the King's most honorable court of Chancery at a certain day, and under a certain pain, by your lordship to be appointed, then and there to answer the premises, and further to abide to such order therein as shall seem to your lordship agreeing to equity and good conscience; and your poor orators shall daily pray for the prosperous estate of your good lordships in honour long to continue.

Answer.

The answer of Thomas Knivet, esquire, to the bill of complaint of Richard Cullyer and John Cullyer, plaintiffs.

The said defendant saith, that the said bill of complaint

is uncertain and untrue in itself, and insufficient in the law to be answered unto, and that the matters therein contained be untruly surmised by the said complainants to the only intent to put the said defendant to vexation, trouble and cost, and is grounded of malice, they the said complainants having no colour of right, title, nor interest unto the said land mentioned in the said bill of complaint; and he, the said defendant, to the matters contained in the same bill, doth think that he by the order of the right honorable court shall not be compelled any further to answer, but be dismissed out of the same for the insufficiency thereof, with his reasonable costs and charges by him sustained in that behalf; Yet nevertheless, if he, the said defendant, shall be compelled any further to answer to the same bill, then he, the same defendant, for further answer saith that the said land, lying in Brawyck Reading mentioned in the said bill of complaint, is and have been time out of mind parcel of the demesnes of the said moiety of the said manor of Cromwell, in Wymondham; and he, the said defendant, for further answer saith, that one Sir Edmund Knyvett, father to the said defendant, and all his ancestors of long time before him, have been seised of one estate of inheritance of the moiety of the said manor, and one-half of the said manor of Cromwell, and that the said Sir Edmund, and all his ancestors, of long time have been seised of the premises with the appurtenances as parcel of the said manor, in their demesne as of fee, and had the possession thereof, and so seised, died thereof by protestation seised; after whose death the premises descended and came and of right ought to descend and come unto the said defendant, as to the son and next heir of the said Sir Edmund, by force whereof he, the same defendant, entered into the premises, and was and is thereof seised in his demesne as of fee; and the same complainants, claiming the premises by force of a surrender made unto them, the said complainants, by one Edmund Mychell in the time of one [*blank*] being guardian of the said Sir Edmund, and having the custody of the body and lands of the said Sir Edmund during his minority, where nothing in right nor law can pass by the same surrender, but the same is utterly void to bind the said defendant, did enter; upon whom the said defendant did re-enter, as it was lawful for him to do, without that the said Edmund Mychell was lawfully seised in his demesne as of fee, of the lands mentioned in the said bill by copy of court roll at will of the lord according to the custom of the said manor, as in the said bill is untruly alleged, or that the said Edmund Mychell had any lawful interest in the same, or could lawfully make any good or effectual surrender of the same to the said complainants, or that the premises have been used to be demitted or be demittable by copy of court roll for term of life or lives, or in fee, to be holden at the will of the lord by copy of court roll, according to the custom of the said manor time out of mind, as in the said bill of complaint is also untruly alleged, for he, the said defendant, saith that by divers ancient precedents and court rolls ready to be shewed to your honourable court it may appear that the same hath been letten for term of years by the lords of the said manor after the time being unto them, by whom the said complainants claim; or that the same Edmund Mychell for a sum of money to him paid by Richard Cullyer, their father, did surrender the premises, as in the same bill is also untruly alleged, for he, the said defendant, saith, that he the same Edmund had no right nor lawful interest to surrender the same; and if any such surrender were, yet the said defendant saith that the same is verily void in law; or that the said complainants paid any fine for the premises, or were admitted tenants to hold at the will of the lord, as in the same bill is also untruly alleged. And if any such were, yet the same being paid unto his father's said guardian, and their admission by the said guardian, the premises being of the demesnes of the said manor, ought not in no wise to bind him; and without that any other thing mentioned in the said bill of complaint here in this answer not sufficiently confessed, and avoided, traversed, or denied, is true or material to be answered unto, all which matters the said defendant is ready to aver and prove, as this right honorable court shall award. Whereupon the said defendant prayeth to be dismissed out of this right honorable court with his reasonable costs and charges by him sustained in that behalf.

Replication

The replication of Richard Cullyer and John Cullyer, to the answer of Thomas Knyvett esquire.

The said complainants by protestation that the said answer is insufficient in the law for further replication say that the said bill of complaint is certain and sufficient in the law to be answered unto, and for further replication say that the said twenty acres mentioned in the said bill is ancient copyhold land, and have been used to be demised by copy of court roll, according to the custom of the said manor of Cromwell time out of remembrance of man, as is alleged in the said bill, and say also that the said twenty acres lieth now enclosed and have lien enclosed by the space of sixty years or thereabout with other lands and tenements holden by copy of court roll of the manor of Gresshawgh in Wymondham aforesaid, which said twenty acres about the first or second year of the reign of King Henry the Seventh, before that time with other of the said lands then also enclosed did lie open as fields, and in the time of the reign of King Edward the Fourth the said twenty acres were holden, used, and occupied by copy of court roll, according to the custom of the said manor, to one Edmund Cullyer and his heirs, by the name of the third part of one enclose called Reading, being bond or customary land in Wymondham aforesaid, to hold the same to the said Edmund and his heirs by copy of court roll, at will of the lord of the said manor according to the custom of the said manor; upon which grant the said Edmund paid a fine to the lord of the said manor and was admitted tenant thereof, by force whereof the said Edmund Cullyer was seised of the said twenty acres in his demesne as of fee by copy of court roll at will of the lord of the said manor, according to the custom of the said manor, and the said Edmund so being seised of the said twenty acres, the same did surrender according to the custom of the said manor to one Thomas Plomer and his heirs, by virtue whereof the said Thomas Plomer was admitted tenant of the said twenty acres, according to the custom of the said manor, and was seised of the said twenty acres in his demesne as of fee according to the custom of the said manor, and paid the accustomable fine thereof for the same to the lord of the said manor, and did the other services and paid the rents thereof according to the custom of the said manor; and the said Thomas Plomer so being seised of the said twenty acres the same did surrender according to the custom of the said manor to the said Edmund Mychell named in the said bill, by virtue whereof the said Edmund Mychell was lawfully admitted tenant to the premises, according to the custom of the said manor, and was seised thereof in his demesne as of fee according to the said custom, and paid the accustomable fine for the same to the lord of the said manor, and did the services and paid also the rents thereof accordingly, and the said Edmund Mychell so being seised of the premises according to the custom of the said manor, the same according to the said custom did surrender to the said complainants, as is alleged in the said bill; by virtue whereof the said complainants were admitted tenants of the premises and paid the fine thereof, and have done all services, and paid the rents and customs pertaining thereto, according to the custom of the said manor of Cromwell, and hath bestowed great costs upon the same, whereby the said twenty acres be much better than they were at such time as the said complainants were admitted tenants thereto, as in the said bill it is further alleged. And the said complainants do further reply and say in all and everything as they before in their said bill have said, without that,[1] that the said land lying in Brawicke Reading mentioned in the said bill is and have been time out of mind of man parcel of demesnes of the moiety of the said manor of Cromwell, or that the said Sir Edmund had the possession of the said twenty acres, or were seised thereof, otherwise than by the payment of the rents of the same by the said complainants and others, that did hold the same by copy of the said Sir Edmund; and without that the said Sir Edmund died seised thereof, or that the same did descend to the said defendant as demesnes of the said manor discharged of the said tenure, by copy of court roll according to the custom of the said manor; for the said complainants say that the said Sir Edmund during all his life did permit and suffer the said complainants to enjoy the premises according to the custom of the said manor, without let or gainsaying, which the said Sir Edmund would not have done if the said complainants had not had a just right and title to have had the same; without that, that the said complainants did claim the premises only by a surrender made to the said Mychell by the guardian of the said Sir Edmund during his minority, or that the surrender made by the said Mychell during the minority of the said Sir Edmund is void by the law or that the law is that nothing can pass by a surrender made during the said minority, or that a surrender made then is

[1] *i.e.* Not admitting.

void, or that the premises have been letten for years as is alleged in the said bill; and the said complainants for replication do reply and say in all and every thing, matter, and sentence as they before in their said bill have said; without that, that any other things in this replication not sufficiently replied unto, denied, traversed, or confessed and avoided is true, all which matters the said complainants are ready to verify as this honorable court will award, and pray as they before have prayed.

4. PETITION IN CHANCERY FOR PROTECTION AGAINST BREACH OF MANORIAL CUSTOMS [*R.O. Chancery Proceedings; Series II, Bundle* 196, *No.* 25], 1568.

To the right honorable Sir Nicholas Bacon, knight, Lord Keeper of the Great Seal of England.

In most humble wise sheweth and complaineth to your good Lordship your daily orators John Wyat, John Blake, John Whittington, Thomas Knight, Thomas Ellis, Thomas Moris, Richard Cooke, Symon Lucas, and Richard Blake, with divers other poor men to the number of forty, customary tenants of the manor of Slindon in the County of Sussex, That where they and their ancestors and those whose estate they have in the said customary tenements, parcel of the said manor (time out of memory of man) have been seised to them and to their heirs for ever according to the custom of the said manor, all and every which customs of late one Anthony Kempe esquire, lord of the said manor, hath diversely, contrary to conscience and equity, devised and imagined by divers indirect means to break, annihilate, and infringe, and your said orators hath diversely vexed and troubled by the order of the common laws and menaceth to expel your said orators out of their several tenements unless they will pay other customs and services than they of right ought to do by the customs of the said manor. For where by the custom of the said manor your Lordship's said orators and those whose estate they or any of them have in the premises, have been lawfully and quietly seised of the said tenements customary in their demesne as of fee according to the custom of the said manor for the several services thereupon due and accustomed, clearly discharged of all day works, licences of marriage or fines for the same, and having always free liberty to let all and singular the premises aforesaid without any licence beforehand to be obtained of the lords of the said manor for the time being, neither have further at any time done any manner of services whatsoever out of the said manor: And also where after the death of every of the said customary tenants, having a whole yardland, there hath been due for heriot only the best beast, and if such have no beast, then 10*s.* in money only; and after the death of every tenant holding half a yardland 6*s.* 8*d.* for relief only, and after the death of every cottager 6*d.* only, and at every alienation of a yardland 10*s.* in money, and at every alienation of a half yardland 6*s.* 8*d.* in money, and at the alienation of every cottage 6*d.*, and at the death and alienation of every tenant one whole year's rent only for and in the name of a fine, over and besides the only heriot or relief aforesaid, and suit of court and other services in this bill specified: And where by the further custom of the said manor the lords of the said manor for the time being by the custom of the said manor should make no seizure or forfeiture for waste done in their cottages customary, unless the same be severally presented at the several Courts to be holden one half year after another, and the same yet then not reformed within one month after; And where the cutting down of any the woods standing and growing upon their several tenements customary for house-bote, fire-bote, plough-bote, cart-bote, gate-bote and hedge-bote, and such like hath not heretofore been taken for waste but always as lawful to do by the custom of the said manor; And where also by the further custom of the said manor, where any forfeiture is committed, perpetrated or done for any offence whatsoever whereby there is given cause of seizure and forfeiture to the lord of the manor for the time being, yet by the custom of the same manor, the said forfeiture notwithstanding, they to whom the same so forfeited should descend, remain, come, or grow after the death of such tenant so offending, should and may lawfully claim all and singular such tenements so forfeited or seized after the death of such offender, as though no such forfeiture had been made; And where by the custom of the said manor all and every the tenants of the said manor should and ought to have from time to time in the woods of the lord of the said manor sufficient timber for reparations of their said tenements customary at the assignment of the lord or his officers, and if the lord the same refuse to do upon reasonable request being thereof made to the said lord or his steward of his court for the time being, if then their said tenements decay, or fall down in default of reparations, there shall nor ought any forfeiture or seizure to be made for any such waste; And where the widows of the tenants customary of the said manor should and ought by the custom of the said manor have their widow's estate for one penny only; And where by their further custom the eldest son, brother or next cousin, male or female, should inherit and have the said customaries and after the decease of their ancestors only; And where by the custom of the said manor it is lawful for the said tenants as aforesaid to assign and demise the several tenements for years to any person or persons at their will and pleasure, yet nevertheless by the custom of the said manor it hath been lawful for the lord of the said manor misliking the said undertenant upon one year's warning to expel and put out such tenant, after which it shall be lawful for the said tenants that so did demise or let their tenements to re-enter and the same to enjoy as before, and after to let the same as before to any person or persons in manner and form aforesaid, until such person shall be by the lord misliked and expulsed as aforesaid; And where by the further custom of the said manor the said tenants and every of them and their heirs and assigns should and ought to have the masting of their own hogs in the time of mast in the north woods of the said manor of Slindon, and likewise the pasturing of their cattle and sheep in the said woods and in all other the lord's commons of the said manor, paying for the ovissing[1] and masting of every hog 2*d.* only; And whereas by the further custom of the said manor the tenants aforesaid have and may at their will and pleasure surrender into the hands of two tenants of the said manor out of the court, or into the hands of the lord or his steward in the court, to the use of any person or person of such estate as they shall declare and limit upon the said surrender, yet nevertheless by the custom of the said manor it is not lawful for any tenant of the said manor to convey, surrender or alienate any one part, parcel or piece of their tenement customary, unless he give and surrender the whole to the use of one only person in possession; And where the

[1] *i.e.* Pasturing.

youngest tenant of any customary tenement for the time being ought to be crier in the lord's court by the custom of the said manor: All which customs are not only to be proved to be the old and ancient customs of the said manor, but also now of late the said Anthony Kempe hath by his deed indented declared the same to be true in manner and form as it is before alleged; And where by the said Indenture the said Anthony Kempe hath further, for and in consideration of a further and a new rent of eight pounds to him granted, and for and in consideration of twenty pounds to him paid, and for and in consideration to make a perpetual and final end of all controversies heretofore moved and after to be moved, doth further covenant and grant in the said indenture that it shall be lawful for the customary tenants and copyholders of the said manor to enclose, and sever, and severally to hold to them and to their heirs and assigns forever six score acres of land, parcel of the wastes of the lords of the said manor, wherein they now have common, in such place convenient to be limited before the feast of Easter next coming, by consent of two persons to be named by the said Anthony Kempe and two other persons by the said tenants; All the which premises notwithstanding, the said Anthony Kempe doth against all conscience utterly deny unto your Lordship's said orators their said customs and the aforesaid further agreement according to the said indenture, and doth daily vex your said orators quietly to have and enjoy their said customary tenants [*sic*] with their appurtenances according to the customs aforesaid. May it therefore please your good lordship the premises favourably tendering to grant the Queen's Majesty's writ of *subpœna* to be directed to the said Anthony Kempe commanding him thereby personally to appear in this honourable Court at a day certain in the said writ of *subpœna* mentioned, then and there upon his corporal oath to answer to the premises and to abide such order therein as to your Lordship shall upon the truth of the matter appearing seem according to equity; and your said poor orators shall daily pray to God for the continual preservation of your honor. EDWARD FENNER.

5. Lease[1] of the Manor of Ablode to a Farmer [*Rolls Series. Historia et Cartularium Monasterii Gloucestriæ, Vol. III, pp.* 291–5], 1516.

This indenture made on the 5th day of October in the seventh year of King Henry VIII between William . . . Abbot of St. Peter . . . of the one part and Richard Cockes and Catharine his wife . . . and William and John, sons of the said Richard and Catharine, of the other part, witnesseth, that the aforesaid Abbot and Convent . . . have leased, demised, and to farm let to Richard, Catharine, William, and John, the site of their Manor of Ablode, situated in the county of Gloucester, with all its houses, buildings, arable lands, meadows, feedings and pastures, dovecotes, weir, waters, fishpools, and rabbit warrens, with all and everything thereto pertaining. And the said abbot and convent have leased to the aforesaid . . . divers goods and chattels, moveable, and immoveable, pertaining to the said manor. . . . Moreover the said abbot and convent have leased to the said . . . 320 sheep remaining for stock on the said manor, priced per head at 16*d.*, which amounts in all to the sum of 21*l.* 6*s.* 8*d.*, together with their meadows, pastures and all easements . . . needed for the support of the said sheep. . . . Furthermore the said abbot and convent have leased to the aforesaid . . . divers lands and demesne meadows belonging to the said manor, when the reversion thereof shall in any way have occurred, which lands and demesne meadows are now occupied by the customary tenants of the lord, as is plain from the rental drawn on the back of the present indenture. . . . And it shall be lawful for the aforesaid Richard, Catharine, William and John, or any of them to introduce at their pleasure new tenants on all those demesne lands aforesaid, now in the hands of the tenants there, whenever the aforesaid reversion shall have fallen in.

[1] The most interesting clauses in the lease are (*a*) that which relates to the leasing of the stock of the manor ("Stock and land lease"); (*b*) the last, which shows how the practice of leasing a manor to one large farmer replaced the earlier practice of leasing parts of it to numerous small tenants.

6. Lease of the Manor of South Newton to a Farmer [*Roxburghe Club, Surveys of the lands belonging to William Earl of Pembroke*], 1568.

John Rabbett holds to himself and his assigns, by an indenture dated November 28 in the fourth year of Elizabeth, at a fine of £120, the whole site of the farm of the Manor of South Newton in the county of Wilts., all its demesne lands, meadows, marshes, pastures, commons, fisheries, and the customary works of the tenants in South Newton, Stovord, and Childhampton, with all and singular their appurtenances in the above-mentioned South Newton belonging to the site and the farm or of old demised to farm with the above-mentioned site, as fully as Lewis ap Jevan had and occupied it, and also one virgate of land and one ham of meadow, lying in the afore-mentioned South Newton, called the Parson's yardland and ham with a sheep pasture, . . . excepted and altogether reserved to the lord and his heirs the advowson of the vicarage there ; the said John Rabbett and his assigns to have and to hold the aforesaid . . . from Michaelmas before this indenture for the full term of 21 years, paying thence yearly to the lord for the aforesaid farm and site with its appurtenances

per bs. 12*d.* 4*l.*	per bs. 8*d.* 106*s.* 8*d.*	per bs. 3*d.* 26*s.* 8*d.*
10 quarters of wheat	20 quarters of barley,	[*sic*]
prec. cap. 4*d.* 6*s.* 8*d.*	prec. cap. 4*d.* 6*s.* 8*d.*	10 quarters of oats
20 capons,	20 pigeons,	prec. cap. 4*d.* 4*s.*
		12 great fish called great Trouts.

and for the aforesaid virgate of land . . . 13*s.* at the usual terms, with all other clauses and agreements, as is set forth at length in the indenture placed in the register. And be it known that the grain, capons, and pigeons and fish are valued at the rate written above the head of each kind. And there belong to the farm of arable land 55 acres in Middlefield, 60 acres in Westfield, and 60 acres in Eastfield, and one meadow called Long Ham lying in a close and containing 11½ acres, and the cropping of one meadow called Duttenham lying in the west part of Wishford containing 10½ acres, one meadow called Beymeade containing 4½ acres lying on the north-west side of South Newton, and one curtilage near the barn containing 2 acres, and a hill called the Down estimated to contain 100 acres, and it is able to keep 500 sheep, 36 cattle, and 12 horses. And there belong to the aforesaid virgate of land, called the Parson's Yardland, of arable land in Southfield 6½ acres, in Middlefield 8½ acres, in Northfield 6 acres, and one ham of meadow, pasture for 10 cows, 1 bull, and 120 sheep with the farmer, 14*s.*

4*l.*
Wheat 10 qrs.
106*s.* 8*d.*
Barley 20 qrs.
26*s.* 8*d.*
Oats 10 qrs.
6*s.* 8*d.*
Capons 20.
6*s.* 8*d.*
Pigeons 20.
4*s.*
Fish 12.

7. The Agrarian Programme of the Pilgrimage of Grace [*Gairdner, Letters and Papers, Hen. VIII, Vol.* xi, 1246], 1536.

9. That the lands in Westmoreland, Cumberland, Dent, Sedbergh, Furness, and the abbey lands in Mashamshire, Kyrkbyshire, Notherdale, may be by tenant right, and the Lords to have, at every change, 2 years rent for gressum, according to the grant now made by the Lords to the Commons there. This is to be done by Act of Parliament.

13. The statute for enclosures and intacks to be put in execution, and all enclosures and intacks since 4 Hen. VII to be pulled down, except mountains, forests, and parks.

8. The Demands of the Rebels led by Ket [*Harl. MSS.* 304, *f.* 75. *Printed by Russell, Ket's Rebellion in Norfolk, p.* 48], 1549.

We pray your grace that where it is enacted for enclosing that it be not hurtful to such as have enclosed saffron grounds, for they be greatly chargeable to them, and that from henceforth no man shall enclose any more.[1]

We certify your grace that whereas the lords of the manors hath been charged with certe free rent, the same lords hath sought means to charge the freeholders to pay the same rent, contrary to right.

We pray your grace that no lord of no manor shall common upon the commons.

We pray that priests from henceforth shall purchase no lands neither free nor Bondy, and the lands that they have in possession may be letten to temporal men, as they were in the first year of the reign of King Henry the VII.

We pray that reed ground and meadow ground may be at such price as they were in the first year of King Henry the VII.

We pray that all marshes that are holden of the King's Majesty by free rent or of any other, may be again at the price that they were in the first year of King Henry VII.

We pray that all bushels within your realm be of one stice, that is to say, to be in measure viii gallons.

We pray that [priests] or vicars that be [not able] to preach and set forth the word of God to his parishioners may be thereby put from his benefice, and the parishioners there to choose another, or else the patron or lord of the town.

We pray that the payments of castleward rent, and blanch farm and office lands, which hath been accustomed to be gathered of the tenements, whereas we suppose the lords ought to pay the same to their bailiffs for their rents gathering, and not the tenants.

We pray that no man under the degree of a knight or esquire keep a dove house, except it hath been of an old ancient custom.

We pray that all freeholders and copyholders may take the profits of all commons, and there to common, and the lords not to common nor take profits of the same.

[1] Some doubt has been expressed as to the interpretation of these words. They should probably be read as referring to enclosures made not by lords or by large farmers, but by the peasants themselves. The rebels point out that a considerable number of people have spent capital on hedging and ditching their lands for the better cultivation of saffron, and therefore ask that, while other enclosures should be pulled down, a special exception may be made in favour of this particular kind of enclosure.

We pray that no feodary within your shires shall be a councillor to any man in his office making, whereby the King may be truly served, so that a man being of good conscience may be yearly chosen to the same office by the commons of the same shire.

We pray your grace to take all liberty of let into your own hands whereby all men may quietly enjoy their commons with all profits.

We pray that copyhold land that is unreasonably rented may go as it did in the first year of King Henry VII, and that at the death of a tenant or at a sale the same lands to be charged with an easy fine as a capon or a reasonable [sum] of money for a remembrance.

We pray that no priest [shall be chaplain] nor no other officer to any man of honour or worship, but only to be resident upon their benefices whereby their parishioners may be instructed with the laws of God.

We pray that all bond men may be made free, for God made all free with his precious blood-shedding.

We pray that rivers may be free and common to all men for fishing and passage.

We pray that no man shall be put by your escheator and feodary to find any office unless he holdeth of your Grace in chief or capite above xl.*l* by year.

We pray that the poor mariners or fishermen may have the whole profits of their fishings as porpoises, grampuses, whales or any great fish, so it be not prejudicial to your Grace.

We pray that every proprietary parson or vicar having a benefice of xv.*l* or more by year shall either by themselves or by some other person teach poor men's children of their parish the book called the catechism and the primer.

We pray that it be not lawful to the lords of any manor to purchase lands freely and to let them out again by copy of court roll to their great advancement and to the undoing of your poor subjects.

We pray that no proprietary parson or vicar, in consideration of avoiding trouble and suit between them and their poor parishioners which they daily do precede and attempt, shall from henceforth take for the full contentation [*i.e.* satisfaction] of all the tenths which now they do receive but viiid of the noble in the full discharge of all other tithes.

We pray that no man under the degree of [*blank*] shall keep any conies upon any of their own freehold or copyhold unless he pale them in so that it shall not be to the commons' nuisance.

We pray that no person, of what estate, degree or condition he be, shall from henceforth sell the wardship of any child, but that the same child if he live to his full age shall be at his own chosen concerning his marriage, the King's wards only except.

We pray that no manner of person having a manor of his own shall be no other lord's bailiff but only his own.

We pray that no lord knight nor gentleman shall have or take in farm any spiritual promotion.

We pray that your Grace to give license and authority by your gracious commission under your great seal to such commissioners as your poor commons hath chosen, or as many of them as your Majesty and your council shall appoint and think meet, for to redress and reform all such good laws, statutes, proclamations, and all other your proceedings, which hath been hidden by your justices of your peace, sheriffs, escheators, and other your officers from your poor commons, since the first year of the reign of your noble grandfather King Henry VII.

We pray that those your officers that hath offended your Grace and your commons, and so proved by the complaint of your poor commons, do give unto these poor men so assembled iiijd. every day so long as they have remained there.

We pray that no lord, knight, esquire nor gentleman do graze nor feed any bullocks or sheep if he may spend forty pounds a year by his lands, but only for the provision of his house.

By me, Robt. Kett.

" " Thomas Aldryche. Thomas Cod.

9. Petition to Court of Requests from Tenants Ruined by Transference of a Monastic Estate to Lay Hands[1] [*R.O. Requests Proceedings, Bundle* 23, *No.* 13], 1553.

Inhabitants of Whitby *v.* York.

To [the] Queen's Highness our most dread Sovereign Lady and to her most honorable Council.

1553. Lamentably complaining sheweth unto your Highness and to . . . Council your poor obedient subjects and daily orators, poor husbandmen the . . . of Halkesgarthe and Senseker in Whitby Strand in the County of York, that the said inhabitants, late being tenants of the dissolved Monastery of Whitby [afore]said, after it was come into the hands of our late sovereign lord King Henry . . . and after that it did come to the hands and possession of the late Duke of Northumb[erland] and of late purchased of him by one Sir John Yorke, knight, who is now in possession of the premises; which said Sir John Yorke hath lately been there and kept court on the said premises at two sundry times; which said Sir John Yorke of his extort power and might, and by great and sore threatenings of the said tenants and inhabitants there, and by other means, hath gotten from them all the leases [that were in their] custodies and possession, and unreasonably hath raised and . . . rents and excessively hath gressomed, fined, pilled and . . . maketh inquiry all about for your poor orators with great . . . do suppose if he could find them, he would lay the . . . because they should not be able to exhibit this their bill of c[omplaint] . . . and your said Council, how he hath fined them and raised . . . and yearly rents, if your said orators should still bear and pay, appear by a bill hereunto annexed your orators hands or marks thereto . . . of the old [rents] the [ne]w by them . . . to be paid unto the said Sir John Yorke . . . thereby shall be utterly undone in this world . . . favour, help and succour with speedy [remedy] . . . consideration of the premises and forasmuch as your said orators and ancestors of your said poor orators have holden and enjoyed the premises according to the

[1] This document, though very imperfect, is interesting as illustrating (*a*) the land speculation which followed the dissolution of the monasteries, (*b*) the rack-renting of tenants which such speculation naturally produced.

old ancient custom, old rents and old fines, as hereunder it may plainly appear, without enhancing, or raising, without vexation or trouble, and in consideration also that the said Sir John Yorke is a man of power and might, lands, goods, and possessions . . . greatly friended, and your poor orators being sore afraid to be imprisoned by him, and also very poor men, and not able to sue against him, nor hath no remedy but only to sue . . . Majesty of your most gracious goodness . . . said Council, to call before your Majesty and your said C[ouncil] . . . and to take order in the premises, that your poor orators according to justice, right, and good conscience may peaceably enjoy all the premises, paying their old accustomed rents and fines, according as they and their ancestors have done, time out of mind of man. And your said poor orators shall daily pray to God for the prosperous preservation of your Majesty in your most Royal Estate long to reign, and for your most honourable Council long to continue.

Endorsed . . .

21 October.

The tenants and inhabitants of Senseker and Halkesgarthe in Whitby Strand in the County of York desire to have Sir John Yorke called before the Council and to take order that your orators may have . . .

The Names of the tenants of Halkesgarthe and Senseker.

	The old rent.	The new rent.	And the fine.
First John Coward ..	24*s*.	3*l*. 16*d*.	33*s*. 4*d*.
From Henry Russell ..	42*s*. 11½*d*.	4*l*. 7*s*. 3*d*.	3*l*. 6*s*. 8*d*.
From Elisabeth Postgate, widow	18*s*. 10*d*.	41*s*. 5*d*.	18*s*.
From Thomas Robynson	12*s*. 11½*d*.	40*s*. 7*d*.	33*s*. 4*d*.
From John Robynson ..	10*s*. 2*d*.	33*s*. 4*d*.	33*s*. 4*d*.
From James Browne ..	16*s*. 1*d*.	36*s*. 10*d*.	24*s*. 6*d*.
From Robert Lyne ..	16*s*. 4*d*.	33s. 10*d*.	13*s*. 4*d*.
From John Nattris ..	7*s*. 8*d*.	15*s*.	10*s*.
From Robert Stor ..	23*s*. 5*d*.	50*s*. 2*d*.	15*s*.
From Thomas Coward ..	14*s*. 9*d*.	31*s*.	2*s*. 6*d*.
From Thomas Hodshon	20*s*. 5*d*.	50*s*. 8*d*.	24*s*.
From William Walker ..	7*s*. 3*d*.	17*s*.	5*s*.
From Henry Tomson ..	11*s*. 3½d.		

	The old rent.	The new rent.	And the fine.
From Henry Coverdaill..	15*s.*	36*s.*	11*s.* 8*d.*
From Nicholas Grame ..	22*s.* 6*d.*	46*s.* 8*d.*	3*s.*
From William Postgate	28*s.* 7*d.*	3*l.* 6*s.* 8*d.*	23*s.* 6*d.*
From William Brown ..	13*s.* 4*d.*	26*s.* 8*d.*	24*s.* 10*d.*
From Robert Jefrayson..	14*s.*	30*s.*	3*s.* 4*d.*
From William Bois and Robert Jefrason ..	34*s.* 8*d.*	3*l.* 6*s.* 8*d.*	13*s.* 4*d.*
From Robert Barker ..	14*s.* 6*d.*	30*s.*	2*s.* 8*d.*
From Christofer Jefrayson	10*s.* 8*d.*	26*s.* 8*d.*	3*s.* 4*d.*
From Richard Colson and Isabell Colson, widow..	31*s.*	3*l.* 2*s.*	
From Robert Sutton and Kateryn Sutton, widow	23*s.* 4*d.*	53*s.* 4*d.*	36*s.* 8*d.*
From Thomas Postgate, younger, and Henry Russell	27*s.* 6*d.*	3*l.* 6*s.* 8*d.*	37*s.*
From Thomas Postgate the elder, Suthwait house..	18*s.* 3*d.*	46*s.* 8*d.*	23*s.* 4*d.*
From Robert Huntrodes	50*s.* 2*d.*	5*l.* 16*s.* 8*d.*	7*s.*

At Lammas last past my Lady Yorke at Whitby earnestly demanded of the said Robert Michaelmas farm before hand, insomuch he durst not hold it but paid it to her, the sum of .. .. 58*s.* 4*d.*

From William Jakson, likewise paid 20*s.* for his farm afore hand.

From Maryon Huntrodes, widow	50*s.* 2*d.*	5*l.* 16*s.* 8*d.*	7*s.*
	Sum :— 28*l.* 19*s.* 8½*d.*	Sum :— 64*l.* 9*s.* 9*d.*	Sum :— 23*l.* 15*s.* 8*d.*

[Endorsed.] Bill versus Yorke.

Orders and Decrees.

24th day of October in the first year of the reign of Queen Mary.

Be it remembered that the cause brought afore the Queen's Council in Her Majesty's Court of Requests at the suit as well of Robert Stor as William Poskett and William Browne, tenants to Sir John Yorke, knight, in the Lordship of Whitby in the County of York, is now ordered by the said Council by the agreement of the said Sir John, who hath promised that the said parties afore named, and every of them, shall have and quietly enjoy their tenements and holds during the years and terms in their leases and copies yet enduring, paying their rents and farms accustomed without any interruption to the contrary or any other by him or in his name or procurement.

10. Petition to Court of Requests to Stay Proceedings Against Tenants Pending the Hearing of their Case Before the Council of the North [*R.O. Requests Proceedings. Bundle III, No.* 24], 1576.

To the Queen's most excellent Majesty.

In most humble wise sheweth unto your Majesty your poor subject Thomas Langhorne, and other the inhabitants and residents of the lordship of Thornthwaite in your county of Westmoreland, that whereas your suppliant and other of the inhabitants and residents of the lordship aforesaid, and their ancestors time out of memory of man, have quietly had and enjoyed from heir to heir according to their ancient custom in consideration of their service to be in readiness with horse,[1] harness and other furniture to serve your Majesty at their own costs and charges in defence of your realm against the Scots, which custom hath been sufficiently approved and allowed before your Majesty's President and Council at York, as by a decree ready to be shewed more at large it may appear. But so it is, and if it please your Majesty, that Sir Henry Curwyn, knight, lord of the lordship aforesaid, hath since the beginning of your Majesty's reign expelled out of one piece of Shapps parish within the said lordship, where there was but thirteen tenants, twelve of them he hath expelled and taken their land from them and enclosed it into his demesnes, whereby your Majesty's service for the same is utterly taken away: and also the said Sir Henry Curwyn, lord of the lordship aforesaid, hath of late surrendered over the same lordship to Nicholas Curwyn, gentleman, his son and heir, which Sir Henry and Nicholas do excessively fine the poor tenants and specially your orator, who was forced to pay them for the fine of his

[1] For this form of customary tenure, "border tenure," see *Northumberland County History, passim.*

tenement, being but 13*s.* 10*d.* by year, 31*l.* 6*s.* 8*d.*, and was admitted tenant to the said Nicholas Curwyn, who notwithstanding hath contrary to all right and conscience granted a lease of your subject's tenement to one Henry Curwyn, servant to the same Nicholas, in the nature of an *ejection firm*[1] here at the common law, and hath by your Majesty's writ arrested your orator to appear in your Highness' Bench at Westminster to the utter undoing of your said poor subject, his wife and five children for ever, being not able to defend his rightful cause: May it therefore please your most excellent Majesty that order may be set down by your Majesty and your most honourable council that none of the lordship aforesaid may be expelled out and from their tenant rights until their said custom shall be tried and examined before the Lord President of York for the time being, and that your Majesty's said subject may not be constrained to answer any suit here at the Common Law concerning their tenant right. And your said orators shall according to their bounden duties pray to God for the preservation of your most Royal Majesty long to live and reign over us.

[Endorsed.] 18 May, 1586.

Your humble subject Thomas Langhorne, one of the tenants of the lordship of Thornthwaite in the county of Westmoreland, being molested in their tenant right by one Henry Curwyn, servant unto Nicholas Curwyn, lord of the said manor, desire most humbly that all actions at the Common Laws here at Westminster might be stayed and the full hearing of the matter reserved to the Lord President at York.

25 May, 18 Elizabeth.

Writ of injunction granted, as appears, etc.

11. Petition from Freeholders of Wootton Bassett for Restoration of Rights of Common [*Topographer and Genealogist, Vol. III*], *temp.* Charles I.

To the Right Honourable House of Parliament now assembled, the humble petition of the Mayor and Free Tenants of the Borough of Wootton Basset in the County of Wilts.

Humbly showeth to this Honourable House,

That whereas the Mayor and Free Tenants of the said

[1] *i.e.* an *ejectio firmae*, an action of ejectment. See Pollock and Maitland, *History of English Law*, Vol. II, p. 109.

Borough, by relation of our ancient predecessors, had and did hold unto them free common of pasture for the feeding of all sorts of other beasts, as cows, etc., without stint, be they never so many, in and through Eastern Great Park, which said park contained by estimation 2000 acres of ground or upwards; and in the second and third year of the reign of King Philip and Queen Mary the manor of Wootton Basset aforesaid came by patent into the hands and possession of one Sir Francis Englefield, knight, who, in short time after he was thereof possessed, did enclose the said park; and in consideration of the common of pasture that the free tenants of the borough had in the said park did grant, condescend and lease out unto the said free tenants of the said borough to use as common amongst them that parcel of the said Great Park which formerly was and now is called by the name of Wootton Lawnd, which was but a small portion to that privilege which they had before it, [and] doth not contain by estimation above 100 acres; but the free tenants being therewith contented, the mayor and free tenants did equally stint the said ground or common, as followeth:—that is to say to the mayor of the town for the time being two cows feeding, and to the constable one cow feeding, and to every inhabitant of the said borough, each and every of them, one cow feeding and no more, as well the poor as the rich, and every one to make and maintain a certain parcel or bound set forth to every person; and ever after that inclosure for the space of fifty and six years or thereabouts any messuage, burgage or tenement that was bought or sold within the said borough did always buy and sell the said cows-leaze together with the said messuage or burgage as part member of the same, as doth and may appear by divers deeds which are yet to be seen; and about which time, as we are informed and do verily believe, that Sir Francis Englefield, heir of the aforesaid Sir Francis Englefield, did by some means gain the charter of our town into his hands, and as lately we have heard his successor now keepeth it; and we do believe that at the same time he did likewise gain the deed of the said common, and he thereby knowing that the town had nothing to show for their rights of common but by prescription, did begin suits in law with the said free tenants for their common, and did vex them with so many suits in law for the space of seven or eight years at the least, and never suffer anyone to come to trial in all that space, but did divers times attempt to gain his possession thereof by putting in of divers sorts of cattle, in so much that at length, when his servants did put in cows by force into the said common, many times and present upon the putting of them in, the Lord in his mercy did send thunder and lightning from heaven, which did make the cattle of the said Francis Englefield to run so violent out of the said ground that at one time one of the beasts was killed therewith; and it was so often that people that were not there in presence to see it, when it thundered, would say Sir Francis Englefield's men were putting in their cattle into the Lawnd, and so it was, and as soon as those cattle were gone forth it would presently be very calm and fair, and the cattle of the town would never stir but follow their feeding as at other times, and never offer to move out of the way but did follow their feeding. And this did continue so long, he being too powerful for them, that the said free tenants were not able to wage law any longer; for one John Rous, one of the free tenants, was thereby enforced to sell all his land (to the value of £500) with following the suits in law, and many others were thereby impoverished and were thereby forced to yield up their right and take a lease of their said common of the said Sir Francis Englefield for term of his life. And the said mayor and free tenants hath now lost their right of common in the said Lawnd near about twenty years, which this Sir Francis Englefield, his heirs and his trustees, now detaineth from them. Likewise the said Sir Francis Englefield hath taken away their shops or shambles standing in the middle of the street in the market-place from the town, and hath given them to a stranger that liveth not in the town. . . . And he hath altered and doth seek ways and means to take the election of the mayor of our town to himself; for whereas the mayor is chosen at the law-day and the jury did ever make choice of two men of the town and the lord of the manor was to appoint one of them to serve, which the lord of the manor refused, and caused one to stay in two years together divers times, which is a breach of our custom.

And as for our common we do verily believe that no corporation in England so much is wronged as we are. For we are put out of all the common that ever we had and have not so much as one foot of common left unto us, nor never shall have any. We are thereby grown so in poverty, unless it please

God to move the hearts of this Honourable House to commiserate our cause, and to enact something for us, that we may enjoy our right again. And your orators shall be ever bound to pray for your health and prosperity to the Lord.

[here follow 23 signatures.]

Divers hands more we might have had, but that many of them doth rent bargains of the lord of the manor, and they are fearful that they shall be put forth of their bargains ; and then they shall not tell how to live. Otherwise they would have set to their hands.

12. PETITION TO CROWN OF COPYHOLDERS OF NORTH WHEATLEY (*S.P.D. Charles I, Vol.* 151, *No.* 38], 1629.

To the King's most Excellent Majesty.

The humble petition of your Majesty's poor and distressed tenants of your manor of North Wheatley in the county of Nottingham belonging to your Majesty's Duchy of Lancaster.

Most humbly shewing : That your poor subjects have time out of mind been copyholders of lands of inheritance to them and their heirs for ever of the manor aforesaid, and paid for every oxgang of land xvi*s.* viii*d.* rent, and paid heretofore upon every alienation xii*d.* for every oxgang, but now of late, about 4º Jacobi by an order of the Duchy Court they pay xi*s.* vi*d.* upon every alienation for every acre, which amounteth now to 45*s.* an oxgang.

And whereas some of your tenants of the said manor have heretofore held and do now hold certain oxgangs of lands belonging to the said manor by copy from 21 years to 21 years, and have paid for the same upon every copy 2*s.*, and for every oxgang 16*s.* 8*d.* per annum, they now of late, by an order in the Duchy Court, hold the same by lease under the Duchy Seal, and pay 6*l.* 13*s.* 4*d.* for a fine upon every lease and 16*s.* 8*d.* rent with an increase of 6*s.* 8*d.* more towards your Majesty's provision.

And whereas in 11º Edw. 4ⁱ, your petitioners did by copy of court roll hold the demesnes of the said manor for term of years at 9*l.* 6*s.* 8*d.* per annum, they afterwards in 6º Eliz. held the same demesnes by lease under the seal of the Duchy for 21 years, at the like rent. And ten years before their lease was expired, they employed one Mr. Markham in trust to get their lease renewed, who procured a new lease of the demesnes in his own name for 21 years at the old rent, and afterwards, contrary to the trust committed to him, increased and raised the rent thereof upon the tenants to his own private benefit to 56*l.* per annum.

And whereas the woods belonging to the said manor hath within the memory of man been the only common belonging to the said town, paying yearly for the herbage and pannage thereof 6*s.* 8*d.*, they now also hold the same under the Duchy Seal at 16*l.* 16*s.* 2*d.* per annum.

And whereas the court rolls and records of the said manor have always heretofore been kept under several locks and keys, whereof your Majesty's stewards have kept one key and your Majesty's tenants (in regard it concerned their particular inheritances) have kept another key; but now they are at the pleasure of the stewards and officers transported from place to place, and the now purchasers do demand the custody of them, which may be most prejudicial to your Majesty's poor tenants.

Now forasmuch as your Majesty hath been pleased to sell the said manor unto the City of London, who have sold the same unto Mr. John Cartwright and Mr. Tho. Brudnell, gent.; and for that your petitioners and tenants there (being in number two hundred poor men, and there being 11 of your Majesty's tenants there, that bear arms for the defence of your Majesty's realm, and 12 that pay your Majesty subsidies, fifteens, and loans) are all now like to be utterly undone, in case the said Mr. Cartwright and Mr. Brudnell should (as they say they will) take away from your tenants the said demesnes and woods after the expiration of their leases, and that your poor tenants should be left to the wills of the purchasers for their fines, or that the records and court rolls should not be kept as in former times in some private place, where the purchasers and tenants may both have the custody and view of them as occasion shall serve;

May it therefore please your sacred Majesty that such order may be taken in the premises for the relief of your poor tenants of the manor aforesaid, that they may not be dispossessed of the demesnes and leases, and that they may know the certainty of their fines for the copyhold, demesnes and leases, and may have the court rolls and records safely kept as formerly they have been, and that your Majesty will be further pleased to refer the consideration, hearing, ordering and determination of the premises unto such noblemen, or other four gentlemen of esteem in the country, whom your Majesty shall be pleased to appoint, that are neighbours unto your tenants, and do best know their estate and grievances. That they or any two or three of them may take such order, and so settle the business between the purchasers and your poor tenants, as they in their wisdom and discretion shall judge to be reasonable and fitting, or to certify your Majesty how they find the same and in whose default it is they cannot determine thereof. And your poor tenants as in all humble duty bound will daily pray for your Majesty.

Whitehall, this 10th of November, 1629.

His Majesty is graciously pleased to refer the consideration of this request to the commissioners for sale of his lands, that upon the report unto his Majesty of their opinion and advice his Majesty may give further order therein.

DORCHESTER.

13. AN ACT AVOIDING PULLING DOWN OF TOWNS [7 *Hen. VIII. c.* 1. *Statutes of the Realm, Vol. III, pp.* 176–7], 1515.

The King our Sovereign Lord calling to his most blessed remembrance that where great inconveniences be and daily increase by dislocation, pulling down, and destruction of houses and towns within this realm, and laying to pasture lands which customably have been manured and occupied with tillage and husbandry, whereby idleness doth increase, for where in some one town 200 persons, men and women and children, and their ancestors out of time of mind, were daily occupied and lived by sowing corn and grains, breeding of cattle, and other increase necessary for man's sustenance, and now the said persons and their progenies be minished and decreased, whereby the husbandry which is the greatest commodity of this realm for sustenance of man is greatly decayed, Churches destroyed, the service of God withdrawn, Christian people there buried not prayed for, the patrons and curates wronged, cities, market towns brought to great ruin and decay, necessaries for man's sustenance made scarce and dear, the people sore minished in the realm, whereby the power and defence thereof is enfeebled and impaired, to the high displeasure of God and against his laws and to the subversion of the common weal of this realm and dislocation of the same, if substantial and speedy remedy be not thereof provided; wherefore the King our Sovereign Lord, by the advice and assent of the Lords Spiritual and Temporal, and the Commons, in this present Parliament assembled, and by the authority of the same, ordaineth, stablisheth and enacteth, that all such towns, villages, boroughs and hamlets, tything houses and other habitations in any parish or parishes within this realm, whereof the more part the first day of this present parliament was or were used and occupied to tillage and husbandry, [as] by the owner or owners thereof for their singular profit, avail, and lucre wilfully since the said first day be or hereafter shall be suffered or caused to fall down and decay, whereby the husbandry of the said towns, villages, boroughs, hamlets, tithings houses and other habitations and parishes within this realm been or hereafter shall be decayed, and turned from the said use and occupation of husbandry and tillage into pasture, shall be by the said owner or owners, their heirs, successors or assigns or other for them, within one year next after such wilful decay, re-edified and made again meet and convenient for people to dwell and inhabit in the same, and to have use and therein to exercise husbandry and tillage as at the said first day of this present parliament or since was there used, occupied and had, after the manner and usage of the country where the said land lieth, at the cost and charges of the same owner or owners, their heirs, successors or assigns. And if since the said first day of this present parliament any lands which at the same first day or since were commonly used in tillage, been enclosed or from henceforth shall be enclosed and turned only to pasture, whereby any house of husbandry within this realm is or shall be hereafter decayed, that then all such lands shall be by the same owner or owners, their heirs, successors or assigns or other for them, within one year next ensuing the same decay, put in tillage, and exercised, used and occupied in husbandry and tillage, as they were the first said day of this present parliament or any time since, after the manner and usage of the country where such land lieth; and if any person or persons do contrary to the premises or any of them, that then it be lawful to the King, if any such lands or houses be holden of him immediately, after office or inquisition found thereof comprehending the same matter of record, or to the lords of the fees, if any such lands or houses [have] been holden of immediately, without office or inquisition thereof had, to receive yearly half the value of the issues and profits of any such lands whereof the house or houses of husbandry be not so maintained and sustained, and the same half deal of the issues and profits to have, hold and keep to his or their own use without anything thereof to be paid or given, to such time as the same house or houses be sufficiently re-edified, built or repaired again, for the exercising and occupying of husbandry; and immediately after that, as well the interest and title given by this Act to our Sovereign Lord the King as to the lords of the fee to cease and no longer to endure; and that it shall be lawful to the owner and owners of such lands, house or houses holden immediately of our said Sovereign Lord the King to have and enjoy the same and to take the issues and profits thereof as if no such office or inquisition had never been had nor made; and that no manner of freehold be in the King nor in any such lord or lords by virtue of this act or taking of any such profits of or in any such lands in no manner of form, but only the King and the said lord or lords have power to take, receive and have the said issues and profits as is abovesaid, and therefore the King or the said lord or lords to have power to distrain for the same issues and profits to be had and perceived by them in form abovesaid by authority of this present act. . . .

14. The Commission[1] of Inquiry Touching Enclosures [*Patent Roll* 9 *Hen. VIII*, *p.* 2, *m.* 6*d.*], 1517.

The King to his beloved and faithful John Veysy, dean of our Chapel, Andrew Wyndesore, knight, and Roger Wegeston, late of Leicester, greeting. Whereas of late in times past divers our lieges, not having before their eyes either God or the

[1] Similar letters are addressed to other Commissioners directing them to make similar inquiries in other parts of the country. The Commission was appointed by Wolsey. Its returns are important as a source of information both on the said conditions of the period and on the administrative methods of the Tudor statesmen (see Leadam, *Domesday of Enclosures*) and subsequent Commissions were appointed in 1548, 1566, 1607, 1632, 1635, and 1636, the last three being prompted partly by the desire to raise money by means of fines.

benefit and advantage of our realm or the defence of the same, have enclosed with hedges and dykes and other enclosures certain towns, hamlets and other places within this our realm of England, where many of our subjects dwelt and there yearly and assiduously occupied and exercised tillage and husbandry, and have expelled and ejected the same our subjects dwelling therein from their holdings and farms, and have reduced the country round the houses, towns and hamlets aforesaid, and the fields and lands within the same, to pasture and for flocks of sheep and other animals to graze there for the sake of their private gain and profit, and have imparked certain great fields and pasture and woods of the same in large and broad parks, and certain others in augmentation of parks for deer only to graze there, whereby the same towns, hamlets and places are not only brought to desolation, but also the houses and buildings of the same are brought to so great ruin, that no vestige of the same at the present is left, and our subjects, who have dwelt in the said places and there occupied and exercised tillage and husbandry, are now brought to idleness, which is the step-mother of virtues, and daily live in idleness, and the crops and breeding of cattle that were bred and nourished by the same tillers and husbandmen dwelling in the same towns, hamlets and places for human sustenance, are withdrawn and entirely voided from the same places, and the churches and chapels there hallowed are destroyed and divine services there taken away, and the memory of souls of Christians buried there utterly and wholly perished, and many other inestimable damages grow therefrom and daily hereafter will grow, to the greatest desolation and undoing of our realm and diminution of our subjects, unless an opportune remedy for the reformation of the same be swiftly and speedily applied: We, as we are duly bound, desiring to reform the aforesaid and wishing to be certified touching the same, what and how many towns and hamlets and how many houses and buildings have been thrown down from the feast of St. Michael the Archangel in the fourth year of the reign of the most illustrious lord Henry, late King of England, the Seventh, our father, and how many and how great lands which were then in tillage are now enclosed and converted to pasture, and how many and how great parks have been imparked for the feeding of deer since the same feast, and what lands have been enclosed in any parks or any park, which then were or was, for the amplifying and enlarging of such parks, have therefore appointed you and two of you to enquire by oath of good and lawful men of the counties of Oxford, Berks, Warwick, Leicester, Bedford, Buckingham, and Northampton, as well within liberties as without, and by other ways, manners and means whereby you shall or may the better learn the truth, what and how many towns, how many houses and buildings have been thrown down from the aforesaid feast, and how many and how great lands which were then in tillage are now converted to pasture, and how many and how great parks have been enclosed for the feeding of deer on this side the same feast, and what lands have been enclosed in any parks or any park, which then were or was, for the enlargement of such parks, and by whom, where, when, how and in what manner, and touching other articles and circumstances in any wise concerning the premises, according to the tenour and effect of certain articles specified in a bill to these presents annexed. And therefore we command you that you attend diligently to the premises and do and execute the same with effect. And by the tenour of these presents we command our sheriffs of the counties aforesaid that at certain days and places, which you shall cause them to know, they cause to come before you or two of you as many and such good and lawful men of their bailiwick by whom the truth of the matter may the better be known and enquired of; and that you certify us in our Chancery of what you shall do in the premises in three weeks from the day of St. Michael next coming, together with this commission. In witness whereof, etc. Witness the King at Westminster, the 28th day of May.

15. An Act Concerning Farms and Sheep [25 *Hen. VIII*, *c.* 13. *Statutes of the Realm, Vol. III*, *p.* 451], 1533–4.

Forasmuch as divers and sundry [persons] of the king's subjects of this realm, to whom God of his goodness hath disposed great plenty and abundance of moveable substance, now of late within few years have daily studied, practised and invented ways and means how they might accumulate and gather together into few hands as well great multitude of farms as great plenty of cattle and in especial sheep, putting such lands as they can get to pasture and not to tillage, whereby they have not only pulled down churches and towns and enhanced the old rates of their rents of the possessions of this realm, or else brought it to such excessive fines that no poor man is able to meddle with it, but also have raised and enhanced the prices of all manner of corn, cattle, wool, pigs, geese, hens, chickens, eggs and such other almost double above the prices which hath been accustomed, by reason whereof a marvellous multitude and number of people of this realm be not able to provide meat, drink and clothes necessary for themselves, their wives and children, but be so discouraged with misery and poverty that they fall daily to theft, robbery and other inconvenience, or pitifully die for hunger and cold; and as it is thought by the King's most humble and loving subjects that one of the greatest occasions that moveth and provoketh those greedy and covetous people so to accumulate and keep in their hands such great portions and parties of the grounds and lands of this realm from the occupying of the poor husbandmen, and so to use it in pasture and not in tillage, is only the great profit that cometh of sheep, which now be coming to a few persons' hands of this realm in respect of the whole number of the King's subjects, that some have 24 thousand, some 20 thousand, and some more and some less, by which a good sheep for victual that was accustomed to be sold for 2*s.* 4*d.* or 3*s.* at the most, is now sold for 6*s.*, 5*s.* or 4*s.* at the least; and a stone of clothing wool that in some shires of this realm was accustomed to be sold for 18*d.* or 20*d.* is now sold for 4*s.* or 3*s.* 4*d.* at the least, and in some countries where it hath been sold for 2*s.* 4*d.* or 2*s.*, or 3*s.* at the most, it is now sold for 5*s.* or 4*s.* 8*d.* at the least, and so raised in every part of this realm; which things thus used be principally to the high displeasure of Almighty God, to the decay of the hospitality of this realm, to the diminishing of the King's people, and to the hindrance of the clothmaking, whereby many poor people hath been accustomed to be set on work, and in conclusion if remedy be not found it may turn to the utter destruction and dislocation of this realm, which God defend; it may therefore please the King's Highness of his most gracious and godly disposition, and the Lords Spiritual and Temporal of their goodness and charity, with the assent of the Commons in this present parliament assembled, to ordain and enact by authority of the same, that no person or persons from the feast of St. Michael the Archangel which shall be in the year of Our Lord God 1535 shall keep occupy or have in his possession in his own proper lands, nor in the possession, lands or grounds of any other which he shall have or occupy in farm, nor otherwise have of his own proper cattle in use, possession or property, by any manner of means, fraud, craft or covyn, above the number of 2,000 sheep at one time within any part of this realm of all sorts and kinds, upon pain to lose and forfeit for every sheep that any person or persons shall have or keep above the number limited by this act, 3*s.* 4*d.*, the one half to the King our Sovereign Lord, and the other half to such person as will sue for the same. . . . It is also further enacted by authority aforesaid that no manner person after the said feast of the nativity of Our Lord shall receive or take for term of life, years or at will, by indenture, copy of court roll or otherwise, any more houses, tenements of husbandry, whereunto any lands are belonging in town, village, hamlet or tithing within this realm above the number of two such holds or tenements; and that no manner person shall have or occupy any such holds so newly taken to the number of two as is before expressed, except he or they be dwelling within the same parishes where such holds be, upon the pain of forfeiture for every week that he or they shall have, occupy, or take any profits of such holds contrary to this act 3*s.* 4*d.*, the moiety of which forfeiture to be to the King our Sovereign Lord and the other moiety to the party that will sue for the same. . . . .

16. Intervention of Privy Council under Somerset to Protect Tenants[1] [*Acts of Privy Council, p.* 540], 1549.

28 June, 1549.

An Order taken upon complaint made to the Lord Protector and other of the King's Majesty's Privy Council for the town of Godmanchester.

First, all and every person within the said town having any

[1] For Somerset's popular agrarian policy, see Pollard, *The Protector Somerset*, and, especially, the introduction to the *Commonwealth of this Realm of England* (edited by Lamond).

more houses of habitation than one in his possession, or any site of a house whereupon a house of habitation hath been with [in] [*blank*] years standing, shall at and before the Feast of St. Michael in the year of our Lord God 1549 let or demise every the said house with the land thereto accustomed, besides one, to a convenient person, if any that shall require, upon the usual rent, and upon every site now having no house of habitation shall before the said Feast of St. Michael in the same year build a house for habitation and thereto allot so much as thereto was heretofore belonging, and the same shall let and demise, if any that will hire, upon the accustomed rent.

Item, every person having converted any house or habitation unto any other use shall before Michaelmas next coming revert to the use of habitation as it was before, and the same shall let to any which that require upon the accustomed rent, and every person forthwith shall for every house of habitation, decayed site of habitation, and for every house of habitation converted to other use during the time of his possession, maintain and keep the King's watch and other common charges of the town in like manner as hath been heretofore of them used.

Item, whereas there is a great number of acres, lately belonging to certain gilds there, it is ordered that the same shall be divided to the inhabitants thereof in this manner; that is to say, to every plough-land 5 acres, and to every cottage or artificer there dwelling, or which hereafter upon the houses to be new builded shall dwell, one acre; and if the number do not extend, then every plough-land 4, and so for lack of that rate every plough-land 3; and the residue of the said acres falling after that rate to be divided amongst the cottages, paying for every of the said acres 3*s.* 4*d.* and above.

Item, also whereas there be certain groves of wood destroyed and turned to pasture in the same town, every such grove being so altered shall be by the owner thereof again (having been so altered within this 20 years before Michaelmas next coming) enclosed and preserved for wood, saving so much of the same to be reserved for a high way for the owner as in those cases the like is there used, the same high way to be severed by hedge from the rest of the grove; and where the groves be so destroyed that there remaineth no hope of growth, the owner thereof shall before the next season following meet for the same set it with wood or sow it with acorns or otherwise as the same may best be for growth of wood.

Provided nevertheless if any manner person have converted any house of habitation or any site of habitation to his necessary use about his own house, so that the same should be great inconvenience to be reverted to the first and old use, then in that case the owner shall be discharged if he for every such habitation so altered do build a like house in some other convenient like place, and the same to use to all purposes as before is said of the like.

The bailiffs be commanded to bring their grant by charter to the Lord Protector at All Hallow tide next coming.

For the observation of which orders the bailiffs and others of that town be bound in recognisance before the said Protector and Council.

Henry Frear Thomas Trecy John Clark	Have acknowledged and each of them has acknowledged that they owe to the Lord the King by themselves 100*l*. sterling.

Upon condition to perform the articles above mentioned.

17. An Act for the Maintenance of Husbandry and Tillage [39 *Eliz. c.* 2, *Statutes of the Realm, Vol. IV., Part II. pp.* 893-96], 1597-8.

Whereas the strength and flourishing estate of this kingdom hath been always and is greatly upheld and advanced by the maintenance of the plough and tillage, being the occasion of the increase and multiplying of people both for service in the wars and in times of peace, being also a principal means that people are set on work, and thereby withdrawn from idleness, drunkenness, unlawful games and all other lewd practices and conditions of life; and whereas by the same means of tillage and husbandry the greater part of the subjects are preserved from extreme poverty in a competent estate of maintenance and means to live, and the wealth of the realm is kept dispersed and distributed in many hands where it is more ready to answer all necessary charges for the service of the realm; and whereas also the said husbandry and tillage is a cause that the realm doth more stand upon itself, without depending upon foreign countries either for bringing in of corn in time of scarcity, or for vent and utterance of our own commodities being in over great abundance; and whereas from the 27th year of King Henry VIII of famous memory, until the five and thirtieth year of Her Majesty's most happy reign, there was always in force some law which did ordain a conversion and continuance of a certain quantity and apportion of land in tillage not to be altered; and that in the last parliament held in the said five and thirtieth year of her Majesty's reign, partly by reason of the great plenty and cheapness of grain at that time within this realm, and partly by reason of the imperfection and obscurity of the law made in that case, the same was discontinued; since which time there have grown many more depopulations, by turning tillage into pasture, than at any time for the like number of years heretofore: Be it enacted . . . that whereas any lands or grounds at any time since the seventeenth of November in the first year of Her Majesty's reign have been converted to sheep pastures or to the fattening or grazing of cattle, the same lands having been tillable lands, fields or grounds such as have been used in tillage by the space of twelve years together at the least next before such conversion, according to the nature of the soil and course of husbandry used in that part of the country, all such lands and grounds as aforesaid shall, before the first day of May which shall be in the year of Our Lord God 1599, be restored to tillage, or laid for tillage in such sort as the whole ground, according to the nature of that soil and course of husbandry used in that part of the country, be within three years at the least turned to tillage by the occupiers and possessors thereof, and so shall be continued for ever.

And be it further enacted by the authority aforesaid, that all lands and grounds which now are used in tillage or for tillage, having been tillable lands, fields or grounds, such as next before the first day of this present parliament have been by the space of twelve years together at the least used in tillage or for tillage, according to the nature of the soil and course of husbandry used in that part of the country, shall not be converted to any sheep pasture or to the grazing or fattening of cattle by the occupiers or possessors thereof, but shall, according to the nature of that soil and course of husbandry used in that part of the country, continue to be used in tillage or for tillage for corn or grain, and not for waste. . . . And be it enacted by the authority aforesaid, that if any person or body politic or corporate shall offend against the premises, every such person or body politic or corporate so offending shall lose and forfeit for every acre not restored or not continued as aforesaid, the sum of twenty shillings for every year that he or they so offend ; and that the said penalties or forfeitures shall be divided in three equal parts, whereof one third part to be to the Queen's Majesty, her heirs and successors to her and their own use (and) one other third part to the Queen's Majesty, her heirs and successors for relief of the poor in the parish where the offence shall be committed. . . . and the other third part to such person as will sue for the same in any court of record at Westminster. . . . Provided also, that this act shall not extend to any counties within this realm of England, but such only as shall be hereafter specified ; that is to say, the counties of Northampton, Leicester, Warwick, Buckingham, Bedford, Oxford, Berkshire, the Isle of Wight, Gloucester, Worcester, Nottingham, Hampshire, Wiltshire, Somerset, Dorset, Derby, Rutland, Lincoln, Hereford, Cambridge, Huntingdon, York, Pembroke in South Wales, and the Bishopric of Durham and Northumberland, and the counties of all the cities and corporations lying situate and being within the counties aforesaid, or confining to the same, and the Ainsty of the county of the city of York.

18. Speech in House of Commons on Enclosures [*Hist. MSS. Com. MSS. of Marquis of Salisbury, Part VII, pp.* 541–3], 1597[1].

But now, as if all these wrongs should be redressed, and all the cries and curses of the poor should be removed, it hath pleased you, Mr. Speaker, to exhibit this bill to our view as a complete remedy. I will not say 'it is worse than the disease.' But this I may truly say, 'It is too weak for the disease ! ' Three things I find exactly and providently respected. First, that the law is general, without exception, drawing in the purchaser as well as the first offender, whereat, howsoever some may shake their heads, as pressed with their own grief, yet is there no new imposition charged upon them, but such as is grounded upon the common law. For being without contra-

[1] Two Acts against depopulation were passed in this year, 39 Eliz., c. 1, and 39 Eliz., c. 2 (see No. 17 of this section). The name of the member making the following speech is not known.

diction that this turning of the earth to sloth and idleness, whereby it cannot fructify to the common good, is the greatest and most dangerous nuisance and damage to the common people, the law hath provided that the treasure of wickedness shall profit nothing, but that the nuisance shall be reformed in the hands of the people that come in upon the best consideration. . . . And 26 Eliz. in the Exchequer, in Claypole's case, an exhibition was exhibited upon the Statute of 4 Hen. VII[1] against a purchaser for converting of tillage into pasture, and adjudged good, though the purchaser were not the converter, but only a contriver of the first conversion. So as this new law tends but for an explanation of the old, that every one by the eye may be informed what ought by the hand to be amended. Nay, though it be not fit, Mr. Speaker, to be published among the ruder sort, who, if they were privy to their own strength and liberty allowed them by the law, would be as unbridled and untamed beasts, yet is it not unfit to be delivered in this place of council, that is, that where the wrong and mischief spreads to an universality, there the people may be their own justices, as in 6 Ed. II and 8 Ed. III Ass. 154 and 447 it is adjudged that if a wall be raised atraverse the way that leadeth to the Church all the parishioners may beat it down, and 9 Ed. IV 145, if the course of a water that runs to a town be stopped or diverted all the inhabitants may break it down. Are the people thus interested in the Church wherein their souls are fed, and shall we not think them to be as deeply interested in the corn and increase of the earth that feeds and maintains their bodies? Therefore most wisely hath the gentleman that penned the law pressed the case upon the purchaser that he plough, lest the people plot to circumvent him.

The second thing so well provided is . . . that it turns one eye backward to cure the ancient complaints and old festered disease of dearth and scarcity that hath been so long among us, and turns the other eye forward to cut out, as it were, the core that might draw on hereafter mischiefs of the same nature; where the gentleman that framed this bill hath dealt like a most skilful chirurgien, not clapping on a plaster to cover

[1] 4 Hen. VII, c. 19, by which all occupiers of 20 acres and upwards which have been tilled for the last three years are to maintain them in tillage.

the sore that it spread no further, but searching into the very depths of the wound, that the life and strength which hath so long been in decay by the wasting of towns and countries may at length again be quickened and repaired.

The third thing most politicly respected is the intercourse and change of ground to be converted into tillage, keeping a just proportion. For it fareth with the earth as with other creatures that through continual labour grow faint and feeble-hearted, and therefore, if it be so far driven as to be out of breath, we may now by this law resort to a more lusty and proud piece of ground while the first gathers strength, which will be a means that the earth yearly shall be surcharged with burden of her own excess. And this did the former law-makers overslip, tyeing the land once tilled to a perpetual bondage and servitude of being ever tilled.

But this threefold benefit I find crossed and encountered with a fourfold mildness and moderation fit to have a keen edge and sharpness set upon it, wherein I acknowledge my master that drew this project to have shewed himself like a tender-hearted physician, who coming to a patient possessed and full of corrupt and evil humours, will not hastily stir the body, but apply gentle and easy recipes. But surely, Mr. Speaker, a desperate disease must have a desperate medicine, and some wounds will not be healed but by incision.

The first moderation I mislike in this new law is that the most cunning and skilful offender shall altogether slip the collar; for if a man have decayed a whole town by enclosures, and hath rid his hand of it by exchange with Her Majesty, taking from her ancient enclosed pastures naturally yielding after the rate that his forced enclosed ground can yield upon such corrupt improvement, and to justify the true value shall take a lease back again of the Queen, the man is an occupier within the words of this law. But by your favour, Mr Speaker, not within the intent of this law to plough this new enclosure, because Her Majesty is in reversion, and this law doth not extend neither to her nor to her farmers. And that none might escape it were good that all of this kind might be enforced either to a contribution toward the poor,[1] who are chiefly wronged, or to the breaking up of the grounds he

[1] For the exaction of such a contribution see Section IV, No. 20 of this Part.

received from Her Majesty because they come in lieu of the former.

The second moderation that would be amended is in the imposition of the pain . . . which is but 10*s.* yearly for every acre not converted. By your favour, Mr. Speaker, it is too easy: and I will tell you, Sir, the ears of our great sheep-masters do hang at the door of this house, and myself have heard since this matter grew in question to be reformed, that some, enquiring and understanding the truths of the penalty, have prepared themselves to adventure 10*s.* upon the certainty of the gain of 30*s.* at the least. The third moderation is in the exception that exempts grounds mown for hay to be converted into tillage. And, if it please you, Sir, the first resolutions our enclosed gentlemen have is to sort and proportion their grounds into two divisions, the one for walks whereon their sheep may feed in the fresh summer, the other for hay whereon their sheep may feed in the hard winter; so that these grounds that carry hay have been as oil to keep the fire flaming and therefore no reason why they should be shielded and protected from the ploughshare.

The fourth moderation is that after this reconversion there is no restraint, but that every one may keep all the land ploughed in his own hands; whereupon will follow that as now there is scarcity of corn and plenty of such as would be owners, so then there will be plenty of corn, but scarcity of such as can be owners. For until our gentlemen that now enclose much, and then must plough much, shall meet with more compassion toward the poor than they have done, their small will be as small as it hath been, and then every one will be either an engrosser under false pretence of large housekeeping, or else a transporter by virtue of some license he will hope to purchase. And therefore it were good that every one should be rated how much he should keep in his own hands, and that not after the proportions of his present estimation; as, if a man hath lifted up his countenance by reason of this unnatural and cruel improvement after the rate of a gentleman of a thousand pounds by year, where the same quantity of land before would yield but a hundred pounds by year, I would have this man ruled after his old reckoning. . . .

We sit now in judgment over ourselves: therefore as this bill entered at first with a short prayer, 'God speed the plough,' so I wish it may end with such success as the plough may speed the poor.

(Endorsed: 1597. To Mr. Speaker against enclosures.)

19. SPEECHES IN HOUSE OF COMMONS ON ENCLOSURES [*D'Ewes Journal, p.* 674], 1601.[1]

The points to be considered of in the continuance of Statutes were read, and offered still to dispute whether the Statute of Tillage should be continued.

Mr. Johnson said, In the time of Dearth, when we made this statute, it was not considered that the hand of God was upon us; and now corn is cheap; if too cheap, the Husbandman is undone, whom we must provide for, for he is the staple man of the kingdom. And so after many arguments he concluded the Statute to be repealed.

Mr. Bacon said the old commendation of Italy by the Poet was *potens viris atque ubere glebae*, and it stands not with the policy of the State that the wealth of the kingdom should be engrossed into a few graziers' hands. And if you will put in so many provisoes as be desired, you will make it useless. The Husbandman is a strong and hardy man, the good footman. Which is a chief observation of good warriors, etc. So he concluded the statutes not to be repealed.

Sir Walter Raleigh said, I think the law fit to be repealed; for many poor men are not able to find seed to sow so much as they are bound to plough, which they must do, or incur the penalty of the law. Besides, all nations abound with corn. France offered the Queen to serve Ireland with corn for 16*s.* a quarter, which is but 2*s.* the bushel; if we should sell it so here, the ploughman would be beggared. The low countryman and the Hollander, which never soweth corn, hath by his industry such plenty that they will serve other nations. The Spaniard, who often wanteth corn, had we never so much plenty, will not be beholding to the Englishman for it. . . .

And therefore I think the best course is to set it at liberty, and leave every man free, which is the desire of a true Englishman.

Mr. Secretary Cecil said, I do not dwell in the country. I am not acquainted with the plough. But I think that whosoever doth not maintain the plough destroys this king-

[1] No action was taken to amend or repeal existing laws. For Bacon's views see his *History of King Henry* VII.

dom. . . My motion therefore shall be that this law may not be repealed, except former laws may be in force and revived. Say that a glut of corn should be, have we not sufficient remedy by transportation, which is allowable by the policy of all nations? . . . I am sure when warrants go from the Council for levying of men in the countries, and the certificates be returned unto us again, we find the greatest part of them to be ploughmen. And excepting Sir Thomas More's Utopia, or some such feigned commonwealth, you shall never find but the ploughman is chiefly provided for, the neglect whereof will not only bring a general, but a particular damage to every man. . . . If we debar tillage, we give scope to the depopulator; and then if the poor being thrust out of their houses go to dwell with others, straight we catch them with the Statute of Inmates; if they wander abroad they are within danger of the Statute of the Poor to be whipped.

20. Return to Privy Council of Enclosers Furnished by Justices of Lincolnshire [*S.P.D. Charles I, Vol.* 206, *No.* 7], *c.* 1637.

Lincoln.—An abstract of such depopulators as have been hitherto dealt withal in Lincolnshire, and received their pardon.

The persons in number	9
The sum of their fines	300*l.*
The number of houses by bond to be erected	33
The time for the erection, within one year..	
The number of farms to be continued that are now standing	22
The fines are already paid.	

Sir Charles Hussey, knt. Fine 80*l.*

Bond of 200 marks, with condition to set up in Honington 8 farmhouses with barns, etc., and to lay to every house 30 acres of land, and to keep 10 acres thereof yearly in tillage.

Sir Henry Ayscough, knt. Fine 20*l.*

Bond 200 marks. To set up 8 farmhouses in Blibroughe with 30 acres to every farm, and 12 thereof to be kept yearly in tilth.

Sir Hamond Whichcoote, knt. Fine 40*l.*

Bond 200 marks. To set up 8 farmhouses, etc., in Harpswell, with 40 acres to every house; and 16 thereof in tillage.

Sir Edward Carre, knt. Fine 30*l.*

Bond 100*l.* To set up 2 farmhouses in Branswell, and 1 in Aswarby with 40 acres to every house, 16 in tillage.

Sir William Wraye, knt. Fine 30*l.*

Bond 100*l.* To set up in Gaynesby 2 farmhouses with 2 acres at least to either, 10 in tillage, and to continue 2 farms more in Grainsby and 3 in Newbell and Longworth, with the same quantity, as is now used there, a third part in tilth.

Sir Edmund Bussye, knt. Fine 10*l.*

Bond 100*l.* To set up one farmhouse in Thorpe with 40 acres, 14 thereof in tillage, and to continue 14 farms in Hedor, Oseby, Aseby, and Thorpe, as they now are, with a third part in tillage.

Richard Rosetor, esqr. Fine 10*l.*

Bond 50*l.* To set up one farm in Limber with 40 acres, 16 in tillage, and to continue 1 farm in Limber, and 2 in Sereby, *ut sup.*

Robert Tirwhitt, esqr. Fine 10*l.*

Bond 50*l.* To set up one farm in Cameringham with 40 acres, 16 in tillage.

John Tredway, gent. Fine 10*l.*

Bond 40*l.* To set up one farm in Gelson with 30 acres, 10 thereof in tillage.

[Endorsed.] Lincoln Depopulators fined and pardoned and the reformations to be made.

21. Complaint of Laud's Action on the Commission for Depopulation [*S.P.D. Charles I, Vol.* 497, *No.* 10], 1641.

That upon the Commission of enquiry after depopulation, the Lord Archbishop of Canterbury and other the Commissioners, at the solicitation of Tho. Hussey, gent, did direct a letter in nature of a Commission to certain persons within the County of Wilts, to certify what number of acres in South Marston in the parish of Highworth were converted from arable to pasture, and what number of ploughs were laid down, etc.

Whereupon the Archdeacon with two others did return certificate, to the Lord Archbishop, etc.

Upon this certificate, Mr. Anth. Hungerford, Mr. Southby, with 15 others, were convented before his Grace and the other Commissioners at the Council Board, where, being charged with conversion;

Mr. Anth. Hungerford and Mr. Southby with some others did aver that they had made no conversion, other than they had when they came to be owners thereof.

His Grace said that they were to look no further than to the owners. And certificate was returned that so many acres were converted and so many ploughs let down.

They alleged that this certificate was false and made without their privity, and therefore Mr. Hungerford in the behalf of the rest did desire that they might not be judged upon that certificate; but that they might have the like favour as Mr. Hussey had, to have certificates of the same nature directed to other Commissioners, or a Commission, if it might be granted, to examine upon oath whereby the truth might better appear.

His Grace replied to Mr. Hungerford, "Since you desire it and are so earnest for it you shall not have it."[1]

They did offer to make proof that since the conversion there were more habitations of men of ability and fewer poor, and that whereas the King had before 4 or 5 soldiers of the trained band he had now 9 there; that the impropriation was much better to be let.

His Grace said to the rest of the Lords, "We must deal with these gentlemen as with those of Tedbury, to take 150*l* fine, and to lay open the enclosures."

Which they refusing to do they were there threatened with an information to be brought against them in the Star Chamber. And accordingly were within a short time after by the said Mr. Hussey served with *subpœnas* at Mr. Attorney his suit in the Star Chamber: And this, as Mr. Hussey told Mr. Hungerford, was done by my Lord Archbishop his command.

[Endorsed.] Depopulation. Mr. Hungerford and Mr. Southby. (1641.)

[1] See Clarendon, *History of the Rebellion I*, 204.
"And the revenue of too many of the Court consisted principally in enclosures, and improvements of that nature, which he [*i.e.*, Laud], still opposed passionately except they were founded upon law; and then, if it would bring profit to the King, how old and obsolete soever the law was, he thought he might justly advise the prosecution. And so he did a little too much countenance the Commission for Depopulation, which brought much charge and trouble upon the people, which was likewise cast upon his account."

SECTION II

TOWNS AND GILDS

1. A Protest at Coventry against a Gild's Exclusiveness, 1495—2. A Complaint from Coventry as to Inter-municipal Tariffs, 1498—3. The Municipal Regulation of Wages at Norwich, 1518—4. The Municipal Regulation of Markets at Coventry, 1520—5. The Municipal Regulation of Wages at Coventry, 1524—6. An Act for Avoiding of Exactions taken upon Apprentices in Cities, Boroughs, and Towns Corporate, 1536—7. An Act whereby certain Chantries, Colleges, Free Chapels, and the Possessions of the same be given to the King's Majesty, 1547—8. Regrant to Coventry and Lynn of Gild Lands Confiscated under 1 Ed. VI, c. 14 (the preceding Act), 1548.—9. A Petition of the Bakers of Rye to the Mayor, Jurats, and Council to Prevent the Brewers taking their trade, 1575—10. Letter to Lord Cobham from the Mayor and Jurats of Rye concerning the Preceding Petition, 1575—11. The Municipal Regulation of the Entry into Trade at Nottingham, 1578–9—12. The Municipal Regulation of Markets at Southampton, 1587—13. The Municipal Regulation of Wages at Chester, 1591—14. The Company of Journeymen Weavers of Gloucester, 1602—15. Petition of Weavers who are not Burgesses, 1604–5—16. Extracts from the London Clothworkers' Court Book, 1537–1627—17. The Feltmakers' Joint-Stock Project, 1611—18. The Case of the Tailors of Ipswich, 1615—19. The Grievances of the Journeymen Weavers of London, *c.* 1649.

The documents in this section illustrate certain aspects of the life of towns and gilds from 1485–1660. In the first half of the sixteenth century two important changes in the legal position of gilds were made by Act of Parliament. (i) Owing to the growing complaints of their exclusiveness (Nos. 1 and 6). Parliament had already by 15 Hen. VI, c. 6, and 19 Hen. VII, c. 7, compelled gilds to submit their ordinances to the approval of extra-municipal authorities before they became valid (Nos. 6 and 17). By 22 Hen. VIII it fixed 2*s.* 6*d.* as the maximum fee to be charged persons entering and 3*s.* 4*d.* as the maximum fee for persons leaving their apprenticeship. By 28 Hen. VIII c. 5 it forbad restrictive agreements designed to prevent apprentices or journeymen starting in trade on their own account (No. 6). (ii.) By 37 Hen. VIII c. 4 and 1 Ed. VI. c. 14 (No. 7) Parliament confiscated for the benefit of the Crown that part of gild property which was applied to religious purposes. The latter Act was, however, strongly opposed in the House of Commons, and the confiscated estates were restored to two towns, Coventry and King's Lynn (No. 8).

Apart from these changes towns and gilds pursued in the sixteenth century much the same economic policy as in earlier ages. They imposed inter-municipal tariffs (No. 2), and regulated markets (Nos. 4 and 12), wages (Nos. 3, 5, and 13), apprenticeship and the entry into trades (Nos. 1, 9, 10, 11, 15) on high moral grounds (No. 10), but sometimes with consequences unpleasant to those who were excluded (Nos. 1 and 15). Indeed their anxiety to preserve their monopoly occasionally brought them into conflict with the law, which "abhors all monopolies" (No. 18). Inside the gilds, however, a momentous change was going on. The fifteenth century had seen the rise within gilds of "yeomanry" organizations consisting of journeymen, of which an example is given below (No. 14, and Part I, Section V, No. 16). In the sixteenth and seventeenth centuries the gilds, at least in the larger towns, represented a wide range of interests, from the mercantile capitalist to the industrial small master, and it was often of such small masters, whose numbers appear to have increased in the sixteenth century, that the "yeomanry" then consisted (No. 16). They tended, however, to be at the mercy of the large capitalists, and occasionally under the first two Stuarts, who favoured them, they endeavoured to protect themselves by joint-stock enterprise (No. 17). In the middle of the seventeenth century a reverse movement was taking place. Small masters were becoming journeymen, and in London journeymen were engaged under the Commonwealth in active agitation. Their organization was that of an embryo trade union; their doctrine the application to industrial affairs of the theory of the social contract (No. 19).

AUTHORITIES

The more accessible of the modern writers dealing with the subject of this section are Cunningham, *English Industry and Commerce, Modern Times*, Vol. I; Ashley, *Economic History*, Vol. I, Part II, Chap. I and II; Gross, *The Gild Merchant*; Abram, *Social England in the Fifteenth Century*; Mrs. Green, *English Town Life in the Fifteenth Century*; Dunlop and Denman, *English Apprenticeship and Child Labour*; Unwin, *Industrial Organization in the Sixteenth and Seventeenth Centuries*, and *The Gilds and Companies of London*; Webb, *English Local Government, The Manor and Borough*; Brentano, *Gilds and Trade Unions*; Toulmin Smith, *English Gilds*; Rogers, *Six Centuries of Work and Wages.*

Bibliographies are given in Gross, *op. cit.* (the most complete); Cunningham *op. cit.*, Vol. II, pp. 943–998; Ashley, *op. cit.*, pp. 3–5 and 66–68; Abram, *op. cit.*, pp. 229–238; Dunlop and Denman, *op. cit.*, pp. 355–363; Unwin, *Industrial Organization in the Sixteenth and Seventeenth Centuries*, pp. 263–270.

The student may also consult the following:—

(1) *Documentary Authorities*:—The records of numerous towns and gilds have been published, and only a few can be mentioned here:—Stevenson, Records of Nottingham; Tingey, Records of Norwich; Bateson, Records of Leicester; Morris, Chester in the Plantagenet and Tudor Reigns; Turner, Select Records of Oxford; Harris, The Coventry Leet Book (E.E.T.S.); Bickley, The Little Red Book of Bristol; Guilding, Records of the Borough of Reading; Publications of the Historical Manuscripts Commission, Report 14, App. viii (Bury St. Edmunds); 15, App. x (Coventry), 12, App. ix (Gloucester), 13, App. iv (Hereford); 9, App. i (Ipswich); 14, App. viii (Lincoln); 15, App. x (Shrewsbury).

(2) *Literary Authorities*:—The number of contemporary writers dealing with gild and town life is not large. The most important are: Drei Volkswirthschaftliche Denkscriften aus der Zeit Heinrich VIII, von England, edited by Pauli; Starkey, A Dialogue Between Cardinal Pole and Thomas Lupset (E.E.T.S.); England in the Reign of King Henry VIII; The Commonwealth of this Realm of England (edited by Lamond); Crowley, Select Works (E.E.T.S.); Lever's Sermons (in Arber Reprints: where criticisms will be found on the confiscation of gild property); Harrison, A Description of Britain; Roxburghe Club, A Dialogue or Confabulation Between two Travellers.

1. A Protest at Coventry against a Gild's Exclusiveness [*Coventry Leet Book, Vol. II, pp.* 566–7], 1495.

1495. Mem.: that within vii days after Lammas there was a bill set upon the north church door in St. Michael's Church by some evil disposed person unknown, the tenor whereof hereafter ensueth:—

Be it known and understand
This city should be free and now is bond.

Dame Good Eve made it free,
And now there be customs for wool and drapery.

Also it is made that no prentice shall be
But xiii pennies pay shall he.

That act did Robert Green,[1]
Wherefore he had many a curse, I ween.

2. A Complaint from Coventry as to Intermunicipal Tariffs [*Coventry Leet Book, Part I, p.* 592], 1498.

Oct. 18th, 1498 . . . And on the morrow the Mayor presented a bill to the said Prince desiring by the same that he would please to desire the prior of Coventry to pay at his desire the murage money which he had withdrawn the space of 20 years, and also showed his Grace by the same bill how the citizens of Coventry were troubled by their merchandizes in Bristol, Gloucester, and Worcester, and compelled to pay toll and other customs contrary to their liberties. Upon which bill letters went out to Bristol, Gloucester, and Worcester, desiring by the same that the said citizens of Coventry might pass free without any custom paying after their liberty, or else they appear in London *crastino St. Martini* then next following.

3. The Municipal Regulation of Wages at Norwich [*Tingey. Selected Records of Norwich, II, p.* 110], 1518.

Sept. 21st, 1518. It is agreed that from henceforth no artificer shall employ apprentice working by the day, viz.,

[1] Robert Green was chosen Mayor of Coventry in 1494.

carpenters, masons, tilers, reeders, by taking for the wage of such an apprentice more than one penny a day until he has been appointed to better wages or salary by the headman of that craft in the presence of the Mayor for the time being. And if any one shall do contrary, he shall forfeit 12*d.*, to be levied from the goods of the master of that apprentice.

4. The Municipal Regulation of Markets at Coventry (*Coventry Leet Book, Part III, pp.* 674–5], 1520.

October 10, 1520. Memorandum that the Xth day of October and in the [eleventh] year of the reign of King Henry VIII, then Master John Bond being Mayor of the City of Coventry, the price of all manner of corn and grain began to rise. Whereupon a view was taken by the said Mayor and his brethren what stores of all manner of corn, and what number of people was then within the said city, men, women and children, etc.

. . . .[1]

Summa Totalis of the people then being within the city, of men women and children.	Summa Totalis 6601 persons.	In Malt, 2405 qrs. In Rye and Mastlin, 100 qrs. 1 strike. In wheat, 47 qrs. In Oats, 39 qrs. 2 strike. In Pease, 18 qrs. 2 strike.

Also a view by him taken what substance of malt was then brewed within the city weekly by the common brewers that brewed to sell. . . . The number of all the common brewers in the city . . . . 68. Item, they brewed weekly in malt 146 qrs. 1 bus.

Mem., that there was brought into this said city the Friday before Christmas Day in the year of the said John Bond then being Mayor, by his labour and his friends, to help sustain the city with corn, of all manner of grain Summa 97 qrs. 6 strike.

Mem., that there was at that time 43 bakers within the city, which did bake weekly amongst all 120 qrs. of wheat and 12, besides pease and rye.

[1] Here follow particulars of the number of persons and amount of grain in each ward.

5. The Municipal Regulation of Wages at Coventry [*Coventry Leet Book, Part III, pp.* 688–9], 1524.

[Enacted] that the weavers of this city shall have for the weaving of every cloth, to the making whereof goeth and is put 80 and 8 lb. of wool or more to the number of 80 lb. and 16, 5*s.* for the weaving of every such cloth; and if the said cloth contain above the said number then the weaving to be paid for as the parties can agree, and if the cloth contain under the said number, then the owner to pay for weaving but 4*s.* 6*d.* And if the cloth be made of rests or green wool, then to pay as the parties can agree; and the payment to be made in ready moncy and not in wares as it is wont to be, and who refuses thus to do, and so proved before Master Mayor, to forfeit for every said default 3*s.* 4*d.*, to be levied by the searchers of the said craft of weavers, with an officer to them appointed by the said Mayor, to the use of the common box. [Enacted] that every clothier within this city shall pay for walking of every cloth of green wool or middle work, 3*s.* 4*d.*, and for every cloth of fine wool as the clothier and walker can agree, and that the clothier do pay therefore in ready money and not in wares.

6. An Act for Avoiding of Exactions Taken Upon Apprentices in Cities, Boroughs and Towns Corporate [28 *Hen. VIII, c.* 5. *Statutes of the Realm, Vol. IV, Part I, pp.* 286–8], 1536.

Where in the parliament begun at London the third of November in the 21st year of the reign of our most dread Lord King Henry the eight, and from thence adjourned and prorogued to Westminster the 16 day of January in the 22 year of the reign of our said Sovereign Lord and there then also holden, it was and it is recited, that where before that time it was established and enacted in the 19 year of our late Sovereign Lord King Henry the VIIth, that no masters, warden and fellowship of crafts, or any of them, nor any rulers of guilds or fraternities, should take upon them any acts or ordinances nor to execute any acts or ordinances by them before that time made or then hereafter to be made, in disheritance or diminution of the prerogative of the King nor of other nor against the common profit of the people, but if the same acts or ordinances were examined or approved by the chancellor, treasurer of England or chief justice of either bench or 3 of them, or before the justices of assize in their circuit or progress in the shire where such acts or ordinances be made, upon pain of forfeiture of £40 for every time that they do the contrary, as more plainly in the said act doth appear; since which time divers wardens and fellowships have made acts and ordinances, that every apprentice should pay at his first entry in their common hall to the wardens of the same fellowship some of them 40*s.*, some 30*s.*, some 20*s.*, some 13*s.* 4*d.*, some 6*s.* 8*d.*, some 3*s.* 4*d.* after their own sinister minds and pleasure, contrary to the meaning of the said act made in the said 19 year of the reign of the said late King Henry the VIIth and to the great hurt of the King's true subjects putting their children to be apprentices: It was therefore in the said parliament holden at Westminster in the said 22 year of the reign of King Henry the eight, established and enacted by the King our Sovereign Lord by the advice of his Lords, Spiritual and Temporal, and of the Commons in the same parliament assembled and by the authority of the same, that no master, wardens or fellowships of crafts or masters or any of them, nor any rulers of fraternities should take from thenceforth of any apprentice or of any other person or persons for the entry of any apprentice into their said fellowship above the sum of 2*s.* 6*d.*, nor for his entry when his years and term is expired and ended, above 3*s.* 4*d.* upon pain of forfeiture of £40 for every time that they do to the contrary. . . . Since which said several acts established and made (as is aforesaid), divers masters, wardens and fellowships of crafts have by cautell and subtil means compassed and practised to defraud and delude the said good and wholesome statutes, causing divers apprentices or young men immediately after their years be expired, or that they may be made free of their occupation or fellowship, to be sworn upon the Holy Evangelist at their first entry that they nor any of them after their years or term expired shall not set up or open any shop, house nor [cellar] nor occupy as free men, without the assent and licence of the master, wardens or fellowships of their occupations, upon pain of forfeiting their freedom or other like penalty; by reason whereof the said apprentices and journeymen be put to as much or more charges thereby than they beforetime were put unto for the obtaining and entering of their freedom, to the great hurt and impoverishment of the said apprentices and journeymen and other their friends; For remedy whereof be it now by the authority of this present parliament established, ordained and enacted, that no master, wardens or fellowships of crafts nor any of them, nor any rulers of guilds fraternities or brotherhoods, from henceforth compel or cause any apprentice or journeyman, by oath or bond heretofore made or hereafter to be made or otherwise, that he after his apprenticeship or term expired, shall not set up nor keep any shop house nor cellar, nor occupy as a freeman without licence of the masters, wardens or fellowships of his or their occupation for and concerning the same; nor by any means exact or take of any such apprentices or journeyman nor any other occupying for themselves, nor of any other persons for them, after his or their said years expired, any sum of money or other things for or concerning his or their freedom or occupation, otherwise or in any other manner than before is recited limited and appointed in the said former act made in the said 22 year of the reign of King Henry the eight; upon the pain to forfeit for every time that they or any of them shall offend contrary to this act £40. . . . .

7. An Act Whereby Certain Chantries, Colleges, Free Chapels, and the Possessions of the Same be Given to the King's Majesty [1 *Ed. VI*, c. 14. *Statutes of the Realm, Vol. IV, Part I, p.* 24], 1547.

The King's most loving subjects, the Lords Spiritual and Temporal, and the Commons, in this present parliament assembled, considering that a great part of superstition and errors in Christian religion hath been brought into the minds and estimation of men, by reason of the ignorance of their very true and perfect salvation through the death of Jesus Christ, and by devising and phantasing vain opinions of purgatory and masses satisfactory to be done for them which be departed, the which doctrine and vain opinion by nothing more is maintained and upholden than by the abuse of trentalls, chantries and other provisions made for the continuance of the said blindness and ignorance; and further considering and understanding that the alteration, change and amendment of the same, and converting to good and godly uses, as in erecting of grammar schools to the education of youth in virtue and godliness, the further augmenting of the universities and better provision for the poor and needy, cannot in this present parliament be provided and conveniently done, nor cannot nor ought to any other manner person be committed than to the King's Highness, whose Majesty with and by the advice of his Highness most prudent council can and will most wisely and beneficially both for the honour of God and the weal of this his Majesty's realm, order, alter, convert and dispose the same. . . .

[Clause reciting 37 Hen. VIII, c. 4.][1]

. . . It is now ordained and enacted by the King our Sovereign Lord, with the assent of the Lords and Commons in this present parliament assembled, and by the authority of the same, that all manner of colleges, free chapels and chantries, having been or *in esse* within five years next before the first

[1] This and the following document deal with the confiscation of that part of the property of gilds which was devoted to religious purposes. The Act printed above was a re-enactment with some important variations of an Act of 1545 (37 Hen. VIII, c. 4). For its object and effect see Ashley, *Economic History*, Vol. I, part 11, pp. 142–145, and pp. 184–187, who gives reasons for disagreeing with the statement of Thorold Rogers (*Six Centuries of Work and Wages*, pp. 347–350, and *The Economic Interpretation of English History*, p. 15) that the Act "suppressed" the craft gilds; Pollard, *The Political History of England* 1547–1603, pp. 17–20 ("the greatest educational opportunity in English history was lost, and the interests of the nation were sacrificed to those of its aristocracy")· Leach, *English Schools at the Reformation*, p. 68; Toulmin Smith's *English Gilds*. Lever (*Sermons* 1550, Arber's Reprints, pp. 32, 73, and 81) complains bitterly of the use to which the confiscated property was put. "For in suppressing of abbeys, cloisters, colleges, and chantries, the intent of the King's Majesty that dead is, was, and of this our King now is, very godly. . . . Howbeit covetous officers have so used this matter that even those goods which did serve to the relief of the poor, the maintenance of learning, and to comfortable necessary hospitality in the Commonwealth, be now turned to maintain worldly, wicked, covetous ambition." . . . "Your Majesty hath had given and received by Act of Parliament, colleges, chantries, and gilds for many good considerations, and especially, as appeareth in the same Act, for erecting of grammar schools to the education of youth in virtue and godliness, to the further augmenting of the Universities, and better provision for the poor and needy. But now many grammar schools, and much charitable provision for the poor be taken, sold, and made away, to the great slander of you and your laws, to the utter discomfort of the poor, to the grievous offence of the people, to the most miserable drowning of youth in ignorance, and for decay of the Universities."

day of this present parliament, which were not in actual and real possession of the said late king, nor in the actual and real possession of the king our sovereign lord that now is, nor excepted in the said former act in form abovesaid, other than such as by the king's commissions in form hereafter mentioned shall be altered, transposed or changed, and all manors, lands, tenements, rents, tythes, pensions, portions and other hereditaments and things above-mentioned belonging to them or any of them, and also all manors, lands, tenements, rents and other hereditaments and things above-mentioned, by any manner of assurance, conveyance, will, devise or otherwise had, made, suffered, acknowledged or declared, given, assigned, limited or appointed to the finding of any priest to have continuance for ever, and wherewith or whereby any priest was sustained, maintained or found, within five years next before the first day of this present parliament, which were not in the actual and real possession of the said late King, nor in the actual and real possession of our Sovereign Lord the King that now is, and also all annual rents, profits, and emoluments, at any time within five years next before the beginning of this present parliament employed, paid or bestowed toward or for the maintenance, supportation or finding of any stipendiary priest intended by any act or writing to have continuance for ever, shall by the authority of this present parliament, immediately after the feast of Easter next coming, be adjudged and deemed and also be in very actual and real possession and seisin of the King our Sovereign Lord and his heirs and successors for ever; without any office or other inquisition thereof to be had or found, and in as large and ample manner and form as the priests, wardens, masters, ministers, governors, rulers or other incumbents of them or any of them at any time within five years next before the beginning of this present parliament had occupied or enjoyed, or now hath, occupieth or enjoyeth the same; and as though all and singular the said colleges, free chapels, chantries, stipends, salaries of priests and the said manors, lands, tenements and other the premises whatsoever they be, and every of them, were in this present act specially, particularly, and certainly rehearsed, named and expressed, by express words, names and surnames, corporations, titles and faculties, and in their natures, kinds and qualities. . .

And over that be it ordained and enacted by the authority

of this present parliament, that where any manors, lands, tenements, tythes, pensions, portions, rents, profits, or other hereditaments, by any manner of assurance, conveyance, will, devise or otherwise at any time heretofore had, made, suffered, acknowledged or declared, were given assigned or appointed to or for the maintenance, sustentation or finding of any priest or divers priests for term of certain years yet continuing, and that any priest hath been maintained, sustained or found with the same or with the revenues or profits thereof within five years last past, that the king from the said feast of Easter next coming shall have and enjoy in every behalf for and during all such time to come every such and like things, tenements, hereditaments, profits and emoluments as the priest or priests ought or should have had for or toward his or their maintenance, sustenance or finding, and for no longer or further time, nor for any other profit, advantage or commodity thereof to be taken. . . .

. . . And be it ordained and enacted by the authority of this present parliament, that the King our Sovereign Lord, his heirs and successors, from the said feast of Easter next coming, shall have hold, perceive and enjoy for ever, all lands, tenements, rents and other hereditaments which, by any manner of assurance, conveyance, wills, will, devise or otherwise at any time heretofore had made suffered, acknowledged, or declared, were given, assigned or appointed to go or be employed wholly to the finding or maintenance of any anniversary or obit or other like thing, intent, or purpose, or of any light or lamp in any church or chapel to have continuance for ever, which hath been kept or maintained within five years next before the said first day of this present parliament.

. . . And furthermore be it ordained and enacted by the authority aforesaid, that the King our Sovereign Lord shall from the said feast of Easter next coming have and enjoy to him, his heirs and successors for ever, all fraternities, brotherhoods and guilds being within the realm of England and Wales and other the king's dominions, and all manors, lands, tenements and other hereditaments belonging to them or any of them, other than such corporations, guilds, fraternities, companies and fellowships of mysteries or crafts, and the manors, lands, tenements, and other hereditaments pertaining to the said corporations, guilds, fraternities, companies and fellowships of mysteries or crafts above mentioned, and shall by virtue of this act be judged and deemed in actual and real possession of our said Sovereign Lord the King, his heirs and successors from the said feast of Easter next coming for ever, without any inquisitions or office thereof to be had or found. . . .

And also be it ordained and enacted by the authority aforesaid, that our said Sovereign Lord the King, his heirs and successors, at his and their will and pleasure, may direct his and their commission and commissions under the great seal of England to such persons as it shall please him, and that the same commissioners, or two of them at the least, shall have full power and authority by virtue of this Act and of the said commission, as well to survey all and singular lay corporations, guilds, fraternities, companies and fellowships of mysteries or crafts incorporate, and every of them, as all other the said fraternities, brotherhoods and guilds within the limit of their commission to them directed, and all the evidences, compositions, books of accounts and other writings of every of them, to the intent thereby to know what money and other things was paid or bestowed to the finding or maintenance of any priest or priests, anniversary, or obit or other like thing, light or lamp, by them or any of them; as also to enquire, search and try, by all such ways and means as to them shall be thought meet and convenient, what manors, lands, tenements, rents and other hereditaments, profits, commodities, emoluments and other things be given, limited, or appointed to our said Lord the King by this act, within the limits of their commission: and also that the same commissioners or two of them at the least, by virtue of this act and of the commission to them directed, shall have full power and authority to assign and shall appoint, in every such place where guild, fraternity, the priest or incumbent of any chantry *in esse* the first day of this present parliament, by the foundation, ordinance, [the] first institution thereof should or ought to have kept a grammar school or a preacher, and so hath done since the feast of St. Michael the Archangel last past, lands, tenements and other hereditaments of every such chantry, guild and fraternity to remain and continue in succession to a schoolmaster or preacher for ever, for and toward the keeping of a grammar school or preaching, and for such godly intents and purposes and in such manner and form as the same commissioners or two of them at the least shall assign or appoint: and also to make and ordain a vicar to have perpetuity for ever in every parish church, the first day of this present parliament being a college, free chapel, or chantry, or appropriated and annexed or united to any college, free chapel, or chantry that shall come to the king's hands by virtue of this act, and to endow every such vicar sufficiently, having respect to his cure and charge; the same endowment to be to every vicar and to his successors for ever, without any other license or grant of the King, the bishop, or other officers of the diocese: . . .

. . . And also be it ordained and enacted by the authority of this present parliament that our Sovereign Lord the King shall have and enjoy all such goods, chattels, jewels, plate, ornaments and other moveables, as were or be the common goods of every such college, chantry, free chapel, or stipendiary priest belonging or annexed to the furniture or service of their several foundations, or abused of any of the said corporations in the abuses aforesaid, the property whereof was not altered nor changed before the 8 day of December in the year of our Lord God 1547. . . .

8. Regrant to Coventry and Lynn of Gild Lands Confiscated under I Ed. VI, c. 14. [*Acts of the Privy Council, New Series, pp.* 193–5], 1548.

At Westminster, Sunday, the vith of May, 1548

Whereas in the last parliament, holden at Westminster in November, the first year of the King's Majesty's reign, among other articles contained in the act for colleges and chantry lands, etc., to be given unto his Highness, it was also inserted that the lands pertaining to all guilds and brotherhoods within this realm should pass unto his Majesty by way of like gift, at which time divers then being of the lower house did not only reason and argue against that article made for the guildable lands, but also incensed many others to hold with them, among the which none were stiffer nor more busily went about to impugn the said articles than the burgesses for the town of Lynn, in the county of Norfolk, and the burgesses of the city of Coventry, in the county of Warwick; the burgesses of Lynn alleging that the guild lands belonging to their said town were given for so good a purpose (that is to say, for the maintenance and keeping up of the pier and seabanks there, which being untended to would be the loss of a great deal of low ground of the country adjoining), as it were great pity the same should be alienated from them as long as they employed it to so necessary an use ; and semblably they of Coventry declaring that where that city was of much fame and antiquity, some times very wealthy though now of late years brought into decay and poverty, and had not to the furniture of the whole multitude of the Commons there, being to the number of xi or xii thousand housling people, but two churches wherein God's service is done, whereof the one, that is to say, the church of Corpus Christi, was specially maintained of the revenues of such guild lands lying only in houses and tenements within the town as had been given heretofore by diverse persons to that use and others no less beneficial to the supporting of that city ; if therefore now by the act the same lands should pass from them it should be a manifest cause of the utter desolation of the city, as long as the people, when the churches were no longer supported, nor God's service done therein, and the other uses and employments of those lands omitted, should be of force constrained to abandon the city and seek new dwelling places, which should be more loss unto the King's Majesty by losing so [much] of the yearly fee farm there, and subversion of so notable a town, than the accruing of a sort of old houses and cottages pertaining to the guilds and chantries of the said cities, should be of value or profit to his Majesty, as long as his Highness should be at more cost with the reparations of the same than the yearly rents would amount unto.

In respect of which their allegations and great labour made herein unto the House, such of his Highness Council as were of the same House there present thought it very likely and apparent that not only that article for the guildable lands should be dashed, but also that the whole body of the act might either sustain peril or hindrance being already engrossed, and the time of the Parliament Prorogation hard at hand, unless by some good policy the principal speakers against the passing of that article might be stayed ; whereupon they did anticipate this matter with the Lord Protector's Grace and others of the Lords of his Highness Council, who, pondering on the one part how the guildable lands throughout this realm amounted to no small yearly value, which by the article aforesaid were to be accrued to his Majesty's possessions of the Crown; and on the other part weighing in a multitude of free voices what moment the labour of a few setters on had been of heretofore in like cases, thought it better to stay and content them of Lynn and Coventry by granting to them to have and enjoy their guild lands, etc., as they did before, than through their means, on whose importune labour and suggestion the great part of the Lower House rested, to have the article defaced, and so his Majesty to forego the whole guild lands throughout the realm; and for these respects and also for avoiding of the proviso which the said burgesses would have had added for the guilds to this article, which might have ministered occasion to others to have laboured for the like, they resolved that certain of his Highness' Councillors being of the Lower House should persuade with the said burgesses of Lynn and Coventry to desist from further speaking or labouring against the said article, upon promise to them that if they meddled no further against it, his Majesty, once having the guildable lands granted unto him by the act as it was penned unto him, should make them over a new grant of the lands pertaining then unto their guilds, etc., to be had and used to them as afore. Which thing the said Councillors did execute as was devised, and thereby stayed the speakers against it, so as the act passed with the clause for guildable lands accordingly.

And now seeing that the Mayors and others of the said city of Coventry and town of Lynn by reason of that promise so made unto them have humbly made suit unto the Lord Protector's Grace and Council aforesaid that the same may be performed unto them, which promise his Grace and the said Council do think that his Highness is bound in honour to observe, although it were not so that indeed those lands which belonged to the guild at Lynn cannot well be taken from them, being so allotted and employed to the maintenance of the pier and seabanks there, which of necessity as was alleged, require daily reparations, no more than the guild and chantry lands at Coventry upon the foresaid considerations could conveniently (as was thought) be taken from them without putting the said city to apparent danger of desolation; it was therefore this day ordained, and by the accord and assent of the Lord Protector's Grace and others of his Highness

Council decreed, that letters patents should be made in due form under the King's Majesty's Great Seal of England whereby the said guild lands belonging to the two churches at Coventry should be newly granted unto them of the city for ever, and the lands lately pertaining to the guild of Lynn also granted unto that town for ever, to be used to such like purpose and intent as aforetimes by force of their grants they were limited to do accordingly.

9. A PETITION OF THE BAKERS OF RYE TO THE MAYOR, JURATS AND COUNCIL TO PREVENT THE BREWERS TAKING THEIR TRADE [*Hist. MSS. Com, Thirteenth Report, App. Part IV, p.* 45], 1575.

Whereas, as well in ancient time as now of late days, good and wholesome laws have been by the State of this realm devised, ordained, and enacted for the better maintenance of the subjects of the same; amongst which laws it is ordained how each sort of people, being handicraftsmen or of occupation, should use the trade and living wherein they have been lawfully trained up and served for the same as the said laws do appoint; nevertheless, it may please your worships, divers persons do seek unto themselves by sinister ways and contrary to those good laws certain trades to live by, and not only to live by but inordinately to gain, to the utter overthrow of their neighbours which have lawfully used those occupations, and served for the same according to the said laws. Amongst which sort of people certain of the brewers of this town use the trade and occupation of bakers, not having been apprentices to the same, nor so lawfully served in the same trade as they thereby may justly challenge to use the said occupation of baking, to the utter impoverishment of the bakers of the said town, their wives, children, and families, and contrary to the law, equity, and good conscience; whereby we whose names are underwritten shall be constrained to give over, and for themselves to seek some other means to live, and to leave our wives and children, if in time remedy be not provided by your worships for the same.

James Welles.
John Mylles.
Edward Turner.
Philip Caudy.
William Gold.

10. LETTER TO LORD COBHAM FROM THE MAYOR AND JURATS OF RYE CONCERNING THE PRECEDING PETITION [*ibid., pp.* 47–8], 1575.

Upon the lamentable complaint of our poor neighbours the bakers, we did with good and long deliberation consider of their cause, and finding that their decay is such as without speedy reformation they shall not have wherewith to maintain their wives, children, and family, which are not few in number, a thing in conscience to be lamented, and we for remission in duty to be greatly blamed; and since the overthrow of these poor men is happened by reason of the brewers (who ought by the laws of this realm not to be bakers also) have by our sufferance (but the rather for that Robert Jackson is towards your Lordship) used both to bake and brew of long time, whereby Robert Jackson (God be thanked) is grown to good wealth, and the whole company of the bakers thereby utterly impoverished, and finding that by no reasonable persuasion from us, neither with the lamentable complaint of the bakers, those brewers would leave baking, we were driven by justice and conscience to provide for their relief the speedier. Whereupon we did, with consent of Mayor, Jurats, and Common Council, make a certain decree, lawful, as we think, for the better maintenance of them, their wives, children and family, a matter in civil government worth looking into when the state of a common weal is preferred before the private gain of a few, which decree we required Mr. Gaymer to acquaint your Honour with, at his last being with you, who upon his return advertised us that your Lordship had the view thereof, and also of your Honour's well liking of the same, humbly beseeching your good Lordship's aid and continuance therein, whereof we have no doubt, being a matter that doth concern (and that according to the laws of the realm) the relief of those who are brought to the brink of decay.

11. THE MUNICIPAL REGULATION OF THE ENTRY INTO TRADES AT NOTTINGHAM [*Stevenson, Nottingham Records, Vol. IV, p.* 186], 1578–9.

1578–9, March 9. Memorandum also, that all manner of prentices already bound and to be bound to bring their indentures to be enrolled before May day next, or else every master to forfeit 12*d*. And the Mayor to admit no burgess but by consent of the Wardens of the occupation in default of the Wardens; and to have a special regard that such have been and served as apprentices and been enabled, according to the statute of anno 5 of Queen Elizabeth.

12. MUNICIPAL REGULATION OF MARKETS AT SOUTHAMPTON [*Hearnshaw, Southampton Court Leet Records, Vol. I, Part II, p.* 256], 1587.

Item we present that Mr. Brawycke, who, it is said . . . was bound unto your worships for the serving of the inhabitants of this town with candles at 2*d*. the lb., having all the tallow of the victuallers to this town at a price reasonable to his good liking and great commodity many years, restraining all others from having any part thereof by virtue of his grant from your worships as aforesaid, a scarcity of tallow now happening for one year, doth presently refuse to serve the inhabitants at any reasonable price, and the best cheap that is to be had is 3*d*., and many times 4*d*. the lb.; a happy man that can make his bargain so well to take it when there is profit and refuse to serve when the profit faileth, and to raise it at his own will for his best advantage, and to tie all men and himself to be at liberty; the artificers and the poorer sort of people are most of all pinched, wherewith they, with the rest, find themselves aggrieved, so desire your worships thoroughly to consider thereof.

13. THE MUNICIPAL REGULATION OF WAGES AT CHESTER [*Morris, Chester in the Plantagenet and Tudor Reigns, p.* 436], 1591.

30 July, 33 Eliz. And at the same assembly Mr. Mayor delivered the corporation of the wrights and slaters, letting to understand of their great exactions of the citizens and servants, whereby they deserved to be disfranchised and their corporations dissolved. Whereupon it was thought most meet that Mr. Mayor do call before him the aldermen and stewards thereof, and take them in bond for redress and remedy of all such wrongs . . . and in the meantime their corporation to be retained and also receive and give from time to time such wages as shall be appointed by the Mayor for the time being.

14. The Company of Journeymen Weavers of Gloucester [*Hist. MSS. Com., Twelfth Report, App. Part IX, pp.* 416–418], 1602.

Thos. Machyn, Mayor of the City of Gloucester, to all to whom, etc. Know ye that there came this day into the Court of the aldermen there divers of the journeymen weavers of the said city in the name of their whole fellowship of journeymen, and signified by their petition that whereas before this time sundry good ordinances have been made and granted by, and agreed upon by and between the master weavers of the said city, known by the name of the Warden and Fraternity of St. Anne of the weavers in the town of Gloucester, and the said journeymen, for the good order and government of man and for their better relief; and some disuse of the same has been of late years through the negligence of some of the said journeymen, and upon this untrue intendment that some of the said ordinances were not warrantable by the laws of this realm, nor convenient for the public good of the said city; it has therefore seemed fit to us, the Mayor and Aldermen, not only thoroughly to consider the said articles, but also to consider such books of compositions as have been heretofore given to the said company or fraternity of weavers, either by our predecessors or by the justices of assize of the county of the city; we have therefore called before us the Wardens and Stewards of the said fraternity or company to hear what they could or would say thereupon for our better information, requiring them further to shew us their books of compositions; who very willingly and orderly brought before us the several books hereafter mentioned; one book approved by the Justices of Assize, dated 10 Nov., 24 Henry VII, another book granted by our predecessors, also allowed by the Justices of Assize, dated 13 March, 4 Edward VI. We, having fully considered the said books, are pleased, with the consent of the present Warden and Stewards of the said Company of Weavers and of others the masters of the said Company occupying the trade of weaving within the said city, to allow that the journeymen of the said trade in the said city may in quiet and orderly sort at any time hereafter congregate and meet together at any fit place within the said city and such time of the day, between the hours of seven of the clock in the forenoon and four of the clock in the afternoon, as to them shall be thought fit and convenient, ever giving notice to the Warden of the said Company of weavers or, in his absence, to one of the stewards of the said fraternity one day before, at the least, of their meaning and purpose to meet, to the intent that if the said Warden or any of the said Company of the master weavers shall think or know anything meet to be considered of and conferred of between them, that the same might be proposed and so concluded of as might stand with equity and good order, and to the end that a quiet and peaceable demeanour with orderly and civil usage may be by and among the said whole company of journeymen at all times hereafter observed, and that the one to the other of them may give that brotherly aid and Christian relief as best may be for their helps, some of them being young men and bachelors having neither houses of their own or family, and some others of great years burdened with the charge of wife and many children; it is therefore thought good by us, with the assent of the said master-weavers, that they the said journeymen shall and lawfully may yearly, on the day of Saint Peter the Apostle, meet together and choose two honest and discreet journeymen of the elder and discreetest sort of them to be their Stewards for the year ensuing, which Stewards shall have power and authority to assemble and call together all the journeymen of the said art or others whatsoever professing and using the trade of weaving in the said city or suburbs of the same not being masters, and they so being assembled to confer among themselves of all such good means and orders as best may be for the good of their society and to the only ends and purposes before mentioned; which said journeymen being so chosen shall take upon them the said office of Stewardship and shall execute all and singular the following ordinances, either of them refusing the said office to forfeit 40*s.*; and the said Stewards shall be yearly presented on St. Ann's day by six of the elder and better sort of their Company of journeymen unto the Warden and Stewards of the said Company of Weavers at such time and place as shall be by them appointed, there to understand what to them doth pertain as servants of the said trade of weaving, or by virtue of their composition or grants made heretofore, or hereafter to be made, etc., all of which they shall faithfully promise by giving of their hands to perform and cause to be performed, on pain of 20*s.*

[Detailed ordinances follow. They require journeymen

who are strangers to produce a certificate of apprenticeship and testimony of good behaviour, and to pay on admission 8*d.* to the fellowship of journeymen. Other journeymen are to pay 4*d.* on admission, and all are to pay 1*d.* per quarter "to the relief of the poorer sort of the said fellowship." Journeymen embezzling yarn are to be expelled, and those absent from the election of new stewards are to be fined 3*s.* 4*d.* The company of journeymen shall do nothing prejudicial "towards the Warden and his Company . . . of the said art . . . of weavers, either by raising . . . their wages or otherwise."]

15. A Petition of Weavers who are not Burgesses [*Nottingham Records*, *Vol. IV*, *pp.* 274–5], 1604–5.

To the worshipful master mayor and his brethren.

Be it known, Right Worshipful, that we be a certain number of poor weavers who do use our trade within this town of Nottingham, thereby to maintain ourselves our wives and children, according to the laws of God and the King's Majesty's laws. It is not unknown unto your worship how the burgess weavers have sought, and at this present do seek, to put us down from working, thereby to work the utter undoing of us and of our poor families. We humbly do entreat your Worships' favours with equity to consider of our poor estates, who do not offend them nor work within their freedom or composition, if they have any. Your Worships may understand they do trouble us more of malice than for any hindrance they receive by us, for that we see men of other trades, both in this corporation and others, not being burgesses, yet work in manner as we do, unmolested or troubled. Therefore we beseech your Worships that we may have liberty to use our trades for the maintenance of ourselves, our wives, and children, and if there be anything due either to Master Mayor or any of his Worships' officers we are ready to discharge it; but as for the weavers, we know no reason or authority they have to claim anything of us, neither do we find ourselves able to bear so heavy a burden as they would lay upon us.

16. Extracts from the London Clothworkers' Court Book [*Unwin, Industrial Organization in the Sixteenth and Seventeenth Centuries, pp.* 229–234], 1537–1627.

July 13, 1 Mary. All the company had warning to keep their servants from unlawful assemblies and that they have no talk of the council's matters as they will answer at their uttermost perils.

January 16, 1-2 Mary. The wardens of the yeomanry brought into the hall a new chest with iii locks and iii keys to serve to put their money in, wherein was by them put in ready money xiiij*l.* vis. xi*d.*, the Mr. of the Company having one key, the upper warden of the yeomanry another key, and one of the assistants of the yeomanry to have the third key.

Also it was agreed that the said Wardens of the Yeomanry shall have such orders as hath been here taken, concerning such articles as they ought amongst themselves to observe, to be entered in their book to the intent they may better keep them.

July 13, 2 Mary. It is agreed that from henceforth all such apprentices as shall come out of their years, being of the handicraft, shall before they be sworn be tried and seen by the Wardens of the Yeomanry, whether they be workmen able to serve in the common weal or not.

. . . . .

November 29, 1567. This day the whole company of the handicraftsmen were warned to be here according to the order taken by the last court day, and these articles following were read unto them, and they all with one voice consented to every of the said articles, and made humble request with willing hearts as they professed that these said orders may be forthwith put in execution with diligence, affirming the same orders to be profitable to them all.

Item that there shall be eight or ten persons elected and chosen by the wardens and assistants to have the view of all the merchants' cloths hereafter to be wrought within the company, and that no person of this company to fold, take, or press or to deliver to the owner any merchant's cloth before the same cloth be viewed and seen by two of the said persons so appointed. And the said cloths so by them seen and found truly wrought, that is to say rowed, barbed, first-coursed and shorn from the one end to the other according to the statute last made, they to set the common seal of the house to every such cloth in token of true workmanship done upon the same. And every such cloth as shall be by the said searchers or any of them found faulty in workmanship, or that shall be folded, tacked, pressed, or delivered to the owner before it be viewed and sealed in form aforesaid, every workman of such cloth or cloths to pay for a fine of every such cloth xx*s*. . . .

. . . .

December 6, 1591. This day also at the earnest suit and request and upon the full agreement of those of the assistants and livery of the Company being of the handicraft, the Wardens of the Yeomanry, their assistants and xxiiij more of the said yeomanry, it was by this Court fully ordered and agreed that there shall be four of the said yeomanry appointed to be sealers to seal all such woollen cloth as the merchants or any of them shall appoint and deliver to any of this company to be dressed to the intent to be transported over sea, etc. . . . and that every clothworker shall send for the sealers when his cloth is ready.

January 16, 1610–11. The humble suit of your worships servants of the yeomanry.

First, we entreat your worship that the upper Warden of the Yeomanry's account may be yearly audited according to an old custom carefully provided for by your worships predecessors, (that is to say) by two from your worships Court of Assistants and two of our Ancients of the yeomanry.

Secondly, we humbly entreat your worship that the remainder of the quarterage, your worships' officers being paid, may remain in the yeomanry's chest according to an old custom, our worshipful Master of this Company for the time being to keep one key, the upper Wardens of the Yeomanry to keep another key, and one of the Ancients of the Assistants of the Yeomanry to keep the third key.

Thirdly, we desire of your worship that the upper warden of the yeomanry may have one of his Ancients last being in his place to sit by him and assist him in his accompts and to show him wherein the Company is wronged.

Fourthly, we desire that when we shall find our officer of the yeomanry to be slack and remiss in doing of his duty in his service which he ought to do for the good of the Company, and the same duly proved against him, that we of the yeomanry may have full authority to dismiss him at our own discretion, but not without the consent of the Master and Wardens and Assistants of this Company for the time being first had and obtained in that behalf.

These Petitions and requests of the yeomanry were granted and agreed upon by the Master, Wardens and Assistants present at the said court holden the said sixteenth day of January 1610 aforesaid.

. . . . . .

June 13, 1627. Whereas . . . Suit was commenced in Court of King's Bench at Westminster by the Wardens of Yeomanry in the name of Master and Wardens against divers Merchant Adventurers upon viii Elizabeth, which yet dependeth in the said court undetermined, and the said Wardens of Yeomanry considering that the proceedings in like suits formerly commenced have been stopped by some special command of the King and State upon the solicitation of the said Merchant Adventurers being strong in purse and friends, have bethought themselves of a way or mean to prevent the said Merchant Adventurers from the like, and to that purpose have dealt with a Gentleman named Mr. George Kirke of the King's Majesty's Bedchamber, very gracious with his Majesty, who for a fourth part of this moiety of all penalties, forfeitures which shall be obtained or gotten upon any recovery to be had against any of the said Merchant Adventurers upon any action or suit brought or to be brought, sued, commenced, etc., hath undertaken to do his best and to use all the credit and means he can to his Majesty that there be no stop or stay in course of law for the solicitation or procurement of the said Merchant Adventurers in suits already brought or to be brought.

[The Wardens of Yeomanry ask that the Court may record the agreement.]

17. The Feltmakers' Joint-Stock Project[1] [*Cotton MSS. Titus B.V.* 117], *c.* 1611.

The state of the Feltmakers' Case, with some propositions on their part to remedy the mischiefs they now are constrained to endure.

The feltmakers were by decrees in Star Chamber united to the Company of the Haberdashers, London, and did sit

[1] Unwin, *Industrial Organization in the Sixteenth and Seventeenth Centuries*, pp. 240-42.

with them in their hall for government of the trade, till they, finding themselves rather oppressed by them than any way cherished or abuses reformed, thereupon by suit obtained a charter from his Majesty by which they were incorporated a body of themselves by the name of Master, Wardens and Commonalty of the Art and Mystery of Feltmakers of London and 4 miles compass.

Hereupon by allowance of the Lord Mayor they published their charter, took them a hall, and accordingly did and do govern their company. Afterwards considering that they were a trade and company of themselves by whom many thousands do live besides their company, namely, the hat trimmers, band makers, hat dyers and hat sellers, which are the haberdashers, and yet nevertheless they were extremely kept under by the haberdashers engrossing the commodity of wools brought in merely for their trade of hatmaking and for no other use, and by that means having both the means of the feltmakers' trade (for wool) and the means of their maintenance (for buying their wares being made) all in their power, by which the feltmakers in general (except some few in particular) do find themselves much wronged, and by means of it and their daily threats did fear the overthrow of their trade: whereupon the generality petitioning to the company of the hard case they lived in, notwithstanding their extreme sore labour, besought them to provide some means for their relief and prevention of what might ensue. The company then by means made them a stock to buy the wools imported for the company at the best hand; but being opposed by the haberdashers, the prices by that means were enhanced, and yet the sale of their wares made kept in bondage as before, whereby many of their trade have been impoverished, many forced to leave their trade, and many to forsake the city, by which means all that now live of feltmaking as pickers, carders, trimmers, bandmakers, dyers and hatsellers are much hindered, the trade being drawn into the country.

Hereupon the company became (as often before) humble suitors for their freedom, which by opposition of the Company of Haberdashers and their false suggestions to the court, they could not obtain—howbeit a Committee of Aldermen have certified it to be fit—neither are suffered to have liberty to search for the abuses of their trade under warrant from the

Lord Mayor, which formerly they have often done; besides, their shops threatened to be shut up, notwithstanding their inhabiting of the city many years.

Now the company seeing the extreme malice of the haberdashers, and that the sale of their wares lieth solely in them, whereby many are forced to hawk their hats made contrary to the statutes, and sell at far less rates than they can truly afford them, only to buy victual, whereby if some redress be not had many will be undone or forced to go into the country, to the great damage of the trade in general and overthrow of the corporation which they much desire to support: they have considered to raise them a stock to take in all men's wares when they be made, to avoid hawking, and to encourage men to follow their trade and continue within the corporation, for the benefit of all parties, the city, the trade and company, and all that trim and sell hats and live by that trade, without desire of enhancing the price of anything or damage to any man.

The stock they purpose to be 25,000*l.*, to be resident in some convenient place of the suburbs, where men may take notice to have money for their wares if they will bring them, being made good and at such rates as they may well be afforded, by judgment of sworn men of the trade, who shall rate them both inward and outward, so as the poor shall sell much better than they have done the other sort, howbeit they sell cheaper by 2*s.* in the pound than for the most part they have done; yet having a certain market and ready money to buy wool again; and, in that then they shall be in no hazard of loss by trusting, as now they do, their gain will be much more.

1. The corporation will flourish.

2. Felts will be better made in that every man shall have price for his ware as his workmanship is.

3. The trade, being much used in the country, will revert into the city, to the benefit of the city and all that live by the trade.

4. The haberdasher shall buy good wares more generally than now and at as cheap rates as he now usually buyeth (the times of the year and prices of wool considered), and be sorted with much more ease and content than now he is.

5. The haberdasher of mean estate shall be in much better

case than now, for that every man shall have good wares without culling according to their sorts.

6. The commonwealth shall be better served in that now they shall have good wares for their money.

7. The stock cannot but be gainful to the stockers, in that the hats, according to their goodness, shall come in at 2*s.* in the pound profit upon the sale, merely out of the feltmaker's labour, who is equally benefited by the certain stock. Besides, the often return of the stock at 2*s.* in the pound cannot but give content to the stockers.

8. The stock shall be sufficiently secured were it never so much, in that they shall deliver no money without a sufficient value of wares. Their sale will be certain in that without buying the haberdashers cannot uphold their trade. Besides, no man shall have benefit of the stock except he will bring all the ware he makes to it (except it be a hat or two specially made, and that with the privilege of the stockers). Besides, if at any time the stock shall be full of ware and want money, the company by a general consent can forbear bringing in or slack their making for a time. But so it is that once in a year all felts will off, of what nature soever.

9. The wares being of necessity to be bought, the stockers will need not trust except they will but upon good security, which will make men more wary in buying.

18. The Case of the Tailors of Ipswich[1] [*Coke's Reports, Part XI, pp.* 53–55], 1615.

Trin. II, Jac. Reg. King's Bench.

[The Master, Wardens, and Community of the Tailors and Workers of cloth of the town of Ipswich in the County of Suffolk brought an action for 13*l.* 13*s.* 4*d.* against William Sheninge. They allege

(i) that by the letters patent incorporating them they had power to make reasonable rules and ordinances and to impose fines for breach of them;

(ii) that they had made a rule that no person occupying any of the said trades in Ipswich should keep any shop or chamber, or exercise the said faculties, or any of them, or take an apprentice or journeyman, till he should present himself to the Master and Wardens of the

[1] This case is important as an illustration of the attitude of the Common Law Courts towards rules made in restraint of trade. See below, section III of this Part, Nos. 17 and 24.

said society, should prove that he had served an apprenticeship, and should be admitted as a sufficient workman, on pain of 5 marks fine;

(iii) that in accordance with 19 Hen. vii., cap. 7, they had submitted these rules to the justices of assize, who had allowed them;

(iv) that William Sheninge had worked 20 days as a tailor without complying.

The defendant pleaded he was an apprentice by the space of 7 years, that he had been retained as domestic servant for a year and that as such he made garments for him, his wife, and children, which is the same use and exercise wherein the plaintiffs demur.]

And in this case upon argument at the Bar and Bench, divers points were resolved—

1. That at the Common Law no man could be prohibited from working in any lawful trade, for the law abhors idleness . . . and especially in young men, who ought in their youth . . . to learn lawful trades and sciences which are profitable to the common weal. . . . And therefore the law abhors all monopolies, which prohibit any from working in any lawful trade. And that appears in 2 H. 5, 56. A dyer was bound that he should not use the dyers' craft for 2 years, and there Hull holds that the bond was against the common law, and by God if the plaintiff was here he should go to prison till he paid a fine to the king; so for the same reason, if an husbandman is bound that he shall not sow his land, the bond is against the common law. . . . And if he who undertakes upon him to work is unskilful, his ignorance is a sufficient punishment to him . . . and if any one takes him to work and spoils it, an action on the case lies against him. And the Statute of 5 Eliz. 4, which prohibits every person from using or exercising any craft, mystery, or occupation unless he has been an apprentice by the space of 7 years was not enacted only to the intent that workmen should be skilful, but also that youth should not be nourished in idleness, but brought up and educated in lawful sciences and trades: and therefore it appears that without an Act of Parliament none can be prohibited from working in any lawful trade. Also the common law doth not prohibit any person from using several Arts or mysteries at his pleasure. . .

2. That the said Restraint of the defendant for more than the said Act of 5 Eliz. has made was against law, and therefore for as much as the Statute has not restrained him who has

served as an apprentice for seven years from exercising the trade of a tailor, the said ordinance can't prohibit him from exercising his trade till he has presented himself before them, or till they allow him to be a workman; for these are against the liberty and freedom of the subject, and are a means of extortion in drawing money from them, either by delay or some other subtil device or by oppression of young Tradesmen by the old and rich of the same Trade, not permitting them to work in their trade freely; and all this is against the Common Law and the commonwealth. But ordinances for the good order and government of men of Trades and Mysteries are good, but not to restrain any one in his lawful mystery.

3. It was resolved that the said branch of the Act of 5 Eliz. is intended of a public use and exercise of a trade to all who will come, and not of him who is a private cook, tailor, brewer, baker, etc., in the house of any for the use of a family, and therefore the said ordinance had been good and consonant to law. Such a private exercise and use had not been within it, for every one may work in such a private manner, although he has never been an apprentice in the trade.

4. It was resolved that the Statute of 19 H. 7, cap. 7, doth not corroborate any of the ordinances made by any corporation, which are so allowed and approved as the Statute speaks, but leaves them to be affirmed as good, or disaffirmed as unlawful, by the law; the sole benefit which the corporation obtains by such allowance is that they shall not incur the penalty of 40*l.* mentioned in the Act, if they put in use any ordinances which are against the king's prerogative, or the common profit of the people. Judgment for defendant.

19. THE GRIEVANCES OF THE JOURNEYMEN WEAVERS OF LONDON [*Gildhall Library. The case of the Commonalty of the Corporation of Weavers of London truly stated*],[1] *c.* 1649.

Humbly presented to the consideration of the honourable House of Commons.

All legal jurisdictions over a number of people or society of men must either be primitive or derivative. Now primitive

[1] Part of this document is quoted by Unwin, *Industrial Organization in the Sixteenth and Seventeenth Centuries*, pp. 205–6.

jurisdiction is undoubtedly in the whole body, and not in one or more members, all men being by nature equal to other; and all jurisdictive power over them, being founded by a compact and agreement with them, is invested in one or more persons, who represent the whole, and by the consent of the whole are empowered to govern by such rules of equality towards all, so that both governor and governed may know certainly what the one may command and what the other must obey; without the performance of which mutual contract all obligations are cancelled, and that jurisdictive power returns unto its first spring (the people) from whence it was conveyed.

And doubtless whatever power our Governors of the Corporation of Weavers may pretend and plead for, if they had any rationally, they had it at first from the whole body, as it stands incorporated into a civil society of men walking by such rules, established for the preservation of the trade, advancement and encouragement of the profession thereof.

And if it be objected that they had a charter granted them by the King, wherein they are invested that power they challenge, we answer that there is not any one liberty that is granted to them but that is also granted to the meanest member of the said company. The words of the charter are these :—

[Here follows a copy of the charter granted by King Henry II to the Weavers of London.]

So that it is clear that this grant was not to so many particular men, but to the whole society; and what power soever any person or persons were afterwards invested withall must of necessity be by the consent, election, and approbation of the whole body; and if our Egyptian taskmasters have any further commission for their usurped power over us, why do they not produce it? Certainly, if they could, they would. But having none they plead custom and precedents, both which they will find but broken reeds to lean upon, but rotten props to support their worm-eaten sovereignty.

1. For first, there must be these two things to make a custom valid: (i) Usage; (ii) Time. Yet that time must be such whereof there is no memory of man, and the usage must be peaceable, without interruption. But both these are wanting

to strengthen their claim to their pretended power over us.
. . . . . .

2. Suppose there were a custom, and that it had been time out of mind also, yet if long usurpations of power could make the exercise thereof legal, the very foundation of just government were subverted.

3. No custom against an Act of Parliament is valid in law. But the custom claimed by our governors is against the very fundamental constitutions both of all civil societies and of several Acts of Parliament, which ordain that all elections shall be free, chiefly 3 of Ed. I, chap. 5, by virtue of which the people choose all their officers and magistrates in the several parishes and precincts in this kingdom. And if it be according to law in the major, the commonwealth, it must consequently hold in the minor, a particular corporation or civil society of men, as we are, etc.

4. But customs are only valid when reasonable. . . . Now nothing in the world can be more unreasonable than that such a number of men as 16 should have liberty to exercise a power over as many thousands, without, nay against, their wills, consent, or election . . . , the challenge and exercise of such a power over a people being the perfectest badge of slavery that men can be subjected to.

But we shall proceed in a discovery of those oppressions and abuses which we complain so much against in our governors.

1st Charge. They have admitted aliens to be members for sums of money, contrary to the statutes of the realm, orders of the Lord Mayor and Court of Aldermen, customs of the city, and ordinances of the company. . . . They have brought in by their own confession three hundred and twelve strangers to be masters of the said company, and have taken for their admittance 5*l.* a man, which amounted to 1,560*l.*, or thereabouts. . . . They object that the strangers admitted are broad weavers and deal not in the commodities that we trade in, viz., ribbon, lace, etc.

The objection is false; for most of us can, and many of us have wrought, as good broad stuffs as are nowadays made, and would do still, were it not for the vast number of strangers (which have engrossed the trade). . . And if it be demanded how or by what means they got the trade into their hands, we answer that at the beginning of the war many of us and our servants engaged for the Parliament, and, in our absence, they, being generally malignant, staying at home, and keeping servants all of their own country, never employing any English, as they by law ought, by degrees got all the trading, so that now the war is ended, and we returned to follow our callings, we can get no employment. By which means many hundreds have been forced to leave the trade, as to be porters, labourers, water-bearers, etc., and many forced to take relief from the several parishes wherein they dwell. . . .

2nd Charge. They have admitted natives to weave and set up weaving in their gild, without serving seven years, contrary to the statutes, orders and customs aforesaid, as hath been proved by several witnesses before the Committee of the honourable House.

3rd Charge. They exact extraordinary fees of those persons that they make free or admit, taking a silver spoon of an ounce and a half weight, and five shillings and eightpence in money, contrary to the Statute of 22 of Hen. VIII, chap. 4, and 28 of Hen. VIII, chap. 5. . . .

4th Charge. They have deprived the commonalty of their rights in their first ordinance, which saith the bailiffs are to be chosen by the bailiffs, wardens, assistants, and commonalty, which ordinance is grounded upon the Statute of 3rd of Ed. I, chap. 5, which saith elections ought to be free, etc.

As touching the right of election, sufficient hath been spoken in the preamble before these charges; only give us leave to insert a few particulars in answer to their objection.

1. Whereas they object, that the commonalty are represented in the livery of the said company, we answer :—Legal representatives must be legally chosen by the persons represented, or else they cannot, or at least ought not, to be bound by their determinations. But the livery-men of our company are chosen by the bailiffs and governors, and not by the commonalty, so may properly be called the governors' representatives and not ours, we being never called upon to give our voice in their elections. Neither are they, indeed, elected, but brought in for 5*l.* a man. In lieu whereof they are invested with a peculiar privilege above others, by being empowered to keep more servants than ordinary, by which means the commonalty is destroyed also. . . .

5th Charge. They have dismissed the yeomanry contrary to six several orders made with their consent by the Lord Mayor and Court of Assistants.

But they object that they have not dismissed them, etc. If they had not dismissed them, what needed so many several orders to be made to the contrary? But we desire you to take notice that the yeomanry did consist of sixteen persons which were authorized by the aforesaid six several orders to search and find out the abuses in trade, viz., intruders that had not served seven years, and that none but serviceable goods might be made for the commonwealth. Now, because these governors gain by intruders, making them pay for their permission, and driving the greatest trade, making much light and deceitful work, therefore they have dismissed the said yeomanry, by reason whereof both the said evils are continued. Besides, the yeomanry by the said orders were to have the journeymen's quarteridges for their pains, but now being by them dismissed they gather the quarteridges and share it among themselves.

6th Charge. That they have wasted the treasure and stock of the company in byways, and have not made that provision for the poor members of the company as by their trust they ought to have done.

So that what with their feastings, defending vexatious suits contrary to law, purchasing a monopoly, large fees for councillors, bills, demurrers, suits against weavers of other companies, etc., they have in one year out of the company's stock and income (which amounted but to 791*l.* 5*s.* 5*d.*) spent 566*l.* 19*s.* 8*d.*, which year's account agrees with their disbursements other years also; and for 200*l.* given by one Mr. Ralph Hamon to purchase land for the poor, they have purchased none to this day, but have shared the money among themselves. . . .

The premises considered, and all other circumstances duly weighed, our desires for the freedom of elections being both legal and rational, our sufferings and abuses under usurping pretended governors so abusive and offensive, our wants so great, company so numerous, trading so little, and that too devoured by strangers, . . . we therefore hope that all these things put together will be of such weight with all conscientious, godly men in this honourable House of Commons, as that we shall not need to fear your willing assistance for the redressing of these great evils and granting our just desires. The speedy performance whereof will not only gain unto you the prayers of many thousand persons who are ready to perish for want of trading, but also engage them, as heretofore, so for the future, to stand by you in your greatest necessities, for the strengthening your hands in the execution of justice and judgment, and redress of the oppressions of the nation.

SECTION III

THE REGULATION OF INDUSTRY BY THE STATE

The documents in this section illustrate the regulation of industrial relationships by the government of the Tudors and of the first two Stuarts. The principal aims of their policy were to check the movement of the textile industries from the town to country districts (Nos. 3 and 6), to prevent the concentration of industry in the hands of capitalists (Nos. 3 and 11), or the creation of a necessitous proletariat (No. 4), to exercise a police supervision over the movement of labour (Nos. 6, 7 and 14), to maintain the quality of English goods (No. 2), to prevent class encroaching on class (Nos. 5 and 6) either through the wage earner demanding excessive wages (No. 5) or through the employer beating them down unduly (Nos. 8, 10, 19, 20), in short to crystallize existing relationships with such changes only as the economic developments of recent years, particularly the fall in the value of money (No. 6), and the spread of the textile industries into rural districts (No. 3) made inevitable.

The system was developed in numerous Acts, of which the most important are given below (Nos. 3, 6 and 10). The most comprehensive measure was the Statute of Artificers of 1563 (No. 6). There was little original in this Act. Just as the Statutes forbidding depopulation (Part II, section I) really only developed manorial customaries into a national system, and the Poor Law Statutes (Part II, section IV) were based on the experiments of municipal authorities, so the Statute of Artificers was based partly on the practices of gilds (Part II, section II), partly on the mediæval Statutes of Labourers (see Part I, section VI, Nos. 12–19). Indeed, Cecil's original proposal (No. 5) seems to have been to re-enact 12 Richard II, cap. 3, which the rise in prices had made out of date. If seriously entertained, this idea must have been discarded. The most important innovation introduced by the statute in its final form was the substitution of a system of industrial regulation applying to almost the whole country for regulations applying to particular localities and particular trades.

The most important parts of the Statute of Artificers were those relating to apprenticeship and to the assessment of wages. The former, if we may judge by the proceedings of the County Justices (Nos. 11 & 15) and of municipal authorities

(Part II, section II, Nos. 9, 10, 11, 15), seem to have been administered with considerable strictness, which was only to be expected in view of the interest which gilds, boroughs, traders and craftsmen generally had in seeing that they were carried out. Judicial interpretations seem, however, to have begun at an early date to whittle them away to some extent (No. 17), for the Judges disliked rules "in restraint of trade" (No. 24 and section II, No. 18).

The wage clauses of the Statute present a more difficult problem. There is no doubt that their object was to fix a maximum (not a minimum) wage for agricultural labour (Nos. 6 and 14), which, however, should move with movements in prices. This policy was not so oppressive as it appears to us, because of the wide distribution of landed property, the consequent fact that comparatively few rural workers depended entirely upon wages for their living, and the relatively small difference between the social position of the small farmer or master craftsman and the hired persons whom they employed. In a colony like Massachusetts, where the policy of fixing maximum wages was adopted, its motive was seen in the simplest form (No. 21). Even in England, however, the same motives were at work to a less degree (Nos. 5, 22 and 23). The policy of fixing a maximum wage was, in fact, on a par with that of fixing prices, and probably popular with the small masters and small landholders, who formed a large proportion of the urban and rural population. It did not come to an end with the destruction of the absolute monarchy, but continued, with fair regularity, down to 1688, and, after that, with much less regularity, at any rate to 1762.

The regulation of wages did not, however, only aim at fixing a maximum. It also aimed on some, perhaps rare, occasions at fixing a minimum, at any rate for workers in the textile industries. These latter were treated in a special way, because the development of capitalism in the textile industries (Nos. 2, 3, 8, 16 and 19) had created a wage problem of a modern kind, at any rate in the south and east of England, such as did not yet exist in agriculture. Municipal authorities had in the past fixed minimum rates for textile workers (section II, No. 5). In 1593 four Bills were drafted which proposed to do the same by legislation, of which one is printed below (No. 8), and in 1603–04 an Act (No. 10) was passed to this effect. Two examples of the establishment of minimum rates are given from the proceedings of the Wiltshire Quarter Sessions, in 1602 and 1623. In the former case (No. 9) a piece list was drafted by a committee of clothiers and weavers, which was subsequently issued without alteration by the Justices (No. 13). In the latter case (No. 18) the textile workers of Wiltshire asked the Justices to enforce the assessment of wages on their employers, and the Justices complied by ordering the rates to be published at Devizes. This shows that the regulation of wages did in some cases protect the workers. Naturally, however, the Justices required stimulating in this part of their duties, and during the period of Charles I's personal government the Privy Council intervened to compel them to fix rates, as it did to compel them to administer the Poor Laws. In 1630 it received a petition from the textile workers of Suffolk and Essex complaining that their wages had been reduced, and appointed commissioners to investigate the matter (No. 19), who compelled the employers to raise wages (No. 20). The policy of fixing *minimum* rates seems to have come to an end with the fall of the absolute monarchy in 1640, though it was occasionally revived by Parliament in the sixteenth century. (Part III, section III, Nos. 3, 4 and 15).

AUTHORITIES

The more accessible of the modern writers dealing with the subject of this section are :—Cunningham, *English Industry and Commerce, Modern Times,* Part I ; Ashley, *Economic History,* Vol. I, Part II, Chap. iii ; Unwin, *Industrial Organisation in the Sixteenth and Seventeenth Centuries* ; Abram, *Social England in the Fifteenth Century* ; Dunlop and Denman, *English Apprenticeship and Child Labour* ; Rogers, *Six Centuries of Work and Wages* ; Hewins, *English Trade and Finance in the Seventeenth Century* ; Schanz, *Englische Handelspolitik Gegen Ende des Mittelalters* ; Tawney in *Die Vierteljahrschrift für Sozial und Wirtschaftsgeschichte,* Band

XI and XII, Heft 8 and 9; Macarthur, in E. H. R., Vols. IX, XIII and XV; Hewins in *Economic Journal*, Vol. VIII; Hutchins, *ibid*, Vol. X.

Bibliographies are given by Cunningham, *op. cit.*, pp. 943-998; Unwin, *op. cit.*, pp. 263–270; Ashley, *op. cit.*, pp. 190–1, 243–8; Abram, *op. cit.*, pp. 229–238; Dunlop & Denman, *op. cit.*, pp. 355–63; the student may also consult the following:—

(1) *Documentary authorities*, 1485–1660:—The most important printed sources of information for the administration of the industrial legislation of the 16th century are Town Records (see bibliographies, especially those of Unwin and of Dunlop & Denman), and the Proceedings of the County Justices contained in the following works:—Hamilton, Devonshire Quarter Sessions from Queen Elizabeth to Queen Anne; Atkinson, Quarter Session Records of the North Riding of Yorkshire; Willis Bund, Worcester County Records, division 1; Cox, Three Centuries of Derbyshire Annals; Hardy, Hertford Quarter Session Records; Hardy & Page, Bedfordshire County Quarter Sessions; volumes published by the Historical MSS. Commission, especially Vol. I; Victoria County History, *passim*.

(2) *Literary authorities*.—The law is explained by numerous writers of legal text books, *e.g.*, Fitzherbert, The Book Belonging to a Justice of the Peace; Lambard, Eirenarcha; Sheppard, Whole Office of the County Justice of the Peace. Cases before the courts concerning apprenticeship are quoted in the Reports of Coke and Croke. Sidelights on contemporary opinion may be obtained from Rotuli Parliamentorum III, 269, 330, 352; IV, 330–331, 352; V, 110; More, Utopia; Starkey, A Dialogue between Cardinal Pole and Thomas Lupset (Early English Text Society, England in the Reign of King Henry VIII); Forest, The Pleasant Poesy of Princely Practice (*ibid.*); The Commonweal of this Realm of England (edited by E. R. Lamond); King Edward's Remains, a Discourse about the Reformation of many abuses (printed in Burnet's History of the Reformation); Winthrop's Journal; Petty, A Treatise of Taxes and Contributions, Chapter I, Section 4.

1. Proposals for the Regulation of the Cloth Manufacture[1] [*Brit. Mus. Cotton MSS.*, *Titus B. I*, *fol.* 189], *temp.* Hen. VIII.

Articles to be certified to my lord privy seal according to his letter for the complaint of the weavers in the seven hundreds in the country of Kent.

First, that no clothier, that hath not had exercise in his youth by the space of two years at the least in the craft of

[1] Quoted Schanz, Vol. II, pp. 660–1.

weaving, use or have in his house or at his commandment any loom.

Item, that no clothier weaver using to make coloured clothes shall use, have, or occupy in his house or at his assignment any more than one loom.

Item, that if the clothmaker have cause to complain upon the weaver for not duly and truly working of their clothes or the weaver cause to complain upon the clothier for not paying him his duty for the said weaving, that then the party grieved shall complain to the next justice of peace, and he shall assign one indifferent weaver and one indifferent clothier to examine the cause of variance and to assess what amends the party grieved shall have. And the party to stand and abide the order so made.

Item, where it is ordered by the statute of anno 4 E. 4 *capitulo primo*, that the clothier shall pay ready money to the weavers and spinners and other their artificers, that the said statute shall be put in due execution.

Item, if any clothier, tailor, cordwainer or other artificer, by what name or names soever he or they be called, that hereafter shall fortune to come out of any shire other than out of the said shire of Kent into any of the 7 hundreds there to seek service and to have work, that then he or they that will or shall happen to take him or them into his or their service or services, shall before one of the justices of the peace be bound unto the king by way of recognisance in such sum as by the discretion of the said justice shall be appointed; that the said person so by him taken into service shall be of good behaviour during the time that he shall be in his service, and that the said justice be not compellable to certify the same recognisance, unless the same recognisance be forfeited. And this to be done from time to time, as often as the justice of the peace shall think convenient. And if any man retain any man in his service without putting in surety, as is above said, that then the justice of the peace to have authority to commit such person or persons to ward, there to remain by his discretion.

EDWARD WOTTON.
THOMAS WYLFFORD.

2. Administrative Difficulties in the Regulation of the Manufacture of Cloth [1] [*Brit. Mus. Cotton MSS. Titus B. V, fol.* 187], 1537.

Before my right hearty commendations to your good lordship. It may please the same to understand, that divers of the clothmakers in these parts have been with me, declaring unto me, that in case they shall be compelled to make cloth from Michaelmas forwards according to the king's act, it shall cause them and other of their occupation to cease and forbear clothmaking, saying, that it is impossible to keep the breadth of the cloth limited by the act, and also that the weavers, being very poor men, have not nor be able to provide looms and sleys to weave clothes according to the act. Whereunto I answered them, that there is much slander in outward parts for false clothmaking, and for remedy thereof this act was provided; and or ever the act was made, there were divers clothmakers spoken with, who affirmed, that it was reasonable; wherefore I told them that I thought that they did rather seek occasion to continue still false clothmaking, than put their good endeavour to make true cloth according to the act; and also I shewed to them, that the King's Highness had suspended the same act by a long time by his proclamation, to the intent that they might provide looms and other necessaries for the making of true cloth according to the act, wherefore I marvelled much that they had been so negligent in the provision thereof, declaring unto them, that I thought that the King's Highness would not defer the execution of the act any longer; which it seemed to me they lamented very sorely, saying that they would leave their occupying for the time; for they could not by no possible means make cloth according to the act, and specially for their breadth; and I bade them take heed and beware, for I thought, they might perform the act, if they had good will and good zeal to the common weal; and if they by obstinacy or wilfulness would leave clothmaking, whereby percase might grow murmur and sedition among the people for lack of work, that then it would be laid to their charges, to their perils and utter undoings. Whereunto they said obediently, that they would do that lay in their possible powers, but more they could not, beseeching

[1] Schanz, Vol. 11, pp. 662–3.

me, that I would be a means to the King's Highness once again to suspend the act, which I would not promise them to do, and so left them for this time in despair of this matter; and so now advertise your good lordship thereof, to the intent that, if it seem by your wisdom convenient, ye may move the King's Majesty hereof to the intent, his Grace's pleasure may be known, whether his Highness of his goodness would yet suspend the act for one other year, which in my poor opinion, if so may stand with his Grace's pleasure, shall not be much amiss, beseeching your good lordship, that I may be advertised hereof as soon as you conveniently may; for Michaelmas is the last day of the old proclamation for this matter; and thus fare your good lordship as heartily well as I would myself. Written at Terlyng the 23rd day of September.

Your[s] assuredly to his
preservation (?)
THOMAS AUDELEY,
lord chancellor.

3. AN ACT TOUCHING WEAVERS[1] [2 *&* 3 *Phil. & Mary, c.xi. Statutes of the Realm, Vol. IV, Part I, p.* 286-87], 1555.

Forasmuch as the weavers of this realm have, as well at this present parliament as at divers other times, complained that the rich and wealthy clothiers do many ways oppress them, some by setting up and keeping in their houses divers looms, and keeping and maintaining them by journeymen and persons unskilful, to the decay of a great number of artificers which were brought up in the said science of weaving, their family and household, some by ingrossing of looms into their hands and possession, and letting them out at such unreasonable rents as the poor artificers are not able to maintain themselves, much less their wives, family and children, some also by giving much less wages and hire for the weaving and workmanship of [cloth] than in times past they did, whereby they are enforced utterly to forsake their art and occupation wherein they have been brought up: It is therefore, for remedy of the premises, and for the avoiding of a great number of inconveniences which may grow (if in time it be not foreseen)

[1] This Act suggests that something like a factory system may have been growing up in the sixteenth century: See Ashley, *Economic History*, Vol. II, The Woollen Industry.

ordained, established and enacted, by authority of this present parliament, that no person using the feat or mistery of clothmaking and dwelling out of a city, borough, market town or corporate town, shall from the feast of St. Michael the Archangel now next ensuing, keep, retain or have in his or their house or possession any more or above one woollen loom at one time, nor shall by any means directly or indirectly receive or take any manner profit, gain or commodity by letting or setting any loom, or any house wherein any loom is or shall be used and occupied, which shall be together by him set or let, upon pain of forfeiture for every week that any person shall do contrary to the tenour and true meaning hereof 20*s*.

And be it further ordained and enacted by like authority, that no woollen weaver using or exercising the feat or mistery of weaving, and dwelling out of city, borough, market town or town corporate, shall after the said feast have or keep at any time above the number of two woollen looms, or receive any profit, gain or commodity, directly or indirectly as is aforesaid, by any more than two looms at one time, upon pain to forfeit for every week that any person shall offend or do to the contrary 20*s*.

And it is further ordained and enacted by like authority, that no person which shall after the said feast, use, exercise or occupy only the feat or mistery of a weaver, and not clothmaking, shall during the time that he shall use the feat or mistery of a weaver, keep or have any tucking mill, or shall use or exercise the feat or mistery of a [tucker] or dyer, upon pain to forfeit for every week that he shall so do 20*s*.

And it is further enacted by like authority, that no person which after the said feast shall use, exercise or occupy the feat or mistery of a tucker or fuller, shall during the time that he shall so use the said feat or mistery, keep or have any loom in his house or possession, or shall directly or indirectly take any profit or commodity by the same, upon pain to forfeit for every week 20*s*.

And it is further ordained and enacted by like authority, that no person whatsoever, which heretofore hath not used or exercised the feat, mistery or art of clothmaking, shall after the said feast, make or weave or cause to be made or woven any kind of broad white woollen cloths, but only in a city, borough, town corporate or market town, or else in such place or places where such cloths have been used to be commonly made by the space of ten years next before the making this act; upon pain of forfeiture for every cloth otherwise made five pounds.

Provided always and be it further enacted by the authority aforesaid, that it shall not be lawful to any person or persons being a weaver, or that doth or shall use the art or mistery of a weaver or weaving, dwelling out of a city, borough, town corporate or market town, to have in his and their service any more or above the number of two apprentices at one time; upon pain to forfeit for every time that he shall offend or do contrary to this branch or article the sum of ten pounds.

And further be it enacted by the authority aforesaid, that it shall not be lawful to or for any person or persons to set up the art or mistery of weaving, after the said feast of St. Michael, unless the same person or persons so setting up the same art or mistery of weaving, have been apprentice to the same art or mistery, or exercised the same, by the space of 7 years at the least; upon pain of twenty pounds to be forfeited to the King and Queen's Majesties, her Grace's heirs or successors, the one moiety of all which forfeitures shall be to the King and Queen's Highnesses, heirs [and] successors, and the other moiety to him or them that will sue for the same in any court of record by action of debt, bill, plaint or information, wherein no wager of law, essoigne or protection shall be admitted or allowed for the defendant.

. . . Provided always, and be it enacted by the authority aforesaid, that this act or anything therein contained shall [not] in any way extend or be prejudicial to any person or persons that doth or shall dwell in the counties of York, Cumberland, Northumberland or Westmoreland; but that they and every of them shall and may have and keep looms in their houses, and do and exercise all and every thing and things for or concerning spinning, weaving, clothworking and clothmaking in the said counties, as they or any of them might have done or exercised lawfully before the making of this statute; anything contained in this statute to the contrary in any way notwithstanding.

4. Enactment of Common Council of London as to Age of Ending Apprenticeship[1] [*Arber, Stationers' Records, I, p. xli*],[2] 1556.

For as much as great poverty, penury, and lack of living hath of late years followed, . . . and one of the chiefest occasions thereof, as it is thought, . . . is by reason of the over hasty marriages and over soon setting up of households of and by the youth and young folks of the said city [of London], which hath commonly used, and yet do, to marry themselves as soon as ever they come out of their apprenticehood, be they ever so young and unskilful, yea, and often times many of them so poor that they scantily have of their proper goods wherewith to buy their marriage apparel . . . and forasmuch as the chiefest occasion of the said inconveniences, as it is very evident, is by reason that divers and sundry apprentices, as well of the said artificers as also of other citizens of the said city, are commonly bound for so few years that their terms of apprenticeability expireth and endeth oversoon, and that they are there upon incontinently made free of the said city; . . . for remedy, stay, and reformation whereof it is ordained . . . that no manner of persons . . . shall be any manner of ways or means made free of the said city . . . until such time as he and they shall severally attain to the age of 24 years.

5. William Cecil's Industrial Programme[3] [*Hist. MSS. Com. MSS. of the Marquis of Salisbury, Part I, pp.* 162–3], 1559. Considerations delivered to the Parliament, 1559.

1. *Vagabonds.*—That the statute 1 Edward VI, Chap. viii., concerning idle persons and vagabonds being made slaves, now repealed, be revived with additions.

2. *Labourers and Servants.*—That the Statutes 12 Richard

[1] This enactment is interesting as offering a precedent followed in the Statute of Artificers (No. 6 of this section), and as showing one of the social reasons for compulsory apprenticeship, which probably somewhat postponed the age of marriage. (See No. 11 of this section.)

[2] Quoted Dunlop and Denman, *English Apprenticeship and Child Labour*, pp. 52-3.

[3] Compare this with the following document (No. 6). It will be observed that Cecil's proposals as to wages are more drastic than the actual provision of the Statute of Artificers.

II, Chap. iii, "that no servant or labourer at the end of this term depart out of the hundred or place where he dwells," etc., and 13 Richard II, Chap. viii., ordering the Justices at every session to appoint by proclamation the wages of workers, etc., be confirmed with the addition "that no man hereafter receive into service any servant without a testimonial from the master he last dwelt with, sealed with a Parish Seal kept by the constable or churchwarden, witnessing he left with the free license of his master, penalty £10. So, by the hands of the masters, servants may be reduced to obedience, which shall reduce obedience to the Prince and to God also; by the looseness of the time no other remedy is left but by awe of law to acquaint men with virtue again, whereby the Reformation of religion may be brought in credit, with the amendment of manners, the want whereof has been imputed as a thing grown by the liberty of the Gospel, etc.

3. *Husbandry.*—That the Statutes, 4 Hen VII, Chap. 9, "for re-edifying houses of husbandry, and to avoid the decay of towns and villages," and 5 Edward VI, Chap. 5, "for maintenance of husbandry and tillage," be put in execution.

4. *Purchase of Lands.*—No husbandman, yeoman or artificer to purchase above 5*l.* by the year of inheritance, save in cities, towns and boroughs, for their better repair; one mansion house only to be purchased over and above the said yearly value. The common purchasing thereof is the ground of dearth of victuals, raising of rents, etc.

5. *Merchants.*—No merchant to purchase above £50 a year of inheritance, except aldermen and sheriffs of London, who, because they approach to the degree of knighthood, may purchase to the value of £200.

6. *Apprentices.*—None to be received apprentice except his father may spend 40*s.* a year of freehold, nor to be apprenticed to a merchant except his father spend £10 a year of freehold, or be descended from a gentleman a merchant. Through the idleness of these professions so many embrace them that they are only a cloak for vagabonds and thieves, and there is such a decay of husbandry that masters cannot get skilful servants to till the ground without unreasonable wages, etc.

. . .

6. AN ACT TOUCHING DIVERS ORDERS FOR ARTIFICERS, LABOURERS, SERVANTS OF HUSBANDRY AND APPRENTICES [5 *Eliz. c. iv. Statutes of the Realm, Vol. IV, Part I, pp.* 414–22], 1563.

I. Although there remain in force presently a great number of statutes concerning . . . apprentices, servants and labourers, as well in husbandry as in divers other . . . occupations, yet partly for the imperfection and contrariety . . . in sundry of the said laws, and for the variety and number of them, and chiefly for that the wages and allowances limited in many of the said statutes are in divers places too small . . . respecting the advancement of prices . . . . the said laws cannot conveniently without the greatest grief and burden of the poor labourer and hired man be put in due execution; and as the said statutes were at the time of the making of them thought to be very good and beneficial . . . , as divers of them yet are, so if the substance of as many of the said laws as are meet to be continued shall be digested and reduced into one sole law, and in the same an uniform order prescribed . . . , there is good hope that it will come to pass that the same law, being duly executed, should banish idleness, advance husbandry and yield unto the hired person both in the time of scarcity and in the time of plenty a convenient proportion of wages: Be it therefore enacted. . . . That as much of the statutes heretofore made as concern the hiring, keeping, departing, working, wages or order of servants, workmen, artificers, apprentices and labourers . . . shall be from and after the last day of September next ensuing repealed. . . .

II. No person after the aforesaid last day of September . . . shall be retained, hired or taken into service to work for any less time than for one whole year in any of the sciences . . . or arts of clothiers, woollen cloth weavers, tuckers, fullers, cloth workers, shearmen, dyers, hosiers, tailors, shoemakers, tanners, pewterers, bakers, brewers, glovers, cutlers smiths, farriers, curriers, sadlers, spurriers, turners, cappers, hat-makers or feltmakers, bowyers, fletchers, arrowhead-makers, butchers, cooks, or millers.

III. Every person being unmarried and every other person being under the age of thirty years that after the feast of Easter next shall marry, and having been brought up in any of the said arts [etc.] or that hath exercised any of them by the space of three years or more, and not having lands, tenements [etc.] copyhold or freehold of an estate of inheritance or for term of lives of the clear yearly value of 40*s*. nor being worth of his own goods the clear value of 10*l*., . . . , not being retained with any person in husbandry or in any of the aforesaid arts . . . nor in any other art, nor in household or in any office with any nobleman, gentleman or others, . . ., nor having a convenient farm or other holding in tillage whereupon he may employ his labour, shall (during the time that he shall so be unmarried or under the age of 30 years), upon request made by any person using the art or mystery wherein the said person so required hath been exercised as is aforesaid, be retained and shall not refuse to serve according to the tenor of this Statute upon the pain and penalty hereafter mentioned.

IV. No person which shall retain any servant shall put away his said servant, and no person retained according to this Statute shall depart from his master, mistress or dame before the end of his term, upon the pain hereafter mentioned, unless it be for some reasonable cause to be allowed before two Justices of Peace, or one at the least, or before the mayor or other chief officer of the city, borough or town corporate wherein the said master [etc.] inhabiteth, to whom any of the parties grieved shall complain; which said justices or chief officer shall have the hearing and ordering of the matter between the said master [etc.] and servant, according to the equity of the cause; and no such master [etc.] shall put away any such servant at the end of his term, or any such servant depart from his said master [etc.] at the end of his term, without one quarter warning given . . . upon the pain hereafter ensuing.

V. Every person between the age of 12 years and the age of 60 years not being lawfully retained nor apprentice with any fisherman or mariner haunting the seas, nor being in service with any carrier of any corn, grain or meal for provision of the city of London, nor with any husbandman in husbandry, nor in any city [etc.] in any of the arts . . . appointed by this Statute to have apprentices, nor being retained . . . for the digging . . . melting . . . making of any silver [or other metals, coal, etc.], nor being occupied in the making of any glass, nor being a gentleman born, nor being a student or scholar in any of the universities or in any school, nor having [lands or goods, as above, section 3], nor having a father or mother then living or other ancestor whose heir apparent he is then having lands [etc.] of the yearly value of £10 or above, or goods or chattels of the value of 40*l.*, nor being a necessary or convenient officer or servant lawfully retained as is aforesaid, nor having a convenient farm or holding . . . nor being otherwise lawfully retained according to the true meaning of this Statute, shall . . . . by virtue of this Statute be compelled to be retained to serve in husbandry by the year with any person that keepeth husbandry and will require any such person so to serve.

VI. [Penalty on masters unduly dismissing servants, 40*s.*: on servants unduly departing or refusing to serve, imprisonment.]

VII. None of the said retained persons in husbandry or in any of the arts or sciences above remembered, after the time of his retainer expired, shall depart forth of one city, town or parish to another nor out of the . . . hundred nor out of the county where he last served, to serve in any other city . . . or county, unless he have a testimonial under the seal of the said city or of the constable or other head officer and of two other honest householders of the city, town or parish where he last served, declaring his lawful departure, . . . , which testimonial shall be delivered unto the said servant and also registered by the parson of the parish where such master [etc.] shall dwell. . . .

VIII. [Penalty on a servant departing without such testimonial, imprisonment or whipping; on any one hiring him, 5*l.*]

IX. All artificers and labourers being hired for wages by the day or week shall betwixt the midst of the months of March and September be at their work at or before 5 of the clock in the morning, and continue at work until betwixt 7 and 8 of the clock at night, except it be in the time of breakfast, dinner or drinking, the which times at the most shall not exceed above 2½ hours in the day . . . and all the said artificers and labourers between the midst of September and the midst of March shall be at their work from the spring of the day in the morning until the night of the same day, except it be in time afore appointed for breakfast and dinner, upon pain to forfeit one penny for every hour's absence to be deducted out of his wages.

X. [Penalty on artificers, etc., breaking contract with employers, imprisonment and fine of 5*l.*]

XI. And for the declaration what wages servants, labourers and artificers, either by the year or day or otherwise, shall receive, be it enacted, That the justices of the peace of every shire . . . within the limits of their several commissions . . . and the sheriff of that county if he conveniently may, and every mayor, bailiff or other head officer within any city . . . wherein is any justice of peace, within the limits of the said city . . . shall before the 10th day of June next coming, and afterward yearly at every general sessions first to be holden after Easter, or at some time convenient within six weeks next following Easter, calling unto them such discreet and grave persons of the said county or city as they shall think meet, and conferring together respecting the plenty or scarcity of the time and other circumstances necessary to be considered, have authority within the limits of their several commissions to rate and appoint the wages as well of such of the said artificers . . . or any other labourer, servant or workman whose wages in time past hath been by any law rated and appointed, as also the wages of all other labourers, artificers [etc.] which have not been rated, as they shall think meet to be rated [etc.] by the year or by the day, week, month or other wise, with meat and drink or without meat and drink, and what wages every workman or labourer shall take by the great for mowing, reaping or threshing [and other agricultural employment] and for any other kind of reasonable labours or service, and shall yearly, before the 12th day of July next after the said assessment made, certify the same . . . with the considerations and causes thereof into the Court of Chancery[1]; whereupon it shall be lawful to the Lord Chancellor of England [or] Lord Keeper upon declaration thereof to the Queen's Majesty . . . or to the Lords and others of the Privy Council to cause to be printed and sent down before the 1st day of September next after the said certificate into every county . . . proclamations containing the several rates appointed . . . with commandment . . . to all persons . . . straitly to observe the same, and to all Justices [etc.] to see the same duly and severely observed . . .; upon receipt whereof the said

[1] This provision was repealed in 1597.

Sheriffs, Justices [etc.] shall cause the same proclamation to be entered of record . . . and shall forthwith in open markets upon the market days before Michaelmas then ensuing cause the same proclamation to be proclaimed . . . and to be fixed in some convenient place . . . : and if the said sheriffs, justices [etc.] shall at their said general sessions or at any time after within six weeks . . . think it convenient to retain for the year then to come the rates of wages that they certified the year before or to change them, then they shall before the said 12th day of July yearly certify into the said Court of Chancery their resolutions, to the intent that proclamations may accordingly be renewed and sent down, and if it shall happen that there be no need of any alteration . . . then the proclamations for the year past shall remain in force. . . .

XII. [Penalty on Justices absent from sessions for rating wages, 5*l*.]

XIII. [Penalty for giving wages higher than the rate, ten days' imprisonment and fine of 5*l*.; for receiving the same, twenty-one days' imprisonment.] NB

XIV. [Penalty on servants, etc., assaulting masters, etc., one year's imprisonment.]

XV. Provided that in the time of hay or corn harvest the Justices of Peace and also the constable or other head officer of every township upon request . . . may cause all such artificers and persons as be meet to labour . . . to serve by the day for the mowing. . . or inning of corn, grain and hay, and that none of the said persons shall refuse so to do, upon pain to suffer imprisonment in the stocks by the space of two days and one night. . . .

XVI. [Proviso for persons going harvesting into other counties.]

XVII. Two justices of peace, the mayor or other head officer of any city (etc.] and two aldermen or two other discreet burgesses . . . if there be no aldermen, may appoint any such woman as is of the age of 12 years and under the age of 40 years and unmarried and forth of service . . . to be retained or serve by the year or by the week or day for such wages and in such reasonable sort as they shall think meet; and if any such woman shall refuse so to serve, then it shall be lawful for the said justices [etc.] to commit such woman to ward until she shall be bounden to serve as aforesaid.

XVIII. And for the better advancement of husbandry and tillage and to the intent that such as are fit to be made apprentices to husbandry may be bounden thereunto, . . . every person being a householder and having half a ploughland at the least in tillage may receive as an apprentice any person above the age of 10 years and under the age of 18 years to serve in husbandry until his age of 21 years at the least, or until the age of 24 years as the parties can agree . . .

XIX. Every person being an householder and 24 years old at the least, dwelling in any city or town corporate and exercising any art, mistery or manual occupation there, may after the feast of St. John Baptist next coming . . . retain the son of any freeman not occupying husbandry nor being a labourer and inhabiting in the same or in any other city or town incorporate, to be bound as an apprentice after the custom and order of the city of London for 7 years at the least, so as the term of such apprentice do not expire afore such apprentice shall be of the age of 24 years at the least.

XX. Provided that it shall not be lawful to any person dwelling in any city or town corporate exercising any of the misteries or crafts of a merchant trafficking into any parts beyond the sea, mercer, draper, goldsmith, ironmonger, embroiderer or clothier that doth put cloth to making and sale, to take any apprentice or servant to be instructed in any of the arts [etc.] which they exercise, except such servant or apprentice be his son, or else that the father or mother of such apprentice or servant shall have . . . lands, tenements (etc.] of the clear yearly value of 40*s*. of one estate of inheritance or freehold at the least. . . .

XXI. From and after the said feast of St. John the Baptist next, it shall be lawful to every person being an householder and 24 years old at the least and not occupying husbandry nor being a labourer dwelling in any town not being incorporate that is a market town . . . and exercising any art, mistery or manual occupation . . . to have in like manner to apprentices the children of any other artificer not occupying husbandry nor being a labourer, which shall inhabit in the same or in any other such market town within the same shire, to serve as apprentices as is aforesaid to any such art [etc.]

as hath been usually exercised in any such market town where such apprentice shall be bound.

XXII. Provided that it shall not be lawful to any person dwelling in any such market town exercising the art of a merchant trafficking into the parts beyond the seas, mercer [etc. as above, section XX] to take any apprentice or in any wise to instruct any person in the arts [etc.] last before recited, after the feast of St. John Baptist aforesaid, except such servant or apprentice shall be his son, or else that the father or mother of such apprentice shall have lands [etc.] of the clear yearly value of 3*l.* of one estate of inheritance or freehold at the least. . . .

XXIII. From and after the said feast it shall be lawful to any person exercising the art of a smith, wheelwright, ploughwright, millwright, carpenter, rough mason, plaisterer, sawyer, lime-burner, brickmaker, bricklayer, tiler, slater, healyer, tilemaker, linen-weaver, turner, cooper, millers, earthen potters, woollen weaver weaving housewives' or household cloth only and none other, cloth-fuller otherwise called tucker or walker, burner of ore and wood ashes, thatcher or shingler, wheresoever he shall dwell, to have the son of any person as apprentice . . . albeit the father or mother of any such apprentice have not any lands, tenements or hereditaments.

XXIV. After the first day of May next coming it shall not be lawful to any person, other than such as now do lawfully exercise any art, mistery or manual occupation, to exercise any craft now used within the realm of England or Wales, except he shall have been brought up therein seven years at the least as apprentice in manner abovesaid, nor to set any person on work in such occupation being not a workman at this day, except he shall have been apprentice as is aforesaid, or else having served as an apprentice will become a journeyman or be hired by the year; upon pain that every person willingly offending shall forfeit for every default 40*s.* for every month.

XXV. Provided that no person exercising the art of a woollen cloth weaver, other than such as be inhabiting within the counties of Cumberland, Westmoreland, Lancaster, and Wales, weaving friezes, cottons or housewives' cloth only, making and weaving woollen cloth commonly sold by any clothier, shall have any apprentice or shall instruct any person in the science of weaving aforesaid in any place (cities, towns corporate, and market towns only except), unless such person be his son, or else that the father or mother of such apprentice or servant shall . . . have lands [etc.] to the clear yearly value of 3*l*. of an estate of inheritance or freehold . . . upon pain of forfeiture of 20*s*. for every month.

XXVI. Every person that shall have three apprentices in any of the said crafts of a cloth-maker, fuller, shearman, weaver, tailor or shoemaker shall keep one journeyman, and for every other apprentice above the number of the said three apprentices one other journeyman, upon pain of every default therein, 10*l*.

XXVII. [Proviso for worsted-makers of Norwich.]

XXVIII. If any person shall be required by any householder having half a ploughland at the least in tillage to be an apprentice and to serve in husbandry, or in any other kind of art before expressed, and shall refuse so to do, then upon the complaint of such housekeeper made to one Justice of Peace of the county wherein the said refusal is made, or of such householder inhabiting in any city, town corporate, or market town to the mayor, bailiffs or head officer of the said city [etc.] . . . they shall have full power to send for the same person so refusing; and if the said Justice or head officer shall think the said person meet to serve as an apprentice in that art . . . the said Justice or head officer shall have power . . . to commit him unto ward, there to remain until he will be bounden to serve . . . and if any such master shall evil entreat his apprentice . . . or the apprentice do not his duty to his master, then the said master or apprentice being grieved shall repair unto one Justice of Peace within the said county or to the head officer of the place where the said master dwelleth, who shall . . . take such order and direction between the said master and his apprentice as the equity of the case shall require; and if for want of good conformity in the said master the said Justice or head officer cannot compound the matter between him and his apprentice, then the said Justice or head officer shall take bond of the said master to appear at the next sessions then to be holden in the said county or within the said city [etc.] . . . and upon his appearance and hearing of the matter . . . if it be thought meet unto them to discharge the said apprentice, then the said Justices or four of them at the least, whereof one to be of the quorum, or the said head officer, with the consent of three other of his brethren or men of best reputation within the said city [etc.] shall have power . . . to pronounce that they have discharged the said apprentice of his apprenticehood . . .: and if the default shall be found to be in the apprentice, then the said Justices or head officer, with the assistants aforesaid, shall cause such due punishment to be ministered unto him as by their wisdom and discretions shall be thought meet.

XXIX. Provided that no person shall by force of this Statute be bounden to enter into any apprenticeship, other than such as be under the age of 21 years.

XXX. And to the end that this Statute may from time to time be . . . put in good execution . . . be it enacted, That the Justices of Peace of every county, dividing themselves into several limits, and likewise every mayor or head officer of any city or town corporate, shall yearly between the feast of St. Michael the Archangel and the Nativity of our Lord, and between the feast of the Annunciation of our Lady and the feast of the Nativity of St. John Baptist . . . make a special and diligent inquiry of the branches and articles of this Statute and of the good execution of the same, and where they shall find any defaults to see the same severely corrected and punished without favour . . . or displeasure.

XXXI. . . . Every Justice of Peace, mayor, or head officer, for every day that he shall sit in the execution of this Statute, shall have allowed unto him 5*s.* to be paid . . . of the fines [etc.] due by force of this Statute. . . .

XXXII. [Procedure for recovery of penalties.]

XXXIII. Provided always that this Act shall not be prejudicial to the cities of London and Norwich, or to the lawful liberties [etc.] of the same cities for the having of apprentices.

XXXIV. [Contracts of apprenticeship contrary to this Act to be void, and a penalty of 10*l.*]

XXXV. [Contracts of apprenticeship to hold good though made while the apprentice is under age.]

7. Proposals for the Better Administration of the Statute of Artificers [*S.P.D., Eliz., Vol.* 88, *No.* 11], 1572.

Whereas there passed an act in the Parliament holden at Westminster in the fifth year of the reign of our most gracious

Sovereign Lady the Queen's Majesty that now is, touching divers good and laudable orders for artificers, labourers, servants of husbandry, and apprentices; in the which act, amongst divers and sundry good branches therein contained, there are two specially to be noted, which, as it should seem, were then and therein specially enacted for the only means of the better maintaining of the same act in the full strength and virtue, according to the true meaning thereof: which have been, and yet daily are, as well by the subtle devices of some lewd servants, as also by the disorderly dealings of some masters, mistresses, and dames, not only neglected, but also wilfully violated and broken, whereby the true, good and godly meaning of the same act, for so good and laudable an order provided in that behalf, doth and will daily grow to be accounted as frustrate and of none effect: and as it now already is the chief, or only, cause of the great number of idle vagabonds, wherewith the realm at this present is so replenished: so, without it shall please the Queen's Majesty by good advice to provide some speedy remedy therefore, it will not only be a means of the increasing of them but also of their maintenance.

The two branches to be noted are these:—

The points wherein the masters, mistresses, dames, and servants do so abuse the two foresaid branches, that they be in a manner as frustrate.

It is too manifest, that divers and sundry servants, retained as well in husbandry as in other the arts and sciences aforesaid, and others out of those sciences throughout the whole Realm, do daily, notwithstanding this act, and without any fear of the penalty thereof, at their pleasures before the time of their covenanted service be expired, either purloin somewhat from their masters, mistresses, and dames, and so suddenly run away, or else, not willing to be rebuked for their faults, do quarrel with them, and so boldly depart away without any certificate[1] or testimonial for their discharge: and being thus disorderly departed do forge a testimonial, or get one to forge it for them, although they give 12*d.* or 2*s.* for the doing thereof, whereas, if they had orderly departed, [it] should have cost them but 2*d.*: and with such testimonial dare boldly pass from one shire to another, yea some time from

[1] For the working of the system of certificates. see No. 14, pp. 352–3.

one parish to another, and there be retained till they find the like means, or pick the like occasion to depart in like disorder. And the very cause why they dare thus boldly and disorderly depart, leaving their masters, mistresses, and dames destitute in their most need, is for that no order is kept, according to the Statute, in the making, signing, and delivering of the testimonials: but [they] be made by the masters themselves or by some other in their houses that can write, and being so disorderly made, do, as disorderly, sign and deliver the same without calling either parson, vicar, or other officer to the same: which is a very good cause for a very simple servant, seeing how slight a testimonial will serve him to pass with, to move him to forge the like at all times after to serve his turn. And yet if they were orderly made, signed, and delivered, according to Statute, it could no better serve his turn to pass with than one of these: for if he pass a shire or two off from the place where he last served, neither the marks nor names thereunto signed be there known scarce to one among a thousand.

For the second branch.—It is likewise too manifest, that there be many masters, mistresses and dames, knowing how much the order of these certificates or testimonials be abused, which have not letted to retain such servants so departed without showing any certificates or testimonials at all, willing for necessity's sake to retain rather a simple vagabond coming without his certificate, than a subtle vagabond coming with his forged testimonials, as he doubteth, and yet perchance is true indeed. But that is too hard for them to know, for that the names therein are to them unknown, and the places, far asunder, not easy to be tried: and so sometime an honest poor servant indeed passeth unhired for want of good order keeping in these testimonials, and a very vagabond indeed is some time hired in hope of his simplicity. And the masters, mistresses, and dames be commonly deceived by both kinds when they stand in most need of their service.

The cause why these good and laudable orders run to such decay by the foresaid abuses, is, for that no one person hath any benefit, worth the pains, and charges, to look to the redress hereof: the same being so hard and painful a matter to be done throughout the realm, and therewithall so chargeable.

Therefore if it may please the Queen's Majesty of her Highness' most gracious benignity, for the better and speedier reformation hereof, to appoint and give authority by her Majesty's Letters Patents for term of years unto us, her Highness' most humble subjects, Richard Carmarden and Edmond Mathew, our deputies and assigns, to give out one uniform order of testimonials to every shire and parish throughout the realm at our only costs and charges, taking therefore in recompense as well of our said costs and charges, as also for our travails which we shall bestow therein, no more than is already limited by the said Statute, which is but two pence for every testimonial:[1] and that also these articles here following may be annexed to the said Statute by this Parliament.

First, That there be no other certificates or testimonials used in the realm, to be delivered to any servants by any person or persons, but only such as shall be made and delivered by such as her Majesty hath or shall appoint by her Highness' Letters Patents to do the same.

Secondly, That every servant so departing and having received one of the same certificates or testimonials, and seeking again to serve, shall first deliver, to such as shall be there appointed to be the officer's deputies, his old testimonial cancelled, before he be again retained.

And thirdly, That none of the said certificates or testimonials, so orderly delivered to any servant, shall be any discharge for him to pass with for any longer time than for one month after the date thereof: and if any person be taken with any testimonial, the date thereof being so expired, then to be lawful for every head officer to take the said testimonial from him, and to deliver the same cancelled to the officer's deputy and to force him to serve or to be, etc.

8. Draft of a Bill Fixing Minimum Rates for Spinners and Weavers [*S.P.D., Eliz., Vol.* 244, *No.* 129], 1593.

An Act as well to avoid deceits done by spinners of woollen yarn, and weavers of woollen cloths, and to increase their wages, as also to reform the great abuses and oppressions done to her Majesty's good subjects by regrators of woollen yarn, commonly called yarn choppers or jobbers of yarn.

[1] For this method of delegating administration to private speculators see Section V of this Part, Nos. 14 and 22.

Forasmuch as divers Laws and Statutes have been heretofore ordained for the true making of woollen cloths, and divers penalties, in some cases of money, and in some other cases of the cloths themselves, are by the same Laws and Statutes imposed upon clothiers, by whom many thousands of her Majesty's subjects are set to work, and maintained; and that it falleth out many times, that divers faults punishable even with the loss of their cloths without the clothiers' fault are voluntarily committed by their spinners and weavers, by the one's deceitful spinning their yarn, and by the other's false weaving the same into cloth; and forasmuch as necessity doth partly enforce them thereunto, for lack of sufficient wages and allowance for their workmanship at the hands of the clothier, whereby to sustain the poor estate of themselves, their wives and children; at the humble petition as well of the said clothiers, as also of their said spinners and weavers, and first for the avoiding of all deceitful dealing between the clothiers and their weavers, Be it enacted by the Queen's most excellent Majesty, the Lords Spiritual and Temporal, and the Commons, in this present parliament assembled, and by the authority of the same:—That all wool which, after the feast of Easter next, shall be delivered for or by any clothier to any person or persons to be spun, shall be delivered by true and lawful weight, and that all and every spinner and spinners shall deliver again to or for such clothier yarn of the same wool by the same true and lawful weight (all necessary waste thereof excepted) without concealing any part thereof, or deceitfully putting thereunto any oil, water, or other thing, upon pain that every spinner doing the contrary shall forfeit four times the value that such deceit by any such spinner committed or done shall amount unto. And for the better relief of all and every the said spinner and spinners, be it further enacted by the authority aforesaid, that after the said feast all and every clothier and clothiers and spinsters to the market shall pay for the spinning of every pound weight of the best sorting warp three pence, of every pound weight of the second warp two pence halfpenny, of every pound weight of the worst warp to be used in sorting cloths two pence farthing, of every pound weight of the best abbs[1] two pence halfpenny, of every pound weight of the best sorting abbs two pence, and of every pound weight of the worst sorting abbs to be used

[1] *i.e.*, wefts.

in sorting cloths three halfpence farthing, of every pound weight of single list three halfpence, upon pain to forfeit for every penny that any such clothier shall withhold or detain from any spinner contrary to the charitable intent of this statute twelve pence.

To avoid all evil and corrupt dealing between clothiers and their weavers, be it enacted by the authority aforesaid:—That all and every weaver and weavers which after the said feast, shall have the weaving of any woollen yarn to be webbed into cloth, shall weave, work, and put into the web, for cloth to be made thereof, as much and all the same yarn, as any clothier, or any other person for or in the behalf of any clothier, shall deliver to the same weaver with his used mark put to the same, without changing, or any parcel thereof leaving out of the same web, or else shall restore to the same clothier the surplusage of the same yarn, if any shall be left not put into the same web, without deceitfully putting of any deceivable brine, moisture, sand, dust, or other thing thereunto, upon pain to forfeit four times the value that such deceit by any such weaver committed or done shall amount unto. And for the better relief of all and every the said weaver and weavers be it further enacted by the authority aforesaid, that after the said feast all and every clothier and clothiers shall pay for the weaving of every ell[1] containing three pounds weight in yarn, of every broad listed cloth, as it shall be laid upon the bar and which shall be woven in a fourteen hundred sley, sixteen pence, for the weaving of every ell, containing three pounds weight and three-quarters in yarn of every broad listed cloth, as it shall be laid upon the bar and which shall be woven in a thirteen hundred sley, fourteen pence, and for every beer[2] between thirteen hundred and fourteen hundred twelve pence,

[1] The words from "ell" to "fourteen hundred" have been crossed out in the original, and the rest of the passage as far as the end of the paragraph (p. 339) is bracketed as if for cancellation. Interlined is the following substituted clause, to be read after the words "for the weaving of every":—"of their best fine cloths vj*s.* viij*d.*, and for their second sort of fine cloths iiij*s.*, and for their least sort of fine cloths iij*s.*, and for the best sort of sorting cloths ij*s.*, and for the middle and least sort of sorting cloths or pack cloths with narrow lists, xviij*d.*, more than was given by any clothier in any of the said counties or elsewhere of like making for the weaving of every or any of the said sorts of cloths at or before the feast of Xmas last past."

[2] *i.e.*, the (variable) number of ends into which a warp is divided in the process of warping.

for the weaving of every ell containing three pounds weight and three-quarters at the least in yarn of every broad listed cloth as it shall be laid upon the bar and which shall be woven in a twelve hundred sley, ten pence, and for every beer between twelve hundred and thirteen hundred two shillings, for weaving of every ell containing three pounds weight and an half at the least in yarn of every broad listed cloth as it shall be laid upon the bar and which shall be woven in a eleven hundred sley, eight pence, and for every beer between eleven hundred and twelve hundred, twelve pence, for weaving of every ell containing three pounds weight and an half at the least in yarn of every broad listed cloth as it shall be laid upon the bar and which shall be woven in a ten hundred sley, six pence, and for every beer between ten hundred and eleven hundred twelve pence, for weaving of every broad listed cloth, that shall be woven in a sley under a ten hundred, and that shall contain thirty ells as it shall be laid upon the bar, twelve shillings, for the weaving of every broad listed cloth that shall be woven in a sley under a ten hundred, and that shall contain eight and twenty ells as it shall be laid upon the bar, ten shillings, for weaving of every narrow listed sorting cloth that shall be woven in a ten hundred sley, ten shillings, for the weaving of every narrow listed sorting cloth that shall be woven in a nine hundred sley, nine shillings, for the weaving of every narrow listed sorting cloth that shall be woven in an eight hundred sley, eight shillings, and for the weaving of every beer over and above in any of the said sleys of the said narrow listed cloths three pence, upon pain to forfeit for every penny that any clothier shall withhold or detain from any weaver contrary to the true intent of this act twelve pence.

And be it further enacted by the authority aforesaid that wheresoever any greater wages hath been heretofore usually given for spinning any of the sorts of yarn aforesaid or for weaving any of the sorts of cloths aforesaid, that there and in all such place the same wages or greater shall after the said feast be given without any diminution thereof, upon pain that every clothier shall forfeit for every penny that he or she shall so detain from any spinner or weaver contrary to the true intent of this act twelve pence, any the rate or wages before in this act particularly limited and appointed to weavers notwithstanding. And be it further enacted by the said authority, that after the said feast no clothier, for the weaving of any his or her white cloths, shall use or cause to be used any sley of less breadth than eleven quarters and three nails of the yard in white work beside the list, upon pain to forfeit for every such default ten shillings. And be it further enacted by the authority aforesaid that after the said feast no clothier shall use any warping bar that shall contain any greater length than three yards from one pin to another upon pain to forfeit for every such default ten shillings. And further be it enacted by the authority aforesaid that justices of assize in their circuits, justices of peace in their sessions, sheriffs in their turns, stewards in their leets and lawdays, mayors, sheriffs, and bailiffs of cities, boroughs and towns corporate in their courts, shall and may inquire, hear, and determine from time to time all and every the said offences committed and done within the limits of their several jurisdictions and authorities.

[Here follow provisions as to the division of fines.]

And forasmuch as divers evil-disposed persons commonly called yarn choppers or jobbers of woollen yarn, wanting the fear of God, and caring only for their own private gain without having any regard to the maintenance of the commonwealth, using no trade either of making woollen cloths, or of any other thing made of woollen yarn, inverting the true intent of the statute made in the eighth year of our late Sovereign Lord King Henry the sixth among other things especially to destroy the falsity of regrators of yarn called yarn choppers, to their own malicious purpose, do in every fair and market buy up and get into their hands so great quantities of woollen yarn, that the clothiers and others using lawful trade wherein woollen yarn must need be occupied, and by which trade many thousands of her Majesty's poor subjects are relieved, are driven for their necessity sake to buy the same at their hands deceitfully handled and at such unreasonable price as they list to set upon the same, whereby the clothiers and others using divers lawful ways and means for the employment of woollen yarn, are very greatly hindered, and such drones, idle members and evil weeds in a commonwealth by such oppressions maintained and greatly enriched, for remedy whereof be it enacted established and ordained by the authority aforesaid :—That no manner of person or persons shall after the said feast of Easter next buy, bargain, take, or make any promise for bargain or sale of or for any woollen yarn but only such person or persons as are known to be makers of woollen cloth or other thing made of woollen yarn or mixed with woollen yarn, his or their wife or wives or his or their children, apprentices or servants, inhabiting in his or their mansion house or houses, and who shall or may lawfully make of the said woollen yarn any kind of bayes, knit hose, arras, tapestry, coverlets, or any other thing or things used to be made of woollen yarn or mixed with woollen yarn, upon pain of forfeiture of all woollen yarn to be bought, or whereof any promise for bargain or sale thereof shall be taken or made contrary to the true meaning of this act, in whose hands soever any such woollen yarn shall be found, and further to incur all the pains and penalties limited to yarn choppers by the said act made in the eighth year of King Henry the sixth.

[Here follows provisions as to the division of fines.]

9. Draft Piece-list Submitted for Ratification to the Wiltshire Justices by Clothiers and Weavers [*Hist. MSS. Com., Vol. I, p.* 162, *The Records of Quar'er Sessions in the County of Wiltshire*], 1602.

Apud Trowbridge, 30 December A.o. xlv^to^ Eliza bethae Reginae.

The just proportions of the several works put forth by the Clothiers of the County of Wilts both to the Weavers and Spinners, with the valuation of the wages according as every sorts of work do deserve by reason of the fineness of the wool and spinning of every sort of work; as also by reason of the hard working of every sort with the usual numbers of hundreds, beers[1] and abbs which is commonly put forth to every several cloth, which is the best rate by which we can keep apportion, set down by us the clothiers of the said county.

Imprimis we think a weaver is worth to have for the weaving of a cloth of 700	vii*s*.
And for every beer above 700 and under 800 ..	iid.
The spinning of these sorts of warp is worth the pound	ii*d*.
And the spinning of the abb is worth the pound	1*d*. *ob*.
Item, one of 800 of white work is worth the weaving	viii*s*.
And for every beer above 800 and under 900[2] ..	ii*d*. *ob*.

[1] For the meaning of "beer" and "abb" see notes to document No. 8.
[2] Instead of "about 800 under 900," as printed in *op. cit.*

The spinning of these sorts of warp worth the pound	ii*d*. *ob*.
The spinning of the Abbe worth the pound ..	i*d*. *ob*.
These sorts of broad lists are more worth than the narrow lists by the cloth	xii*d*.
The hanking is worth	xii*d*.

[Scales are also given for 900, 1000, 1100, and 1200 lbs. A graduated rise in price varying from xii*d*. in the case of a cloth of 900 lbs. to ii*s*. for a cloth of 1100 to 1200 lbs. is awarded ; for every beere i*d*. up to vi*d*., and for every pound of abbe above 54 and not above 60 xviii*d*, and above 60 lbs. xx*d*.]

Clothiers Signing—

William Yerbury.
Nicholas Phippe.
John Usher.
Walter Yerbury.
John Yewe.
Edward Cogswell.
Richard Dycke.

Weavers Signing—

Hugh Watts.
Henry Cappe.
William Rundell.
Henry Prior.
Thomas Lavington.
Bartholomew Skege.

10. An Act Empowering Justices to Fix Minimum Rates of Payment [1 *James I, c.* 6. *Statutes of the Realm, Vol. IV, Part II, pp.* 1022–24], 1603–04.

. . . And whereas the said act [*i.e.* 5 Eliz., c. iv] hath not, according to the true meaning thereof, been duly put in execution, whereby the rates of wages for poor artificers, labourers and other persons whose wages were meant to be rated by the said act, have not been rated and proportioned according to the plenty, scarcity, necessity, and respect of the time, which was politicly intended by the said act, by reason that ambiguity and question have risen and been made whether the rating of all manner artificers, workmen and workwomen, his and their wages, other than such as by some statute and law have been rated, or else such as did work about husbandry, should or might be rated by the said law; Forasmuch as the said law hath been found beneficial for the commonwealth, be it enacted by authority of this present parliament, that the said statute, and the authority by the same statute given to any person or persons for assessing and rating of wages, and the authority to them in the said act committed, shall be expounded and construed, and shall by force of this act give authority to all persons having any such authority to rate wages of any labourers, weavers, spinsters, and workmen or workwomen whatsoever, either working by the day, week, month, year, or taking any work at any person or persons' hands whatsoever, to be done in great or otherwise. . . .

And furthermore be it enacted by the authority aforesaid, that if any clothier or other shall refuse to obey the said order, rate or assessment of wages as aforesaid, and shall not pay so much or so great wages to their weavers, spinsters, workmen or workwomen as shall be so set down rated and appointed, according to the true meaning of this act, that then every clothier and other person and persons so offending shall forfeit and lose for every such offence, to the party aggrieved, ten shillings: and that if the said offence and offences of not paying so much or so great wages to their said workmen, workwomen and others shall be confessed by the offender, or that the same shall be proved by two sufficient and lawful witnesses before the justices of peace in their quarter sessions of the peace, the justices of assize in their sessions, or before any two justices of the peace, whereof one to be of the quorum; that then every such person shall forthwith stand and be in law convicted thereof; which said forfeiture of ten shillings shall be levied by distress and sale of the offenders goods, by warrant from the said justices before whom any such conviction shall be had; which sale shall be good in law against any such offender or offenders. . . .

Provided nevertheless and be it enacted by the authority aforesaid, That no clothier, being a justice of peace in any precinct or liberty, shall be any rater of any wages for any weaver, tucker, spinster, or other artizan that dependeth upon the making of cloth; and in case there be not above the number of two justices of peace within such precinct or liberty but such as are clothiers, that in such case the same wages shall be rated and assessed by the major part of the common council of such precinct or liberty, and such justice or justices of peace (if any there be) as are not clothiers.

11. ADMINISTRATION IN WILTSHIRE OF ACTS REGULATING THE MANUFACTURE OF CLOTH [*Hist. MSS. Com., Vol. I, pp.* 74–5], 1603.

Orders agreed upon for the occupation of weavers.[1]

First, that no person using the trade of weaving woollen cloth be suffered to keep more looms than that the statute made a° v^{to} Elizabethae alloweth. 2. *Item*, that all such persons as are now permitted to be master weaver, and themselves have not served their full term of apprenticeship, whether he be above or under the age of xxxtie years and married or unmarried, shall not make or take any apprentice to serve him as apprentice hereafter, neither shall any serve him as an apprentice. 3. *Item*, that every such person permitted to be a master weaver which hath not served his full years of apprenticeship shall not keep above one loom going; and no apprentice to work with him but a journeyman or journeymen. 4. *Item*, none hereafter to be made apprentice to the art of weaving broad cloth but according to the form of the statute *ut supra*. 5. *Item*, that all such as are now allowed to be apprentices, their names to be registered, and none hereafter to be made apprentices but such persons as are appointed overseers of the said occupation to be first made acquainted thereof, to the end no abuse may be suffered, nor unlawful shift used to defraud the true meaning of the said statute. 6. *Item*, that no weaver shall sell his apprentice and take another before the first have served seven years. 7. *Item*, that none shall work as a journeyman except he bring certificate that he hath served full seven years, or his master to testify the same. 8. *Item*, that no clothman shall keep above one loom in his house, neither any weaver that hath a ploughland shall keep more than one loom in his house. 9. *Item*, that no weaver shall keep two apprentices in one loom working except one of them be in his last year. 10. *Item*, that no apprentice shall come forth of his covenant of apprenticeship before he be four and twenty years of age, to avoid young marriages and the increase of poor people. 11. *Item*, that no person or persons shall keep any loom or looms going in any other house or houses beside

[1] The original heading, for which that above was afterwards substituted, runs:—"A table to be presented for and concerning the occupation of weaving by the sworn men unto Henry Priour authorized for that purpose." It is probable that the "sworn men" were clothiers and weavers (see No. 9), and that Henry Priour was a justice.

their own, or maintain any to do the same. 12. *Item*, that all those that have entered into the trade of broad weaving contrary to the statute within these two years may be expelled and put from the same trade, and all those that are journeyman (*sic*) and have not served their time, if they be not married, may return and serve their seven years out, or else to be put from their occupation. 13. *Item*, that all those that are entered in contrary to the statute, having other things to live upon, may be expelled, and put from the trade. 14. *Item*, that all weavers dwelling in any town corporate, borough, or market town, may call into their fellowship all weavers dwelling within three miles compass of any of the said towns, as well journeymen and [as ?] masters, and that there may be so many overseers of these said companies as may be fit for the same. 15. *Item*, that every master weaver of these several companies may have a meeting once every quarter, whereby they may have the examination of those things that may be amiss amongst them, to the end no disorder rise amongst them as in time past hath been, and that every broad weaver keeping a loom may give quarterly iv*d*. towards the relief of their poor brethren that shall need. 16. *Item*, that the master of every several company may call before them every particular offender in matters pertaining to their occupation, whether it be master or journeyman or apprentice, to the end that drunkenness, idleness, or pilfering of their masters' stuff may be punished by laws fit for any of these offences. 17. *Item*, that any of those that shall disobey any of these good orders that are set down, that there may be such penalties inflicted upon any such persons as may be able to suffice them, and shall be agreeable with the laws of the realm, and by such persons as are thereunto authorised by the statutes and laws.

James Martin.	Hen. Poole.
Henry Martyn.	James Ley.
G. Tooker.	Thos. Hungerforde.
	Edmund Lamberte.

12. Assessment made by the Justices of Wiltshire, Dealing Mainly with other than Textile Workers [*Hist. MSS. Com., Vol. I, pp.* 162–167, *The Records of Quarter Sessions in the County of Wilts*], 1604.

. . . third day of May in the first year of our Sovereign

Lord James by the grace of God King of England . . . Defender of the Faith, and upon diligent respect and consideration by . . . for the time . . . according to the form of a statute made in the first[1] year of the reign of our late Sovereign Lady Queen . . . hereafter particularly ensueth.

Wages by the year for husbandry.

A bailiff of husbandry shall not take by the year of wages above liii*s*. iiii*d*. and a livery or x*s*. for the same.

A chief shepherd which keepeth one thousand sheep and above shall not take by the year of wages above xl*s*., and a livery or viii*s*. for the same, and pasture or feeding for xx*ti* sheep all the year or xii*d*. for every of them.

A shepherd which keepeth six hundred sheep shall not take of wages above xxiii*s*. iii*d*., and a livery or vi*s*. for the same, and feeding for ten sheep all the year or xii*d*. for every of them.

A chief hind of husbandry and a chief carter shall not take by the year of wages above xl*s*. and a livery or viii*s*.

A common servant of husbandry and a common shepherd above the age of xxi years shall not take by the year [either of] them of wages above xxxiii*s*. iiii*d*. and a livery or vi*s*. viii*d*. for the same.

All other servants and shepherds under xxi years and above xvi years shall not take by the year of wages above xx*s*. and a livery or v*s*. for the same.

A chief woman servant shall not take by the year of wages above xxx*s*. and a livery or vi*s*. for the same.

Every other woman servant above xvi years of age shall not take by the year of wages above xx*s*. and a livery or v*s*. for the same.

Wages by the day for labourers in harvest and at all other times of the year in husbandry.

Mowers of grain by the day with meat and drink shall not take of wages above v*d*. and without meat and drink not above x*d*.

Men labourers in haymaking or gripping of lent corn shall not take by the day with meat and drink of wages above iiii*d*. and without meat and drink not above viii*d*.

Women labourers in haymaking or gripping of lent corn shall

[1] A mistake for fifth (see No. 6).

not take by the day with meat and drink of wages above iii*d.* and without not above vi*d.*

Mowers of corn shall not take by the day with meat and drink of wages above v*d*, and without meat and drink not above x*d.*

Men reapers of wheat and rye shall not take by the day with meat and drink of wages not above v*d.* and without meat and drink not above x*d.*

Women reapers of wheat and rye shall not take by the day with meat and drink not above iiii*d.* and without meat and drink not above ix*d.*

Every hedger, ditcher, thresher and other like labourer in husbandry not afore named shall not take by the day from Michaelmas to the Annunciation of our Lady of wages with meat and drink not above iii*d.*, and without meat and drink not above vii*d.*, and that at the election of the hirer; and from the Annunciation of our Lady unto Michaelmas of wages by the day with meat and drink not above iiii*d.*, and without meat and drink not above viii*d.*, and that at the election of the hirer.

Wages for Taskwork without Meat and Drink.

For reaping and binding of wheat, rye, or beans, for every acre by the lug not above xx*d.*

Mowing of barley for every acre by lug not above v*d.*

Mowing of oats for every acre by lug not above iiii*d.*

Hacking or hawming of pease or fatches for every acre by lug not above xii*d.*

Mowing of grass for every acre by lug not above x*d.*

Making of hay for every acre by lug not above ix*d.*

Threshing of wheat, rye, pease, beans, or fatches, for every quarter, not above x*d.*

Threshing of barley or oats for every quarter not above vi*d.*

Ditching, planting, and hedging of a perch containing sixteen foot and a half in length, three foot in depth, and five foot in breadth in gravel or stony ground, and setting the same with two chests of plants and making hedge for every perch, not above vi*d.*

Ditching, planting, and hedging after the same order in other sandy or easy grounds, by the lug of like awise not above v*d.*

Making of hedge for every perch not above 1*d.*

Making of plaisted hedge and other fenced hedge more strong and scouring of the ditch, for every perch not above ii*d.*

Paling and railing with one rail, felling and clearing of timbe and digging of the holes for the posts, for every perch not above x*d*.

Railing with double rails with felling and clearing of timbe and digging of the holes for the posts, for every perch not abov v*d*.

Railing with single rail after the same sort, for every perc not above iii*d*.

Sawing of board or timber for every hundred not above xvii*d*

Wages by the day for these artificers following.

For a Master Carpenter ..
For a Master Free Mason
For a Master rough Mason
For a Master Bricklayer ..
For a Master Plumber ..
For a Master Glazier ..
For a Master Carver ..
For a Master Joiner ..
For a Master Millwright ..
For a Master Wheelwright
For a Master Plasterer ..

None of these shall take by th day from Michaelmas to th Annunciation of our Lady wit meat and drink of wages no above v*d*., and without meat an drink not above x*d*. And from the Annunciation o our Lady to Michaelmas no above vi*d*. with meat and drink and without meat and drink no above xi*d*. by the day.

For every common workman or journeyman of thes sciences from Michaelmas to the Annunciation of our Lady c wages by the day with meat and drink not above iii*d*., an without meat and drink not above vii*d*.; and from the Annun ciation of our Lady to Michaelmas with meat and drink no above iiii*d*., and without meat and drink not above vii*d*.

For every apprentice of these sciences and for every laboure to attend to serve them, from Michaelmas to the Annunciatio of our Lady with meat and drink not above ii*d*., and withou meat and drink not above v*d*., and from the Annunciatio of our Lady to Michaelmas with meat and drink not abov iii*d*., and without meat and drink not above vii*d*.

Wages by the day for these occupations following:—

For a chief ploughwright by the day from Michaelmas t the Annunciation of our Lady with meat and drink not abov iiii*d*., and without meat and drink not above viii*d*.; and fro the Annunciation of our Lady to Michaelmas with meat an drink not above v*d*., and without meat and drink not above x

For sawyers the couple from Michaelmas to the Annunciatio of our Lady with meat and drink not above viii*d*., and witho meat and drink not above xvi*d.*; and from the Annunciation of our Lady to Michaelmas with meat and drink not above x*d.*, and without meat and drink not above xviii*d.* So always that the owner of the saw do have for every day 1*d.* more than his fellow.

For a Hellyer or Tiler ..	Every one of these to take by the day from Michaelmas to the Annunciation of our Lady with meat and drink not above iii*d.*, and without meat and drink not above vii*d.*
For a Shingler	
For a Brickmaker ..	
For a Limeburner ..	
For a Lathmaker ..	
For a Quarrier ..	
For a Pavier or Pitcher	
For a Collier	And from the Annunciation of our Lady to Michaelmas with meat and drink not above iiii*d.*, and without meat and drink not above viii*d.*
For a Bondcaster ..	
For a Thatcher ..	
For a Chandler ..	
For a Tinker	
For a Painter	

Wages by the year for the journeymen of these occupations following with meat and drink.

For a miller by the year with meat and drink of wages not bove xl*s.* and a livery, or vi*s.* viii*d.* for the same.

For a loader to the mill of wages not above xxvi*s.* viii*d.* and livery, or vi*s.* for the same.

For a dyer, for a brewer, for a tanner, for a linen weaver, he chiefest to take by the year of wages not above l*s.*, and ll other common workmen of the same occupation of wages y the year not above xl*s.* without any livery.

Shoemaker ..	The chiefest of these to take by the year of wages not above xl*s.*
Currier	
Woollen Weaver..	
Tucker	
Fuller	
Shearman ..	
Clothworker ..	
Hosier	and every common workman of the same occupations to take by the year of wages not above xxvi*s.* viii*d.*
Tailor	
Baker	
Glover	
Girdler	

A Spurrier .. ..
A Capper .. ..
A Hatter .. ..
A Feltmaker ..
A Bowyer .. ..
A Fletcher .. ..
An Arrowhead-maker
A Butcher .. ..
A Fishmonger ..
A Pewterer ..
A Cutler .. ..
A Smith .. ..
A Sadler .. ..
A Furrier or Skinner
A Parchment-maker
A Cooper .. ..
A Earthen Potmaker
A Turner .. ..

The chiefest of these to take by the year of wages not above xl*s.*

and every common workman of the same occupations to take by the year of wages not above xxvi*s.* viii*d.*

Every master weaver or chief workman in that trade, working duly and truly, shall have of wages for weaving of a cloth of what sort soever after the rate of [*blank*] the day and every other ordinary workman of that trade, working as aforesaid, shall have for weaving of a cloth of what sort soever after the rate of [*blank*]; but they shall not take their wages for every day that they shall be about the making of a cloth, but only for so many days as good workmen of that trade following their labour duly and painfully may, if they will, make such a cloth.

Every master tucker, following his labour duly and painfully, shall take of wages by the week not above [*blank*], and every ordinary workman of the same trade, following his labour as aforesaid, shall take of wages by the week not above [*blank*]. Every woman spinner's wage shall be such as, following her labour duly and painfully, she may make it account to [*blank*] the day.

James Mervin.
Wm. Eyre.
Edw. Penruddock.
Jasper More.
John Dauntsey.
Alexander Tutt.
Jo. Ernlle.
James Ley.
Henry Martyn.

13. Assessment Made by the Justices of Wiltshire, Dealing Mainly with Textile Workers [*Hist. MSS. Com., Vol. I, pp.* 167-168, *The Records of Quarter Sessions in the County of Wilts*], 1605.

Wiltshire.—The declaration of the general rates of wages of servants, labourers, artificers, handycraftsmen, weavers, spinsters, workmen and workwomen within the foresaid county assessed and rated by the Justices of the Peace of the foresaid county, whose hands and seals are hereunder to these presents set, at the General Sessions of the Peace of the said county holden at the Devizes in the said county the ninth day of April in the year of the reign of our Sovereign Lord James by the grace of God, etc. . . ., according to the Statutes in that case made and provided.

Imprimis, that the rates of the wages of servants, labourers, artificers, and handicraftsmen within the said county shall continue and be for this year now next ensuing in all respects as they were rated and assessed the last year next before.

Item that the rates of wages of the weavers and spinsters shall be for this year now next ensuing as follows, viz. :—

	A weaver for weaving a cloth of 700 ..	vii*s.*
	And for every beer[1] above 700 and under 800	ii*d.*
700	A spinner for spinning of a pound of these sorts of warp shall have	ii*d.*
	And for a pound of abb spinning ..	i*d.* ob.
	Item for weaving of a cloth of 800 ..	viii*s.*
	And for every beer above 800 and under 900	ii*d.* ob.
800	A spinner for spinning of a pound of these sorts of warp shall have	ii*d.* ob.
	And for a pound of abb	i*d.* ob.
	For a weaving of a broad listed white of this making	ix*s.*
	For the hanking thereof	xii*d.*
	Item for weaving of a cloth of 900 ..	ix*s.*
	For every beer above 900 and under 1000 ..	iii*d.*
900	A spinner for spinning of a pound of these sorts of warp shall have	ii*d.* ob. q.
	For the spinning of a pound of abb of that sort	i*d.* ob. q.
	And for every pound of abb wrought into a cloth above 54 and not above 60 ..	xii*d.*

[1] For the meaning of "beer" and "abb" see notes to document No. 8.

	Item for weaving of a cloth of 1000 ..	x*s*.
	For every beer above 1000 and under 1100	iiii*d*.
1000	For every pound of abb above 54 and not above 60	xii*d*.
	For every pound of abb above 60 ..	xvi*d*.
	A spinner for spinning of a pound of these sorts of warp shall have	iii*d*. ob.
	And for a pound of abb	ii*d*.
	Item for weaving of a cloth of 1100 being narrow listed with 54*li* of abb	xii*s*.
	For every beer above 1100 and not above 1200	vi*d*.
	For every pound of abb above 54 and not above 60	xviii*d*.
1100	For every pound of abb above 60 pound	xx*d*.
and	A spinner for spinning a pound of these	
1200	sorts of warp shall have	iiii*d*.
	And for a pound of abb.	ii*d*. ob.
	For weaving of the broad listed whites of the three sorts of cloth next before mentioned	xiii*s*. vi*d*.
	For the hanking of them	xii*d*.

James Mervin.
Wa. Longe.
Wm. Eyre.
Jo. Ernele.
Jaspar More.
Edward Penrudock.
H. Sadler.
Jo. Dauntesey.
John Hungerford.
Wm. Bayles.
Jo. Warneford.

W. Blacker.
Edw. Rede.
Henry Martyn.
G. Tooker.
Anth. Hungerford.
La. Hyde.

14. Administration of the Wage Clauses of the Statute of Artificers [*Atkinson, North Riding Quarter Sessions, Vol. I, pp.* 27, 60, 69, 99, 105], 1605–8.

Jan. 17th, 1605. [Presented by the Jury.] John Bulmer of West Cottam, husbandman, for hiring servants without recording their names and salaries before the Chief Constable, *contra formam statuti*, etc., and also Rob. Harrison and Will Keldell both of the same, for the like. . . .

Helmesly, Jan. 8, 1606. The inhabitants of Thirkleby, (Great and Little), for refusing to give the names of their servants and their wages to the constables of the said town or to the Head Constables. The inhabitants of Kilbornes, Over and Nether, for the like and for giving their servants more wages than the statute doth allow.

Thomas Gibson, of Easingwold, for retaining and accepting into his service one Will Thompson without shewing to the Head Officer, Curate or Churchwarden any lawful testimonial.

Will Burnett, of Bawker, for refusing to pay pence for entering his servants' names; Cuthbert Ivyson, of Awdwarke, husbandman, for retaining Tim Johnson, servant, at husbandry for 46*s*., contrary to the rates assessed by the Justices.

Thirske, April 14, 1607. Thomas Grange of East Harlesey, for refusing to give a note of his servants and their wages.

Malton, Jan. 12, 1607. Jane Kay of Fawdington within the constabulary of Bagby, for denying to give the names of her servants, nor tickets nor rates of her servants.

Malton, Jan. 12, 1607. Alice Sharrow, of New Milnes in Seazey parish, for taking more wages of Will Bell of Rascall than, etc.

Malton, Jan. 12, 1607. Thos. Wawne of Thorp Rawe, yeoman, for giving wages to . . . Rymer his servant, exceeding the rate set down by the Justices.

15. Administration of the Apprenticeship Clauses of the Statute of Artificers [*Atkinson, North Riding Quarter Sessions, Vol. I, pp.* 106 and 121], 1607–8.

Malton, Jan. 12, 1607. [Presented by the Jury.] Thomas Cooke, . . . webster, for trading, having never served vii years' apprentice. . . .

Rob. Pybus of Beedall, for buying barley to malt to sell without license, and also useth the trade of malting, he being a very young man, unmarried, which is contrary to the statute.

Helmesley, July 12, 1608. Rob. Richardson of Sawdon, carpenter, for using that trade, having been but two years apprentice.

Fr. Storry of Gristropp, carpenter, for retaining one John Milborne and John Palmer as apprentices without indenture.

16. The Organisation of the Woollen Industry[1] [*S.P.D. James I, Vol.* LXXX, 13], 1615.

The breeders of wool in all countries are of three sorts—

1. First those that are men of great estate, having both grounds and stock of their own, and are beforehand in wealth. These can afford to delay the selling of their wools and to stay the clothiers' leisure for the payment to increase the price. The number of these is small.

2. Those that do rent the king's, noblemen's and gents' grounds and deal as largely as either their stock or credit will afford. These are many and breed great store of wool; most of them do usually either sell their wools beforehand, or promise the refusal of them for money which they borrowed at the spring of the year to buy them sheep to breed the wool, they then having need of money to pay their Lady-day rent and to double their stock upon the ground as the spring time requireth, and at that time the clothiers disburse their stock in yarns to lay up in stock against hay-time and harvest when their spinning fails. So that then farmers and clothiers have greatest want of money at one time.

3. The general number of husbandmen in all the wool countries that have small livings, whereof every one usually hath some wool, though not much. They are many in numbers in all countries and have great store of wool, though in small parcels. Many of these also do borrow money of the wool merchant to buy sheep to stock their commons. Their parcels being so small, the times of selling so divers, the distance of place so great between the clothier and them, it would be their undoing to stay the clothier's leisure for the time of their sale, or to be subject to him for the price. . . .

These wools are usually converted by four sorts of people.

1. The rich clothier that buyeth his wool of the grower in the wool countries, and makes his whole year's provision beforehand and lays it up in store, and in the winter time hath it spun by his own spinsters and woven by his own weavers and fulled by his own tuckers, and all at the lowest rate for wages. These clothiers could well spare the wool buyers that they might likewise have wool at their own prices, and the rather because

[1] Quoted Unwin, *Industrial Organization in the Sixteenth and Seventeenth Centuries*, App. A, II.

many of them be brogging clothiers and sell again very much, if not most, of the wool they buy.

2. The second is the meaner clothier that seldom or never travels into the wool country to buy his wool, but borrows the most part of it at the market, and sets many poor on work, clothes it presently, and sells his cloth in some countries upon the bare thread, as in Devonshire and Yorkshire, and others dress it and sell it in London for ready money, and then comes to the wool market and pays the old debt and borrows more. Of this sort there are great store, that live well and grow rich and set thousands on work; they cannot miss the wool chapman, for if they do they must presently put off all their work-folk, and become servants to the rich clothier for 4*d.* or 6*d.* a day, which is a poor living.

3. The third sort are such clothiers that have not stock enough to bestow, some in wool and some in yarn, and to forbear some in cloth as the rich clothiers do, and they buy but little or no wool, but do weekly buy their yarn in the markets, and presently make it into cloth and sell it for ready money, and so buy yarn again; which yarn is weekly brought into the markets by a great number of poor people that will not spin to the clothier for small wages; but have stock enough to set themselves on work, and do weekly buy their wool in the market by very small parcels according to their use and weekly return it in yarn, and make good profit thereof, having their benefit both of their labour and of the merchandise, and live exceeding well. These yarn-makers are so many in number that it is supposed by men of judgment that more than half the cloths that are made in Wilts, Gloucester, and Somersetshire is made by the means of these yarn-makers and poor clothiers that depend weekly upon the wool chapman, which serves them weekly with wool either for money or credit.

4. The fourth sort is of them of the new drapery, which are thousands of poor people inhabiting near the ports and coasts from Yarmouth to Plymouth and in many great cities and towns, as London, Norwich, Colchester, Canterbury, Southampton, Exeter and many others. These people by their great industry and skill do spend a great part of the coarse wools growing in the kingdom, and that at as high a price or higher than the clothiers do the finest wools of this country, as appeareth by a particular hereunto annexed. . . .

17. PROCEEDINGS ON APPRENTICESHIP CLAUSES OF 5 ELIZ., c. 4 [*Reports of Special Cases Touching Several Customs and Liberties of the City of London, collected by Sir H. Calthrop*, 1655], 1615.

Hil. 12, *Iac.* 1 [Tolley's case]. It was agreed and resolved that an upholsterer is not a trade within that Stat. For first it is not a trade that is mentioned in any of the branches of the Statute, howsoever in all parts of the Statute there is mention made of 61 several trades and misteries. And if the artizans which at that time were assistants unto the committees for the expressing of all manner of trades had thought that the trade of an upholsterer had been such a trade that required art and skill for the encouraging of it, they would not have failed to make mention of it. . . . Thirdly the trade of an upholsterer doth not require any art or skill for the exercizing of it, inasmuch as he hath all things made to his hand, and it is only to dispose them in order after such time as they are brought to him. . . . and so he is like Aesop's bird which borroweth of every bird a feather, his art resting merely in the overseeing and disposition of such things which other men work, and in the putting of feathers into tick, and sewing them up when he hath done, the which one that hath been an apprentice unto it but seven days is able to perform. And the intent of this Statute was not to extend unto any other trade but such as required art and skill for the managing of them; and therefore it was adjudged in the Exchequer upon an information against one in the 42nd year of the late Queen Eliz. that a costermonger was not a trade intended by the Statute of 5 Eliz., because his art was in the selling of apples, which required no skill or experience for the exercise of it. So an husbandman, tankardbearer, brickmaker, porter, miller, and such like trades are not within the Statute of 5 Eliz., cap 4, so as none may exercize them but such a one as hath been an apprentice by the space of 7 years; for they are arts which require ability of body rather than skill.

18. A PETITION TO FIX WAGES ADDRESSED TO THE JUSTICES BY THE TEXTILE WORKERS OF WILTSHIRE [*Historical MSS. Commission, Vol. I, p. 94. The Records of Quarter Sessions in the County of Wilts.*], 1623.

May it please you to be informed of the distressed estate

of most of the weavers, spinners, and others that work on the making of woollen clothes, that are not able by their diligent labours to get their livings, by reason that the clothiers at their will have made their work extreme hard, and abated wages what they please. And some of them make such their work-folks to do their household businesses, to trudge in their errands, spool their chains, twist their list, do every command, without giving them bread, drink, or money for many days' labour. May it please you therefore, for the redressing of these enormities done by the clothiers, to appoint certain grave and discreet persons to view the straitness of works, to assess rates for wages according to the desert of their works, now especially in this great dearth of corn, that the poor artificers of these works of woollen cloth may not perish for want of food, while they are painful in their callings, so shall many families be bound to pray for your worships' happiness and eternal felicity.

Order signed by nine justices.

The petitioners to set down their names to this petition, and the place of their dwelling, and the clothiers dwelling next to the places of their habitations to be warned to be at Devizes the Thursday in the next Whitsun week, to confer with us hereabouts, that they call others grieved herein to attend us at that time.[1]

19. Appointment by Privy Council of Commissioners to Investigate Grievances of Textile Workers in East Anglia [*Privy Council Register. Charles I, Vol.* 6, *pp.* 350-1], 1630.

At Whitehall the 16th February, 1630.

Present:

Lord Treasurer.	Lord V. Wentworth.
Lord Privy Seal	Lord V. Falkland.
Lord High Chamberlain.	Lord Bishop of Winton.
Earl Marshall.	Lord Newburgh.
Earl of Dorset.	Mr. Treasurer.
Lord V. Dorchester.	Mr. Comptroller.

Mr. Secretary Coke.

Whereas a petition was this day presented to the Board

[1] The final result of the meeting was that the Justices ordered the rates fixed to be published on market day at Devizes.

by Sylvia Harbert, widow, on the behalf of herself and divers others, showing that the poor spinsters, weavers and combers of wool in Sudbury and the places near adjoining thereunto, in the counties of Suffolk and Essex, are of late by the clothiers there (who are now grown rich by the labours of the said poor people) so much abridged of their former and usual wages, that they (who in times past maintained their families in good sort) are now in such distress by the abatement of their wages in these times of scarcity and dearth, that they are constrained to sell their beds, wheels and working tools for want of bread, as by the petition itself doth more at large appear, wherein the petitioners humbly sought to be relieved by some directions from this Board :—their Lordships upon consideration had thereof, have thought fit and ordered that the petition being first signed by the Clerk of the Council attendant shall be recommended to Sir Robert Crane, Bart., Sir Thomas Wiseman, Sir William Maxey, Sir Drewe Deane, Kt., Thomas Eden, Doctor of the Civil Law, Henry Gent, Esq., and Robert Warren, Justices of the Peace of the counties aforesaid, Richard Skinner and Benjamin Fisher, Aldermen of Sudbury, or to any four of them, whereof one Justice of the Peace of each county, and one of the said aldermen, to be three, who are hereby authorised and required to call before them such persons on either side, as they think fittest to inform them of the true state of these complaints, and thereupon to settle such a course for the relief of the petitioners by causing just and orderly payment to be made them of their due and accustomed wages, as that they may have no further cause to complain, nor the Board be further troubled herewithall. And in case any particular person shall be found (either out of the hardness of his heart towards the poor, or out of private ends or humours) refractory to such courses as the said commissioners shall think reasonable and just, that then they bind over every such person to answer the same before the Board.

20. Report to Privy Council of Commissioners Appointed Above[1] [*S.P.D. Charles I, Vol.* 189, *No.* 40], 1630.

Right Honourable and our very good Lord,

We have according to your lordship's order from the Council Board, dated the 16th day of February, 1630, under the hand

[1] No. 19.

of the Clerk of the Council, called before us the saymakers, spinsters, weavers and combers, of Sudbury and the towns adjoining, and have examined the cause of the saymakers abating the wages of the spinsters, weavers and combers; and asking the saymakers why they did so abate, their answer was that all of that trade in other parts of the Kingdom did the like; but if it might be reformed in all other parts, they were content to give such wages as we should set down. Whereupon we did order, with the good liking of all parties, as in this enclosed paper is set down. We therefore humbly pray your lordships that the like order may be taken throughout all the kingdom with men of that trade, by way of His Majesty's proclamation, or any other order which may seem best to your lordships' wisdoms; for if the like order be not more general than to Sudbury and the towns adjacent, it must necessarily be their ruin and utter undoing. And so commending the same to your lordships' further direction, we humbly rest, your lordships' in all services to be commanded.

This xxvith of April, 1631.

Dra Deane.
Tho. Wyseman. He. Gent.
Willi. Maxey. R. Wareyn.
Richard Skynner.
Ben Fissher.

Endorsed,

27 April, 1631.

from the Justices of the Peace in the county of Essex concerning the Saymakers, Spinsters, Weavers and Combers of Sudbury.

Essex. An order made at our meeting at Halsted in the said county the eighth day of April Anno domini 1631 by virtue of an order from the Lords of the Council.

It is ordered and agreed upon by us whose names are hereunder written, that the saymakers within the town of Sudbury in Suffolk shall pay unto the spinsters for spinning of every seven knots, one penny, and to have no deduction of their wages, and that the reel whereon the yarn is reeled to be a yard in length, and no longer, and we do further order, that for all the white sayes under five pounds weight the saymaker shall give unto the weaver twelve pence the pound for the weaving thereof, and for the sayes that shall be above five pounds and under ten pounds to give twelve pence the pound, abating six pence in the piece for the weaving thereof, and for the mingled sayes containing eight or nine pounds, nine shillings, and so proportionably as it shall contain more or less in weight. This our order to continue until the 15th day of May next ensuing, except from the Council there shall be other order taken.

Thos. Wyseman.	R. Wareyn.
Willi. Maxey.	Ri. Skynner.
Dra. Deane.	Beniamine Fissher.

21. High Wages in the New World [*Winthrop's Journal, Vol. II, p.* 220], 1645.

The war in England kept servants from coming to us, so as those we had could not be hired, when their times were out, but upon unreasonable terms, and we found it very difficult to pay their wages to their content (for money was very scarce). I may upon this occasion report a passage between one Rowley and his servant. The master, being forced to sell a pair of his oxen to pay a servant his wages, told his servant he could keep him no longer, not knowing how to pay him the next year. The servant answered he would serve him for more of his cattle. 'But how shall I do' (saith the master) 'when all my cattle are gone?' The servant replied, 'You shall then serve me, and so you may have your cattle again.'

22. Young Men and Maids Ordered to Enter Service [*Hist. MSS. Com., Vol. I., p.* 132], 1655.

At an adjourned sessions on 5 June an order was made that, whereas the rate of wages fixed for servants and labourers had been proclaimed, but young people, both men and maids, fitting for service, will not go abroad to service without they may have excessive wages, but will rather work at home at their own hands, whereby the rating of wages will take little effect, therefore no young men or maids fitting to go abroad to service (their parents not being of ability to keep them) shall remain at home, but shall with all convenient speed betake themselves to service for the wages aforesaid, which if they refuse to do the Justices shall proceed against them.

23. Request to Justices of Grand Jury of Worcestershire to Assess Wages [*Hist. MSS. Com., Vol. I, p.* 322], 1661.

Presentments by the Grand Jury. 1661, Ap. 23. We desire that the overseers of parishes may not be hereafter compelled to provide houses for such young persons as will marry before they have provided themselves with a settling. We desire that servants' wages may be rated according to the statute, for we find the unreasonableness of servants' wages a great grievance so that the servants are grown so proud and idle that the master cannot be known from the servant except it be because the servant wears better clothes than his master.[1] We desire that the statute for setting poor men's children to apprenticeship be more duly observed, for we find the usual course is that if any are apprenticed it is to some petty trade, and when they have served their apprenticeship they are not able to live by their trades, whereby not being bred to labour they are not fit for husbandry. We therefore desire that such children may be set to husbandry for the benefit of tillage and the good of the commonwealth.

24. Proceedings on Apprenticeship Clauses of Statute of Artificers[2] [*Privy Council Register, Oct.* 29, 1669].

Upon reading this day at the board the humble Petition of Francis Kiderbey of Framlingham . . . draper, setting forth that he served his apprenticeship for 7 years in the City of London to a Tailor, whereby he came to the knowledge and skill of all sorts of cloth, and used and exercised the same for a long time; that the petitioner's occasions calling him to live in Framlingham aforesaid, and that town wanting one that dealt in cloth, the petitioner set up a shop for selling the same, and thereby got a good livelihood for himself and family; yet some, out of malice, hath caused three bills of Indictment to be presented against him at the sessions held at Woodbridge for that county upon the Statute made 5 Eliz. c. 4, whereby it is provided that none shall use any manual occupations but he that hath been bound seven years an apprentice to the

[1] The last clause is scratched through in the original.

[2] Quoted Unwin, *Industrial Organization in the Sixteenth and Seventeenth Centuries*, App. A, VII.

same, which Statute, though not repealed, yet has been by most of the Judges looked upon as inconvenient to trade and to the increase of inventions; that the Petitioner hath removed the said indictments into the Court of King's Bench, where judgment will be given against him, that statute being still in force, and therefore praying that his Majesty will be pleased to give order to his Attorney-General to enter a *non prosequi* for stopping proceedings against him. It was ordered by his Majesty in Council that it be and it is hereby referred to Mr. Attorney-General to examine the truth of the Petitioner's case, and upon consideration thereof to report to his Majesty in Council his opinion thereupon, and how far he conceives it may be fit for his Majesty to gratify the Petitioner in his said request.

[On Dec. 17, 1669, the Attorney-General reported that Kiderbey was liable to the penalty of the Statute, but that the indictments being in the King's name, his Majesty might order a *non processe* to be entered; which was ordered to be done.]

SECTION IV

THE RELIEF OF THE POOR AND THE REGULATION OF PRICES

1. Regulations made at Chester as to Beggars, 1539—2. A Proclamation Concerning Corn and Grain to be brought into open Markets to be sold, 1545—3. Administration of Poor Relief at Norwich, 1571—4. The first Act Directing the Levy of a Compulsory Poor Rate, 1572—5. The first Act Requiring the Unemployed to be set to Work, 1575–6—6. Report of Justices to Council Concerning Scarcity in Norfolk, 1586—7. Orders devised by the Special Commandment of the Queen's Majesty for the Relief and Ease of the Present Dearth of Grain Within the Realm, 1586—8. The Poor Law Act of 1601—9. A note of the Grievances of the Parish of Eldersfield, 1618—10. Petition to Justices of Wiltshire for Permission to Settle in a Parish, 1618—11. Letter from Privy Council to Justices of Cloth-making Counties, 1621–2—12. Letter from Privy Council to the Deputy Lieutenants and Justices of the Peace in the Counties of Suffolk and Essex concerning the Employment of the Poor, 1629.—13. The Licensing of Badgers in Somersetshire, 1630—14. Badgers Licensed at Somersetshire Quarter Sessions, 1630—15. The Supplying of Bristol with Grain, 1630–1—16. Proceedings against Engrossers and other Offenders, 1631—17. Order of Somersetshire Justices Granting a Settlement to a Labourer, 1630–1—18. Report of Derbyshire Justices on their Proceedings, 1631—19. Letter from Privy Council to Justices of Rutlandshire, 1631—20. Judgment in the Star Chamber against an Engrosser of Corn, 1631.

The national system of Poor Relief which was built up in the course of the sixteenth century was composed of three elements, experiments of municipal authorities, Parliamentary legislation, supervision and stimulus supplied by the Privy Council. The first step taken by towns was usually to organize begging by granting licences to certain authorized beggars, while punishing the idler (No. 1); the next to provide establishments where necessitous persons could be set to work on materials provided at the public expense (No. 3). The action of the State followed the same lines of development. During the first three quarters of the sixteenth century it (*a*) left the provision of the funds needed for relief to private charity, (*b*) directed the relief of the "impotent poor," but treated all able-bodied persons in one category, that of "sturdy rogues." But in 1572 it recognized the inadequacy of voluntary contributions by directing the levy of a compulsory poor rate (No. 4), and in 1576 made the important innovation of discriminating between persons unemployed because they could not get work and persons unemployed because they did not want work, by enacting that the former should be set to work on materials provided for them, and that the latter should be committed to the House of Correction (No. 5). The system was completed by the Act for the Relief of the Poor of 1601 (No. 8). Its administration was in the hands of the Justices of the Peace, who were much occupied with questions of settlement (Nos. 9, 10, 17), with carrying out instructions sent to them by the Privy Council for relieving distress (Nos. 12 and 19), and with making reports to the Privy Council of their proceedings (No. 18).

The provision of relief was never intended to be, and down to 1640 was not, the sole method of coping with problems of distress. It was in its origin associated with measures of a preventive character, attempts to prevent the eviction of peasants (Part II, Section I, Nos. 9, 10, 13–17, 20 and 21), occasional attempts to raise wages (Part II, section III, Nos. 10, 18, 19 and 20), attempts to prevent employers dismissing workpeople in times of trade depression (No. 11), attempts to regulate the price of food stuffs and to secure adequate supplies for the markets (Nos. 2, 6, 7, 13, 14, 15, 16, 20). In the latter matter, as in many others, the Tudor governments tried to make a regularly administered national system out of what had for centuries been the practices of local bodies. The Justices of the Peace were required in 1545 to inspect barns and to compel the owners of supplies of grain to sell it in open market (No. 3). Under Elizabeth the system was elaborated. The Justices from time to time made returns to the Privy Council of the stocks of grain available (No. 6), and of the prices ruling (No. 18); and extremely detailed instructions for their guidance were drawn up by Burleigh in 1586 (No. 7). The licensing of "Badgers," or dealers in corn, was part of their regular business (Nos. 13 and 14); the movement of grain from one district to another was carefully supervised (No. 15); and engrossers and regrators were frequently brought before them (No. 16). The efficiency of the system depended very largely on the close supervision of local government and economic affairs by the Privy Council, and on the fact that offenders against public policy could be tried before the Court of Star Chamber. One case before that Court is printed below (No. 20). It is interesting as showing both the economic ideas upon which the policy of regulating prices was based, and the way in which attempts to supervise economic relationships brought the government into collision with the interests of the middle and commercial classes.

AUTHORITIES

The only modern English writer who deals adequately with the subject of this section is Miss E. M. Leonard, *The Early History of English Poor Relief*. Short accounts of different aspects of the subject are given by Cunningham, *English Industry and Commerce, Modern Times*, Part I; Ashley, *Economic History*, Chap. V; Nicholls, *History of the Poor Law*; Rogers, *Six Centuries of Work and Wages*; Tawney, *The Agrarian Problem in the Sixteenth Century*; Gasquet, *Henry VIII and the English Monasteries; Oxford Historical and Literary Studies*, I, *Elizabethan Rogues and Vagabonds and their Representation in Contemporary Literature*, by Frank Aydelotte; *Oxford Studies in Social and Legal History*, Vol. III, *One Hundred Years of Poor Law Administration in a Warwickshire Village*, by A. W. Ashby. The student may also consult the following:—

(1) *Documentary authorities*:—Municipal Records (see bibliographies and references under section II) and Quarter Sessions Records (see bibliographies and references under section III); the Statutes of the Realm, Acts of the Privy Council, Calendars of State Papers Domestic, especially under Elizabeth; Reports of the

Historical Manuscripts Commission, especially Vol. I (containing Quarter Sessions Proceedings of Wiltshire and Worcestershire), the volumes containing a report on the papers of the Marquis of Salisbury (in particular Part VII), and a report on the papers of the Marquis of Lothian (pp. 76–80).

(2) Reference to questions of pauperism and prices will be found in contemporary literary authorities set out under section I, in particular in the works of More, Crowley, Lever, Stubbes, Harrison, Bacon and Moore, and in the Commonwealth of this realm of England. Awdeley, Fraternity of Vagabonds (1561, Early English Text Society), gives an amusing account of the habits of vagrants.

1. Regulations made at Chester as to Beggars [*Morris. Chester in the Plantagenet and Tudor Reigns, pp.* 355, 356], 1539.

Henry Gee, Mayor, 31 Henry VIII. [1539]. Forasmuch as by reason of the great number of multitude of valiant idle persons and vagabonds which be strong and able to serve and labour for their livings, and yet daily go on begging within the same city, so that the poor impotent and indigent people and inhabiting within the same city and having no other means to get their living but only by the charitable alms of good Christian people daily want and be destitute of the same, to the great displeasure of Almighty God and contrary to good conscience and the wholesome statute and laws of our sovereign Lord the King in such case made and provided ; for reformation whereof it is ordained and established by the said city . . . that the number and names of all indigent and needy mendicant people shall be searched, known and written, and thereupon divided in xv parts, and every of them assigned to what ward they shall resort and beg within the said city, and in no other place within the same, and their names to be written in a bill and set up in every man's house within every ward for knowledge to whom they shall give their alms and to no other. And if any other person or persons come to any man or woman's door, house or person to beg, not having his name in the bill within that man's or woman's houses, then the same man or woman to give unto the same beggar no manner alms or relief but rather to bring or send him to the stocks within the same ward, or else to deliver him to the constable of the same ward or the alderman's deputy within the same ward, and he to put him in the stocks, there to remain by the space of a day and a night; and yet, every man and woman that shall offend in using themselves contrary to this ordinance concerning such valiant beggars shall for every such offence forfeit xii*d.* to be levied to the use of the common box by the commandment of the alderman of the same ward, and for default of payment thereof the same man or woman so offending to be committed to the ward by the mayor till it be paid.

And if any of the indigent and poor needy beggars [beg] at any time in any other place within this city out of the ward to them assigned as is aforesaid, then the same beggar so offending to be punished by the mayor's discretion. And further it is ordered that all manner of idle persons, being able to labour abiding within the said city and not admitted to live by alms within the said city, shall every workday in the morning in the time of winter at vi of the clock, and in time of summer at iiii of the clock, resort and come unto the high cross of the said city, and there to offer themselves to be hired to labour for their living according to the king's laws and his statutes provided for labourers; and if any person or persons do refuse so to do, then he or they so refusing to be committed to ward by the mayor of the said city for the time being, there to remain unto such time he or they so refusing hath found sufficient sureties to be bound by recognisance before the said mayor in a certain sum, so to [do] accordingly to the King's laws and statutes aforesaid.

2. A Proclamation . . . concerning Corn and Grain to be Conveyed and Brought into Open Markets to be Sold [*Br. M. Harleian MSS.* 442, *fo.* 211[1]], 1545.

Forasmuch as it is come to the knowledge of our Sovereign Lord the King, how that divers persons, as well his own subjects as others, having more respect to their own private lucre and advantage than to the common weal of this his Highness's realm, have by divers and sundry means accumulated and got into their hands and possession a great number and multitude of corn and grain, far above the necessary finding of their households, sowing of their lands, paying their rent-corn and performing of their lawful bargains of corn without fraud or

[1] Quoted Schanz, *op. cit.*, Vol. II, pp. 669–671.

intrigue; and the same of their covetous minds do wilfully detain and keep in their possessions without bringing any part or parcel thereof into any market to be sold, intending thereby for to cause the prices of corn to rise, so that they may sell their corn and grain at such unreasonable prices as they will themselves; by reason whereof the prices of corn and grains . . . be raised to such excessive and high prices, that his Majesty's loving subjects cannot gain with their great labours and pains sufficient to pay for their convenient victuals and sustenance, and worse are like to be hereafter, unless speedy remedy be provided in that behalf; his Highness, therefore, by the advice of his said most honourable council, and by authority of the said act of parliament made in the said 31st year of his Majesty's reign, straightly chargeth and commandeth all justices of peace . . . within 20 days next ensuing the publishing of this proclamation according to the said act, and oftener after that by their discretions, to assemble themselves together . . . and that the said justices . . . or two of them at the least, shall with all convenient speed search the houses, barns and yards of such persons as have been accustomed or used to sell corn and grain, and have abundance of corn and grain more than shall be necessary for the sowing of their lands, paying their rent-corn, performing their said lawful bargains of corn, and finding of their houses until the feast of All Saints next coming; and where they shall find any such abundance or surplus, shall by their discretions straightly . . . command in the name of our said sovereign lord the king the owner or owners thereof to convey and bring or cause to be brought such part and portion of their said corn and grain unto the market or markets there near adjoining, or to have such other market or markets, where they afore time have used or accustomed to sell their corn there to be sold at, and during such time as shall be thought meet by the said justices of the peace or two of them at the least; the same justices delivering unto every of the said owner and owners a bill subscribed with their hands, mentioning and declaring the days, places, number and certainty of the bringing of the said corn and grain to the said market and markets to be sold, as is aforesaid, according to their said commandments and appointments; and if any person or persons do wilfully refuse to convey or bring or cause to be brought unto the said market or markets to be sold such part or portion of any such corn and grain as by the said justices or two of them at the least, shall be to him and them limited and appointed as is aforesaid, that then every such person and persons so offending shall lose and forfeit for every bushel . . . 3*s.* and 4*d.* . . . This proclamation to continue and endure until the feast of All Saints next coming and no longer. . . .

3. Administration of Poor Relief at Norwich [*Leonard, Early History of English Poor Relief, pp.* 311–314], 1571.

[It is ordered] 1. First, that no person or persons old or young shall be suffered to go abroad after a general warning given, or be found a-begging in the streets at the sermon or at any man's door or at any place within the city, in pain of six stripes with a whip.

2. That not any person or persons shall sustain or feed any such beggars at their doors, in pain of such fine as is appointed by statute, and further to pay for every time fourpence, to be collected by the deacons, and to go to the use of the poor of the said City.

3. Item that at the house called the Normans in the convenientest place therefore, shall be appointed a working place, as well for men as for women, viz. for the men to be prepared fourteen malt querns to grind malt and such exercises; and for the women to spin and card and such like exercises.

Which working place shall contain to set twelve persons or more upon work, which persons shall be kept as prisoners to work for meat and drink for the space of twenty and one days at the least, and longer if cause serve, and they shall not eat but as they can earn (except some friend will be bound for them), that the city shall no more be troubled with them; with this proviso that such persons as shall be thither committed shall be such as be able to work and daily notwithstanding will not work but rather beg, or be without master or husband, or else be vagabonds or loiterers.

Which persons shall begin their works at five of the clock in summer, viz. from our Lady the Annunciation until Michel mas, and shall end their works at eight of the clock at night, and in Winter to begin at six of the clock from Michelmas to our Lady, and to end at seven of the clock at night or half an hour past, with the allowance of one half hour or more to eat and a quarter of an hour to spend in prayer.

And every one sent thither shall be by warrant from the mayor or his deputy or deputies to the bailiff there, upon which warrant the bailiff shall be bound to receive everyone so sent and set them a-work.

And those that shall refuse to do their works to them appointed or keep their hours, to be punished by the whip at the discretion of the wardens or bailiff of the house.

. . . . . .

For the bailiff of Bridewell.

Item, upon the said authority be also appointed another officer, to be called the bailiff of Bridewell, who is also to be resident there with his wife and family, who shall take the charge by inventory from the wardens of all bedding and other utensils delivered unto him to the use of the workfolks, who shall yearly account with the wardens for the same.

And also shall take charge of such vagabonds, men and women, as to them shall be committed, enforcing them to work by the hours aforesaid. The men to grind malt and other works, and the women to use their hand-deed and, except that they work, not to eat.

And to take of them for their victual, and fuel, or other necessaries as the price shall be rated and there set up. And to allow them for their work by the pound (or otherwise) as shall be rated and set up, and shall use such correction as is aforesaid.

And also shall receive all stuff thither brought and see the same truly and well used and safely delivered.

And he to provide him of such servants as in his absence or his wife's shall see the works done as it ought to be, and to do the house business, as washing, making of beds, baking and also to be expert in hand-deed to spin, card, etc.

And also to provide one officer surveyor, to go daily about the city, with a staff in his hand, to arrest whom that is apt for Bridewell and bring them to master mayor or to any of the committees be commanded thither.

And as he goeth abroad he shall certify how the works in every ward are ordered and occupied, and shall inform master mayor, the committees or his master thereof.

And he shall resort to the deacons in every ward, and be aiding unto them to bring such as be new comers into the city to master mayor, the same presently to be sent away again to the place they came from. And likewise shall bring all disordered persons to be punished to Bridewell if such shall dwell in any ward, and shall give his whole attendance thereupon.

And the said bailiff shall be allowed for himself, his wife, servants and surveyors, (if he shall be charged with his whole number of prisoners,) for meat, drink and wages thirty pounds by year, whereof he shall pay forty shillings a year to a priest to minister service to them twice a week, or else, if he have less charge, to have after the rate as by the discretion of the committees and wardens of Bridewell shall be thought convenient or as they can agree. . . .

. . . .

Orders for children and others in wards.

Item, that there be also appointed by the committees or commissioners for every single ward so many select women as shall suffice to receive of persons within that ward, viz. of women, maidens or children that shall be appointed unto them by the committees or deacons, to work or learn letters in their house or houses, of the most poorest children whose parents are not able to pay for their learning or of women and maids that live idly or be disordered to the number of six, eight, ten or twelve at the most in any one of their houses.

The same to be driven to work and learn, by the hours appointed in Bridewell and with such corrections, till their hands be brought into such use and their bodies to such pains as labour and learning shall be easier to them than idleness, and as they shall of themselves be able to live of their own works with their families as others do.

And every such select woman appointed to take charge of such aforesaid, shall see that such as to them be committed shall do their works truly and workmanly and be learned profitably, or else to lay sharp correction upon them; and every such select woman doing her duty to teach or cause to be taught or set a-work, to have for her pains in that behalf twenty shillings by year every one of them so appointed and nominated.

And whosoever select woman so appointed shall refuse the

same being thereunto appointed, shall suffer imprisonment by the space of twenty days at the least.

4. The First Act Directing the Levy of a Compulsory Poor Rate [14 *Eliz. c.* 5. *Statutes of the Realm, Vol. IV, Part I, pp.* 590–98], 1572.

. . . And when the number of the said poor people forced to live upon alms be by that means truly known, the said justices, mayors, sheriffs, bailiffs and other officers shall within like convenient time devise and appoint, within every their said several divisions, meet and convenient places by their discretions to settle the same poor people for their habitations and abidings, if the parish within the which they shall be found shall not or will not provide for them; and shall also within like convenient time number all the said poor people within their said several limits, and thereupon (having regard to the number) set down what portion the weekly charge towards the relief and sustentation of the said poor people will amount unto within every their said several divisions and limits; and that done, they . . . shall by their good discretions tax and assess all and every the inhabitants, dwelling in all and every city, borough, town, village, hamlet and place known within the said limits and divisions, to such weekly charge as they and every of them shall weekly contribute towards the relief of the said poor people, and the names of all such inhabitants taxed shall also enter into the said register book together with their taxation, and also shall by their discretion within every their said divisions and limits appoint or see collectors for one whole year to be appointed of the said weekly portion, which shall collect and gather the said proportion, and make delivery of so much thereof, according to the discretion of the said justices . . . and other officers, to the said poor people, as the said justices . . . and other officers shall appoint them: and also shall appoint the overseers of the said poor people by their discretions, to continue also for one whole year; and if they do refuse to be overseers, then every of them so refusing to forfeit ten shillings for every such default.

5. The First Act Requiring the Unemployed to be Set to Work [18 *Eliz. c.* 3. *Statutes of the Realm, Vol. IV, Part I, pp.* 610-13], 1575-6.

. . . Also to the intent youth may be accustomed and brought up in labour and work, and thus not like to grow to be idle rogues, and to the intent also that such as be already grown up in idleness and so [be] rogues at this present, may not have any just excuse in saying that they cannot get any service or work, and then without any favour or toleration worthy to be executed, and that other poor and needy persons being willing to work may be set on work: be it ordered and enacted by the authority aforesaid, that in every city and town corporate within this realm, a competent store and stock of wool, hemp, flax, iron or other stuff, by the appointment and order of the mayor, bailiffs, justices or other head officers having rule in the said cities or towns corporate (of themselves and all others the inhabitants within their several authorities to be taxed, levied and gathered), shall be provided. . . . Collectors and governors of the poor from time to time (as cause requireth) shall and may, of the same stock and store, deliver to such poor and needy person a competent portion to be wrought into yarn or other matter within such time and in such sort as in discretions shall be from time to time limited and prefixed, and the same afterwards, being wrought, to be from time to time delivered to the said collectors and governors of the poor, for which they shall make payment to them which work the same according to the desert of the work, and of new deliver more to be wrought; and so from time to time to deliver stuff unwrought and receive the same again wrought as often as cause shall require; which hemp, wool, flax or other stuff wrought from time to time, shall be sold by the said collectors and governors of the poor either at some market or other place, and at such time as they shall think meet, and with the money coming of the sale, to buy more stuff in such wise as the stocks or store shall not be decayed in value. . . .

6. Report of Justices to Council concerning Scarcity in Norfolk[1] [*S.P.D. Eliz., Vol.* 191, *No.* 12], 1586.

May it please your honours, after the remembrance of our

[1] Quoted Leonard, *Early History of English Poor Relief*, pp. 316-17.

humble duties to be advertized; that for a further proceeding in the accomplishment of your honourable letters concerning the furnishing of the markets with corn, we have according to our former letters of the ixth of June last, met here together this day for conference therein. And perusing all our notes and proceedings together, we find that throughout this shire by such order as we have taken with owners and farmers and also badgers and buyers of corn and grain, the markets are by them plentifully served every market day with corn, and the same sold at reasonable rates, viz. wheat at xxii*s.* the quarter, rye at xvi*s.*, malt at xiiii*s.* and barley at xii*s.*, of which kinds of corn the poorer sort are by persuasion served at meaner prices. And so we doubt not but it shall likewise continue according to our direction until it shall please God that new corn may be used. And hereof thinking it best in performance of our duties to advertize your honours, we humbly take our leave. From Attlebrigge the xith of July 1586.

Your ho: humble at commandment. . . .

[Signature of Justices.]

7. ORDERS DEVISED BY THE SPECIAL COMMANDMENT OF THE QUEEN'S MAJESTY FOR THE RELIEF AND EASE OF THE PRESENT DEARTH OF GRAIN WITHIN THE REALM [*Lansdowne MSS.*, 48, *f.* 128, *No.* 54[1]], 1586.

That the sheriffs and justices of the peace by speedy warning of the sheriff shall immediately upon receipt of these orders assemble themselves together, and shall take amongst them into their charge by several divisions all the hundreds, rapes, or wapentakes of the said county.

Item, every company so allotted out shall forthwith direct their precepts unto the said sheriff to warn the high constables, under-constables, and others the most honest and substantial inhabitants . . . to appear before them, . . . and upon the appearance of the said persons they shall divide them into so many juries as they shall think meet, giving instruction to the said sheriff to return as few of such as be known great farmers for corn or have store of grain to sell as he can; . . .

[1] Quoted Leonard, *Early History of English Poor Relief*, pp. 318–26.

Item, they shall first declare the cause why they are sent for . . and then they shall give them the oath following :—

The Juries' Oath.

You shall swear, etc., that you shall enquire and make true and due search and trial what number of persons every householder that hath corn in their barns, stacks or otherwhere, as well justices of the peace as others whatsoever within the parish of . . . , have in their houses ; what number of acres they have certainly to be sown this year with any manner of grain ; what bargains they have made with any persons for any kind of grain to be sold by or to them ; to whom and by whom and upon what price they have made the same, and what quantity of any manner of grain they or any other have in their barns, garners, lofts, cellars or floors or otherwise to be delivered unto them upon any bargain.

Item, what number of badgers, kidders, broggers or carriers of corn do inhabit within the said parish, and whither they do use to carry their corn they buy, and where they do usually buy the same and what their names be, and how long they have used that trade, and by whose license, and to see the same licenses of what tenor they are of.

Item, what number of maltmakers, bakers, common brewers or tipplers dwell within the said parish, and who they are by name, and how long they have used that trade, and how much they bake or brew in the week, and what other trade they have whereby otherwise to live.

Item, who within the same parish be the great buyers of corn, or do buy, or have bought any corn or grain, to sell again, or have sold it again since midsummer last.

Item, who within the same parish buyeth or have bought or sold any corn upon the ground, of whom and to whom hath the same been bought or sold and at what prices, and to certify unto us of the premises and of every part thereof. . . .

That the said justices of the peace, having received . . . the verdicts of the said juries, . . . shall call . . . such persons before them of every parish as upon the presentment so made shall appear to have corn to spare, and upon due consideration of the number of persons which each hath in his house according to their qualities, and of the quantity of grain the party hath toward the finding of the same or otherwise to be spent in his house and sowing of his grounds, allowing to every householder for his expenses in his house for every person thereof according to their quality sufficient corn for bread and drink, between this and the next harvest, and for their seed after the rate of the sowing of that country upon an acre ; and (*sic*) that they shall bind all such as shall appear to have more of any kind of grain than shall serve to uses above mentioned, as well justices of the peace as other, by recognizance in some good reasonable sums of money to observe the orders ensuing, viz., . . .

You shall bring or cause to be brought weekly so many quarters or bushels of corn as wheat, rye, barley, malt, peas, beans, or other grain, or so much thereof as shall not be directly sold to the poor artificers or day labourers of the parish within which you dwell by order of the justice of the peace of the division within which you do dwell or two of them, to the market of . . ., there to be by you or at your assignment sold unto the Queen's subjects in open market by half quarters, two bushels, one bushel or less as the buyer shall require of you, and not in greater quantity, except it be a badger or carrier of corn admitted according to the statute, or to a common known brewer or baker, . . . and you shall not willingly leave any part of your corn unsold if money be offered to you for the same by any that are permitted to buy the same after the usual price of the market there that day, neither shall you from the beginning of the market to the full end thereof keep or cause to be kept any part of your said corn out of the open sight of the market. . . .

Ye shall buy no corn to sell it again.

Ye shall neither buy nor sell any manner of corn but in the open market, unless the same be to poor handicraftsmen or day-labourers within the parish where you do dwell that cannot conveniently come to the market towns by reason of distance of place, according to such direction as shall be given unto you in that behalf by the justices of the peace of that division within which you do dwell, or two of them, and to none of these above one bushel at a time.

That the justices of the peace within their several divisions have special regard that engrossers of corn be carefully seen unto and severely punished according to the law, and where such are found, to make certificate thereof and of the proofs to the Queen Majesty's attorney general for the time being, who is directed speedily to inform against them for the same, and to see also that none be permitted to buy any corn to sell again but by special license.

That they take order with the common bakers for the baking of rye, barley, peas, and beans for the use of the poor, and that they appoint special and fit persons diligently to see their people well dealt withall by the common bakers and brewers in all towns and places in their weight and assize, and effectually to enquire for and search out the default therein, and thereupon to give order for punishment of the offenders severely according to the law, and where any notable offence shall be in the bakers, to cause the bread to be sold to the poorer sort under the ordinary prices in part of punishment of the baker.

That no badgers of corn, bakers or brewers, do buy any grain, or covin or bargain for the same, but in the time of open market, and that but by license under the hand of the justices of the division where they do dwell, or three of them, and that they weekly bring their license with them to the market where they do either buy or sell, and that the license contain how much grain of what kind and for what place they are licensed to buy and carry, that there be set down upon the license the day, place, quantity and price the corn is bought at, that they take but measurably for the carriage, baking and brewing thereof, that they show their book weekly to such as the justice of the division wherein they dwell shall appoint, being no bakers or badgers of corn. And that those persons every 14 days make report to the justice of the division wherein they dwell how the people are dealt withall by the badgers, bakers and brewers. And that such as have otherwise sufficient to live on, or that are known to be of any crime or evil behaviour, be not permitted to be badgers of corn, nor any badgers to be permitted but such as the statute doth limit, and that none be permitted to buy or provide corn in the market in gross as badger or baker and such like, upon pain of imprisonment, until one hour after the full market be begun, that the poor may be first served.

That the said justices, or two or one of them, at the least, in every division, shall be personally present at every market within their several divisions to see the orders to be taken by the authority hereof to be well observed, and the poor people provided of necessary corn, and that with as much favour in the prices as by earnest persuasion of the justices may be obtained; . . .

That all good means and persuasions be used by the justices in their several divisions that the poor may be served of corn at convenient and charitable prices.

That there be no buying or bargaining for any kind of corn but in open market, and that the justices in their several divisions restrain common maltsters of making barley-malt in those countries and places where there be oats sufficient to make malt of for the use of the people, and to restrain as well the brewing of barley-malt by or for ale houses or common tipplers in those countries and places, as also the excess use of any kind of malt by all common brewers in all alehouses and common tippling houses wheresoever, and that sufficient bonds be taken of all common brewers, maltsters and common tipplers, according to the true meaning of this article, and that the unnecessary number of alehouses and common tipplers be forthwith suppressed in all places, and that direction be given to all tippling houses, taverns and alehouses not to suffer any persons to repair thither to eat and drink at unseasonable times.

That the justices use all other good means that are not mentioned in these orders that the markets be well served and the poor relieved in their provisions during this time of dearth, and that no expense of any grain meet for bread to feed men be wasted upon feeding of beasts, neither that any be spent in making of a stuff called starch, as of late there hath been discovered great quantity expended in that vain matter being in no sort to be suffered to continue.

That the justices be straightly commanded to see by all good means that the able people be set on work, the houses of correction provided and furnished, and there idle vagabonds to be punished.

That the justices do their best to have convenient stock to be provided in every division or other place, according to the statute for setting the poor awork, and the justices to use all other good and politic means within their several divisions to continue and maintain the poor people in work within the parish, or at the furthest, within the hundred or division.

That the maimed or hurt soldiers and all other impotent persons be carefully seen unto to be relieved within their several parishes, hundreds or divisions, according to the law therefor provided, and that where the provisions formerly made be not sufficient it may be now for this time of dearth increased; and where one parish is not able to give sufficient relief to such their poor, that parish to have the supply of such parishes near adjoining as have fewer poor and are better able to give relief, and that no vagabond or sturdy beggar, or any that may otherwise get their living by their labours, be not suffered to wander abroad under colour of begging in any town or highway, and that the justices do presently give order that there be persons sufficiently weaponed to assist the constables of every town to attach such vagabonds both in their town-side and highways, and to commit them to prison without bail, but as two of the justices of the peace near that division shall order, and if the township shall not observe this order for the attaching and punishment of the said vagabonds, then the justices shall see due punishment by fine upon the whole township, or upon such parties in the town as shall be found in fault.

That the justices of the peace do once every month certify their doings and proceedings by force of these instructions unto the sheriff of the said county, in which certificate they shall also make certificate of such justices as shall be absent from any of these services, and the true cause of their absence, and shall also certify the usual prices of all kinds of grain in their markets for that month past, of all which the same sheriff to certify the Privy Council once in every forty days at the farthest, so as that default in any justice that shall be absent may be duly considered and corrected by authority of his Majesty's council as reason shall require, and so as such persons as are placed as justices for their credit may not continue in those rooms, wherein they shall be found not disposed to attend such a necessary and godly service as this is, but others of better disposition may supply those rooms, if there shall be need of any such number, as in most places is thought not very needful, the number being in common opinion more hurtful than profitable to justice.

And if any shall offend against the true meaning of these instructions, or any part thereof, or shall use any sinister means to the defrauding thereof, that such be severely punished according to the laws, and for such obstinate persons as shall not conform themselves the justices shall at their pleasure bind to appear before the Queen Majesty's Privy Council by a day certain, there to be further dealt with by severe punishment for the better ensample of all others. . . .

8. The Poor Law Act of 1601 [43 *and* 44 *Eliz. c.* 2. *Statutes of the Realm, Vol. IV, Part II, pp.* 962–5], 1601.

Be it enacted by the authority of this present parliament, that the churchwardens of every parish, and four, three or two substantial householders there as shall be thought meet, having respect to the apportion and greatness of the same parish or parishes, to be nominated yearly in Easter week or within one month after Easter, under the hand and seal of two or more justices of the peace in the same county, whereof one to be of the *quorum*, dwelling in or near the same parish or division where the same parish doth lie, shall be called overseers of the poor of the same parish: and they or the greater part of them shall take order from time to time, by and with the consent of two or more such justices of peace as is aforesaid, for setting to work of the children of all such whose parents shall not by the said churchwardens and overseers or the greater part of them be thought able to keep and maintain their children; and also for setting to work all such persons married or unmarried having no means to maintain them, [or] use no ordinary and daily trade of life to get their living by; and also to raise weekly or otherwise, by taxation of every inhabitant parson, vicar and other, and of every occupier of lands, houses, tithes impropriate or propriations of tythes, coal mines or saleable underwoods, in the said parish, in such competent sum and sums of money as they shall think fit, a convenient stock of flax, hemp, wool, thread, iron and other necessary ware and stuff to set the poor on work, and also competent sums of money for and towards the necessary relief of the lame, impotent, old, blind and such other among them being poor and not able to work, and also for the putting out of such children to be apprentices, to be gathered out of the same parish according to the ability of the same parish; and to do and execute all other things as well for the disposing of the said stock as otherwise concerning the premises as to them shall seem convenient: which said churchwardens and overseers so to be nominated, or such of them as shall not be let by sickness or other just excuse to be allowed by two such justices of peace or more as aforesaid, shall meet together at the least once every month in the church of the said parish, upon the Sunday in the afternoon after Divine Service, there to consider of some good course to be taken and of some meet order to be set down in the premises, and shall within four days after the end of their year and after other overseers nominated as aforesaid, make and yield up to such two justices of peace as is aforesaid a true and perfect account of all sums of money by them received, or rated and assessed and not received, and also of such stock as shall be in their hands or in the hands of any of the poor to work, and of all other things concerning their said office; and such sum or sums of money as shall be in their hands shall pay and deliver over to the said churchwardens and overseers newly nominated and appointed as aforesaid; . . . .

And be it further enacted that it shall be lawful for the said churchwardens and overseers, or the greater part of them, by the assent of any two justices of the peace aforesaid, to bind any such children as aforesaid to be apprentices, where they shall see convenient, till such man-child shall come to the age of four and twenty years, and such woman-child to the age of one and twenty years, or the time of her marriage; the same to be as effectual to all purposes as if such child were of full age, and by indenture of covenant bound him or herself.

And the said justices of peace or any of them to send to the house of correction or common gaol such as shall not employ themselves to work, being appointed thereunto as aforesaid.

9. A Note of the Grievances of the Parish of Eldersfield [*Hist. MSS. Com. Vol. I, pp.* 298-299], 1618.

There are divers poor people in the said parish which are a great charge. Giles Cooke, not of our parish, married a widow's daughter within our parish, which widow is poor and lives in a small cottage, which is like to be a charge. Joan Whiple had lived 40 years and upward in the parish with a brother, as a servant to him; and now that she has grown old and weak he has put her off to the parish; she was taken begging within the parish and was sent to Teddington, where she said she was born, but that parish has sent her back again. Elzander Man, born in Forthampton, in the county of Gloucester, married a wife within the parish, who was received by her mother till she had two children ; the said wife is now dead, and he is gone into Gloucestershire and has left his children to the keeping of the parish. Thomas Jones, born at Harfield, in the county of Gloucester, married a wife within the parish, and has two children ; the said Jones being now gone, the parishioners would know if they might send the woman to her husband, or to the place where she or her husband was born. . . . . Francis Gatfield has gone from the parish, leaving his child and some goods and money; the child is left in charge of the parish and the goods with his brother and sister; the parishioners desire to know whether they may not avoid keeping the child or seize the said goods towards its maintenance.

10. Petition to Justices of Wiltshire for Permission to Settle in a Parish [*Hist. MSS. Com., Vol. I, p.* 298], 1618.

Petitioner doth give you to understand that he was born in Stockton within this county, and has been bred up in the same parish, and most of my time in service; and have taken great pains for my living all my time since I was able, and of late I fortuned to marry with an honest young woman, and my parishioners not willing that I should bring her in the parish, saying we would breed a charge among them. Then I took a house in Bewdley, and there my wife doth yet dwell and in confines thereabouts, and I send or bring my wife the best relief I am able, and now the parish of Bewdley will not suffer her to dwell there for doubt of further charge. Right worshipful, I most humbly crave your good aid and help in this my distress, or else my poor wife and child are like to perish without the doors. And this, right worshipful, I do humbly crave, that by your good help and order to the parish of Stockton I may have a house there to bring my wife and child unto, that I may help them the best I can.

11. Letter from Privy Council to Justices of Cloth-making Counties[1] [*Privy Council Register, Feb. 9th,* 1621–2], 1621–2.

We do hereby require you to call before you such clothiers

[1] Quoted Leonard, *Early History of English Poor Relief*, pp. 147–8.

as you shall think fitting, and to deal effectually with them for the employment of such weavers, spinners and other persons as are now out of work, where we may not omit to let you know, that as we have employed our best endeavours in favour of the clothiers both for the vent of their cloth and for moderation in the price of wool (of which we hope they shall speedily find the effects), so may we not endure that the clothiers in that or any other county should at their pleasure, and without giving knowledge thereof unto this Board, dismiss their workfolks, who, being many in number and most of them of the poorer sort, are in such cases likely by their clamours to disturb the quiet and government of those parts wherein they live. And if there shall be found greater numbers of poor people than the clothiers can receive and employ, we think it fit and accordingly require you to take order for putting the statute in execution, whereby there is provision made in that behalf by raising of public stocks for the employment of such in that trade as want work. Wherein if any clothier shall after sufficient warning refuse or neglect to appear before you, or otherwise shall obstinately deny to yield to such overtures in this case as shall be reasonable and just, you shall take good bonds of them for refusing to appear before us, and immediately certify their names unto this Board . . .; this being the rule by which both the woolgrower, the clothier and merchant must be governed, that whosoever had a part of the gain in profitable times since his Majesty's happy reign, must now in the decay of trade . . . bear a part of the public losses as may best conduce to the good of the public and the maintenance of the general trade.

12. Letter from Privy Council to the Deputy Lieutenants and Justices of the Peace in the Counties of Suffolk and Essex concerning the Employment of the Poor[1] [*Privy Council Register, Chas. I, Vol. V, f.* 263], 1629.

Whereas we by special directions of his Majesty did lately commend unto your care the present state of those parts of your county where the poor clothiers and their workmen at present destitute of work might some other way be employed,

[1] Quoted Leonard, *Early History of English Poor Relief, pp.* 336–7.

or for the time be relieved till some obstructions to trade were removed, as also to keep in order those that are loose and ill disposed people; to which end his Majesty, by advice of his Privy Council and the Judges, hath lately published a proclamation declaring his pleasure and command in what manner the truly poor and impotent should be relieved, those of able bodies should be set on work and employed in honest labour, and the sturdy, idle and dangerous rogues and vagabonds should be repressed and punished, which proclamation you shall herewith likewise receive; now, because we understand that in your county there is more than ordinary occasion to use all diligence and industry at this time, we have thought fit to put you more particularly in mind thereof, and in answer of your letters to let you know that it is the resolution of all the judges, that by the law you have sufficient power and ought to raise means out of the several parishes, if they be of ability, or otherwise in their defect, in their several hundreds, lathes or wapentakes, and for want of their ability (to set your poor on work and to relieve the aged and impotent not able to work) in the whole body of the county; wherefore his Majesty commands that the ways provided by law in these cases be duly followed with all diligence and possible speed. You are required to understand the true state of the country from the ministers, churchwardens and overseers of the several parishes within your several divisions. And what rests herein to be done by order at the quarter sessions, the judges advise that for this purpose you may call the quarter sessions sooner then the ordinary set times, and do that which in this case is so requisite.

Further we let you to know, that such hath been his Majesty's care and personal pains taken to remove these impediments that of late have been to trade, and to open a free vent to the commodities of your country, that yourselves will shortly see the fruits of it to your comforts; nevertheless in the meantime these things provided by the law, and the helps that by your care may be added, are in no sort to be neglected, but exactly pursued; of which your proceedings we are to be advertised that so we may render account thereof to his Majesty.

And so, etc.

13. THE LICENSING OF BADGERS IN SOMERSETSHIRE [*Somerset Quarter Sessions Records, Vol.* 24, *p.* 120], 1630.

This Court taking notice of the great prices of corn and butter and cheese and all other commodities, it was ordered that from henceforth no badger whatsoever be licensed but in open sessions, and shall first enter into recognizance and be entered by the clerk of the peace into his book of records, and also that all maltsters do the like before any justice do sign and seal his licence.

14. BADGERS LICENSED AT SOMERSETSHIRE QUARTER SESSIONS [*Somerset Quarter Sessions Records, Vol.* 24, *p.* 119], 1630.

To Edith Doddington of Hilbishopps, widow, to be a badger of butter and cheese and to carry the same into the counties of Wilts, Hampshire, Dorset and Devon, and to return again laden with corn, and to sell it again in any fair or market within this county during one whole year now next ensuing; and she is not to travel with above three horses, mares, or geldings at the most part; for performance whereof Mr. Symes is to take her recognizance, granted by John Horner, John Symes, John Harington.

To Thomas Rawlings of Lympsham to buy corn in the counties of Wilts and Somerset to sell the same again in the city of Bristol, Mr. Harington to take the recognizance. Ro. Phelipps, Pa. Godwyn.

To Anthony Banbury of Pitney to buy barley and oats, and the same to convert into malt, and to sell again in any fair, and to travel not with above two horses, geldings or mares at the most. Ro. Phelipps, He. Berkley, Pa. Godwyn, John Harington.

15. THE SUPPLYING OF BRISTOL WITH GRAIN [*Somerset Quarter Sessions Records, Vol.* 24, *pp.* 145–6, *No.* 33], 1630–1.

Whereas it is entreated on the behalf of the city of Bristol that their purveyors, drivers, and higglers may buy and carry away for the necessary provision of the said city such quantities of corn as may be conveniently spared within the markets of this county, and that they may freely carry through the said county such corn and grain as they shall buy in the counties adjacent: It is therefore thought fit and ordered, that these purveyors, drivers and higglers may buy, drive, and carry in and through the said county such proportions thereof as shall by us the justices of peace in our several divisions be thought convenient to be bought, driven, and carried and no more, so as the said purveyors, drivers and higglers be lawfully licensed so to do; and this our order to stand in force for the space of forty days, that in the mean time a joint conference may be had according to his Majesty's directions in that behalf with some of the magistrates of the said city and of the justices of such adjacent counties as the premises shall concern, and this Bench doth depute Sir Henry Berkeley, Sir John Horner, Kts., Robte Hopton, Esqr., and Sir Ralph Hopton, Knight, or any three or two of them to meet, treat and conclude with them in the said conference.

16. PROCEEDING AGAINST ENGROSSERS AND OTHER OFFENDERS [*Somerset Quarter Sessions Records, Vol.* 24, *p.* 152, *No.* 19], 1631.

General Sessions of the Peace held at Ivelchester the 19th, 20th, 21st and 22nd days of April, 7 Charles (1631).

Richard Granger maketh oath against William Hurde of Walton, yeoman, James Hurde of the same, Richard Pinckard of the same, yeoman, for buying corn in ground; against Jacob Hill of Halse, using a trade of clothing not being apprentice, William Rowswell of Wellington for regrating of cheese, Jacob Androwse of Bridgwater and Thomas Prinne of Somerton, partners, for buying corn in ground, John Durston of Wilton for buying and selling within five weeks, George Thorne of Stogursey and John Brewer of Combwitch for the same offence, Edmund Galle of Bridgwater for taking extortion, Richard Barker of Godnye in the parish of Meare for maintaining a cottage that hath not four acres of land.

17. ORDER OF SOMERSETSHIRE JUSTICES GRANTING A SETTLEMENT TO A LABOURER [*Somerset Quarter Sessions Records, Vol.* 24, *p.* 139, *No.* 4], 1630–1.

General Sessions of the Peace held at Wells the 11th, 12th, 13th and 14th days of January, 6 Charles.

Lyonell Wills having petitioned this Court, showing that

whereas he hath remained in the parish of Tintenhull for the space of five years now last past, three years whereof he served as a labouring servant, and the two last years as a married man, although not with the consent of some of the parish, and during the said two latter years after he became a married man he endeavoured to take a house within the said parish for his money without any charge to the said parish; and some of the said parish hath forbidden him to remain there any longer and threateneth him, and those that would set or let him any house, to impose great pains on them that shall receive him or let him any house, whereby he is inforced to travel from place to place with his wife and children, and thereby doubteth that he shall in the end be taken as a vagrant; which, the Court taking into consideration, have thought fit to order that the said Lionell Wills be settled at Tintenhull, as they conceiveth by law he ought to be, if his petition be true. And that the said parishioners upon sight of this order do there receive him, and suffer him to be and abide, until they shall show good cause to the contrary to this Court. And that they do suffer him to take a house for his money within the said parish, which if they shall refuse to do, or impose any fines or pains upon those that shall set or let any house unto him or shall be willing thereunto, that then upon complaint thereof made unto Sir Robte Phelipps, Knight, or Thomas Lyte, Esqr., or either of them, they finding his petition to be true will be pleased to bind all such parties to the next Sessions as shall refuse thus to receive him or to trouble any that shall let set them a house to dwell in.

18. Report of Derbyshire Justices on their Proceedings [*S.P.D.*, *Charles I*, *Vol.* 202, *No.* 54], 1631.

Wirksworth Wapentake.

To Francis Bradshawe, Esq., High Sheriff of the County of Derby.

Sir,

In pursuit of the orders and directions given us in command as well by the printed book as also by several letters sent unto us from the right honourable the lords of her Majesty's most honourable Privy Council, we, whose names are hereunder written, having within our allotment the wapentake or hundred of Wirksworth, have had monthly meetings within the said hundred and have summoned both the high constable, petty constables, churchwardens, and overseers of the poor within that division and hundred to appear before us.

1. And first we have made diligent inquiry how all the said officers and others have done their duties in execution of the laws mentioned in the Commission, and what persons have offended against any of them, and punished such as we have found faulty.

2. We have taken care that the lords and parishioners of every town relieve the poor thereof, and they are not suffered to straggle or beg up and down either in their parishes or elsewhere. But such poor as have transgressed have been punished according to law, and the impotent poor there are carefully relieved. We have also taken especial care that both the stewards of leets and ourselves in particular have taken care for the reformation of abuses in bakers, alehouse-keepers, breaking of assize, forestallers and regrators, against tradesmen of all sorts for selling with underweight, and have made search in market towns and other places and taken away and burned very many false weights and measures, and taken order for the punishing of the said offenders.

3. We have made special inquiry of such poor children as are fit to be bound apprentices to husbandry and otherwise, and of such as are fit to take apprentices, and therein we have taken such course as by law is required. And we find none refuse to take apprentices, being thereunto required.

4. We do not find upon our inquiry that the statute for labourers and ordering of wages is deluded, and the common fashion of none essoyning of course is restrained.

5. The weekly taxations for relief of the poor in these times of scarcity is raised to higher rates, and we have further observed the course appointed in the fifth article.

6. We have taken order the petty constables within our said division are chosen of the ablest parishioners.

7. Watches in the night and warding by day are appointed in every town for apprehension of rogues and for good order, and we have taken order to punish such as we have found faulty.

8. We have taken care that the high constable doth his duty in presenting to us the defaults of the petty constables

for not punishing the rogues and in presenting to us the defaulters.

9. We find none presented to us that live out of service and refuse to work for reasonable wages.

10. We have one House of Correction at Ashborn within our wapentake, which is near the town prison, where such as are committed are kept to work.

11. We have punished several persons for harbouring rogues in their barns and outhouses, and have observed the further directions of the 11th article.

12. We have had care to see that all defects and defaults in the amending of highways be redressed, and the defaulters have been presented to the next quarter sessions and punished.

And as touching their lordships' letters and orders directed concerning corn and enclosures, we do at our monthly meetings take a strict account that the former orders therein taken by us in pursuit thereof be duly observed and put in execution, and particularly none sell such corn (as they are appointed to sell out of the market) but to the poor of the said parish. And neither the petty constable nor any other officer can (as they inform us) present any engrossers of corn, etc., or forestallers of markets.

The prices of corn (considering the times) are not on our markets in our opinion unreasonable, but are as follow, viz., wheat for the strike 5*s.*, four peck making a strike, rye 4*s.*, barley 3*s.* 4*d.*, malt 5*s.*, peas 4*s.*, oats 2*s.* 6*d.*

We have made especial inquiry touching enclosures made within these two years, but find very few within our division, for the most of our wapentake hath been long since enclosed. Howsoever some few hath been presented, which we have commanded to throw down, and have stayed the proceedings of such enclosures as have been lately begun and are not finished.

We have no maltmakers in this wapentake but for their own use.

We have put down a full third part of all the alehouses within this wapentake; yet there are so great a multitude of poor miners within this wapentake that we are enforced to leave more alehousekeepers than otherwise we would.

We have taken order for the binding all cooks, alehousekeepers, victuallers and butchers within this hundred that they neither dress nor suffer to be dressed or eaten any flesh during the time of Lent or other days prohibited, and our recognizances to that purpose do remain with the Clerk of the Peace, to be by him certified according to the statute.

John Fitzherbert.
Chr. Fulwood.

19. LETTER FROM PRIVY COUNCIL TO JUSTICES OF RUTLANDSHIRE[1] [*Privy Council Register, Vol. VI, f.* 345], 1631.

Whereas we have been made acquainted with a letter written by John Wildbore, a Minister in and about Tinwell within that county, to a friend of his here, wherein after some mention by him made of the present want and misery sustained by the poorer sort in those parts through the dearth of corn and the want of work, he doth advertize in particular some speeches uttered by a shoemaker of Uppingham (whose name we find not) tending to the stirring up of the poor thereabout to a mutiny and insurrection; which information was as followeth, *in hæc verba:* "Hearest thou ?" saith a shoemaker of Uppingham to a poor man of Liddington, "If thou wilt be secret I will make a motion to thee." "What is your motion ?" saith the other. Then said the shoemaker, "The poor men of Okeham have sent to us poor men of Uppingham, and if you poor men of Liddington will join with us, we will rise, and the poor of Okeham say they can have all the armour of the country in their power within half an hour, and in faith (saith he) we will rifle the churls." Upon consideration had thereof, however this Board is not easily credulous of light reports nor apt to take impression from the vain speeches or ejaculations of some mean and contemptible persons; yet because it sorts well with the care and providence of a state to prevent all occasions which ill-affected persons may otherwise lay hold of under pretence and colour of the necessity of the time, we have thought good hereby to will and require you, the Deputy Lieuts. and Justices of peace next adjoining, forthwith to apprehend and take a more particular examination as well of the said shoemaker as of such others as you shall think fit concerning the advertizement aforesaid and that you take especial care that the arms of that county in and about those parts be safely disposed of; and likewise

[1] Quoted Leonard, *Early History of English Poor Relief*, pp. 338–9.

(which is indeed most considerable and the best means to prevent all disorders in this kind) that you deal effectually in causing the market to be well supplied with corn and the poor to be served at reasonable prices and set on work by those of the richer sort, and by raising of stock to relieve and set them on work according to the laws. All which we recommend to your especial care, and require an account from you of your doings and proceedings herein with all convenient expedition.

And so, etc.

20. JUDGMENT IN THE STAR CHAMBER AGAINST AN ENGROSSER OF CORN [*Camden Society. Cases in the Courts of Star Chamber and High Commission, edited by S. R. Gardiner*], 1631.

In Camera Stellata, Michaelmas, 7° Caroli.

One Archer of Southchurch in Essex was brought *ore tenus*, being then charged by Mr. Attorney-General for keeping in his corn, and consequently for enhancing the price of corn the last year, which offence Mr. Attorney affirmed to be of high nature and evil consequence, to the undoing of the poor and *malum in se*, and then desired his examination taken before the Lord Keeper might be read. His examination purported that he had seen at the time of his examining a presentment that was made against him by the Grand Jury at the last Assizes in Essex before Justice Vernon for the said offence of keeping in his corn and enhancing; and for that he had made a bargain to sell the poor of the town where he dwelled rye for 7*s*. a bushell, and afterwards refused to perform his bargain unless he might have nine shillings a bushell: he denied his bargain, but for his excuse said, he sold to the towns about him for the poor, wheat at 7*s*. and 8*s*. a bushell, and at the latter end of the year for 5*s*., and rye for 7*s*. and 6*s*., etc., and some for 3*s*. and 6*d*. the bushell. He confessed he kept in his corn till June, and that he had 8 quarters of wheat, 60 quarters of rye, and 100 quarters of oats, and that his family were himself and his wife and daughters, two maids, and a man; he confessed that he sold none or very little of his corn in Rochford hundred where he dwelt, though he were commanded so to do by the Earl of Warwick; yet for his defence he further alleged that his barn was not visited by any justices or officers according to his Majesty's late proclamation and orders for that purpose, and that he had no notice of the said proclamation and orders ; lastly, he confessed he sold most of his corn at London and Chelmsford, and that he bought his seed corn out of market, etc. His examination aforesaid was shewed to him and he confessed it to be true, and acknowledged his hand thereunto subscribed before it was read in court ; and it being read, the Lord Keeper demanded of Archer what he could there say for himself, and what answer he would make to this accusation. The said Archer saith that he could make no other answer than he had made in his examination, and submitted himself to the mercy of the Court.

Mr. Attorney desired that their Lordships would proceed to sentence the said Archer according to his desert, and withall prayed that a precedent of a sentence given in the Star Chamber in the 29 and 30 of Queen Elizabeth against one Framingham of Norfolk in the like case might be read before their Lordships gave their sentence in this cause ; and it was read. The said Framingham was accused upon his own confession in this Court *ore tenus* for destroying of husbandry in making cottages of his tenants' houses, taking away the land and letting it lie to pasture in his own hands, and letting the cottages at dear rates, and forstalling the markets, and enhancing the prices of corn, whereupon he was fined 500*l.* to the Queen, and ordered to pay 40*l.* to the poor, and to stand upon a stool in Cheapside with a paper on his head declaring his offence, and to lay his land again to the cottages, and to let them at reasonable rates.

Justice Harvey delivered his opinion, that whereas it hath pleased God to send a plentiful year, and yet the price of corn continued very high, himself and the rest of the Justices of the Peace that were in the last Quarter Sessions in Hertfordshire assembled, did advise among themselves how they might deal with the country to bring down the price, but they were afraid to meddle with any thing upon experience of their ill-taking what was so well intended by his Majesty, that by the late orders, thereupon taking occasion to go on and raise the prices of corn higher ; he was of opinion that this man's punishment or example will do a great deal more good than all their orders which they might have made at the Sessions ;

and therefore he declared his offence to be very great, and fit to be punished in this Court; and adjudged him to pay 100 marks fine to the King, and 10*l.* to the poor, and to stand upon the pillory in Newgate Market an hour with a paper, wherein the cause of his standing there was to be written, put upon his hat, "For enhancing the price of corn"; and then to be led through Cheapside to Leadenhall Market, and there likewise to stand upon the pillory one hour more with the same paper upon his hat, and after this to be sent to Chelmsford, and there likewise in the market to stand upon the pillory.

Sir Thomas Richardson affirmed this offence to be an offence at the common law long before the King's proclamation and orders, and also against some statutes, that his keeping in his corn and not bringing it into the next markets by little and little as he ought to have done, and selling it at other markets when the price was as high as he would have it, was an enhancing the price of corn, and that the Justices in Essex did at the common law inquire of such enhancing the price of any victuals, and corn was certainly victual, bread the staff of man's life, and that keeping in of his corn in this manner was enhancing the prices of corn, which is punishable by the statute as well as forestallings, and approved of his Majesty's pious and honourable care for his people. Also he observed in the defendant's confession that he was guilty of forestalling the market, in buying seed corn out of market and not bringing so much of his own to supply the same in the next market. He therefore condemned the said Archer to be guilty of the said offences, and agreed in his said fine to the King, and would have him pay as much to the poor as the 100 marks wanted of 100*l.*

The Bishop of London[1] observed with Mr. Attorney that this was *malum in se*, and that this Archer was guilty of a most foul offence, which the Prophet hath in a very energetical phrase, "grinding the faces of the poor." He commended highly that speech of Justice Harvey, that this last year's famine was made by man and not by God, solicited by the hard-heartedness of men, and commended this observation as being made by his Majesty. And thereupon undertook to clear the wisdom of the Church, in ordaining to pray to God that he would be pleased to turn his scarcity and dearth, which cruel men (but He never) made, through His goodness

[1] *i.e.* Laud.

and mercy into cheapness and plenty. He said that God taketh away the hardness and cruelty of men's hearts, which was the cause of the famine or scarcity, and He only; and therefore the Church hath very wisely ordained as aforesaid. He is glad to hear it declared to be an offence against the common law of this realm; and, therefore, seeing it had pleased God to load the earth so richly, and also to send so dry a time for the inning the same in the harvest, for, if that had wanted, all that abundance had been but an uncomfortable load, as we by our sins had deserved and was threatened, and yet for all this plenty corn was at an extreme rate, and they boast among themselves now they can keep their corn as long as they list and no fear of moulding, he thinks fit this man be made an example that others may fear to offend in the like kind. And assenteth to his fine to be 100 marks, and thinks fit, seeing he hath ground the faces of the poor, he should therefore help to seal them again, and pay 10*l.* to the poor; and the rest of the former sentence he assented unto. The Earl of Danby consented to the sentence in all, adding that he should pay but 10*l.* to the poor, and to stand likewise upon the pillory at the Palace, because some of all countries might take notice thereof.

The Earl of Dorset concurred in his sentence with the Earl of Danby, and commended my Lord Keeper and Mr. Attorney for their care and pains in bringing him to justice, and wished that inquiry should be made if the Justices of the Peace had made default in not visiting the said Archer's barns. But as for the Earl of Warwick, Sir Thomas Richardson had well declared that Lords and Peers of the Parliament were exempted from the services of the said orders, and yet that the Lord of Warwick out of his care had admonished him, etc.

Lord Privy Seal gave his sentence in few words, that Archer was guilty by his own confession of a very great offence, and well worthy the sentence aforesaid, and in full consented to it.

The Lord Keeper did affirm that it was indeed a good work to bring this man forth to be here sentenced, but that it was brought about by means of Justice Vernon, who informed him of the said Archer as being the only man presented in all his circuit for offending in this kind, and that to him this was to be attributed. He was of opinion, that the said Archer was guilty of enhancing the price of corn by keeping in his corn, as is confessed, in this time of scarcity, which was not a scarcity made by God (for there was enough to be had at dear prices and high rates). He affirmed the same to be an offence as well against the common law as against some statutes, and also he would not leave out against his Majesty's proclamation and orders, for his Lordship held there was an aggravation to his offence. And his Lordship declared further (and wished it might be taken notice of, as well as of what had already been spoken, for that much had been said that day of singular use and benefit for the commonwealth), that these were no new opinions. And to that purpose showed that in the old charge to the quest of inquiry in the King's Bench, this enhancing the prices, not only of corn but of any other commodities, was inquirable and to be there punished; also [he] cited a statute whereby those that agree to keep up the price of any commodities, agreeing to sell all at one price, and those that raise false news to bring down the price of any commodities from what they are justly worth, are punishable; as those that raised news that there were great wars beyond sea, and there would be no vent for cloth, and told the same in the country at Coxsall, for that the prices of wools fell there, and they were punished for it. And his Lordship vouched a precedent of one for procuring the raising the price of a certain commodity, for which he was informed against in the King's Bench, and though his Counsel alleged that he had done nothing, he had but spoken, and his offence was in words only, yet he was adjudged an enhancer for but advising the same. And [he] vouched a statute or proclamation in the time of H. 8 for setting the prices on corn, and the like orders and proclamations in the times of E. 6, Queen Eliz. and King James, and agreed it to be well spoken by the Earl of Dorset, that if any shall do any thing tending to depopulation, over and besides his punishment, he shall be enjoined to populate as much, as the said Framingham was: and vouched a book case, where one complaining against another for letting down a sea wall, so that not only his, but diverse other men's grounds were surrounded, the judgment was given in the common pleas that the plaintiff should recover his damages, and the defendant should also make up the said wall at his costs and charges. And thereupon his said Lordship consented to the highest censure against the said Archer for his forestalling the market and keeping in his corn to the enhancing of the price, to the great hurt of the common people, especially the poor labourer: and committed Archer to the Fleet from whence he came.

SECTION V

THE ENCOURAGEMENT OF INDUSTRY AND COMMERCE

1. Letters Patent granted to the Cabots by Henry VII, 1496—2. The Merchant Adventurers' Case for Allowing the Export of Undressed Cloth, 1514–36—3. The Rise in Prices, the Encouragement of Corn growing, and the Protection of Manufactures, *c.* 1549—4. Sir Thomas Gresham on the Fall of the Exchanges, 1558—5. The Reasons why Bullion is Exported [*temp. Eliz.*] —6. The Italian Merchants Explain the Foreign Exchanges, 1576—7. An Act Avoiding divers Foreign Wares made by Handicraftsmen Beyond the Seas, 1562—8. An Act Touching Cloth Workers and Cloth Ready Wrought to be Shipped over the Sea, 1566—9. Incorporation of a Joint Stock Mining Company, 1568.—10. An Act for the Increase of Tillage, 1571—11. Instructions for an English Factor in Turkey, 1582—12. The Advantages of Colonies, 1583—13. Lord Burghley to Sir Christopher Hatton on the State of Trade, 1587 14. A List of Patents and Monopolies, 1603—15. Instructions Touching the Bill for Free Trade, 1604—16. The Establishment of a Company to Export Dyed and Dressed Cloth in Place of the Merchant Adventurers, 1616—17. Sir Julius Cæsar's proposals for Reviving the Trade in Cloths, 1616—18. The Grant of a Monopoly for the Manufacture of Soap, 1623—19. The Statute of Monopolies, 1623–4—20. An Act for the Free Trade of Welsh Cloths, 1623–4—21. The Economic Policy of Strafford in Ireland, 1636—22. Revocation of Commissions, Patents, and Monopolies Granted by the Crown, 1639 —23. Ordinance Establishing an Excise, 1643.

The attempts made between 1405 and 1660 to develop industry and commerce are usually known as "the Mercantile System." But the name is an unfortunate one. The mercantile system was not specially mercantile; for, as preceding sections have shown, government interference was not confined to matters of commerce; nor was it a system, but a collection of opportunist expedients, nearly all of which had been tried in preceding centuries. It is true, however, that after the accession of Elizabeth, the efforts already made under Henry VII and Henry VIII to foster commerce (*see* Schanz, *Englische Handelspolitik gegen Ende des Mittelalters*) were carried on with greater persistency and deliberation. It is from this period, therefore, that the documents in this section are principally drawn.

The most pressing economic problem in the middle of the sixteenth century was the fall in the value of money, caused, principally, by the influx of silver from America, but to a less extent by the debasement of the currency, which led to a rise in prices (No. 3), and a disturbance of the foreign exchanges (Nos. 4 and 5), and which could be met to some small extent by calling in the base coin (Nos. 4 and 5). This the government did in 1560. In 1570, in its anxiety to prevent the efflux of bullion, it took steps to impose a special tax on all exchange transactions, but such a tax was really a tax on banking, and its consequences, according to the business houses concerned, were disastrous (No. 6). The most certain way, however, of securing adequate supplies of bullion was thought to consist in checking imports and encouraging exports (Nos. 3 and 5) ; and the policy was strengthened by other considerations (No. 3). The general policy under Elizabeth was to discourage imports in order to prevent unemployment at home (Nos. 3 and 7), to encourage corn-growing by allowing the export of wheat, except in times of scarcity, on payment of a small duty (Nos. 3 and 10), and to encourage the export of manufactured articles rather than of raw materials, especially the export of dyed and finished cloth (Nos. 3, 8, 11 and 12), any interruption of which caused distress (No. 13). The policy which had been pursued under Henry VIII threatened the vested interests of the Merchants Adventurers, who complained that they could not find markets for finished cloth (No. 2). In the reign of James I a more ambitious attempt was made in the same direction, and in 1614, when the abrupt dissolution of Parliament had left the government in financial difficulties, a plan was initiated for preventing the exportation of cloths not dyed and dressed in England. As the Merchant Adventurers refused to be a party to it, a new company was established to carry on the desired trade, and was granted a charter in 1616 (No. 16). The result of this policy was a tariff war with the Netherlands and acute distress at home, and, after various suggestions for reviving trade had been made (No. 17), the abandonment of the undertaking. The political motives of mercantilism, as well as its economic aims, are illustrated by Strafford's account of his policy in Ireland (No. 21). Of more enduring importance, perhaps, than mercantilist schemes were the development of Joint-Stock Companies (No. 9), the expansion of commercial enterprize (No. 11), and the attempts to establish colonies (No. 12).

Among the methods for fostering industry, and incidentally for raising an unparliamentary revenue, the granting of patents and monopolies holds an important place. These patents ranged from grants of the sole conduct of important industries (Nos. 14 and 18) to grants of trifling offices of profit and pensions (Nos. 14 and 22). The reaction against the interference of the Crown with trade is excellently expressed in the report of the Committee on "the Bill for Free Trade" (No. 15), a document which, in spite of the fact that the Bill was dropped, is of the highest economic and constitutional importance (*see* Gardiner, Vol. 1, pp. 188–190). It is concerned primarily with monopolies enjoyed by trading companies, such as the Company of Merchant Adventurers, the Eastland Company, and the Russia Company. But its arguments apply *a fortiori* to patents granted to individuals, and throw much light on the nature of the economic opposition to the Stuarts. The effect of the attitude of Parliament was seen later in the Act abolishing internal and local restrictions on the trade in woollen cloths (No. 20), in the Statute of Monopolies (No. 19), and in the revocation by Charles in 1639 of patents granted during the period of personal government (No. 22). The place occupied by monopolies in the Stuarts' fiscal system was later, when the Civil War began, partially filled by the Excise (No. 23).

AUTHORITIES

There is no book covering the commercial history of the whole period. The most useful works are :—Schanz, *Englische Handelspolitik gegen Ende des Mittelalters*; Cunningham, *English Industry and Commerce, Modern Times,* Part I; Scott, *Constitution and Finance of English Joint Stock Companies*; Busch, *England Under the Tudors*; Gardiner, *History of England* 1603–1642; Unwin, *Industrial Organization in the Sixteenth and Seventeenth Centuries*; Rogers, *English Industrial and Commercial Supremacy*, and *The Economic Interpretation of History*; Ehrenberg, *Das Zeitalter der Fugger;* Price, *The English Patents of Monopoly*; Hewins, *English Trade and Finance in the Seventeenth Century*; Kennedy, *English Taxation,* 1640–1799; Schmoller, *Mercantilism* (translated by Ashley); Keith, *Commercial Relations Between England and Scotland*; Murray, *Commercial Relations Between England and Ireland*; Beer, *The Old Colonial System*; Durham, *Relations of the Crown to Trade under James I* (Trans. R.H.S., New Series, Vol. XIII).

The student may also consult the following :—

(1) *Documentary Sources* :—Gairdner, Letters and Papers of Henry VIII; S.P. Dom. from 1558 to 1660; The Acts of the Privy Council; The Commons Journals; and the Statutes of the Realm, which are particularly instructive on the subject of commercial policy. An invaluable collection of documents is given by Schanz, *op. cit.*, Vol. II; and useful, though smaller ones, by Scott, Price, Cunningham, and Unwin.

(2) *Literary Sources* :—Starkey, Dialogue Between Cardinal Pole and Thomas Lupset; The Italian Narration of England (Camden E.E.T.S. Society, 1847); Dudley, The Tree of Commonwealth (1509); Drei Volkswirtschaftliche Denkschriften aus der Zeit Heinrich VIII von England, edited by Pauli; The Commonwealth of this Realm of England; Wilson, Discourse upon Usury (1572); Malynes, A Treatise of the Canker of England's Commonwealth (1601); Wheeler, Treatise of Commerce (1601); Malynes, Consuetudo vel Lex Mercatoria (1622); Misselden, Free Trade (1622); Bacon, History of King Henry VII (1622); Knowler, Letters and Despatches of Thomas Wentworth, Earl of Strafford; Robinson, England's Safety in Trade's Increase (1641).

I. Letters Patent Granted to the Cabots by Henry VII [*R.O. Pat.* 4 *Ed. VI*, *p.* 6], 1496.

The King to all to whom, etc., greeting. It is manifest to us by inspection of the rolls of our Chancery that the lord Henry the Seventh, late King of England, our dearest grand father, caused his letters patent to be made in these words:

Henry by the grace of God King of England and France and Lord of Ireland, to all to whom the present letters shall come, greeting. Be it known and manifest that we have given and granted, and by these presents we do give and grant for us and our heirs to our beloved John Cabot, citizen of Venice, and Lewis, Sebastian and Sanctus, sons of the said John, and the heirs and deputies of them and every of them, full and free authority, faculty and power to sail to all parts, regions and gulfs of the sea, east, west and north, under our banners, standards, and ensigns, with five ships or boats of whatsoever portage or kind they be, and with as many sailors and men as they wish to take with them in the said ships at their own and the others' costs and expenses, to find, discover and search out any isles, countries, regions or provinces of heathens and infidels whomsoever set in any part of the world soever, which have been before these times unknown to all Christians. We have granted also to the same and to every of them and to the heirs and deputies of them and every of them, and given licence for them to affix our aforesaid banners and ensigns in any town, castle, isle or solid land soever newly found by them; and that the aforenamed John and his sons or heirs and the deputies of the same may subjugate, occupy and possess any such towns, castles and islands found by them which can be subjugated, occupied and possessed, as our vassals and governors, lieutenants and deputies of the same, acquiring for us the lordship, title and jurisdiction of the same towns, castles, islands and solid land so found; so, nevertheless, that of all fruits, profits, emoluments, commodities, gains and obventions arising from such voyages, the aforesaid John and his sons and heirs and their deputies be held and bound to pay to us for every voyage, as often as they touch at our port of Bristol, at which alone they are held and bound to touch, after deducting the necessary costs and expenses made by them, a fifth part of their capital gain made whether in wares or in money; giving and granting to them and their heirs and deputies that they be free and immune from all payment of customs on all and singular goods and wares which they bring back with them from those places so newly found. And further we have given and granted to the same and to their heirs and deputies that all lands, farms, isles, towns, castles and places whatsoever found by them, as many as shall be found by them, may not be frequented or visited by any other our subjects soever without licence of the aforesaid John and his sons and their deputies, under pain of loss as well of the ships or boats as of all goods whatsoever presuming to sail to those places so found; willing and most straitly commanding all and singular our subjects set as well on land as on sea that they give good assistance to the aforesaid John and his sons and deputies and show all their favour and aid as well in manning the ships or boats as in provision of equipment and victuals to be bought for their money and all other things to be provided for them to be taken for the said voyage. In witness whereof we have caused these our letters patent to be made. Witness myself at Westminster, 5 April in the 11th year of our reign.

And we, because he le ters aforesaid have been lost by mischance, as the aforesaid Sebastian, appearing in person before us in our Chancery, has taken a corporal oath, and that he will restore those letters to us into the same our Chancery to be cancelled there, if he shall find them hereafter, have deemed fit to exemplify by these presents the tenour of the enrolment of the letters aforesaid, at the request of the same Sebastian. In witness whereof these our letters, etc. Witness the King at Westminster, 4 June.

2. The Merchant Adventurers' Case for Allowing the Export of Undressed Cloth [*Br. M. Cotton MS. Tib. D. VIII, f.* 40[1]], 1514-1536.

Considerations alleged by the governor and fellowship of merchant adventurers to prove how it were more for the universal wealth of the realm of England to convey and send over the sea to the markets accustomed cloths of all prices, not dressed nor shorn, than cloths dressed and shorn.

First it is to be noted, marked and considered, that in few years after the act of Parliament made, that no sort of cloths draped and made within the realm of England being above the price of five marks sterling the piece should be conveyed over the sea undressed and unshorn, the same sort of cloths, which at that day were bought for five marks, be now at this present day by the industry of the said merchants uttering

[1] Quoted Schanz, Vol. II, pp. 571-3.

the said cloths sold within the realm for four pounds sterling, which is a great enriching of the whole realm, so that the said merchants think it to stand with reason and conscience, that those sort of cloths, of four pounds the piece, ought to be reputed and taken, in regard of the act, after cloths of five marks the piece.

Item the merchants of those parts buying English cloths will in no wise meddle with any cloths, that be dressed, unless they may have them at a price far under the foot; for it is in experience daily, that the merchants of England conveying over the sea a sort of cloths every of them being of like length and goodness, whereof the one half of them have dressed and shorn and the other half undressed and unshorn, the said merchants shall sell those cloths being undressed five shillings dearer in every cloth, than those that be dressed; also those cloths undressed be meet and ready for every man and the other dressed but only for one man, so that against one cloth dressed the merchants of England shall sell five hundred undressed, whereby it appeareth, that it were for the common weal and great enriching to the realm of England to send over into those parts all sorts of cloths undressed and but a singular and private wealth to dress any such cloths; for there be many more in number, that live by making of cloths and selling of the same, than there be that live by dressing of cloths.

Item the common people of those parts, by whom the most part of those cloths be consumed, do use in their garments sundry colours not accustomed to be worn here in England, which colours cannot be made, unless they buy their cloths undressed; for the dressing of cloths here and there vary and alter so much, that the dressing will take in manner none of their colours. And in case the merchants of England should bring over such cloths dressed, they should not only be undone in the sale of them, but also it were to be doubted, that in brief time after they would wholly relinquish the buying and wearing of any English cloths in those parts, which God defend.

Item there be certain coarse cloths named long Glemsters, and notwithstanding their coarseness the King's Grace is paid for a cloth and a third part in his custom; and if the buyer will cut off 6 or 8 yards of the said cloth, he may lawfully convey it over notwithstanding the act, which should be a great loss in the sale and an occasion that the strangers should not buy them, wherefore the said governor and merchants say, that the said cloths ought of right to pass for cloths under five marks the piece.

Item at this present day, our Lord be thanked, there is shipped and conveyed out of England into those parts more number of cloths of all sorts and there uttered sold and consumed, than ever hath been in memory of man ; and considering, cloth is now there in such high estimation and hath so good vent, the said merchants think, under correction, that it were not necessary, but an utter peril and danger, to attempt them to any other purpose to alter them out of this good trade, which our Lord continue.

Item the inhabitants of those parts by the make of English cloths in frieze consume, waste and spend a great quantity and number of them, which frieze undoubtedly after their using and wearing cannot be made of English cloths dressed here, so that by the only means thereof it should be a great diminution and decay to the common weal of this realm, if the said act for dressing of cloths should take place or effect.

Item the inhabitants of the realm of England have the buying and selling of the wool, one with another, they have also the carding, spinning, weaving, fulling and the first sale of such cloths, and the inhabitants of those parts have only the dressing and shearing of certain of the said cloths, whereby the inhabitants there been a little relieved and a few number of them for a time set to work ; yet by means thereof the rulers and honest burgesses of the towns be desirous to have the nation of England to haunt their said towns, and entertain them with much familiarity and friendship. And it is much to be feared and doubted, that if the realm of England should all covet and they to have no relief nor comfort by the same, that they of Antwerp and other places, studying their common weal, would not only find means ways and occasions to expel the nation from them, but also that no English cloths should be there consumed nor sold, which our Lord defend.

3. The Rise in Prices, the Encouragement of Corn-growing, and the Protection of Manufactures [*The Commonweal of this Realm of England*], c. 1549.

f. 17*b*–*f.* 20.

Knight. How can that be ? What maketh it the matter

what sort of coin we have amongst ourselves, so it be current from one hand to another, yea, if it were made of leather?

Doctor. Ye see, men commonly say so; but the truth is contrary; as not only I could prove by common reason, but also that proof and experience hath already declared the same. But now we do not reason of the causes of these griefs, but what state of men be grieved indeed by this dearth of things; and albeit I find every man grieved by it in one thing or other, yet considering that, as many of them as have wares to sell, do enhance as much in the price of all things that they sell as was enhanced before in the price of things that they must buy; as the merchant, if he buy dear, he will sell dear again. So the artificers, as cappers, clothiers, shoemakers and farriers, have respect large enough, in selling their wares, to the price of victual, wool and iron, which they buy. I have seen a cap for 14*d.*, as good as I can get now for 2*s.* 5*d.*; of cloth ye have heard how the price is risen. Then a pair of shoes costeth me 12*d.* now, that I have in my days bought a better for 6*d.* Then I can get never a horse shod under 10*d.* or 12*d.* [now], where I have seen the common price was 6*d.* for shoeing of a horse round, yea, and 8*d.* (at the most) till now of late. I cannot, therefore, understand that these men have greatest grief by this common and universal dearth, but rather such as have their livings and stipends rated at a certainty, as common labourers at 6*d.* the day, journeymen of all occupations, serving men [at] 40*s.* the year, and gentlemen whose lands are let out by them or their ancestors either for lives or for term of years, so as they can not enhance the rent thereof though they would, and yet have the price enhanced by them of every thing that they buy. Yea the King's Highness, whereof we spake nothing all this while, as he hath most of yearly revenues and that certain, so hath he most lost by this dearth, and by the alteration especially of the coin. For like as a man, that hath a great number of servants under him, if he would grant that they should pay him [pins] weekly where [before] they paid him [pence], I think he should be most loser himself. So we be all but gatherers for the King's Majesty, that be his subjects; we have but every man a poor living; the clear gains cometh for the most [part] to the King's grace. Now if his Grace do take of us the overplus of our getting in this new coin, where he was wont to be paid in other good coin, I report me to you whether that will go as far as the other, in proportion of his necessaries and of the Realm. I think plainly no; for though his Highness might, within his own realm, have things at his own price, as his Grace can not indeed without great grudge of his magistrates and subjects; yea, since his Majesty must have from beyond the seas many things necessary not only for his Grace's household and ornaments, as well for his grace's person and family, as of his horses, which [percase] might be by his Grace somewhat moderated, but also for the furniture of his wars, which by no means can be spared; as armour, and all kinds of artillery, anchors, cables, pitch, tar, iron, steel, handguns, gunpowder, and many other things more than I can reckon, which his Grace must needs buy from beyond the seas, at the price the stranger will set him them at. I pass over the enhancement of the charges of his Grace's household, which is common to his grace with all other noble men. [Therefore], I say, his Majesty hath most loss, by this common dearth, of all other; and not only loss, but danger to the Realm and all his subjects, if his Grace should want treasure to purchase the said habiliments and necessaries for war, or to find soldiers in time of need, which passeth all other private losses that we spake of.

Capper. We hear say, that the King's Majesty maketh up his losses that way by the gains which he hath by the mint another way. If that be too short, he supplieth that lack by subsidies and impositions of his subjects, so as his Grace can not lack, so long as his subjects have it.

Doctor. You say well there. So long as the subjects have it, so it is meet the King should have it; but what and they have it not? for they cannot have it, when there is no treasure left within the realm. And as touching the mint I account the profit much like as if a man would take his wood up by the roots, to make [the more profit thereof at one time, and ever after to lose] the profit that might grow thereof yearly, or to pull the wool of his sheep by the root. And as for the subsidies; how can they be large when the subjects have little to depart with? and yet that way of gathering treasure is not always most safe for the prince's surety; for we see many times the profits of such subsidies spent in appeasing of the people that are moved to sedition partly by occasion of the same. . . .

. . . .

. . . .

f. 31*b*–*f.* 34.

Doctor. Mary, the first way [*sc.* to equalize the profits of tillage and pasture-farming] is to make that wool be of as base a price [to] the breeder thereof as the corn is ; and that shall be, if you make alike restraint of wools, for passing over the sea unwrought, as ye make of corn. Ye have a law made that no corn shall pass over and it be above a noble a quarter ; if it be under ye give free liberty for it to pass over ; let wool be restrained likewise, for passing over, so long as it is above 12*s.* 4*d.* the tod ; and when it is under let it have free passage ; that is one way. Another is, to increase the custom of wool that passeth over unwrought ; and by that the price of it shall be based to the breeders, and yet the price over the sea shall be never the less. But that is increased in the price thereof [on] strangers shall come unto the King's Highness ; which is as profitable to the Realm as though it came to the breeders, and might relieve them of their subsidies. Thus far as touching the bringing down the price of wools ; now to the enhancing of the same price in corn, to be as equivalent to the husbandman as wool should be. And that might be brought to pass if ye will let it have as free passage over sea at all times, as ye have now for wool.

Merchant. By the first two ways men would send less wool over sea than they do now ; and, by that way, the King's customs and profits of his staple should be minished ; by your latter way, the price of corn should be much enhanced, wherewith men should be much grieved.

Doctor. I wot well it would be dear at the first ; but if I can persuade you that it were reasonable it were so, and that the same could be no hindrance to the Realm universally, but great profit to the same, then I think we would be content it should be so ; and as touching the King's custom, I will speak afterward.

Merchant. I will grant, if you can show me that.

Doctor. I will essay it, albeit the matter be somewhat intricate, and as I showed you before, at the first face will displease many ; for they will say, Would you make corn dearer than it is ? Have you dearth enough else without that ? Nay I pray you find means to have it better cheap, if it may be, it is dear enough already ; and such other like reasons would be said. But now let the husbandman answer such men again. Have not the grazers raised the price of your wools and pelts ? and you merchant men, clothiers and cappers, raised the price of your merchandize and wares over it was wont to be in manner double ? Is it not as good reason then I should raise the price of my corn ? What reason is it that you should be at large, and I to be restrained ? Either let us all be restrained together, or else let us all be at like liberty. Ye may sell [your wool] over the sea, your fells, your tallow, your cheese, your butter, your leather, which riseth all by grazings, at your pleasure, and that for the dearest penny ye can get for them. And I shall not send out my corn, except it be at 10*d.* the bushel or under. That is as much to say, as we that be husbandmen should not sell our wares, except it be for nothing, or for so little we shall not be able to live thereof. Think you that if the husbandman here did speak these words, that he did not speak them reasonable ?

Husbandman. I thank you with all my heart ; for you have spoken in the matter more than I could do myself, and yet nothing but that is true. We felt the harm, but we wist not what was the cause thereof ; many of us saw, 12 years ago, that our profits was but small by the ploughs ; and therefore divers of my neighbours that had, in times past, some two, some three, some four ploughs of their own, have laid down, some of them [part, and some of them all] their teams, and turned either part or all their arable ground into pasture, and thereby have waxed very rich men. And every day some of us encloseth a [plot] of his ground to pasture ; and were it not that our ground lieth in the common fields, intermingled one with another, I think also our fields had been enclosed, of a common agreement of all the township, long ere this time. And to say the truth, I, that have enclosed little or nothing of my ground, could [never be able] to make up my lord's rent were it not for a little breed of neat, sheep, swine, geese, and hens that I do rear upon my ground ; whereof, because the price is somewhat round, I make more clear profit than I do of all my corn ; and yet I have but a bare living, by reason that many things do belong to husbandry which now be exceeding chargeable over they were in times past.

Capper. Though this reason of master doctor's here doth please you well that be husbandmen, yet it pleaseth us that be artificers nothing at all, which must buy both bread, corn and malt for our penny. And whereas you, master doctor, say it were as good reason that the husbandman would raise the price of his corn, and have as free vent of the same over sea as we [do and have of our wares], I cannot greatly deny that; but yet I say, that every man hath need of corn, and so they have not of other wares so much.

Doctor. Therefore the more necessary that corn is, the more be the men to be cherished that reared it; for if they see there be not so much profit in using the plough as they see in other feats, think you not that they will leave that trade, and fall to the other that they see more profitable? as ye may perceive by the doings of this honest man's neighbours, which have turned their arable land to pasture, because they see more profit by pasture than by tillage. Is it not an old saying in [Latin], *honos alit artes*, that is to say, profit or advancement nourisheth every faculty; which saying is so true, that it is allowed by the common judgement of all men. We must understand also that all things that should be done in a common wealth be not to be forced, or to be constrained by the straight penalties of the law; but some so, and some other by allurement and rewards rather. For what law can compel men to be industrious in travail, and labour of their bodies, or studious to learn any science or knowledge of the mind? to these things they may be well provoked, encouraged, and allured, if they that be industrious and painful be well rewarded for their pains, and be suffered to take gains and wealth as reward of their labours. And so likewise [they] that be learned, if they be advanced and honoured according to their forwardness in learning, every man will then study either to be industrious in bodily labour, or studious in things that pertain to knowledge. Take this reward from them, and go about to compel them by laws thereto, what man will plough or dig the ground, or exercise any manual occupation wherein is any pain? Or who will adventure over seas for any merchandise? or use any faculty wherein any peril or danger should be, seeing his reward shall be no more than his that sitteth still ? But ye will percase answer me, that all their rewards shall not be taken away, but part of it. Yet then you must grant me, that as if all their rewards were taken from them, all these faculties must needs decay ; so if part of that reward be minished, the use of those faculties shall minish withall, after the rate ; and so they shall be the less occupied, the less they be rewarded and esteemed. But now to our purpose ; I think it more necessary to devise a mean how husbandry might be more occupied, rather than less, which I cannot perceive how it may be brought to pass, but as men do see the more gains therein, the gladder they will occupy the feat. And this to be true [that] some things in a common wealth must be forced with pains and some by rewards allured [may appear] by that that the wise and politic senator Tully writeth, saying, that it was the words of Solon, which was one of the seven men of Greece, and of those seven the only man that made laws, that a common wealth was holden up by things chiefly, that is, by reward and pain ; of which words I gather that men should be provoked to good deeds by rewards and price, and [to] abstain from evil doings by pains. Trow you, if husbandmen be not better cherished and provoked than they be to exercise to plough, but in process of time so many ploughs will be laid down (as I fear me there be already) that if an unfruitful year should happen amongst us, as commonly doth once in seven years, we should then not have only dearth, but also such scarceness of corn, that we should be driven to seek it from outward parts, and pay dear for it. . . .

. . . . . .

. . . . . .

f. 34*b*–*f.* 38.

Doctor. You have heard that by the free vent and sale of corn, the husbandman's profit is advanced. Then it is showed how every man naturally will follow that wherein he seeth most profit. Therefore men will the gladder occupy husbandry. And the more do occupy husbandry, the more plenty of corn must needs be ; and the more plenty of corn there is, thereof better cheap ; and also the more will be spared over that that shall suffice the realm ; and then, that may be spared in a good year shall bring us again other corn, or else the commodities of other countries necessary for us.

Then the more husbandry is occupied, the more universal breed should be of all victuals, as of neat, sheep, swine, geese, eggs, butter, and cheese, for all these are reared much of corn.

Knight. If men should sell, when a good reasonable year is, all that is overplus when the realm is served, what should we do if a barren year should happen, when no store of corn is left of the good year before?

Doctor. First, you must consider that men be sure they will keep enough to serve themselves within the realm, or they sell any forth of the same; and having liberty to sell at their pleasure, doubt ye not, but they had liefer sell their corn 2*d.* or 4*d.* better cheap within the realm, than to be at charges with carrying, and peril of adventure, in sending it over the sea, and sell it dearer (except it be for much more gains). And thus men, being provoked with lucre, will keep the more corn, looking for a dear year in the country, whereby must need be the greater store. And though they did not so, but should sell over the sea all that they might spare over that serveth the realm when the year is plentiful, yet by reason that, through the means aforesaid, more ploughs are set to work than would suffice the realm in a plentiful year, if a scarce year should fall after, the corn of so many ploughs, as in a good year would be more than enough, in [an unfruitful] year at the least should be sufficient to serve the realm. And so should the realm be served with enough of corn in a scarce year, and in a plenteous year no more than enough, which might be sold over the sea for great treasure or other commodities; where now, in a plentiful year, we seek to have as much as may suffice the realm. Then if a scarce year should happen, we must needs lack of our own to serve, and be driven to buy from beyond the sea. And then, if they were as envious as we are, might they not say, when we required any corn of them, that seeing they could get none from us, when we had plenty, why should they let us have any corn when we have scarcity? Surely common reason would that one region should help another when it lacketh. And therefore God hath ordained that no country should have all commodities; but that, that one lacketh, another bringeth forth, and that, that one country lacketh this year, another hath plenty thereof the same year, to the intent that one may know they have need of another's help, and thereby love and society to grow amongst all the more. But here we will do as though we had need of no other country in the earth, but to live all of ourselves; and [as] though we might make the market of all things as we list ourselves; for though God is bountiful unto us and sendeth us many great commodities, yet we could not live without the commodities of others. And, for an ensample, of iron [and] salt, though we have competently thereof, yet we have not the third part to suffice the realm; and that [can] in no wise be spared if we will occupy husbandry. Then tar, resin, pitch, oil, steel, we have none at all; as for wines, spices, linen cloth, silks, and collars, though we might live so without them, yet far from any civility should it be. As I deny not [but many things we might have here sufficiently that we buy now beyond the seas, and] many things we might spare wholly; whereof, if time shall serve, I will talk more hereafter. But now to return to the first point that I spake of before, to be one of the means to bring husbandry up, that is by abasing the estimation of wool and fells; though I take not that way to be as good as the other, for I do not allow that mean that may base any of our commodities except it be for the enhancement of a better commodity, but if both commodities may be enhanced together, as by the last device I think they might be, I allow that way better; nevertheless whereas you, brother merchant, showed before that either by restraining of wools or other commodities, till they were equivalent within the realm after the rate of the corn, or by enhancing the custom of wool and other the said commodities, were brought like to the corn in proportion, the King's Highness' custom should be minished, I think not so. For the one way, as much as he should have for the more wool vented over, so much should he have for the less wool at a greater custom vented over. And the other way is, as much as his Grace should lose by his custom of wool, so much or more should his Grace win by the custom of clothes made within the realm. But one thing I do note by this latter device, that if they should take place, we must do; that is, if we keep within us much of our commodities, we must spare many other things that we have now from beyond the seas; for we must always take heed that we buy no more of strangers than we sell them [for so we should empoverish ourselves and enrich them]. For he were no good husband that hath no other yearly revenues but of husbandry to live on, that will buy more in the market than he selleth again. And that is a point we might save much by of our treasure, in this realm, if we would. And I marvel no man taketh heed unto it, what number first of trifles cometh hither from beyond the seas, that we might either clean spare, or else make them within our own realm, for the which we pay inestimable treasure every year, or else exchange substantial wares and necessary for them, for the which we might receive great treasure. Of the which sort I mean glasses, as well looking as drinking, as to glass windows, dials, tables, cards, balls, puppets, penhorns, inkhorns, toothpicks, gloves, knives, daggers, pouches, brooches, agletes, buttons of silk and silver, earthen pots, pins, points, hawk's bells, paper both white and brown, and a thousand like things, that might either be clean spared, or else made within the realm sufficient for us. And as for some things, they make it of our own commodities and send it us again; whereby they set their people on work, and do exhaust much treasure out of this realm. As of our wool they make cloth, caps, and carses; of our fells they make Spanish skins, gloves, girdles; of our tin, salts, spoons and dishes; of our broken linen cloth and rags, paper both white and brown. What treasure, think you, goeth out of this realm for every of these things? And then for all together it exceedeth my estimation. There is no man that can be contented with any other gloves than is made in France or in Spain; or carse, but it must be of Flanders dye; nor cloth, but it must be of French dye or fresadow; nor brooch nor aglet, but of Venice making or Milanese; nor dagger, sword, nor girdle, or knife, but of Spanish making; no, not so much as a spur, but it must be fetched at the milliner's hand. I have seen within these twenty years, when there were not of these haberdashers that sell French or Milan caps, glasses, as well looking as drinking, yea, all manner vessels of the same stuff; painted cruses, gay daggers, knives, swords, and girdles that is able to make any temperate man to gaze on them, and to buy somewhat, though it serve to no purpose necessary. What need they beyond the sea to travel to Peru or such far country, or to try out the sands of the river Tagus in Spain [Pactolus] in Asia and Ganges in India, to get amongst them small sparks of gold, or to dig the bowels of the earth, for the mine of silver and gold, when they can of unclean clay, not far sought for, and of [pebble] stones and fern roots make [good] gold and silver more than a great many of gold mines would make. I think not so little as a hundred thousand pound a year is fetched of our treasure for things of no value of themselves, but only for the labours of the workers of the same, which are set on work all of our charges. What grossness be we of, that see it and suffer such a continual spoil to be made of our goods and treasure, by such means and specially, that will suffer our own commodities to go, and set strangers on work, and then to buy them again at their hands; as of our wool they make and dye carses, fresadows, broadcloths, and caps beyond the seas, and bring them hither to be sold again; wherein note, I pray you, what they do make us pay at the end for our stuff again, for the stranger custom, for the workmanship, and colours, and lastly for the second custom in the return of the wares into the realm again; whereas, with working the same within our realm, our own men should be set on work at the charges of strangers; the custom should be borne all by strangers to the king, and the clear gains to remain within the realm. . . .

. . . . . .

f. 53*b*–*f.* 55.

And now, because we are entered into communication of artificers, I will make this division of them. Some of them do but bring money out of the country; some other, that which they do get, they spend again in the country; and the third sort of artificers be they that do bring treasure into the country. Of the first, I reckon all mercers, grocers, vintners, haberdashers, milliners, and such as do sell wares growing beyond the seas, and do fetch out our treasure of the same. Which kind of artificers, as I reckon them tolerable, and yet are not so necessary in a commonwealth but they might be best spared of all other; yet if we had not other artificers, to bring in as much treasure as they bring forth, we should be great losers by them. Of the second sort be these: shoemakers, tailors, carpenters, masons, tilers, butchers, brewers, bakers, victuallers of all sorts, which like as they get their living in the country, so they spend it; but they bring in no treasure unto us. Therefore we must [cherish] well the third sort; and these be clothiers, tanners, cappers, and worsted makers only that I know, [which] by their misteries and faculties, do bring in any treasure. As for our wool, fells, tin, lead, butter and cheese, these be the commodities that the ground bears, requiring the industry of a few persons; and if we should only trust to such, and devise nothing else to occupy ourselves, a few persons would serve us for the rearing of such things, and few also [it would] find; and so should the realm be like a [grange], better furnished with beasts than with men; whereby it might be subject to the spoil of other nations about. Which is the more to be feared and eschewed, because the country of his own kind is apt to bring forth such things, as is said before, for the breed of cattle, than for such things as [be] for the nourishment of men, if Pomponius Mela be to be believed, which describing the island, saith thus: *plana, ingens, fecunda, verum iis que pecora quam homines benignius alunt.* That is to say, it is plain, large and plentiful, but of those things that nourisheth beasts more kindly than men. So many forests, chases, parks, marshes and waste grounds, that be more here than most commonly elsewhere, declare the same not to be all in vain that he affirms; that hath not so much arable ground, vines, olives, fruits, and such as be most necessary for the food of men. And as they require many hands in the culture, so they find most persons food; as France, Spain and divers other countries have. Therefore as much ground, as here is apt for those things, would be [turned] (as much as may be) to such uses as may find most persons. And over that, towns and cities would be replenished with all kinds of artificers; not only clothiers which as yet were our natural occupation, but with cappers, glovers, paper makers, glasiers, pointers, goldsmiths, blacksmiths of all sorts, coverlet makers, needle makers, pinners and such other; so as we should not only have enough of such things to serve our realm, and save an infinite treasure that goeth now over for so many of the same, but also might spare of such things ready wrought to be sold over, whereby we should fetch again other necessary commodities and treasures. And thus should be both replenished the realm of people able to defend it, and also win much treasure to the same. Such occupations alone do enrich divers countries, that be else barren of themselves; and what riches they bring to the country where they be well used, the country of Flanders and Germany do well declare; where, through such occupations, it hath so many and wealthy cities, that were incredible in so little ground to be. Wherefore in my mind they are far wide of right consideration, that would have none or less clothing within the realm, because it is sometimes occasion of business or tumults, for lack of vent. There is nothing every way so commodious or necessary for men's use, but it is sometime by ill handling occasion of displeasure; no, not fire and water, that be so necessary as nothing can be more.

4. Sir Thomas Gresham on the Fall of the Exchanges [*Burgon's Life and Times of Sir Thomas Gresham, Vol. I, Appendix No. XXI, pages* 483–486]. 1558.

To the Queen's most excellent Majesty.

It may please your Majesty to understand, that the first occasion of the fall of the exchange did grow by the King's Majesty, your late father, in abasing his coin from vi ounces fine to iii ounces fine. Whereupon the exchange fell from xxvi*s.* viii*d.* to xiii*s.* iv*d.* which was the occasion that all your fine gold was conveyed out of this your realm.

Secondly, by the reason of his wars, the King's Majesty fell into great debt in Flanders. And for the payment thereof they had no other device but pay it by exchange, and to carry over his fine gold for the payment of the same.

Thirdly, the great freedom of the Steelyard and granting of licence for the carrying of your wool and other commodities out of your realm, which is now one of the chief points that your Majesty hath to foresee in this your common weal; that you never restore the steads called the Steelyard again to their privilege, which hath been the chief point of the undoing of this your realm, and the merchants of the same.

Now, for redress of these things, in an. xvcli [1551] the King's Majesty, your late brother, called me to be his agent, and reposed a more trust in me, as well for the payment of his debts beyond the seas, as for the raising of the exchange, being then at xv*s.* and xvi*s.* the pound; and your money current, as it is at this present, being not in value x*s.* First, I practised with the King and my lord of Northumberland to overthrow the Steelyard, or else it could not be brought to pass, for that they would keep down the exchange by this consideration; whereas your own merchants payeth outwards xiv*d.* upon a cloth custom, they pay but ix*d.*; and likewise, for all such wares as was brought into your realm, your own mere merchants payeth xii*d.* upon the pound, the Steelyard paid but iii*d.* upon the pound, which is v*s.* difference upon the hundredth: and as they were men that ran all upon the exchange for the buying of their commodities, what did they pass to give a lower price than your own merchants, when they got v*l.* in the hundred by your custom? Which in process of time would have undone your whole realm, and your merchants of the same.

Secondly, I practised with the King's Majesty, your brother, to come in credit with his own mere merchants: and when time served, I practised with them at a set shipping, the exchange being still at xvi*s.*, that every man should pay the King xv*s.* upon a cloth in Antwerp, to pay at double usage xx*s.* in London; which the King's Majesty paid them royally, which did amount to the sum of lxm*l.* And so, vi months after, I practised the like upon their commodities for the sum of lxxm*l.* [£70,000] to pay for every pound sterling xxii*s.*: so by this means, I made plenty of money, and scarcity, and brought into the King's hands, which raised the exchange to xxiii*s.* iv*d.* And by this means I did not only bring the King's Majesty, your brother, out of debt, whereby I saved him vi or vii*s.* upon the pound, but saved his treasure within the realm, as therein Mr. Secretary Cecil was most privy unto.

Thirdly, I did likewise cause all foreign coins to be unvalued, whereby it might be brought into the mint to his Majesty's most fordle[1]; at which time the King your brother died, and for my reward of service, the Bishop of Winchester sought to undo me, and whatsoever I said in these matters I should not be credited: and against all wisdom, the said Bishop went and valued the French crown at vi*s.* iv*d.*, and the pistole at vi*s.* ii*d.*, and the silver royal at vi*d.* *ob.* Whereupon, immediately, the exchange fell to xx*s.* vi*d.* and xxi*s.*, and there hath kept ever since. And so consequently after this rate and manner, I brought the Queen's Majesty, your sister, out of debt of the sum of ccccxxxvm*l.* [£435,000].

Fourthly, by this it may plainly appear to your Highness, as the exchange is the thing that eats out all princes, to the whole destruction of their common weal, if it be not substantially looked unto, so likewise the exchange is the chief and richest

[1] *i.e.* Fordeal, or advantage.

thing only above all other, to restore your Majesty and your realm to fine gold and silver, and is the mean that makes all foreign commodities and your own commodities with all kind of victuals good cheap, and likewise keeps your fine gold and silver within your realm. As, for example to your Highness, the exchange being at this present at xxii*s*., all merchants seek to bring into your realm fine gold and silver; for if he should deliver it by exchange, he disburses xxii*s*. Flemish to have xx*s*. sterling: and to bring it in gold and silver he shall make thereof xxi*s*. iv*d*.—whereby he saves viii*d*. in the pound: which profit, if the exchange should keep but after this rate of xxii*s*. in few years you should have a wealthy realm, for here the treasure should continue for ever; for that all men should find more profit by v*l* in the hundred to deliver it per exchange, than to carry it over in money. So consequently the higher the exchange riseth, the more shall your Majesty and your realm and common weal flourish, which thing is only kept up by art and God's providence; for the coin of this your realm doth not correspond in fineness not x*s*. the pound.

Finally, and it please your majesty to restore this your realm into such state, as heretofore it hath been; first, your Highness hath no other ways, but when time and opportunity serveth, to bring your base money into fine of xi ounces fine, and so gold after the rate.

Secondly, not to restore the Steelyard to their usurped privileges.

Thirdly, to grant as few licences as you can.

Fourthly, to come in as small debt as you can beyond seas.

Fifthly, to keep up your credit, and specially with your own merchants, for it is they must stand by you at all events in your necessity. And thus I shall most humbly beseech your Majesty to accept this my [poor writing in good] part; wherein I shall from time to time, as opportunity doth serve, put your Highness in remembrance, according to the trust your Majesty hath reposed in me; beseeching the Lord to give me the grace and fortune that my service may always be acceptable to your Highness; as knoweth our Lord, whom preserve your noble Majesty in health, and long to reign over us with increase of honour.

By your Majesty's most humble and faithful obedient subject, THOMAS GRESHAM, *Mercer*.

5. The Reasons Why Bullion is Exported [*Br. M. Cotton Ms. Otho. E. x., f.* 145[1]], *temp.* Elizabeth.

Where the Queen's Majesty is moved, that for the staying of the transportation of gold she will be pleased either to call in all gold by proclamation and then to coin it anew again with more alloy, or else that her Majesty should call in no gold, but coin new and utter them at higher rate than now, it seemeth the matters intend, that it is transported for the richness only, and, being either based by alloy or dearly priced, no more would be transported.

But if all the true causes of this late transportation be considered, that will not be sufficient to stay gold within.

The true causes, that it is transported, be these with others :

1. Some is carried into the Low Countries, because the exchange hath been high and the gold of greater prices there than here.

2. These dear years much hath been carried out to buy corn with, wherein somewhat endeavour hath been, because the return paid no custom.

3. Very much hath been transported to provide foreign commodities, because this realm spendeth more of them, than the same commodities transported amount unto, as it is supposed and as may be perceived by the wines, silks, lawns, gold-lace, silver-lace and such like here spent.

4. Much is conveyed by strangers, that bring in their country commodities and will not employ the price in English commodities, because their customs be great.

5. The like is sometimes done by English merchants for the paying of debts or providing of foreign commodities, for the saving of custom outward being also great.

6. Much bullion hath been transported, because the merchants and goldsmiths could not of long time have it coined and delivered in due time out of the mint.

7. Some by captains, soldiers and others, that might not be searched.

8. Some by the help of the mintmen in thirty-shilling-pieces upon pretence to make great gain thereof to her Majesty.

The second cause will now cease of itself ; the fourth, fifth, sixth and eighth may be removed by good orders to be taken ;

[1] Quoted Schanz, *op. cit.*, Vol. II, pp. 648–9.

the seventh by peace amongst princes; the first will never be taken away further than shall please the bankers and rich merchants of the Low Countries, who joining with the rich Flemings dwelling will be able with their money and cunning to make the exchange to rise and fall, as they shall think good for their gain or our loss. And the governors there, finding by their mint-masters and merchants the alteration of the English standards and values of gold, being more vigilant, provident and skilful in such matters than the English, will at their pleasures cry up and down the currency of English coin, be it never so base, at such times and in such manner as [the]y will, draw it from home to their . . . lnes and melt it or return it back at their pleasures for their own gain and our loss, unless they will agree and take order, that it shall be always current there at the same value that it is here, without alteration.

But the third *causa causarum* being taken away, which is to be wished for, although not to be hoped for in haste, all the rest and all other like causes of transportation must need cease withall or at the least do little hurt; for if England would spend less of foreign commodities than the home commodities will pay for, then the remain must of necessity be returned of silver or gold; but if otherwise, then it will fare in England in short time as it doth with a man of great yearly living, that spendeth more yearly than his own revenue, and spendeth of the stock besides.

And so it is concluded, that for these reasons neither the baseing of the standards nor the raising of the values of the coin of gold is like to stay it from transportation.

6. The Italian Merchants Explain the Foreign Exchanges to Sir Thomas Gresham and Other Royal Commissioners [*Ms. of Lord Calthorpe, Vol. XX, f.* 68[1]], 1576.

Forasmuch as your worships have required, that we, the merchants Italians, should show present your worships with more brevity, than we have done afore, in what points doth grieve us the new imposition and order, that hath been set upon

[1] Quoted Schanz, *op. cit.*, pp. 642–6. It will be observed that the Italian merchants' knowledge of English is apparently somewhat defective.

the exchange, although it is not easily utter it in few words, nevertheless we have set it forth as briefly as we can.

Therefore it may please your worships to understand, that the chiefest living and maintenance that we have is upon the commissions that are sent unto us of our friends from beyond the seas to sell foreign wares here in London and buy English wares for to send over.

The trade of the foreign wares for England will much decay because of the imposition and difficulty upon the exchange; for such our friends, that did send such commodities as alum, woad, canvas, silks, wines and other necessary things for the intent to reiterate shortly after the sending hither such commodities, so soon as they knew they were here arrived, did use to take up money by exchange for London; and if the said wares were not sold or money not due, they gave here commission to their factors to take it up by rechange again; and so in time of an usage or double usage of Antwerp, an usage or a fair at Lyons, this matter might be well compassed without any great loss, and by this mean they might help themselves with their money of their wares a great while before that it were money in deed; but now that they shall know, that the exchange will give them such loss by the payment of this fee besides the ordinary interest that is used to come upon the exchange, they shall not be able to continue this trade nor to reiterate so often the same. Therefore there shall ensue a great diminishing of the Queen's custom inwards, and that the English people shall pay the dearer for the necessary foreign commodities, and we particularly shall remain destitute of these commissions and factories.

We say likewise of the trade of others our commissioners, that did use to send for English commodities as cloths and others being not forbidden and inward, they send nothing or very little; for those, that ought here to buy for themselves, might in two manners furnish the money, the one causing money to be remitted unto them from beyond the seas, and the other in taking money here in London by exchange. Touching the first manner they shall lack much of that help; for money shall not be remitted unto them, for because in foreign places there shall be found no man that will take up money by exchange for London, knowing that it shall be more damageable unto them than other places as much as this fee doth import, which will always fall upon the debtor, and he shall scarcely find money here in London to take up by exchange; so little will be exchange that hereafter will be made, therefore our commission outward will fail unto us, as we have said above of these inward, and the Queen's customs outwards also will much decay, and the English people, that did utter at good prices the commodities and handicrafts, shall not be able to do it as afore they were, they shall suffer much damage and discommodity. Besides this the free exchange hath been an instrument whereby the merchants might pay honourably their debts at their day; for if one ought, for a manner of an example, this day a sum of money, it should be a dishonour unto him to desire his creditors to tarry a seven night, a fortnight or 20 days, until he should retain money for debts due unto him. But to pay his said debt, he might presently take up money by exchange to Lyons, Antwerp and then, after he had received his money, he might remit there for the same time that he took it up, and so with little loss compass his business. But now in such case considering that he shall be forced to pay two times this imposition one in the taking and the other in the delivering so shortly after, the interest of few days will cost him too much; therefore he shall be fain to restrain his trade and shall not be able to accept his friends' debts and changes he did before.

Likewise those of us shall find too much charges, that made double exchanges for service of the English merchants, as for example they took money of your vintners for Bordeaux, and to the intent that the said money might be ready there, they did exchange it for Lyons or other places being content of any small profit; now that they must pay two times this imposition and that the ordinary brokerage, that often times they did save, they now shall not save, they shall need to make their reckoning and ask greater price of the vintners, the which peradventure will find it so heavy beside his part of the fee which he must pay, that he might take an evil occasion to send over the money.

We made also oftentimes amongst us double exchanges without any broker, which was, for a manner of example, that one of us had money in Venice and would bring into this realm French wares, and another hath money in Lyons and would bring wares out of Italy, and so they did agree together to give one to another mutual letters of exchange the one for Lyon and the other for Venice ; and whereas such double exchange of the value of 100*li.* had no charge at all, now it shall have charge 35*s.*, for the fee shall be paid for every one of the 2 bills of exchange, which is 25*s.* and 10*s.* brokerage, that now is not to be escaped, maketh up the 35*s.*, so that we shall be fain utterly to leave of these double exchanges, that we made as well for the commodity of the merchants of your nation as of ourselves to the intent still to serve to the ease and trade of merchandise.

But[1] the order yet is of more trouble and impediment, than the very imposition ; for though the fee were in a manner but a penny in every hundredth pound, it were needful to find a means that the Queen's Majesty should not be defrauded of the same, the which we cannot invent or imagine, without that register shall be kept of all our doings and that our books shall be seen and our letters opened, the which thing will be an extreme prejudice unto our occupations, and we would have taken pain more at large to express the same, if that your worships had not the experience and knowledge better than us of this matter.

Touching the standard of the English money, that you complain of is kept low by reason of the free exchange, we can say nothing but that our exchanges are made with a mutual consent between merchant and merchant, and that the abundance of the deliverers or of the takers make the exchange rise or fall; and this occasion doth counterpoise this place of London with the others ; for if you will compel a needful person to take up for exchange for Antwerp at 26*s.* Flemish for every pound sterling, when the exchange is there at 24*s.*, he shall leave off to take it, but will cause money to be remitted to him from thence according to the course of the exchange there.

But some do complain of some strangers, that bring into England merchandises for more value than that they send out. We say, that the cause of this is the inequalities of the customs outwards ; for a stranger cannot send into Flanders or into France a piece of cloth or kersey, except it should stand him dearer than he might have them there in those places at an Englishman's hands. Besides that it is to be considered, that the most part of commodities of this realm,

[1] "Bothe" in MS.

that in times before might be transported out, now they be utterly forbidden as well corn, leather, tallow, or else charged with great licence as undressed cloths and others, so that it is not possible for strangers to meddle there withall; nevertheless we do deny, that the overplus of the amounting of the strange wares should be sent over by us in ready money, but we deliver it by exchange unto your English merchants, that may better traffic outwardly, and if we do at lower price than the value of the standard, we are very sorry and we would very gladly it were otherwise.

That be the damages difficulties and inconveniences, that by this order shall happen, that is to say, for our part the whole destitution of all our friends' commission, whereupon was grounded our living and maintenance; damage unto Queen's Majesty for the diminishing of her customs for greater sum than the importance of the rent of this fee, though that exchanges should be in such frequency and number as they have been heretofore; the which thing cannot be, for very few exchange will be made; damage also to the common weal, for they shall pay dear for foreign wares for the scarcity that shall be here of the same, and they shall not so well sell the commodities of the realm, as they have done afore; and finally a dangerous occasion may be presented to some to carry away the money out of the realm, the which thing the free exchange doth avoid, and for this intent it is to be thought that it was instituted.

Therefore we, considering that among all restraints, troubles or impediments, that ever was set against the trade of merchants in any place, this is the troublesomest, we beseech your worships to examine it and to report to her Majesty and to her honourable council upon this matter even as God Almighty shall inspire you for the common profit and wealth of this realm.

7. An Act Avoiding Divers Foreign Wares Made by Handicraftsmen Beyond the Seas [5 *Eliz. c.* 7, *Statutes of the Realm, Vol. IV, Part I, pp.* 428–429], 1562.

Whereas heretofore the artificers of this realm of England (as well within the city of London as within other cities, towns and boroughs of the same realm) that is to wit, girdlers, cutlers, saddlers, glovers, point-makers, and such like handicraftsmen, have been in the said faculties greatly wrought, and greatly set on work, as well for the sustentation of themselves, their wives and families, as for a good education of a great part of the youth of this realm in good art and laudable exercise, besides the manifold benefits, that by means or by reason of their knowledges, inventions, and continual travel, daily and universally came to the whole estate of the commonwealth of this said realm:

II. Yet notwithstanding so now it is, that by reason of the abundance of foreign wares brought into this realm from the parts of beyond the seas, the said artificers are not only less occupied, and thereby utterly impoverished, the youth not trained in the said sciences and exercises, and thereby the said faculties, and the exquisite knowledges thereof, like in short time within this realm to decay; but also divers cities and towns within this realm of England much thereby impaired, the whole realm greatly endamaged, and other countries notably enriched, and the people thereof well set on work, to their commodities and livings, in the arts and sciences aforesaid, and to the great discouragement of skilful workmen of this realm, being in very deed nothing inferior to any stranger in the faculties aforesaid.

III. For reformation whereof, be it enacted by our sovereign lady the Queen's Highness, and by the Lords Spiritual and Temporal, and the Commons of this present parliament assembled and by the authority of the same, that no person or persons whatsoever, from or after the feast of the Nativity of St. John Baptist now next ensuing, shall bring or cause to be brought into this realm of England from the parts of beyond the seas, any girdles, harness for girdles, rapiers, daggers, knives, hilts, pummels, lockets, chapes, dagger-blades, handles, scabbards, and sheaths for knives, saddles, horse-harness, stirrups, bits, gloves, points, leather-laces or pins, being ready made or wrought in any parts of beyond the seas, to be sold, bartered or exchanged within this realm of England or Wales; upon pain to forfeit all such wares so to be brought contrary to the true meaning of this act, in whose hands soever they or any of them shall be found, or the very value thereof. This act to continue and endure to the end of the next parliament.

8. An Act Touching Cloth-Workers and Cloths Ready Wrought to be Shipped Over the Sea [8 *Eliz. c.* 6, *Statutes of the Realm, Vol. IV, Part I, p.* 489], 1566.

For the better employment and relief of great multitudes of the Queen's Majesty subjects, using the art and labour of cloth-working, it may please the Queen's most excellent Majesty, at the most humble suit of her said subjects, that it be enacted, and be it enacted by the authority of this present parliament:—That from henceforth for every nine clothes unwrought, hereafter to be shipped or carried into any the parts beyond the seas, contrary to the form of any statute heretofore made and now remaining in strength, by force of any licence hereafter to be granted, the party that shall ship and carry over the same, shall ship and carry over also one like woollen cloth of like sort, length, breadth and goodness, ready wrought and dressed; that is to say, rowed, barbed, first coursed and shorn from the one end to the other, so that every tenth cloth passing over the seas in form aforesaid may and shall be dressed within this realm, before the same shall be shipped or transported over, upon pain to forfeit for every such nine clothes so to be shipped or transported contrary to the meaning of this act, ten pounds. Provided always, that every such tenth cloth so to be transported ready wrought, shall not be accounted any of the clothes permitted to be transported by force of such licence, but that such person as shall have such licence may transport according to such licence the full number of clothes unwrought mentioned in the same licence, over and above the number of such tenth clothes which they shall be compelled to ship and carry over by force of this statute. And be it further enacted by authority aforesaid, that from the last day of February now next coming, no person shall ship or carry into the parts beyond the seas, contrary to the form of any statute heretofore made now remaining in force, any cloth commonly called Kentish cloth or Suffolk cloth, made or to be made in the counties of Kent or Suffolk, unwrought and undressed within this realm; that is to say, not rowed, barbed, first coursed and shorn; upon pain to forfeit for every such cloth, commonly called Kentish or Suffolk cloth, made or to be made in either of the said counties, so to be shipped or transported contrary to the form of this statute, forty shillings; and that no licence for transporting of any cloth or clothes shall be construed or expounded to extend to any such Kentish or Suffolk cloth, made or to be made in either of the said counties to be from henceforth transported. . . . .

9. Incorporation of a Joint-Stock Mining Company [*Patent Rolls*,[1] 10 *Eliz.*, *Part V*], 1568.

Elizabeth by the Grace of God, etc. To all unto whom these presents shall come, greeting.

Whereas we . . . have . . . given and granted full power, license and authority to Thomas Thurland, clerk, . . . and to Daniel Houghsetter, a German born . . . to search . . . for all manner of monies or ores of gold, silver, copper, or quicksilver, within our counties of York, Lancaster, Cumberland, Westmoreland, Cornwall, Devon, Gloucestershire and Worcestershire, and within our principality of Wales, or in any of them, and the same to try out, convert, and use to their most profit and commodity. . . .

And whereas our pleasure, intent, and meaning in our said Letters Patent was that, for the better help and more commodity of the said Thomas Thurland and Daniel Houghsetter and their several assignees, they . . . might . . . grant . . . parts and portions of the said licenses . . . and thereupon their several assignees have . . . granted . . . to . . . William, Earl of Pembroke, and Robert, Earl of Leicestershire, and to . . . James, Lord Mountjoy, and to Sir William Cecil, knight, our principal secretary, and John Tamworth and John Dudley, esquires, Leonell Duchet, citizen and alderman of London, Benedict Spynola, of London, merchant, John Lover, William Winter, Anthony Duchett, of the County of Westmoreland, gentlemen . . . Daniel Ulstett, a German born [and ten others], divers parts and portions of the licenses, powers, authorities, privileges, benefits and immunities aforesaid ;

By force whereof the said Thomas Thurland and Daniel Houghsetter . . . have travailed in the search, work and experiment of the mines and ores aforesaid . . . and have now brought the said work to very good effect, whereby great benefit is like to come to us and this our Realm of England, which also will the rather come to pass if the persons

[1] Printed by the Selden Society, Vol. 28, pp. 4–15.

. . . . having interest in the privileges aforesaid might by our grant be incorporated and made a perpetual body politic; . . .

Know ye, therefore, that we . . . . do give and grant to the aforenamed William Earl of Pembroke [and the others as above] that they by the name of Governor, Assistants, and Commonalty for the Mines Royal shall be from henceforth one body politic in itself incorporate, and a perpetual society of themselves both in deed and name. . . .

And, further, we . . . will and grant . . . that they . . . shall and may not only admit into the said corporation and society such and as many persons as by the statutes . . . shall be prescribed . . . so that every such person . . . shall . . . have for the term of his life at the least the benefit of a quarter of one four-and-twenty part of the licenses, powers, authorities, privileges, benefits and communities aforesaid, . . . but also shall and may minister to every such person to be admitted an oath tending to the due performing and keeping of the rules, statutes, and ordinances in form aforesaid to be made . . .

10. An Act for the Increase of Tillage [13 *Eliz. c.* 13. *Statutes of the Realm, Vol. IV, Part I, pp.* 547-48], 1571.

For the better increase of tillage, and for maintenance and increase of the navy and mariners of this realm, be it enacted, that from and after the feast of the Nativity of St. John Baptist next coming, it shall be lawful to all and every person and persons being subjects of the Queen's Majesty, her heirs and successors, and inhabiting within her highness' realms and dominions, only out of such ports and creeks where are or shall be resident a customer or collector of subsidy of tonnage and poundage, or one of their deputies, and not elsewhere, to load, carry or transport any wheat, rye, barley, malt, peas or beans into any parts beyond the seas, being in amity with this realm, and not prohibited by any restraint or proclamation, only to sell as a merchandize in ships carriers or other vessels bearing cross sails, whereof any English born subjects inhabiting within her Highness' realms and dominions then shall be the only owners, at all such times as the several prices thereof shall be so reasonable and moderate in the several counties where any such transportation shall be intended as that no prohibition shall be made, either by the Queen's Majesty, her heirs or successors, by proclamation to be made in the shire-town or in any port towns of the county, or else by some order of the lord president and council in the north, or the lord president and council in Wales, within their several jurisdictions, or of the justices of assizes at their sessions in other shires out of the jurisdiction of the said two presidents and councils, or by the more part of the justices of the peace of the county at their quarter sessions, in this manner following; that is, the said lord president and councils of the shires within their jurisdiction, the justices of assize at their several sessions in other shires out of the said jurisdictions belonging to the said councils in the north and in Wales, yearly shall, upon conference had with the inhabitants of the country of the cheapness and dearth of any the said kinds of grain within the countries within jurisdictions of the said councils, or in the other countries within the limits of the said justices of assize, by their discretion determine whether it shall be meet at anytime to permit any grain to be carried out of the realm by any port within the said several jurisdictions or limits, and so shall in writing under their hands and seals cause and make a determination either for permission or prohibition, and the same cause to be by the sheriff of the counties published and affixed in as many accustomed market towns and ports within the said shire as they shall think convenient, and in such manner as the Queen's Majesty's proclamations are usually published and affixed; which determination of the said presidents and councils in their jurisdictions, and of the justices of assize in their limits, shall continue in force for the time, place, and manner therein expressed until the said presidents and councils shall otherwise order, or until the justices of assize at their being in their said circuits in every of the said counties shall alter or otherwise order the same, except the same shall be otherwise in the mean time altered or countermanded by the Queen's Majesty, her heirs or successors, or by some order of the justices of the peace in the counties situated out of the jurisdictions of the said two councils in their quarter sessions to be holden in the mean-time, or the greater part of them, shall find the same determination of the justices of assize to be hurtful to the county by means of dearth, or to be a great hindrance to tillage by means of too much cheapness, and shall by their writings under their hands and seals make any determination to the contrary, either for permission or prohibition of carrying of any kind of grain out of the realm; . . . . .

. . . Provided nevertheless, that neither any of the said presidents and councils, nor the said justices of assize nor the said justices of peace above mentioned, shall publish any their determinations above mentioned until the same shall be first by writing notified to the Queen's Majesty or to her privy council, and by her Majesty or her privy council shall be liked and allowed.

Provided also, that the Queen's Majesty, her heirs and successors, shall have and receive by the customers and officers of her ports for the custom or poundage of every quarter of wheat to be transported by force of this statute, twelve pence, and of every quarter of any other grain, eight pence, and of every quarter of wheat that shall be by any special licence hereafter to be granted transported out of the realm, and not by force of this statute, two shillings, and of every quarter of other grain, sixteen pence, notwithstanding any manner of words that shall be contained or inserted in any licences to the contrary; which said several sums, so to be had or taken as custom or poundage, to be in full satisfaction of all manner of custom or poundage for the said corn or grain by any constitution, order, statute, law or custom heretofore made, used, or taken for transporting of any such manner of corn or grain.

Provided also and be it enacted by the authority of this present parliament, that the Queen's Majesty, her heirs and successors, may at all times by her writ of proclamation to be published generally in the whole realm, or in the counties of this realm where any port towns are, command that no person shall by virtue of this act transport or carry out any manner of grain to any parts out of her dominions, either generally out of any port in the realm, or particularly out of any special ports to be in the same proclamation named; and that it shall not be lawful for any person to carry out any such grain contrary to the tenor of the same proclamation, upon such pains as by the laws of the realm are and have been provided.

11. Instructions for an English Factor in Turkey [*Hakluyt. The Principal Voyages of the English Nation*], 1582.

. . . And for that of many things that tend to the common benefit of the State, some tend more and some less, I find that no one thing, after one another, is greater than clothing, and the things incident to the same. And understanding that you are of right good capacity, and become a factor at Constantinople, and in other parts of Turkey, I find no man fitter of all the English factors there than you. And therefore I am so bold to put you in mind and to tell you wherein with some endeavour you may chance to do your country much good, and give an infinite sort of the poor people occasion to pray for you here throughout the realm. This that I mean is in matter of cloth, etc.

1. First, you cannot deny but that this realm yieldeth the most fine wool, the most soft, the most strong wool, the most durable in cloth, and most apt of nature of all others to receive dye, and that no island or any one kingdom so small doth yield so great abundance of the same. . . .

2. There is no commodity of this realm that may set so many poor subjects on work, as this doth, that doth bring in so much treasure, and so much enrich the merchant, and so much employ the navy of this realm, as this commodity of our wool doth.

Ample and full vent of this noble and rich commodity is it that the commonweal of this realm doth require.

Spain now aboundeth with wool, and the same are clothed. Turkey hath wools, and so have divers provinces of Christendom and of heatheners, and cloth is made of the same in divers places.

1. But if England have the most fine and the most excellent wools of the world in all respects (as it cannot be denied but it hath). 2. If there may be added to the same excellent artificial, and true making, and excellent dyeing. 3. Then no doubt but that we shall have vent for our cloths, though the rest of the world did abound much more with wool than it doth. . . .

But if foreign nations turn their wools, inferior to ours, into truer and more excellent made cloth, and shall dye the same in truer, surer, and more excellent and more delectable colours, then shall they sell and make ample vent of their cloths, when the English cloth of better wool shall rest unsold, to the spoil of the merchant, of the clothier, and of the breeder of the wool, and to the turning to bag and wallet of the infinite number of the poor people employed in clothing in several degrees of labour here in England.

Which things weighed, I am to tell you what things I wish you in this realm, and after in Turkey, to endeavour from time to time, as your leisure may permit the same.

Before you out of the realm, that you learn:

1. To know wool, all kinds of cloth made in this realm, and all other employments of wool, home or foreign. . . . All the deceits in clothmaking. . . . The faults in weaving. The faults in walking, rowing, burling, and in racking the cloth above measure upon the tenters. . . .

2. Then to learn of the dyers to discern all kinds of colours, as which be good and sure, and which will not hold; which be fair, and which not. . . .

3. Then to take the names of all the materials and substances used in this city or in the realm in dyeing of cloth or silk. . . .

4. These things superficially learned in the realm before you go, you are fitter in foreign parts to serve your country. . . .

What you shall do in Turkey, besides the business of your factorship.

1. Forasmuch as it is reported that the woollen cloths dyed in Turkey be most excellently dyed, you shall send home unto this realm certain . . . . pieces of shred, to be brought to the Dyers' Hall, there to be shewed, partly to remove out of their heads the too great opinion they have conceived of their own cunning, and partly to move them for shame to endeavour to learn more knowledge, to the honour of their country of England and to the universal benefit of the realm.

2. You shall devise to amend the dyeing of England, by carrying hence an apt young man brought up in the art, or by bringing one or other from thence of skill, or rather to devise to bring one for silks, and another for wool and for woollen cloth. . . .

3. Then to learn to know all the materials and substances that the Turks use in dyeing, be they of herbs, simple or

compound, be they plants, barks, wood, berries, seeds, grains, or mineral matter. . . .

5. And in any wise, if anile that coloureth blue be a natural commodity of those parts, and if it be compounded of an herb, to send the same into this realm by seed, or by root in barrel of earth, with all the whole order of sowing, setting, planting, replanting, and with the compounding of the same, that it may become a natural commodity in this realm, as woad is, to this end, that the high price of foreign woad (which devoureth yearly great treasure) may be brought down. . . .

8. The wools being natural, and excellent colours for dyeing by this means here also natural, in all the art of clothing then we want but one only special thing. For in this so temperate a climate our people may labour the year throughout . . . and the people of this realm by the great and blessed abundance of victual are cheaply fed, and therefore may afford their labour cheap. And where the clothiers in Flanders, by the flatness of their rivers, cannot make water-mills for their cloths, but are forced to dress and thicken all their cloths by the foot and by the labour of men, whereby their cloths are raised to an higher price, we in England have in all shires store of mills upon falling rivers. . . . Then we have also, for scouring our cloths, earths and clays. . . . Then also have we some reasonable store of alum and copperas here, made for dyeing. . . . Then we have many good waters apt for dyeing, and people to spin and to do the rest of all the labours we want not. So as there wanteth, if colours might be brought in and made natural, but only oil; the want whereof if any man could devise to supply at the full with anything that might become natural in this realm, he, whatsoever he were that could bring it about, might deserve immortal fame in this our commonwealth. . . .

10. And if you shall find that they make any cloth of any kind not made in this realm, that is there of great use, then to bring of the same into this realm some "mowsters,"[1] that our people may fall into the trade, and prepare the same for Turkey. For the more kinds of cloth we can devise to make, the more ample vent of our commodity we shall have, and the more sale of the labour of our poor subjects that else for lack of labour become idle and burdenous to the commonweal, and hurtful to many. And in England we are in our clothing

[1] *i.e.* Samples.

trade to frame ourselves according to the desires of foreign nations, be it that they desire thick or thin, broad or narrow, long or short, white or black.

11. But with this proviso always, that our cloth pass out with as much labour of our people as may be, wherein great consideration ought to be had. For (if vent might so admit), as it were the greatest madness in the world for us to vent our wool not clothed, so were it madness to vent our wool in part or on the whole turned into broad cloth, if we might vent the same in kersies; for there is a great difference to our people between the clothing of a sack of wool in the one and the like sack of wool in the other, of which I wish the merchant of England to have a great care as he may for the universal benefit of the poor; and the turning of a sack of wool into bonnets is better than both, etc. And also not to carry out of the realm any cloth white, but dyed, if it may be, that the subjects of this realm may take as much benefit as is possible, and rather to seek the vent of the cloths dyed with the natural colours of England than such as be dyed with foreign colours.

Thus giving you occasion, by way of a little remembrance, to have desire to do your country good, you shall, if you have any inclination to such good, do more good to the poor ready to starve for relief than ever any subject did in this realm by building of almshouses, and by giving of lands and goods to the relief of the poor. Thus may you help to drive idleness, the mother of most mischief, out of the realm, and win you perpetual fame, and the prayer of the poor, which is more worth than all the gold of Peru and of all the West Indies.

12. THE ADVANTAGES OF COLONIES [*A True Report of the late Discoveries and Possession Taken in the Right of the Crown of England of the Newfound Lands by . . . Sir Humfrey Gilbert*[1]*; Hakluyt's Principal Voyages of the English Nation*], 1583.

. . . The fourth chapter sheweth how that the trade, traffic, and planting in these countries is likely to prove very profitable to the whole realm in general.

Now to show how the same is likely to prove very profitable

[1] Gilbert was drowned in the "Squirrel" on September 9th, 1583. The above document purports to have been written after the return of the "Golden Hind," but before the loss of the "Squirrel" was certainly known.

and beneficial generally to the whole realm. It is very certain that the greatest jewel of this realm, and the chiefest strength and force of the same, for defence or offence in martial matter and manner, is the multitude of ships, masters, and mariners ready to assist the most stately and royal navy of her Majesty, which by reason of this voyage shall have both increase and maintenance. And it is well known that in sundry places of this realm ships have been built and set forth of late days for the trade of fishing only; yet, notwithstanding, the fish which is taken and brought into England by the English navy of fishermen will not suffice for the expense of this realm four months, if there were none else brought of strangers. And the chiefest cause why our English men do not go so far westerly as the especial fishing places do lie, both for plenty and greatness of fish, is for that they have no succour and known safe harbour in those parts. But if our nation were once planted there or thereabouts, whereas they now fish but for two months in the year, they might then fish for so long as pleased themselves . . . which being brought to pass shall increase the number of our ships and mariners. . . .

Moreover, it is well known that all savages . . . . will take marvellous delight in any garment, be it never so simple, as a shirt, a blue, yellow, red, or green cotton cassock, a cap, or such like, and will take incredible pains for such a trifle, . . . which being so, what vent for our English cloths will thereby ensue, and how great benefit to all such persons and artificers, whose names are quoted in the margin, I leave to such as are discreet. . . .

To what end need I endeavour myself by arguments to prove that by this voyage our navy and navigation shall be enlarged, when as there needeth none other reason than the manifest and late example of the near neighbours to this realm, the Kings of Spain and Portugal, who, since the first discovery of the Indies, have not only mightily enlarged their dominions, greatly enriched themselves and their subjects, but have also, by just account, trebled the number of their ships, masters and mariners, a matter of no small moment and importance?

Besides this, it will prove a general benefit unto our country, that, through this occasion, not only a great number of men which do now live idly at home, and are burdenous, chargeable, and unprofitable to this realm, shall hereby be set on work, but also children of twelve or fourteen years of age, or under, may be kept from idleness, in making of a thousand kinds of trifling things, which will be good merchandise for that country. And, moreover, our idle women (which the realm may well spare) shall also be employed on plucking, drying, and sorting of feathers, in pulling, beating, and working of hemp, and in gathering of cotton, and divers things right necessary for dyeing. All which things are to be found in those countries most plentifully. And the men may employ themselves in dragging for pearl, working for mines, and in matters of husbandry, and likewise in hunting the whale for trane, and making casks to put the same in, besides in fishing for cod, salmon and herring, drying, salting and barrelling the same, and felling of trees, hewing and sawing of them, and such like work, meet for those persons that are no men of art or science.

Many other things may be found to the great relief and good employment of no small number of the natural subjects of this realm, which do now live here idly, to the common annoy of the whole State. Neither may I here omit the great hope and likelihood of a passage beyond the Grand Bay into the South Seas, confirmed by sundry authors to be found leading to Cataia, the Moluccas and Spiceries, whereby may ensue as general a benefit to the realm, or greater than yet hath been spoken of, without either such charges or other inconveniences, as, by the tedious tract of time and peril, which the ordinary passage to those parts at this day doth minister. . . .

I must now, according to my promise, show forth some probable reasons that the adventurers in this journey are to take particular profit by the same. It is, therefore, convenient that I do divide the adventurers into two sorts, the noblemen and gentlemen by themselves, and the merchants by themselves. For, as I do hear, it is meant that there shall be one society of the noblemen and gentlemen, and another society of the merchants ; and yet not so divided, but that each society may freely and frankly trade and traffic one with the other.

And first to bend my speech to the noblemen and gentlemen, who do chiefly seek a temperate climate, wholesome air, fertile soil, and a strong place by nature whereupon they may fortify, and there either plant themselves or such other persons as they shall think good to send to be lords of that place and country :—To them I say that all these things are very easy to be found within the degrees of 30 and 60 aforesaid, either by south or north, both in the continent and in islands thereunto adjoining, at their choice . . . and in the whole tract of that land, by the description of as many as have been there, great plenty of mineral matter of all sorts, and in very many places both stones of price, pearl and chrystal, and great store of beasts, birds, and fowls, both for pleasure and necessary use of man are to be found. . . .

And now for the better contemplation and satisfaction of such worshipful, honest-minded and well-disposed merchants as have a desire to the furtherance of every good and commendable action, I will first say unto them, as I have done before to the noblemen and gentlemen, that within the degrees aforesaid is doubtless to be found the most wholesome and best temperature of air, fertility of soil, and every other commodity or merchandise, for the which, with no small peril, we do travel into Barbary, Spain, Portugal, France, Italy, Muscovy and Eastland, and yet, to the end my argument shall not altogether stand upon likelihoods and presumptions, I say that such persons as have discovered and travelled those parts do testify that they have found in those countries all these things following, namely :—[a list of beasts, birds, fishes, trees, minerals, etc.] . . .

Now for the trial hereof, considering that in the articles of the society of the adventurers in this voyage there is provision made that no adventurer shall be bound to any further charge than his first adventure, and notwithstanding keep still to himself, his children, his apprentices and servants, his and their freedom for trade and traffic, which is a privilege that adventurers in other voyages have not ; and in the said articles it is likewise provided that none other than such as have adventured in the first voyage, or shall become adventurers in this supply, at any time hereafter are to be admitted in the said society, but as redemptionaries, which will be very chargeable ; therefore, generally, I say unto all such, according to the old proverb, " Nothing venture, nothing have " . . .

The sixth chapter sheweth that the traffic and planting in

those countries shall be unto the savages themselves very beneficial and gainful. . . .

. . . First and chiefly, in respect of the most happy and gladsome tidings of the most glorious gospel of our Saviour Jesus Christ, whereby they may be brought from falsehood to truth, from darkness to light, from the highway of death to the path of life, from superstitious idolatry to sincere Christianity, from the devil to Christ, from hell to heaven. And if in respect of all the commodities they can yield us (were they many more) that they should but receive but this only benefit of Christianity, they were more than fully recompensed.

But hereunto it may be objected that the Gospel must be freely preached, for such was the example of the apostles. . . . Yet for answer we may say with St. Paul : If we have sown unto you heavenly things, do you think it much that we should reap your carnal things ? And withal, The workman is worthy of his hire. These heavenly tidings which those labourers our countrymen (as messengers of God's great goodness and mercy) will voluntarily present unto them, do far exceed their earthly riches. . . .

13. LORD BURGHLEY TO SIR CHRISTOPHER HATTON ON THE STATE OF TRADE [*Sir H. Nicholas, Memoirs of Sir Christopher Hatton, pp.* 470–2], 1587.

TO THE LORD CHANCELLOR.

My Lord,

I am sorry that my pains are such as I cannot attend on you to-day in the Star Chamber, having yesterday, by more zeal of service in the Exchequer Chamber than of regard to my harms, so weakened and pained my leg, as I cannot stir it out of my bed ; but this my declaration of my state is to no purpose to occupy your Lordship withal. This great matter of the lack of vent, not only of clothes, which presently is the greatest, but of all other English commodities which are restrained from Spain, Portugal, Barbary, France, Flanders, Hamburgh, and the States, cannot but in process of time work a great change and dangerous issue to the people of the realm, who, heretofore, in time of outward peace, lived thereby, and without it must either perish for want, or fall into violence to feed and fill their lewd appetites with open spoils of others, which is the fruit of rebellion; but it is in vain to remember this to your Lordship, that is so notorious as there need no repetition thereof. The evil being seen and like daily to increase beyond all good remedies, it is our duties that are Councillors to think of some remedies in time, before the same become remediless; and briefly the best means of remedy must follow the consideration of the causes of this evil, and so *contrariis contraria curare.* The original cause is apparently the contentions and enmities betwixt the King of Spain and his countries, and her Majesty and her countries. The reduction hereof to amity betwixt the Princes, and to open traffic according to the ancient treaties of intercourse, would be the sovereign remedy; but this may be wished sooner than speedily effectuated. But yet, seeing there is a signification notified of the good inclination of both the Princes, and a great necessity to press them both thereto for the suagement of their people, it were pity any course should be taken either to hinder this or not to hasten it, which surely in the Low Countries would be done, with whatsoever a reasonable cost may be, to keep the enemy from victuals, and to withstand his enterprises against our friends until this next harvest; and by this proceeding against him, there is no doubt but he will yield to all reasonable conditions meet both for her Majesty and her protected friends; otherwise, if the good fortune of our friends do decay, and the enemy recover that which he now lacketh, that is store of victuals, he will either underhand make peace with our friends, whom he shall find both weak and timorous, and leave her Majesty in danger for recovery of all that she hath spent, and in greater charges to maintain her two cautionary towns against the whole Low Countries than two Boulognes were, or else he will, being puffed with pride, make a very Spanish conquest of Holland and Zealand,—a matter terrible to be thought of, but most terrible to be felt. But to insist upon this remedy is as yet in vain, and therefore such other poor helps are to be thought of as may somewhat mitigate the accidents present, and stay the increase thereof, whereof when I do bethink myself, I find no one simple remedy, but rather compounded of divers simples, and to say truly they are but simple remedies, until peace may ensue, which is the sovereign sole medicine of all. To have vent increase, there must be more buyers and shippers than there are, and seeing our merchants say that they cannot have sales sufficient,

1. It were good that the Steelyard men were licensed to trade as they were wont to do, with condition upon good bonds that our merchants adventurers shall have their former liberties in Hamburgh ;

2. These Steelyard merchants must also have a dispensation to carry a competent number of unwrought cloths that are coarse, which are the cloths whereof the great stay is in the Realm.

3. Beside this, the merchant strangers might have a like dispensation for the buying and shipping of a competent number of like white coarse cloths.

4. And if her Majesty, for some reasonable time, would abate only 2s. upon a cloth, I think there would grow no loss to her Majesty, having respect to the multitude of the cloths that should be carried, whereas now the strangers carry few, but upon licences, for which her Majesty hath no strangers' customs, but English.

5. The strangers also must have liberty to buy in Blackwell Hall, or else there may be a staple set up in Westminster, out of the liberties of the City of London, which, rather than London would suffer, I think they will grant liberty to strangers in respect to the hallage money which they shall lease. Notwithstanding all these shows of remedies, I could wish that our merchants adventurers were made acquainted herewith, and to be warned, that if they shall not amend the prices to clothiers for their coarse cloths, whereby the clothiers may be reasonably apparent gainers, and that to be put in practice this next week, that then her Majesty will give authority to put the former helps in practice. Thus, my good Lord, because I understand you are to go to the Court this afternoon, I have thought good to scribble, as I do (lying in pain) these few cogitations, submitting them to a more mature disquisition.

Your Lordship's most assured,

W. BURGHLEY.

14. A LIST OF PATENTS AND MONOPOLIES [*Lodge. Illustrations of British History, Vol. III, pp.* 159,[1] *ff.*]

33. Eliz.—A grant to Reynold Hopton only, and no other,

[1] Quoted, *English Patents of Monopoly*, Appendix c, W. H. Price, 1603.

to make flasks, touch-boxes, powder-boxes, and bullet-boxes, for 15 years.

34 Eliz.—A grant to Simon Farmer and John Craford only, and no other, to transport list shreds of woollen cloth, and all manner of horns, for 21 years.

35 Eliz.—A grant to Bryan Annesley, solely, and no other, to buy and provide steel beyond sea and sell the same within this realm for 21 years.

36 Eliz.—A grant to Robert Alexander only, and no other, to buy and bring in anise-seeds, sumach, etc., for 21 years.

39 Eliz.—A grant to John Spillman only, and no other, to buy linen rags, and to make paper.

40 Eliz.—A grant to Ede Schetts, and his assignees only, and no other, to buy and transport ashes and old shoes for 7 years.

36 Eliz.—A grant to [*blank*] only, and no other, to provide and bring in all Spanish wools for making of felt hats, for 20 years.

34 Eliz.—A grant that Sir Jerome Bowes, and no other, shall make glasses for 12 years.

42 Eliz.—A grant made to Harding and others only, concerning saltpeter.

41 Eliz.—A grant that Brigham and Wimmes shall only have the pre-emption of tin.

Other Monopolies for one man only and no other—

To register all writings and assurances between merchants, called policies.

To make spangles.

To print the Psalms of David.

To print Cornelius Tacitus.

To sow woad in certain numbers of shires.

To print grammars, primers, and other school books.

To print the law.

To print all manner of songs in parts.

To make mathematical instruments.

To plainish and hollow silver vessels.

That one man and no other shall make writs of *subpœna* in Chancery, Sir Thomas George.

To write all writs of supplication and *supersedeas* for the peace and good behaviour, and all pardons of outlawry, George Carew.

To draw leases in possession made by the King, Sir Edward Stafford.

To engross all leases by the great seal.

Licenses and Dispensations to one man only, of the Penalty of Penal Laws, and Power given to license others—

[18] Eliz.—A license to Sir Edward Dyer, to pardon and dispense with tanning of leather, contrary to the statute of 5 Eliz., and to license any man to be a tanner.

30 Eliz.—A patent to Sir Walter Raleigh, to make licenses for keeping of taverns and retailing of wines throughout England.

31 Eliz.—The grant to John Ashley and Thomas Windebank, to have all forfeitures and penalties for burning of timber trees to make iron, contrary to the statute of 1 Eliz.

36 Eliz.—A license to Roger Bineon, and others, to take the whole forfeiture of the statute of 5th and 6th of Edw. VI, for pulling down gig-mills.

37 Eliz.—A license to William Smith only, and no others, to take the benefit of the statute of 5 Eliz. for gashing of hides, and barking of trees.

38 Eliz.—A license to Thomas Cornwallis only, and no other, to make grants and licenses for keeping of gaming-houses, and using of unlawful games, contrary to the statute of 33 Henry VIII.

39 Eliz.—A license to William Carre, for nine years, to authorize and license any person to brew beer to be transported beyond sea.

40 Eliz.—A license to Richard Coningsby, to give license for buying of tin throughout England.

41 Eliz.—A license to Richard Carnithen only, to bring in Irish yarn for seven years.

Impositions.

41 Eliz.—A grant to Bevis Bulmer to have an imposition of sea-coal, paying £6,200 rent for 21 years.

36 Eliz.—A grant made to John Parker, Esq., to have twelvepence for filing of every bill in Chancery in respect whereof the subject is to be discharged of payment of anything of search.

41 Eliz.—A license to trade the Levant Seas with currants only, paying £4,000 per annum.

Particular licenses to transport certain numbers of pelts of sheep-skins and lamb-skins.

Certain numbers of woollen cloths.

Certain numbers of dickers of calf-skins.

New Inventions.

Only and no other, so as they were never used in England before.

To inn and drain [*blank*] grounds.

To take water fowl.

To make devices of safe-keeping of corn.

To make a device for soldiers to carry necessary provisions.

15. INSTRUCTIONS TOUCHING THE BILL FOR FREE TRADE [*Journals of the House of Commons, Vol. I, p.* 218], 1604.

The Committees from the House of the Commons sat five whole afternoons upon these Bills ; there was a great concourse of clothiers and merchants, of all parts of the realm, and especially of London ; who were so divided, as that all the clothiers, and, in effect, all the merchants of England, complained grievously of the engrossing and restraint of trade by the rich merchants of London, as being to the undoing, or great hindrance, of all the rest ; and of London merchants, three parts joined in the same complaint against a fourth part ; and of that fourth part, some standing stiffly for their own company, yet repined at other companies. Divers writings and informations were exhibited on both parts ; learned Counsel was heard for the Bill, and divers of the principal Aldermen of London against it ; all reasons exactly weighed and examined ; the Bill, together with the reasons on both sides, was returned and reported by the Committees to the House ; where, at the third reading, it was three several days debated, and in the end passed with great consent and applause of the House (as being for the exceeding benefit of all the land) scarce forty voices dissenting from it.

The most weighty reasons for the enlargement of trade were these :

Natural Right.—All free subjects are born inheritable, as to their land, so also to the free exercise of their industry in those trades, whereto they apply themselves and whereby they are to live. Merchandize being the chief and richest of all other, and of greater extent and importance than all the rest, it is against the natural right and liberty of the subjects of England to restrain it into the hands of some few, as now it is; for although there may be now some five or six thousand persons, counting children and prentices, free of the several Companies of the Merchants, in the whole; yet apparent it is, that the Governors of these Companies, by their monopolizing orders, have so handled the matter, as that the mass of the whole trade of all the realm is in the hands of some two hundred persons at the most, the rest serving for a shew only, and reaping small benefit.

Judgement of Parliament.—The law stands for it; and a law made 12th of Henry the Seventh, never repealed by Parliament, only restrained since by charters, unduly, or by untrue suggestions, procured (by which means all other monopolies have had their original) and the first of those charters since the making of that statute (which was purchased in the end of the reign of Henry the Seventh, at what time Empson and Dudley were instruments of so much wronging and oppressing the people) yet doth in no wise restrain this liberty of free trade, but expressly allow it (with a reverence unto that very act in the 12th of this reign) and so continued till the reign of Queen Elizabeth.

Examples of Nations.—The example of all other nations generally in the world, who avoid in themselves, and hate in us, this monopolizing way of traffic; for it cannot be otherwise counted than a monopoly, when so large a commodity is restrained into the hands of so few in proportion, to the prejudice of all other who by law and natural right might have interest therein. And whereas some allege that there are like Companies in other countries, as of the East Indies in Lesbone, the House of Contraction there, the Fontego at Venice, the Travesana at Noremberg, these allegations are either untrue or unproper. There are places of assembly for merchants, and to consult for good orders in all other countries, but without restraint of trading from any man; and how traffic, by this freedom, doth flourish in other countries, and principally in the Low Countries, far more than in ours, is apparent to all the world.

Wealth.—The increase of the wealth generally of all the land by the ready vent of all the commodities to the merchants at higher rate; for where many buyers are, ware grows dearer; and they that buy dear at home, must sell dear abroad: this also will make our people more industrious.

Equal Distribution.—The more equal distribution of the wealth of the land, which is a great stability and strength to the realm, even as the equal distributing of the nourishment in a man's body; the contrary whereof is inconvenient in all estates, and oftentimes breaks out into mischief, when too much fullness doth puff up some by presumption, and too much emptiness leaves the rest in perpetual discontent, the mother of desire of innovations and troubles: and this is the proper fruit of monopolies. Example may be in London, and the rest of the realm: The custom and impost of London come to a hundred and ten thousand pound a year, and of the rest of the whole realm but to seventeen thousand pound.

Strength.—The increase of shipping, and especially of mariners, in all ports in England. How greatly the mariners of the realm have decayed in all places of latter times, and with how great danger of the state in these late wars, is known to them who have been employed in that kind of service; who do also attribute the cause thereof to this restraint of trade; free traffic being the breeder and maintainer of ships and mariners, as by memorable example in the Low Countries may be seen.

Profit of the Crown.—The increase of custom and subsidy to the King, which doth necessarily follow the increase of foreign traffic and wealth. And they which say otherwise, will dare to say anything. These reasons are in great part set down in the Act of the 12th of Henry VIIth; other particular reasons there are, which this present time doth not yield.

Opportunity Abroad.—Under our gracious Salamon, a Prince of wisdom and peace, we are like to be in league or amity with all nations; whereby, as there will be greater freedom abroad to trade to all places, so fit to have greater at home for all persons to trade. This alteration of times may make that fit now, which in times of hostility might have seemed unfit.

Necessity at Home.—And as there will be greater opportunity abroad, so also much greater necessity at home; for what else shall become of gentlemen's younger sons, who cannot live by arms when there is no wars, and learning preferments are common to all and mean? So that nothing remains fit for them, save only merchandize (and such is the use of other politic nations) unless they turn serving men, which is a poor inheritance.

The general reasons to continue the restraint of trade, and the answer to them, were these:

Imputation of the State.—It is a taint to the King and State, that these restrained companies should be called or counted monopolies; and by this Act we insist and strengthen the complaint of the Haven Towns and other nations against the State for suffering such companies.

Answer.—The same reason doth justify all the monopolies that ever were. It is no touch to the State if abuses creep in, but if reformation, desired by parliament, be denied. But surely this taint doth no ways attaint his Majesty, who hath declared himself a just enemy to all these unjust monopolies.

Not Monopolies.—These Companies are not monopolies; for a monopoly is, when liberty of selling, due to all men by right, is restrained to one, with prejudice of all others.

Answer.—The name of monopoly, though taken originally for personal unity, yet is fitly extended to all improportionable paucity of the sellers in regard of the ware which is sold. If ten men had the only sale of all the horses in England, this were a monopoly; much more the Company of Merchant Adventurers, which, in effect not above two hundred, have the managing of the two third parts of the clothing of this realm, which might well maintain many thousand merchants more. And with how great prejudice this is sundry ways to all the land, let example suffice; let the cry of all the clothiers of England testify, and the utter overthrow of infinite poor persons, which live by them and their works. For the clothiers having no utterance of their cloth but to the merchant adventurers, they, by complot among themselves, will buy but at what time, what quality, and what price themselves list; whereby the clothiers are fain often to return with loss, to lay their cloths to pawn, to slack their trade, to the utter ruin of their poor workmen, with their wives and children.

Keeping up our Commodities.—These Companies keep up the price of our commodities abroad, by avoiding an over-glut of our commodities in places whereto they trade. And this experience doth witness; for our cloth is of late years much dearer than in former times; whereas contrarywise, when trade is free, many sellers will make ware cheap and of less estimation.

Answer.—It is true that all monopolies keep up their commodities for their own private lucre; but they do it unjustly, and to the discontent of all other men; which hath been the cause of so many edicts of the Empire against the Company of Merchant Adventurers, which hath driven them so often to shift their marts; and is the cause, that our merchants are so generally hated, no other nation Christian either using or enduring such restrained Companies in matter of merchandizes. Howbeit both by reason and experience we may conjecture that there is no greater [*blank*] that if trade be made free, our commodities will much abate their price abroad; for the merchants must first buy their commodities at home; and where many buyers are, wares will grow dearer; and buying dear at home, he must sell dear abroad. For it is not true that there will be a greater glut of our commodities in foreign parts; the sellers will be more, but the wares sold will be much the same, especially in those principal commodities, which grow out of the land. It is the store of the merchandize, not the multitude of merchants, which doth make things cheaper. Besides, when trade is free, it is likely that many young men will seek out new places, and trade further for great benefit; whereby the glut in the former places will be less.

The weakness of their argument of experience is plain; for not cloth only, but all other things in the world are risen greatly in price; and in France, where there is no Companies, our kerseys are sold at exceeding good price, and as dear, in proportion, as broad cloths by the Merchant Adventurers. But if it were so, that they kept up our commodities abroad, so do they, by the same skill, foreign commodities at home: so a few rich men do gain by their out-going, and the whole land doth lose much more by their return. They say that they gain little by return of foreign commodities. There lieth a mystery, for it is true, and will be avowed upon certain knowledge, that upon the arrival of the Merchant Adventurers' fleet, the commodities, on the other side, are ordinarily raised at least twenty in the hundred; for so do they quit one wrong with another. But hereby the loss still falls heavy on the subject, who is damnified now again in the commodities returned, as he was before in the engrossing of those which were issued.

Venting all Now.—The Companies that now are, do vent all the commodities of the land, and yet are they hardly able to live one by another.

Answer.—It is not all vented, which the land might spare; and that by reason of the courses held by these Companies, to their own excessive gain, and certain loss of all other men: besides, when traffic shall flourish with us, as doth in other countries, where trade is free, and namely in the Low Countries, who thereby have supported the huge charge of their long wars, things merchantable will increase daily by this encouragement to the subjects' industry, even as there they do; for natural commodities are more than trebled by access of art and industry; and howsoever, yet the division of wealth will be more equal; for now, by the plotting of the governor of these Companies, some few overgrown men devour the wealth, and make merry, whilst the rest, even of their own Companies, do want and weep.

Prenticeship Necessary.—This Act makes it lawful to become merchants without prenticeship; which is an injury to them which have served, and hurt to them that serve not; who, venturing unskilfully, shall be sure of loss.

Answer.—The loss of new merchants, it may be, is as much the desire, as fear of the objectors; but they that have served, have their skill for their labour; and they that serve not, must be at charge of a factor, or join with their friends, and learn skill by them; or at least wise men adventure their stocks with other men, after the fashion of the Low Countries, and other places, where trade doth flourish. By the same reason young gentlemen might be kept from their lands, for want of skill to govern them.

Dissolving Companies.—This Act, by enlarging the Companies, and giving free access to all men, doth in effect dissolve them; for hardly are they able to govern those that are in already; and where government faileth, there will be certain confusion.

Answer.—This Act dissolveth no Company, taketh away

no good government. Those orders in Companies, which tend to monopoly, it abrogateth: orders for necessary contribution to public charges it establisheth; the rest it leaves as it found them, neither in worse state, nor better. It is weakness to say, that a greater multitude cannot be governed; for so neither Kings in their Dominions and subjects, nor cities in their amplitude should increase. If for matter of merchandize there were no such government at all, nor more than there is for our merchants in France, or hath been at Stade, for divers years past, or than there is in the Low Countries, where are the best merchants in the world; yet provident men would consult and join together in that which were for their common benefit, ease, and safety. Such Companies there are in other countries, but no such monopolies as ours are.

Joint Stock Necessary.—This Act is against trading in a joint stock together, which in long and dangerous voyages (as to Musco, and especially the East Indies) is necessary; for in that voyage one alone will not adventure; besides the merchants must keep some port there amongst the infidels.

Answer.—It is true that it is fit to trade to the East Indies with a joint stock, and so do the Hollanders; this Act therefore doth not forbid men to trade in a joint stock, if they list, and see it fit; only forbiddeth to constrain men to trade so against their wills; which heretofore in other trades, and at this day in the Muscovie trade, doth turn to the great damage both of the Commonwealth and of the particular persons so constrained to trade. The Muscovie Company, consisting of eight score, or thereabouts, have fifteen directors, who manage the whole trade; these limit to every man the proportion of stock which he shall trade for, make one purse and stock of all, and consign it into the hands of one agent at Musco, and so again, at their return, to one agent at London, who sell all, and give such account as they please. This is a strong and a shameful monopoly—a monopoly in a monopoly—both abroad and at home. A whole Company, by this means, is become as one man, who alone hath the uttering of all the commodities of so great a country. The inconveniences, which have ensued thereof, are three apparent.

First, by this means they vent less of our commodities; for, by reason of the one agent, they vent all through his hands;

by which means the Hollanders have come in between us; who, trading thither in several with our own English commodities (which are most proper for that country) utter much more than our own merchants, and make quicker return; which has occasioned many Englishmen to join in trade with the Hollanders, to the detriment of the King's Majesty in his customs. And by this means that trade is like utterly to decay; for the Hollanders have grown in short time from two ships to above twenty; this spring they are gone to Muscovie with near thirty ships, and our men but with seven. The like fell out in the Turkie Company, when they constrained men to a joint stock; since the breaking of which combination, there go four ships for one.

Secondly, in their return with Muscovie commodities, they greatly prejudice the Commonwealth and State. Example in cordage, which they bring home in such scarcity, and sell so dearly, as that they have raised it in short time from twenty to thirty shillings; yea, to sell their ware dear, they have contracted with the buyer not to bring any more of that commodity within three years after.

Thirdly, this is hurtful to all the young merchants of their own Company, who cannot forbear their stock so long as now they do, and desire to employ their own industry in managing it, and having oftentimes been all damnified by the breaking of that general factor.

Public Charges.—In divers places, as namely, in Turkey and Muscovy, the merchants are at charge of sending presents, maintaining ambassadors, consuls, and agents, which are otherwise also necessary for the service of his Majesty, and of the State; these charges are now defrayed by these Companies.

Answer.—This matter is expressly provided for by this Act, that all that trade to those places shall be contributory to those charges.

The New Merchants will give over.—The like attempt for free trade was in Anno 1588, at what time liberty being given to all men to buy cloths at Westminster, the Merchant Adventurers gave over to trade at all; whereby the cloth of the land lying on the clothier's hands, they were forced, by petition, to get the former restraint restored.

Answer.—This is true, and the same mischief were likely to ensue again; for it is said, that the same policy is now in speech in their Company. But the times being well altered from war to peace, this mischief would be but short, and other merchants soon grow to take their places, if they should, as (being rich) they may, forsake them. But it were to be trusted that this stomachness, being to their own loss, would not long continue. Howsoever, it doth not stand with the dignity of parliament either to fear or favour the frowardness of any subject.

The Rich will eat out the Poor.—If poor merchants should trade together with the rich, the rich beyond the seas would buy out the poor, being not able to sell at the instant, to make themselves savers; and so there would grow a monopoly *ex facto.*

Answer.—This reason sheweth thus much, that a crafty head, with a greedy heart, and a rich purse, is able to take advantage of the need of his neighbour (which no man doubteth of); but if the difficulties and dishonesties should deter men from action, and not rather increase their diligence and wariness, then should there be no trading at all in any sort.

Strangers will eat out the English.—If all men may be merchants, the sons of strangers denized will, in time, eat out the natural merchants of this kingdom.

Answer.—If the sons of strangers become natural English, why should they not [have] a subject's part? And more they cannot reap. If any further mischief should grow, it might at all times by a new Act be easily remedied.

All Men may go out of the Realm.—If trade be free for all men, then all may become merchants, and under that pretext any may go out of the realm; which will be good news for the papists.

Answer.—This conceit is weak; for so it may be said that all men may become mariners, and so quit the kingdom; and it is provided by express words of the bill that they may not go out of the realm but for their present traffic.

Against London.—This Act is against London, and the wealth thereof, which is necessary to be upheld, being the head city of the kingdom.

Answer.—Nay, it is for London, unless we will confine London into some two hundred men's purses; the rest of the City of London, together with the whole realm, sue mainly for this bill; and they cry, they are undone, if it should be crossed.

Hurt to the King's Customs.—It will be prejudicial to the King's customs, who in other parts will easier be deceived than here in London.

Answer.—Nothing can be more clear than that if transport and return of merchandize will increase by this Act, also the King's customs, which depend thereon, must withal increase: And if this Bill may pass, if the King be pleased to let his custom to farm, to give 5,000*l.* a year more than, *communibus annis*, hath been made these last years. The deceiving of the King is now, when, for want of this freedom, men are enforced to purchase the vent of their commodities out of creeks, because they cannot be admitted to public trade; whereas otherwise they should have no reason to hazard their whole estate, for the saving of so reasonable a duty. As for faults in officers, they may as well happen in London, as in any other place.

Decay of Great Ships.—During freedom of trade, small ships would be employed to vent our commodities, and so our great ships, being the guard of the land, would decay.

It is war, more than traffic that maintaineth great ships; and therefore, if any decay grow, it will be chiefly by peace, which the wisdom of the State will have a regard of; but for as much depends of traffic, no doubt the number of smaller ships will grow by this freedom, and especially mariners, whereof the want is greatest, and of whom the smallest vessels are the proper nurseries. But that the great ships will decay, doth not necessarily follow; for the main trade of all the white cloth, and much of other kind, is shipped from the Port of London, and will be still, it being the fittest Port of the kingdom for Germanie and the Low Countries, where the Merchant Adventurers' trade only lieth; who shall have little cause to alter their shipping. Then the Levent Sea, Muscovy, and East Indies, whither we trade with great ships, the employing of them will be still requisite in the merchants' discretion; for otherwise both the commodity of the returned will be less, and the adventure too great in so rich lading not to provide for more than ordinary assurance against the common hazard at sea.

Other particular reasons there are, for restraint of trade in favour of certain Company.

Merchant Adventurers.—The Company of Merchant Adventurers is very ancient, and they have heretofore been great credit to the Kings, for borrowing money in the Low Countries and Germany.

Answer.—The Company indeed is as ancient as Thomas of Beckett, their founder, and may still continue. Their restraining of others, which this Bill doth seek to redress, is not so ancient, and was so disallowed by parliament in the twelfth year of Henry the seventh; which Act stands impeached by particular charter, but never by consent of the realm repealed. But in truth this Company, being the spring of all monopolies, and engrossing the grand staple commodities of cloth into so few men's hands, deserves least favour. The credit of the King hath been in the cloth (not in their persons) which will be as much hereafter, as heretofore.

Muscovy Company.—The Muscovy Company, by reason of the chargeable invention of that trade two and fifty years since, and their often great loss, was established by Act of Parliament in the eighth year of Queen Elizabeth.

Answer.—The chargeable invention hath been a reason worthy of respect thirty or forty years ago, when the inventors were living, and their charge not recompensed by countervailable gain; which since it hath been their loss, hath been their own fault, in employing one factor, who hath abused them all. Private Acts for favour, when the cause thereof is ceased, are often revoked. Howbeit this Bill dissolveth no Company, only enlargeth them, and abrogateth their unjust orders for monopolies.

An Argument Unanswerable.—Another argument there is, not to be answered by reason, but by their integrity and love of their country, who shall be assaulted with it. In sum, the Bill is a good Bill, though not in all points, perhaps, so perfect as it might be; which defects may be soon remedied and supplied in future parliament.

* * * *

Sir Edward Sandys proceeded in the report, and delivered in the two Bills for free trade; the first (being the principal Bill) with amendments; which were twice read; and the Bill, upon question, ordered to be ingrossed.

16. The Establishment of a Company to Export Dyed and Dressed Cloth, in place of the Merchant Adventurers[1] [*Pat. Rolls*, 13 *James I*, *p.* 2], 1616–17.

James by the Grace of God, etc.:

We have often and in divers manners expressed ourselves . . . what an earnest desire and constant resolution we have that, as the reducing of wools into clothing was the act of our noble Progenitor King Edward the Third, so the reducing of the trade of white cloths, which is but an imperfect thing towards the wealth and good of this our Kingdom, unto the trade of cloths dyed and dressed, might be the work of our time,

To which purpose we did first invite the ancient Company of Merchant Adventurers to undertake the same, who upon allegation or pretence of impossibility refused.

Whereupon nevertheless not discouraged but determined to maintain our princely resolution against impediments and difficulties in a work so excellent, We did find means to draw and procure divers persons of good quality within our City of London and elsewhere with great alacrity and commendable zeal to give a beginning to this our purpose,

In respect whereof, for that above all things We were to take a princely care that between the cessation of the old trade and the inception and settling of the new there should not be any stand of cloth nor failing or deadness in the vent thereof, whereby this work which is so good for the future might prove dangerous in the entrance thereof, we were inforced to grant several licences under our Great Seal unto the said persons for a trade of whites to be temporary and in the interim until this work by due and seasonable degrees without inconvenience of precipitation might be happily accomplished, giving them likewise some powers of assembling, keeping of Courts and the like, but yet without any actual incorporation of them,

But notwithstanding, having evermore in contemplation our first end, We have still provoked and urged on the said persons unto whom the trade is now transferred to some certainty of offer and undertaking concerning a proportion of cloths dressed and dyed to be annually exported, and the same proportion to increase and multiply in such sort as may be a

[1] Printed in the publications of the Selden Society, Vol. 28, pp. 78–98.

fruitful beginning of so good a work and also an assured pledge of the continuation thereof in due time.

Whereupon the said persons or new Company have before the Lords of our Privy Council absolutely condescended and agreed at a Court holden the seventeenth day of June one thousand six hundred and fifteen, that thirty-six thousand cloths shall be dressed and dyed out of such cloths white as were formerly used to be shipped out by the old Company undressed and undyed. . . .

. . . And did further promise and profess with all cheerfulness to proceed as it shall please God to give ability and the trade encouragement to the settling of the whole trade of cloths dressed and dyed, which is the end desired.

Wherefore We, in our princely judgement foreseeing that as long as the said new Company shall remain not incorporated it doth much weaken both the endeavour and expectation which belongeth to this work, as if it were a thing but only in deliberation and agitation and not fully and thoroughly established, have thought it now a fit time to extend our princely grace unto them for their incorporation and to indue and invest them with such liberties and privileges as the old Company formerly had, with such additions and augmentations as the merit of concurrence to so good an end may require, with this, nevertheless, that because the nature of the present liberties and privileges must of necessity differ from those which shall be fit and requisite when the whole trade shall be overcome and settled, there be therefore a power in Us to revoke or alter the same.

Know ye therefore that We . . . by these presents have given, granted and confirmed, and for Us our heirs and successors do give, grant and confirm, unto our right trusty and right well beloved Cousin and Counsellor Thomas, Earl of Suffolk, Lord High Treasurer of England [and others named], and to every of them, and to all and every such person and persons whatsoever our loving subjects as shall, between this and the feast of St. Michael the Archangel next ensuing come in, subscribe, and be admitted of their Society, That they and every of them, their and every of their sons and apprentices according to the constitutions and ordinances hereafter by the Company to be made and presented, shall be one Fellowship and Commonalty and one body corporate and politic in deed and in name, by the name of Governor, Assistants, and Fellowship of the King's Merchants Adventurers of the New Trade of London.

[Power to have common seal, etc.]: [There shall be one Governor, William Cokayne, Alderman of our City of London, to be the first and present Governor, to continue till June 24 next] and from thence until the said William Cokayne or some other of the said Fellowship or Company shall in due manner be chosen and sworn to the said office according to the ordinances and provisions hereafter in these presents expressed and declared, if he the said William Cokayne shall so long live:

[And further] there shall be from henceforth for ever hereafter one or more, not exceeding the number of six, of the said Company or Fellowship to be elected and chosen, which shall be called the Deputy or Deputies of the said Company or Fellowship: . . .

And furthermore We for Us, our heirs and successors, do by these presents grant and confirm to the said [Fellowship] and their successors that it shall and may be lawful to and for them and every of them, and their successors for ever, hereafter to trade, traffic, and occupy and use the trade and feat of merchandise unto, from and with the Town of Callice in the Realm of France and the marches thereof, and into, from and with all and every the countries of Holland, Zeland, Brabant, Flaunders, West Frizeland and all other the countries nigh thereunto adjoining heretofore under the obeisance of the Dukes of Burgundy, or into East Frizeland and Hamborough and the Territories of the same, and into from and with the countries of Germany and all the Territories, Provinces, Cities and Towns thereof with all manner of woollen cloths, kersies, wares, commodities and merchandises whatsoever not prohibited, without any let contradiction or interruption of Us, our heirs or successors, or of any other person or persons whatsoever:

And our will and pleasure is, and We do hereby for Us, our heirs and successors, grant and confirm unto the said [Fellowship &c.], that the said Governor or Deputy and the said Assistants or the more part of them for the time being, being at least thirteen, shall from henceforth for ever have, use and exercise full jurisdiction, power and authority lawfully to rule and govern the same Company or Fellowship and their successors, and all and every merchants and members of the same, in all their private causes, suits, quarrels, misdemeanours, offences and complaints among them touching the said trade, as well here in England as beyond the seas in Callice and the marches thereof, and also in the Countries and Towns of Holland [etc. Germany, etc., as above] rising, moved and to be moved. . .

And moreover We . . . do by these presents grant unto the said [Fellowship, etc.] that the said Governor, Deputy and Assistants, or thirteen of them at the least, and their successors for the time being from time to time and at all times from henceforth, shall and may enact, establish, allow and confirm, and also revoke, disannul and repeal all and every act and acts, laws, and ordinances heretofore had or made by the said [Fellowship, etc.] or by what name or names or additions soever, and also shall and may from henceforth from time to time and at all times hereafter for ever enact, make, ordain and establish acts, laws, constitutions and ordinances [for the good government of the Fellowship] and of every merchant and peculiar member of the same Fellowship or body corporate [and also of all our subjects] intermeddling exercising or using the feat or trade of the said [Fellowship] by any means, as well here in England as in the said countries towns and places beyond the seas, so that the said acts laws [etc.] be not hurtful to any the rights of our Crown, honour, dignity royal or prerogative, or to the diminution of the common weal of this our Realm or contrary to any our laws and statutes. . . . And that the said [Fellowship, or thirteen as aforesaid] shall and may take order with every the subject or subjects of Us our heirs and successors, not being of the said Company and trading or haunting the said countries or places beyond the seas or any of them for merchandise, and compel every of them by fines, forfeitures, penalties, imprisonments or otherwise to obey, hold and perform all such orders, acts and ordinances that hereafter shall be ordained, made, allowed or confirmed by the said [Fellowship or majority as above] for the good government, rule, order and condition of the said subject or subjects, so as the state of the said Company be not by them impeached or hindered but by all means and ways maintained and continued. And that all such forfeitures fines [etc.] so as aforesaid to be levied and taken shall be for evermore to the use and behoof of the said [Fellowship, etc.]

. . . And also We will, and for Us, our heirs and successors, by these presents do grant to the said [Fellowship] that the said [Fellowship or a majority, thirteen at least, as above] shall have full and whole power and authority to impose and lay, and also to take and levy, all reasonable impositions and sums of money whatsoever as well upon all persons trading into the said countries as also upon the merchandise to be transported and carried into the countries, towns, provinces and territories before rehearsed or any of them either by water or land. . . .

And, for the better encouragement of the said Company or Fellowship . . . We do hereby for Us our heirs and successors straitly charge and command all and singular the customers, comptrollers, searchers, surveyors, waiters and all others the officers and ministers of Us our heirs and successors for the time being in all every or any of our ports, havens, creeks and the members of the same within our Realms and Dominions . . . that they and every of them . . . shall not at any time or times hereafter wilfully permit or suffer any of the subjects of Us our heirs or successors or any aliens denizens or strangers to freight, lade or ship out in any ship, crayer, lighter or other vessel whatsoever any goods wares or merchandises whatsoever (being native commodities of this Realm) for any of the said territories, countries and towns before-mentioned wherein the said [Fellowship etc.] according to the intent of these presents are to trade and traffic, but such goods, wares and merchandises only whose entries shall be subscribed and allowed by the Governor or Deputy of the said Company for the time being by bill or writing subscribed with his or their hand or hands, or such other person or persons as by the said Governor or Company shall be thereunto named and appointed, and in such ship or ships or other vessel or vessels only as shall be named in such bills or writings. . . .

And for the better encouragement of the said [Fellowship] to proceed in exportation of cloths dressed and dyed here in this our Realm, which will tend so much to the common weal of the same, and which by the said Company or Fellowship cannot as yet in such full manner be perfected as that they can have sufficient vent for the said dressed and dyed cloths in foreign parts without a temporary liberty to export cloths white, until by continuance of time they shall be further enabled and encouraged, We do by these presents . . . give and grant unto the said [Fellowship etc.] full and free liberty, licence, power, privilege, authority and immunity that they or any of them, by themselves or by their or any of their servants, factors or agents, at their or any of their liberties and pleasures yearly and every year shall and may provide and buy, or cause to be provided and bought, within this our Realm of England and other our Dominions for their or any of their proper use or uses the number of thirty thousand woollen cloths unrowed unbarbed and unshorn and not fully and ready dressed and wrought, of which said number of thirty thousand cloths yearly five and twenty thousand shall be every cloth above the value or price of six pounds of lawful money of England, and the number of five thousand cloths residue of the said yearly number of thirty thousand cloths uncoloured or white above the value or price of four pounds of lawful money of England, or of any higher or greater prices whatsoever, . . . and the same from this our Realm of England into the towns of Callice and the marches thereof in the Realm of France and into the countries and towns of Holland [etc., as above] to transport, send, convey, ship and carry over or cause to be transported, sent, shipped, conveyed and carried over there to be by them unladen, discharged, vented, sold . . . or otherwise disposed . . . and from thence to freight, lade, ship, return, import and bring back into this our said Kingdom or into any part thereof all such wares, commodities, goods and merchandises already not prohibited as to them or any of them their servants, factors or agents shall seem good, paying to Us our heirs and successors our duties and customs due and to be paid for the same, and further paying unto our trusty and well-beloved Cousin the Earl of Cumberland, his executors or assigns, for every white unwrought or undressed woollen cloth so to be by them or any of them shipped or transported out of this Realm under the warrant of his present licence over and above the said thirty thousand cloths two shillings and eight pence. . . .

And our will and pleasure is, and We do hereby declare our Royal intent and meaning to be, and the said [Fellowship, etc.] do covenant, promise and agree to and with Us our heirs and successors by these presents, that they and their successors shall from time to time and at all times do their utmost endeavours that after the end and expiration of the said three years ensuing, during which the proportion of thirty-six thousand cloths are undertaken to be exported as is before in these presents expressed, that their trade of exporting and merchandising into the foresaid countries, provinces, towns and places aforesaid of woollen cloths may be wholly reduced unto the venting of such cloths only as shall be dyed and dressed here within this our Realm and other our Dominions, so far forth as it shall please God to give them and their successors ability and the trade encouragement, anything in these presents contained to the contrary notwithstanding: . . .

. . . Provided also that these our Letters Patents or any matter or thing therein contained shall not extend to give authority or power to the said [Fellowship of the King's Merchants, etc.] or to any member or person of the said Company to transport or carry out of the realm any cloths, kersies, wares, commodities or merchandises whatsoever, which by the laws and statutes of this Realm are restrained or prohibited to be transported or carried over the seas, otherwise than according to the true intent and meaning of these presents, unless they shall obtain and procure licence for the same.

17. Sir Julius Caesar's Proposals for Reviving the Trade in Cloths [*Lansdowne MSS.*,[1] *clii.* 56, *f.* 271], 1616.

Means to avoid the present stand of cloth—

(1) Commissioners honest and substantial and sufficient for skill to be presently appointed for the view of the cloth weekly to Blackwell Hall, and the faulty cloth to be returned upon the clothier with imprisonment till he put in security to answer it in the law; and the good to be justly valued, according to the usual prices for these two years past, and the new Merchant Adventurers enforced to buy the same.

(2) So many of the new Merchant Adventurers as shall refuse to lay out for cloth such sums as they have subscribed for to be presently committed, to abide the censure of the Star Chamber for abusing of his Majesty and the State in so desperate and dangerous a case as this is.

[1] Quoted, Unwin, *Industrial Organization in the Sixteenth and Seventeenth Centuries*, pp. 192–3.

(3) The fines of them to be employed in the buying of cloth for the riddance of the market.

(4) So many in London as are thought worth 10,000*l* to be moved by my Lord Mayor to buy up clothes for 1,000*l*. at the least; especially all woollen drapers of half that worth, viz., 5,000*l*.

(5) Express commandment and present example of King's Counsellors and Courtiers and all their servants to wear nothing but broad cloth in their gowns, cloaks, girths, robes or breeches till Easter next, to the end that woollen drapers may be encouraged to buy the cloth made or to be made before that day; or else on pain of imprisonment not to come into Court.

. . .

(10) And if it be doubtful whether these proceedings agree with law, the answer is that they do, for the law giveth place to parlous cases of State and leaveth them to be provided for by the wisdom of the King and his Counsellors; and *Salus reipublicæ suprema lex est*, which is a sufficient answer to all cavillers and peevish lawyers.

18. The Grant of a Monopoly for the Manufacture of Soap [*W. H. Price, The English Patents of Monopoly, Appendix W.*], 1623.

James, by the grace of God, etc., to all to whom these presents shall come, greeting.

Whereas We, by our letters patents . . . did give and grant unto our well-beloved subjects Roger Jones and Andrew Palmer, their executors, administrators, and assigns, full and free liberty, license, power, privilege, and authority that they . . . and none other, by themselves, their deputies, servants, factors, or workmen, should or might at all and every time and times thereafter, and from time to time, during the term of twenty and one years next ensuing the date of the said letters patents, . . . use, exercise, practice, and put in use . . . the mistery, art, way, means, and trade of "making of hard soap with the material called barilla, and without the use of any fire in the boiling and making thereof, and also of the making of soft soap without the use of fire in the boiling thereof," with such privileges and clauses as in said letters patents are contained and may more at large appear: And whereas since the granting of the said letters patents the said Roger Jones and Andrew Palmer, and such others, their assistants, as by great expense and travail have aided and assisted them in perfecting the said invention, have found out and added to their former invention many particulars conducing much to the profitableness and perfection of the work, both in the use of native and home commodities of this kingdom in the working and composition of the said soaps, and thereby in sparing and saving many thousands yearly which are now expended on foreign commodities bought and brought from beyond the seas, and employed here in the making of soap, in the manner now ordinarily used; . . . Forasmuch as such profitable inventions are not at once and at the first brought to their full perfection, We hold it fit in justice and honour to give all encouragement to such our loving subjects as shall employ their travails, industries, and purses to the furthering of the common good, and to reward them to the full with the fruits of their own labours; and forasmuch also as the said Roger Jones and Andrew Palmer have now approved their inventions and skill to be such as deserveth encouragement, their soap, made (*blank*) the material of our kingdom only, being found to be as sweet and good as the best soft soap now already made, and to extend further in the use thereof, as they in the behalf of themselves and their assistants have also made offer unto us to respect our own particular profit, in such measure as that the loss we may receive in our customs and other duties by the not importing of foreign commodities for the making of soap as in former times, shall by their industries be recommended unto us, our heirs, and successors, in certainty with good advantage; and our loving subjects, who have long complained of the bad and stinking soap now ordinarily in use, shall have good, sweet, and serviceable soap for their money, and yet shall not have the price thereof raised upon them above the usual rate of the best sweet soap now made and sold by the soap-boilers.

Know ye, that We, for the considerations aforesaid, of our especial grace, certain knowledge, and mere motion, have given and granted, and by these presents, for us, our heirs and successors, do give and grant unto the said Roger Jones and Andrew Palmer on the behalf of themselves and their assistants, full and free liberty, license, power, privilege and authority that they, the said Roger Jones and Andrew Palmer, their executors, administrators, and assigns, by themselves or their deputies, servants, factors, or workmen, and none other, shall and may at all and every time and times hereafter, and from time to time during the term of twenty and one years next ensuing the date of these presents, at their own proper costs and charges, use, exercise, practice, and put in use, within our said realms of England and Ireland and dominion of Wales, and our town of Berwick, at their liberty and pleasure, the mistery, art, way and means of making of hard soap and soft soap, as well with the materials and in such manner as in the said former letters patents are expressed, as also of burning and preparing of bean-straw, pea-straw, kelp, fern, and other vegetables to be found in our own dominions, into ordinary ashes or into potashes, and with the said materials of the ashes of bean or pea straw, and kelp, fern, and all other vegetables whatsoever not formerly and ordinarily used or practised within these our realms and dominions to make soap hard or soft, at their will and pleasure, and in such way or form as they have invented or devised; and also of the using of the assay glass for trying of their lye and making of hard and soft soap by their said new inventions, in the way of making of the said soaps by sundry motions, and not boiling of the same with the expense of much fuel, in such sort as was formerly accustomed by such as now usually make soap in and about our city of London and elsewhere in our said dominions; . . . and to the end that this our pleasure may be the better effected, and the said Roger Jones and Andrew Palmer may the more fully enjoy the benefit of this our grant, We will, and for us, our heirs and successors, do straightly charge, inhibit, and command, and do also of our especial grace, certain knowledge, and mere motion, for us, our heirs and successors, grant to the said Roger Jones and Andrew Palmer, their executors, administrators, and assigns, that no person or persons whatsoever born within any our realms or dominions, nor any other person or persons whatsoever, either denizens or strangers born in any foreign realm or country whatsoever, of what estate, degree, or condition soever he or they be or shall be, other than the said Roger Jones and Andrew Palmer, their executors, administrators, and assigns or such as shall by them or some of them be set on work or authorised, shall or may, at any time or times during the said term of one and twenty years hereby granted or mentioned, or intended to be granted, practice, use, exercise, or put in use the said mistery, art, way, means, or trade of making the said hard or soft soaps with any the materials aforesaid, . . . And to the end it may the better appear when any such soap shall be made contrary to the true intent and meaning of these presents, for us, our heirs, and successors, give and grant full liberty, power, and authority unto the said Roger Jones and Andrew Palmer, their executors, administrators, and assigns, that a stamp or stamps, seal or seals, to be engraven with a rose and crown, shall be stamped, sealed, or marked on all the soaps by them or any of them to be made in manner and form before declared, the better to distinguish their said soap from all counterfeit soap, either hard or soft, made or to be made by any person or persons contrary to the true intent and meaning of these presents or of the letters patents before recited, which seal or stamp so to be made as aforesaid We do by these presents will and command be set upon the hard soap, and upon the firkins, barrels, and other vessels containing the said soft soap so to be made, and shall not be set upon soaps hard or soft made by any other person or persons whatsoever contrary to the true intent of these presents, but shall be set and fixed only upon such soap as shall be from time to time made by the said Roger Jones and Andrew Palmer, their executors, administrators, or assigns, according as is herein before set down, and no other; and further, We do by these presents grant that it shall and may be lawful to and for the said Roger Jones and Andrew Palmer, their executors, administrators, or assigns, or any of them, by himself or themselves, or by his, their, or any of their deputies, factors, or servants, at any time or times convenient, and from time to time during the said term of one and twenty years, with assistance of a constable or some other officer, to enter into all and every place and places, house and houses, where they or any of them shall have any just cause to suspect any such hard soap or soft soap, or soap-ashes, or potashes, to be made or endeavoured to be made or stamped or sealed, or to be sold or uttered or set to sale, contrary to the true intent and meaning of these presents or of the letters patents before recited, or any vessels, engines, or instruments to be erected, framed, or used contrary to the true meaning hereof, . . . and finding any such, to seize the hard soaps and soft soaps, and potashes, and other ashes hereby granted so made to the use of us, our heirs, and successors: . . . And forasmuch as the public having an interest herein, which by the enhancing of the prices of the commodities aforesaid may be prejudiced and damnified, our will and pleasure is, and we do hereby straightly charge and command, that they the said Roger Jones and Andrew Palmer, their executors, administrators, and assigns, or any other person or persons by them to be authorised for the making of the said hard soap or soft soap, shall not, at any time during the said term of one and twenty years, sell, or cause to be sold, the said hard soap or soft soap, by them or any of them to be made as aforesaid, at any higher or dearer rates and prices than hard soap and soft soap of the best sorts and kinds were most usually sold for, within the space of seven years now last past before the date of these presents. And further, We do hereby charge and command all and singular justices of peace, mayors, sheriffs, constables, headboroughs, comptrollers, customers, searchers, waiters, and all other officers and ministers to whom it shall or may appertain, to be aiding and assisting in all lawful and convenient manner unto the said Roger Jones and Andrew Palmer, their executors, administrators, deputies, and assigns, in the due execution of these our letters patents, as they tender our pleasure and will avoid our indignation and displeasure in the contrary. . . .

. . . . . .

19. THE STATUTE OF MONOPOLIES [21 *James I*, c. 3, *Statutes of the Realm, Vol. IV, Part. II, pp.* 1212–14], 1623–4.

Forasmuch as your most excellent Majesty, . . ., did, in the year of our Lord God one thousand six hundred and ten, publish in print to the whole realm and to all posterity, that all grants of monopolies and of the benefit of any penal laws, or of power to dispense with the law, or to compound for the forfeiture, are contrary to your Majesty's laws . . . ; and whereas your Majesty was further graciously pleased expressly to command that no suitor should presume to move your Majesty for matters of that nature: yet nevertheless upon misinformations and untrue pretences of public good, many such grants have been unduly obtained and unlawfully put in execution, . . .; for avoiding whereof and preventing of all the like in time to come, may it please your Majesty, at the humble suit of the Lords Spiritual and Temporal and the Commons in this present Parliament, that all monopolies and all commissions, grants, licenses, charters, and letters patents heretofore made or granted to any person or persons, bodies politic or corporate whatsoever, of or for the sole buying, selling, making, working, or using of anything within this realm or the dominion of Wales . . . are altogether contrary to the laws of this realm, and so are and shall be utterly void and of none effect, and in no wise to be put in use or execution.

II. And be it further declared and enacted by the authority aforesaid that all monopolies and all such commissions, grants, licenses, charters, letters patents, proclamations, inhibitions, restraints, warrants of assistance, and all other matters and things tending as aforesaid and the force and validity of them and every of them ought to be, and shall be forever hereafter examined, heard, tried, and determined by and according to the common law of this realm and not otherwise.

III. And be it further enacted by the authority aforesaid that all person and persons, bodies politic and corporate whatsoever, which now are or hereafter shall be, shall stand and be disabled and incapable to have, use, exercise, or put in use any monopoly or any such commission, grant, license, charters, letters patents, proclamations, inhibition, restraint, warrant of assistance, or other matter or thing tending as aforesaid, or any liberty, power, or faculty grounded or pretended to be grounded upon them or any of them.

IV. [Persons aggrieved by monopolists to recover at Common Law treble the damages incurred.]

V. Provided nevertheless, and be it declared and enacted that any declaration before mentioned shall not extend to any letters patents, and grants of privilege, for the term of one and twenty years or under, heretofore made of the sole working or making of any manner of new manufacture within this realm, to the first and true inventor or inventors of such manufactures which others at the time of making of such letters patent and grants did not use, so they be not contrary to the law nor mischievous to the state, by raising of the prices of commodities at home, or hurt of trade, or generally inconvenient, but that the same shall be of such force as they were or should be if this act had not been made, and of none other: and if the same were made for more than one and twenty years, that then the same for the term of one and twenty years only, to be accounted from the date of the first letters patents and grants thereof made, shall be of such force as they were or should have been if the same had been made but for the term of one and twenty years only, and as if this act had never been had or made, and of none other.

VI. Provided also, and be it declared and enacted, that any declaration before mentioned shall not extend to any letters patents and grants of privileges for the term of fourteen years or under, hereafter to be made of the sole working or making of any manner of new manufactures within this realm, to the true and first inventor and inventors of such manufactures which others at the time of making such letters patents and grants shall not use, so as also they be not contrary to the law nor mischievous to the state, by raising prices of commodities at home, or hurt of trade, or generally inconvenient, the said fourteen years to be accounted from the date of the first letters patents or grants of such privilege hereafter to be made, but that the same shall be of such force as they should be if this act had never been made and of none other.

VII. [This Act not to be prejudicial to grants conferred by Act of Parliament.]

VIII. [This Act not to extend to warrants directed to judges to compound for forfeitures under penal statutes.]

IX. Provided also, and it is hereby further intended, declared, and enacted that this act or anything therein contained shall not in any wise extend or be prejudicial unto the city of London, or to any city, borough, or town corporate within this realm, for or concerning any grants, charters, or letters patents to them or any of them made or granted, or for or concerning any custom or customs used by or within them or any of them or unto any corporations, companies, or fellowships of any art, trade, occupation, or mistery, or to any companies or societies of merchants within this realm, erected for the maintenance, enlargement, or ordering of any trade of merchandise, but that the same charters, customs, corporations, companies, fellowships and societies, and their liberties, privileges, powers and immunities shall be and continue of such force and effect as they were before the making of this act, and of none other: anything before in this act contained to the contrary in any wise notwithstanding.

X. [This Act not to extend to grants relating to printing, the manufacture of saltpetre or gunpowder, the casting of ordnance or shot, or to offices other than those created by royal proclamation.]

XI. [This Act not to extend to grants relating to alum or alum-mines.]

XII. [This Act not to extend to the fellowship of the Hostmen of Newcastle-upon-Tyne, or to grants or commissions relating to the licensing of taverns.]

XIII. [This Act not to extend to any grant or privilege concerning the manufacture of glass given to Sir Robert Mansell, or to a grant for the transportation of calf-skins made to James Maxwell.]

XIV. [This Act not to extend to a grant concerning the making of smalt made to Abraham Baker, nor to a grant concerning the melting and casting of iron ore made to Edward, Lord Dudley.]

20. AN ACT FOR THE FREE TRADE OF WELSH CLOTHES,[1] [2 *James I*, *c.* 9, *Statutes of the Realm*, *Vol. IV*, *Part II*, *pp.* 1218–19], 1623–4.

Whereas the trade of making of Welsh clothes, friezes, linings and plains within the principality and dominion of Wales, is and hath been of long continuance, in the using and exercising whereof many thousands of the poorer sort of the inhabitants there in precedent ages have been set on work in spinning, carding, weaving, fulling, cottoning and shearing, whereby they (having free liberty to sell them to whom and where they would) not only relieved and maintained themselves and their families in good sort, but also grew to such wealth and means of living as they were thereby enabled to pay and discharge all duties, mizes, charges, subsidies and taxations which were upon them imposed or rated in their several counties, parishes and places wherein they dwelled, for the relief of the poor,

[1] This Act should be read in connection with the Statute of Monopolies (No. 19) and with the Instructions touching the Bill for Free Trade (No. 15), as representing the ideas of parliament as to the desirability of Free Trade within the country.

and the service of the King and the commonwealth; and whereas also the drapers of the town of Shrewsbury, in the county of Salop, have of late obtained some orders of restraint, whereby the inhabitants of Wales find themselves much prejudiced in the freedom of their markets for buying and selling of their clothes, to their great damage, as was verified by the general voice of the knights and burgesses of the twelve shires of Wales and of the county of Monmouth: for remedy whereof, be it declared and enacted by the King's most excellent Majesty, the Lords Spiritual and Temporal, and Commons in this present parliament assembled, and by the authority of the same, that it shall and may be lawful to and for all and every his Majesty's subjects inhabiting or dwelling, or which at any time shall inhabit or dwell within the said dominion of Wales, or any part thereof, freely to sell by way of barter or otherwise, all or any their Welsh clothes, cottons, friezes, linings or plains, at their wills and pleasures, to any person or persons who lawfully by the laws and statutes of this realm may buy the same; and that it shall and may also be lawful for any person and persons who by the laws or statutes of this realm may lawfully buy such clothes, and other the premises, freely to buy the same of any person or persons inhabiting or dwelling, or which hereafter shall inhabit or dwell, within the said dominion of Wales: any charter, grant, act, order or any thing else heretofore made or done, or hereafter to be made or done, to the contrary notwithstanding.

And be it further enacted by the authority aforesaid, that it shall and may be lawful to and for any person or persons using or which shall use the trade of merchandize, to transport into any the parts beyond the seas any of the said Welsh clothes, cottons, friezes, linings and plains, out of any ports or havens within this realm of England or dominion of Wales, or out of any the members thereof, where his majesty, his heirs or successors, have or shall then have officers attending to search, view and control the same, and to receive the King's Majesty's customs and other duties due and payable for the same; so as always the customs and other duties payable for such clothes and other premises so to be transported, shall be justly and duly paid for the same; and so as always the said Welsh clothes, cottons, friezes, linings and plains, before the transporting thereof, shall be fulled, cottoned and sheared as in former times they have used to be; and that no person shall transport the said clothes in other manner than as aforesaid, upon pain to forfeit the whole value of such clothes so to be transported contrary to the true meaning of this act. . . .

Provided always, that this act or anything therein contained, shall not give power or authority to any foreigner or foreigners to buy and sell by way of retail any the said Welsh clothes, cottons, friezes, linings or plains within the town of Shrewsbury, or in any other corporate town or privileged place, contrary to any lawful charter, grant, custom, privilege or liberty in the same town or place now being or used.

21. THE ECONOMIC POLICY OF STRAFFORD IN IRELAND [*Knowler, Letters and Despatches of Thomas Wentworth, Earl of Strafford, Vol. II, pp.* 19, 20, *Letters of Strafford to the Master of the Rolls, July* 25, 1636], 1636.

The last of my generals was that of trade, which I discoursed in this manner; I let them see how the merchants trading thither had been spoiled by the pirates before my coming, as well in his Majesty's harbours, as at sea, a ship fired in the port of Dublin, in sight of His Majesty's Castle, and there continued burning, and the pirate lading and returning from the ship two days together to the mighty scandal of the State; that the shipping for want of money came so late in the year, that all the mischief was done before they came, which commonly was not before the latter end of July, but that now the monies duly answered unto the Exchequer here, the ships had been for these two last years upon the coast by the beginning of March, five or six of the *Biscayners* taken within the Channel, imprisoned, and after released upon their promise not to exercise any hostility hereafter within the Channel; a great ship of the Duke of *Macqueda* taken on the west coast, and thereby so discouraged them, that the merchant hath not lost anything since my arrival there, nor were so much as heard of a *Biscayner* these last two summers. This hath been a means that Trade hath increased exceedingly, and so will still (if we have peace), to the honour of his Majesty, and the enriching of his people.

That the trade here was not only much greater, but rightly conditioned, the native commodities exported being in value at least a third, if not double, the value to the foreign commodities imported; a certain sign that the Commonwealth gathers upon their neighbours.

That there was little or no manufacture amongst them, but some small beginnings towards a clothing trade, which I had and so should still discourage all I could, unless otherwise directed by his Majesty and their lordships, in regard it would trench not only upon the clothings of England, being our staple commodity, so as if they should manufacture their own wools, which grew to very great quantities, we should not only lose the profit we made now by indraping their wools, but his Majesty lose extremely by his customs, and, in conclusion, it might be feared they would beat us out of the trade itself, by underselling us, which they were well able to do. Besides in reasons of State so long as they did not indrape their own wools, they must of necessity fetch their clothing from us, and consequently in a sort depend upon us for their livelihood, and thereby become so dependent upon this Crown as they could not depart from us without nakedness to themselves and children. Yet have I endeavoured another way to set them on work, and that is by bringing in the making and trade of linen cloth, the rather in regard the women are all naturally bred to spinning, that the Irish earth is apt for bearing of flax, and that this manufacture would be in the conclusion rather a benefit than other to this Kingdom. I have therefore sent for the flax seed into Holland, being of a better sort than we have any, sown this year a thousand pounds worth of it (finding by some I sew the last year, that it takes there very well), I have sent for workmen out of the Low Countries and forth of France, and set up already six or seven looms, which, if please God to bless us this year, I trust so to invite them to follow it, when they see the great profit arising thereby, as that they shall generally take to it and employ themselves that way, which if they do I am confident it will prove a mighty business, considering that in all probability we shall be able to undersell the linen cloths of Holland and France at least twenty in the hundred.

My humble advice in the conclusion for the increase of trade was, that his Majesty should not suffer any act of hostility to be offered to any merchants or their goods within the Channel, which was to be preserved and privileged, as the greatest of his Majesty's ports, in the same nature and property as the

Venetian State do their Gulf, and the King of Denmark his Sound, and therefore I humbly besought his Majesty and their lordships that it might accordingly be remembered and provided for in all future treaties with foreign princes.

Upon the summing up of all which, I did represent that Kingdom to his Majesty and the lords as a growing people that would increase beyond all expectation if it were now a little favoured in this their first spring, and not discouraged by harder usage than either English or Scotch found. The instances I gave were the imposition upon coals, wherein the Irish were not treated as English, but as foreigners, by imposing four shillings upon a tun, which was full as much as either French or Dutch paid; next, that excessive rate set upon a horse or mare to be transported forth of this Kingdom, so as I did not know how the army should be provided for the King's service, there not being in that Kingdom of their own breed to furnish those occasions; and lastly eighteenpence set upon every live beast that comes thence, all which will be a great discouragement for any to transplant themselves and children into a country where they shall presently be dealt withal as aliens, be denied the favours and the graces afforded to other subjects, and utterly quell and cut off any increase of trade by nipping it and overburdening it thus in the bud.

22. Revocation of Commissions, Patents and Monopolies Granted by the Crown [*Soc. Ant. Proc. Coll.*,[1] *April* 15, 1639].

Whereas divers grants, licenses, privileges, and commissions have been procured from his Majesty, . . . , which since upon experience hath been found prejudicial and inconvenient to his people, contrary to his Majesty's gracious intention in granting the same; And whereas also upon like suggestions, there hath been obtained from his Majesty, the lords and others of his Privy Council, divers warrants and letters of assistance for the execution of those grants, licenses, privileges, and commissions according to his Majesty's good intention and meaning therein.

Forasmuch as his most excellent Majesty (whose royal ear and providence is ever intent on the public good of his people)

[1] Quoted, W. H. Price, *English Patents of Monopoly*, Appendix B.

doth now discern that the particular grants, licenses, and commissions hereafter expressed, have been found in consequence far from those grounds and reasons wherefore they were founded, and in their execution have been notoriously abused, he is now pleased of his mere grace and favour to all his loving subjects (with the advice of his Privy Council) by his regal power to publish and declare the several commissions and licenses hereafter following, whether the same have passed his great seal, privy seal, signet, and sign manual, or any of them, to be from hence utterly void, revoked, and hereby determined.

That is to say:—

A commission for cottages and inmates touching scrivenors and brokers.

A commission for compounding with offenders touching tobacco.

A commission for compounding with offenders touching butter.

A commission for compounding with offenders touching logwood.

A commission for compounding with sheriffs for selling under-sheriffs' places.

A commission for compounding with offenders for destruction of woods for iron-works.

A commission for concealments and encroachments within 20 miles of London.

A license to transport sheep and lambskins.

A commission to take men bound to dress no venison, pheasants, or partridges in inns, alehouses, ordinaries, and taverns.

A commission touching licensing of wine-casks.

A commission for licensing of brewers.

A license for sole transporting of lamperns[1] and all proclamations, warrants, or letters of assistance for putting in execution of the said commissions or licenses be from henceforth declared void, determined, and hereby revoked to all intents and purposes.

And his Majesty in like favour and ease to his subjects is further pleased to declare his royal will and pleasure to be, that the particular grants hereafter mentioned (upon feigned suggestions, obtained from him, to public damages) whereby

[1] *i.e.* lampreys.

the same have passed his Majesty's great seal, privy seal, signet, or sign manual or any of them, shall not hereafter be put in execution, viz.:

A grant for weighing of hay and straw in London and Westminster and 3 miles compass.

An office of register to the commission for bankrupts in divers counties of the realm.

An office or grant for gauging of red herrings.

An office or grant for the marking of iron made within the realm.

An office or grant for sealing of bone lace.

A grant for making and gauging of butter casks.

A grant of privilege touching kelp and seaweed.

A grant for sealing of linen cloth.

A grant for gathering of rags.

An office or grant of factor for Scottish merchants.

An office or grant for searching and sealing of foreign hops.

A grant for sealing of buttons.

All grants of fines, penalties, and forfeitures before judgment granted, or mentioned to be granted, by letters patents, privy seals, signet, sign manual, or otherwise.

All patents for new inventions not put in practice within 3 years next after the date of the said grants.

And the several grants of incorporation made unto—

Hatband-makers.

Gutstring-makers.

Spectacle-makers.

Comb-makers.

Tobacco-pipe-makers.

Butchers and Horners.

And his Majesty doth further require and command that there shall be a proceeding against the said patentees by *quo warranto* or *scire facias* to recall the said grants and patents, unless they will voluntarily surrender and yield up the same: and also all proclamations, warrants, or letters of assistance obtained from his Majesty or the lords and others of his Privy Council for execution thereof, from henceforth utterly to cease and be determined, and are hereby absolutely revoked and recalled.

And his Majesty doth further expressly charge and command all and singular the patentees, grantees, or others any ways interested or claiming under the aforenamed grants, licenses, or commissions, or any of them and their deputies, that they or any of them do not at any time hereafter presume to put in use or execution any of the said grants, commissions, or licenses, or any thing therein contained, or any proclamations, warrants, or letters of assistance obtained in that behalf, upon pain of his Majesty's indignation, and to be proceeded against as contemners of his Majesty's royal commands, whereof he will require a strict account. Given at our Manor of York the 9th of April in the 15th year of our reign, 1639.

23. ORDINANCE ESTABLISHING AN EXCISE [*Firth and Rait, Acts and Ordinances of the Interregnum, Vol. I, pp.* 202–14], 1643.

An ordinance for the speedy raising and levying of monies, set by way of charge or new impost, on the several commodities mentioned in the schedule hereunto annexed ; as well for the securing of trade as for the maintenance of the forces raised for the defence of the King and Parliament, both by sea and land, as for and towards the payments of the debts of the commonwealth, for which the public faith is, or shall be, given.

The Lords and Commons now assembled in Parliament, taking into their serious consideration the great danger that this kingdom lyeth under, through the implacable malice and treachery of Papists and other wicked persons ; . . . And forasmuch as many great levies have been already made . . . which the well-affected party to the Protestant religion have hitherto willingly paid, to their great charge, and the malignants of this kingdom have hitherto practised by all cunning ways and means how to evade and elude the payment of any part thereof; By reason whereof the Lords and Commons do hold it fit that some constant and equal way for the levying of monies for the future maintenance of the Parliament forces . . . may be . . . established, whereby the said malignants and neutrals may be brought to and compelled to pay their proportionable parts of the aforesaid charge. . . .

I. Be it therefore ordered, ordained and declared by the said Lords and Commons, that the several rates and charges in a schedule hereunto annexed and contained shall be set and laid . . . . upon all and every the commodities in the said schedule particularly expressed. . . .

II. Be it further ordained . . . that . . . an office . . . shall be . . . erected . . . in the City of London, called . . . by the name of the Office of Excise or New Impost, whereof there shall be eight Commissioners to govern the same. . . .

V. That the like office and so many of such officers shall be . . . erected . . . in all the counties of the realm of England, dominion of Wales, and town of Berwick, and all other the cities . . . as the said eight Commissioners . . . think fit to nominate . . .

VII. That the said office in all places where it shall be placed shall be kept open in the week days from eight . . . till eleven, and from two till five . . ., for the entering and registering the names and surnames, as well of the sellers, buyers and makers of all and every the commodities in the said schedule mentioned, and of the several qualities thereof, as for the receiving of all monies as shall be due upon the sale. . . .

XI. That if any of the sellers of the said commodities shall refuse or neglect to make a true entry of the said commodities . . . that then he or they . . . shall forfeit to the use of the commonwealth four times the true value of the goods and commodities so by him or them neglected to be entered or delivered. . . .

XV. That this ordinance shall begin to take place and effect from the 25th of July, 1643, and from thence to continue only for three years then next ensuing, unless both Houses of Parliament, during that time, shall declare that it shall continue for any longer time. . . .

In this schedule is contained the charge and excise which . . . is set and imposed, to be paid on the several commodities hereafter mentioned.

[Here follows schedule of rates and commodities.]

PART III: 1660–1846

SECTION I

INDUSTRIAL ORGANISATION AND SOCIAL CONDITIONS

1. Defoe's Account of the West Riding Cloth Industry, 1724—2. Defoe's Account of the Woollen Trade, *temp.* George II:—3 Defoe's Account of the Corn Trade; *temp.* George II.—4. Defoe's Account of the Coal Trade, *temp.* George II.—5. A Description of Middlemen in the Woollen Industry, 1739.—6. Report on the Condition of Children in Lancashire Cotton Factories, 1796—7. The Newcastle Coal Vend, 1771–1830—8. The old Apprenticeship System in the Woollen Industry, 1806—9. A Petition of Cotton Weavers, 1807—10. Depression of Wages and its Causes in the Cotton Industry, 1812—11. Evidence of the Condition of Children in Factories, 1816—12. Change in the Cotton Industry and the Introduction of Power-loom Weaving, 1785–1807—13. Evidence by Factory Workers of the Condition of Children, 1832—14. Women's and Children's Labour in Mines, 1842—15. Description of the Condition of Manchester by John Robertson, Surgeon, 1840.

THE documents in this section are intended to illustrate changes in industry and their effects on social conditions between 1660 and 1846. Eight extracts illustrate the condition of industries in the period, their structure, organisation and methods (Nos. 1 to 5, 7, 8 and 12). The first five refer to the early part of the eighteenth century and have a double interest. They record the old conditions in the woollen industry and the wool, corn and coal trades, and enable us to estimate the completeness of the change which was coming (Nos. 1, 2, 3, 4, 5). They show also how far advanced already was the organisation of markets and middlemen, and vertical control. A description of the conditions of the old apprenticeship system in the woollen industry is added (No. 8). Evidence before Committees on the Coal Trade gives an account of the important monopoly agreements and limitations of output which the peculiar conditions of the industry produced (No. 7). An example of the mechanical inventions which revolutionised industry at the close of the period is taken from an autobiographical pamphlet by a pioneer in power-loom cotton weaving (No. 12).

The pressure of industrial change on human life had been felt for some time before the application of new motive-power to machinery took full effect. The fluctuations of the cotton weaving industry and the depression of wages, aggravated by the French wars and trade restrictions, are illustrated by a petition of weavers (No. 9) and by evidence before a committee on the Orders in Council (No. 10). The rest of the extracts refer chiefly to the employment of children under the new industrial conditions. The report of Dr. Perceval in 1796 (No. 6) helped to produce the original Factory Act (See Pt. III, Section III, No. 9). The evidence of Peel and Owen before the committee of 1816 is given as the testimony of exceptional employers (No. 11). It supplements the picture painted by children, parents and overseers before Sadler's committee (No. 13). The Commission of 1842 (No. 14) supplies evidence of the conditions under which women and children worked in the coal mines. A brief description by a surgeon of the condition of Manchester in 1840 is added as giving some indication of the part played by housing conditions in the Industrial Revolution (No. 15).

AUTHORITIES

On Industrial Organisation the principal modern writers are Unwin, *Industrial Organisation in the Sixteenth and Seventeenth Centuries*; Cunningham, *English Industry and Commerce, Modern Times*; Mantoux, *La Révolution Industrielle*; Toynbee, *The Industrial Revolution*; Marx, *Capital*, Vol. II; Hobson, *The Evolution of Modern Capitalism*, *Social England* (edited Traill); H. Levy, *Monopoly and Competition.* Consult also Smiles, *Lives of the Engineers*, *Lives of Boulton and Watt*, *Industrial Biography*; Meteyard, *Life of Wedgwood*; Chapman, *The Cotton Industry*; Galloway, *Annals of Coalmining*; Boyd, *History of the Coal Trade*; Lloyd, *The Cutlery Trades*; Leone Levi, *History of British Commerce*; Porter,

The Progress of the Nation, and *The Victoria County History, passim* (articles on social and economic history and on industries). For social conditions and changes consult Mantoux, Cunningham, Marx, and other writers above-mentioned, and Hutchins, *The Public Health Agitation*; Cooke Taylor, *The Factory System* and *Introduction to the Factory System*; Webb, *History of Trade Unionism.*

Bibliographies are given by Cunningham, *op. cit.*, Part II; Unwin, *op. cit.*; Mantoux, *op. cit.*; *Social England*; Hutchins and Harrison, *History of Factory Legislation*; Webb, *op. cit.*; Cambridge Modern History, Vol. X.

Contemporary.—(1) The chief printed documentary evidence is to be found in the numerous reports of Committees and Commissions. For children's employment see the following Reports: on the State of Children in Manufactories, 1816 (III); on the Bill to regulate the labour of Children, 1832; on Children in Factories, 1833 (XX and XXI); on Children in Mines and Manufactories, 1842 (XV, XVI, XVII); on Children's Employment, 1843 (XII–XV). On conditions of wages and employment see Reports on Petitions; of Framework Knitters, 1778–1779; of Woolcombers, 1794; of Calico Printers, 1804 (V) and 1806 (III); of Hand-loom Weavers: 1834 (X) and 1835 (XIII), 1839 (XIII) and 1840 (XXII and XXIV); also Reports on the Apprenticeship Laws, 1813 (IV); on the Woollen Manufacture, 1806 (III); on Silk and Ribbon Weavers, 1818 (X). The organisation of the Coal Industry is described in Reports on the Coal Trade. See also the Letter Books of Holroyd and Hill (ed. Heaton, Halifax Bankfield Museum Notes, Series II, No. 3).

(2) Contemporary literary evidence for the earlier part of the period is to be found in Defoe, A Tour through the Whole Island of Great Britain, and The Complete English Tradesman; Smith, Memoirs of Wool (a collection); Young, Tour through the North of England, gives a brief survey of the Country in 1770. The changes in industrial methods are described in W. Radcliffe, Origin of the New System of Manufacture, commonly called Power-loom Weaving, Memoir of Edmund Cartwright, and Histories of the Cotton Manufactures by Ure and Baines. Life under the new conditions is described by Gaskell, The Manufacturing Population, and Artizans and Machinery, and Owen, Observations on the Manufacturing System. See also G. Dyer, The Complaints of the Poor People of England; C. Hall, The Effects of Civilisation; J. Brown, Memoir of Robert Blincoe (a child factory-worker); and, for public health, Kay, Moral and Physical Condition of the Working Classes; Richardson, The Health of Nations (Chadwick's writings); Reports 1800 (X) and 1830 (VII); Sanitary Conditions in large towns are described in Reports on Health of Towns, 1840 (XI) and 1845 (XVIII), and on Sanitary Conditions, 1844 (XVII).

1. Defoe's Account of the West Riding Cloth Industry [*D. Defoe, A Tour Through Great Britain, Vol. III, pp.* 144–146, *Ed.* 1769], 1724.

From Blackstone Edge to Halifax is eight miles; and all the way, except from Sowerby to Halifax, is thus up hill and down; so that, I suppose, we mounted up to the clouds, and descended to the water-level, about eight times in that little part of the journey.

But now I must observe to you, that after we passed the second hill, and were come down into the valley again; and so still the nearer we came to Halifax, we found the houses thicker, and the villages greater in every bottom; and not only so, but the sides of the hills, which were very steep every way were spread with houses; for the land being divided into small inclosures, from two acres to six or seven each, seldom more, every three or four pieces of land had an house belonging to them.

In short, after we had mounted the third hill we found the country one continued village, though every way mountainous, hardly an house standing out of a speaking distance from another; and as the day cleared up, we could see at every house a tenter, and on almost every tenter a piece of cloth, kersie, or shalloon; which are the three articles of this country's labour.

In the course of our road among the houses, we found at every one of them a little rill or gutter of running water; if the house was above the road, it came from it, and crossed the way to run to another; if the house was below us, it crossed us from some other distant house above it; and at every considerable house was a manufactory; which not being able to be carried on without water, these little streams were so parted and guided by gutters or pipes, that not one of the houses wanted its necessary appendage of a rivulet.

Again, as the dyeing-houses, scouring-shops, and places where they use this water, emit it tinged with the drugs of the dyeing vat, and with the oil, the soap, the tallow, and other ingredients used by the clothiers in dressing and scouring, etc., the lands through which it passes, which otherwise would be exceeding barren, are enriched by it to a degree beyond imagination.

Then, as every clothier must necessarily keep one horse, at least, to fetch home his wool and his provisions from the market, to carry his yarn to the spinners, his manufacture to the fulling-mill, and when finished, to the market to be sold, and the like; so every one generally keeps a cow or two for his family. By this means, the small pieces of inclosed land about each house are occupied; and, by being thus fed, are still farther improved from the dung of the cattle. As for corn, they scarce sow enough to feed their poultry.

Such, it seems, has been the bounty of nature to this county, that two things essential to life, and more particularly to the business followed here, are found in it, and in such a situation as is not to be met with in any part of England, if in the world beside; I mean coals, and running water on the tops of the highest hills. I doubt not but there are both springs and coals lower in these hills; but were they to fetch them thence, it is probable the pits would be too full of water: it is easy, however, to fetch them from the upper parts, the horses going light up, and coming down loaden. This place, then, seems to have been designed by providence for the very purposes to which it is now allotted, for carrying on a manufacture, which can nowhere be so easily supplied with the conveniences necessary for it. Nor is the industry of the people wanting to second these advantages. Though we met few people without doors, yet within we saw the houses full of lusty fellows, some at the dye-vat, some at the loom, others dressing the cloths; the women and children carding, or spinning; all employed from the youngest to the oldest; scarce any thing above four years old, but its hands were sufficient for its own support. Nor a beggar to be seen, nor an idle person, except here and there in an alms-house, built for those that are ancient, and past working. The people in general live long; they enjoy a good air; and under such circumstances hard labour is naturally attended with the blessing of health, if not riches.

From this account, you will easily imagine, that some of these remote parts of the North are the most populous places of Great Britain, London and its neighbourhood excepted.

2. Defoe's Account of the Wool Trade and Woollen Industries [*D. Defoe, The Complete English Tradesman, Ed.* 1841, *Vol. II, pp.* 188–93], *temp.* George II.

First, the wool itself, being taken from the sheep's back, either by the shearer, the farmer, or by the fellmonger from the skin, becomes a subject of trade; and is either sold to the stapler, or wool merchant, and by him to the manufacturer, or is carried by the farmer and fellmonger, as is sometimes the case, to the particular counties where it is consumed.

These staplers and wool dealers are scattered all over the kingdom, and are a very important and considerable sort of tradesmen, being the first tradesmen into whose hands the said wool comes for sale: the principal towns in England where they are found to be in any numbers together, are in London, or Southwark rather, being principally in Barnaby Street, and the town of Blandford in Dorsetshire; there are also some in Norwich and in Lincolnshire, and in Leicestershire a great many.

Stourbridge fair is famous for the great quantity of wool sold there, and which goes beyond any other fairs or markets in all the north or east parts of England.

But wherever the wool is carried, and by whomsoever it is sold, this of course brings it to the first part of its manufacturing; and this consists of two operations:

1. Combing. 2. Carding.

The combers are a particular set of people, and the combing a trade by itself; the carding, on the other hand, is chiefly done by workmen hired by the clothiers themselves; the combers buy the wool in the fleece or in the pack, and when it is combed, put it on to the next operation on their own account. The carding is generally done by hired servants, as above; these operations hand on the wool to the next, which is common to both, viz., the spinning.

But before it comes this length, it requires a prodigious number of people, horses, carts or wagons, to carry it from place to place; for the people of those countries where the wool is grown, or taken as above, are not the people who spin it into yarn.

On the contrary, some whole counties and parts of counties are employed in spinning, who see nothing of any manufacture among them, the mere spinning only excepted.

Thus the weavers of Norwich and of the parts adjacent, and the weavers of Spitalfields in London, send exceeding great quantities of wool into remote counties to be spun, besides what they spin in both those populous counties of Norfolk and Suffolk; particularly they employ almost the whole counties of Cambridge, Bedford, and Hertford; and besides that, as if all this part of England was not sufficient for them, they send a very great quantity of wool one hundred and fifty miles by land carriage to the north, as far as Westmoreland, to be spun; and the yarn is brought back in the same manner to London and to Norwich.

This vast consumption of wool in Norfolk and Suffolk is supplied chiefly out of Lincolnshire, a county famous for the large sheep bred up for the supply of the London markets, as the western manufacturers are supplied from Leicestershire; of which in its place.

Nor is all this sufficient still; but as if all England was not able to spin sufficient to the manufacture, a very great quantity of yarn, ready spun, is brought from Ireland, landed at Bristol, and brought from thence by land carriage to London, and then to Norwich also.

The county of Essex, a large and exceedingly populous county, is chiefly taken up with the great manufacture of bays and perpets; the consumption of wool for this manufacture is chiefly bought of the staplers in London; the sorting, oiling, combing, or otherwise preparing the wool, is the work of the master manufacturer or bay maker; and the yarn is generally spun in the same county, the extent of it being not less than between fifty and sixty miles' square, and full of great and populous towns, such as Colchester, Braintree, Coggeshall, Chelmsford, Billericay, Bishop Stortford, Saffron Walden, Waltham, Romford, and innumerable smaller but very populous villages, and, in a word, the whole county full of people.

The western part of England, superior both in manufactures and in numbers of people also, are not to be supplied either with wool or with spinning, among themselves, notwithstanding two such articles in both, as no other part of England can come up to by a great deal, viz.:

1. Notwithstanding the prodigious numbers of sheep fed upon those almost boundless downs and plains in the counties of Dorset, Wilts, Gloucester, Somerset, and Hampshire, where the multitudes, not of sheep only, but even of flocks of sheep, are not to be reckoned up; insomuch that the people of Dorchester say there are six hundred thousand sheep always feeding within six miles round that one town.

2. Notwithstanding the large and most populous counties of

Wilts, Somerset, Gloucester, and Devon, in which the manufacture being so exceeding great, all the women inhabitants may be supposed to be thoroughly employed in spinning the yarn for them, and in which counties are, besides, the populous cities of Exeter, Salisbury, Wells, Bath, Bristol, and Gloucester; I say besides these, the greatest towns, and the greatest number of them that any other part of the whole kingdom of Great Britain can show, some of which exceed even the great towns of Leeds, Wakefield, Sheffield, etc., in the North; such as Taunton, Devizes, Tiverton, Crediton, Bradford, Trowbridge, Westbury, Froome, Stroud, Biddeford, Barnstaple, Dartmouth, Bridgewater, Mynhead, Poole, Weymouth, Dorchester, Blandford, Wimbourn, Sherbourne, Cirencester, Honiton, Warminster, Tewksbury, Tedbury, Malmsbury, and abundance of others, too many to set down; all which I mention, because those who pretend to have calculated the numbers of people employed in these four counties assure me that there are not so few as a million of people constantly employed there in spinning and weaving for the woollen manufacture only; that besides the great cities, towns, and seaports, mentioned above, there are not less than one hundred and twenty market towns, six large cities, and fifteen hundred parishes, some of which are exceeding full of people.

And yet, notwithstanding all this, such is the greatness of this prodigious manufacture, that they are said to take yearly thirty thousand packs of wool, and twenty-five thousand packs of yarn ready spun from Ireland.

From hence, take a short view of the middle part of England: Leicester, Northampton, and Warwick shires have a prodigious number of large sheep, which, as is said of Lincolnshire, are bred for the London markets; the wool, consequently, is of an exceeding long staple, and the fineness is known also to be extraordinary.

This wool is brought every week, Tuesday and Friday, to the market at Cirencester, on the edge of Gloucester and Wilts; the quantity is supposed to be at least five hundred packs of wool per week.

Here it is bought by the woolcombers and carders of Tedbury, Malmsbury, and the towns on all that side of Wilts and Gloucester, besides what the clothiers themselves buy; these carry it out far and near among the poor people of all the adjacent countries, for the spinning; and having made the yarn, they supply that manufacture as far as Froome, Warminster, and Taunton; and thus the west country is furnished

The north requires another inspection; the rest of the Leicestershire wool merchants, who do not bring their wool southward, carry it forward to the north, to Wakefield, Leeds, and Halifax; here they mix it with, and use it among the northern wool, which is not esteemed so fine.

Not forgetting, notwithstanding, that they have a great deal of very fine wool, and of a good staple, from the wolds or downs in the East Riding of Yorkshire, and from the bishoprick of Durham, more especially the banks of the Tees, where, for a long way, the grounds are rich, and the sheep thought to be the largest in England.

Hither all the finest wool of those countries is brought; and the coarser sort, and the Scots' wool, which comes into Halifax, Rochdale, Bury, and the manufacturing towns of Lancashire, Westmoreland, and Cumberland, are employed in the coarser manufactures of those countries, such as kerseys, half-thicks, yarn stockings, duffields, rugs, Turkey work, chairs, and many other useful things, which those countries abound in.

3. Defoe's Account of the Corn Trade [*D. Defoe, The Complete English Tradesman, Ed.* 1841, *Vol. II, pp.* 177–182], *temp.* George II.

As the corn trade is of such consequence to us, for the shipping off the overplus, so it is a very considerable business in itself; the principal people concerned in it, as a trade, are, though very numerous, yet but of four denominations;—

1. Cornfactors; 3. Maltsters;
2. Mealmen; 4. Carriers.

1. Cornfactors; these, as corn is now become a considerable article of trade, as well foreign as inland, are now exceeding numerous; and though we had them at first only in London, yet now they are also in all the great corn markets and ports where corn is exported through the whole island of Britain; and in all those ports they generally correspond with the corn factors in England.

Those in the country ride about among the farmers, and buy the corn even in the barn before it is threshed; nay, sometimes they buy it in the field standing, not only before it is reaped, but before it is ripe. This subtle business is very profitable; for, by this means, cunningly taking advantage of the farmers, by letting them have money before-hand, which they, poor men, often want, they buy cheap when there is a prospect of corn being dear; yet sometimes they are mistaken too, and are caught in their own snare; but indeed, that is but seldom; and were they famed for their honesty, as much as they generally are for their understanding in business, they might boast of having a very shining character.

2. Mealmen; these generally live either in London or within thirty miles of it, that employment chiefly relating to the markets of London; they formerly were the general buyers of corn, that is to say, wheat and rye, in all the great markets about London, or within thirty or forty miles of London, which corn they used to bring to the nearest mills they could find to the market, and there have it ground, and then sell the meal to the shopkeepers, called mealmen, in London.

But a few years past have given a new turn to this trade, for now the bakers in London, and the parts adjacent, go to the markets themselves, and have cut out the shopkeeping mealmen; so the bakers are the mealmen, and sell the fine flour to private families, as the mealmen used to do. And as the bakers have cut out the meal shops in London, so the millers have cut out the mealmen in the country; and whereas they formerly only ground the corn for the mealmen, they now scorn that trade, buy the corn, and grind it for themselves; so the baker goes to the miller for his meal, and the miller goes to the market for the corn.

It is true, this is an anticipation in trade, and is against a stated wholesome rule of commerce, that trade ought to pass through as many hands as it can; and that the circulation of trade, like that of the blood, is the life of the commerce. But I am not directing to what should be, but telling what is; it is certain the mealmen are, in a manner, cut out of the trade, both in London and in the country, except it be those country mealmen who send meal to London by barges, from all the countries bordering on the Thames, or on any navigable river running into the Thames west; and some about Chichester,

Arundel, and the coast of Sussex and Hampshire, who send meal by sea; and these are a kind of meal merchants, and have factors at London to sell it for them—either at Queenhithe, the great meal-market of England, or at other smaller markets.

By this change of the trade, the millers, especially in that part of England which is near the Thames, who in former times were esteemed people of a very mean employment, are now become men of vast business; and it is not an uncommon thing to have mills upon some of the large rivers near the town, which are let for three or four hundred pounds a year rent.

3. Maltsters; these are now no longer farmers, and, as might be said, working labouring people, as was formerly the case, when the public expense of beer and ale, and the number of alehouses, was not so great, but generally the most considerable farmers malted their own barley, especially in the towns and counties, from whence they supplied London, and almost every farmhouse of note.

As the demand for malt increased, those farmers found it for their purpose to make more and larger quantities of malt, than the barley they themselves sowed would supply; and so bought the barley at the smaller farms about them; till at length the market for malt still increasing, and the profits like-wise encouraging, they sought far and near for barley; and at this time the malting trade at Ware, Hertford, Royston, Hitchin, and other towns on that side of Hertfordshire, fetch their barley twenty, thirty, or forty miles; and all the barley they can get out of the counties of Essex, Cambridge, Bedford, Huntingdon, and even as far as Suffolk, is little enough to supply them; and the like it is at all the malt-making towns upon the river of Thames, where the malt trade is carried on for supply of London, such as Kingston, Chertsey, Windsor, High Wycombe, Reading, Wallingford, Abingdon, Thame, Oxford, and all the towns adjacent; and at Abingdon in particular, they have a barley market, where you see every market-day four or five hundred carts and wagons of barley to be sold at a time, standing in rows in the market-place, besides the vast quantity carried directly to the maltsters' houses.

The malt trade thus increasing, it soon came out of the hands of the farmers; for either the farmers found so much business, and to so much advantage, in the malting-trade, that they left off ploughing, and put off their farms, sticking wholly to the malt; or other men, encouraged by the apparent advantage of the malting-trade, set it up by itself, and bought their barley, as is said above, of the farmers, when their malt trade first increased; or both these together, which is most probable; and thus malting became a trade by itself.

Again, though the farmers then generally left off malting in the manner as above, yet they did not wholly throw themselves out of the profit of the trade, but hired the making of their own malt; that is, to put out their barley to the malt-houses to be made on their account; and this occasioned many men to erect malthouses, chiefly to make malt only for other people, at so much per quarter, as they could agree; and at intervals, if they wanted full employ, then they made it for themselves; of these I shall say more presently.

Under the head of corn factors, I might have taken notice, that there are many of those factors who sell no other grain than malt; and are, as we may say, agents for the maltsters who stay in the country, and only send up their goods; and assistants to those maltsters who come up themselves.

The mentioning these factors again here, naturally brings me to observe a new way of buying and selling of corn, as well as malt, which is introduced by these factors; a practice greatly increased of late, though it is an unlawful way of dealing, and many ways prejudicial to the markets; and this is buying of corn by samples only. The case is thus:—

The farmer, who has perhaps twenty load of wheat in his barn, rubs out only a few handfuls of it with his hand, and puts it into a little money-bag; and with this sample, as it is called, in his pocket, away he goes to market.

When he comes thither, he stands with his little bag in his hand, at a particular place where such business is done, and thither the factors or buyers come also; the factor looks on the sample, asks his price, bids, and then buys; and that not a sack or a load, but the whole quantity; and away they go together to the next inn, to adjust the bargain, the manner of delivery, the payment, etc. Thus the whole barn, or stack, or mow of corn, is sold at once; and not only so, but it is odds but the factor deals with him ever after, by coming to his house; and so the farmer troubles the market no more.

This kind of trade is chiefly carried on in those market-towns which are at a small distance from London, or at least from the river Thames; such as Romford, Dartford, Grayes, Rochester, Maidstone, Chelmsford, Malden, Colchester, Ipswich, and so down on both sides the river to the North Foreland, and particularly at Margate and Whitstable, on one side; and to the coast of Suffolk, and along the coast both ways beyond, and likewise up the river. Also,

At these markets you may see, that, besides the market-house, where a small quantity of corn perhaps is seen, the place mentioned above, where the farmers and factors meet, is like a little exchange, where all the rest of the business is transacted, and where a hundred times the quantity of corn is bought and sold, as appears in sacks in the market-house; it is thus, in particular, at Grayes, and at Dartford: and though on a market-day there are very few wagons with corn to be seen in the market, yet the street or market-place, nay, the towns and inns, are thronged with farmers and samples on one hand, and with mealmen, London bakers, millers, and cornfactors, and other buyers, on the other. The rest of the week you see the wagons and carts continually coming all night and all day, laden with corn of all sorts, to be delivered on board the hoys, where the hoymen stand ready to receive it, and generally to pay for it also: and thus a prodigious corn trade is managed in the market, and little or nothing to be seen of it.

4. Defoe's Account of the Coal Trade [*D. Defoe, The Complete English Tradesman, Ed.* 1841, *Vol. II, pp.* 172–173], *temp.* George II.

The Newcastle coals, brought by sea to London, are bought at the pit, or at the steath or wharf, for under five shillings per chaldron; I suppose I speak with the most; but when they come to London, are not delivered to the consumers under from twenty-five to thirty shillings per chaldron; and when they are a third time loaded on board the lighters in the Thames, and carried through bridge, then loaded a fourth time into the great west country barges, and carried up the river, perhaps to Oxford or Abingdon, and thence loaded a fifth time in carts or wagons, and carried perhaps ten or fifteen, or twenty miles to the last consumer; by this time they are sometimes sold from forty-five to fifty shillings per chaldron; so that the five shillings first cost, including five shillings tax, is increased to five times the prime cost. And because I have mentioned the frequent loading and unloading the coals, it is necessary to explain it here once for all, because it may give a light into the nature of this river and coast commerce, not in this thing only, but in many others ; these loadings are thus :—

1. They are dug in the pit a vast depth in the ground, sometimes fifty, sixty, to a hundred fathoms ; and being loaded (for so the miners call it) into a great basket or tub, are drawn up by a wheel and horse, or horses, to the top of the shaft, or pit mouth, and there thrown out upon the great heap, to lie ready against the ships come into the port to demand them.

2. They are then loaded again into a great machine called a wagon ; which by the means of an artificial road, called a wagon-way, goes with the help of but one horse, and carries two chaldron, or more, at a time, and this, sometimes, three or four miles to the nearest river or water carriage they come at ; and there they are either thrown into, or from, a great storehouse, called a steath, made so artificially, with one part close to or hanging over the water, that the lighters or keels can come close to, or under it, and the coals be at once shot out of the wagon into the said lighters, which carry them to the ships, which I call the first loading upon the water.

5. A Description of Middlemen in the Woollen Industry [*J. Smith, The Memoirs of Wool, Vol. II, pp.* 310–313, 1747], 1739.

The Tyranny of the Blackwel-Hall Factors.

The sufferings of the poor employed in working up Spanish wool, are not owing to the unmercifulness of the clothiers, but the tyranny of Blackwel-Hall factors ; who though originally but the servants of the makers, are now become their masters, and not only theirs, but the wool merchants and drapers too.

Perhaps, sir, you may ask how it is possible that these men, who style themselves but factors or agents, could find means to lord it as tyrants over their employers ? Why thus : they have managed it so, that the merchant dare not sell his wool to the clothier, nor the clothier presume to buy it of the merchant. On this grand point their whole power is founded. To make this clear, sir, you are to understand, that in the year

1695, the clothiers finding themselves in much the same circumstances they are at present, by their credit given to the drapers on one hand, and their being obliged to purchase wool of the factors, on the other, applied in a body to parliament for relief, and an act was accordingly past for restoring to them Blackwel-Hall for a market, limiting the credit to be given for their goods, to six months ; obliging the factor to demand notes of hand of the draper, payable in that term, for the use of the clothier, on penalty of forfeiting double the value of the debt ; and in case the draper refused to give such notes, so demanded, fining him 20*s.*

For a little while, this act had its desired effect ; these notes were immediately returned to the clothier, who carried them to market for wool, etc., and by that means, made them answer in trade almost as well as cash itself. The factors thus stripped of the most valuable part of their business, immediately concerted such measures as rendered the whole act ineffectual, and put it in their power to tyrannize over the clothiers as much as ever. This was done, by tampering with those of the trade, whose circumstances were most precarious, who induced by the promise of a speedy sale for their goods, prior to those of any other maker, were easily prevailed upon to forego the advantage of the notes granted them by Parliament. This fatal precedent being once set, the factors instantly exacted a like compliance from all the rest ; and if any refused not one piece of their cloth was sold. By which means, being obliged to keep their workmen employed in the interval, their whole stock, though ever so large, was exhausted ; and the more stock they had, the more it became their interest to truckle to their old oppressors, and again take off their wool on what terms they pleased.

This important point carried, like true politicians, they resolved to pursue their blow, and add some new acquisitions to what they possessed before. Accordingly, they again allowed the drapers such unreasonable credit, that it was impossible for the most substantial clothier to carry on the trade, while the returns were so slow and precarious. On an universal complaint therefore of this grievance, they graciously condescended to insure the debt to be paid, twelve months after it was contracted ; but in return of so great a favour, insisted on two and a half per cent. as a reward ; and if any was rash or stubborn enough to disrelish or oppose this new imposition, he had the mortification to wait six months longer for his money, that is to say, a year and a half in all; which, together with the three months the cloth is in making, and three that (one piece with another) it continues in the hall, before it is sold off, make two years in the whole. Now let any one judge how large a stock is absolutely necessary to carry on a trade, under all these disadvantages, particularly when 'tis recollected, that the clothier is obliged to pay his workmen ready money all this while, whether his goods are vended or no; and that the modest factor always insists on his being paid for his wool, with the first money he receives for the cloth.

Neither is even this all. But if the clothier, hard drove by so vast and so continued a charge, should be compelled, as too many are, to draw upon the factor for money before 'tis due, according to their calculation, one misfortune makes way for another; and he must pay an extravagant premium for the advance, probably, of his own money. Nor are you to wonder, sir, that these worthy gentlemen are so solicitous to monopolise the whole market of Spanish wool; since, on a medium, they get four pounds on every pack. Now a considerable clothier may be supposed to work up 80 packs a year; which is in a manner a rent charge of 320*l.* to the factor annually; for it is more than probable that this very wool is purchased with the clothiers' cash; and while the factor grows rich without any risk, and with very little trouble the clothier is doubly excised, both for what he receives, and what is not only withheld, but employed so manifestly to his prejudice.

'Tis farther to be observed, that as by far the greatest part of a clothiers' stock must of necessity be lodged in the factors hands, if he (the clothier) happens to break, or die insolvent (as in spite of a whole life of toil and industry, many of them do) the factor immediately seizes on the whole; it being (says he) a pledge for money advanced, wool sold, etc., so that the rest of the creditors seldom receive a farthing, while he, to whom the poor man's calamity is principally owing, runs away with all.

Besides these capital grievances, there are several others, which though inferior in degree, are, when added together, no small increase of the load; such as the factors lumping the charges for warehouse-room in the hall, porterage, pressing, packing, etc., every article of which ought to be particular; as likewise sending out cloths to the drapers at the expense of the clothier, not for sale; but one would be almost tempted to think, to supply the shops with the paper and packthread they are secured with; since they are returned stripp'd of both, tumbled from end to end, exposed to all weather and accidents, and in such a condition as renders it absolutely necessary to have them cleaned, pressed, and packed anew. And all this, after they have been out of the hall six or eight weeks; though the above quoted act of Parliament provides that every cloth shall be reputed sold, after it hath been detained eight days.

One would think, sir, I had already mentioned grievances enough, not only to justify the clothier, but to excite the concern of the whole people in their favour, and the aid of the legislature in their redress. But there is yet another behind, which ought not to be omitted. It is this. These worthy factors, not content with all these various methods of oppression, to crown the whole, often set up people to act as master clothiers, on their stock, during any little glut of business; and as it is easy to imagine, give all the cloth so made, the preference of the market, though perhaps in all respects, least deserving of it. Hence, those that trade on their own bottoms, and employ the poor in good and bad times alike, are liable to all the disadvantages of the one, with little or no share in the benefits of the other. And hence, more people are admitted into trade, than the trade can possibly maintain; which opens a new door to the tumults and riots so lately felt.

6. Report on the Condition of Children in Lancashire Cotton Factories [*Report of Committee on State of Children in Manufactories*, 1816 (*III*), *pp.* 139–140], 1796.

Resolutions for the consideration of the Manchester Board of Health, by Dr. Perceval, January 25, 1796.

It has already been stated that the objects of the present institution are to prevent the generation of diseases; to obviate the spreading of them by contagion; and to shorten the duration of those which exist, by affording the necessary aids and comforts to the sick. In the prosecution of this interesting undertaking, the Board have had their attention particularly directed to the large cotton factories established in the town and neighbourhood of Manchester; and they feel it a duty incumbent on them to lay before the public the result of their inquiries :—

1. It appears that the children and others who work in the large factories, are peculiarly disposed to be affected by the contagion of fever, and that when such infection is received, it is rapidly propagated, not only amongst those who are crowded together in the same apartments, but in the families and neighbourhoods to which they belong.

2. The large factories are generally injurious to the constitution of those employed in them, even where no particular diseases prevail, from the close confinement which is enjoined, from the debilitating effects of hot or impure air, and from the want of the active exercises which nature points out as essential in childhood and youth, to invigorate the system, and to fit our species for the employments and for the duties of manhood.

3. The untimely labour of the night, and the protracted labour of the day, with respect to children, not only tends to diminish future expectations as to the general sum of life and industry, by impairing the strength and destroying the vital stamina of the rising generation, but it too often gives encouragement to idleness, extravagance and profligacy in the parents, who, contrary to the order of nature, subsist by the oppression of their offspring.

4. It appears that the children employed in factories are generally debarred from all opportunities of education, and from moral or religious instruction.

5. From the excellent regulations which subsist in several cotton factories, it appears that many of these evils may, in a considerable degree, be obviated; we are therefore warranted by experience, and are assured we shall have the support of the liberal proprietors of these factories, in proposing an application for Parliamentary aid (if other methods appear not likely to effect the purpose), to establish a general system of laws for the wise, humane, and equal government of all such works.

7. The Newcastle Coal Vend

[*Reports from Committees on the Coal Trade*, 1800 (*X*), *p.* 540, *and* 1830 (*VIII*), *pp.* 6 *and* 254–5], 1771–1830.

(*a*) 1800.

Evidence of Francis Thompson (*formerly manager of Washington colliery*).

Is there any regulation or limit as to price they[1] may give to the coal-owners?

In August, September, and October, 1771, I found great irregularities in the Coal Trade, particularly with respect to the measure. I communicated my sentiments to two of the most respectable agents of the owners . . .; upon which it was agreed that a meeting should be had of the coal owners belonging to Sunderland, to be convened by me, and the coal-owners at Newcastle, to be convened by a Mr. Gibson and Mr. Morrison, which was done; and we had three or four meetings, and I was appointed Secretary. . . . Since that time, according to the best enquiries I have been able to make, the coal owners have had frequent meetings for the purpose of stipulating the vends[2]; that is, that five of the collieries of the best coals, viz., Walls End, Walker, Wellington, Hebburn, and Heyton, are permitted to vend the greatest proportion, and at the best price; after that there is a second class, which sells one shilling per chaldron lower, being coals of an inferior quality, and also less in proportion as to quantity; there is likewise a third class, at a shilling less than the second, and who are allowed to sell a still less proportion as to quantity.

By what means do you understand those vends have been limited? By the meetings of the coal owners frequently for the purpose of ascertaining the vends.

Was there any positive agreement for that purpose? That cannot be well known, being contrary to Act of Parliament.

(*b*) 1830.[3]

The proprietors of the best coals are called upon to name the price at which they intend to sell their coals for the succeeding twelve months; according to this price, the remaining

[1] The fitters or agents between coal-owners and ship-owners.
[2] The name by which the agreements as to output were known.
[3] Report from Committee on the Coal Trade, 1830 (VIII), p. 6.

proprietors fix their prices; this being accomplished, each colliery is requested to send in a statement of the different sorts of coals they raise, and the powers of the colliery; that is, the quantity that each particular colliery could raise at full work; and upon these statements the committee, assuming an imaginary basis, fix the relative proportions, as to quantity, between all the collieries, which proportions are observed, whatever quantity the markets may demand. The committee then meet once a month, and according to the probable demand of the ensuing month, they issue so much per 1000 to the different collieries; that is, if they give me an imaginary basis of 30,000 and my neighbour 20,000, according to the quality of our coal and our power of raising them in the monthly quantity; if they issue 100 to 1000, I raise and sell 3,000 during the month, and my neighbour 2,000; but in fixing the relative quantities, if we take 800,000 chaldrons as the probable demand of the different markets for the year; if the markets should require more, an increased quantity would be given out monthly, so as to raise the annual quantity to meet that demand, were it double the original quantity.

Evidence of Robert William Brandling.[1]

What means have been resorted to in the north of England, with a view to keep the price of coal at such a rate as should compensate the owners of these collieries in which the expense of raising is the greatest?

We have entered into a regulation at different times, which regulation is in existence now, and which has for its object to secure us a fair uniform remunerating price, and enables us to sell our coals at the port of shipment under our immediate inspection, instead of being driven by a fighting trade, to become the carrier of our coals, and to sell them by third persons in the markets to which they are consigned; thereby trusting our interests to those over whom we have no direct control whatever.

So that practically the real quantity to be sold is fixed with reference to each colliery each month?

Yes. The basis originally fixed, is the proportion taken between all the collieries?

[1] *Ibid.* pp. 254-5.

It is merely an imaginary quantity to fix the relative proportions.

Has the scale of prices now in operation been varied materially from that which was adopted when the regulation of the vend was last on ?

I have already stated in my evidence that ours is a competition price, that we endeavour to get the best price we can, which is a little below what the consumer can get the same article for elsewhere. In the regulation in 1828 we found we had fixed our prices too high ; the consequence was, it created an immediate influx of coals from Scotland, Wales and Yorkshire, and more especially from Stockton ; so that when the coal-owners met together, to enter into another arrangement last year, we were obliged to fix our prices a little lower.

8. The Old Apprenticeship System in the Woollen Industry [*Report of Committee on the Woollen Industry*, 1806 (*III*), *p.* 5], 1806.

Evidence of Mr. James Ellis,[1] 18 *April*, 1806.

Do you instruct this apprentice in the different branches of the trade ?

As far as he has been capable I have done.

Will you enumerate the different branches of the trade which you yourself learnt, and in which you instruct your apprentice ?

I learnt to be a spinner before I went apprentice ; my apprentice was only eleven years old when I took him ; when I went apprentice I was a strong boy, and I was put to weaving first ; I never was employed in bobbin winding myself while I was apprentice ; I had learned part of the business with my father-in-law before I went ; I knew how to wind bobbins and to warp ; after that I learned to weave ; we had two apprentices, and after I had been there a little while we used to spin and weave our webs ; while one was spinning the other was weaving.

Did you also learn to buy your own wool ?

Yes ; I had the prospect of being a master when I came out

[1] A clothier of Harmley, near Leeds, working with an apprentice, two hired journeymen and a boy, and giving some work out.

of my time, and therefore my master took care I should learn that.

Does that branch require great skill?

Yes, it does; I found myself very deficient when I was loose.

Different sorts of wool are applicable to different dyes and different manufactures?

Yes; I was frequently obliged to resort to my master for information as to the dyeing and buying wool.

Does it not require great skill to dye according to pattern, even when you have bought wool?

Yes.

Were you also instructed in that?

Yes; I kept an account all the time I was apprentice of the principal part of the colours we dyed, and practised the dyeing: I always assisted in dyeing; I was not kept constantly to weaving and spinning; my master fitted me rather for a master than a journeyman.

And you instruct your apprentice in the same line?

Yes; we think it a scandal when an apprentice is loose if he is not fit for his business; we take pride in their being fit for their business, and we teach them all they will take.

9. A Petition of Cotton Weavers [*House of Commons Journals*, 47 *Geo. III*, 1807, *Feb.* 26], 1807.

A petition of the several Journeymen Cotton Weavers resident in the counties of Lancaster, Chester, York, and Derby, was presented and read; setting forth, That the petitioners suffer great hardships by the reduction of their wages, and that whenever the demand for goods becomes slack, many master manufacturers adopt the expedient of reducing wages, thereby compelling the petitioners, in order to obtain a livelihood, to manufacture greater quantities of goods at a time when they are absolutely not wanted, and that great quantities of goods so manufactured are sacrificed in the market at low prices, to the manifest injury of the fair dealer, and the great oppression of the petitioners, who are reduced one half of the wages they are justly entitled to, and in many cases, are not able to earn more than nine shillings per week: And therefore praying, That leave may be given to bring in a bill to regulate, from time to time, the wages of the petitioners.

10.—Depression of Wages and its Causes in the Cotton Industry [*Report of Committee on Orders in Council, 1812 (III), pp.* 218 *and* 267–272], 1812.

Thursday, May 14, 1812.

Evidence of James Kay (cotton and woollen manufacturer, of Bury).

What used to be the price of cotton per piece in 1807?—I took out the manufacturing prices for three years before 1807, and four years since. Those are minutes from your own books?—Yes, in May, 1805, for the quality goods called Blackburn supers we gave six shillings; in May, 1806, we gave the same; in May, 1807, we gave the same; in November, 1807, we dropped them to 5*s.* 6*d.*; in December, 1807, to 5*s.*; in January 1808 to 4*s.* 6*d.*; in May 1808 they were at 4*s.*; it was at the time they were very much distressed, and rioting. In May, 1809, we gave 4*s.*, in March, 1810, we gave 7*s.*; in April, 6*s.*; and in May the same. In May, 1811, we again gave 4*s.*; and at the present time we give 4*s.* 6*d.*

Evidence of Jeremiah Bury (cotton manufacturer of Stockport).

Friday, May 15, 1812.

What might a man make at weaving, in the year 1810?—A man weaving plain work, in the year 1810, might make probably from 12*s.* to 15*s.* a week.

At plain work now what may a person earn?—The same man now would not make more than ten or twelve shillings.

What might a man in full employment, in 1810, make in spinning?—. . . I apprehend that a man might make from fifteen to twenty-five shillings a week in spinning.

What will the same man make now?—I think a man now might make from thirteen or fourteen to eighteen shillings.

Do you ever recollect so great distress as there is at present?—Never; I have known the trade these thirty years, but I never knew anything like it.

Your manufactures went to the Continent pretty extensively till the year 1807?—Yes, we sold to the merchants who sent to the Continent.

Can you tell what interrupted that trade?—We had no further trade when the Continent was shut up.

To what is the want of trade owing?—The want of market for our goods.

To what is the want of market owing?—It is impossible for me to say, but I believe if we had an opening in America, we should have sufficient market for our goods; when we lost the Continental trade we had America to depend upon, now we have lost America we have no regular markets to depend upon.

11.—Evidence of the Condition of Children in Factories

[*Report of Committee on Children in Manufactories*, 1816 (*III*), *pp.* 89 *and* 132–133], 1816.

Mr. Robert Owen, again called in, and examined.

Have you anything to add to your evidence of yesterday?—Some questions were put to me yesterday respecting the early age at which children are employed at Stockport; I knew I had made a memorandum at the time, but I could not then put my hand upon it; I have since found it; and I can now reply to the questions regarding those cases. Mr. George Oughton, secretary to the Sunday school in Stockport, informed me about a fortnight ago, in the presence of an individual, who will probably be here in the course of the morning, that he knows a little girl of the name of Hannah Downham, who was employed in a mill at Stockport at the age of four. Mr. Turner, treasurer to the Sunday school, knows a boy that was employed in a mill at Stockport when he was only three years old. Mr. Turner and Mr. Oughton, if they were sent for would, I have no doubt, state these cases before the Committee.

They were mentioned to you as a rare instance?—They were mentioned to me in the midst of a very numerous assembly of very respectable people; I inquired of them whether they knew, as they were surrounded with, I believe, two or three thousand children at the time, what was the age at which children were generally admitted into cotton mills; their answer was, Some at five, many at six, and a greater number at seven. I have also received very important information from a very respectable individual at Manchester, relative to the age at which children are employed, the hours they are kept to work, and a variety of other particulars from very authentic sources.

Name those sources ?—Mr. Nathaniel Gould and Mr. George Gould.

Does the information you propose to give come from the manufactory to which it relates ?—No manufacturer would give information against himself.

State what you know relative to the number of hours which children and others are employed in their attendance on mills and manufactories ?—About a fortnight ago I was in Leeds ; and in conversation with Mr. Gott, whose name is well-known to many gentlemen in this room, he stated to me that it was a common practice, when the woollen trade was going on well, to work sixteen hours in the day : I was also informed by Mr. Marshall, who is another principal, and considered a highly respectable manufacturer in Leeds, that it was a common practice to work at flax-mills there sixteen hours a day whenever the trade went well : I was also informed by Mr. Gott, that when the Bill, generally known by the name of Sir Robert Peel's Bill, was brought in last session of Parliament, the night-work at Leeds was put an end to. In Stockport, on Sunday fortnight, I saw a number of small children going to the church ; they appeared to me to be going from a Sunday school ; the master was with them ; I stopped the master, and asked him what he knew of the circumstances of the manufacturers in Stockport ; he said he knew a great deal, because he himself had formerly, for many years, been a spinner in those mills ; his name is Robert Mayor, of the National School in Stockport ; he stated that he was willing to make oath that mills in Stockport, within the last twelve months, had been worked from three and four o'clock in the morning until nine at night, that he himself has frequently worked those hours.

Sir Robert Peel, Bart.

The house in which I have a concern gave employment at one time to near one thousand children of this description. Having other pursuits, it was not often in my power to visit the factories, but whenever such visits were made, I was struck with the uniform appearance of bad health, and, in many cases, stinted growth of the children ; the hours of labour were regulated by the interest of the overseer, whose remuneration depending on the quantity of the work done, he was often induced to make the poor children work excessive hours, and to stop their complaints by trifling bribes. Finding our own factories under such management, and learning that the like practices prevailed in other parts of the kingdom where similar machinery was in use, the children being much over-worked, and often little or no regard paid to cleanliness and ventilation in the buildings; having the assistance of Dr. Percival and other eminent medical gentlemen of Manchester, together with some distinguished characters both in and out of Parliament, I brought in a Bill in the Forty-second year of the King, for the regulation of factories containing such parish apprentices. The hours of work allowed by that Bill being fewer in number than those formerly practised, a visible improvement in the health and general appearance of the children soon became evident, and since the complete operation of the Act contagious disorders have rarely occurred.

Diffident of my own abilities to originate legislative measures, I should have contented myself with the one alluded to, had I not perceived, that, owing to the present use of steam power in factories, the Forty-second of the King is likely to become a dead letter. Large buildings are now erected, not only as formerly on the banks of streams, but in the midst of populous towns, and instead of parish apprentices being sought after, the children of the surrounding poor are preferred, whose masters being free from the operation of the former Act of Parliament are subjected to no limitation of time in the prosecution of their business, though children are frequently admitted there to work thirteen to fourteen hours per day, at the tender age of seven years, and even in some cases still younger. I need not ask the Committee to give an opinion of the consequence of such a baneful practice upon the health and well-being of these little creatures, particularly after having heard the sentiments of those eminent medical men who have been examined before us; but I most anxiously press upon the Committee, that unless some parliamentary interference takes place, the benefits of the Apprentice Bill will soon be entirely lost, the practice of employing parish apprentices will cease, their places will be wholly supplied by other children, between whom and their masters no permanent contract is likely to exist, and for whose good treatment there will not be the slightest security. Such indiscriminate and unlimited employment of the poor, consisting of a great proportion of the inhabitants of trading districts, will be attended with effects to the rising generation so serious and alarming, that I cannot contemplate them without dismay, and thus that great effort of British ingenuity, whereby the machinery of our manufactures has been brought to such perfection, instead of being a blessing to the nation, will be converted into the bitterest curse.

Gentlemen, if parish apprentices were formerly deemed worthy of the care of Parliament, I trust you will not withhold from the unprotected children of the present day an equal measure of mercy, as they have no masters who are obliged to support them in sickness or during unfavourable periods of trade.

12.—Change in the Cotton Industry and the Introduction of Power-Loom Weaving [*William Radcliffe, The Origin of Power-Loom Weaving*, 1828, *pp.* 9–10, *etc.*], *c.* 1785–1807.

The principal estates being gone from the family, my father resorted to the common but never-failing resource for subsistence at that period, viz., the loom for men, and the cards and hand-wheel for women and boys. He married a spinster (in my etymology of the word) and my mother taught me (while too young to weave) to earn my bread by carding and spinning cotton, winding linen or cotton weft for my father and elder brothers at the loom, until I became of sufficient age and strength for my father to put me into a loom. After the practical experience of a few years, any young man who was industrious and careful, might then, from his earnings as a weaver, lay by sufficient to set him up as a manufacturer, and though but few of the great body of weavers had the courage to embark in the attempt, I was one of the few. Availing myself of the improvements that came out while I was in my teens, by the time I was married (at the age of 24, in 1785), with my little savings, and a practical knowledge of every process from the cotton-bag to the piece of cloth, such as carding by hand or by the engine, spinning by the hand-wheel or jenny, winding, warping, sizing, looming the web, and weaving either by hand or fly-shuttle, I was ready to commence business for myself; and by the year 1789, I was well established, and employed many hands both in spinning and weaving, as a master manufacturer.

From 1789 to 1794, my chief business was the sale of muslin warps, sized and ready for the loom (being the first who sold cotton twist in that state, chiefly to Mr. Oldknow, the father of the muslin trade in our country). Some warps I sent to Glasgow and Paisley. I also manufactured a few muslins myself, and had a warehouse in Manchester for my general business.

. . . . . .

At Midsummer, 1801, on taking[1] stock very accurately we[2] found we had upwards of £11,000 in our concern ; I had also a landed estate in Mellor, in which was comprehended Podmore, where my father was born, with a rent roll, and good tenants of upwards of £350 per annum, charged with about £1,800 on mortgage. Mr. Ross's father was a merchant and magistrate in Montrose, and rich, and, my partner being an only son, could at any time lend us a few thousands, which he afterwards did to the amount of £6,000, including the £2,500 paid down on the formation of our partnership. With this real capital —an unlimited credit (£5,000 with our bankers amongst the rest), an excellent trade, and every prospect of its continuing so for a time, we came to the conclusion of purchasing the premises in the Hillgate, from Mr. Oldknow and Mr. Arkwright, then standing empty, which I never should have thought of for a moment, but from what had passed at the Castle Inn, for the sole purpose of filling them with looms, etc., on some new plan, and just so much spinning machinery as would supply the looms with weft. But beyond the common warping, sizing, weaving, etc., all was a chaos before me ; yet so confident was I, that with such assistance as I could call in, we should succeed, that before I began I laid a trifling wager with my partner, that in two years from the time I commenced, I produced 500 pieces of 7-8ths and 9-8ths printing cambrics, all wove in the building in one week by some new process, which I won easily. And as the price for weaving alone when we began was 17*s.* per piece, and had never been below 16*s.* at any time, we thought we were justified in what we were doing, even if little improvement could be found. And if the goods made abroad from the annually increasing export of twist,

[1] *Ibid.* pp. 15-16. [2] Radcliffe and his partner Ross.

and their prohibitions of our goods in consequence, had not gradually reduced this price of weaving from 17*s*. (with a profit of 10 to 20 per cent. to the master), to 4*s*. to the weaver (and no profit to the master !), we should have been handsomely rewarded by our trade. But to return from this digression, we concluded our contract about Michaelmas with Messrs. Oldknow and Arkwright, for the premises above mentioned ; and I brought my family to Stockport in the latter end of December, 1801. I must here observe that we had at that time a large concern in Mellor, that with its various branches for putting out work, employing upwards of 1000 weavers, widely spread over the borders of three counties, in a vast variety of plain and fancy goods, all of which had been raised (like a gathering snowball) from a single spindle, or single loom by myself, and was then upon such a system as apparently might go on without my personal attention.

. . . . . .

I shut myself up (as it were) in the mill on the 2nd January, 1802,[1] and with joiners, turners, filers, etc., etc., set to work ; my first step was some looms in the common way in every respect, which I knew would produce the cloth so much wanted, and in some degree cover our weekly expenses.

Before the end of the month I began to divide the labour of the weavers, employing one room to dress the whole web, in a small frame for the purpose, ready for the looms in another room, so that the young weaver had nothing to learn but to weave ; and we found this a great improvement, for besides the advantage of learning a young weaver in a few days, we found that by weaving the web as it were back again, the weft was driven up by the reed the way the brushes had laid the fibres down with the paste, so that we could make good cloth in the upper rooms with the dressed yarn quite dry, which could not be done in the old way of dressing, when the weft was drove up against the points of the fibres, which shewed us the reason why all weavers are obliged to work in damp cellars, and must weave up their dressing, about a yard long, before the yarn becomes dry, or it spoils.

This accomplished, I told my men I must have some motion attached to either traddles or the lathe, by machinery, that would take up the cloth as it was wove, so that the shed might

[1] *Ibid*. pp. 20-21.

always be of the same dimensions, and of course the blow of the lathe always moving the same distance, would make the cloth more even than could possibly be done in the old way, except by very skilful and careful weavers.

This motion to the loom being at length accomplished to our satisfaction, I set Johnson to plan for the warping and dressing, suggesting several ideas myself. His uncommon genius led him to propose many things to me, but I pointed out objections to them all, and set him to work again. His mind was so teased with difficulties, that he began to relieve it by drinking for several days together (to which he was too much addicted) but for this I never upbraided him, or deducted his wages for the time, knowing that we were approaching our object; at length we brought out the present plan, only that the undressed yarn was all on one side, and the brush to be applied was first by hand, then by a cylinder, and lastly the crank motion.

. . . . . .

The partnership being thus dissolved,[1] I proceeded in my business with a double prospect of success; first, by the real business I was doing weekly, of 6 to 700 pieces per week, of printing cambrics, mostly woven in the factory, and the other part in weaving-families in the neighbourhood, on the small looms I had furnished to them, delivering them dressed warps on the beam, and pin-cops for the weft. This system had now become practicable, and was so greatly approved of by the weavers, that, had I weathered the calm, which soon after came upon my credit, I might, in a short time, have had all my looms in the dwellings of the operative weavers on the plan I had been driving at from the first, and from the superior advantage of machine dressing. The evenness produced by this mode of preparation, and the working in my loom, not only rendered these goods of ready sale, but gave me a weekly profit of 90*l.* to 100*l.*, which, along with the second branch of income that formed my double prospect, viz., the premiums of licenses under patent rights beginning to pour in from the first houses in the trade, to the amount of 1,500*l.*, in the eight months from the first of July, 1806, to March, 1807, when my vessel became quite becalmed.

. . . . . .

In the year 1770,[2] the land in our township was occupied by

[1] *Ibid.* p. 41. [2] *Ibid.* pp. 59-60.

between fifty to sixty farmers ; rents, to the best of my recollection, did not exceed 10*s*. per statute acre, and out of these fifty or sixty farmers, there were only six or seven who raised their rents directly from the produce of their farms ; all the rest got their rent partly in some branch of trade, such as spinning and weaving woollen, linen, or cotton. The cottagers were employed entirely in this manner, except for a few weeks in the harvest. Being one of those cottagers, and intimately acquainted with all the rest, as well as every farmer, I am the better able to relate particularly how the change from the old system of hand-labour to the new one of machinery operated in raising the price of land in the sub-division I am speaking of. Cottage rents at that time, with convenient loomshop and a small garden attached, were from one and a half to two guineas per annum. The father of a family would earn from eight shillings to half a guinea at his loom, and his sons, if he had one, two, or three alongside of him, six or eight shillings each per week ; but the great sheet anchor of all cottages and small farms was the labour attached to the hand-wheel, and when it is considered that it required six to eight hands to prepare and spin yarn, of any of the three materials I have mentioned, sufficient for the consumption of one weaver,—this shews clearly the inexhaustible source there was for labour for every person from the age of seven to eighty years (who retained their sight and could move their hands) to earn their bread, say one to three shillings per week, without going to the parish.

. . . .

From the year 1770 to 1788[1] a complete change had gradually been effected in the spinning of yarns. That of wool had disappeared altogether, and that of linen was also nearly gone ; cotton, cotton, cotton, was become the almost universal material for employment. The hand-wheels, with the exception of one establishment, were all thrown into lumber-rooms, the yarn was all spun on common jennies, the carding for all numbers, up to 40 hanks in the pound, was done on carding engines ; but the finer numbers of 60 to 80 were still carded by hand, it being a general opinion at that time that machine-carding would never answer for fine numbers. In weaving no great alteration had taken place during these eighteen years, save the introduction of the fly-shuttle, a change in the woollen

[1] *Ibid.* pp. 61-62.

looms to fustians and calico, and the linen nearly gone, except the few fabrics in which there was a mixture of cotton. To the best of my recollection there was no increase of looms during this period,—but rather a decrease.

I shall confine myself to the families in my own neighbourhood.[1] These families, up to the time I have been speaking of, whether as cottagers or small farmers, had supported themselves by the different occupations I have mentioned in spinning and manufacturing, as their progenitors from the earliest institutions of society had done before them. But the mule-twist now coming into vogue, for the warp, as well as weft, added to the water-twist and common jenny yarns, with an increasing demand for every fabric the loom could produce, put all hands in request of every age and description. The fabrics made from wool or linen vanished, while the old loom-shops being insufficient, every lumber-room, even old barns, cart-houses, and outbuildings of any description were repaired, windows broke through the old blank walls, and all fitted up for loom-shops. This source of making room being at length exhausted, new weavers' cottages with loomshops rose up in every direction; all immediately filled, and when in full work the weekly circulation of money, as the price of labour only, rose to five times the amount ever before experienced in this sub-division, every family bringing home weekly 40, 60, 80, 100, or even 120 shillings per week!!!

13. Evidence by Factory Workers of the Condition of Children [*Report of Committee on Factory Children's Labour*, 1831–2 (*XV*), *p.* 192, *etc.*], 1832.

Evidence of Samuel Coulson.

5047. At what time in the morning, in the brisk time, did those girls go to the mills?

In the brisk time, for about six weeks, they have gone at 3 o'clock in the morning, and ended at 10, or nearly half past at night.

5049. What intervals were allowed for rest or refreshment during those nineteen hours of labour?

Breakfast a quarter of an hour, and dinner half an hour, and drinking a quarter of an hour.

[1] *Ibid.* p. 65.

5051. Was any of that time taken up in cleaning the machinery?

They generally had to do what they call dry down; sometimes this took the whole of the time at breakfast or drinking, and they were to get their dinner or breakfast as they could; if not, it was brought home.

5054. Had you not great difficulty in awakening your children to this excessive labour?

Yes, in the early time we had them to take up asleep and shake them, when we got them on the floor to dress them, before we could get them off to their work; but not so in the common hours.

5056. Supposing they had been a little too late, what would have been the consequence during the long hours?

They were quartered in the longest hours, the same as in the shortest time.

5057. What do you mean by quartering?

A quarter was taken off.

5058. If they had been how much too late?

Five minutes.

5059. What was the length of time they could be in bed during those long hours?

It was near 11 o'clock before we could get them into bed after getting a little victuals, and then at morning my mistress used to stop up all night, for fear that we could not get them ready for the time; sometimes we have gone to bed, and one of us generally awoke.

5060. What time did you get them up in the morning?

In general me or my mistress got up at 2 o'clock to dress them.

5061. So that they had not above four hours' sleep at this time?

No, they had not.

5062. For how long together was it?

About six weeks it held; it was only done when the throng was very much on; it was not often that.

5063. The common hours of labour were from 6 in the morning till half-past eight at night?

Yes.

5064. With the same intervals for food?

Yes, just the same.

5065. Were the children excessively fatigued by this labour?

Many times; we have cried often when we have given them

the little victualling we had to give them; we had to shake them, and they have fallen to sleep with the victuals in their mouths many a time.

5066. Had any of them any accident in consequence of this labour?

Yes, my eldest daughter when she went first there; she had been about five weeks, and used to fettle the frames when they were running, and my eldest girl agreed with one of the others to fettle hers that time, that she would do her work; while she was learning more about the work, the overlooker came by and said, "Ann, what are you doing there?" she said, "I am doing it for my companion, in order that I may know more about it," he said, "Let go, drop it this minute," and the cog caught her forefinger nail, and screwed it off below the knuckle, and she was five weeks in Leeds Infirmary.

5067. Has she lost that finger?

It is cut off at the second joint.

5068. Were her wages paid during that time?

As soon as the accident happened the wages were totally stopped; indeed, I did not know which way to get her cured, and I do not know how it would have been cured but for the Infirmary.

5069. Were the wages stopped at the half-day?

She was stopped a quarter of a day; it was done about four o'clock.

5072. Did this excessive term of labour occasion much cruelty also?

Yes, with being so very much fatigued the strap was very frequently used.

5073. Have any of your children been strapped?

Yes, every one; the eldest daughter; I was up in Lancashire a fortnight, and when I got home I saw her shoulders, and I said, "Ann, what is the matter?" she said, "The overlooker has strapped me; but," she said, "do not go to the overlooker, for if you do we shall lose our work"; I said I would not if she would tell me the truth as to what caused it. "Well," she said, "I will tell you, father." She says, "I was fettling the waste, and the girl I had learning had got so perfect she could keep the side up till I could fettle the waste; the overlooker came round, and said, "What are you doing?" I said, "I am fettling while the other girl keeps the upper end up"; he said, "Drop it this minute;" she said, "No, I must go on with this"; and because she did not do it, he took a strap, and beat her between the shoulders. My wife was out at the time, and when she came in she said her back was beat nearly to a jelly; and the rest of the girls encouraged her to go to Mrs. Varley, and she went to her, and she rubbed it with a part of a glass of rum, and gave her an old silk handkerchief to cover the place with till it got well.

5080. What was the wages in the short hours?

Three shillings a week each.

5081. When they wrought those very long hours what did they get?

Three shillings and sevenpence halfpenny.

5082. For all that additional labour they had only 7½*d.* a week additional?

No more.

5083. Could you dispose of their wages, when they had received them, as you wished: did you understand that?

They never said anything to me; but the children have said, "If we do not bring some little from the shop I am afraid we shall lose our work." And sometimes they used to bring a bit of sugar or some little oddment, generally of their own head.

5084. That is, they were expected to lay out part of their wages under the truck system?

Yes.

5086. Had your children any opportunity of sitting during those long days of labour?

No; they were in general, whether there was work for them to do or not, to move backwards and forwards till something came to their hands.

5118. At the time they worked those long hours, would it have been in their power to work a shorter number of hours, taking the 3*s.*?

They must either go on at the long hours, or else be turned off.

Evidence of Gillett Sharpe.[1]

5484. Have you had any children, yourself, working at these mills?

Yes.

5488. What sort of mill did she go to?

[1] *Ibid.* p. 209, Numbers 5484, 5488, 5492.

To a worsted manufactory; but it so happened with her that her stepmother dying, I took her away to manage the affairs of my house; she was very young to be sure, but she did what I had to do, except what I hired out, and she is very healthy and strong; but with regard to my boy, Edwin, he was a proverb for being active and straight before he went; there is a portion of ground of considerable extent, opposite to a building in our neighbourhood, and that boy would run seven times round that piece of ground, and come in without being much fatigued; but when he had gone to the mill some time, perhaps about three years, he began to be weak in his knees; and it went on to that degree, that he could scarcely walk; I had three steps up into my house, and I have seen that boy get hold of the sides of the door to assist his getting up into the house; many a one advised me to take him away; they said he would be ruined, and made quite a cripple; but I was a poor man, and could not afford to take him away, having a large family, six children, under my care; they are not all mine, but I have to act as a father to them; he still continued to go, but during the last six or seven months the factory has been short of work; they spin for commission; and it has so happened that they have worked less hours since last November than they formerly did, not being able to obtain so much work; and he is very much improved in that time with regard to the strength of his knees, and it has been observed by the neighbours that he grows a little, but he is bent in one knee.

5492. Have you had any other children on whom this labour has had a similar effect?

Yes, I have a daughter Barbara; she went to the mill between 7 and 8 years of age; she was straight then, but, however, a few years back, about three years since, she fell weak and lame in one of her knees, and she was off her work in consequence; but, however, in a few weeks she got a little recovered and went to the mill again, and she has continued to go there ever since, and she has got very much bow-legged, the legs are bent outwards.

Evidence of Elizabeth Bentley.[1]

5127. What age are you?

Twenty-three.

[1] *Ibid.* p. 195, Numbers 5127-5219.

5128. Where do you live?

At Leeds.

5129. What time did you begin to work at a factory?

When I was six years old.

5130. At whose factory did you work?

Mr. Busk's.

5131. What kind of mill is it?

Flax-mill.

5132. What was your business in that mill?

I was a little doffer.

5133. What were your hours of labour in that mill?

From 5 in the morning till 9 at night, when they were thronged.

5134. For how long a time together have you worked that excessive length of time?

For about half a year.

5214. You are considerably deformed in your person in consequence of this labour?

Yes, I am.

5215. At what time did it come on?

I was about 13 years old when it began coming, and it has got worse since; it is five years since my mother died, and my mother was never able to get me a pair of good stays to hold me up, and when my mother died I had to do for myself, and got me a pair.

5216. Were you perfectly straight and healthy before you worked at a mill?

Yes, I was as straight a little girl as ever went up and down town.

5217. Were you straight till you were 13?

Yes, I was.

5218. Have you been attended to by any medical gentleman at Leeds or the neighbourhood?

Yes, I have been under Mr. Hares.

5219. To what did he attribute it?

He said it was owing to hard labour, and working in the factories.

Evidence of Mr. Charles Stewart.[1]

8094. Does that length of standing and of exertion tend to deform the limbs of the children so employed?

[1] *Ibid.* p. 353, Numbers 8094-8103.

Yes, that is my opinion; I took an examination of those that were employed under me in that flat.

8095. In which of Mr. Boyack's mills are you employed?

In a tow-mill.

8097. The New Ward Mill, is it?

Yes; there are fifty hands in the room altogether, old and young; and I found that out of that fifty there were nine who had entered the mill before they were nine years of age, who are now above thirteen years of age.

8098. Having been at that employment then, four years?

Yes; and out of those nine, there were six who were splay-footed, and three who were not; the three who were not splay-footed were worse upon their legs than those who were; and one was most remarkably bow-legged; she informed me she was perfectly straight before she entered the mills.

8099. What was that girl's name?

Margaret Webster.

8100. You say she was remarkably bow-legged, was it very observable?

Very observable; I can hardly describe the woman's deformity, from the way in which she walks; but I have passed by, and thought that I was far from her, and have got on her shins as I was going past her.

8103. Have you made any other examination?

I have examined those who had not entered the mills till after twelve years of age, and found that out of fifty there were fourteen of this class; two of them were splay-footed, and one with her ankle a little wrong; the others were all perfectly straight.

14.—Women's and Children's Labour in Mines [*Children's Employment Commission, Mines,* 1842 (*XV*), *p.* 24, *etc.*], 1842.

Sex: Employment of Girls and Women in Coal Mines. Districts in which Girls and Women are Employed Underground.

119. In England, exclusive of Wales, it is only in some of the colliery districts of Yorkshire and Lancashire that female children of tender age and young and adult women are allowed to descend into the coal mines and regularly to perform the

same kinds of underground work, and to work for the same numbers of hours, as boys and men; but in the East of Scotland their employment in the pits is general; and in South Wales it is not uncommon.

120. West Riding of Yorkshire: Southern Part.—In many of the collieries in this district, as far as relates to the underground employment, there is no distinction of sex, but the labour is distributed indifferently among both sexes, excepting that it is comparatively rare for the women to hew or get the coals, although there are numerous instances in which they regularly perform even this work. In great numbers of the coal-pits in this district the men work in a state of perfect nakedness, and are in this state assisted in their labour by females of all ages, from girls of six years old to women of twenty-one, these females being themselves quite naked down to the waist.

121. "Girls," says the Sub-Commissioner, "regularly perform all the various offices of trapping, hurrying, filling, riddling, tipping, and occasionally getting, just as they are performed by boys. One of the most disgusting sights I have ever seen was that of young females, dressed like boys in trousers, crawling on all fours, with belts round their waists and chains passing between their legs, at day pits at Hunshelf Bank, and in many small pits near Holmfrith and New Mills: it exists also in several other places. I visited the Hunshelf Colliery on the 18th of January: it is a day pit; that is there is no shaft or descent; the gate or entrance is at the side of a bank, and nearly horizontal. The gate was not more than a yard high, and in some places not above two feet. When I arrived at the board or workings of the pit I found at one of the side-boards down a narrow passage a girl of fourteen years of age, in boy's clothes, picking down the coal with the regular pick used by the men. She was half sitting, half lying, at her work, and said she found it tired her very much, and "of course she didn't like it." The place where she was at work was not two feet high. Further on were men at work lying on their sides and getting. No less than six girls out of eighteen men and children are employed in this pit. Whilst I was in the pit the Rev. Mr. Bruce, of Wadsley, and the Rev. Mr. Nelson, of Rotherham, who accompanied me, and remained outside, saw another girl of ten years of age, also dressed

in boy's clothes, who was employed in hurrying, and these gentlemen saw her at work. She was a nice-looking little child, but of course as black as a tinker, and with a little necklace round her throat."

Conclusions.[1]

From the whole of the evidence which has been collected, and of which we have thus endeavoured to give a digest, we find—

In regard to Coal Mines—

1. That instances occur in which children are taken into these mines to work as early as four years of age, sometimes at five, and between five and six, not unfrequently between six and seven, and often from seven to eight, while from eight to nine is the ordinary age at which employment in these mines commences.

2. That a very large proportion of the persons employed in carrying on the work of these mines is under thirteen years of age; and a still larger proportion between thirteen and eighteen.

3. That in several districts female children begin to work in these mines at the same early ages as the males.

7. That the nature of the employment which is assigned to the youngest children, generally that of "trapping," requires that they should be in the pit as soon as the work of the day commences, and, according to the present system, that they should not leave the pit before the work of the day is at an end.

8. That although this employment scarcely deserves the name of labour, yet, as the children engaged in it are commonly excluded from light and are always without companions, it would, were it not for the passing and re-passing of the coal carriages, amount to solitary confinement of the worst order.

9. That in those districts in which the seams of coal are so thick that horses go direct to the workings, or in which the side passages from the workings to the horseways are not of any great length, the lights in the main ways render the situation of these children comparatively less cheerless, dull, and stupefying; but that in some districts they remain in solitude and darkness during the whole time they are in the pit, and,

[1] *Ibid.* p. 255, etc.

according to their own account, many of them never see the light of day for weeks together during the greater part of the winter season, excepting on those days in the week when work is not going on, and on the Sundays.

10. That at different ages, from six years old and upwards, the hard work of pushing and dragging the carriages of coal from the workings to the main ways, or to the foot of the shaft, begins; a labour which all classes of witnesses concur in stating requires the unremitting exertion of all the physical power which the young workers possess.

11. That, in the districts in which females are taken down into the coal mines, both sexes are employed together in precisely the same kind of labour, and work for the same number of hours; that the girls and boys, and the young men and young women, and even married women and women with child, commonly work almost naked, and the men, in many mines, quite naked; and that all classes of witnesses bear testimony to the demoralizing influence of the employment of females underground.

13. That when the workpeople are in full employment, the regular hours of work for children and young persons are rarely less than eleven; more often they are twelve; in some districts they are thirteen; and in one district they are generally fourteen and upwards.

14. That in the great majority of these mines night-work is a part of the ordinary system of labour, more or less regularly carried on according to the demand for coals, and one which the whole body of evidence shows to act most injuriously both on the physical and moral condition of the workpeople, and more especially on that of the children and young persons.

15. Description of the Condition of Manchester by John Robertson, Surgeon [*Report of Committee on Health of Towns*, 1840 (*XI*), *pp*. 221–222, *App. II*], 1840.

Until twelve years ago there was no paving and sewering Act in any of the townships; even in the township of Manchester, containing in the year 1831 upwards of 142,000 inhabitants, this was the case; and the disgraceful condition of the streets and sewers on the invasion of the cholera you have no doubt learned from Dr. Kay's able and valuable pamphlet.[1] At the present time the paving of the streets proceeds rapidly in every direction, and great attention is given to the drains. Upon the whole, it is gratifying to bear testimony to the zeal of the authorities in carrying on the salutary improvements, especially when it is known that no street can be paved and sewered without the consent of the owners of property, unless a certain large proportion of the land on either side is built upon. Owing to this cause several important streets remain to this hour disgraceful nuisances.

Manchester has no Building Act, and hence, with the exception of certain central streets, over which the Police Act gives the Commissioners power, each proprietor builds as he pleases. New cottages, with or without cellars, huddled together row behind row, may be seen springing up in many parts, but especially in the township of Manchester, where the land is higher in price than the land for cottage sites in other townships is. With such proceedings as these the authorities cannot interfere. A cottage row may be badly drained, the streets may be full of pits, brimful of stagnant water, the receptacle of dead cats and dogs, yet no one may find fault. The number of cellar residences, you have probably learned from the papers published by the Manchester Statistical Society, is very great in all quarters of the town; and even in Hulme, a large portion of which consists of cottages recently erected, the same practice is continued. That it is an evil must be obvious on the slightest consideration, for how can a hole underground of from 12 to 15 feet square admit of ventilation so as to fit it for a human habitation?

We have no authorised inspector of dwellings and streets. If an epidemic disease were to invade, as happened in 1832, the authorities would probably order inspection, as they did on that occasion, but it would be merely by general permission, not of right.

So long as this and other great manufacturing towns were multiplying and extending their branches of manufacture and were prosperous, every fresh addition of operatives found employment, good wages, and plenty of food; and so long as the families of working people are well fed, it is certain they

[1] J. P. Kay. *Moral and Physical Condition of the Working Classes in Manchester*, 1832.

maintain their health in a surprising manner, even in cellars and other close dwellings. Now, however, the case is different. Food is dear, labour scarce, and wages in many branches very low; consequently, as might be expected, disease and death are making unusual havoc. In the years 1833, 1834, 1835, and 1836 (years of prosperity), the number of fever cases admitted into the Manchester House of Recovery amounted only to 1,685, or 421 per annum; while in the two pinching years, 1838 and 1839, the number admitted was 2,414, or 1,207 per annum. It is in such a depressed state of the manufacturing districts as at present exists that unpaved and badly sewered streets, narrow alleys, close, unventilated courts and cellars, exhibit their malign influence in augmenting the sufferings which that greatest of all physical evils, want of sufficient food, inflicts on young and old in large towns, but especially on the young.

Manchester has no public park or other grounds where the population can walk and breathe the fresh air. New streets are rapidly extending in every direction, and so great already is the expanse of the town, that those who live in the more populous quarters can seldom hope to see the green face of nature. . . . In this respect Manchester is disgracefully defective; more so, perhaps, than any other town in the empire. Every advantage of this nature has been sacrificed to the getting of money in the shape of ground-rents.

SECTION II

AGRICULTURE AND ENCLOSURE

1. Enclosure Proceedings in the Court of Chancery, 1671—2. Advice to the Stewards of Estates, 1731—3. Procedure for Enclosure by Private Act, 1766—4. Farming in Norfolk, 1771—5. A Petition against Enclosure, 1797—6. Extracts on Enclosure from the Surveys of the Board of Agriculture, 1798–1809—7. Arthur Young's Criticism of Enclosure, 1801—8. Enclosure Consolidating Act, 1801—9. General Enclosure Act, 1845.

Progress in methods of agriculture (No. 4) and the movement towards enclosure and consolidation (Nos. 1–3 and 5–9) are the subjects illustrated in this section. Great advances were made in the science and practice of farming between the end of the Commonwealth and the repeal of the Corn Laws. But the controversial subject of enclosure overshadows everything else. And, as is shown by the extract from Arthur Young's account of the famous Norfolk farming, agricultural progress was closely connected with enclosure and consolidation (No. 4). Specimens are given of two stages of enclosure proceedings (No. 1 and No. 3), which suggest that voluntary agreements ratified in Chancery gradually merged in enclosure by Act, compulsory upon a dissatisfied minority. The Awards, on which the justice or injustice of the settlement would in some degree depend, are generally too long for quotation. But the General Act of 1801 (No. 8) was an attempt to codify the best existing practice, and gives a general view of the practice of the best Commissioners.

A mass of controversial literature on both sides deals with the reasons and effects of the enclosures. The advantages, from the point of view of a large landowner, are set out in a text book for land stewards (No. 2). The reverse side, as it appeared to the small holder, is given in a petition, which was fruitless, against the enclosure of a Northamptonshire village (No. 5). Arthur Young's criticism of the way in which the process was carried out is of great importance, because he had been the most strenuous advocate of enclosing and because he had had unrivalled opportunities of judging the change, both as an independent traveller and as secretary of the Board of Agriculture (No. 7). The best printed material for an independent judgment is to be found in the surveys made by this, a semi-official Society of Agriculture, whose agents, with easily recognisable degrees of impartiality, describe the objects, methods and results of the enclosing movement in different counties. Extracts are given from their reports (No. 6), together with the first real reform of procedure, made when the nineteenth century was far advanced, so as to safeguard the interests of the peasantry (No. 9).

AUTHORITIES

The most important modern books on the subject are:—Hammond, *The Village Labourer*; Gonner, *Common Land and Inclosure*; Prothero, *English Farming Past and Present*; Hasbach, *The English Agricultural Labourer*; Levy, *Large and Small Holdings*; Johnson, *The Disappearance of the Small Landowner*; Slater, *The English Peasantry and the Enclosure of the Common Fields*; Ashby, *One Hundred Years of Poor Law Administration in a Warwickshire village* in *Oxford Studies in Social and Legal History*, Vol. III; Leonard in *Transactions of the Royal Historical Society*, 3rd Series, Vol. XIX.

Bibliographies in Hasbach, Hammond, Levy, and Cunningham, *English Industry and Commerce, Modern Times*, Part II.

Contemporary (1).—Records of late seventeenth century enclosures may be found in Chancery Enrolled Decrees, and Enclosures Awards in Proceedings in Chancery (Public Record Office, and some copies in Durham Court of Chancery). Eighteenth century material includes petitions in Journals of the House of Commons; proceedings in Parliament, ditto; Awards, in custody of Clerks of the Peace and of County Councils—a Return of Commons (Inclosure Awards) to the House of Commons, 1904, shows where they are to be found. There are reports of Committees on Cultivation of Waste, etc., 1795 (IX), ditto, 1797 (IX), ditto, 1800 (IX); on Inclosure, 1844 (V), on Allotments, 1843 (VII).

Contemporary (2) *Literary Authorities.*—The best descriptions of agriculture are to be found in Arthur Young's various Tours (1768–71) in The Annals of Agriculture (1784–1815), and in the Reports made to the Board of Agriculture; Reports on individual counties (partial list in Hasbach's bibliography), a General Report (1808), and Reviews of Reports for different sections of the country (by William Marshall, 1808–17). Cobbett's Rural Rides are more literary and political and less official (1830). For agricultural progress, see J. Tull, The New Horse-hoeing Husbandry (1731), and Young *passim*; for the legal aspect, The Law of Commons (1698); for contemporary opinion, D. Davies, The Case of Labourers in Husbandry (1795), Young, An Enquiry into the Propriety of Applying Wastes, etc. (1802), and a long list of pamphlets (bibliography in Hasbach).

1. ENCLOSURE PROCEEDINGS IN THE COURT OF CHANCERY [*Entry Book on the Division of Commons, etc., in the Durham Court of Chancery, Book M, No.* 482, 1671–1676 (*Original in Public Record Office*)], 1671.

Division of the Town Fields of Bishop Auckland, October, 1671

Forasmuch as heretofore by order and decree of this Court bearing date the fifteenth day of September last past, made between the parties above named, for the reasons then appearing to this Court it was then ordered and decreed by the consent of all the said parties . . . that all the lands and grounds lying and being in the three common fields called the Hitherfield, Midlefield and Fairfield lying at Bishop Auckland, therein mentioned should . . . be forthwith measured and divided according to the agreements and consents of the said parties, . . . and also that every of the said parties should have his and their particular shares, parts, and proportions therein particularly allotted and set forth in severalty unto him and them, to be by them respectively hedged, fenced, enclosed and enjoyed in severalty for ever thenafter for the better husbandry and improvement thereof. . . . And now upon the motion of Mr. William Brabart . . . alleging that since the making of the said decree several of the parties thereunto, perceiving that some of the defendants, formerly being the chief opposers of the said intended division, have obtained their shares in the premisses to be in such part thereof as themselves desired, their said parts being small and inconsiderable, they have therefore of late descended from their shares and parts of the premisses formerly by them desired or consented unto and do now endeavour to have their proportionate parts to lie in other parts and places of the premisses, to the great decay, hindrance, and obstruction of the said division, notwithstanding their former consents thereunto. It was therefore humbly prayed by the said Counsel that a Commission might be awarded out of this Court to indifferent Commissioners . . . as well for the hearing of all the said objections . . . as also to view and divide all the said premisses and to appoint and set forth to every of the said parties their proportionable parts therein.

[*August*, 1672, *Decree of the Court.*]

Forasmuch as . . . every owner's share hath been duly set out . . . and yet nevertheless one of the said defendants hath endeavoured to obstruct the said division . . . it is therefore now thought fit and so ordered by the Right Honourable Sir Francis Goodriche Knight, Chancellor of the County of Durham and Sadberge, that the Award . . . shall stand absolutely confirmed and decreed unless good cause be shown to the contrary at the next sitting at Durham.

2. Advice to the Stewards of Estates [*Edward Lawrence, The Duty and Office of a Land Steward, 3rd Ed.*, 1731, *pp.* 25, 26, *and* 39], 1731.

A Steward should not forget to make the best enquiry into the disposition of any of the freeholders within or near any of his Lord's manors to sell their lands, that he may use his best endeavours to purchase them at as reasonable a price, as may be for his Lord's advantage and convenience—especially in such manors, where improvements are to be made by inclosing commons and common-field; which (as every one, who is acquainted with the late improvement in agriculture, must know) is not a little advantageous to the nation in general, as well as highly profitable to the undertaker. If the freeholders cannot all be persuaded to sell, yet at least an agreement for inclosing should be pushed forward by the steward, and a scheme laid, wherein it may appear that an exact and proportional share will be allotted to every proprietor; persuading them first, if possible, to sign a form of agreement, and then to choose commissioners on both sides.

If the Steward be a man of good sense, he will find a necessity for making a use of it all, in rooting out superstition from amongst them, as what is so great a hindrance to all noble improvements? The substance of what is proper for the proprietors to sign before an inclosure is to be made, may be conceived in some such form as followeth.

"Whereas it is found, by long experience, that common or open fields, wherever they are suffered or continued, are great hindrances to a public good, and the honest improvement which every one might make of his own, by diligence and a seasonable charge: and, whereas the common objections hitherto raised against inclosures are founded on mistakes, as if inclosures contributed either to hurt or ruin the poor; whilst it is plain that (when an enclosure is once resolved on) the poor will be employed for many years, in planting and preserving the hedges, and afterwards will be set to work both in the tillage and pasture, wherein they may get an honest livelihood: And whereas all or most of the inconveniences and misfortunes which usually attend the open wastes and common fields have been fatally experienced at ——, to the great discouragement of industry and good husbandry in the freeholders, viz., that the poor take their advantage to pilfer, and steal, and trespass; that the corn is subject to be spoiled by cattle, that stray out of the commons and highways adjacent; that the tenants or owners, if they would secure the fruits of their labours to themselves, are obliged either to keep exact time in sowing and reaping or else to be subject to the damage and inconvenience that must attend the lazy practices of those who sow unseasonably, suffering their corn to stand to the beginning of winter, thereby hindering the whole parish from eating the herbage of the common field till the frosts have spoiled the most of it," etc., etc.

. . . . . .

To conclude this article upon commons,[1] I would advise all noblemen and gentlemen, whose tenants hold their lands by Copy of Court Roll for three lives, not to let them renew, except they will agree to deliver up their Copy, in order to alter the tenure by converting it to leasehold on lives. This method will put a stop to that unreasonable custom of the widow holding a life by her free-bench, which is a fourth life, not covenanted for in the Copy, but only pretended to by custom; which deprives the lord of an undoubted right of making the best, and doing what he will with his own.

[1] p. 39.

3. Procedure for Enclosure by Private Act, *January &c.*, 1766 [*Commons Journals, Vol.* XXX, 1765–6, *p.* 459, *etc.*], 1766.

A Petition of Stephen Croft, the Younger, Esquire, Lord of the manor of Stillington, in the county of York, and owner of several estates, within the said manor and parish of Stillington, and also Impropriator of the Great Tithes there; of the Reverend James Worsley, Clerk, Prebandary of the Prebend of Stillington aforesaid, patron of the Vicarage of Stillington aforesaid, of the Reverend Lawrence Sterne, Clerk, Vicar of the said parish,[1] and of William Stainforth, Esquire, and of several other persons, whose names are thereunto subscribed, being also owners of copyhold messuages, cottages, estates, and other properties, within the said parish; was presented to the House and read; setting forth, that, within the said manor and parish, is a common, or waste, called Stillington Common, and also open fields and ings,[2] which, in their present situation, are incapable of improvement; and that it would be of great advantage to the several persons interested in the said common, fields and ings, if they were enclosed and divided into specific allotments, and all rights of common and average thereon, or upon any other commonable lands in the said parish, were extinguished, or if the said common was so inclosed, and a power given to the several proprietors and owners of estates in the said fields and ings, to flat and inclose the same, first making satisfaction to the improprietor upon the tithes thereof; and after the flatting and inclosing the same, all right of common, or average, was to cease; and therefore praying, that leave may be given to bring in a Bill for the purposes aforesaid, or any of them, in such manner, and under such regulations, as the House shall deem meet.

Ordered, That leave be given to bring in a Bill pursuant to the prayer of the said petition: and that Mr. Cholmley, Sir George Savile, and Sir Joseph Mawbey, do prepare and bring in the same.

[*February* 3.—Bill presented to the House and read a first time.]

February 10, 1766.[3] A Bill for inclosing and dividing the common waste grounds, open fields, open meadows, grounds,

[1] Author of *Tristram Shandy*. [2] *i.e.* Meadows. [3] *Ibid.* p. 522.

and ings, within the parish of Stillington, in the county of York, was read a second time.

Resolved, That the Bill be committed to Mr. Cholmley, Mr. Fonereau, Sir John Taines [etc., etc.]; and all the members who serve for the counties of York, Nottingham, Northumberland, and Durham: and they are to meet this afternoon, at five of the clock, in the Speaker's Chamber.

February 27.[1] Mr. Cholmley reported from the Committee, to whom the Bill for inclosing and dividing the common waste grounds [etc.] within the parish of Stillington, in the county of York, was committed. That the Committee had examined the allegations of the Bill; and found the same to be true; and that the parties concerned had given their consent to the Bill, to the satisfaction of the Committee, except the proprietors of sixty acres of land in the said fields and ings, who refused their consent to the inclosure, and the proprietors of twenty seven acres of land, who were not at home when application was made for their consents; and that the whole of the said fields and ings contain six hundred acres or thereabouts; and also, except the proprietors of eight common rights, who refused to consent, and the proprietors of seven common rights, who were from home when application was made for their consents; and that the whole number of common rights are eighty-nine; and that no person appeared before the Committee to oppose the Bill; and that the Committee had gone through the Bill, and made several amendments thereunto; which they had directed him to report to the House; and he read the report in his place; and afterwards delivered the Bill, with the amendments, in at the Clerk's Table; where the amendments were once read throughout; and then a second time, one by one; and, upon the Question severally put thereon, were agreed to by the House; and several amendments were made, by the House, to the Bill. Ordered, that the Bill, with the amendments be ingrossed.

[*March* 3. The Bill read a third time and passed. Sent to the House of Lords.

[1] *Ibid.* p. 610.

March 18. Reported that the Lords agreed to the Bill without amendment.

The King's Assent given to the Bill.]

4. FARMING IN NORFOLK [*A. Young, The Farmer's Tour,* 1771, *Vol. II, Letter XIV, pp.* 150, 156, 161], 1771.

As I shall presently leave Norfolk it will not be improper to give a slight review of the husbandry which has rendered the name of this county so famous in the farming world. Pointing out the practices which have succeeded so nobly here, may perhaps be of some use to other countries possessed of the same advantages, but unknowing in the art to use them.

From forty to fifty years ago, all the northern and western, and a part of the eastern tracts of the county, were sheep walks, let so low as from 6*d.* to 1*s.* 6*d.* and 2*s.* an acre. Much of it was in this condition only thirty years ago. The great improvements have been made by means of the following circumstances.

First. By inclosing without the assistance of parliament.

Second. By a spirited use of marl and clay.

Third. By the introduction of an excellent course of crops.

Fourth. By the culture of turnips well hand-hoed.

Fifth. By the culture of clover and ray-grass.

Sixth. By landlords granting long leases.

Seventh. By the country being divided chiefly into large farms.

• • • • • •

The Course of Crops.[1]

After the best managed inclosure, and the most spirited conduct in marling, still the whole success of the undertaking depends on this point: No fortune will be made in Norfolk by farming, unless a judicious course of crops be pursued. That which has been chiefly adopted by the Norfolk farmers is,

1. Turnips.
2. Barley.
3. Clover: or clover and ray-grass.
4. Wheat.

• • • • •

[1] *Ibid.* p. 156.

Large Farms.[1]

If the preceding articles are properly reviewed, it will at once be apparent that no small farmers could effect such great things as have been done in Norfolk. Inclosing, marling, and keeping a flock of sheep large enough for folding, belong absolutely and exclusively to great farmers. . . . Nor should it be forgotten that the best husbandry in Norfolk is that of the largest farmers. . . . Great farms have been the soul of the Norfolk culture : split them into tenures of an hundred pounds a year, you will find nothing but beggars and weeds in the whole county.

5. A Petition Against Enclosure [*Commons Journals*,[2] *July* 19, 1797], 1797.

A Petition of the hereunder-signed small Proprietors of Land and Persons entitled to Rights of Common [at Raunds, Northamptonshire].

That the petitioners beg leave to represent to the House that, under the pretence of improving lands in the same parish, the cottagers and other persons entitled to right of common on the lands intended to be enclosed, will be deprived of an inestimable privilege, which they now enjoy, of turning a certain number of their cows, calves, and sheep, on and over the said lands ; a privilege that enables them not only to maintain themselves and their families in the depth of winter, when they cannot, even for their money, obtain from the occupiers of other lands the smallest portion of milk or whey for such necessary purpose, but in addition to this, they can now supply the grazier with young or lean stock at a reasonable price, to fatten and bring to market at a more moderate rate for general consumption, which they conceive to be the most rational and effectual way of establishing public plenty and cheapness of provision ; and they further conceive, that a more ruinous effect of this enclosure will be the almost total depopulation of their town, now filled with bold and hardy husbandmen, from among whom, and the inhabitants of other open parishes, the nation has hitherto derived its greatest strength and glory, in the supply of its fleets and armies, and driving them, from necessity and want of employ, in vast

[1] *Ibid*, p. 161. [2] Quoted Hammond, *The Village Labourer*, pp. 39-40.

crowds, into manufacturing towns, where the very nature of their employment, over the loom or the forge, soon may waste their strength, and consequently debilitate their posterity, and by imperceptible degrees obliterate that great principle of obedience to the Laws of God and their country, which forms the character of the simple and artless villagers, more equally distributed through the open counties, and on which so much depends the good order and government of the state. These are some of the injuries to themselves as individuals, and of the ill consequences to the public, which the petitioners conceive will follow from this, as they have already done from many enclosures, but which they did not think they were entitled to lay before the House (the constitutional patron and protector of the poor) until it unhappily came to their own lot to be exposed to them through the Bill now pending.

6. Extracts on Enclosure from the Surveys of the Board of Agriculture, 1798–1809.

Somersetshire [*J. Billingsley, Somerset*, 1798, *pp.* 48–50 *and* 52].

Let us begin with taking a view of the objections which have been started to this species of improvement, and see if we cannot prove them to be for the most part either false or frivolous.

1st. Invasion of the rights and interest of the cottagers.

. . . . . .

The foremost of these objections carries with it the appearance of a humane attention to the comfort of the poor; but a brief investigation will lessen its influence, if not totally refute it.

There are but two modes of enclosing commons. First, by unanimous consent of the parties claiming rights, who delegate power to commissioners, chosen by themselves, to ascertain their validity, and divide them accordingly, under covenants and agreements properly drawn and executed for the purpose. Or secondly, by act of parliament obtained by the petition of a certain proportion of the commoners, both in number and value, whereby a minority, sanctioned only by ignorance, prejudice, or selfishness, is precluded from defeating the ends of private advantage and public utility.

In point of economy, the first of these methods is most eligible, as it saves the expense of an act of parliament, with an equal security to the proprietors. But it is seldom practised unless in commons on a small scale, from the difficulty of procuring the consent of every individual claimant, without which it cannot be accomplished.

In either of these methods, it is manifest that the right of the cottager cannot be invaded; since with respect to legal or equitable construction, he stands precisely on the same ground with his more opulent neighbours; and as to his interest, I can truly declare that, in all cases which have fallen within my observation, inclosures have meliorated his condition, by exciting a spirit of activity and industry, whereby habits of sloth have been by degrees overcome, and supineness and inactivity have been exchanged for vigour and exertion.

. . . . . .

Besides, moral effects of an injurious tendency accrue to the cottager from a reliance on the imaginary benefits of stocking a common. The possession of a cow or two, with a hog, and a few geese, naturally exalts the peasant, in his own conception, above his brothers in the same rank of society. It inspires some degree of confidence in a property, inadequate to his support. In sauntering after his cattle, he acquires a habit of indolence. Quarter, half, and occasionally whole days are imperceptibly lost. Day labour becomes disgusting; the aversion increases by indulgence; and at length the sale of a half-fed calf, or hog, furnishes the means of adding intemperance to idleness. The sale of the cow frequently succeeds, and its wretched and disappointed possessor, unwilling to resume the daily and regular course of labour, from whence he drew his former subsistence, by various modes of artifice and imposition, exacts from the poor's rate the relief to which he is in no degree entitled.

Lincolnshire [*Arthur Young*, *Lincoln*, 1799, *pp.* 85–6].

[Evidence of Elmhurst, a Commissioner under Enclosure Act.]

Another observation I at the first made, and ever after put in practice, was this, always to begin to line out and allot for the smallest proprietors first (whether rich or poor) in every parish, so as to make such allotment as proper and convenient for the occupation of such, or their tenant (as that might be) to occupy; and so on, from the smallest to the greatest: for it is for the advantage of the greatest and most opulent proprietors that a bill is presented and act passed; and at their requests, and not the small ones; and, as the little ones would have no weight by opposition, they must submit, was it ever so disadvantageous to them; as it very often happens; and, therefore, there can be no partiality in defending those who cannot help or defend themselves; and a little man may as well have nothing allotted to him, as to have it so far off, or so inconvenient for him, that it is not worth his having, as it would prevent his going to his daily labour; and, therefore, he must sell his property to his rich and opulent adjoining neighbours; and that, in some measure, decreases population.

Norfolk [*Young, Norfolk*, 1804, *pp.* 82, 86, 94, 135, 156].

Bintrey and Twiford.[1] Enclosed 1795.

Poor. There were 20 acres allotted for fuel, let by the parish. There were 46 commonable rights; the whole divided according to value; very few little proprietors; but small occupiers suffered.

Brancaster.[2] Enclosed 1755.

Poor. Very well off; Barrow-hills, a common of 65 acres, allotted to them; and each dwelling-house has a right to keep the two cows or heifers; or a mare and foal; or two horses; and also to cut furze.

Cranworth, Remieston, Southborough.[3] Enclosed 1796.

Poor. They kept geese on the common, of which they are deprived. But in fuel they are benefited; an allotment not to exceed $\frac{1}{20}$ let, and the rent applied in coals for all not occupying above 5*l.* a year: this is to the advantage of those at Southborough, having enough allowed for their consumption; at Cranworth the poor are more numerous, and the coals of little use.

Ludham.[4]

The commons were enclosed in 1801: all cottagers that claimed had allotments; and one for fuel to the whole; but the cottages did not belong to the poor; the allotments in general went to the larger proprietors, and the poor consequently were left, in this respect, destitute; many cows were

[1] p. 82. [2] p. 86. [3] p. 94. [4] p. 135.

kept before, few now. All the poor very much against the measure.

Sayham and Ovington.[1] Enclosed 1800.

Poor.—An allotment of not less than 50*l.* a year, for distributing to the poor in coals, was ordered by the act; it let for 98*l.* There were 100 commonable right houses. They used to sell a cottage of 3*l.* a year, with a right, for 80*l.* For each, four acres were allotted: and the cottage with this allotment would now sell for 160*l.* And what is very remarkable, every man who proved to the Commissioners that they had been in the habit of keeping stock on the common, was considered as possessing a common-right and had an allotment in lieu of it. Nor was it an unpopular measure, for there were only two men against it from the first to the last.

Gloucestershire [*Thomas Rudge, Gloucester*, 1807, *pp.* 92–93].

In all Acts of Inclosure, it might perhaps be proper, as it would certainly be equitable, to relieve the pressure which weighs on small proprietors, in a degree not proportioned to the advantages they derive from them: for it should be remembered, that the expence of fencing a small allotment is considerable greater than that of a larger one, according to the quantity; that is, a square piece of land containing ten acres will cost half as much as forty, though only of one-fourth value. This disproportion occasions much reluctance in the class of proprietors before-mentioned; and though it is frequently overcome by the superior influence of the great landholders, yet the injustice of it cannot but strike the considerate mind with conviction.[2]

Leicestershire [*William Pitt, Leicester*, 1809, *pp.* 15, 16 *and* 166].

The enclosure of this vale[3] has not at all, I believe, hitherto lessened the number of its inhabitants, as the farms are small, and few changes of tenantry have taken place. The farmer and his family take a hand in the business, yet few can do without a male and female servant, and labourer, who may

[1] p. 156.

[2] The expenses of enclosure of an average amount were calculated by the Board of Agriculture at 497*l.* for the Act, 259*l.* for the Survey, 344*l.* for the Commissioners, 550*l.* 7*s.* 6*d.* for fencing, etc. General Report on Enclosures, 1808.

[3] Belvoir.

have a family: these with the necessary mechanics, blacksmith, wheelwright, tailor, weaver, etc., form a considerable population in each village, I should suppose about 10 or 12 to every 100 acres. . . . As the tendency of the country is to pasture and feeding, the rejected occupier and his family must emigrate into towns, or elsewhere, for employ.

The management of the Duke of Rutland's property has always been conducted in the most liberal and benevolent manner; yet I think the enclosure of a rich district, and converting it to grass, has a natural tendency to decrease the population of that district; less corn is certainly now raised in Belvoir than in its open state.

Mr. Ainsworth complains that labourers have not in general sufficient gardens, nor even cottages, for want of which they are driven into towns; and that in many cases by enclosures the cottages have been suffered to go to decay, as the land would let for as much rent without them to the larger farmers, and by turning it to grass, fewer labourers' cottages are wanting.

Northamptonshire [*William Pitt, Northampton*, 1809, *p.* 70].

From the observations I have made in this county, I have no doubt but, if the average produce of common fields be three quarters per acre, the same land will, after a little rest as grass, and the improvements to be effected by enclosure, produce, on an average, four quarters per acre; and I believe that the produce of every common field may be increased in a like proportion by enclosure and an improved cultivation.

7. ARTHUR YOUNG'S CRITICISM OF ENCLOSURE [*Young, An Inquiry into the Propriety of Applying Wastes, etc.*, 1801, *pp.* 13 *and* 42], 1801.

Go to an alehouse kitchen of an old enclosed country, and there you will see the origin of poverty and poor rates. For whom are they to be sober? For whom are they to save? (Such are their questions.) For the parish? If I am diligent, shall I have leave to build a cottage? If I am sober, shall I have land for a cow? If I am frugal, shall I have half an acre of potatoes? You offer no motives; you have nothing but a parish officer and a workhouse! Bring me another pot.

• • • • • •

Objection VIII. Wastes are as much property as my house. Will a farmer give up his right of commonage ?

I will not dispute their meaning[1]; but the poor look to facts, not meanings : and the fact is, that by nineteen enclosure bills in twenty they are injured, in some grossly injured. It may be said that commissioners are sworn to do justice. What is that to the people who suffer ? It must be generally known that they suffer in their own opinions, and yet enclosures go on by commissioners, who dissipate the poor people's cows wherever they come, as well those kept legally as those which are not. What is it to the poor man to be told that the Houses of Parliament are extremely tender of property, while the father of the family is forced to sell his cow and his land because the one is not competent to the other ; and being deprived of the only motive to industry, squanders the money, contracts bad habits, enlists for a soldier, and leaves the wife and children to the parish ? If enclosures were beneficial to the poor, rates would not rise as in other parishes after an act to enclose. The poor in these parishes may say, and with truth, *Parliament may be tender of property* ; *all I know is, I had a cow, and act of Parliament has taken it from me.* And thousands may make this speech with truth.

8.—Enclosure Consolidating Act [*Statutes* 41, *Geo. III*, 109], 1801.

An Act for consolidating in one act certain provisions usually inserted in acts of inclosure ; and for facilitating the mode of proving the several facts usually required on the passing of such acts.

II. No commissioner shall be capable of being a purchaser of any part or parts of the lands, tenements, or hereditaments within any parish in which the lands and grounds intended to be inclosed are situate, either in his own name, or in the name or names of any person or persons, until five years after the date and execution of the award to be made by any such commissioner or commissioners.

IV. And be it further enacted, that a true, exact, and particular survey, admeasurement, plan, and valuation, of all the lands and grounds to be divided, allotted, and inclosed

[1] *Ibid.* p. 42.

by any such act, and also of all the messuages, cottages, orchards, gardens, homesteads, ancient inclosed lands and grounds, within any such parish or manor, shall be made and reduced in writing, by such commissioner or commissioners, or by such other person or persons as he or they shall nominate and appoint, as soon as conveniently may be, for the purposes of such act.

VI. And be it further enacted, that all persons, and bodies corporate or politic, who shall have or claim any common or other right to or in any such lands so to be inclosed, shall deliver or cause to be delivered to such commissioner or commissioners, or one of them, at some one of such meetings as the said commissioner or commissioners shall appoint for the purpose (or within such further time, if any, as the said commissioner or commissioners shall for some special reason think proper to allow for that purpose) an account or schedule in writing, signed by them, or their respective husbands, guardians, trustees, committees, or agents, of such their respective rights or claims, and therein describe the lands and grounds, and the respective messuages, lands, tenements, and hereditaments, in respect whereof they shall respectively claim to be entitled to any and which of such rights in and upon the same or any part thereof, with the name or names of the person or persons then in the actual possession thereof, and the particular computed quantities of the same respectively, and of what nature and extent such right is, and also in what rights, and for what estates and interests, they claim the same respectively, distinguishing the freehold from the copyhold or leasehold; or on non-compliance therewith, every of them making default therein shall, as far only as respects any claim so neglected to be delivered, be totally barred and excluded of and from all right and title in or upon such lands so to be divided respectively, and of and from all benefit and advantage in or to any share or allotment thereof.

[All objections must be delivered in writing to the commissioners before the meeting appointed to consider objections.]

VII. Provided also, and be it further enacted, that nothing herein contained shall authorise such commissioner or commissioners to hear and determine any difference or dispute which may arise, touching the right or title to any lands, tenements, or hereditaments, but such commissioner or commissioners shall assign and set out the several allotments directed to be made unto the person or persons, who, at the time of the division and inclosure, shall have the actual seisin or possession of the lands, tenements, or hereditaments, in lieu or in right whereof such allotment shall be respectively made.

[VIII. Commissioners, before making any allotments, to appoint public carriage roads, and prepare a map thereof to be deposited with their clerk, and give notice thereof, and appoint a meeting, at which, if any person shall object, the commissioners, with a justice of the division, shall determine the matter.]

XII. And be it further enacted, that such commissioner or commissioners in making the several allotments directed by any such act, shall have due regard as well to the situation of the respective houses or homesteads of the proprietors, as to the quantity and quality of the lands and grounds to be allotted to them respectively, so far as may be consistent with the general convenience of the said proprietors; and that such commissioner or commissioners in making the said allotments shall have particular regard to the convenience of the owners or proprietors of the smallest estates in the lands and grounds directed to be allotted and exchanged.

XIV. And be it further enacted, that the several shares of and in any lands or grounds shall, when so allotted, be and be taken to be in full bar of and satisfaction and compensation for their several and respective lands, grounds, rights of common, and all other rights; and that from and immediately after the making the said division and allotments, and the execution of the award, all rights whatsoever, by such act intended to be extinguished, belonging to or claimed by any person or persons whomsoever, bodies politic or corporate, in, over, or upon such lands or grounds, shall cease, determine, and be for ever extinguished.

[XXIV and XXIX. If allotments are not enclosed and fenced within an appointed time the commissioners may have the work done and charge the expense to the proprietor or let the allotment and apply the rents till the expenses are paid. If it has been provided by an act that the expenses of obtaining and executing it are to be shared among the proprietors of allotments the commissioners may levy them by distress and sale of the goods of those who fail to pay at the appointed times.]

XXXII. And be it further enacted, that in case it shall be provided by any such act, that the expenses attending the same shall be paid by sale of any part of the land so to be inclosed, the said commissioner or commissioners shall mark and set out such part or parts of the said waste or commonable lands, as in his or their opinion will by sale thereof raise a sum of money sufficient to pay and discharge all such charges and expenses as may by any such act be directed to be paid and discharged out of the same; and the said commissioner or commissioners shall sell such part or parts of the said lands to any person or persons for the best price or prices that can be gotten for the same.

XXXV. And be it further enacted, that as soon as conveniently may be after the division and allotment of the said lands and grounds shall be finished, pursuant to the purport and directions of this or any such act, the said commissioner or commissioners shall form and draw up, or cause to be formed and drawn up, an award in writing, which shall express the quantity of acres, roods, and perches, in statute measure, contained in the said lands and grounds, and the quantity of each and every part and parcel thereof which shall be so allotted, assigned, or exchanged, and the situations and descriptions of the same respectively, and shall also contain a description of the roads, ways, footpaths, watercourses, watering places, quarries, bridges, fences, and land marks, set out and appointed by the said commissioner or commissioners respectively as aforesaid, and all such other rules, orders, agreements, regulations, directions, and determinations, as the said commissioner or commissioners shall think necessary, proper, or beneficial to the parties; which said award shall be fairly ingrossed or written on parchment, and shall be read and executed by the commissioner or commissioners, in the presence of the proprietors who may attend at a special general meeting called for that purpose, of which ten days' notice at least shall be given in some paper to be named in such act and circulating in the county, which execution of such award shall be proclaimed the next Sunday in the church of the parish in which such lands shall be, from the time of which proclamation only, and not before, such award shall be considered as complete.

XL. And be it further enacted and declared that nothing in such act contained shall lessen, prejudice, or defeat the right, title, or interest of any lord or lady of any manor or lordship, or reputed manor or lordship, within the jurisdiction or limits whereof the lands and grounds thereby directed to be divided and allotted are situate, lying, and being of, in, or to the seigniories, rights, and royalties incident or belonging to such manor or lordship, or reputed manor or lordship, or to the lord or lady thereof, or to any person or persons claiming under him or her, but the same (other than and except the interest and other property as is or are meant or intended to be barred by such act) shall remain, in as full, ample, and beneficial manner, to all intents and purposes, as he or she might or ought to have held or enjoyed such rights before the passing of such act, or in case the same had never been made.

9. General Enclosure Act [*Statutes*, 8 *and* 9 *Victoria*, 118], 1845.

An act to facilitate the inclosure and improvement of commons and lands held in common, the exchange of lands, and the division of intermixed lands ; to provide remedies for defective or incomplete executions, and for the non-execution of the powers of general and local inclosure acts ; and to provide for the revival of such powers in certain cases.

. . . Be it therefore enacted . . . that it shall be lawful for one of her Majesty's principal secretaries of State to appoint any two fit persons to be commissioners under this act . . . and the commissioners shall, with the first commissioner of her Majesty's woods, forests, land reserves, works and buildings for the time being, be the commissioners for carrying this act into execution.

[Assistant commissioners may be appointed to whom powers may be delegated.

Village greens may not be enclosed. Land near towns and land subject to unlimited rights of pasture, etc., may not be enclosed without special direction of parliament.]

XXX. And be it enacted, that in the provisional order of the commissioners concerning the enclosures under the provisions of this act of any waste land of any manor on which the tenants of such manor have rights of common, or of any other land subject to rights of common which may be exercised all times of the year, and which shall not be limited by number or stints, it shall be lawful for the commissioners to require . . . the appropriation of an allotment for the purpose of exercise and recreation for the inhabitants of the neighbourhood [10 acres for a population of 10,000 ; 8 for 5,000 to 10,000, etc.]

XXXI. [In similar cases the commissioners may order the appropriation of such an allotment for the labouring poor as the commissioners shall think necessary.]

L. All encroachments and enclosures, other than enclosures duly authorised by the custom of the manor of which such land shall be parcel . . . within twenty years next before the first meeting for the examination of claims . . . shall be deemed parcel of the land subject to be enclosed ; provided always that in case . . . it shall appear to the commissioners just or reasonable that rights or interests in the lands to be enclosed should be allowed to the persons in possession of such encroachments, it shall be lawful for the commissioners . . . to direct what rights shall be allowed.

[Encroachments of twenty years standing to be deemed old enclosures.]

SECTION III

GOVERNMENT REGULATION OF WAGES, CONDITIONS OF EMPLOYMENT, AND PUBLIC HEALTH

1. An Act against Truck, 1701—2. A Wages Assessment at a Warwickshire Quarter Sessions, 1738—3. Spitalfields Weavers Act, 1773—4. A Middlesex Wages Assessment under the Spitalfields Act, 1773—5. Agricultural Labourers' Proposals for a Sliding Scale of Wages, 1795—6. Debates on Whitbread's Minimum Wage Bill, 1795–6—7. Arbitration Act for the Cotton Industry, 1800—8. Amendment of the Arbitration Act, 1804—9. The First Factory Act, 1802—9A. Minutes of Committee on Children in Factories—10. Calico Printers' Petition for Regulation, 1804—11. Report on Calico Printers' Petition, 1806—12. Cotton Weavers' Petition against the Repeal of 5 Elizabeth c. 4, 1813—13. Debates on the Regulation of Apprentices, 1813–1814—14. Resolutions of the Watchmakers on Apprenticeship, 1817—15. Report of Committee on the Ribbon Weavers, 1818—16. The Cotton Factory Act of 1819—17. Oastler's First Letter on Yorkshire Slavery, 1830—18. Factory Act, 1833—19. Proposals for a Wages Board for Hand-loom Weavers, 1834—20. Coal Mines Regulation Act, 1842—21. Debate on Factory Legislation, 1844—22. Factory Act, 1844—23. Recommendations of the Commission on the Health of Towns, 1845.

THE eighteenth century was nearly a blank period in the history of direct regulation of industrial conditions by the State. There was no systematic intervention on the scale of Tudor or Victorian times; and political opinion hardened against the principle and destroyed the machinery which had been inherited from the sixteenth century. Such machinery, for the regulation of wages, was still occasionally used in the early part of the eighteenth century, as is shown by occasional examples of wages assessments at Quarter Sessions (No. 2). Acts were passed for individual trades forbidding the practice of paying wages in truck (No. 1). Local pressure even obtained a special Act providing for the regulation of London silk-weavers' wages (No. 3, No. 4). This Spitalfields Act was used as a precedent for the proposals to extend the policy of regulation, which began to fill the Journals of the House of Commons during the period when the new machinery and methods and the French wars dislocated employment and wages. Examples are given of petitions asking that wages should be regulated and that the limitation of apprentices should be enforced under the statute 5 Elizabeth c. 4, to which attention had been called (Nos. 10, 11, 12 and 14). Independent attempts were made to set up a minimum wage, directly and through wages-boards (Nos. 5, 6 and 19). All these applications ended in complete failure. Parliament provided a system of arbitration for the cotton industry (Nos. 7 and 8), but repealed both the wages and apprenticeship clauses of the Elizabethan Act. Contemporary opinion in Parliament relied on the working of free bargaining and economic forces (Debates on Whitbread's Bill and on Apprenticeship, Nos. 6 and 13).

The history of Factory legislation (Nos. 9, 16, 17, 18, 20, 21, 22) shows how the policy of non-interference was abandoned in another field. The employment of children in the new factories was one result of the eighteenth century system of Poor relief. It produced horrors which the first Factory Act was designed to remedy (No. 9). But the use of steam-power and the growth of big industrial districts led to the wholesale employment of children not under the Poor Law. Public opinion was at last aroused by the campaigns of Oastler and others, who pointed to the contrast between the Anti-Slavery agitation and the conditions of the English mills (No. 17). The successive Acts of 1819, 1833, 1842 and 1844 (Nos. 16, 18, 20, 22) show how legislators were forced to extend the principle of regulation from children to young persons and women, and from cotton mills to other textile factories and to mines. In the debate on the

Act of 1844 the respective points of view of the Tory philanthropist, the political economist, and the manufacturer, were dramatically contrasted (No. 21). The last extract is from one of a series of reports on the condition of great industrial towns (No. 23), by which Chadwick, a disciple of Bentham and a champion of the new Poor-law, forced Parliament to interfere in the economic control of town life.

AUTHORITIES

For modern writers on general conditions, see Authorities for Section I. The history of agitation for Factory legislation is to be found in Hutchins and Harrison, *History of Factory Legislation*; Von Plener *Die Englische Fabrikgesetzgebung*; Alfred (S. Kydd), *The Factory Movement*; Cooke Taylor, *The Factory System and the Factory Acts*; Keeling, *Child Labour in the United Kingdom*, Part I. Details of the agitation are given in Hodder, *Life of Shaftesbury*; Podmore, *Life of Owen*; Hutchins, *The Public Health Agitation*; Greenwood, Richard Oastler. A general view is given in Dicey, *Law and Opinion in England*; Kirkman Gray, *Philanthropy and the State*; Held, *Zwei Bücher zur Sozialen Geschichte Englands*.

Bibliographies are in Hutchins and Harrison, *op. cit.*; Cunningham, *op. cit.*; and Cambridge Modern History, Vol. XII.

Contemporary.—See Authorities for Section I. In addition, for Wages Assessments under the Spitalfields Act in 1784 and 1795, see collection in British Museum, 1029, p. 4. The Reports of Factory Inspectors are valuable sources after 1833. See also Hansard Parliamentary Debates on Wages, and Factory Legislation, 1795, 1813–14, 1816, 1832–3, 1844, 1846.

The chief contemporary literary sources for general conditions are given under Section I. The Factory legislation movement is described by some of the actors: Owen, Observations on the Manufacturing System; Oastler, Yorkshire Slavery, Life and Opinions, Letters from the Fleet, etc.; Memoir of the Life and Writings of Michael Sadler; Nassau Senior, Letters on the Factory Act; L. Horner, On the Employment of Children in Factories.

1. An Act Against Truck [*Statutes*, 1 *Anne* 2, 18], 1701.

An act for the more effectual preventing the abuses and frauds of persons imployed in the working up the woollen, linen, fustian, cotton, and iron manufactures of this kingdom.

. . . .

III. And to prevent the oppression of the labourers and workmen imployed in the woollen, linen, fustian, cotton and iron manufacture, be it enacted by the authority aforesaid, That all payments and satisfactions hereafter to be made to any of the same labourers and workmen, for any work by them done in the same manufacture, shall be by the lawful coin of this realm, and not by any cloth, victuals, or commodities, in lieu thereof: and all wool delivered out to be wrought up, shall be so delivered, with declaration of the true weight thereof, on pain that every offender, in either of the said cases, shall forfeit and pay to such labourer or worker, double the value of what shall be due for such work by him, her, or them done; and if any such labourer or worker shall be guilty of any such fraud or default in the work by him, her, or them done, then such labourer or worker shall allow and answer to the owner of such work double the damages thereby sustained.

[*Cf.* 12 Geo. I. c. 34, sec. iii.—"every clothier, sergemaker or woollen or worsted stuffmaker, or person concerned in making any woollen cloths, serges or stuffs, or any wise concerned in employing woolcombers weavers or other labourers in the woollen manufactory, shall . . . pay unto all persons by them employed . . . the full wages or other price agreed on in good and lawful money of this kingdom; and shall not pay the said wages . . . or any part thereof, in goods or by way of truck."]

2. A Wages Assessment at Warwickshire Quarter Sessions [*Ashby, The Poor Law in a Warwickshire Village* (*Oxford Studies in Social and Legal History, Vol. III, p.* 175)], 1738.

The particular rate of wages of all manner of artificers, labourers, and servants, as well by the day with meat and drink as without, as also by the whole year in gross or by task, made and provided, having a special regard and consideration to the prices of provisions and all other circumstances necessary to be considered at this time. April, 1738.

	£	s.	d.
Every servant in husbandry by the year	5	10	0
Second servant	4	0	0
Servant boy from 14 to 18 years of age	2	10	0
Servant boy from 11 to 14	1	0	0

	£	s.	d.
Every head servant maid by the year	3	0	0
Second maid servant	2	10	0
Labourers from Martinmas to March 25 by the day..	0	0	8
From March 25 to harvest and after harvest to Martinmas	0	0	9
Every mower of grass by the day, with drink ..	0	1	0
,, without drink	0	1	2
Every woman in haymaking, with drink	0	0	5
,, without drink	0	0	6
Every woman in corn harvest, with drink	0	0	6
,, without drink	0	0	7
Every carpenter by the day, March 25 to St. Michael's, with drink..	0	1	0
,, without drink	0	1	2
From Michaelmas to Lady Day, with drink ..	0	0	10
,, without drink	0	1	0
Every mason by the day in summer, with drink ..	0	0	10
,, without drink	0	1	0
Every mason by the day in winter, with drink ..	0	0	10
,, without drink	0	1	0
Thatcher by day, summer and winter	0	1	0
Weeders of corn by the day	0	0	4

[This was still in force in 1773.]

3. Spitalfields Weavers Act [*Statutes*, 13 *Geo. III*, 68], 1773.

An Act to impower the magistrates therein mentioned to settle and regulate the wages of persons employed in the Silk Manufacture within their respective jurisdictions.

Whereas it would be for the benefit of persons employed in the Silk Manufacture, if the magistrates were impowered to settle, between the master weavers and their journeymen, the price of labour in the several branches of the said manufacture; be it therefore enacted by the King's most excellent Majesty, by and with the advice and consent of the Lords spiritual and temporal, and Commons, in this present Parliament, assembled and by the authority of the same, that from and after the first day of July, one thousand seven hundred and seventy-three, the wages and prices for work of the journeymen weavers within the city of London shall be settled, regulated, and declared, by the Lord Mayor, Recorder and Aldermen, of the said city; and in all places in the county of Middlesex, by the Justices of the Peace for the said county; and in all places within the city and liberty of Westminster, at the General Quarter Sessions of the peace holden in and for the said city and liberty; and in all places within the liberty of the Tower of London, at the General Quarter Sessions of the Peace holden in and for the said liberty, at their General Quarter Sessions of the Peace respectively; and the Lord Mayor, Recorder and Aldermen of the city of London, and the said Justices of the Peace, are hereby respectively authorised and impowered, from time to time, upon application being made to them for that purpose, to settle, regulate, order, and declare the wages and prices of work of the journeymen weavers working within their respective jurisdictions as aforesaid; and shall and may, within the space of fourteen days next after the making every such order, cause the same to be printed and published, at the reasonable expense of the person or persons applying for the same, three times, in any two daily newspapers published in London or Westminster; which publication shall be deemed and allowed to be sufficient notice and publication thereof; and from and after publication thereof, all weavers, and their journeymen, are hereby strictly required to observe the same.

And be it further enacted, that if after the said first day of July, one thousand seven hundred and seventy-three, any master weaver, within either of the aforesaid districts, shall give more or less wages, or pay larger or less prices, to any of the journeymen weavers aforesaid, for their work, than shall be settled or allowed as aforesaid, and shall be convicted of the said offences before any two of His Majesty's Justices of the Peace, within either of the districts or jurisdictions aforesaid where the said offence shall be committed, on the oath or oaths of one or more credible witness or witnesses, he shall forfeit the sum of fifty pounds; to be levied by distress and sale of the offender's goods; and the said penalty, when recovered, shall be paid into the hands of the Master of the Weavers' Company, first deducting the expense of such prosecution, to be distributed by him, in conjunction with the Wardens of the said company, to any distressed journeymen weavers or their families, who shall have been last employed in either of the aforesaid jurisdictions, at their discretion.

And be it further enacted, that if any journeyman weaver or weavers within the districts aforesaid, shall ask, receive, or take more or less wages, or larger or less prices for their work than shall be settled by the respective quarter-sessions, as aforesaid ; or shall enter into any combination to raise the wages or prices of the said work, or for this purpose shall decoy, solicit, or intimidate, any journeyman or journeymen weavers within the districts aforesaid, so that he or they quit their masters, for whom they shall then be employed ; or shall assemble themselves in any numbers exceeding the number of ten, in order to frame or deliver petitions or other representations, touching their wages or prices of work, except to the said Justices of the Peace, or to the Lord Mayor, Recorder, and Aldermen of the city of London, at their respective Quarter Sessions, and shall be convicted of any of the said offences, on the oath or oaths of one or more credible witness or witnesses, before any two or more of His Majesty's Justices of the Peace, within either of the districts or jurisdictions aforesaid where the offence shall be committed, [he or they] shall forfeit a sum not exceeding forty shillings : And if the said forfeiture be not immediately paid, it shall and may be lawful for the said Justices to commit the said offender to the House of Correction, to hard labour, for any time not exceeding three months; the said forfeiture, when recovered, to be applied in the same manner as the forfeiture of fifty pounds afore-mentioned.

And be it further enacted, that it shall and may be lawful for any two Justices of the Peace, within the limits and jurisdictions aforesaid, on information upon oath made before them by any person or persons whatsoever, that there is reason to suspect that any master or journeyman weaver, within the districts or jurisdictions aforesaid, hath been guilty of any of the offences aforesaid, at request of such informant, to issue their summons, in writing, signed by any such two Justices, requiring any clerk, foreman, apprentice, servant, or other person or persons employed or retained by such person so suspected to have offended, or any other person or persons whatsoever, whose attendance shall appear necessary for the purpose of giving evidence in the premises, to attend and testify concerning the premises : And if any person so summoned shall not attend, and proof shall be made of the service of such summons either personally or by leaving the same at the last or usual place of abode of such person, it shall be lawful for such two Justices, or any other two Justices of the Peace acting for such county or place, and they are hereby required (unless a reasonable excuse be made for such non-attendance to the satisfaction of such justices) to issue their warrant, under their hands and seals, for the apprehending and bringing him or her before them, or some other two or more Justices of the Peace acting for such county or place, to be examined touching the premises; and if any such person so attending or being brought before such Justices, shall refuse to be examined or give their testimony touching the premises, such person shall by the said justices be committed to the House of Correction for one month, there to remain, unless he or she shall sooner submit to be examined and give testimony as the law requires.

And be it further enacted, that if any master weaver residing within the limits aforesaid, shall, directly or indirectly, in any manner whatsoever, retain or employ any journeyman weaver out of or beyond the limits aforesaid, with intent or design to elude or evade this act, or shall give, allow, or pay, or cause to be given, allowed, or paid, to such journeyman, any more or less wages than shall be settled, as aforesaid, every such person shall, for every such offence, forfeit fifty pounds; to be sued for by action of debt, in any of His Majesty's Courts of Record at Westminster, wherein no essoin, protection, or wager of law, or more than one imparlance, shall be allowed, and wherein the ordinary costs of the suit shall be paid; one moiety of which said forfeiture, when recovered, shall belong and be paid to His Majesty and His successors, and the other moiety to the person who shall sue for the same.

Provided always, and be it further enacted, that nothing in this act contained shall extend, or be construed to extend, to fix, control, or regulate, the wages or allowances to be paid to servants in the said business of a weaver, *bona fide* retained and employed as foreman.

And be it further enacted by the authority aforesaid, that from and after the passing of this act, no person or persons, being silk weavers, residing within the districts aforesaid, shall have in his or their service at any one time more than two apprentices, upon pain of forfeiting for every offence the sum of twenty pounds; to be levied by distress and sale of the offender's goods and chattels, upon conviction, on the oath or oaths of one or more credible witness or witnesses, before two Justices of the Peace within either of the jurisdictions aforesaid where the said offence shall be committed, and the said penalty, when recovered, shall be paid into the hands of the Master of the Weavers' Company, to be applied by him, as aforesaid, and the said Justices are hereby authorised and required to discharge every such apprentice or apprentices exceeding the number of two.

4. A Middlesex Wages Assessment under the Spitalfields Act [*Public Record Office, H.O.* 86, 26], 1773.

Sir John Fielding presents his respects to the Earl of Suffolk and acquaints him that he had the pleasure yesterday of assisting at the general Quarter Sessions for the county of Middlesex to carry into execution the late Act of Parliament for the regulating of the wages of journeymen weavers in Spitalfields, etc., and the wages were then settled by a numerous and unanimous bench to the entire satisfaction of those masters and journeymen weavers who appeared there in behalf of their respective bodies, and I sincerely hope that this step will prove a radical cure for all tumultuous assemblies from that quarter so disrespectful to the King and so disagreeable to Government, as it will amply reward your Lordship's judicious attention to a matter so conducive to peace and good order, for by this statute your Lordship has conveyed contentment to the minds of thousands of his Majesty's subjects. The Act for the appointment of clergymen with proper salaries agreeable to my proposals was also carried into execution to attend the gaols, and this preventive step will, I am persuaded, be attended with very salutary effects; and as the important business of the sessions is over, I hope your Lordship will take the advantage of my Lord North's leisure to settle the affair regarding my general prevention plan which now lies before him for his Majesty's approbation.

I am, with unfeigned truth, my Lord,

Your Lordship's respectful and the public's faithful

Servant.

Sir John Fielding,

9th July, 1773.

5. AGRICULTURAL LABOURERS' PROPOSALS FOR A SLIDING SCALE OF WAGES [*Annals of Agriculture, Vol. XXV, p.* 503[1]], 1795.

At a numerous meeting of the day labourers of the little parishes of Heacham, Snettisham, and Sedgford, this day, 5th November, in the parish church of Heacham, in the county of Norfolk, in order to take into consideration the best and most peaceable mode of obtaining a redress of all the severe and peculiar hardships under which they have for many years so patiently suffered, the following resolutions were unanimously agreed to :—1st, That *the labourer is worthy of his hire*, and that the mode of lessening his distresses, as hath been lately the fashion, by selling him flour under the market price, and thereby rendering him an object of a parish rate, is not only an indecent insult on his lowly and humble situation (in itself sufficiently mortifying from his degrading dependence on the caprice of his employer) but a fallacious mode of relief, and every way inadequate to a radical redress of the manifold distresses of his calamitous state. 2nd, That the price of labour should, at all times, be proportioned to the price of wheat, which should invariably be regulated by the average price of that necessary article of life; and that the price of labour, as specified in the annexed plan, is not only well calculated to make the labourer happy without being injurious to the farmer, but it appears to us the only rational means of securing the permanent happiness of this valuable and useful class of men, and, if adopted in its full extent, will have an immediate and powerful effect in reducing, if it does not entirely annihilate, that disgraceful and enormous tax on the public—the Poor Rate.

Plan of the Prices of Labour Proportionate to the Price of Wheat.

	per last.		per day
When wheat shall be	14*l*.	the price of labour shall be	1*s*. 2*d*.
,, ,, ,,	16	,, ,, ,,	1*s*. 4*d*.
,, ,, ,,	18	,, ,, ,,	1*s*. 6*d*.
,, ,, ,,	20	,, ,, ,,	1*s*. 8*d*.
,, ,, ,,	22	,, ,, ,,	1*s*. 10*d*.
,, ,, ,,	24	,, ,, ,,	2*s*. 0*d*.
,, ,, ,,	26	,, ,, ,,	2*s*. 2*d*.

[1] Quoted Hammond, *The Village Labourer*, pp. 137–9.

	per last.		per day.
When wheat shall be	28*l*.	the price of labour shall be	2*s*. 4*d*.
,, ,, ,,	30	,, ,, ,,	2*s*. 6*d*.
,, ,, ,,	32	,, ,, ,,	2*s*. 8*d*.
,, ,, ,,	34	,, ,, ,,	2*s*. 10*d*.
,, ,, ,,	36	,, ,, ,,	3*s*. 0*d*.

And so on, according to this proportion.

3rd. That a petition to parliament to regulate the price of labour, conformable to the above plan, be immediately adopted; and that the day labourers throughout the county be invited to associate and co-operate in this necessary application to parliament, as a peaceable, legal, and probable mode of obtaining relief; and, in doing this, no time should be lost, as the petition must be presented before the 29th January, 1796.

4th. That one shilling shall be paid into the hands of the treasurer by every labourer, in order to defray the expenses of advertising, attending on meetings, and paying counsel to support their petition in parliament.

5th. That as soon as the sense of the day labourers of this county, or a majority of them, shall be made known to the clerk of the meeting, a general meeting shall be appointed, in some central town, in order to agree upon the best and easiest mode of getting the petition signed: when it will be requested that one labourer, properly instructed, may be deputed to represent two or three contiguous parishes, and to attend the above intended meeting with a list of all the labourers in the parishes he shall represent, and pay their respective subscriptions; and that the labourer, so deputed, shall be allowed two shillings and sixpence a day for his time, and two shillings and sixpence a day for his expenses.

6th. That Adam Moore, clerk of the meeting, be directed to have the above resolutions, with the names of the farmers and labourers who have subscribed to and approved them, advertised in one Norwich and one London paper; when it is hoped that the above plan of a petition to parliament will not only be approved and immediately adopted by the day labourer of this county, but by the labourers of every county in the kingdom.

7th. That all letters, *post paid*, addressed to Adam Moore, labourer, at Heacham, near Lynn, Norfolk, will be duly noticed.

6. Debates on Whitbread's Minimum Wage Bill [*Parliamentary History, Vol. XXXIII, cols.* 700–15], 1795–6.

Debate in the Commons on Mr. Whitbread's Bill to regulate the wages of Labourers in Husbandry. December 9. Mr. Whitbread presented to the House a bill "to explain and amend so much of the act of the 5th of Elizabeth, intituled: 'An act containing divers orders for artificers, labourers, servants of husbandry and apprentices,'" as empowers justices of the peace, at, or within six weeks after, every general quarter sessions held at Easter, to regulate the wages of labourers in husbandry. The bill was read a first time. On the motion for the second reading, Mr. Whitbread said, that he had brought forward this bill under the idea that it was possible, by adopting its regulations, to give great relief to a very numerous and useful class of the community. The act of Elizabeth empowered justices of the peace to fix the maximum of labour. This bill went only to empower them to fix the minimum. However the House might decide with respect to his bill, he trusted at least that the act of Elizabeth would be repealed.

Mr. Fox said, that the bill was undoubtedly a bill of great delicacy and importance, and with respect to which, he admitted that, to a considerable extent, there might exist a rational difference of opinion. The act of Elizabeth, as his hon. friend had truly stated, empowered the justices to fix the highest price of labour, but it gave them no power to fix the lowest. It secured the master from a risk that could but seldom occur, of being charged exorbitantly for the quantity of service; but it did not authorise the magistrate to protect the poor from the injustice of a griping and avaricious employer, who might be disposed to take advantage of their necessities, and undervalue the rate of their service. If the price of labour was adequate to the support of the poor at ordinary times, though not equal to the accidental high price of provisions at the present moment, it might be contended that there was less necessity for any new legislative regulation. But, taking the average price of labour for some years past, including that period during which the scarcity had operated, no man could deny that the price of labour was greatly disproportionate to the rate of provisions. That the general price of labour should be adequate to the support of the general mass of the community was indisputably a right principle. They all knew that a very extensive tax was exacted from the country, under the denomination of poor-rates, and that such a tax must be continued. It was understood that to this fund none could apply, but those few to whom, from particular circumstances, their labour might not be sufficiently productive to secure an adequate support. But he feared that the reverse was the case; that the exception was with respect to the few who derived sufficient means of subsistence from their labour, and that the great mass of the labouring part of the community were under the necessity of applying to this fund for relief. If the House, as was proposed, were to form an association, in order to pledge themselves to use only a particular sort of bread, with a view to diminish the pressure of the scarcity, ought they not at the same time to form an association in order to raise the price of labour to a rate proportionate to the price of articles of subsistence? With this view, he called upon the House to consider the principle of the bill, and its provisions. He would call upon them also to attend to the subject, in a constitutional view, though he could not hope, from the complexion of recent transactions, that this was a view of the subject which would have great weight. It was not fitting in a free country that the great body of the people should depend upon the charity of the rich. In the election of members of Parliament, all those were strictly excluded from exercising any franchise, with a very few exceptions, who had at any time received relief from the parish. Was it becoming in a country like this, that the general mass of the labouring part of the community, excepting those who derived relief from the bounty and generosity of individuals, should be excluded from the exercise of their most important privilege as freemen? He admitted many of the rich to be humane and charitable; but he could not allow that those who were the most useful and industrious members of society should depend upon a fund so precarious and degrading, as the occasional supplies derived from their bounty. If the price of provisions had for two years been such as to put every poor man under the necessity of applying for the aid of parocial charity, and if that circumstance constituted a positive disqualification with respect to the exercise of a constitutional right, what, he asked, was the state of a country which first compelled every poor man to dependence, and then reduced him to servitude? If they were to go into associations, pledging themselves to use a particular sort of bread, with a view to alleviate the scarcity, it was surely of more importance that they should associate in order to redress the more material grievance, and strike at the fundamental source of the evil. With this view he should be glad to see an association in order to put the price of labour upon a footing adequate to the rate of provisions. If the regulations of the present bill should not be adopted, he should be happy that any other legislative enactments should be brought forward in order to afford relief and protection to the poor.

The bill was ordered to be read a second time on the 3rd of February, and to be printed.

February 12th, 1796. The order of the day being read for the second reading of the bill,

Mr. Whitbread said, that ample time had been given for members to consider maturely its object and regulations, and to collect from their constituents such information as they might require. For his own part, every inquiry he had instigated, convinced him of the necessity of remedying the grievances of the industrious poor by some legislative provisions. Whether those which he had suggested were the most proper to be adopted, was a question for the decision of the House? Having bestowed considerable pains in drawing up the bill, he might have left it for their consideration upon its merits alone, did not the novelty of the measure demand a few words in explanation. He felt as much as any man how greatly it was to be desired that there should be no legislative interference in matters of this nature, and that the price of labour, like every other commodity, should be left to find its own level. From reasonings upon the subject, the result was, that it always would find its level. But the deductions of reason were confuted by experience; for he appealed to the sense of the House, whether the situation of the labouring poor in this country was such as any feeling or liberal mind would wish? He did not mean that the wages of the labourer were inadequate for his subsistence and comfort in times of temporary scarcity, and unusual hardship; but even at the period preceding such distress, the evil had prevailed. In most parts of the country, the labourer had long been struggling with increasing misery, till the pressure had become almost too grievous to be endured, while the patience of the sufferers under their accumulated distresses had been conspicuous and exemplary. And did not such distress, supported with so much fortitude, merit relief from the legislature ? Were it necessary to refer to any authority, he would quote the writings of Dr. Price, in which he showed that in the course of two centuries, the price of labour had not increased more than three or at most four-fold ; whereas the price of meat had increased in the proportion of six or seven ; and that of clothing, no less than fourteen or fifteen-fold in the same period. The poor-rates, too, had increased since the beginning of the century from £600,000, at which they were then estimated, to upwards of three millions. Nor was this prodigious increase in the poor rates to be ascribed to the advance of population ; for it was doubtful whether any such increase had taken place. At the present period the contrary seemed to be the case. By the pressure of the times, marriage was discouraged ; and among the laborious classes of the community, the birth of a child, instead of being hailed as a blessing, was considered as a curse. For this serious evil a remedy was required, and to this the bill was directed. It was his wish to rescue the labouring poor from a state of slavish dependence ; to enable the husbandman, who dedicated his days to incessant toil, to feed, to clothe, and to lodge his family with some degree of comfort ; to exempt the youth of the country from the necessity of entering the army or the navy, and from flocking to great towns for subsistence ; and to put it in the power of him who ploughed and sowed and threshed the corn, to taste of the fruits of his industry, by giving him a right to a part of the produce of his labour. Such were the grounds upon which the bill in question was built. To those who dreaded everything that wore the aspect of innovation, and reprobated every measure that was new, he would say that here there was no departure from established precedents, no introduction of unknown principles. The statute of the 5th of Elizabeth was enacted expressly for the purpose of regulating the price of labour. This statute was acted upon for forty years, when it was afterwards amended by a subsequent one in the reign of James the 1st, bearing a similar title. He would not be understood as commending the principle of these statutes : on the contrary, he was of opinion that they operated as a clog to industry, by permitting justices to fix the maximum of labour. But so late as the 8th of his majesty, justices were empowered to regulate the wages of tailors, and even now the lord mayor and council of London control those of the silk weavers. To those who were afraid of entrusting justices with power, he should only say, that he left the power where he found it. At present they were possessed of the power to oppress the labourer; and this bill only invested them with the additional power to redress his grievances. By fixing the minimum of the wages of labour, a comfortable subsistence was secured to industry, and at the same time greater exertions were prompted by the hope of greater reward. To some, perhaps, the time of bringing this subject forward might appear exceptional. There were those who would say, if the labourers were not distressed, why agitate a question for which no necessity calls, and awaken desires which are not felt? Others would maintain, that it was unseasonable to direct the public attention to such a subject, while the pressure of distress might excite discontents, or raise improper expectations. To these he could only answer, that he was not one who could see wise and salutary measures sacrificed to the pretended inconvenience of the times; and that he was of opinion that what was proper to be done could scarcely be done out of season. He then moved, "that the bill be now read a second time."

Mr. Pitt said, that in the interval which had taken place since the first reading of the bill, he had paid considerable attention to the subject, and endeavoured to collect information from the best sources to which he had access. The evil was certainly of such a nature as to render it of importance to find out a proper remedy, but the nature of the remedy involved discussions of such a delicate and intricate nature, that none should be adopted without being maturely weighed. The present situation of the labouring poor in this country was certainly not such as could be wished, upon any principle, either of humanity, or policy. That class had of late been exposed to hardships which they all concurred in lamenting, and were equally actuated by a desire to remove. He would not argue how far the comparison of the state of the labourer, relieved as it had been by a display of beneficence never surpassed at any period, with the state of this class of the community in former times, was just, though he was convinced that the representations were exaggerated. At any rate, the comparisons were not accurate, because they did not embrace a comprehensive view of the relative situations. He gave the hon. gentleman ample credit for his good intentions in bringing the present bill into parliament, though he was afraid that its provisions were such as it would be impolitic, upon the whole, to adopt; and such as, if adopted, would be found to be inadequate to the purposes proposed. The authority of Dr. Price had been adduced to show the great advance that had taken place on every article of subsistence, compared with the slow increase of the wages of labour. But the statement of Dr. Price was erroneous, as he compared the earnings of the labourer at the period when the comparison is instituted, with the price of provisions, and the earnings of the labourer at the present day, with the price of the same articles, without adverting to the change of circumstances, and to the difference of provisions. Corn, which was then almost the only food of the labourer, was now supplied by cheaper substitutions, and it was unfair to conclude that the wages of labour were so far from keeping pace with the price of provisions, because they could no longer purchase the same quantity of an article for which the labourer had no longer the same demand. The simple question now to be considered was, whether the remedy for the evil, which was admitted to a certain extent to exist, was to be obtained by giving to the justices the power to regulate the price of labour, and by endeavouring to establish by authority, what would be much better accomplished by the unassisted operation of principles? It was unnecessary to argue the general expediency of any legislative interference, as the principles had been perfectly recognised by the hon. gentleman himself. The most celebrated writers upon political economy, and the experience of those states where arts had flourished the most, bore ample testimony of their truth. They had only to enquire, therefore, whether the present case was strong enough for the exception, and whether the means proposed were suited to the object intended? The hon. gentleman imagined that he had on his side of the question the support of experience in this country, and appealed to certain laws upon the statute-book, in confirmation of his proposition. He did not find himself called upon to defend the principle of these statutes, but they were certainly introduced for purposes widely different from the object of the present bill. They were enacted to guard the industry of the country from being checked by a general combination among labourers; and the bill now under consideration was introduced solely for the purpose of remedying the inconveniences which labourers sustain from the disproportion existing between the price of labour and the price of living. He had the satisfaction to hear the hon. gentleman acknowledge, that if the price of labour could be made to find its own level, it would be much more desirable than to assess it by arbitrary statute, which in the execution was liable to abuse on the one hand, and inefficacy on the other. If the remedy succeeded according to the most sanguine expectations, it only established what would have been better effected by principle; and if it failed, on the one hand it might produce the severest oppression, and on the other hand encourage the most profligate idleness and extravagance. Was it not better for the House, then, to consider the operation of general principles, and rely upon the effects of their unconfined exercise? Was it not wiser to reflect what remedy might be adopted, at once more general in its principles, and more comprehensive in its object, less exceptional in its example, and less dangerous in its application? They should look to the instances where interference had shackled industry, and where the best intentions have often produced the most pernicious effects. It was indeed the most absurd bigotry, in asserting the general principle, to exclude the exception; but trade, industry and barter would always find their own level, and be impeded by regulations which violated their natural operation, and deranged their proper effect. This being granted, he appealed to the judgment of the House, whether it was better to refer the matter entirely to the discretion of a magistrate, or to endeavour to find out the causes of the evil, and by removing the causes, to apply a remedy more justifiable in its principle, more easy in the execution, more effectual in its operations, in fine, more consonant to every sound and rational policy. The evil, in his opinion, originated in a great measure in the abuses which had crept into the poor-laws of this country, and the complicated mode of executing them. The poor-laws of this country, however wise in their original institution, had contributed to fetter the circulation of labour, and to substitute a system of abuses, in room of the evils which they humanely meant to redress, and by engrafting upon a defective plan defective remedies produced nothing but confusion and disorder. The laws of settlements prevented the workman from going to that market where he could dispose of his industry to the greatest advantage, and the capitalist from employing the person who was qualified to procure him the best returns for his advances. These laws had at once increased the burthens of the poor, and taken from the collective resources of the state to supply wants which their operation had occasioned, and to alleviate a poverty which they tended to perpetuate. Such were the institutions which misguided benevolence had introduced, and, with such warnings to deter, it would be wise to distrust a similar mode of conduct, and to endeavour to discover remedies of a different nature. The country had not yet experienced the full benefit of the laws that had already been passed to correct the errors which he had explained. From the attention he had bestowed upon the subject, and from the enquiries he had been able to make of others, he was disposed to think we had not yet gone far enough, and to entertain an opinion that many advantages might be derived, and much of the evil now complained of removed, by an extension of those reformations in the poor-laws which had been begun. The encouragement of friendly societies would contribute to alleviate that immense charge with which the public was loaded in the support of the poor, and provide by savings of industry for the comfort of distress. Now the parish officer could not remove the workman, merely because he apprehended he might be burthensome, but it was necessary that he should be actually chargeable. But from the pressure of a temporary distress might the industrious mechanic be transported from the place where his exertions could be useful to himself and his family, to a quarter where he would become a burthen without the capacity of even being able to provide for himself. To remedy such a great striking grievance, the laws of settlement ought to undergo a radical amendment. He conceived, that to promote the free circulation of labour, to remove the obstacles by which industry is prohibited from availing itself of its resources, would go far to remedy the evils, and diminish the necessity of applying for relief to the poor-rates. In the course of a few years, this freedom from the vexatious restraint which the laws imposed would supersede the object of their institutions. The advantages would be widely diffused, the wealth of the nation would be increased, the poor man rendered not only more comfortable, but more virtuous, and the weight of poor-rates, with which the landed interest is loaded, greatly diminished. He should wish, therefore, that an opportunity were given of restoring the original purity of the poor laws, and of removing those corruptions by which they had been obscured. He was convinced, that the evils which they had occasioned did not arise out of their original constitution, but coincided with the opinion of Blackstone, that, in proportion as the wise regulations that were established in the long and glorious reign of Queen Elizabeth, have been superseded by subsequent enactments, the utility of the institution has been impaired, and the benevolence of the plan rendered fruitless. While he thus had expressed those sentiments which the discussion naturally prompted, it might not, perhaps, be improper, on such an occasion, to lay before the House the ideas floating in his mind, though not digested with sufficient accuracy, nor arranged with a proper degree of clearness. Neither what the hon. gentleman proposed, nor what he himself had suggested, were remedies adequate to the evil it was intended to remove. Supposing, however, the two modes of remedying the evil were on a par in effect, the preference in principle was clearly due to that which was least arbitrary in its nature; but it was not difficult to perceive that the remedy proposed by the hon. gentleman would either be completely ineffectual, or such as far to over-reach its mark. As there was a difference in the numbers which compose the families of the labouring poor, it must necessarily require less to support a small family. Now by the regulations proposed, either the man with a small family would have too much wages, or the man with a large family, who had done most service to his country, would have too little. So that were the minimum fixed upon the standard of a large family, it might operate as encouragement to idleness on one part of the community; and if it were fixed on the standard of a small family, those would not enjoy the benefit of it for whose relief it was intended. What measure then could be found to supply the defect? Let us, said he, make relief in cases where there are a number of children, a matter of right and an honour, instead of a ground for opprobrium and contempt. This will make a large family a blessing, and not a curse; and this will draw a proper line of distinction between those who are able to provide for themselves by their labour, and those who, after having enriched their country with a number of children, have a claim upon its assistance for their support. All this, however, he would confess, was not enough, if they did not engraft upon it resolutions to discourage relief where it was not wanted. If such means could be practised as that of supplying the necessities of those who required assistance by giving it in labour or affording employment, which is the principle of the act of Elizabeth, the most important advantages would be gained. They would thus benefit those to whom they afforded relief, not only by the assistance bestowed, but by giving habits of industry and frugality, and, in furnishing a temporary bounty, enable them to make permanent provision for themselves. By giving effect to the operation of friendly societies, individuals would be rescued from becoming a burthen upon the public, and, if necessary, be enabled to subsist upon a fund which their own industry contributed to raise. These great points of granting relief according to the number of children, preventing removals at the caprice of the parish officer, and making them subscribe to friendly societies, would tend, in a very great degree, to remove every complaint to which the present partial remedy could be applied. Experience had already shown how much could be done by the industry of children and the advantages of early employing them in such branches of manufacture as they are capable to execute. The extension of schools of industry was also an object of material importance. If any one would take the trouble to compute the amount of all the earnings of the children who are already educated in this manner, he would be surprised, when he came to consider the weight which their support by their own labours took off the country, and the addition which, by the fruits of their toil, and the habits to which they were formed, was made to its internal opulence. The suggestion of these schools was originally drawn from Lord Hale and Mr. Locke, and upon such authority he had no difficulty in recommending the plan to the encouragement of the legislature. Much might be effected by a plan of this nature susceptible of constant improvement. Such a plan would convert the relief granted to the poor into an encouragement to industry, instead of being, as it is by the present poor laws, a premium to idleness and a school for sloth. There were also a number of subordinate circumstances to which it was necessary to attend. The law which prohibits giving relief where any visible property remains should be abolished. That degrading condition should be withdrawn. No temporary occasion should force a British subject to part with the last shilling of his little capital, and compel him to descend to a state of wretchedness from which he could never recover, merely that he might be entitled to a casual supply. Another mode also of materially assisting the industrious poor was, the advancing of small capitals, which might be repaid in two or three years, while the person who repaid it would probably have made an addition to his income. This might put him who received them in the way of acquiring what might place him in a situation to make permanent provision for himself. These were the general ideas which had occurred to him upon the subject; if they should be approved of by any gentleman in the House, they might perhaps appear at a future time in a more accurate shape than he could pretend to give them. He could not, however, let this opportunity slip without throwing them out. He was aware that they would require to be very maturely considered. He was aware also of a fundamental difficulty, that of insuring the diligent execution of any law that should be enacted. This could only be done by presenting to those who should be entrusted with the execution motives to emulation, and by a frequent inspection of their conduct as to diligence and fidelity. Were he to suggest an outline, it would be this. To provide some new mode of inspection by parishes, or by hundreds—to report to the magistrates at the petty sessions, with a liberty of appeal from them to the general quarter sessions, where the justice should be empowered to take cognizance of the conduct of the different commissioners, and to remedy whatever defects should be found to exist. That an annual report should be made to parliament, and that parliament should impose upon itself the duty of tracing the effect of its system from year to year, till it should be fully matured. That there should be a standing order of the House for this purpose, and in a word, that there should be an annual budget opened, containing the details of the whole system of poor-laws, by which the legislature would show that they had a constant and a watchful eye upon the interests of the poorest and most neglected part of the community. He was not vain enough to imagine that these ideas were the result of his own investigations, but he was happy to say that they arose from a careful examination of the subject, and an extensive survey of the opinions of others. He would only add that it was a subject of the utmost importance, and that he would do everything in his power to bring forward or promote such measures as would conduce to the interest of the country. He gave the hon. gentleman every possible credit for his humane and laudable motives, yet seeing the subject in the light in which he did, he was compelled to give his negative to the motion.

Mr. Lechmere said, that the bill was not only founded in humanity, but policy also. The late alarming scarcity ought to induce every man who wished to encourage the industrious poor, to promote every plan of relief for them at such a crisis. No agricultural labourer could at present support himself and his family with comfort; for a barley loaf was at the enormous price of $12\frac{1}{2}d.$, while the whole of the labourer's daily wages amounted to no more than one shilling. *Haud ignara mali, miseris succurrere disco*, was a noble sentiment; but he would rather have the labourer enjoy the honest fruits of his industry, than be obliged to receive his due as an eleemosynary gift. It appeared to him that the minimum of agricultural labour should be fixed.

Mr. Buxton said, that the bill did not appear likely to be of much service, for if the price of labour were to be fixed by the justices of peace, he feared many industrious people would be thrown out of employ, and become a burthen to their respective parishes. The people he alluded to were those who by sickness or old age were rendered incapable of doing so much as a common labourer, and who consequently would be rejected for persons of more strength and activity. He had consulted with various well informed farmers and gentlemen in Norfolk who unanimously concurred in opinions that the bill would be injurious.

Mr. Vansittart commended the hon. gentleman who introduced the bill, for his humane intentions, but he had no hesitation in voting against it, because he thought any arbitrary regulations of the justices of the peace, in the price of labour, would be a greater evil than that already complained of. The bill appeared to him unnecessary, as the law since the reign of James I, enabled the magistrate the fix the price of labour.

Mr. Burdon did not think that the industrious poor were in that wretched situation stated by some gentlemen. The industrious labourer, in many instances, was able to support his family, and lay up something for his old age. From the average price of labour for some years, the House must perceive that the wages of the labourer were considerably increased. The friendly societies, if they continued to extend, would be productive of infinite good. As to the bill, he was convinced of its inadequacy to correct the abuses of which it complained. He recommended rather to repeal the act of Elizabeth than set it up as a precedent to act upon.

Mr. Fox said that no man was more against the idea of compulsion as to the price of labour than he was. The question now was, not on the general principle, but on that particular state of the law, which rendered some measure necessary to be adopted for the relief of the labouring poor, while the law, as it stood, was saddled with so many restrictions. He approved of the bill proposed by his hon. friend, as calculated to correct that which was bad in its present operation, and to secure at least to the labourer the means of partial relief. But if the House objected to the measure as improper, if they were of the opinion that it was not the most judicious or desirable that might be applied, he hoped they would go to the root of the evil, and provide some remedy adequate to the extent of the grievance. If, therefore, they should give a negative to the second reading of the bill, he should consider that by so doing they pledged themselves to take the subject into their early and most serious consideration. If what his hon. friend had brought forward should induce the House to go into a full examination of the subject, and to provide a remedy commensurate to the evil, he would not only have accomplished his own benevolent intentions, but would have done a much greater service to the country, than even if the bill which he had now brought forward were adopted.

Mr. Whitbread said:—"I cannot but congratulate the House on the able and eloquent speech of the chancellor of the exchequer. At the same time I must remark that if the poor laws were actually such, as the right hon. gentleman has stated they ought to be, it would not have been necessary for me to have brought forward any proposition; but I am afraid that facts and experience will be found undeniably to confirm my assertion, that the poor in this country are in a state scarcely consistent with the character of a civilised country. As to what the right hon. gentleman has stated about the price of labour finding its own level, he does not recollect that, till the level be found, the industrious poor labour under the pressure of immediate suffering. If the expedients he has proposed should succeed, they are matters of future regulation, and not calculated to afford relief which the exigencies of the times so imperiously demand. If it should be possible to a considerable degree to promote industry among the children of the poor, and to destroy the oppressive restrictions with respect to settlements, still it will be a considerable time before the price of labour will have found its level. Even if more effectual regulations should afterwards be adopted, still this bill is eligible as a temporary relief. It does not compel the magistrates to act: it only empowers them to take measures according to the exigency of the times. It has been stated as an objection to the bill, that it goes to fix the price of labour, but gentlemen do not attend to the circumstances, that it does not go to determine what should be the general price of labour, but only what should be the least price of labour under particular circumstances. As to the particular case of labourers, who have to provide for a number of children, the wisest thing for government, instead of putting the relief afforded to such on the footing of a charity, supplied, perhaps, from a precarious fund, and dealt with a reluctant hand, would be at once to institute a liberal premium for the encouragement of large families. There is just one circumstance to which I shall advert, before I conclude, namely, the wretched manner in which the poor are lodged. It is such as ought not to be suffered in a country like this, proud of its freedom, and boasting of the equal rights of all its subjects. The landlord, who lets the ground upon lease to the farmer, does not consider himself as bound to repair the cottages. The farmer, who has only a temporary interest in the property, feels no anxiety on the subject. The cottage, dismantled and mouldering to decay, affords neither warmth nor shelter to the poor inhabitant, who is left exposed to the fury of the elements and the inclemency of every season. If a negative should be put upon the second reading of the bill, I shall then move for leave to bring in a bill to repeal the statute of Elizabeth, and afterwards for a committee to take into consideration the state of the poor laws."

The motion was negatived. After which, the bill was ordered to be read a second time on that day three months.

7. Arbitration Act for the Cotton Industry [*Statutes*, 39 *and* 40 *Geo. III*, 90], 1800.

An act for settling disputes that may arise between masters and workmen engaged in the cotton manufacture in that part of Great Britain called England.

That, from and after the first day of August in the year of our Lord one thousand eight hundred, in all cases that shall or may arise within that part of Great Britain called England, where the masters and workmen cannot agree respecting the price or prices to be paid for work done, or to be done, in the said manufacture, whether such dispute shall happen or arise between them respecting the reduction or advance of wages or any injury or damage done, or alleged to have been done, by the workmen to the work, or respecting any delay, or supposed delay, on the part of the workmen in finishing the work or the not finishing such work in a good and workmanlike manner; and also in all cases where the workmen are to be employed to work any new pattern which shall require them to purchase any new implements of manufacture for the working thereof, and the masters and workmen cannot agree upon the compensation to be made to such workmen for or in respect thereof, and also respecting the length of all pieces of cotton goods, or the wages or compensation to be paid for all pieces of cotton goods that are made of any great or extraordinary length, and respecting the manufacture of cravats, shawls, polycat, romall, and other handkerchiefs, and the number to be contained in one piece of such handkerchiefs, and the wages to be paid in respect thereof, and in all cases of dispute or difference arising or happening by and between the masters and workmen employed in such manufacture, out of, for, or touching such trade or manufacture, which cannot be otherwise mutually adjusted and settled by and between them; it shall and may be lawful, and it is hereby declared to be lawful, for such masters and workmen, between whom such dispute or difference shall arise as aforesaid, or either of them, to demand and have an arbitration or reference of such matter or matters in dispute, and each of them is hereby authorised and empowered forthwith to nominate and appoint an arbitrator for and on his respective part and behalf, to arbitrate and determine such matter or matters in dispute as aforesaid, and such arbitrators so appointed as aforesaid, after they shall have accepted and taken upon them the business of the said arbitration, are hereby authorised and required to summon before them, and examine upon oath the parties and their witnesses (which oath the said arbitrators are hereby authorised and required to administer according to the form set forth in the schedule to this act), and forthwith to proceed to hear and determine the complaints of the parties and the matter or matters in dispute between them, and the award to be made by such arbitrators shall in all cases be final and conclusive between the parties; but in case such arbitrators so appointed cannot agree to decide such matter or matters in dispute so to be referred to them as aforesaid, and do not make and sign their award within the space of three days after the signing of the said submission, that then they shall forthwith, and without delay, go before and attend upon one of his Majesty's justices of the peace acting in and for the county, riding, city, liberty, division, township, or place, and residing nearest to the place where such dispute shall happen and be referred, and state to such justice the points in difference between them the said arbitrators, which points in difference the said justice shall and he is hereby authorised and required to hear and determine, which determination of such justice shall be made and signed within the space of three days after the expiration of the time hereby allowed the arbitrators to make and sign their award, and shall be final and conclusive between the parties so differing as aforesaid.

[In cases of dispute the points of difference shall be stated to a justice whose award shall be final. Justices who are cotton manufacturers cannot act.]

8. Amendment of the Arbitration Act [*Statutes*, 44 *Geo. III*, 87], 1804.

An act to amend an act, passed in the thirty-ninth and fortieth years of his present Majesty, intituled, An act for settling disputes that may arise between masters and workmen engaged in the cotton manufacture in that part of Great Britain called England.

II. And be it further enacted, that, in all cases where an arbitration may be demanded by the said recited act, where the party complaining and the party complained of shall come before or agree, by any writing under their hands, to abide by the determination of any justice of the peace or magistrate of any county, city, town, or place, within which the parties reside, it shall and may be lawful for such justice of the peace or magistrate to hear and finally determine in a summary manner the matter in dispute between such parties; but if such parties shall not come before, or so agree to abide by the determination of such justice of the peace or magistrate, then it shall be lawful for any such justice or magistrate, and such justice of the peace or magistrate is hereby required, on complaint made before him, and proof by the examination of the party, making such complaint, that application has been made to the person or persons against whom such cause of complaint has arisen, or his, her, or their agent or agents, if such dispute has arisen with such agent or agents, to settle such dispute, and that the same has not been settled upon such complaint being made, or where the dispute relates to a bad warp, such cause of complaint shall not be done away within forty-eight hours after such application, to summon before him such person or persons, or agent or agents, on some day not exceeding three days, exclusive of Sunday, before the making such complaint, giving notice to the person making such complaint of the time and place appointed in such summons for the attendance of such person or persons, agent or agents, as aforesaid; and if at such time and place the person or persons so summoned shall not appear by himself, or send some person on his, her, or their behalf, to settle such dispute, or appearing shall not do away such cause of complaint, then and in such case it shall be lawful for such justice, and he is hereby required, at the request of either of such parties, to nominate arbitrators or referees for settling the matters in dispute ; and such justice shall then and there at such meeting propose not less than four nor more than six persons, one-half of whom shall be master-manufacturers or agents or foremen of some master-manufacturer, and the other half of whom shall be weavers in such manufacture (such respective persons residing in or near to the place where such dispute shall have arisen) out of which master-manufacturers, agents, or foremen, the master engaged in such dispute, or his agent, shall choose one, and out of which weavers so proposed, the weaver or his agent, shall choose another, who shall have full power to hear and finally determine such dispute ; and the said justice shall thereupon appoint a place of meeting according to the directions of this act, and also a day for the meeting, notice of which nomination, and of the day of meeting, shall thereupon be given to the persons so nominated arbitrators or referees, and to any party to any such dispute, who may not have attended the meeting before such justice as aforesaid.

[For criticism of the act see Petition of Cotton Weavers, 1813, Pt. III, Section III, No. 12, page 576.]

9. THE FIRST FACTORY ACT [*Statutes*, 42 *Geo. III*, 87], 1802.

An act for the preservation of the health and morals of apprentices and others, employed in cotton and other mills, and cotton and other factories.

. . . All such mills and factories within *Great Britain and Ireland*, wherein three or more apprentices, or twenty or more other persons, shall at any time be employed, shall be subject to the several rules and regulations contained in this act; . . .

II. And be it enacted, that all and every the rooms and apartments in or belonging to any such mill or factory shall, twice at least in every year, be well and sufficiently washed with quick lime and water over every part of the walls and ceiling thereof; and that due care and attention shall be paid by the master or mistress of such mills or factories to provide a sufficient number of windows and openings in such rooms or apartments, to insure a proper supply of fresh air in and through the same.

III. And be it further enacted, that every such master or mistress shall constantly supply every apprentice during the term of his or her apprenticeship with two whole and complete suits of clothing. . . .

IV. And be it further enacted, that no apprentice that now is or hereafter shall be bound to any such master or mistress shall be employed or compelled to work for more than twelve hours in any one day (reckoning from six of the clock in the morning to nine of the clock at night), exclusive of the time that may be occupied by such apprentice in eating the necessary meals: Provided always, that, from and after the first day of June one thousand eight hundred and three, no apprentice shall be employed or compelled to work upon any occasion whatever between the hours of nine of the clock at night and six of the clock in the morning.

VI. And be it further enacted, that every such apprentice shall be instructed, in some part of every working day, for the first four years at least of his or her apprenticeship. . . .

VII. And be it further enacted, that the room or apartment in which any male apprentice shall sleep shall be entirely separate and distinct from the room or apartment in which any female apprentice shall sleep, and that not more than two apprentices shall in any case sleep in the same bed.

VIII. And be it further enacted, that every apprentice, or (in case the apprentices shall attend in classes) every such class, shall for the space of one hour at least every Sunday be instructed and examined in the principles of the Christian religion . . . and such master or mistress shall send all his or her apprentices under the care of some proper person, once in a month at least, to attend during divine service in the church of the parish . . . or in some licensed place of divine worship; and in case the apprentices cannot conveniently attend such church or chapel . . . the master or mistress . . . shall cause divine service to be performed in some convenient room or place in or adjoining to the mill or factory. . . .

IX. And be it further enacted, that the justices of the peace for every county . . . shall . . . appoint two persons, not interested in, or in any way connected with, any such mills or factories, to be visitors . . .; one of whom shall be a justice of peace . . . and the other shall be a clergyman of the Established Church. . . .

9A. Minutes of Committee on Children in Factories, 1816 (III), *p.* 277.

Examination of Richard Arkwright, June 7, 1816.

Q. What is your opinion of the Act known under the name of Sir Robert Peel's Bill ? I could wish to confine myself to facts as much as possible.

What have you known of that Act ? That Act has not been followed up, with respect to the visiting of magistrates, for these thirteen years. I think they visited my mills at Cromford twice.

p. 278.

Are you of opinion that Sir Robert Peel's Bill, which passed in the year 1802, has accomplished much benefit for the children, for whose protection it was intended ?

I certainly thought that the discussions upon that Bill, and the Bill itself, did a great deal of good, but that can be only matter of opinion.

10. Calico Printers' Petition for Regulation [*Commons Journals, Vol. LIX, Feb.* 22, 1804], 1804.

A petition of several journeymen calico printers, and others working in that trade, in the counties of Lancaster, Derby, Chester, and Stafford, in England, and in the counties of Lanark, Renfrew, Dumbarton, Stirling, and Perth in Scotland, was presented to the House, and read ; setting forth that great numbers of the petitioners and other journeymen calico printers have, for a series of years past, been greatly distressed for want of work in their trade, and that this distress has chiefly arisen from a very general, if not universal, practice of the master calico printers in the counties above enumerated, who systematically carry on the said trade by employing in it, in many instances, a greater number of out-door apprentices than of journeymen, and, upon an average, nearly two of such apprentices to three journeymen, a practice of great injury to the petitioners, their families, and, ultimately, even to the apprentices themselves ; and that one of the injurious effects, to the petitioners by this system is, that, in many instances boys are taken as apprentices to the said trade or business on verbal agreement, whereby they are at liberty to absent themselves from the service and control of their masters on any trifling disagreement, and are generally replaced by others, thereby creating an overstock of hands in the said trade: And therefore praying, That leave may be given to bring in a bill to regulate the trade or business of calico printers.

Ordered, that the said petition be referred to the considera tion of a committee.

11. REPORT ON CALICO PRINTERS' PETITION [*Commons Journals, Vol. LXI, July* 17, 1806], 1806.

Your committee have naturally endeavoured to ascertain the cause of those discontents, and, as far as they have been able to collect from the minutes of evidence referred to them, they find it has arisen principally from the multiplication of apprentices. That this has gone to an extent, and that the disproportion of apprentices to journeymen exists to a degree, far beyond that understood to prevail in any other mechanical profession whatever, appears to your committee in several instances. In one instance, that of the shop of Berry and Co. of Lancashire, they find that 55 apprentices were employed, and only two journeymen; in another, that of the shop of Tod and Co. of Dumbarton, there were 60 apprentices, and only two journeymen. Such a disproportion, your committee conceive, must strike as extraordinary any one in the least degree acquainted with the custom of trade.

The practice of introducing such an increased number of apprentices, which commenced about the year 1790, does not appear from the minutes of evidence to have proceeded from any scarcity of hands to supply the demands of the masters, or make up the work required; on the contrary, it appears that in the course of the period when this excessive multiplication of apprentices went on, a number of journeymen were seeking in vain for employment.

With regard to the multiplication of apprentices, while your committee declare that they are not friendly to the idea of imposing any restrictions upon trade, they are ready to state that the inclination of their minds is this, that either all restrictions ought to be abolished, and the masters and journeymen left to settle matters between themselves, or an additional restriction ought to be introduced to counteract the evils obviously resulting from the restrictions which already exist. This restriction your committee mean of course to apply to apprentices; and if a precedent were wanted to justify such a measure, they would refer to the case of the silk weavers, and that of other trades, which are to be found on the Statute Book. In the instance of the silk weavers, no more than two apprentices can be legally taken by any master, whatever may be the number of his journeymen; and yet, since the enactment of this law, no scarcity of hands has ever been complained of in that flourishing branch of trade. Indeed, throughout all the mechanical professions, it is, as far as has come to the knowledge of any of the members of your committee, the general rule, that no master shall have more than two or three apprentices at the most. This general rule is conceived to be established through an understanding between the masters and the journeymen.

The salutary effects of leaving the masters and journeymen to settle their affairs between themselves, is particularly exemplified in the calico printing business: for, although in Lancashire and Derbyshire, etc., where there is nearly a proportion of one apprentice to one journeyman, and between masters and journeymen a consequent jealousy, productive of perpetual variance and confusion; there is in the neighbourhood of London, where a different feeling prevails, and where matters are amicably adjusted between the parties, a very different proportion of apprentices and journeymen. In 14 shops examined by one of the witnesses, in 1803, the number of journeymen were 216, the apprentices only 37.

But to return to the subject of restrictions: your committee are persuaded that as the Legislature has thought proper to interpose its authority, to prevent the journeymen from concerting measures among themselves to settle their affairs with the masters, it would be ready to remove any complaints which might arise from advantage taken by the masters of the existence of such restriction. The wisdom and humanity of Parliament would shrink from sanctioning the Combination Law, if it appeared to them, at the time of its enactment, likely to operate only in favour of the strong, and against the weak; if it had any apparent tendency to secure impunity to oppressors, and to give an undue advantage to the masters, who can combine with little danger of detection, and who can carry their projects into execution with little fear of opposition. The Legislature could never mean to injure the man, whose only desire is to derive a subsistence from his labour, and that indeed is all a journeyman calico printer can look to; for, from the particular nature of his trade, differing much from others, he cannot, from the capital required, ever calculate upon becoming a master.

12. Cotton Weavers' Petition Against the Repeal of 5 Elizabeth c. 4 [*Commons Journals*, *Vol. LXVIII*, *Feb.* 25, 1813], 1813.

A petition of several cotton weavers resident in the division of Bolton Le Moors, in the county of Lancaster, was presented and read; setting forth, that the petitioners are much concerned to learn that a bill has been brought into the House to repeal so much of the Statute 5 Elizabeth, as empowers and requires the magistrates, in their respective jurisdictions, to rate and settle the prices to be paid to labourers, handicrafts, spinners, weavers, etc.; and that the petitioners have endured almost constant reductions in the prices of their labour for many years, with sometimes a trifling advance, but during the last thirty months they have continued, with very little alteration, so low, that the average wages of cotton weavers do not exceed 5*s.* per week, though other trades in general earn from 20*s.* to 30*s.* per week; and that the extravagant prices of provisions of all kinds render it impossible for the petitioners to procure food for themselves and families, and the parishes are so burthened that an adequate supply cannot be had from that quarter; and that, in the 40th year of His present Majesty a law was made to settle disputes between masters and workmen[1]; which law having been found capable of evasion, and evaded, became unavailing: after which, in 1802, 1803, and 1804, applications being made to amend that of the 40th, another law was made, varying in some points from the former; but this also is found unavailing, inasmuch as no one conviction before a magistrate under this law has ever been confirmed at any Quarter Sessions of the Peace; and that several applications have since been made to the House to enact such laws as they would judge suitable to afford relief to the trade, in which masters and workmen joined, but hitherto without any effect; and that, about twelve months since, it was found that the Statute of 5 Eliz. (if acted upon) was com-

[1] See above. Pt. III, Section III, Nos. 7 and 8, p. 568 and p. 570.

petent to afford the desired relief, and it was resorted to in certain cases, but the want of generality prevented its obtaining at that time, especially as it can be acted on only at the Easter Quarter Sessions, or six weeks thereafter; and that, as petitions to the magistrates were almost general at the last Quarter Sessions, and all graciously received at each different jurisdiction, much hope was entertained that at the next Easter sessions the magistrates would settle the wages of the petitioners, and they obtain food by their industry; and that the present bill to repeal the aforesaid law has sunk the spirits of the petitioners beyond description, having no hope left: the former laws made for their security being unavailing, there is no protection for their sole property, which is their labour; and that, although the said law of 5 Eliz. was wisely designed to protect all trades and workmen, yet none will essentially suffer by its repeal save the cotton weavers: the silk weavers have law to secure their prices, as have other artizans; tradesmen generally receive their contracted wages, but cotton weavers, when their work is done, know not what they shall receive, as that depends on the goodness of the employer's heart: And that the petitioners, therefore, most humbly, and earnestly pray, that the House, for the aforesaid reasons, will not repeal the said Statute of 5 Eliz., it being the only law by which they can hope any relief from their present misery; and the existing laws being evaded, this would afford, when acted upon, prices somewhat suitable to the prices of provisions in adverse times; but should the House see it proper to repeal the said law, the petitioners pray, that in that case it will enact a law to secure and grant such wages to the petitioners as will enable them to live by their industry, equally beneficial to masters and workmen.

Ordered, That the said Petition do lie upon the Table.

[The wages clauses of 5 Eliz. 4 were repealed by 53 Geo. III, 40, 1813.]

13. Debates on the Regulation of Apprentices [*Parl. Debates, Series I, Vol. XXV, Cols.* 1120–1131; *XXVII*, 423–425, 563–574, 879–884], 1813-1814.

Apprentices.—*Mr. Rose* adverted to the petition[1] he presented the other day, which was signed by above 800 masters

[1] For enforcing the Statute of Apprentices.

and 13,000 journeymen in London; and by 1,154 masters and 17,517 journeymen in the country; making above 32,000 in all. The policy of the system began in Edward the 3rd. Some had doubted the effects of the law, and deemed all restrictions injurious to commerce: others considered the want of restrictions more dangerous, and contended that the present system had encouraged habits of industry. The courts had, in general, narrowed the spirit and application of the restrictions. He thought that if the existing law was not to be enforced, it ought to be amended or repealed. A petition signed by such a number of tradesmen was deserving the most attentive consideration. He should therefore move that the petition be referred to a committee.

Mr. Serjeant Onslow allowed that the number of signatures to the petition entitled it to a respectful consideration. As to the allegations of the petition, he thought it very extraordinary that the petitioners should really expect that parliament would allow them to bring actions upon this statute, against whom they pleased, well-founded or ill-founded, without being subject to costs in case of failure. From his experience in a certain judicial situation, he could say, and he believed he might appeal to all his professional friends about him for the confirmation of his statement, that he never knew any indictment brought under this statute except against a person of great skill and acquirements. The preamble of the Act stated its object to be "to prevent the introduction of unskilful workmen": and yet no indictments were ever brought against unskilful workmen, but only against very skilful and ingenious men. This shewed pretty clearly the spirit in which such prosecutions were brought.

Mr. D. Giddy said, that he should not vote for the committee, if he did not think it likely that the resolution they would come to would be directly opposite to that which was expected by the petitioners. He certainly did entertain great doubts, whether in the present state of the commercial world there was any use in those apprenticeships, although they might have been necessary in the infancy of commerce. It frequently happened, that a young man had not a talent for that particular business to which he had been bound an apprentice, and was yet possessed of other talents, by the exercise of which he might obtain a most respectable subsistence.

It appeared to him a cruel hardship to fetter the minds and limbs of men, so as to prevent their obtaining a subsistence by the fair exercise of their talents and of their limbs. As to what was said of corporate rights, obtained by apprenticeship, he thought that made it the less necessary to add penalties. If those corporate rights, however, were to be considered of real value, he thought it a great hardship that they could not be obtained in any other way than by serving an apprenticeship.

Mr. Butterworth also felt inclined to disapprove of the Act as highly injurious to trade in general, and to rising talent. In illustration of the hardships of the Act, and of the manner in which it was generally enforced, he mentioned a case which had come within his own immediate observation. In an office of which he had the command, there was a young man of great skill, and consequently of great value to his employers; he, however, had not served the regular apprenticeship, and his fellow-workmen therefore combined against him, demanding his discharge. He (Mr. B.) interfered on behalf of the young man, but in vain; for the conspiracy amongst the workmen attained that height that their request was obliged to be complied with. The young man was discharged, and though skilful in that particular trade, he had been compelled to sell the furniture, the produce of his industry, to support a wife and family, who were dependent on him for support. He did not oppose the committee, because he was convinced that the determination would be in favour of the repeal of the 5th of Elizabeth.

The petition was then referred to a committee.

Wednesday, April 6, 1814.[1]

APPRENTICE LAWS.—*Mr. H. Davis* presented a petition from certain master manufacturers of the city of Bristol, praying that so much of the Act of the 5th of Elizabeth, cap. 4, as inflicted penalties on persons exercising trades to which they had not served regular apprenticeships, should be repealed. Ordered to lie on the table.

Mr. P. Moore presented a petition from the manufacturers of Coventry, praying that that part of the 5th of Elizabeth,

[1] Parliamentary Debates, Series I, Cols. 423-25, Vol. XXVII.

cap. 4, which inflicted penalties on persons exercising trades to which they had not served regular apprenticeships, should be rendered efficient. He should merely move "that the petition do lie on the table"; but, before he sat down, he wished to enquire of the learned gentleman (Mr. Serjeant Onslow) who had given notice of his intention to introduce a Bill on the subject, whether he meant, in his proposed measure, to confine himself merely to the repeal of that part of the 5th of Elizabeth which sanctioned those penalties, or to do away with the Act altogether? He also wished to know whether the learned gentleman intended to push his Bill through the different stages in the present session; or, having introduced it, to let it lie over till the next? In his opinion a committee ought to be appointed, in the first instance, to examine the whole of the petitions that had been presented relative to the 5th of Elizabeth, and also to look into the provisions of that Act.

Mr. Serjeant Onslow said, most unquestionably he did not mean to go beyond the terms of his notice, in the measure he should introduce. He had stated explicitly the part of the Act that he wished to have repealed, and he had not since altered his determination. With respect to the second point of the hon. gentleman's interrogatory, "Whether he intended to hurry the Bill through the House?" he would answer that he certainly did not. But the hon. gentleman seemed to forget that the present period was virtually almost the commencement of the session, and that very important business was yet to come on. He (Serjeant Onslow) certainly did wish to have the sense of the House taken on the Bill, before the session terminated. And this, he thought, could be done without any imputation of hurry. In the last session the Treasurer of the Navy (Mr. Rose) had presented a petition from a great number of persons who were desirous that the penalties should be continued; and moved for a committee to investigate the allegations of the petitioners. A committee was granted—it sat from day to day—and the evidence adduced before it was printed. He (Serjeant Onslow) enquired of that right hon. gentleman whether he intended to found any motion on this evidence? And, understanding that he did not, he stated, at the close of the last session, that he would himself submit a motion on the subject. Soon after parliament met he gave notice of a motion for the 30th of November; but, in consequence of a number of gentlemen who represented large manufacturing districts (particularly the hon. member for Yorkshire) not being then in town, he postponed it till the 22nd of February, and had finally put it off till the 27th of the present month—knowing that a call of the House would take place before that period, which would ensure a full attendance when the proposed measure came to be discussed. That the country was not unprepared for it, was evident from the numerous petitions which had been presented in favour of it. Petitions of that nature had been received from Leeds, Birmingham, Huddersfield, Bristol, and many other populous neighbourhoods. Several petitions had been presented against it. How they were procured he did not know; but the language in all of them appeared nearly the same. With respect to the principal trade carried on by the constituents of the hon. gentleman, it would not be at all affected by the new Bill, because it was already guarded by a variety of enactments totally independent of the 5th of Elizabeth.

Mr. P. Moore said it was very true that his constituents (the freemen of Coventry) were obliged by Act of Parliament to serve a regular apprenticeship, before they could carry on the business alluded to by the learned gentleman. Now they were alarmed lest by the proposed Bill they should be deprived of a right which they had long enjoyed. They therefore were anxious that the Bill should not be hurried through the House.

The petition was ordered to lie on the table.

Wednesday, April 27, 1814.[1]

APPRENTICESHIP LAWS.—*Mr. Serjeant Onslow* rose to move for leave to bring in a Bill to repeal part of an Act, passed in the 5th year of Elizabeth, entitled "An Act containing divers orders for artificers, labourers, servants of husbandry, and apprentices." . . . The reign of Queen Elizabeth, though glorious, was not one in which sound principles of commerce were known; and a perusal of the other clauses of the Act, as well as the one creating the penalties for exercising trades contrary to its provisions, would fully confirm that assertion;

[1] Parliamentary Debates, Series I, Vol. XXVII, Cols. 563-74.

indeed it did not seem to be the object of that statute to favour manufactures; it rather seemed to be intended to make them subservient to a most mistaken notion of favour to the landed interest. So little was political economy then understood that the idea never seemed to have occurred, that agriculture was best promoted by the prosperity of commerce and manufactures; and that restraints on them defeated the end they aimed at, and discouraged that very employment which they ought to promote. . . . Apprenticeships had been looked upon as favourable to the morals of youth, and he was very far from wishing to discourage them; but he did not wish them to be an indispensable qualification for legally carrying on trades. . . . Apprenticeships were as common in trades not within the statute as in those that were within what had been called the protection, but what he thought the curse, of the statute. . . .

Mr. Philips.—The persons most competent to form regulations with respect to trade were the master manufacturers, whose interest it was to have goods of the best fabric; and no legislative enactment could ever effect so much in producing that result, as the merely leaving things to their own course and operation. The proof of this was to be found in the fact that the manufactures for which the country was most famous, were precisely those to which this Act did not apply. If this narrow principle had been carried into every branch of art, the machinery of Sir Richard Arkwright would have been lost to the country—and the genius of Mr. Watt, whose inventions had added more to the productive powers of the empire, than if the population had been increased one half, would have been still unknown. The hon. gentleman then proceeded to point out the evil effects which arose from the system of combination among tradesmen [workmen].

Leave was given to bring in the Bill.

Friday, May 13, 1814.[1]

APPRENTICE LAWS.—*Mr. Serjeant Onslow* moved the second reading of the Bill, which was warmly opposed by

Sir Fred. Flood, who, though a friend to liberty, disliked licentiousness. The Bill went to abrogate that most salutary law of the 5th of Elizabeth, and to revive the practice which

[1] Parliamentary Debates, Series I, Vol. XXVII, Cols. 879-884.

had previously existed from Edward the Third's time. It would be destructive of the interests of persons who served their apprenticeships, and paid for education in their respective trades, and ruinous to the morals of youth. It would be hurtful to commerce, to mechanics, to manufacture and to the Stamp Act. The present law had lasted 220 years. He proposed to postpone the second reading to that day six months.

Mr. Protheroe seconded the motion, as the Bill proceeded on no general comprehensive system, but simply on a repeal without any efficient substitute for what was to be repealed. He objected to the measure in a moral point of view; in which respect he was upheld by the opinions of Lord Coke and Sir Wm. Blackstone. He had heard much of vexatious prosecutions under the Act of Elizabeth; but, on enquiry, he found that at Bristol for the last 20 years, there had not been one such prosecution. If apprenticeships were more encouraged, he was satisfied that combinations among journeymen would almost entirely be put an end to. If the House were to lower its attention down to the humble cottage, they would there see the advantages of this system, in beholding careful masters provided for the youths, who, in addition, were provided with food and clothing, while their morals were protected. He should be happy that the present Bill were withdrawn, and some measure unaccompanied by its disadvantages were introduced.

Mr. Hart Davis could not disguise from himself that the present measure was attended with many difficulties. It would undoubtedly be of great advantage to our manufacturers that the present law should be repealed, and that every restraint should be removed from the rising generation. Supposing a person brought up to a trade for which from his constitution he was not fit, was he to be excluded from pursuing any other pursuit, or occupation whatever? Suppose the trade of button-makers, which was a trade that speedily passed away; or of gun-makers, of whom probably 40,000 might be in a few months thrown out of employment, was it to be held that they could follow no other occupation, but must remain a burden upon the community? The more he considered the present measure, the more he was satisfied of its utility.

Mr. Protheroe explained that he could wish a general review of the whole system.

Mr. Giddy thought if any one measure more than another could be said to involve the general rights of mankind, the present was that measure. What was this but the general right of the inhabitants of this country to employ the energies of their mind and body in the way they themselves pleased? And if a system were to be continued by which men were deprived of this general and undoubted right, it seemed to be incumbent on those who contended for the continuance of such a restriction to shew on what principle it was founded. If gentlemen attended to the time in which the law in question was passed, they would find it was a period in which many ill-advised monopolies had been granted, and one in which remonstrances on that subject had been made by the House of Commons on the impolicy of such a system, which had not been much attended to. Nothing, he was convinced, had contributed so much as the law in question to check the progress in our arts and manufactures.

Sir C. Mordaunt, on the part of his constituents, the manufacturers of Birmingham, was strongly in favour of the present repeal. If the law, as it now stood, were put in force, it would have the effect of imposing the strongest possible fetters upon ingenuity and industry.

Mr. Thompson liked liberty; and doing so, he wished to see every man have the liberty of employing his hands and his genius in the best way he could to his own advantage, and for the benefit of the country. This no man was at liberty to do, so long as the present law remained in force. He wished the law totally repealed, though the Bill did not go so far. The present law was necessarily broken every day. It was clear that the judges always wished to evade it, when they could do so. He knew a case of two men who were prosecuted under the Act for sawing a piece of wood; another, of a good and bad baker in the same town; where the bad one, finding that the good one had not served a regular apprenticeship, had him turned out, and got liberty to poison all his neighbours with his bad bread. Some years ago the printers struck, and there was a difficulty in getting even the parliamentary papers printed. Let those who chose it bind their children as apprentices; but let not others be compelled to do the same.

Instances of the absurdity of the law would be innumerable. It was none the better for the age of it, which the worthy baronet had stated. It was, in fact, superannuated; and it was much the kindest way to let it die quietly, and so confer an advantage both on the country and Ireland. Lord Ellenborough once got the coach-makers out of a scrape ingeniously enough. They were attacked as wheelmakers; but his lordship said that coaches could not have been known in Elizabeth's days, as that queen went to parliament on horseback. He perfectly agreed in the opinion which Lord Mansfield had given, in speaking of the Act of Elizabeth, that "it was against the natural rights of man, and contrary to the common law rights of the land."

Mr. Rose considered this as a subject of extraordinary difficulty. After all that had been said, he could not help thinking that if the Bill were passed into law, it would put an end to apprenticeships altogether; for no person would subject himself to a seven years' servitude when he knew that having fulfilled his indenture, he would only be on a level with a man who perhaps had not been one year at the business. He was willing to examine and improve the 5th of Elizabeth, but would not agree to this unqualified repeal.

Sir J. Newport was surprised that the hon. baronet (Sir F. Flood) should be so anxious to perpetuate a statute which never was law in Ireland; and yet in that country, where no such penalties as those inflicted by the 5th of Elizabeth existed, the system of apprenticeships was freely and voluntarily adopted. He thought, on every principle of justice, that the subject was entitled to make use of his abilities and industry in those pursuits most beneficial to his interests.

Sir S. Romilly had been applied to on the subject of the present Bill, by the constituents of two hon. gentlemen who had already delivered their sentiments on the measure this night (Messrs. Protheroe and Davis). He felt the highest respect for the gentlemen who had so applied to him on the subject of the present Bill; but his opinion of the measure being decidedly opposite to theirs, he thought he should not be acting a manly part were he either to abstain from voting on the Bill, or were he to content himself with a silent vote on this occasion. He was satisfied that there were reasons sufficiently strong to support the system of apprenticeships in those trades in which a number of years were requisite to the acquiring a knowledge of them, without the assistance of the law as it now stood. This law, which went to prohibit a man from the exercise of that trade for which he was fit, he therefore thought ought to be repealed. For what was it but to take from a poor man the only property he possessed —his genius and industry—and to drive him into a workhouse; or to force him to abandon his country, and to forsake his wife and family. These were the moral consequences which the House was to look for from a perseverance in the law as it now stood.

Alderman Atkins hoped that some clause might be introduced into the Bill when it was in the committee, that would give sufficient encouragement to the apprentice system; while, at the same time, the abuses of it might be remedied.

Sir F. Flood, seeing the sense of the House against him, withdrew his amendment.

Mr. Canning wished the Bill to go into the committee. He was aware that the subject was attended with considerable difficulties. The difficulty would be to find the means of doing away the abuses complained of, without doing away the system altogether, which he was convinced was useful to the perfection of our manufactures, and still more useful as affecting the morality of the lower orders.

Mr. Serjeant Best said that if no other member introduced a clause to that effect, he himself should feel it his duty to propose one. He thought the penal clauses of the Act of Elizabeth should certainly be repealed, but that at the same time it was much better that young people should not be left without some control. He thought that at present the masters had much more advantages from the services of the apprentices, than the apprentices had from the instruction of the master, as most of those trades might be learned in a very short time. He therefore wished that part of the earnings might go to the parents, as an encouragement to the system.

Mr. P. Moore opposed the Bill, because he thought that its enactment would operate seriously to the prejudice of our manufactures both in skill and reputation. Indeed, such had been found the effect of the partial repeal of the statute of

Elizabeth with respect to the woollen manufacture.[1] For although the Yorkshire tag had formerly been a sufficient recommendation upon the continent, yet since the repeal alluded to, our pieces of woollen manufactures were examined yard by yard before they were purchased.

Mr. Lockhart expressed his opinion, that this Bill, if enacted, should only operate prospectively; that is, that it should not become effective until a certain period; so that those mechanics who had served apprenticeships upon the faith of the existing law, should not be injured by its operation, by being thrown out of employment at a period of life when they could not devote themselves to any other profession than that to which they had been reared.

Mr. B. Shaw deprecated the idea that morality was likely to be endangered, or our manufactures injured, by the enactment of the Bill under consideration; for Scotland, to which the Act of Elizabeth never extended, was never found in any degree inferior in morality or skill in manufacture.

Mr. W. Smith observed, that he never heard of any proposition of reform which was not likely to be inconvenient to some persons; and therefore he was not surprised at the assertion, that the adoption of the Bill before the House would operate to injure the interests of particular persons. The apprehension of such injury was, however, in his judgment, unfounded. But still, those who expressed the apprehension were entitled to attention; and the objections which certain petitioners urged against this Bill, would, he had no doubt, meet all due consideration in the committee. The fact was, as to the statute of Elizabeth, that its existence served to create monopolies; and the effect of those monopolies was, that when the demand for an article was large, the price was enhanced to the public; while, when the demand became small, many workmen were thrown out of employment. Therefore, the repeal of that statute would tend to serve both the public and the workmen. As to the argument advanced in support of the statute of Elizabeth, merely in consequence of its antiquity, he could not admit that it had any force. He declared that his ears were quite tired of the phrase "the wisdom of our ancestors," which phrase was, in fact, calculated

[1] The apprenticeship regulations in the woollen industries had been set aside by Acts of Parliament, 1803 and 1809.

only to impose upon the superficial. For, after all, what did this phrase mean? The world was younger in the time of our ancestors, although they were older than us. Time, Lord Bacon said, was the greatest innovator; and if, at this advanced time of the world, after all our experience, we could not improve upon the system of our ancestors, our intellects must be what would hardly be asserted, not only quite unequal to theirs, but infinitely inferior. How, then, could it be pretended, that the same legislative arrangements applied in the reign of Elizabeth, when the trade of the whole British Empire was not equal to that of the port of London at this day, was strictly applicable at present, and suited to our improved situation?

Mr. Serjeant Onslow replied, and, observing upon the petitions on the table against the Bill, expressed his conviction that they were not the unsolicited acts of the petitioners; as indeed appeared from several placards about town, inviting signatures to such petitions; and those petitioners, he meant especially the journeymen mechanics, would find the repeal of the Act of Elizabeth rather materially serviceable, than in any degree injurious to their interests.

The Bill was read a second time, and ordered to be committed on Tuesday.

[The apprenticeship regulations of the 5 Eliz. c. 4 were abolished by 54 Geo. III. 96, 1814.]

14. Resolutions of the Watchmakers on Apprenticeship [*Report of Committee on Petitions of the Watchmakers*, 1817 (*VI*)], 1817.

1. That the obvious intention of our ancestors, in enacting the statute of the 5 Elizabeth, cap. 4, was to produce and maintain a competent number and perpetual succession of masters and journeymen, of practical experience, to promote, secure, and render permanent the prosperity of the national arts and manufactures, honestly wrought by their ability and talents, inculcated by a mechanical education, called a seven years' apprenticeship; whereby according to the memorable words of the statute itself " it will come to pass, that the same law (being duly executed) should banish idleness, advance husbandry, and yield unto the hired person, both in time of

scarcity and in time of plenty, a convenient proportion of wages."

2. That it is by apprenticeships, that the practitioners in the arts and manufactures attain the high degree of perfection, whereby British productions have arrived at the great estimation in which they were heretofore held in foreign markets.

8. That the apprenticed artisans have, collectively and individually, an unquestionable right to expect the most extended protection from the Legislature, in the quiet and exclusive use and enjoyment of their several and respective arts and trades, which the law has already conferred upon them as a property, as much as it has secured the property of the stockholder in the public funds; and it is clearly unjust to take the whole of the ancient established property and rights of any one class of the community, unless, at the same time, the rights and property of the whole commonwealth should be dissolved, and parcelled out anew for the public good.

10. That in consequence of too minute a division of labour, injudiciously allowed in several manufactures, the workmen employed are not enabled to make throughout any one article however simple, or even to maintain themselves by their industry.

11. That the unlimited or promiscuous introduction of various descriptions of persons without apprenticeship into the manufactures occasions a surplus of manufacturing poor, and an unnecessary competition, ruinous to the commercial capital and industry of the nation; because the overflow of goods causes all the productions of the manufacturies to fall in price, and be sold to foreigners for less money than they cost in making; which deficiencies are necessarily made up by the ruin of the master manufacturers, bankruptcies, and dividends to creditors; and are the cause of increased parochial and other rates, thus necessarily created, for the support of the poor workmen, who are deprived of the fair price of their honest labour.

17. That the system of apprenticeships, whether considered in a religious, political or moral point of view, is highly beneficial to the State, and from the neglect thereof is to be attributed the great defalcation of public morals, the numerous frauds committed in trade, the increased numbers of juvenile criminals, public trials and executions.

18. That the pretensions to the allowance of universal uncontrolled freedom of action to every individual founded upon the same delusive theoretical principles which fostered the French Revolution, are wholly inapplicable to the insular situation of this Kingdom, and if allowed to prevail, will hasten the destruction of the social system so happily arranged in the existing form and substance of the British constitution, established by law.

19. That the meeting highly approves the proceedings of the 62,875 masters and journeymen, who have already presented petitions, to the House of Commons, praying for leave to bring a Bill into Parliament to amend, extend and make more effectual the statute of apprenticeship, 5 Elizabeth, chap. 4.

21. That the most effectual preventive against and check upon combinations of journeymen, as also of masters in any trade, is for the persons engaged in such trades to take apprentices as required by law.

15. Report of Committee on the Ribbon Weavers [*Report of Committee on the Ribbon Weavers*, 1818 (*IX*)], 1818.

Your Committee also report, That it appears by the examination that the silk, and ribbon weavers in particular, are and have been for some time past suffering great privations and distress, arising out of inadequate wages; that such distress has had the effect of reducing thousands of them to seek parochial aid, and have, in consequence, increased the poor-rate, especially in the parishes of Coventry and in the County of Warwick, where the ribbon trade is the staple manufacture, to an extent too burdensome to be much longer borne.

That the low rate of wages complained of by the Petitioners is not in consequence of the want of trade, it having been proved to your committee that there are as many silk goods, particularly ribbons, now making, as at any former time.

That a system of half-pay apprenticeship has been resorted to, which has been attended with ruinous consequences to the morals of such apprentices, and exceedingly injurious to the trade.

That the evils complained of do not exist in London, Westminster, and Middlesex; which your committee believe to be owing to the provisions of the act called the Spitalfields Act, which extend to those places, the effects of which are fully detailed in the evidence.

That the whole of the masters and weavers in the Ribbon Trade concur in the propriety of an extension of the Spitalfields Act.

Your Committee are, therefore, of opinion, that it is absolutely necessary, for the protection of the weavers in the silk trade, and the ribbon trade in particular, and to enable them to support themselves and families, and also for protecting the parishes in which these trades are carried on, that some legislative interference should take place; and your committee think that a remedy could be found in the extension of the provisions of the Spitalfields and Dublin Acts, or at least a trial of that extension for a period of a few years, by way of experiment.

Your committee cannot but remark, that whilst the Statute of 5th Elizabeth, c. 4, was in force, that the distressing circumstances now complained of, never occurred.

3 June, 1818.

16. The Cotton Factory Act of 1819 [*Statutes*, 59 *Geo. III*, 66], 1819.

An Act to make further Provisions for the Regulation of Cotton Mills and Factories, and for the better Preservation of the Health of young Persons employed therein.

I. No child shall be employed in any description of work, for the spinning of cotton wool into yarn, or in any previous preparation of such wool, until he or she shall have attained the full age of nine years.

II. And be it further enacted, that no person, being under the age of sixteen years, shall be employed in any description of work whatsoever, in spinning cotton wool into yarn, or in the previous preparation of such wool, or in the cleaning or repairing of any mill, manufactory or building, or any millwork or machinery therein, for more than twelve hours in any one day, exclusive of the necessary time for meals; such twelve hours to be between the hours of five o'clock in the morning and nine o'clock in the evening.

III. And be it further enacted, that there shall be allowed

to every such person, in the course of every day, not less than half an hour to breakfast, and not less than one full hour for dinner; such hour for dinner to be between the hours of eleven o'clock in forenoon and two o'clock in the afternoon.

IV. Provided nevertheless, and be it further enacted, that if at any time, in any such mill, manufactory or buildings as are situated upon streams of water, time shall be lost in consequence of the want of a due supply, or of an excess of water, then and in every such case, and so often as the same shall happen, it shall be lawful for the proprietors of any such mill, manufactory or building, to extend the before mentioned time of daily labour, after the rate of one additional hour per day, until such lost time shall have been made good, but no longer.

V. And be it further enacted, that the ceilings and interior walls of every such mill, manufactory, or building shall be washed with quick lime and water twice in every year.

17. OASTLER'S FIRST LETTER ON YORKSHIRE SLAVERY [*The Leeds Mercury, Saturday, October* 16, 1830], 1830.

Slavery in Yorkshire.

To the editors of the Leeds Mercury.

"It is the pride of Britain that a Slave cannot exist on her soil; and if I read the genius of her constitution aright, I find that Slavery is most abhorrent to it—that the air which Britons breathe is free—the ground on which they tread is sacred to liberty."

Rev. R. W. Hamilton's Speech at the Meeting held in the Cloth-Hall Yard, Sept. 22nd, 1830.[1]

Gentlemen,—No heart responded with truer accents to the sounds of liberty which were heard in the Leeds Cloth-hall yard, on the 22nd instant, than did mine, and from none could more sincere and earnest prayers arise to the throne of Heaven, that hereafter Slavery might only be known to Britain in the pages of her history. One shade alone obscured my pleasure, arising not from any difference in principle, but from the want

[1] September 22, 1830, an anti-Slavery meeting at the Coloured Cloth Hall, Leeds, addressed by Lord Morpeth, Henry Brougham, etc., in favour of the abolition of Slavery in the British colonics.

of application of the general principle *to the whole Empire.* The pious and able champions of *Negro* liberty and *Colonial* rights should, if I mistake not, have gone farther than they did; or perhaps, to speak more correctly, before they had travelled so far as the West Indies, should, at least for a few moments, have sojourned in our immediate neighbourhood, and have directed the attention of the meeting to scenes of misery, acts of oppression and victims of Slavery, even on the threshold of our homes!

Let the truth speak out, appalling as the statements may appear. The fact is true. Thousands of our fellow-creatures and fellow-subjects, both male and female, the inhabitants of a *Yorkshire-town*, (Yorkshire now represented in Parliament by the giant of anti-slavery principles,[1]) are at this very moment existing in a state of slavery *more horrid* than are the victims of that hellish system—"*Colonial Slavery.*" These innocent creatures drawl out unpitied their short but miserable existence, in a place famed for its profession of religious zeal, whose inhabitants are ever foremost in *professing* "Temperance" and "Reformation," and are striving to outrun their neighbours in Missionary exertions, and would fain send the Bible to the farthest corner of the Globe—aye in the very place where the anti-slavery fever rages most furiously, her *apparent charity* is not more admired on earth, than her *real* cruelty is abhorred in heaven. The very streets which receive the droppings of an "Anti-Slavery Society" are every morning wet with the tears of innocent victims at the accursed shrine of avarice, who are compelled (not by the cart-whip of the negro slave-driver) but by the dread of the equally appalling thong or strap of the overlooker, to hasten half-dressed, *but not half-fed*, to those magazines of British Infantile Slavery—*the Worsted Mills in the town and neighbourhood of Bradford!!!*

. . . . .

Thousands of little children, both male and female, *but principally female*, from SEVEN to fourteen years, are daily *compelled* to *labour* from six o'clock in the morning to seven in the evening with only—Britons, blush whilst you read it!—*with only thirty minutes allowed for eating and recreation.*

. . . . .

[1] Brougham.

The Blacks may be fairly compared to beasts of burden *kept for their master's use.* The whites to those *which others keep and let for hire*! If I have succeeded in calling the attention of your readers to the horrid and abominable system on which the worsted mills in and near Bradford are conducted, I have done some good. Why should not children working in them be protected by legislative enactments, as well as those who work in cotton mills. Christians should feel and act for those whom Christ so eminently loved and declared that "of such is the kingdom of heaven."

Your insertion of the above in the Leeds Mercury, at your earliest convenience, will oblige, Gentlemen,

Your most obedient servant,

Richard Oastler.

Fixby Hall, near Huddersfield, Sept. 29th, 1830.

18. Factory Act [*Statutes*, 3 *and* 4 *Wm. IV*, 103], 1833.

An Act to regulate the Labour of Children and young Persons in the Mills and Factories of the United Kingdom.

. . . no person under eighteen years of age shall be allowed to work in the night, that is to say between the hours of half-past eight o'clock in the evening and half-past five o'clock in the morning, except as hereinafter provided, in or about any cotton, woollen, worsted, hemp, flax, tow, linen, or silk mill or factory. . . .

II. And be it further enacted, that no person under the age of eighteen years shall be employed in any such mill or factory in such description of work as aforesaid more than twelve hours in any one day, nor more than sixty-nine hours in any one week, except as hereinafter provided.

VI. And be it further enacted, that there shall be allowed in the course of every day not less than one and a half hours for meals to every such person restricted as hereinbefore provided to the performance of twelve hours work daily.

VII. And be it enacted, that from and after the first day of January one thousand eight hundred and thirty-four it shall not be lawful for any person whatsoever to employ in any factory or mill as aforesaid, except in mills for the manufacture of silk, any child who shall not have completed his or her ninth year of age.

VIII. And be it further enacted, that from and after the expiration of six months after the passing of this act, it shall not be lawful for any person whatsoever to employ, keep, or allow to remain in any factory or mill as aforesaid for a longer time than forty-eight hours in any one week, nor for a longer time than nine hours in any one day, except as herein provided, any child who shall not have completed his or her eleventh year of age, or after the expiration of eighteen months from the passing of this act any child who shall not have completed his or her twelfth year of age, or after the expiration of thirty months from the passing of this act any child who shall not have completed his or her thirteenth year of age: Provided nevertheless, that in mills for the manufacture of silk children under the age of thirteen years shall be allowed to work ten hours in any one day.

[XI. No child under thirteen to be employed without a certificate that the child is of normal strength and appearance.]

XVII. . . . it shall be lawful for His Majesty by Warrant under his Sign Manual to appoint during His Majesty's pleasure four persons to be Inspectors of factories and places where the labour of children and young persons under eighteen years of age is employed, . . . and such Inspectors or any of them are hereby empowered to enter any factory or mill, and any school attached or belonging thereto, at all times and seasons by day or by night, when such mills or factories are at work. . . .

XVIII. And be it further enacted, that the said Inspectors or any of them shall have power and are hereby required to make all such rules, regulations, and orders as may be necessary for the due execution of this act, which rules, regulations, and orders shall be binding on all persons subject to the provisions of this act; and such inspectors are also hereby authorised and required to enforce the attendance at school of children employed in factories according to the provisions of this act. . . .

XX. And be it further enacted, that from and after the expiration of six months from the passing of this act, every child hereinbefore restricted to the performance of forty-eight hours of labour in any one week shall, so long as such child shall be within the said restricted age, attend some school. . . .

19. PROPOSALS FOR A WAGES BOARD FOR HAND-LOOM WEAVERS [*First Report from Committee on Hand-loom Weavers' Petitions*, 1834 (*X*), *pp.* 48–9], 1834.

Evidence of Hugh Mackenzie, June 28, 1834.

Have the goodness to explain to the Committee . . . what are the boards of trade for which you have sent up petitions to the House ?

We have endeavoured upon many occasions to make this system of a board of trade, which we pray for, as well understood as possible. . . . Now the old Spitalfields Act every one that is not friendly to the present proposed plans of boards of trade never fails to bring forward as an objection, as a thing which has been practically tried and failed. There is, however, nothing more different. The Spitalfields Act carried its own ruin in its constitution ; it was framed upon the principle of being local, and confined to one place only. It was impossible that such an act could stand long, for whilst competition went on in the country, other manufacturers who were only at ten miles distance, or anywhere where the act did not extend, were at liberty to set up the same kind of work, and pay for it, without any transgression of the law, at a great reduction. This being the case, the trade of Spitalfields then began to spread to different parts of the country where the act did not extend ; the consequence was, that Spitalfields was soon undersold by cheaper goods than it could make itself, and this led to the ruin of the Spitalfields Act. But had the thing been made general, and extended over the whole nation, the towns in the neighbourhood could not have underwrought Spitalfields ; they would have been on the same footing. Had that act been made general, it would have been very good for the country at large ; not the fixed price that the Spitalfields Act contained, but the minimum, the lowest price ; it might rise and fall according to the circumstances of the trade. Now our views of it are exactly and principally founded upon that ; a board of trade that shall extend over the whole nation, and that it shall be under one superintending head. We suppose that that superintending head could be nothing short of His Majesty's Board of Trade in London, and that boards of trade in local places in the country, who are only branches, locally established, not to do as themselves pleased, but they are to be all subordinate to one general board: that these boards shall be at all times guided by the circumstances of the times; and that this data, or lowest minimum of price, shall be taken from what the manufacturer or manufacturers of respectability are able and willing to pay, provided that others were obliged to pay the same prices with him, and that he could not be undersold in the market: that the foreign trade shall by no means be excluded from the consideration of the board; they are to be taken into consideration whether it is expedient that the prices shall be brought down a little, or up a little, just as the nature of trade might require. . . .

Have you any parties introduced in these boards of trade consisting of masters and workmen, who would belong to neither party, who would act in conjunction with them in arbitrating where there was a difference of opinion whether the master paid too little or too much wages? Yes, we had conceived that the self-interest of both parties might induce them to differ, supposing an equal number of manufacturers and weavers composed this board; and one party under such circumstances must of course be in the wrong. Now the only arbiter that could be brought forth under such circumstances must be a neutral, that was pretty well versed in the nature of trade, and that arbitrator could be none other than His Majesty's Board of Trade in London.

In Glasgow or anywhere in Scotland, have you a board of trade in operation upon the principles you approve of, that you think would answer all purposes? It is going on just now; it is working at Paisley very finely, and at Glasgow.

. . . .

Just explain those principles as far as you can? The working of the Paisley board at the present time, and the working of the Glasgow board, are exactly upon the same principles. The principle is this, that for all the species of work made at Paisley, the manufacturers made out a table of prices, and the weavers made out another; they were reciprocally handed to each other for correction, and the result was, they came to a mutual agreement; they entered into a 12 months' agreement, that they would issue no more work out to their workmen below the minimum price fixed, say it was 1*s*. for a certain fabric.[1]

20. Coal Mines Regulation Act [*Statutes* 5 *and* 6, *Victoria* 99], 1842.

An Act to prohibit the employment of women and girls in mines and collieries, to regulate the employment of boys, and to make other provisions relating to persons working therein.

. . . That from and after the passing of this act it shall not be lawful for any owner of any mine or colliery whatsoever to employ any female person within any mine or colliery, or permit any female person to work or be therein, for the purpose of working therein, other than such as were at or before the passing of this act employed within such mine or colliery; and that from and after three calendar months from the passing of this act it shall not be lawful for any owner of any mine or colliery to employ any female person who at the passing of this act shall be under the age of eighteen years within any mine or colliery. . . .

II. . . . That from and after the first day of March, one thousand eight hundred and forty-three, it shall not be lawful for any owner of any mine or colliery to employ any male person under the age of ten years . . . other than such as at the passing of this act shall have attained the age of nine years, and were at or before the passing of this act employed within such mine or colliery.

III. . . . That it shall be lawful for one of Her Majesty's principal Secretaries of State, if and when he shall think fit, to appoint any proper person or persons to visit and inspect any mine or colliery; and it shall be lawful for every person

[1] *Cf.* Fielden's proposals, as reported by the Committee's Second Report, 1835 (XIII), p. 14.

"The principal feature of Mr. Fielden's Bill is, that returns shall be made every three or six months of the prices of weaving paid by the smallest number of manufacturers, who collectively made one-half of the goods of any description in the parish or township whence the returns are sent, and the average of the highest prices paid by a majority of such manufacturers, shall be the lowest price to be paid in such parish or township during the succeeding three or six months. The effects of the measure would be to withdraw from the worst-paying masters the power which they now possess of regulating wages, and to confer it upon those whose object it is to raise the condition and character of the workpeople."

so authorised to enter and examine such mine or colliery . . . at all times and seasons, by day or by night, and to make inquiry touching any matter within the provisions of this act; . . .

[VII. No provision of the Act to affect employment on the surface.]

X. And whereas the practice of paying wages to workmen at public houses is found to be highly injurious to the best interests of the working classes; be it therefore enacted, that from and after the expiration of three months from the passing of this act no proprietor or worker of any mine or colliery, or other person, shall pay or cause to be paid any wages . . . at or within any tavern, public house, beer shop, or other house of entertainment.

[XI. Wages so paid can be recovered as if no payment made.]

21. Debate on Factory Legislation [*Parliamentary Debates, 3rd Series, Vol.* 73, *Cols.* 1073–1151], 1844.

Hours of Labour in Factories. House of Commons in Committee on the Factories Bill. March 15, 1844.

Lord Ashley rose to propose the amendment of which he had given notice—

"That, the word 'night' shall be taken to mean from six o'clock in the evening to six o'clock in the following morning; and the word 'mealtime' shall be taken to mean an interval of cessation from work for the purpose of rest and refreshment, at the rate of two hours a day, with a view to effect a limitation of the hours of labour to ten in the day."

The form of my amendment (said the noble Lord) requires some preliminary explanation. I move it in its present shape at the suggestion of my right hon. friend and the Government, though I fear that in adopting that course I subject myself to some disadvantage. The House will allow me at the outset to explain my amendment. I propose that the word "night," in this clause shall be taken to mean from six o'clock in the evening till six on the following morning, that will leave twelve clear hours during which work shall cease, and I propose further, that out of the twelve hours of day, there shall be two hours during which there shall be a cessation of labour; but that no person shall be affected by this amendment, except those who, under clause ten, are guaranteed against night-work, children, and young persons under thirteen years of age. If I succeed in this amendment it will be necessary to make some corresponding alteration in the eighth clause. The tenth clause I propose to leave, as that will afford an opportunity of giving some relaxation through the summer months. During the winter months, that is from the 15th of October to the 15th of March, hours of labour are not to exceed ten, two being for meals; but during the summer months, that is from the 15th of March to the 15th of October, the hours to be twelve and two for meals, making fourteen in the whole. Now, I would say with a view to conciliate opposition, that though I shall be ready to propose, as I intend to do, to limit the labour of all young persons and children to ten hours in each day, I am yet willing to obtain that object in parts and by degrees; that is, I propose to limit the hours of labour for such persons to eleven hours a day from the 1st of October in the present year, and ten hours a day from the 1st of October, 1845. Nearly eleven years have now elapsed since I first made the proposition to the House which I shall renew this night. Never, at any time, have I felt greater apprehension or even anxiety; not through any fear of personal defeat, for disappointment is "the badge of all our tribe;" but because I know well the hostility that I have aroused, and the certain issues of indiscretion on my part affecting the welfare of those who have so long confided their hopes and interests to my charge.

And here let me anticipate the constant, but unjust, accusation that I am animated by a peculiar hostility against factory masters, and I have always selected them as exclusive objects of attack. I must assert that the charge, though specious, is altogether untrue. I began, I admit, this public movement by an effort to improve the condition of the factories; but this I did, not because I ascribed to that department of industry a monopoly of all that was pernicious and cruel, but because it was then before the public eye, comprised the wealthiest and most responsible proprietors, and presented the greatest facilities for legislation.

As soon as I had the power, I showed my impartiality by moving the House for the Children's Employment Commission. The curious in human suffering may decide on the respective merits of the several reports; but factory labour has no longer an unquestionable pre-eminence of ill fame; and we are called upon to give relief, not because it is the worst system, but because it is oppressive, and yet capable of alleviation. Sir, I confess that ten years of experience have taught me that avarice and cruelty are not the peculiar and inherent qualities of any one class or occupation—they will ever be found where the means of profit are combined with great and, virtually, irresponsible power—they will be found wherever interest and selfishness have a purpose to serve, and a favourable opportunity.

. . . . .

This will conclude the statement that I have to make to the House—and now, sir, who will assert that these things should be permitted to exist? Who will hesitate to apply the axe to the root of the tree, or, at least, endeavour to lop off some of its deadliest branches? What arguments from general principles will they adduce against my proposition? What, drawn from peculiar circumstances? They cannot urge that particular causes in England give rise to particular results; the same cause prevails in various countries; and wherever it is found, it produces the same effects. I have already stated its operation in France, in Russia, in Switzerland, in Austria, and in Prussia; I may add also in America; for I perceive by the papers of the 1st of February, that a Bill has been proposed in the Legislature of Pennsylvania, to place all persons under the age of sixteen within the protection of the "ten hours" limit. I never thought that we should have learned justice from the City of Philadelphia. In October last I visited an immense establishment in Austria, which gives employment to several hundred hands; I went over the whole, and conversed with the managers, who detailed to me the same evils and the same fruits as those I have narrated to the House—prolonged labour of sixteen, and seventeen hours, intense fatigue, enfeebled frame, frequent consumptive disorders, and early deaths—yet the locality had every advantage; well-built and airy houses in a fine open country, and a rural district; nevertheless, so injurious are the effects, that the manager added, stating at the same time the testimony of many others who resided in districts where mills are more abundant, that, in ten years from the time at which he spoke, "there would hardly be a man in the whole of those neighbourhoods fit to carry a musket."

Let me remind, too, the House of the mighty change which has taken place among the opponents to this question. When I first brought it forward in 1833, I could scarcely number a dozen masters on my side, I now count them by hundreds. We have had, from the West Riding of Yorkshire, a petition signed by 300 mill-owners, praying for a limitation of labour to ten hours in the day. Some of the best names in Lancashire openly support me. I have letters from others who secretly wish me well, but hesitate to proclaim their adherence; and even among the members of the Anti-Corn-Law League, I may boast of many firm and efficient friends. Sir, under all the aspects in which it can be viewed, this system of things must be abrogated or restrained—it affects the internal tranquillity of those vast provinces, and all relations between employer and employed—it forms a perpetual grievance and ever comes uppermost among their complaints in all times of difficulty and discontent. It disturbs the order of nature, and the rights of the labouring men, by ejecting the males from the workshop, and filling their places by females, who are thus withdrawn from all their domestic duties and exposed to insufferable toil at half the wages that would be assigned to males, for the support of their families. It affects—nay, more, it absolutely annihilates, all the arrangements and provisions of domestic economy—thrift and management are altogether impossible; had they twice the amount of their present wages, they would be but slightly benefited—everything runs to waste; the house and children are deserted; the wife can do nothing for her husband and family; she can neither cook, wash, repair clothes, nor take charge of the infants; all must be paid for out of her scanty earnings, and, after all, most imperfectly done. Dirt, discomfort, ignorance, recklessness, are the portion of such households; the wife has no time for learning in her youth, and none for practice in her riper age; the females are most unequal to the duties of the men in the factories; and all things go to rack and ruin, because the men can discharge at home no one of the especial duties that Providence has assigned to the females. Why need I detain the House by a specification of these injurious results? They will find them stated at painful length in the Second Report of the Children's Employment Commission. Consider it, too, under its physical aspect! Will the House turn a deaf ear to the complaints of suffering that resound from all quarters? Will it be indifferent to the physical consequences on the rising generation? You have the authority of the Government Commissioner, Dr. Hawkins, a gentleman well skilled in medical statistics—

> "I have never been (he tells you) in any town in Great Britain or in Europe, in which degeneracy of form and colour from the national standard has been so obvious as in Manchester."

I have, moreover, the authority of one of the most ardent antagonists, himself a mighty millowner, that, if the present system of labour be persevered in, the "county of Lancaster will speedily become a province of pigmies." The toil of the females has hitherto been considered the characteristic of savage life; but we, in the height of our refinement, impose on the wives and daughters of England a burthen from which, at least during pregnancy, they would be exempted even in slave-holding states, and among the Indians of America. But every consideration sinks to nothing compared with that which springs from the contemplation of the moral mischiefs this system engenders and sustains. You are poisoning the very sources of order and happiness and virtue; you are tearing up, root and branch, all the relations of families to each other; you are annulling, as it were, the institution of domestic life, decreed by Providence Himself, the wisest and kindest of earthly ordinances, the mainstay of social peace and virtue, and therein of national security.

Right Hon. Sir J. R. G. Graham[1]*:*

Sir, I never rose to discharge any duty in this House which I considered at the same time more painful and more imperative. The pain, I must admit, is considerably increased by the eloquence of the address which my noble friend has just concluded, and especially of the passage which marked the close of his speech. The noble lord has asked whether any man will be found in this House to resist the proposal which he has thought it his duty to make, and he has appealed to considerations of justice and mercy, intimating, if not directly,

[1] *Ibid.* Cols. 1101-2 and 1108-9.

at least by implication, that resistance to his motion is inconsistent both with justice and mercy. I, on the other hand, having due regard to those sacred principles which my noble friend has invoked, am bound, on my own part, and on the part of the Government, to offer to the proposal of the noble Lord my decided opposition.

The noble lord said, the time is come when, in his opinion, it is necessary to lay the axe to the root of the tree. Before we do this let me entreat the Committee carefully to consider what is that tree which we are to lay prostrate. If it be, as I suppose, the tree of the commercial greatness of this country, I am satisfied that although some of its fruits may be bitter, yet upon the whole it has produced that greatness, that wealth, that prosperity, which make these small islands most remarkable in the history of the civilised world, which, upon the whole, diffuse happiness amidst this great community, and render this nation one of the most civilised, if not the most civilised, and powerful on the face of the globe.

* * * * * *

My noble friend stated that he would not enter into the commercial part of the question; but if I can show that the inevitable result of the abridgement of time will be the diminution of wages to the employed, then I say, with reference to the interests of the working classes themselves, there never was a more doubtful question before Parliament than this. The House will remember that the branches of manufacture affected by this Bill are dependent upon machinery. Such is the rapidity with which improvements are made, that no machinery can last more than twelve or thirteen years without alterations; and master manufacturers have been obliged to pull down machinery that was perfectly sound and good to make the necessary alterations which competition forces upon them. Well, then, it is necessary to replace machinery in the course of twelve or thirteen years. You are now discussing whether you shall abridge by one-sixth the period of time in which capital is to be replaced, all interest upon it paid, and the original outlay restored. Such an abridgement would render it impossible that capital with interest should be restored. Then in the close race of competition which our manufacturers are now running with foreign competitors, it must be considered what effect this reduction of one-sixth of the hours of labour would have upon them. The question in its bearing upon competition must be carefully considered ; and I have been informed that in that respect such a step would be fatal to many of our manufacturers—a feather would turn the scale: an extra pound weight would lose the race. But that would not be the first effect. The first effect would fall upon the operative. It is notorious that a great part of the power of the mill-owners, a power which alone justifies such legislation as this, arises from the redundant supply of labour. It follows that when a master is pressed upon by your legislation, he will compensate himself by forcing upon those in his employ a decrease of wages. I believe the large majority of intelligent operatives comprehend that proposition thoroughly. I have seen many, and conversed with them, and they have admitted that the proposal involves a necessary decrease of wages. In the report presented in 1841 by my excellent friend Mr. Horner, who has discharged with the most honourable fidelity the duty of inspector of factories, there is information upon this point, and with the permission of the House I will read a passage—a single passage only—but one which goes to the root of the whole subject. Mr. Horner said:

> "I have made an estimate of the loss a mill would sustain from working eleven hours a day only instead of twelve, and I find it would amount to £850 per annum. If it were reduced to ten hours, it would be about £1,530 per annum. Unless, therefore, the mill-owner can obtain a proportionately higher price for the commodity, he must reduce wages or abandon his trade. I have made some calculations as to the probable reduction of wages, and of the whole loss that would be thrown on the operatives. I make the amount in the case of eleven hours a day to be 13 per cent., and in the case of ten hours a day 25 per cent. at the present average rate of wages."

Now, I believe this to be perfectly accurate. The question then arises, whether you shall create in the manufacturing districts one sudden general fall of wages to the amount of 25 per cent? I believe that the adoption of the motion of my noble friend would produce that effect. Though I am most anxious to take every precaution with regard to infant labour—though I am as firmly resolved as my noble friend to urge upon the House to put a limit upon female labour, still, upon the whole, I cannot recommend the House to adopt an enactment which limits the labour of young persons to a shorter period than twelve hours.

Mr. T. Milner Gibson[1]:

As the right hon. baronet had alluded to the argument of not destroying the profits upon manufactures, he (Mr. Gibson) would read some remarks upon that point by Mr. Senior, a gentleman whose name would be of great weight with hon. members. In 1836 or 1837, Mr. Senior, with some other gentlemen, went into the manufacturing districts with the view of ascertaining the effect of factory legislation, and making observations upon the factory population. Mr. Senior wrote a letter dated the 28th March, 1837, to Mr. Poulett Thomson to the following effect:—

> "Under the present law, no mill in which persons under eighteen years of age are employed (and, therefore, scarcely any mill at all), can be worked more than eleven and a half hours a day, that is twelve hours for five days in a week, and nine on Saturday. The following analysis will show that in a mill so worked the whole net profit is derived from the last hour. I will suppose a manufacturer of 100,000*l*.–80,000*l*. in his mill and machinery, and 20,000*l*. in raw material and wages. The annual return of that mill, supposing the capital to be turned once a year, and gross profits to be 15 per cent., ought to be goods worth 115,000*l*. produced by the constant conversion and re-conversion of the 20,000*l*. circulating capital, from money into goods and from goods into money, in periods of rather more than two months. Of this 115,000*l*., each of the 23 half hours of work produces 5–115ths, or 1–23rd. Of these 23-23rds (constituting the whole 115,000*l*.) 20, that is to say, 100,000*l*. out of the 115,000*l*., simply replace the capital; 1-23rd (or 5,000*l*. out of the 115,000*l*.) makes up for the deterioration of the mill and machinery. The remaining 2–23rds, the last two of the twenty-three half hours of every day, produce the net profit of 10 per cent. If, therefore (prices remaining the same), the factory could be kept at work thirteen hours instead of eleven

[1] *Ibid.* Cols. 1111-2.

and a half, by an addition of about 2,600*l.* to the circulating capital, the net profit would be more than doubled. On the other hand, if the hours of working were reduced by one hour per day (prices remaining the same), net profit would be destroyed; if they were reduced by an hour and a half, even gross profit would be destroyed. The circulating capital would be replaced, but there would be no fund to compensate the progressive deterioration of the fixed capital."

It was clear that this principle of Mr. Senior's was sound, and if hon. gentlemen would consider it carefully they would find it indisputable. The House would consider whether they would not, as the right hon. baronet had expressed it, be affecting the safety and stability of the great staple manufactures, under the impression that they were legislating humanely for the working classes, while, in point of fact, the result would be that by the depreciation of manufactures, the greatest possible injury would be inflicted upon the operatives.

Mr. J. Bright[1] said, It is with unfeigned reluctance that I rise to speak, having so recently addressed the House at some length, but being intimately connected with the branch of industry which is affected by the proposition now under consideration, and having lived all my life among the population most interested in this Bill, and having listened most attentively for more than two hours to the speech of the noble lord, the member for Dorsetshire, I think I am entitled to be heard on the question now under discussion. I have listened to that speech without much surprise, because I have heard or read the same speech, or one very like it, on former occasions, and I did not suppose that any material change had taken place in the opinions of the noble lord. It appears to me, however, that he has taken a one-sided view, a most unjust and unfair view of the question; it may not be intentionally, but still a view which cannot be borne out by facts; a view, moreover, which factory inspectors and their reports will not corroborate, and one which, if it influence the decision of this House, will be most prejudicial to that very class which the noble lord intends to serve. The right hon. baronet, the Secretary for the Home Department, who is, I presume, the promoter of this Bill, should have given the House some reason for the

[1] *Ibid.* Cols. 1132-5, 1148 and 1150-1.

introduction of a new Factory Bill. No such reason has yet been given, and I am at a loss to discover any grounds on which it can with fairness be asserted that the Bill now in operation has failed in its effect. I know the inspectors affirm that it cannot be fully carried out. Every body who knows anything of the manufactories of the North, knew when it was passed that it could not be fully carried out; and the proposition now made, is to render this impracticable Act more stringent. In a trade so extensive, employing so many people, carried on under circumstances ever varying, no Act of Parliament interfering with the minute details of its management, can ever be fully carried out. I am not one who will venture to say that the manufacturing districts of this country are a paradise; I believe there are in those districts evils great and serious; but whatever evils do there exist are referable to other causes than to the existence of factories and long chimneys. Most of the statements which the noble lord has read, would be just as applicable to Birmingham, or to this metropolis, as to the northern districts; and as he read them over, with respect to the ignorance and intemperance of the people, the disobedience of children to their parents, the sufferings of mothers, and the privations which the children endure, I felt that there was scarcely a complaint which has been made against the manufacturing districts of the north of England, which might not be urged with at least as much force against the poorest portion of the population of every large city in Great Britain and Ireland. But among the population of Lancashire and Yorkshire, where towns are so numerous as almost to touch each other, these evils are more observable than in a population less densely crowded together. I can prove, however, and I do not wish to be as one-sided as the noble lord, I can prove from authorities, which are at least as worthy of attention as his, the very reverse in many respects of what he has stated as the true state of those districts. Now the Committee will bear in mind that a large portion of the documents which the noble lord has quoted, have neither dates nor names. I can give dates and names, and I feel confident that the authorities I shall cite are worthy of the deepest attention. I must go over the grounds of complaint which the noble lord has urged, and although I may run the risk of being a little tedious, yet considering that for two hours or more I have listened to the charges which he has made, I do think that, connected as I am most intimately with the population and the district to which the noble lord has alluded, I have a right to an audience for the counter-statement which I have to make. Now, with respect to the health of the persons employed, and I will speak more particularly of the cotton trade, with which I am more immediately connected, Mr. Harrison, the inspecting surgeon for Preston, says :—

> "I have made very particular inquiries respecting the health of every child whom I have examined, and I find that the average annual sickness of each child is not more than four days ; at least not more than four days are lost by each child in a year in consequence of sickness. This includes disorders of every kind, for the most part induced by causes wholly unconnected with factory labour. I have been not a little surprised to find so little sickness which can fairly be attributed to mill work. I have met with very few children who have suffered from injuries occasioned by machinery ; and the protection, especially in new factories, is now so complete, that accidents will, I doubt not, speedily become rare. I have not met with a single instance, out of 1,656 children whom I examined, of deformity that is referable to factory labour. It must be admitted that factory children do not present the same blooming, robust appearance, as is witnessed among children who labour in the open air ; but I question if they are not more exempt from acute disease, and do not, on the whole, suffer less sickness than those who are regarded as having more healthy employments."

This was the statement of a man who had for a long time been inspecting-surgeon in a district where there are a large number of mills, and it may be taken as a fair criterion of the rest. In the analysis of the Factory Report, page 16, I find the following statement :—

> "In conclusion, then, it is proved, by a preponderance of seventy-two witnesses against seventeen, that the health of those employed in cotton mills is nowise inferior to that in other occupations ; and, secondly, it is proved by tables drawn up by the secretary of a sick club, and by the more extensive tables of a London actuary, that

the health of the factory children is decidedly superior to that of the labouring poor otherwise employed."

From the Factory Inspector's Reports in 1834 I have extracted the following testimony, and no doubt this evidence is quite as good as if it had been given this year; for from that time to this there has been a progressive improvement in everything relating to the management of the factories of the north of England.

> "The general tenor of all the medical reports in my possession confirms Mr. Harrison's view of factory labour on the health of the younger branches of working hands. It is decidedly not injurious to health or longevity, compared with other employments." Then, in page 51, Mr. Saunders says, "It appears in evidence, that of all employments to which children are subjected, those carried on in factories are among the least laborious, and of all departments of in-door labour, amongst the least unwholesome." Mr. Horner says, "It is gratifying to be able to state, that I have not had a single complaint laid before me either on the part of the masters against their servants, or of the servants against their masters; nor have I seen or heard of any instance of ill-treatment of children, or of injury to their health by their employment." And on the 21st of July, 1834, speaking on the employment of children, he says: "And as their occupation in the mills is so light as to cause no bodily fatigue, they would pass their eight hours there as beneficially as at home; indeed, in most cases, far more so."

. . . . . .

I think I have now said enough with regard to this part of the subject—apparently too much for hon. gentlemen opposite, who appear only anxious to hear and applaud one side, and many of whom have not even heard that. But notwithstanding all these facts I admit there are evils, serious evils, and much distress in the manufacturing districts; many are still out of employment, and in many branches of trade wages are low. We have violent fluctuations in trade, and periods when multitudes endure great suffering and it becomes this House to inquire why do these fluctuations occur, and what is the great cause of their suffering. I attribute much of this to the mistaken and unjust policy pursued by this House, with respect to the trade and industry of the country. Hitherto manufacturers have had no fair chance: you have interfered with their natural progress, you have crippled them by your restrictions, you have at times almost destroyed them by monopolies, you have made them the sources of your public revenue, and the upholders of your rents, but at your hands they have never to this moment received justice and fair dealing. I do not charge the noble lord with dishonesty, but I am confident if he had looked at this question with as anxious a desire to discover truth, as he has to find materials for his case, he would have found many subjects of congratulation to counterbalance every one which he would have had reason to deplore. The noble lord and hon. gentlemen opposite, when they view from their distant eminence the state of the manufacturing districts, look through the right end of the telescope; what they see is thus brought near to them, and is greatly magnified; but when they are asked to look at the rural districts, they reverse the telescope and then everything is thrown to the greatest possible distance and is diminished as much as possible.

. . . . . .

The noble lord, the Member for Liverpool, says, he is most anxious to improve the condition of the working classes; he points to more education, a higher state of morals, better food and better clothing, as the result of the adoption of the proposition now before the House. But there is one thing that the noble lord has failed to prove; he has failed to show how working only ten hours will give the people more sugar. The noble lord is the representative of the sugar monopolists of Liverpool, and, after voting to deprive the people of sugar, he is perfectly consistent in denying them the liberty even to work. The people ask for freedom for their industry, for the removal of the shackles on their trade; you deny it to them, and then forbid them to labour, as if working less would give them more food, whilst your monopoly laws make food scarce and dear. Give them liberty to work, give them the market of the world for their produce, give them the power to live comfortably, and increasing means and increasing intelligence will speedily render them independent enough and wise enough to bring the duration of labour to that point at which life shall be passed with less of irksome toil of every kind, and more of recreation and enjoyment. It is because I am convinced this project is now impracticable, and that under our present oppressive legislation, it would make all past injustice only more intolerable, that I shall vote against the proposition which the noble lord, the member for Dorset, has submitted to the House.

22. Factory Act [*Statutes* 7 *ana* 8, *Victoria* 15], 1844.

An Act to amend the Laws relating to Labour in Factories.

XX. And be it enacted, that no child or young person shall be allowed to clean any part of the mill-gearing in a factory while the same is in motion for the purpose of propelling any part of the manufacturing machinery; and no child or young person shall be allowed to work between the fixed and traversing part of any self-acting machine while the latter is in motion by the action of the steam engine, water-wheel, or other mechanical power.

XXI. And be it enacted, that every fly-wheel directly connected with the steam engine or water-wheel or other mechanical power, whether in the engine house or not, and every part of a steam engine and water-wheel, and every hoist or teagle, near to which children or young persons are liable to pass or be employed, and all parts of the mill-gearing in a factory, shall be securely fenced; and every wheel-race not otherwise secured shall be fenced close to the edge of the wheel-race; and the said protection to each part shall not be removed while the parts required to be fenced are in motion by the action of the steam engine, water-wheel, or other mechanical power for any manufacturing process.

XXIV. And be it enacted, that one of Her Majesty's principal Secretaries of State, on the report and recommendation of an inspector, may empower such inspector to direct one or more actions to be brought in the name and on behalf of any person who shall be reported by such inspector to have received any bodily injury from the machinery of any factory, for the recovery of damages for and on behalf of such person.

XXIX. And be it enacted, that every child who shall have completed his eighth year, and shall have obtained the surgical certificate required by this act of having completed his eighth year, may be employed in a factory in the same manner and under the same regulations as children who have completed their ninth year; but no child under eight years of age shall be employed in any factory.

XXX. And be it enacted, that no child shall be employed in any factory more than six hours and thirty minutes in any one day, save as herein-after excepted, unless the dinner time of the young persons in such factory shall begin at one of the clock, in which case children beginning to work in the morning may work for seven hours in one day; and no child who shall have been employed in a factory before noon of any day shall be employed in the same or any other factory, either for the purpose of recovering lost time or otherwise, after one of the clock in the afternoon of the same day, save in the cases when children may work on alternate days, or in silk factories more than seven hours in any one day, as herein-after provided.

XXXI. And be it enacted, that in any factory in which the labour of young persons is restricted to ten hours in any one day it shall be lawful to employ any child ten hours in any one day on three alternate days of every week, provided that such child shall not be employed in any manner in the same or in any other factory on two successive days, nor after half past four of the clock in the afternoon of any Saturday: Provided always, that the parent or person having direct benefit from the wages of any child so employed shall cause such child to attend some school for at least five hours between the hours of eight of the clock in the morning and six of the clock in the afternoon of the same day on each week day preceding each day of employment in the factory, unless such preceding day shall be a Saturday, when no school attendance of such child shall be required: Provided also, that on Monday in every week after that in which such child began to work in the factory, or any other day appointed for that purpose by the inspector of the District, the occupier of the factory shall obtain a certificate from a school-master, according to the form and directions given in the schedule (A) to this act annexed, that such child has attended school as required by this act; but it shall not be lawful to employ any child in a factory more than seven hours in any one day, until the owner of the factory shall have sent a notice in writing to the inspector of the district of his intention to restrict the hours of labour of young persons in the factory to ten hours a day, and to employ children ten hours a day; and if such occupier of a factory shall at any time cease so to employ children ten hours a day he shall not again employ any child in his factory more than seven hours in any one day until he shall have sent a further notice to the inspector in the manner herein-before provided.

XXXII. And be it enacted, that no female above the age of eighteen years shall be employed in any factory save for the same time and in the same manner as young persons may be employed in factories; and that any person who shall be convicted of employing a female above the age of eighteen years for any longer time or in any other manner shall for every such offence be adjudged to pay the same penalty as is provided in the like case for employing a young person contrary to law: provided always, that nothing herein or in the Factory Act contained as to certificates of age shall be taken to apply to females above the age of eighteen years.

23. RECOMMENDATIONS OF THE COMMISSION ON THE HEALTH OF TOWNS [*Second Report of Commissioners on State of Large Towns and Populous Districts* (*XVIII*), 1845, *pp.* 13–68], 1845.

That in all cases the local administrative body appointed for the purpose have the special charge and direction of all the works required for sanitary purposes, but that the Crown possess a general power of supervision.

That before the adoption of any general measure for drainage a plan and survey upon a proper scale, including all necessary details, be obtained, and submitted for approval to a competent authority.

That the Crown be empowered to define and to enlarge from time to time the area for drainage included within the jurisdiction of the local administrative body.

That, upon representation being made by the municipal or other authority, or by a certain number of the inhabitants of any town or district, or part thereof, setting forth defects in the condition of such place, as to drainage, sewerage, paving, cleansing, or other sanitary matters, the Crown appoint a competent person to inspect and report upon the state of the defects, and, if satisfied of the necessity, have power to enforce upon the local administrative body the due execution of the law.

That the management of the drainage of the entire area, as defined for each district, be placed under one jurisdiction.

That the construction of sewers, branch sewers, and house drains, be entrusted to the local administrative body.

That the duty of providing the funds necessary to be imposed upon the local administrative body, and that the cost of making the main and branch sewers be equitably distributed among the owners of the properties benefited; and that the expense of making the house-drains be charged upon the owners of the house, to which the drains are attached, etc.

That some restriction be placed on the proportionate rates in the pound to be levied in one year, but if the local administrative body finds that there is need for larger funds, for the immediate execution of works for sanitary measures, than can be provided by such rates, it be empowered to raise, by loan on security of the rates, subject to the approval of the Crown, such sums as may be requisite for effecting the objects in view.

That provision always be made for the gradual liquidation of such debts, within a given number of years.

That the whole of the paving, and the construction of the surface of all streets, courts and alleys be placed under the management of the same authority as the drainage.

That the provisions in local Acts, vesting the right to all the dust, ashes, and street refuse in the local administrative body, be made general; and that the cleansing of all privies and cess-pools at proper times, and on due notice, be exclusively entrusted to it.

That it be rendered imperative on the local administrative body, charged with the management of the sewerage and drainage, to procure a supply of water in sufficient quantities not only for the domestic needs of the inhabitants, but also for cleansing the streets, scouring the sewers and drains, and the extinction of fire. . . .

That measures be adopted for promoting a proper system of ventilation in all edifices for public assemblage and resort, especially those for the education of youth.

That, on complaint of the parish medical or other authorised officer, that any house or premises are in such a filthy and unwholesome state as to endanger the health of the public, and an infectious disorder exists therein, the local administrative body have power to require the landlord to cleanse it properly, without delay; and in case of his neglect or inability, to do so by its own officers, and recover the expense from the landlord.

That the local administrative body have power to appoint, subject to the approval of the Crown, a medical officer properly qualified to inspect and report periodically upon the sanitary condition of the town or district, to ascertain the true causes of disease and death, more especially of epidemics increasing the rates of mortality, and the circumstances which originate and maintain such diseases, and injuriously affect the public health of such town or populous district.

[Provisions for abating factory exhalations and nuisances; for regulating the width of new courts, the accommodation of cellar-dwellings and the sanitation of new houses; for power to buy out new water companies at the end of a term of years; for controlling lodging-houses; for providing public spaces and walks.][1]

[1] The first general Public Health Act (1848) was based on this report and that of the Select Committee on the Health of Towns, 1840 (XI)

SECTION IV

COMBINATIONS OF WORKMEN

1. A Strike of the Journeymen Feltmakers, 1696–99—2. A Petition of Master Tailors against Combination among the Journeymen, 1721—3. A Dispute in the Northumberland and Durham Coal Industry, 1765—4. Sickness and Unemployment Benefit Clubs among the Woolcombers, 1794—5. Combination Act, 1799—6. Combination Act, 1800—7. The Scottish Weavers' Strike, 1812—8. The Repeal of the Combination Acts, 1824—9. A Prosecution of Strikers under the Common Law of Conspiracy, 1810—10. An Act Revising the Law affecting Combinations, 1825—11. The Conviction of the Dorchester Labourers, 1834—12. An Address of the Working Men's Association to Queen Victoria, 1837—13. A Chartist Manifesto on the Sacred Month, 1839—14. The Rochdale Pioneers, 1844.

The history of modern Trade Unions is separated from that of earlier combinations by the industrial changes of the eighteenth century and by the alterations in the law affecting them. Illustrations of combinations are given from the seventeenth century (No. 1), the early middle and later eighteenth century (Nos. 2, 3 and 4) and the early nineteenth century (Nos. 7 and 11). The most important changes in the law were made towards the close of the period (Nos. 5, 6, 8, 10).

The strike of the Journeymen Feltmakers (No. 1) shows a well-organised body of London craftsmen at the end of the seventeenth century fighting the chartered Company on a wages question in a time of rising prices. The struggle was long, and ended, in 1699, in arbitration by Members of Parliament. The Journeymen Tailors' combination against which the Master Tailors appealed to Parliament in 1721 (No. 2) was also a London organisation, and claimed to control the hours of labour as well as wages. The woolcombers (No. 4) were early famous for combined action, and their system was remarkable for the way in which it combined a fighting trade policy with Friendly Benefit. The declaration of the miners in the northern coalfield (No. 3) refers to one of the recurring struggles over the yearly Bindings. The result of the strike is unknown.

The Master Tailors and the employers in some other trades were successful in procuring special Acts of Parliament forbidding combinations (No. 2, note). At the end of the eighteenth century the two general Combination Acts made most kinds of trade union action specifically illegal (No. 5 and No. 6). Combination still survived, but their leaders were always open to attack in emergencies like that of the Scotch weavers' strike (No. 7). Their special liability under the Act of 1800 was removed in 1824, and, though an outburst of strikes led to a revision of the law, the skilled assistance of Francis Place and Hume saved the Trade Unions from being thrust back into their former position (Nos. 8 and 10). But organised striking could also be brought within the common law of conspiracy. Strikers had been proceeded against in this way before (No. 9); and this liability remained after 1825, as well as liability under an Act against oaths of secrecy (No. 11). The case of the Dorchester agricultural labourers (No. 11) also serves to illustrate the great, though short-lived enthusiasm of the Trade Union movement in the 'thirties. Its failure was followed by the rise of Chartism. The immediate objects of the Chartists were political, but their real grievances and ideals were economic, as their early manifestos plainly show (No. 12); and their leaders wavered between political methods and the direct action of the general strike (No. 13). The Rochdale Pioneers co-operative society (No. 14) was founded in the middle of this period of Trade Union and Chartist agitation, and illustrates a third parallel development of working-men's combinations under the stress of the Industrial Revolution.

AUTHORITIES

Modern books: The standard history is S. and B. Webb, *History of Trade Unionism*: for the legal position, Dicey, *Law and Opinion in England*; Schloesser and Clark, *Legal Position of Trade Unions*; for the seventeenth century, Unwin, *Industrial Organization.* Miners' combinations are described in Fynes, *The Miners of Northumberland and Durham,* Tailors' Combinations in Galton, *The Tailoring Trade* (Select Documents, Introduction). Wallas' *Life of Francis Place* gives an account of the repeal of the Combination Acts, Podmore, *Life of Owen,* describes the forward movement among trade unions. For early co-operative history see Holyoake, *The Rochdale Pioneers.* The most complete accounts of the Chartists are in Dolléans' *Chartisme,* and *Beer, Geschichte des Socialismus in England,* Part II, of which an English translation is to appear shortly.

Bibliographies in S. and B. Webb, *op. cit.* and *Industrial Democracy*; Unwin, *op. cit.*, Galton, *op. cit.*. Cunningham *op. cit.*, and Fay, *Co-operation at Home and Abroad.*

Contemporary.—1. *Documentary authorities*: Records of a seventeenth century strike are printed in Unwin, *Industrial Organisation,* App. A. Petitions by weavers, feltmakers, etc., are to be found in the House of Commons Journals, Vols. 27, 36 and *passim.* Galton, *op. cit.*, covers the eighteenth century. For collections of price lists, *e.g.*, tailors, printers, brushmakers, bookbinders, basketmakers, see Webb., *op. cit.* bibliography; also for early rules and minutes of the Unions of keelmen, cotton spinners, miners, etc. Official material for the history of the Combination Acts and their repeal is in the Report from Committee on Artizans and Machinery, 1824 (V), and on Combination Acts, 1825 (IV). There was a Report on Friendly Societies in 1825 (X).

2. *Literary authorities.*—Descriptions by those who were actors in the events of the early nineteenth century are given in the Life of Robert Owen (by himself), in The Life and Struggles of William Lovett (by himself), and The Life of Thomas Cooper (by himself). Early Trade and Chartist Journals are important sources:—The United Trades Co-operative Journal, 1830, The Poor Man's Guardian, 1831-5, The Crisis 1832–4, The Ten Hours' Advocate, 1846–7, The Stone Masons' Circular, 1834. Other material for the early history of combinations is to be found in rare pamphlets, such as A Voice from the Coal Mines, 1825 (see Webb Bibliographies, *op. cit.*).

1. A Strike of the Journeymen Feltmakers[1] [*Feltmakers' Court Book*], 1696–99.

November 16*th*, 1696. It is agreed and ordered by this Court that from and after the 21st day of this present month

[1] Quoted in Unwin, *Industrial Organization in the Sixteenth and Seventeenth Centuries,* App. A, pp. 248-52.

of November until the month of September next coming, the wages to be given by the master workmen of the Mistery living within the city of London and four miles compass of the same to the journeymen of the trade making of hats shall be as followeth (that is to say) :—

	s.	d.	
A Beaver	3	0	with diet.
A hat of any price from 18s. to a Beaver ..	2	6	,, ,,
,, ,, 16s. price	2	4	,, ,,
,, ,, 14s. ,, ...	2	2	,, ,,
,, ,, 12s. ,, ...	1	10	,, ,,
,, ,, 10s. ,, ...	1	6	,, ,,
,, ,, 8s. or any other price up to 10s.	1	2	,, ,,
,, ,, 7s. or 6s.	1	0	,, ,,
,, ,, 5s.	0	9	,, ,,

And also that if the journeymen free of this Company do not accept of the wages before set down and expressed of, and from any workmaster living within the limits aforesaid, then and in such case it shall and may be lawful for all and every workmaster living without the freedom of the city to employ and set to work as a journeyman any person or persons of the Mistery being natives of this kingdom, so as such person or persons in that case to be employed make proof before a Court of Assistants of this Company that he or they have served his or their apprenticeship of seven years in the said Mistery. Upon which proof so made and on payment of the sum of twenty shillings fine to the use of the Company, besides the Clerk and Beadle fees according to ancient custom, such person or persons may be admitted a foreign journeyman or journeymen of this Company, any byelaw or byelaws, ordinance or ordinances of this Company to the contrary thereof in any wise notwithstanding. And it is further ordered that none of the masters or journeymen of the Mistery do give or take more than the rates above mentioned upon pain that the party offending shall forfeit for every time he shall be found to act contrary to the true meaning of the above order such sum of money, not exceeding the sum of 5*l*., as the Court of Assistants of this Company shall think fit to impose on him or them.

. . . . . .

Nov. 30*th*, 1696. Geo. Burkeridge and others to the number of 12 journeymen of the Mistery to this Court on behalf of themselves and all the journeymen of the trade within the limits of the Corporation, that they are come to a resolution among themselves not to accept of any less wages for making of hats than what they formerly received and desire that the late Order for lessening their wages may be set aside.

. . . . . .

June 20th, 1698. George Burkeridge, Thomas Newby and one other journeyman came to this Court on behalf of themselves and the other journeymen for the accommodation of the matters in difference between them and the Company, and offered that in order thereto all matters relating to the trade might stand on the same foot as in 1682 and suits touching the singeing boys to be forborne. After long debate thereupon had, the Court acquainted them, that if they would give an ingenuous account and full discovery of their combinations and collections of money against the Company by Wednesday next, they might expect some favour, which the journeymen promised to comply with.

August 5th, 1698. The Master reported to this Court that the committee appointed last Court to meet several journeymen of the trade with Mr. Cox and Mr. Cholmley in order to accommodate the matters in difference between the masters and journeymen, who had then declared their sorrow for their unlawful combinations to raise their wages and promised to subscribe an Instrument declaring the same, and that they would for the future be obedient to the bye-laws of the Company and discover all such evil practices. And a draft of such Instrument or submission being read, it is ordered that the same be engrossed with such alteration as the Clerk shall think fit and be signed by the persons indicted and fifteen more of such of the journeymen as the Master and Wardens shall direct. And thereupon the prosecutions shall be stayed. [The Instrument.]

We whose hands are hereunto subscribed and set, being journeymen Feltmakers in and about the city of London and borough of Southwark, do hereby acknowledge:—that we with other journeymen of the said trade have held several meetings wherein we have conspired and combined together to enhance the prices for making of hats, for which several of us now stand indicted, and being now greatly sensible and fully convinced of the unlawfulness of such conspiracies do hereby declare our hearty and unfeigned sorrow for the same, and we and every one of us do hereby promise and agree to and with the Master, Wardens and Commonalty of the Company of Feltmakers, London, that neither we nor any of us (nor any other journeyman of the trade with our or any of our privity or consent) shall or will at any time hereafter do any act or thing whatsoever that may in any wise tend to the promoting or encouraging of such conspiracies or combinations. But that we and every of us shall and will do all that in us lieth to discourage and prevent such conspiracies and combinations for the future, and also will endeavour to raise and collect money among the journeymen Feltmakers what they shall freely contribute and pay towards prosecuting the French or any other unlawful workers in the said Trade. And for that purpose shall and will truly pay such money that shall be raised by such contributions into the hands of the Master of the said Company for the time being. And we do further promise that we will for the time to come behave and demean ourselves tractable and conformable to the government and bye-laws of the said Company.

July 3rd, 1699. The Masters reported to this Court that on Tuesday last he attended, with others of the Company, on the Parliament Members for the County of Surrey, according to a Rule of the Court made by the Lord Chief Justice Holt at the last Assizes at Kingston. And after hearing them and the defendants and other journeymen of the trade, they made an award and therein made no other alteration of the rates than 2*d*. allowance on a Beaver, a penny on a 14*s*. hat, and a penny allowance on an 8*s*., and so on to a 10*s*. hat, and they directed the indictment to be discharged and bill in Chancery to be dismissed.

2. A Petition of Master Tailors Against Combination Among the Journeymen[1] [*British Museum, f.* 816 *m.*, 14 (*II*)], 1721.

"The case of the Master Tailors residing within the Cities of London and Westminster, in relation to the great Abuses committed by their Journeymen. Humbly offered to the consideration of Parliament.

The Journeymen Tailors in and about the cities of London

[1] Quoted in F. W. Galton, *The Tailoring Trade*, pp. 1-4.

and Westminster, to the number of seven thousand and upwards, have lately entered into a combination to raise their wages, and leave off working an hour sooner than they used to do ; and for the better carrying on their design, have subscribed their respective names in books prepared for that purpose, at the several houses of call or resort (being public houses in and about London and Westminster) where they use ; and collect several considerable sums of money to defend any prosecutions against them.

At this time there are but few of them come to work at all, and most of those that do, insist upon, and have, twelve shillings and ninepence per week (instead of ten shillings and ninepence per week, the usual wages), and leave off work at eight of the clock at night (instead of nine, their usual hour, time out of mind), and very great numbers of them go loitering about the town, and seduce and corrupt all they can meet: to the great hindrance and prejudice of trade.

Upon complaint made to some of His Majesty's Justices of the Peace, they have issued out their warrants against these offenders as loiterers ; by virtue whereof some of them have been bound over to the Sessions, and others have been taken up, and bound over to appear in His Majesty's Court of King's Bench at Westminster, and the subscription books seized by virtue of the Secretary of State's warrant: Yet they still continue obstinate, and persist not only in putting the abovesaid difficulties upon their masters, to the great prejudice of trade in general ; but also in collecting great sums of money to support their unlawful combinations and confederacies.

This combination of the Journeymen Tailors is and may be attended with many evil consequences : inasmuch as the public is deprived of the benefit of the labour of a considerable number of the subjects of this kingdom, and the families of several of these journeymen thereby impoverished, and likely to become a charge and burden to the public : And the very persons themselves who are under this unlawful combination, choosing rather to live in idleness, than to work at their usual rates and hours, will not only become useless and burdensome, but also very dangerous to the public ; and are of very ill example to journeymen in all other trades ; as is sufficiently seen in the Journeymen Curriers, Smiths, Farriers, Sail-makers, Coach-makers, and artificers of divers other arts and misteries, who have actually entered into confederacies of the like nature ; and the Journeymen Carpenters, Bricklayers and Joiners have taken some steps for that purpose, and only wait to see the event of others.

These Journeymen Tailors, when there is a hurry of business against the King's Birth-day, or for making of mourning or wedding garments (as often happens) or other holidays, and always the summer seasons, are not content with the unreasonable rates they at present insist upon ; but have demanded, and have had three or four shillings a day, and sometimes more ; otherwise they will not work ; and at such times some will not work at all ; which is a great disappointment to gentlemen, and an imposition to the masters ; and, if suffered to go on, must increase the charge of making clothes considerably.

As to the said houses of call, or public-houses, there are a great number of them in London and the suburbs, where these journeymen tailors frequently meet and use, and spend all or the greatest part of the moneys they receive for their wages ; and the masters of these houses of call, support, encourage and abet these journeymen in their unlawful combinations for raising their wages, and lessening their hours.

The laws now in being for regulating of artificers, labourers, and servants, were made in the fifth of Queen Elizabeth, and might well be adapted for these times ; but not altogether so proper for the trade of London and Westminster, &c., as it is now carried on.

Therefore, the masters humbly hope this honourable house will take such measures, by passing of a law for redress of the public grievances aforesaid, or grant such other relief, as in their great wisdom shall seem meet.[1]

[1] A Committee of the House of Commons reported on this petition "that the petitioners have fully proved the allegations," February 16, 1721. The Journeymen petitioned in reply. Stat. 7 Geo. I, 1 c. 3 (1721) declared combinations among the journeymen tailors unlawful in London, Westminster, and the Bills of Mortality, and fixed the hours of labour, thirteen, and the maximum wages, two shillings a day, from the end of March to the end of June, and one and eightpence for the rest of the year. Justices were given power to alter the rates at Quarter Sessions.

3. A Dispute in the Northumberland and Durham Coal Industry [*Newcastle Chronicle, September* 21, 1765], 1765.

Whereas several scandalous and false reports have been and still continue to be spread abroad in the country concerning the Pitmen in the Counties of Durham and Northumberland absenting from their respective employments before the expiration of their Bonds: This is therefore to inform the Public that most of the Pitmen in the aforesaid Counties of Durham and Northumberland were bound the latter end of August, and the remainder of them were bound the beginning of September, 1764, and they served till the 24th or 25th of August, 1765, which they expect is the due time of their servitude; but the honourable Gentlemen in the Coal Trade will not let them be free till the 11th of November, 1765, which, instead of 11 months and 15 days, the respective time of their Bonds, is upwards of 14 months. So they leave the most censorious to judge whether they be right or wrong. For they are of opinion that they are free from any Bond wherein they were bound.—And an advertisement appearing in the newspapers last week commanding all persons not to employ any Pitmen whatever for the support of themselves and families, it is confidently believed that they who were the authors of the said advertisement are designed to reduce the industrious poor of the aforesaid counties to the greatest misery: as all the necessaries of Life are at such exorbitant prices, that it is impossible for them to support their families without using some other lawful means, which they will and are determined to do, as the said advertisement has caused the people whom they were employed under to discharge them from their service:—Likewise the said honourable Gentlemen have agreed and signed an Article, not to employ any Pitmen that has served in any other colliery the year before; which will reduce them to still greater hardships, as they will be obliged to serve in the same colliery for life; which they conjecture will take away the ancient character of this Kingdom as being a free nation.—So the Pitmen are not designed to work for or serve any of the said Gentlemen, in any of their collieries, till they be fully satisfied that the said Article is dissolved, and new Bonds and Agreements made and entered into for the year ensuing.

4. Sickness and Unemployment Benefit Clubs among the Woolcombers [*House of Commons Journals, Vol.* XLIX, *pp.* 323–4], 1794.

March 13, 1794. Report on Woolcombers' Petitions, 323.

William Gates being asked whether it was usual to go from place to place to seek employment, he said it was, and that their clubs or societies subsist them till they get work. . . . And being asked, whether there are any number of woolcombers who do not belong to the societies, he said, "There are some, but not one in one hundred that does not belong to some society."

Jonathan Sowton . . . was asked, of what nature the clubs were. He said, "It is a contribution upon every woolcomber (who is willing to be a member of a club) according to the exigencies of their affairs: the one end of it is to enable the woolcombers to travel from place to place to seek for employment, when work is scarce where he resides; and the other end of it is to have relief when he is sick wherever he may be; and if he should die to be buried by the club; and it is necessary for him, to entitle himself to be relieved by these clubs, to have a certificate from the club to which he belongs, that he has behaved well in and to the woolcombing trade, and that he is an honest man; but if he defrauds anybody, he loses his claim to that certificate, and to the advantages belonging to it."[1]

5. Combination Act [*Statutes*, 39 *Geo. III*, 86], 1799.

. . . All contracts, covenants, and agreements whatsoever, in writing or not in writing, at any time or times heretofore made or entered into by any journeymen manufacturers or other workmen, or other persons within this kingdom, for obtaining an advance of wages of them or any of them, or any other journeymen manufacturers or other workmen, or other persons in manufacture, trade, or business, or for lessening or

[1] *Cf.* A Proclamation against combinations in the Woolcombing Industry (in Notes and Queries, Series III, Vol. 12, September 21, 1867, pp. 224-5) in February, 1718, reciting that their Societies interfered in questions of prices and apprentices and, if a member was thrown out of work on account of such interference, "they fed them with money till they could again get employment, in order to oblige their masters to employ them for want of other hands."

altering their or any of their usual hours or time of working or for decreasing the quantity of work, or for preventing or hindering any person or persons from employing whomsoever he, she, or they shall think proper to employ in his, her, or their manufacture, trade, or business, in the conduct or management thereof, shall be and the same are hereby declared to be illegal, null, and void, to all intents and purposes whatsoever.

[Workmen making such agreements or combinations, or endeavouring to prevent others from hiring themselves or to induce them to quit work, or attending a meeting or persuading others to attend a meeting for such purposes, are made liable to three months imprisonment in common gaol or two months in the house of correction.]

6. Combination Act [*Statutes*, 39 *and* 40 *Geo. III*, *c.* 106], 1800.

An Act to repeal an Act, passed in the last session of Parliament, intituled, An Act to prevent unlawful combinations of workmen; and to substitute other provisions in lieu thereof.

[All contracts heretofore entered into for obtaining an advance of wages, altering the usual time of working, decreasing the quantity of work, &c. (except contracts between masters and men) shall be void.]

II. And be it further enacted, that no journeyman, workman, or other person shall at any time after the passing of this act make or enter into, or be concerned in the making of or entering into any such contract, covenant, or agreement, in writing or not in writing, as is herein-before declared to be an illegal covenant, contract, or agreement; and every journeyman and workman or other person who, after the passing of this act, shall be guilty of any of the said offences, being thereof lawfully convicted, within three calendar months next after the offence shall have been committed, shall, by order of such justices, be committed to and confined in the common gaol, within his or their jurisdiction, for any time not exceeding three calendar months, or at the discretion of such justices shall be committed to some house of correction within the same jurisdiction, there to remain and to be kept to hard labour for any time not exceeding two calendar months.

III. And be it further enacted, that every journeyman or workman, or other person, who shall at any time after the passing of this act enter into any combination to obtain an advance of wages, or to lessen or alter the hours or duration of the time of working, or to decrease the quantity of work, or for any other purpose contrary to this act, or who shall, by giving money, or by persuasion, solicitation, or intimidation, or any other means, wilfully and maliciously endeavour to prevent any unhired or unemployed journeyman or workman, or other person, in any manufacture, trade, or business, or any other person wanting employment in such manufacture, trade, or business, from hiring himself to any manufacturer or tradesman, or person conducting any manufacture, trade, or business, or who shall, for the purpose of obtaining an advance of wages, or for any other purpose contrary to the provisions of this act, wilfully and maliciously decoy, persuade, solicit, intimidate, influence, or prevail, or attempt or endeavour to prevail, on any journeyman or workman, or other person hired or employed, or to be hired or employed in any such manufacture, trade, or business, to quit or leave his work, service, or employment, or who shall wilfully and maliciously hinder or prevent any manufacturer or tradesman, or other person, from employing in his or her manufacture, trade, or business, such journeymen, workmen, and other persons as he or she shall think proper, or who, being hired or employed, shall, without any just or reasonable cause, refuse to work with any other journeyman or workman employed or hired to work therein, and who shall be lawfully convicted of any of the said offences, shall, by order of such justices, be committed to and be confined in the common gaol, within his or their jurisdiction, for any time not exceeding three calendar months; or otherwise be committed to some house of correction within the same jurisdiction, there to remain and to be kept to hard labour for any time not exceeding two calendar months.

IV. And for the more effectual suppression of all combinations amongst journeymen, workmen, and other persons employed in any manufacture, trade or business, be it further enacted, that all and every persons and person whomsoever, (whether employed in any such manufacture, trade, or business, or not), who shall attend any meeting had or held for the purpose of making or entering into any contract, covenant, or agreement, by this act declared to be illegal, or of entering into, supporting, maintaining, continuing, or carrying on any combination for any purpose by this act declared to be illegal, or who shall summons, give notice to, call upon, persuade, entice, solicit, or by intimidation, or any other means, endeavour to induce any journeyman, workman, or other person employed in any manufacture, trade, or business, to attend any such meeting, or who shall collect, demand, ask, or receive any sum of money from any such journeyman, workman, or other person, for any of the purposes aforesaid, or who shall persuade, entice, solicit, or by intimidation, or any other means, endeavour to induce any such journeyman, workman, or other person to enter into or be concerned in any such combination, or who shall pay any sum of money, or make or enter into any subscription or contribution, for or towards the support or encouragement of any such illegal meeting or combination, and who shall be lawfully convicted of any of the said offences, within three calendar months next after the offence shall have been committed, shall, by order of such justices, be committed to and confined in the common gaol within his or their jurisdiction, for any time not exceeding three calendar months, or otherwise be committed to some house of correction within the same jurisdiction, there to remain and be kept to hard labour for any time not exceeding two calendar months.

VI. And be it further enacted, that all sums of money which at any time heretofore have been paid or given as a subscription or contribution for or towards any of the purposes prohibited by this act, and shall, for the space of three calendar months next after the passing of this act, remain undivided in the hands of any treasurer, collector, receiver, trustee, agent, or other person, or placed out at interest, and all sums of money which shall at any time after the passing of this act, be paid or given as a subscription or contribution for or towards any of the purposes prohibited by this act, shall be forfeited, one moiety thereof to his Majesty, and the other moiety to such person as will sue for the same in any of his Majesty's courts of record at Westminster ; and any treasurer, collector, receiver, trustee, agent, or other person in whose hands or in whose name any such sum of money shall be, or shall be placed out, or unto whom the same shall have been paid or given, shall and may be sued for the same as forfeited as aforesaid.

[All contracts between masters or other persons for reducing the wages of workmen or for altering the hours of work or for increasing the quantity of work, are to be void. Masters convicted of such agreements, shall be fined 20*l.*: half to go to the Crown, half to the informer and the poor of the parish.]

XVIII. And whereas it will be a great convenience and advantage to masters and workmen engaged in manufactures, that a cheap and summary mode be established for settling all disputes that may arise between them respecting wages and work; be it further enacted by the authority aforesaid, that, from and after the first day of August in the year of our Lord one thousand eight hundred, in all cases that shall or may arise within that part of Great Britain called England, where the masters and workmen cannot agree respecting the price or prices to be paid for work actually done in any manufacture, or any injury or damage done or alleged to have been done by the workmen to the work, or respecting any delay or supposed delay on the part of the workmen in finishing the work, or the not finishing such work in a good and workmanlike manner, or according to any contract; and in all cases of dispute or difference, touching any contract or agreement for work or wages between masters and workmen in any trade or manufacture, which cannot be otherwise mutually adjusted and settled by and between them, it shall and may be, and it is hereby declared to be lawful for such masters and workmen between whom such dispute or difference shall arise as aforesaid, or either of them, to demand and have an arbitration or reference of such matter or matters in dispute; and each of them is hereby authorized and empowered forthwith to nominate and appoint an arbitrator for and on his respective part and behalf, to arbitrate and determine such matter or matters in dispute as aforesaid by writing, subscribed by him in the presence of and attested by one witness, in the form expressed in the second schedule to this Act; and to deliver the same personally to the other party, or to leave the same for him at his usual place of abode, and to require the other party to name an arbitrator in like manner within two days after such reference to arbitrators shall have been so demanded; and such arbitrators so appointed as aforesaid, after they shall have accepted and taken upon them the business of the said arbitration, are hereby authorised and required to summon before them, and examine upon oath the parties and their witnesses, (which oath the said arbitrators are hereby authorised and required to administer according to the form set forth in the second schedule to this act), and forthwith to proceed to hear and determine the complaints of the parties, and the matter or matters in dispute between them; and the award to be made by such arbitrators within the time being after limited, shall in all cases be final and conclusive between the parties; but in case such arbitrators so appointed shall not agree to decide such matter or matters in dispute, so to be referred to them as aforesaid, and shall not make and sign their award within the space of three days after the signing of the submission to their award by both parties, that then it shall be lawful for the parties or either of them to require such arbitrators forthwith and without delay to go before and attend upon one of his Majesty's justices of the peace acting in and for the county, riding, city, liberty, division, or place where such dispute shall happen and be referred, and state to such justice the points in difference between them the said arbitrators, which points in difference the said justice shall and is hereby authorised and required to hear and determine and for that purpose to examine the parties and their witnesses upon oath, if he shall think fit.[1]

7. THE SCOTTISH WEAVERS' STRIKE [*Report from Committee on Artizans and Machinery*, 1824 (*V*), *pp.* 60–63], 1812.

Evidence of Mr. Alex. Richmond. 23 February, 1824.

Were you one of the delegates appointed by the workmen in Glasgow?

Yes; on the failure of the last application to Parliament the association turned its attention to some Acts of Parliament that were discovered, empowering the justices of the peace to affix rates of wages, with a view to raising the wages; the fact was, fluctuation was a greater evil perhaps, than the lowness of the rate; previous to that period, fluctuations, to the extent of thirty per cent., took place in the course of a

[1] Compare Pt. III. Section III, Nos. 7 and 8 Arbitration Acts, pp. 568 & 570.

month, in the price of labour; an attempt was made to get an extra-judicial arrangement with the masters; the masters were divided in opinion upon the point, some of them were for a regulation, others opposed it; after several ineffectual attempts to come to an arrangement with that part of the masters who opposed it, part of the masters being in the interest of the operatives, at last a process was entered before the quarter sessions.

Will you state how the process proceeded?

The justices of the peace found the rate demanded reasonable; it was amended in some instances, and the masters immediately refused to pay the rate. Our counsel in the process had consented, for the purpose of obviating the difficulties and getting over the objections that might be made against the expediency, to withdraw the imperative part of the prayer; the prayer of the petition originally founded upon, prayed, that they might be compelled to pay the price, but it was only a declaratory decision, as the imperative part was withdrawn, for the purpose of preventing the difficulty; we then, as the masters refused to pay, tried every method of getting an extra-judicial decision. The present Lord Justice Clerk had been a member of the Committee of the House of Commons in 1809, and appeared decidedly opposed to the principle of interference; and we conceived from the sentiments of the court, that though they had decided the law, if we went on the expediency of the case, we might very likely lose, and we determined therefore to try the experiment of striking work.

What was the result of this strike?

About three weeks after the effort commenced, there was a direct interference, on the part of government, to suppress it, by the apprehension of all the parties concerned.

What do you mean by the apprehension of all the parties concerned?

There was a committee of five, who had conducted the process during the whole period, and we were all apprehended and committed to gaol.

You were one of the five?

I was.

Under what law were you apprehended?

There was no specific law. There was a case I might have

mentioned, but as it applies to the combination, I will introduce it here. In 1811, a combination had taken place amongst the cotton spinners; and in a case that was aggravated by assault, that was tried at the Glasgow circuit, the present Lord President Hope, who then presided, stated it as an aggravation of the crime of combination, that there was a clear remedy in law, as the magistrates had full power and authority to affix rates of wages, or settle disputes: that was the ground on which we entered the action in 1812. In the face of this, after having acted upon it on this principle, the mere act of striking work in a body was construed as an infringement of the Combination Law; and after having acted upon the authority of Lord President Hope, we were convicted, on what law I am yet at a loss to know.

Have there been any combinations, or any individuals prosecuted for combinations, since that period?

The only other branch of the cotton trade that ever had an association or combination efficient in Scotland, was the calico printers, and they were the next that were followed by the suppression of the cotton weavers' branch in 1815.

In what manner were they broken up?

By the interference of government; immediately after this case, the Lord Advocate proceeded against them, as public prosecutor in Scotland.

Were they paid higher than other mechanics?

Yes: their wages frequently averaged from forty to fifty shillings a week, previous to that; now they are down from twelve to fifteen shillings.

8. The Repeal of the Combination Acts [*Statutes*, 5 *Geo. IV*, 95], 1824.

An Act to repeal the Laws relative to the Combination of Workman; and for other purposes.

[A large number of statutes, wholly or partly repealed, including 39 & 40 Geo. III., 106, except the arbitration clauses.]

II. And be it further enacted, that journeymen, workmen or other persons who shall enter into any combination to obtain an advance, or to fix the rate of wages, or to lessen or alter the hours or duration of the time of working, or to decrease the quantity of work, or to induce another to depart from his service before the end of the time or term for which he is hired, or to quit or return his work before the same shall be finished, or, not being hired, to refuse to enter into work or employment, or to regulate the mode of carrying on any manufacture, trade or business, or the management thereof, shall not therefore be subject or liable to any indictment or prosecution for conspiracy, or to any other criminal information or punishment whatever, under the common or the statute law.

III. And be it further enacted, that masters, employers or other persons, who shall enter into any combination to lower or to fix the rate of wages, or to increase or alter the hours or duration of the time of working, or to increase the quantity of work, or to regulate the mode of carrying on any manufacture trade or business, or the management thereof, shall not therefore be subject or liable to any indictment or prosecution, or for conspiracy, or to any other criminal information or punishment whatever, under the common or the statute law.

V. And be it further enacted, that if any person, by violence to the person or property, by threats or by intimidation, shall wilfully or maliciously force another to depart from his hiring or work before the end of the time or term for which he is hired, or return his work before the same shall be finished, or damnify, spoil or destroy any machinery, tools, goods, wares or work, or prevent any person not being hired from accepting any work or employment; or if any person shall wilfully or maliciously use or employ violence to the person or property, threats or intimidation towards another on account of his not complying with or conforming to any rules, orders, resolutions or regulations made to obtain an advance of wages, or to lessen or alter the hours of working, or to decrease the quantity of work, or to regulate the mode of carrying on any manufacture, trade or business, or the management thereof; or if any person, by violence to the person or property, by threats or by intimidation, shall wilfully or maliciously force any master or mistress manufacturer, his or her foreman or agent, to make any alteration in their mode of regulating, managing, conducting or carrying on their manufacture, trade or business; every person so offending, or causing, procuring, aiding, abetting or assisting in such offence, being convicted thereof in manner hereafter mentioned, shall be imprisoned only, or imprisoned and kept to hard labour, for any time not exceeding two calendar months.

VI. And be it further enacted, that if any persons shall combine, and by violence to the person or property or by threats or intimidation, wilfully and maliciously force another to depart from his service before the end of the time or term for which he or she is hired, or return his or her work before the same shall be finished, or damnify, spoil or destroy any machinery, tools, goods, wares or work, or prevent any person not being hired from accepting any work or employment; or if any persons so combined shall wilfully or maliciously use or employ violence to the person or property, or threats or intimidation towards another, on account of his or her not complying with or conforming to any rules, orders, resolutions or regulations made to obtain an advance of wages, or to lessen or alter the hours of working, or to decrease the quantity of work, or to regulate the mode of carrying on any manufacture, trade or business, or the management thereof; or if any persons shall combine, and by violence to the person or property, or by threats or intimidation, wilfully or maliciously force any master or mistress manufacturer, his or her foreman or agent, to make any alteration in their mode of regulating, managing, conducting or carrying on their manufacture, trade or business; each and every person so offending, or causing, procuring, aiding, abetting or assisting in such offence, being convicted thereof in manner hereinafter mentioned, shall be imprisoned only, or imprisoned and kept to hard labour, for any time not exceeding two calendar months.

9. A Prosecution of Strikers Under the Common Law of Conspiracy [*The Times, June* 4, 1824], 1810.

To the Editor of the Times.

Sir,—

That the Committee have proceeded, I will not say rashly, but, upon misinformation, will be evident from a slight attention to the evidence of Mr. Richard Taylor, printer.

In reply to some introductory questions, he states that he has been a printer some 20 years—that he has turned his attention to the combination laws—and that his opinion is, that they are of no service. He afterwards states as follows :—

"There were some men imprisoned for combining a great many years ago, and that created a great deal of misunderstanding; for they were some of the most respectable of the workmen—those who had been intrusted by their fellow-workmen at large to negotiate an advance of prices with the masters; and of course the inflicting of imprisonment on men who are generally respected was a thing which created a great deal of ill-blood: a deal of mischief was the consequence of it."

Mr. Richard Taylor, then, here states that a great deal of mischief was effected by that prosecution. But what will the Committee say, if, when that evidence is put right, it shall be found to reflect not upon the Combination Laws now attempted to be repealed, but upon the old common law, which it is intended to leave in force? Mr. Taylor makes a slight mistake as to the fact; which mistake being corrected, the whole tide of his argument is turned away from the Combination Laws, and made to bear upon the common law for conspiracy. . .

. . . How Mr. Taylor, knowing that some of the offenders in that case were sentenced to two years' imprisonment, and knowing, at the same time, that the Combination Laws do not admit of an imprisonment for more than three months, should yet say that those men were tried upon the Combination Laws, is most inconceivable.

I am, Sir, etc.,

J. W.[1]

10. An Act Revising the Law affecting Combinations [*Statutes*, 6 *Geo. IV*, 109], 1825.

An Act to repeal the Laws relating to the combination of Workmen, and to make other Provisions in lieu thereof.

III. And be it further enacted, that from and after the passing of this act, if any person shall by violence to the person or property or by threats or intimidation, or by molesting or in any way obstructing another, force or endeavour to force any journeyman, manufacturer, workman, or other person hired or employed in any manufacture, trade, or business to depart from his hiring, employment, or work, or to return his work before the same shall be finished, or prevent or

[1] John Walter, proprietor of *The Times*.

endeavour to prevent any journeyman, manufacturer, workman, or other person not being hired or employed from hiring himself to or from accepting work or employment from any person or persons; or if any person shall use or employ violence to the person or property of another, or threats or intimidation, or shall molest or in any way obstruct another for the purpose of forcing or inducing such person to belong to any club or association, or to contribute to any common fund, or to pay any fine or penalty, or on account of his not belonging to any particular club or association, or not having contributed or having refused to contribute to any common fund, or to pay any fine or penalty, or on account of his not having complied or of his refusing to comply with any rules, orders, resolutions, or regulations made to obtain an advance or to reduce the rate of wages, or to lessen or alter the hours of working, or to decrease or alter the quantity of work, or to regulate the mode or carrying on any manufacture, trade, or business, or the management thereof; or if any person shall by violence to the person or property of another, or by threats or intimidation, or by molesting or in any way obstructing another, force or endeavour to force any manufacturer or person carrying on any trade or business to make an alteration in his mode of regulating, managing, conducting, or carrying on such manufacture, trade or business, or to limit the number of his apprentices, or the number or description of his journeymen, workmen or servants; every person so offending, or aiding, abetting, or assisting therein, being convicted thereof in manner hereinafter mentioned, shall be imprisoned only, or shall and may be imprisoned and kept to hard labour, for any time not exceeding three calendar months.

IV. Provided always, and be it enacted, that this act shall not extend to subject any persons to punishment who shall meet together for the sole purpose of consulting upon and determining the rate of wages or prices which the persons present at such meeting, or any of them, shall require or demand for his or their work, or the hours or time for which he or they shall work, in any manufacture, trade or business, or who shall enter into any agreement, verbal or written, among themselves, for the purpose of fixing the rate of wages or prices which the parties entering into such agreement, or any of them, shall require or demand for his or their work, or the hours of time for which he or they will work, in any manufacture, trade, or business; and that persons so meeting for the purposes aforesaid, or entering into any such agreement as aforesaid, shall not be liable to any prosecution or penalty for so doing; any law or statute to the contrary notwithstanding.

V. Provided also, and be it further enacted, that this act shall not extend to subject any persons to punishment who shall meet together for the sole purpose of consulting upon and determining the rate of wages or prices which the persons present at such meeting, or any of them, shall pay to his or their journeymen, workmen, or servants for their work, or the hours, or time of working, in any manufacture, trade, or business; or who shall enter into any agreement, verbal or written, among themselves, for the purpose of fixing the rate of wages or prices which the parties entering into such agreement, or any of them, shall pay to his or their journeymen, workmen, or servants for their work, or the hours or time of working, in any manufacture, trade or business; and that persons so meeting for the purposes aforesaid, or entering into any such agreement as aforesaid, shall not be liable to any prosecution or penalty for so doing, any law or statute to the contrary notwithstanding.

11. The Conviction of the Dorchester Labourers [*The Times, March* 20, 1834], 1834.

Spring Assizes, Western Circuit, Dorchester. Monday, March 17. Crown Court (before Baron Williams). Administering unlawful oaths.

James Lovelace, George Lovelace, Thomas Stanfield, John Stanfield, James Hammet, and James Brine were indicted for administering . . . a certain unlawful oath and engagement, purporting to bind the person taking the same not to inform or give evidence against any associate, and not to reveal or discover any such unlawful combination.[1] . . .

John Lock.—I live at Half Puddle. I went to Toli Puddle a fortnight before Christmas. I know the prisoner James Brine. I saw him that evening at John Woolley's. He called me out and I went with him. He took me to Thomas Stanfield's, and asked me if I would go in with him. I refused and

[1] The indictment was framed on 37 Geo. III, 123, against seditious and illegal confederacies.

went away. I saw him in about a fortnight afterwards in a barn. He asked me if I would go to Toll Puddle with him. I agreed to do so. James Hammet was then with him. Edward Legg, Richard Peary, Henry Courtney, and Elias Riggs were with us. They joined us as we were going along. One of them asked if there would not be something to pay, and one said there would be 1*s.* to pay on entering, and 1*d.* a week after. We all went into Thomas Stanfield's house into a room upstairs. John Stanfield came to the door of the room. I saw James Lovelace and George Lovelace go along the passage. One of the men asked if we were ready. We said, yes. One of them said, "Then bind your eyes," and we took out handkerchiefs and bound over our eyes. They then led us into another room on the same floor. Someone then read a paper, but I don't know what the meaning of it was. After that we were asked to kneel down, which we did. Then there was some more reading; I don't know what it was about. It seemed to be out of some part of the Bible. Then we got up and took off the bandages from our eyes. I had then seen James Lovelace and John Stanfield in the room. Some one read again, but I don't know what it was, and then we were told to kiss the book, when our eyes were unblinded, and I saw the book, which looked like a little Bible. I then saw all the prisoners there. James Lovelace had on a white dress, it was not a smock-frock. They told us the rules, that we should have to pay 1*s.* then, and a 1*d.* a week afterwards, to support the men when they were standing out from their work. They said we were as brothers; that when we were to stop for wages we should not tell our masters ourselves, but that the masters would have a note or a letter sent to them.

. . . . . .

Mrs. Francis Wetham.—I am the wife of a painter in the town. In October, last year, James Lovelace and another person came to our shop; he said he wanted something painted from a design he had brought; he had two papers with him, on one was a representation of a skull, and on the other a skeleton arm extended with a scythe; he said it was to be painted on canvas, a complete skeleton on a dark ground, six feet high; over the head, "Remember thine end." I asked him what it was for, whether a flag or a sign; he told me it was a secret for a society, and he would tell me no more; if I wanted further information I was to send to him, "J. Lovelace, Toll Puddle."

. . . . . .

The following letter was then put in and read:—

Bere Heath, Feb. 1, 1834.

Brother,

We met this evening for the purpose of forming our committee. There was 16 present, of whom 10 was chosen—namely, a president, vice-president, secretary, treasurer, warden, conductor, three outside guardians and one inside guardian. All seemed united in heart, and expressed his approval of the meeting. Father and Hallett wished very much to join us, but wish it not to be known. I advised them to come Tuesday evening at 6 o'clock, and I would send for you to come at that time, if possible, and enter them, that they may be gone before the company come. I received a note this morning which gave me great encouragement, and I am led to acknowledge the force of union.

(Signed by the secretary.)

The following rules were then put in and read:—

General Rules.

1. That this Society be called the Friendly Society of Agricultural Labourers.

. . . . . .

20. That if any master attempts to reduce the wages of his workmen, if they are members of this order, they shall instantly communicate the same to the corresponding secretary, in order that they may receive the support of the grand lodge; and in the meantime they shall use their utmost endeavours to finish the work they may have in hand, if any, and shall assist each other, so that they may all leave the place together, and with as much promptitude as possible.

21. That if any member of this society . . . solely on account of his taking an active part in the affairs of this order . . . shall be discharged from his employment . . . then the whole body of men at that place shall instantly leave that place, and no member of this society shall be allowed to take work at such place until such member be reinstated in his situation.

[22. If a member divulge any secret of the society, members throughout the country shall refuse to work with him.]

23. That the object of this society can never be promoted by any act or acts of violence, but, on the contrary, all such proceedings must tend to injure the cause and destroy the society itself. This order therefore will not countenance any violation of the laws.[1]

12. An Address of the Working Men's Association to Queen Victoria [*The Life and Struggles of William Lovett, pp.* 124–8], 1837.

Madam,

While we approach your Majesty in the spirit of plain men seeking their political and social rights, apart from mere names, forms, or useless ceremonies, we yield to none in the just fulfilment of our duties, or in the ardent wish that our country may be made to advance to the highest point of prosperity and happiness. . . .

The country over which your Majesty has been called on to preside, has by the powers and industry of its inhabitants been made to teem with abundance, and were all its resources wisely developed and justly distributed, would impart ample means of happiness to all its inhabitants.

But, by many monstrous anomalies springing out of the constitution of society, the corruptions of government, and the defective education of mankind, we find the bulk of the nation toiling slaves from birth till death—thousands wanting food, or subsisting on the scantiest pittance, having neither time nor means to obtain instruction, much less of cultivating the higher faculties and brightest affections, but forced by their situation to engender enmity, jealousy, and contention, and too often to become the victims of intemperance and crime.

. . . . . .

The exclusive few have ever been intent in keeping the people ignorant and deluded, and have sedulously administered to their vices and fomented their prejudices. Hence the use of their privileges and distinctions to allure the wealthy and

[1] The prisoners were found Guilty. On March 19 they were sentenced to seven years' transportation. April 16, Lord Howick, in answer to a question in Parliament, said that he believed their ship had already sailed. The remainder of their sentence was remitted in 1836.

corrupt the innocent; hence their desire to retain within their own circle all the powers of the Legislative and Executive, all the riches of Church and State. . . .

To this baneful source of exclusive political power may be traced the persecutions of fanaticism, the feuds of superstition, and most of the wars and carnage which disgrace our history. To this pernicious origin may justly be attributed the unremitted toil and wretchedness of your Majesty's industrious people, together with most of the vices and crimes springing from poverty and ignorance, which, in a country blessed by nature, enriched by art, and boasting of her progress and knowledge, mock her humanity and degrade her character.

. . . . . .

We entreat your Majesty that, whoever may be in your ministry, you will instruct them, as a first and essential measure of reform, to prepare a bill for extending the Right of Suffrage to all the adult population of the kingdom; excepting such as may be justly incapacitated by crime or defection of the light of reason; together with such other essential details as shall enable all men to exercise their political rights unmolested.

13. A Chartist Manifesto on the Sacred Month [*William Lovett, Life and Struggles*, p. 214], 1839.

We respectfully submit the following propositions for your serious consideration[1]:—

That at all the simultaneous public meetings to be held for the purpose of petitioning the Queen to call good men to her councils, as well as at all subsequent meetings of your unions or associations up to the 1st of July, you submit the following questions to the people there assembled:—

1. Whether they will be prepared, at the request of the Convention, to withdraw all sums of money they may individually or collectively have placed in savings banks, private banks, or in the hands of any person hostile to their just rights?

2. Whether, at the same request, they will be prepared immediately to convert all their paper money into gold and silver?

[1] Addressed to the Chartist Convention.

3. Whether, if the Convention shall determine that a sacred month will be necessary to prepare the millions to secure the charter of their political salvation, they will firmly resolve to abstain from their labours during that period, as well as from the use of all intoxicating drinks ?

4. Whether, according to their old constitutional right—a right which modern legislators would fain annihilate—they have prepared themselves with the arms of freemen to defend the laws and constitutional privileges their ancestors bequeathed to them ?

14. THE ROCHDALE PIONEERS [*Industrial Co-operation, Ed. Catherine Webb, pp.* 68–9], 1844.

The objects of this Society are to form arrangements for the pecuniary benefit and improvement of the social and domestic condition of its members, by raising a sufficient amount of capital, in shares of one pound each, to bring into operation the following plans and arrangements :—

The establishment of a Store for the sale of provisions clothing, etc.

The building, purchasing, or erecting a number of houses, in which those members desiring to assist each other in improving their domestic and social condition may reside. To commence the manufacture of such articles as the Society may determine upon, for the employment of such members as may be without employment, or who may be suffering in consequence of repeated reductions in their wages.

As a further benefit and security to the members of this Society, the Society shall purchase or rent an estate or estates of land, which shall be cultivated by the members who may be out of employment or whose labour may be badly remunerated.

That, as soon as practicable, this Society shall proceed to arrange the powers of production, distribution, education and government: or, in other words, to establish a self-supporting home colony of united interests, or assist other societies in establishing such colonies.

That, for the promotion of sobriety, a Temperance Hotel be opened in one of the Society's houses as soon as convenient.

SECTION V

THE RELIEF OF THE POOR

THE national organisation of poor-relief was permanently affected by the constitutional troubles of the seventeenth century. Supervision and pressure from a central authority were removed and were not again strongly felt till near the close of this period. This change shows itself in the documentary evidence; national regulation is rare and comes only as the result of a special emergency or panic (Nos. 1, 3, 4, 10). The Settlement Act of 1662 (No. 1), with its successors, was an attempt to meet the special local difficulties which sprang from the want of central control and uniformity. The Act of 1722 provided the machinery for the more drastic treatment of the poor advocated in Defoe's pamphlet (No. 2), by means of a workhouse and a system of tests for relief; for this purpose unions of parishes could be formed (No. 3). Gilbert's Act (No. 4) in the last quarter of the century was a reversion to milder policy; it was intended to distinguish more clearly the different classes of poor relieved, to provide suitable treatment for the old infirm and children in institutions, and to find employment for the able-bodied. It illustrates the growing pressure of industrial changes on the working classes, as well as the current of humanitarian feeling which ran a broken course from this time to the end of the period. It was an adoptive, not a compulsory, Act, and no more legislative changes of the first importance were made till 1834. Meanwhile vast transformations were being made in town and, especially, in country life, and the destitution line was crossed by a whole section of the nation. The Settlement laws were relaxed, but, after Pitt's abortive proposals in 1795, Parliament stood aside. The initiative was thus left to the local authority. The so-called Speenhamland Act of Parliament (No. 5) is the classic instance of the methods of supplementary allowances adopted by the Justices in various counties. Its aim was humane; its effect, to check the pressure for higher wages, was not intended (see No. 5, note).

The eighteenth century system produced great local variety, some examples of which are given from the survey published by Eden in 1797 (Nos. 6 and 7). The official workhouse, the farming of the poor to a contractor, the employment of the poor within the workhouse, and the relief of the rates by the Roundsman system of servile labour are described (Nos. 6 and 7. See also No. 8).

The Poor Law Commission of 1834 (No. 9) was the culminating point of a reaction against the results of the previous half century. Its intention was to make a clean sweep of tradition and to reassert the principle of uniformity. Its authors, in the spirit of their age, hoped to make their reform negatively, by cutting away influences which corrupted human nature. The extracts (No. 9) show their leading principles and recommendations. The Act of 1834 (No. 10) embodied their conclusions, leaving a large discretion to a new central authority. The Regulations and Orders (No. 11) of these Commissioners and their successors, the Poor Law and Local Government Boards, were, henceforward, the chief directing force of Poor Relief policy.

AUTHORITIES

Nicholls' *History of the English Poor Law*, Mackay, ditto (a continuation), and Fowle, *The Poor Law*, are general modern descriptions. Webb, *English Poor Law Policy*, is an historical criticism of the system from 1834; see also Kirkman Gray, *Philanthropy and the State.* The eighteenth century is described in Cunningham, *Growth of English Industry and Commerce, Modern Times*; Webb, *English Local Government, The Parish and the County*; Redlich and Hirst, *Local Government in England*, Vol. I; Hammond, *The Village Labourer*, c. 7; Hasbach, *The English Agricultural Labourer*, c. 3 and c. 4, and Mantoux, *La Révolution Industrielle.* Ashby, *The Poor Law in a Warwickshire Village* (in Oxford Studies in Social and Legal History, Vol. III), provides illustrations.

Bibliographies in Hasbach and Cunningham, *op. cit.*

Contemporary (1) *Documentary Sources.*—The best collection of contemporary statistics, of paupers, diet, cost, etc., in the eighteenth century is given in Eden, The State of the Poor. The Report of the 1834 Commission (XXVII and XXVIII) describes conditions and the new policy. See also Report of Committees on the Poor Law, 1817 (VI) and 1819 (III), and Report of Committee on Labourers' Wages, 1824 (VI).

(2) *Literary authorities.*—Illustrations of contemporary opinion can be found for different periods in Defoe, Giving Alms no Charity, Reports of the Society for Bettering the Condition of the Poor (1795–1808), Rose, Observations on the Poor Law. A municipal system is described in Cary, The Proceedings of the Corporation of Bristol. A general survey was made in the middle of the eighteenth century by Burn, History of the Poor Laws, and at the end by Eden, The State of the Poor.

1. Settlement Law [*Statutes*, 14 *Charles II*, *c.* 12], 1662.

An Act for the better relief of the poor of this kingdom.

Whereas the necessity, number and continual increase of the poor, not only within the Cities of London and Westminster with the liberties of each of them, but also through the whole kingdom of England and Dominion of Wales, is very great and exceeding burdensome, being occasioned by reason of some defects in the law concerning the settling of the poor and for want of a due provision of the regulations of relief and employment in such parishes or places where they are legally settled, which doth enforce many to turn incorrigible rogues and others to perish for want, together with the neglect of the faithful execution of such laws and statutes as have formerly been made for the apprehending of rogues and vagabonds and for the good of the poor. For remedy whereof and for the preventing the perishing of any of the poor, whether old or young, for want of such supplies as are necessary, may it please your most

Excellent Majesty that it may be enacted . . . that whereas by reason of some defects in the law poor people are not restrained from going from one parish to another and therefore do endeavour to settle themselves in those parishes where there is the best stock, the largest commons or wastes to build cottages, and the most woods for them to burn and destroy and when they have consumed it then to another parish, and at last become rogues and vagabonds to the great discouragement of parishes to provide stocks where it is liable to be devoured by strangers . . . it shall and may be lawful upon complaint made by the churchwardens or overseers of the poor of any parish to any Justice of Peace, within forty days after any such person or persons coming so to settle, as aforesaid in any tenement under the yearly value of ten pounds for any two justices of the peace whereof one to be of the Quorum of the division where any person or persons that are likely to be chargeable to the parish shall come to inhabit, by their warrant to remove and convey such person or persons to such parish where he or they were last legally settled either as a native householder sojourner apprentice or servant for the space of forty days at the least unless he or they give sufficient security for the discharge of the said parish to be allowed by the said Justices.

[II. Appeal to Quarter Sessions.

III. Persons allowed to go for the Harvest into another parish if they have a certificate of settlement in their original parish.

IV. Provision for setting up workhouses in London and within the Bills of Mortality.]

[VI. and XXIII. The President and Governors of such workhouses may set rogues and vagrants to work in the workhouse with the consent of the Privy Council. Justices of the Peace may sentence disorderly persons and "sturdy beggars" to transportation not exceeding seven years.

Persons allowed to go for the harvest into another parish if they have a certificate of settlement in their original parish.

Provision made for setting up workhouses in London and within the Bills of Mortality. The President and Governors of such workhouses may set rogues and vagrants to work in the workhouse. Justices of the Peace may, with the leave of the Privy Council, sentence disorderly persons and "sturdy beggars" to transportation not exceeding seven years.][1]

2. DEFOE'S PAMPHLET, "GIVING ALMS NO CHARITY" [*D. Defoe, Giving Alms no Charity, etc.*], 1704.

I humbly crave leave to lay these heads down as fundamental maxims, which I am ready at any time to defend and make out.

1. There is in England more labour than hands to perform it, and consequently a want of people, not of employment.
2. No man in England, of sound limbs and senses, can be poor merely for want of work.
3. All our workhouses, corporations and charities for employing the poor, and setting them to work, as now they are employed, or any Acts ot Parliament, to empower overseers of parishes, or parishes themselves, to employ the poor, except as shall be hereafter excepted, are, and will be public nuisances, mischiefs to the nation which serve to the ruin of families and the increase of the poor.
4. That it is a regulation of the poor that is wanted in England, not a setting them to work.

. . . . . .

The poverty and exigence of the poor in England is plainly derived from one of these two particular causes,

Casualty or Crime.

By Casualty, I mean sickness of families, loss of limbs or sight, and any, either natural or accidental, impotence as to labour.

The crimes of our people, and from whence their poverty derives, as the visible and direct fountains are:

1. Luxury.
2. Sloth.
3. Pride.

[1] Amended by 8 and 9 Wm. and Mary, 30. Persons with certificates from churchwardens of their parishes, acknowledging them to be inhabitants, not to be removed from any other parish till chargeable and then to be chargeable in the parish where the certificates were given. Any one receiving relief to wear a badge. Also by 35 Geo. III, 101. "No poor person shall be removed . . . to the place of his or her last legal settlement, until such person shall have become actually chargeable to the parish."

This is so apparent in every place, that I think it needs no explication; that English labouring people eat and drink, but especially the latter, three times as much in value as any sort of foreigners of the same dimensions in the world.

. . . . .

There is a general taint of slothfulness upon our poor, there is nothing more frequent, than for an Englishman to work till he has got his pocket full of money, and then go and be idle, or perhaps drunk, till it is all gone, and perhaps he himself in debt; and ask him in his cups what he intends, he will tell you honestly, he will drink as long as it lasts, and then go to work for more.

3. THE WORKHOUSE TEST ACT [*Statutes*, 9 *Geo. I c.* 7], 1722.

An Act for amending the laws relating to the settlement, employment and relief of the poor.

IV. And for the greater ease of parishes in the relief of the poor, be it further enacted by the authority aforesaid, that it shall and may be lawful for the churchwardens and overseers of the poor in any parish, town, township or place, with the consent of the major part of the parishioners or inhabitants of the same parish, town, township or place, in vestry, or other parish or public meeting for that purpose assembled, or of so many of them as shall be so assembled, upon usual notice thereof first given, to purchase or hire any house or houses in the same parish, township or place, and to contract with any person or persons for the lodging, keeping, maintaining and employing any or all such poor in their respective parishes, townships or places, as shall desire to receive relief or collection from the same parish, and there to keep, maintain and employ all such poor persons, and take the benefit of the work, labour and service of any such poor person or persons, who shall be kept or maintained in any such house or houses, for the better maintenance and relief of such poor person or persons, who shall be there kept or maintained; and in case any poor person or persons of any parish, town, township or place, where such house or houses shall be so purchased or hired, shall refuse to be lodged, kept or maintained in such house or houses, such poor person or persons so refusing shall be put out of the book or books where the names of the persons who ought to receive collection in the said parish, town, township or place, are to be registered, and shall not be entitled to ask or receive collection or relief from the churchwardens and overseers of the poor of the same parish, town or township; and where any parish, town or township shall be too small to purchase or hire such house or houses for the poor of their own parish only, it shall and may be lawful for two or more such parishes, towns or townships or places, with the consent of the major part of the parishioners or inhabitants, and with the approbation of any justice of peace dwelling in or near any such parish, town or place, signified under his hand and seal, to unite in purchasing, hiring, or taking such house, for the lodging, keeping and maintaining of the poor of the several parishes, townships or places so uniting, and there to keep, maintain and employ the poor of the parishes so uniting, and to take and have the benefit of the work, labour or service of any poor there kept and maintained, for the better maintenance and relief of the poor there kept, maintained and employed; and that if any poor person or persons in the respective parishes, townships or places so uniting, shall refuse to be lodged, kept and maintained in the house, hired or taken for such uniting parishes, townships or places, he, she or they so refusing, shall be put out of the collection-book, where his, her or their names were registered, and shall not be entitled to ask or demand relief or collection from the churchwardens and overseers of the poor in their respective parishes, townships or places: and that it shall and may be lawful for the churchwardens and overseers of the poor, with the consent of the major part of the parishioners or inhabitants, to contract with the churchwardens and overseers of the poor of any other parish, township or place, for the lodging, maintaining or employing, of any poor person or persons of such other parish, township or place, as to them shall seem meet; and in case any poor person or persons of such other parish, township or place, shall refuse to be lodged, maintained and employed in such house or houses, he, she or they so refusing, shall be put out of the collection-book of such other parish, township or place, where his, her or their names were registered, and shall not be entitled to ask, demand or receive any relief or collection from the churchwardens and overseers of the poor of his, her or their respective parish, township or place: provided always, that no poor person or persons, his, her or their apprentice, child or children, shall acquire a settlement in the parish, town or place, to which he, she or they are removed by virtue of this act. No person or persons shall be deemed, adjudged or taken, to acquire or gain any settlement in any parish or place, for or by virtue of any purchase of any estate or interest in such parish or place, whereof the consideration for such purchase doth not amount to the sum of thirty pounds, *bona fide* paid, for any longer or further time than such person or persons shall inhabit in such estate, and shall then be liable to be removed to such parish or place, where such person or persons were last legally settled, before the said purchase and inhabitancy therein.

VI. No person or persons whatsoever, who shall be taxed, rated or assessed to the scavenger or repairs of the highway, and shall duly pay the same, shall be deemed or taken to have any legal settlement in any city, parish, town or hamlet, for or by reason of his, her or their paying to such scavenger's rate or repairs of the highway as aforesaid; any law to the contrary in any wise notwithstanding.

4. Gilbert's Act [*Statutes*, 22 *George III*, *c*. 83], 1782.

An act for the better relief and employment of the poor.

Whereas notwithstanding the many laws now in being for the relief and employment of the poor, and the great sums of money raised for those purposes, their sufferings and distresses are nevertheless very grievous; and, by the incapacity, negligence, or misconduct of overseers, the money raised for the relief of the poor is frequently misapplied, and sometimes expended in defraying the charges of litigations about settlements indiscreetly and unadvisedly carried on. . . .

VII. And be it further enacted, that it shall and may be lawful for two justices of the peace of the limit where such poor house shall be, or be so agreed to be situated, and they are hereby required, as soon as conveniently may be after such agreement shall have been made as aforesaid, upon application to them by two or more of the persons who shall have signed such agreement, and upon producing the same to them, to appoint one of the persons so recommended to be guardian of the poor for each of such parishes, townships, and places, in the form contained in the said schedule, No. VII, or to that or the like effect; and every such guardian shall attend the monthly meetings hereby directed to be holden, and execute the several powers and authorities given to guardians by this act, and shall have, and is hereby invested with, all the powers and authorities given to overseers of the poor by any other act or acts of parliament.

XVII. The guardians of the poor of the several parishes, townships and places which shall adopt the provisions of this act, shall provide a suitable and convenient house or houses, with proper buildings and accommodations thereto, when wanted.

And, to render the provisions of this act more practicable and beneficial, be it further enacted, that no person shall be sent to such poor house or houses, except such as are become indigent by old age, sickness, or infirmities, and are unable to acquire a maintenance by their labour; and except such orphan children as shall be sent thither by order of the guardian or guardians of the poor, with the approbation of the visitor; and except such children as shall necessarily go with their mothers thither for sustenance.

XXX. And, be it further enacted, that all infant children of tender years, and who, from accident or misfortune, shall become chargeable to the parish or place to which they belong, may either be sent to such poor house as aforesaid, or be placed by the guardian or guardians of the poor, with the approbation of the visitor, with some reputable person or persons in or near the parish, township, or place, to which they belong, at such weekly allowance as shall be agreed upon between the parish officers and such person or persons with the approbation of the visitor, until such child or children shall be of sufficient age to be put into service, or bound apprentice to husbandry, or some trade or occupation; and a list of the names of every child so placed out, and by whom and where kept, shall be given to the visitor; who shall see that they are properly treated, or cause them to be removed, and placed under the care of some other person or persons, if he finds just cause so to do; and when every such child shall attain such age, he or she shall be so placed out, at the expense of the parish, township, or place, to which he or she shall belong, according to the laws in being: provided nevertheless, that if the parents or relations of any poor child sent to such house, or so placed out as aforesaid, or any other responsible person, shall desire to receive and provide for any such poor child or children, and signify the same to the guardians at their monthly meeting, the guardians shall, and are hereby required to dismiss, or cause to be dismissed, such child or children from the poor-house, or from the care of such person or persons as aforesaid, and deliver him, her, or them, to the parent, relation, or other person so applying as aforesaid : provided also, that nothing herein contained shall give any power to separate any child or children, under the age of seven years, from his, her, or their parent or parents, without the consent of such parent or parents.

XXXI. And be it further enacted, that all idle or disorderly persons who are able, but unwilling, to work or maintain themselves and their families, shall be prosecuted by the guardians of the poor of the several parishes, townships, and places, wherein they reside, and punished in such manner as idle and disorderly persons are directed to be by the statute made in the seventeenth year of the reign of his late majesty King George the Second ; and if any guardian shall neglect to make complaint thereof, against every such person or persons, to some neighbouring justice of the peace, within ten days after it shall come to his knowledge, he shall, for every such neglect, forfeit a sum not exceeding five pounds, nor less than twenty shillings, one moiety whereof, when recovered, shall be paid to the informer, and the other moiety to be disposed of as the other forfeitures are hereinafter directed to be applied.

XXXII. And be it further enacted, that where there shall be, in any parish, township, or place, any poor person or persons who shall be able and willing to work, but who cannot get employment, it shall and may be lawful for the guardian of the poor of such parish, township or place, and he is hereby required, on application made to him by or on behalf of such poor person, to agree for the labour of such poor person or persons, at any work or employment suited to his or her strength and capacity, in any parish, township or place, near the place of his or her residence, and to maintain, or cause such person or persons to be properly maintained, lodged, and provided for, until such employment shall be procured, and during the time of such work, and to receive the money to be earned by such work or labour, and apply it in such maintenance, as far as the same will go, and make up the deficiency, if any; and if the same shall happen to exceed the money expended in such maintenance, to account for the surplus, which shall afterwards, within one calendar month, be given to such poor person or persons who shall have earned such money, if no further expenses shall be then incurred on his or her account to exhaust the same. And in case such poor person or persons shall refuse to work, or run away from such work or employment, complaint shall be made thereof by the guardian to some justice or justices of the peace in or near the said parish, township, or place; who shall enquire into the same upon oath, and on conviction punish such offender or offenders, by committing him, her, or them, to the house of correction, there to be kept to hard labour for any time not exceeding three calendar months, nor less than one calendar month.

XLI. And whereas it frequently happens that poor children, pregnant women, or poor persons afflicted with sickness, or some bodily infirmity, are enticed, taken, or conveyed by parish officers, or other persons, from one parish or place to another, without any legal order of removal, in order to ease the one parish or place, and to burden the other with such poor person: for remedy thereof, be it further enacted, that, when any guardian, or other person or persons, shall so entice, take, convey, or remove, or cause or procure to be so enticed, taken, conveyed, or removed, any such poor person or persons from one parish or place to another, which shall adopt the provisions of this act, without an order of removal from two justices of the peace for that purpose, every person or persons so offending shall, for every such offence, forfeit a sum not exceeding twenty pounds, nor less than five pounds.

5. Speenhamland "Act of Parliament" [*The Reading Mercury, May* 11, 1795], 1795.

Berkshire, to wit.

At a General Meeting of the Justices of this County, together with several discreet persons assembled by public advertisement,[1] on Wednesday the 6th day of May, 1795, at the Pelican

[1] *Reading Mercury*, May 4, contained an advertisement of a general meeting of justices "to limit, direct, and appoint the wages of day labourers."

Inn in Speenhamland (in pursuance of an order of the last Court of General Quarter Sessions) for the purpose of rating Husbandry Wages, by the day or week, if then approved of, [names of those present] . . . .

Resolved unanimously,

That the present state of the Poor does require further assistance than has been generally given them.

Resolved,

That it is not expedient for the Magistrates to grant that assistance by regulating the Wages of Day Labourers, according to the directions of the Statutes of the 5th Elizabeth and 1st James: But the Magistrates very earnestly recommend to the Farmers and others throughout the county, to increase the pay of their Labourers in proportion to the present price of provisions; and agreeable thereto, the Magistrates now present, have unanimously resolved that they will, in their several divisions, make the following calculations and allowances for relief of all poor and industrious men and their families, who to the satisfaction of the Justices of their Parish, shall endeavour (as far as they can) for their own support and maintenance.

That is to say,

When the Gallon Loaf of Second Flour, weighing 8lb. 11ozs. shall cost 1*s.*

Then every poor and industrious man shall have for his own support 3*s.* weekly, either produced by his own or his family's labour, or an allowance from the poor rates, and for the support of his wife and every other of his family, 1*s.* 6*d.*

When the Gallon Loaf shall cost 1*s.* 4*d.*

Then every poor and industrious man shall have 4*s.* weekly for his own, and 1*s.* and 10*d.* for the support of every other of his family.

And so in proportion, as the price of bread rise or falls (that is to say) 3*d.* to the man, and 1*d.* to every other of the family, on every 1*d.* which the loaf rise above 1*s.*

By order of the Meeting,

W. Budd, Deputy Clerk of the Peace.[1]

[1] Simultaneously the Magistrates published a recommendation to overseers to grow potatoes, setting poor people to work and offering them one-third or one-fourth of the crop, and to sell at 1*s.* a bushel; also to get in a stock of peat, faggots, furze, etc., in the summer and to sell at a loss in the winter.

6. The Workhouse System [*Eden, The State of the Poor, 1797, Vol. II, pp.* 168–9], 1797.

Stanhope (*Durham*).

The poor have been farmed for many years: about fifteen years ago they were farmed for 250*l.*; but the expense has gradually increased since that period: the year before last, the expense was 495*l.*, and last year 494*l.*; and the Contractor says that he shall lose 100*l.* by his last bargain, and will not take the poor this year under 700*l.* Twenty-two poor people are at present in the house, and 100 families receive weekly relief out of it: these out-poor, the Contractor says, will cost him 450*l.* for the year ending at May-day next. The Poor-house was built about fifteen years ago; it is, like most others in the hands of contractors, in a dirty state.

Preston (*Lancashire*)[1].

The number of poor in the workhouse a few weeks ago, was as follows:—

Men	26
Women	39
Boys	47
Girls	40
Total	152

At present there are 158 or 159 in the house. The number of out-poor at present is 70; they cost about 10*l.* a week.

The work-house is built on a tolerable plan, but wants apartments for the sick. There are 4 or 5 beds in a room: the bedsteads are made of iron, and the beds are stuffed with chaff: white-washing and other means of keeping the house clean, seem rather neglected. It is said that about 15 die in a year in the house. About 20 acres of land were inclosed from the common, for the use of the house, for keeping cows horses, and pigs; raising potatoes, etc.: this plot of ground is much improved by cultivation. Nothing is manufactured for the use of the house. The boys and girls are employed in weaving calicoes, till they are able to earn their living elsewhere. Old women wind cotton; a few, who can work,

[1] *Ibid.*, p. 368.

are employed in husbandry, gardening, and other occupations: no account of their earnings could be obtained.

St. Martin-in-the-Fields (*London*)[1].

The poor of this parish are partly relieved at home, and partly maintained in the workhouse in Castle-street, Leicester Fields. There are, at present, about 240 weekly out-pensioners, besides a considerable number of poor on the casual list. Of 573, the number of poor at present in the workhouse, 473 are adults and 100 children; of which 54 are boys, 21 girls, able to work, and 25 infants. Their principal employment is spinning flax, picking hair, carding wool, etc.; their annual earnings, on an average of a few years past, amount to about £150. It was once attempted to establish a manufacture in the house; but the badness of the situation for business, the want of room for workshops, and the difficulty of compelling the able poor to pay proper attention to work, rendered the project unsuccessful. Between 70 and 80 children belonging to this parish are, generally, out at nurse in the country: a weekly allowance of 3*s.* (lately advanced to 3*s.* 6*d.*) is paid with each child.

At 7 or 8 years of age, the children are taken into the house, and taught a little reading, etc., for three or four years, and then put out apprentices.

Bulcamp (*Suffolk*)[2].

The poor of 46 incorporated parishes in the hundred of Blything, are maintained in a house of industry, which is situated on an eminence in the parish of Bulcamp. The expense of erection was 12,000*l.*; the house was opened for the reception of the poor in October, 1766. The whole annual sum, to be paid by the parishes (which was fixed at the average of seven years' expenditure, previous to their incorporation), was 3,084*l.* 12*s.* 8*d.*; in 1780 half the debt was paid off, and the rates reduced one-eighth, or to 2,699*l.* 1*s.* 1*d.*; in June, 1791, the whole debt was discharged. The rates have been continued at the reduced sum of 2,699*l.* 1*s.* 1*d.* In 1793, the corporation found it necessary to apply to Parliament for farther powers, relative to the binding out poor children apprentices, which cost 350*l.* 15*s.*

[1] *Ibid.*, p. 440 [2] *Ibid.*, p. 678.

The work done in this house is chiefly spinning for the Norwich manufacture: clothes and bedding, etc., for the house, are also made at home. The following were the last week's earnings: an account of the annual earnings could not be procured; but it appears that they have been about 8*l*. a week, or 400*l*. a year, for several weeks past.

Worsted spinners	..	4*l*.	3*s*.	1¾*d*.
Tow spinners ..	..	1*l*.	12*s*.	1*d*.
Sempstresses ..	..	0*l*.	7*s*.	3*d*.
Tailors ..	..	0*l*.	9*s*.	0*d*.
Knitters ..	..	0*l*.	8*s*.	0*d*.
Weavers ..	..	0*l*.	7*s*.	0*d*.
Shoemakers ..	..	0*l*.	16*s*.	0*d*.
Total earnings for one week		8*l*.	2*s*.	5¾*d*.

Number of paupers in the house in June, in each of the following years (the average number in the year must, probably, be more), and Table of Mortality:—

Years.	No. of Persons.	Deaths.
1782	297	87
1783	298	69
1784	265	76
1785	295	82
1786	143	70
1787	256	67
1788	290	52
1789	207	37
1790	192	18
1791	235	34
1792	243	9
1793	260	23
1794	270	37
	Average of 13 years ..	50$\frac{11}{13}$

The number at present in the house is 40 men, 60 women, and 255 children: total 355.

The house is very roomy and convenient. The beds are chiefly of feathers: the dormitories and other rooms are kept very clean. More work is done now than formerly; but owing to lowness of wages, the receipts have decreased.

The number of deaths is very great, and, I presume, rather arises from the number of old persons admitted into the house than from any inattention towards the sick.

7. TWO VARIETIES OF THE ROUNDSMAN SYSTEM OF RELIEF [*Eden, The State of the Poor*, 1797, *Vol. II, p.* 29 *and p.* 384], 1797.

(*a*) *Winslow* (*Buckinghamshire*)

There seems to be a great want of employment: most of the labourers are (as it is termed), on the Rounds; that is, they go to work from one house to another round the parish. In winter sometimes 40 persons are on the rounds. They are wholly paid by the parish, unless the householders choose to employ them; and from these circumstances, labourers often become very lazy, and imperious. Children, above ten years old, are put on the rounds, and receive from the parish from 1*s*. 6*d*. to 3*s*. a week.

(*b*) *Kibworth Beauchamp* (Leicestershire)[1].

In the winter, and at other times, when a man is out of work, he applies to the overseer, who sends him from house to house, to get employ: the housekeeper, who employs him, is obliged to give him victuals, and 6*d*. a day; and the parish adds 4*d*. (total, 10*d*. a day) for the support of his family; persons working in this manner are called rounds-men, from their going round the village or township for employ.

8. ANOTHER EXAMPLE OF THE ROUNDSMAN SYSTEM [*Thomas Batchelor, The Agriculture of Bedfordshire* (*Agricultural Surveys*), 1808, *pp.* 608–9], 1808.

Bedfordshire.

The increase of population has caused a deficiency of employment, which is so remarkable in some seasons, that a great proportion of the labourers "go the rounds." This practice is not modern; but as it is not supposed to be sanctioned by law, it may be proper to describe the nature of it, and its general consequences. When a labourer

[1] Eden, *The State of the Poor*, Vol. II, p. 384.

can obtain no employment he applies to the acting overseer, from whom he passes on to the different farmers all round the parish, being employed by each of them after the rate of one day for every 20*l.* rent. The allowance to a labourer on the rounds, is commonly 2*d.* per day below the pay of other labourers, which is found to be a necessary check upon those who love liberty better than labour. Boys receive from 4*d.* to 6*d.* per day on the rounds, the whole of which is often repaid to the farmers by the overseers. About half the pay of the men is returned in the same manner, and the farmers often receive in this way the amount of from 2*d.* to 4*d.* in the pound rent, which consequently causes the apparent expense of the poor to exceed the truth. The practice in question has a very bad effect on the industry of the poor : they are often employed in trivial business; the boys in particular are of little use in the winter season. The men are careful not to earn more than they receive, and seem to think it the safer extreme to perform too little rather than too much.

9. Report of the Poor Law Commission [*Report from Commission on the Poor Laws*, 1834 (*XXVII*), *pp.* 297, 228, 47, 261–262, 306–307], 1834.

We recommend, therefore, the appointment of a Central Board to control the administration of the Poor Laws; with such assistant Commissioners as may be found requisite; and that the Commissioners be empowered and directed to frame and enforce regulations for the government of workhouses, and as to the nature and amount of the relief to be given and the labour to be exacted in them, and that such regulations shall, as far as may be practicable, be uniform throughout the country.

* * * * * *

It may be assumed that in the administration of relief, the public is warranted in imposing such conditions on the individual relieved, as are conducive to the benefit either of the individual himself, or of the country at large, at whose expense he is to be relieved.[1]

The first and most essential of all conditions, a principle which we find universally admitted, even by those whose

[1] *Ibid.*, p. 228.

practice is at variance with it, is that his situation on the whole shall not be made really or apparently so eligible as the situation of the independent labourer of the lowest class. Throughout the evidence it is shown, that in proportion as the condition of any pauper is elevated above the condition of independent labourers, the condition of the independent class is depressed; their industry is impaired, their employment becomes unsteady, and its remuneration in wages is diminished. Such persons, therefore, are under the strongest inducements to quit the less eligible class of labourers and enter the more eligible class of paupers. The converse is the effect when the pauper class is placed in its proper position, below the condition of the independent labourer. Every penny bestowed, that tends to render the condition of the paupers more eligible than that of the independent labourer, is a bounty on indolence and vice. We have found, that as the poor's rates are at present administered, they operate as bounties of this description to the amount of several millions annually.

* * * * * *

Another evil connected with outdoor relief, and arising from its undefined character, is the natural tendency to award to the deserving more than is necessary, or where more than necessary relief is afforded to all, to distinguish the deserving by extra allowances.[1] . . . The whole evidence shows the danger of such an attempt. It appears that such endeavours to constitute the distributors of relief into a tribunal for the reward of merit, out of the property of others, have not only failed in effecting the benevolent intentions of their promoters, but have become sources of fraud on the part of the distributors, and of discontent and violence on the part of the claimants.

* * * * * *

The chief specific measures which we recommend are:[2]—

First, that except as to medical attendance, and subject to the exception respecting apprenticeship hereinafter stated, all relief whatever to able-bodied persons or to their families, otherwise than in well-regulated workhouses (*i.e.*, places where they may be set to work according to the spirit and intention of the 43rd of Elizabeth), shall be declared unlawful, and shall cease, in manner and at periods hereafter specified; and that

[1] *Ibid.*, p. 47. [2] *Ibid.*, pp. 261-2.

all relief afforded in respect of children under the age of 16, shall be considered as afforded to their parents.

At least four classes are necessary:[1]—(1) The aged and really impotent; (2) The children; (3) The able-bodied females; (4) The able-bodied males. Of whom we trust that the two latter will be the least numerous classes. It appears to us that both the requisite classification and the requisite superintendence may be better obtained in separate buildings than under a single roof. . . . Each class might thus receive an appropriate treatment; the old might enjoy their indulgences without torment from the boisterous; the children be educated, and the able-bodied subjected to such courses of labour and discipline as will repel the indolent and vicious.

10. The Poor Law Amendment Act [*Statutes*, 4 *and* 5 *Wm. IV*, 76], 1834.

An Act for the Amendment and better Administration of the Laws relating to the Poor in England and Wales.

Whereas it is expedient to alter and amend the Laws relating to the Relief of poor Persons in England and Wales: Be it therefore enacted . . . that it shall be lawful for His Majesty, His Heirs and Successors, by Warrant under the Royal Sign Manual, to appoint three fit persons to be Commissioners to carry this Act into execution. . . .

XV. And be it further enacted, . . . for executing the powers given to them by this Act the said Commissioners shall and are hereby authorized and required, from time to time as they shall see occasion, to make and issue all such rules, orders, and regulations for the management of the poor, for the government of workhouses and the education of the children therein, and for the management of parish poor children under the provisions of an Act made and passed in the seventh year of the reign of His late Majesty King George the Third, intituled *An Act for the better Regulation of Parish poor Children of the several Parishes therein mentioned within the Bills of Mortality*, and the superintending, inspecting, and regulating of the Houses wherein such poor children are kept and maintained, and for the apprenticing the children of poor persons, and for the guidance and control of all Guardians,

[1] p. 306-7.

Vestries, and Parish officers, so far as relates to the management or relief of the poor, and the keeping, examining, auditing, and allowing of accounts, and making and entering into contracts in all matters relating to such management or relief, or to any expenditure for the relief of the poor, and for carrying this Act into execution in all other respects, as they shall think proper; and the said Commissioners may, at their discretion, from time to time suspend, alter, or rescind such rules, orders, and regulations, or any of them: provided always that nothing in this Act contained shall be construed as enabling the said commissioners or any of them to interfere in any individual case for the purpose of ordering relief.

XXVI. And be it further enacted, that it shall be lawful for the said commissioners, by order under their hands and seal, to declare so many parishes as they may think fit to be united for the administration of the laws for the relief of the poor, and such parishes shall thereupon be deemed a Union for such purpose, . . . but, notwithstanding . . . each of the said parishes shall be separately chargeable with and liable to defray the expense of its own poor, whether relieved in or out of any such workhouse.

XXXVIII. And be it further enacted, that where any parishes shall be united by order or with concurrence of the said commissioners for the administration of the laws for the relief of the poor, a Board of Guardians of the poor for such Union shall be constituted and chosen, and the workhouse or workhouses of such Union shall be governed, and the relief of the poor in such Union shall be administered, by such Board of Guardians; and the said Guardians shall be elected by the ratepayers, and by such owners of property in the parishes forming such Union as shall in manner hereinafter mentioned require to have their names entered as entitled to vote as owners in the books of such parishes respectively.

11. Outdoor Relief Prohibitory Order [11*th Annual Report of the Poor Law Commissioners, pp.* 29–33], 1844.

Amended General Orders.—Regulating the Relief of Able-Bodied Poor Persons.

1. Every able-bodied person, male or female, requiring relief from any parish within any of the said Unions, shall be relieved

wholly in the workhouse of the Union, together with such of the family of every such able-bodied person as may be resident with him or her, and they not be in employment, and together with the wife of every such able-bodied male person, if he be a married man, and if she be resident with him; save and except in the following cases:—

1st. Where such person shall require relief on account of sudden and urgent necessity.

2nd. Where such person shall require relief on account of any sickness, accident, or bodily or mental infirmity affecting such person, or any of his or her family.

* * * * * *

4th. Where such person, being a widow, shall be in the first six months of her widowhood.

5th. Where such person shall be a widow, and have a legitimate child or legitimate children dependent upon her, and incapable of earning his, her, or their livelihood, and have no illegitimate child born after the commencement of her widowhood.

* * * * * *

7th. Where such person shall be the wife, or child, of any able-bodied man who shall be in the service of Her Majesty as soldier, sailor, or marine.

* * * * * *

Given under our hands and Seal of Office, this 21st day of December, in the year of our Lord 1 thousand 8 hundred and 44.

(Signed) Geo. Nicholls.
G. C. Lewis.
Edward W. Head.

SECTION VI

FINANCE AND FOREIGN TRADE

THIS section illustrates various departments of Government policy: taxation and revenue (Nos. 1, 9 and 12), public debts (Nos. 7 and 10), fiscal and trade policy (Nos. 1, 2, 4, 6, 13–17, 19), the coinage (Nos. 3, 5 and 8), and the national Bank (Nos. 7, 11, and 18). The specimens of revenue policy begin with the Act by which Charles II abandoned feudal dues in exchange for a general and hereditary excise (No. 1). The principle involved in this transaction may be compared with Sir Robert Walpole's remarks on the question of justice in taxation (No. 9) and with Pitt's speech on introducing the Income Tax in 1798, which also gives a survey of the whole financial position and a defence of the policy of paying for wars out of hand (No. 12). The opposite policy, of war-loans, had been adopted earlier, and the French wars of the seventeenth and eighteenth centuries established the funding system. An outline is given of the Sinking Fund by which it was supposed that this national liability could be reduced while it was being created

(No. 10). The foundation of the Bank of England (No. 7) was an important step in the policy of national loans as well as an encouragement to the growth of capital and capitalist industry. The French wars at the end of the eighteenth century produced a crisis in the management of the Bank's reserve; an official report explains the causes of the panic which led to the suspension of cash payments and also shows the deliberate policy by which the suspension was continued till 1819 (No. 11). This was the first controversy of great importance on the subject of currency since the seventeenth century, when the government of Charles II had adopted the policy of allowing free export and free coinage of Gold and Silver (Nos. 3 and 5). The gradual deterioration of the coinage which led to the recoinage of 1696 is illustrated by a contemporary description (No. 8). The Bank Charter Act (No. 18) shows the financial aspect of rapid national expansion in the nineteenth century and the method adopted to give stability to credit by limiting the issue of unsupported paper currency, in the period before the triumph of the cheque system.

The Navigation Act of Charles the second's reign (No. 2) formed part of a system by which the State set itself to encourage particular industries and took a part in the struggle for commercial leadership. (See also Nos. 4 and 6. The complications of this policy with considerations of revenue and particular interests rapidly increased, while the manufacturing export trade became more important (No. 13). A reaction led by the Economists had begun in the latter part of the eighteenth century. In the nineteenth century the battle raged over the special protection successfully claimed by the Agricultural Interest in the depression at the end of the Napoleonic wars (No. 15). The debates and petitions (No. 14, No. 16, No. 19) bristle with the new Political Economy. They also give an indication of the new social class created by the Industrial Revolution and of the struggle of the landowners with the North of England manufacturers who founded and financed the Anti-Corn-Law League, the most successful of all political associations for an economic object (No. 17).

AUTHORITIES

The most important modern authorities on taxation and finance are: Dowell, *History of Taxation and Taxes*; Seligman, *The Income Tax*; Kennedy, *English Taxation*, 1640–1799: on currency and banking, Shaw, *History of the Currency*; Andréadès, *History of the Bank of England*; Thorold Rogers, *The First Nine Years of the Bank of England*; Bagehot, *Lombard Street*: on commercial and fiscal policy; Day, *History of Commerce*; Levi, *History of British Commerce*; Hewins, *English Trade and Finance*; Beer, *The Old Colonial System* and *British Colonial Policy*; Hertz, *The Old Colonial System*; Ashley, *Surveys*; Cunningham, *Growth of English Industry and Commerce, Modern Times*, and *Rise and Decline of the Free Trade Movement*; Bruce, *Annals of the East India Company*; Holland, *The Fall of Protection*; Morley, *Life of Cobden*; Trevelyan, *Life of Bright;* Nicholson, *The English Corn Laws.* Smart, *Economic Annals of the Nineteenth Century*, analyses economic debates, legislation and conditions in the early nineteenth century.

Bibliographies in Cunningham, *op. cit.*, Day *op. cit.*, Cambridge Modern History, Vols. VI and X, and Grant Robertson, *England Under the Hanoverians.*

Contemporary.—Parliamentary Paper, **XXXV**, 1869, gives a summary of public revenue and expenditure, 1688–1869. Important documents for financial history are contained in the seventeenth century Treasury Papers (ed. Shaw). The Advice of the Council of Trade on the Exportation of Gold and Silver, 1660, is in McCulloch's Collection of Tracts on Money. The official history of the suspension of cash payments is in the Reports of Committees on the Restriction in Payments, 1797 (XI), on the High Price of Gold, 1810 (III), and on Cash Payments, 1819 (III).

A collection of literary authorities on monetary questions was made by McCulloch, "A Select Collection of Scarce and Valuable Tracts on Money"; it includes Petty's Quantulumcunque, Isaac Newton's Representations, etc. For contemporary opinion on taxation and finance, see Petty, Taxes and Taxation Price; Observations on Reversionary Payments, and The State of the Public Debts; Smith, The Wealth of Nations, and the Speeches of Pitt (Everyman Series), and of Cobden (edited Bright and Rogers). For foreign commerce consult The Diary and Consultation Book of Fort St. George (ed. Pringle), and Reports of Commons Committee on Orders in Council, 1812, together with the pamphlet literature on Colonial policy (see Cunningham *op. cit.* and McCulloch's Select Collection of Tracts on Commerce).

1. Act Abolishing Tenure by Knight Service, etc. [*Statutes*, 12 *Charles II*, 24], 1660.

It is hereby enacted that the Court of Wards and Liveries and all Wardships, Liveries, Primer-Seizins, and Ouster-le-mains, values, and forfeitures of marriages by reason of any tenure of the King's majesty or of any other knight's service, and all mean rates and all other gifts, grants, charges incident or arising for or by reason of wardships [etc.], be taken away and discharged. And that all fines for alienation, seizures, and pardons for alienations, tenure by homage [etc.], also Aide pur file marrier et pur farer fitz chivalier, and all other charges incident thereunto, be likewise taken away and discharged, as from February 24, 1645. And that all tenures by knight's service of the King, or of any other person and by knight service in capite, and by socage in capite of the King, and the fruits and consequents thereof—be taken away and discharged.

And all tenures of any Honours, manors, lands, tenements, or hereditaments of any estate of inheritance at the common law, held either of the King or of any other person or persons, bodies politic or corporate are hereby enacted to be turned into free and common socage to all intents and purposes.

[Purveyance and Pre-emption abolished.]

XIV. And now to the intent and purpose that his Majesty, his heirs and successors, may receive a full and ample recompence—there shall be paid unto the King's majesty his heirs and successors forever hereafter in recompence as aforesaid the several rates [etc.] following :—

[1*s*. 3*d*. a barrel of beer sold above 6*s*. a barrel.
3*d*. a barrel of beer sold at 6*s*. or below 6*s*. a barrel.
2*d*. a gallon of spirits imported.
3*s*. a barrel of beer imported.
1*d*. a gallon of aqua-vitae, etc.]

2. Navigation Act [*Statutes*, 12 *Chas. II*, 18], 1660.

An Act for the encouraging and increasing of shipping and navigation.

For the increase of shipping and encouragement of the navigation of this nation wherein, under the good providence and protection of God, the wealth, safety and strength of this kingdom is so much concerned; be it enacted by the King's most excellent majesty, and by the lords and commons in this present parliament assembled, and by the authority thereof, that from and after the first day of December one thousand six hundred and sixty, and from thenceforward, no goods or commodities whatsoever shall be imported into or exported out of any lands, islands, plantations or territories to his Majesty belonging or in his possession, or which may hereafter belong unto or be in the possession of his Majesty, his heirs and successors, in Asia, Africa or America, in any other ship or ships, vessel or vessels whatsoever, but in such ships or vessels as do truly and without fraud belong only to the people of England or Ireland, dominion of Wales or town of Berwick-upon-Tweed, or are of the built of and belonging to any the said lands, islands, plantations or territories, as the proprietors and right owners thereof, and whereof the master and three-fourths of the mariners at least are English.

And it is further enacted by the authority aforesaid, that no goods or commodities that are of foreign growth, production or manufacture, and which are brought into England, Ireland, Wales, the islands of Guernsey and Jersey, or town of Berwick-upon-Tweed, in English-built shipping, or other shipping belonging to some of the aforesaid places, and navigated by English mariners, as aforesaid, shall be shipped or brought from any other place or places, country or countries, but only from those of the said growth, production or manufacture, or from those ports where the said goods and commodities can only, or are, or usually have been, first shipped for transportation, and from none other places or countries.

3. Proposals for Free Exportation of Gold and Silver [*McCulloch, Tracts on Money*, 1856, *pp.* 145], 1660.

Advice of his Majesty's Council of Trade, concerning the Exportation of Gold and Silver in Foreign Coins and Bullion.

[Concluded Dec. 11, 1660.]

. . . Supposing that it were of absolute necessity to restrain all money and bullion, once imported, to be kept within this kingdom. It then came under consideration whether either the laws hitherto made in that behalf are, or that it be possible to make a law, adequate to prevent the exportation thereof.

And here we were convinced, by experience, that the laws of this kingdom (hitherto made) have been of no effect to the end thereby designed; and looking abroad, as there are nowhere more strict and severe laws against the exportation of coin and bullion than in Spain and France, we found all to be to as little purpose.

We then, thirdly, enquired what loadstone attracted this metal by force of nature to itself, against all human providence or prevention; and soon found that it was alone the present course of trade and traffic throughout the world. . . .

And therefore, in the fourth place, we discovered that, as it is impossible by any laws to restrain money and bullion against the use that traffic finds for the same; so also the adhering to this principle of restraining thereof discourageth, as well all natives as foreigners, to import any money or bullion—where the exportation thereof is forbidden them.

From whence, fifthly, the many advantages (thereby given away clearly to the stranger from the English) present themselves; for the stranger, knowing we must be furnished in one of these places for our occasions, make us pay dearly for our accommodation.

So that, to wind up all that has been said, the result of the several reasons and arguments herein summed up seemed to be this: that time and experience instruct, and the present state of traffic throughout the world require, that, for the increase of the stock of money in these your Majesty's kingdoms, some way of liberty for the exportation, at least of foreign coin and bullion, should be found out, and put in execution; which hath produced the humble advice offered in the preceding paper.

. . . . . .

4. AN ATTACK ON THE NAVIGATION ACT[1] [*P.R.O. Colonial Papers, Vol. XXXVI, No.* 88], *c.* 1663.

To the King's Most Excellent Majesty.

The Humble Remonstrance of John Bland, of London, Merchant, on the behalf of the Inhabitants and Planters of Virginia and Maryland.

[1] Quoted in *The Virginia Magazine of History and Biography*, Vol. I, pp. 142–145.

Most humbly representing unto your Majesty the inevitable destruction of these colonies, if so be that the late Act for increase of trade and shipping be not as to them dispensed with; for it will not only ruinate the inhabitants and planters, but make desolate the largest, fertilist, and most glorious plantations under Your Majesty's Dominion; the which, if otherwise suspended, will produce the greatest advantage to this nation's commerce and considerablest income to Your Majesty's revenue, that any part of the world doth to which we trade. [Rejoinder to argument that the Dutch prohibit English trade with their Indian Dominions. The American colonies are in need of customers. Why should the Dutch be prevented from dealing with them ?]

Virginia and Maryland are colonies, which though capable of better commodities, yet for the present afford only these, tobacco chiefly, then in the next place corn and cattle, commodities almost in every country whatever to be had; withal they are such commodities, that except purchased in these plantations so cheap as not elsewhere so to be had, none would ever go thither to fetch them, no, not we ourselves. Which being so, then certainly it cannot stand with wisdom to hinder the Hollanders from going thither.

Then again, if you keep thence the Hollanders, can it be believed that from England more ships will be sent than are able to bring thence what tobacco England will spend ? If they do bring more, must they not lose both stock and block, principal and charges ? . . .

A further prejudice doth evidently attend the commerce by this Act, not only in debarring Hollanders from trading to these colonies, but thereby we do likewise debar ourselves; for, by the Act, no English ships can load any goods in Virginia and Maryland to transport to any country but our own territories. . . . I demand then, if it would not be better to let our English ships, loading in those colonies, to go whither they please, and pay in the places where they do trade (if it will not be dispensed with otherwise), the same customs to your Majesty as they should have done in England, or give bills from thence to pay it in England ? Certainly this would be more beneficial to the commerce, and security both for the ships and goods, and advantageous to your Majesty; for whilst they are coming to England they might be at the end of their intended voyages and obtain a market, which haply in England could not be had. . . .

If that notwithstanding what is by the foregoing particulars declared, it may seem reasonable that the Act shall stand in force. . . . Then let me on behalf of the said colonies of Virginia and Maryland make these following proposals which I hope will appear but equitable; and I dare undertake for them, that they will be very well satisfied, that those few tobacconists that have engrossed that trade into their hands, shall still continue in it without moving further against them therein.

First, that the traders to Virginia and Maryland from England shall furnish and supply the planters and inhabitants of these colonies with all sorts of commodities and necessaries which they may want or desire, at as cheap rates and prices as the Hollanders used to have when the Hollander was admitted to trade hither.

Secondly, that the said traders out of England to these colonies shall not only buy of the planters such tobacco in the colonies as is fit for England, but take off all that shall be yearly made by them, at as good rates and prices as the Hollanders used to give. . . .

By way of accommodation this I propose. Let all Hollanders and other nations whatsoever freely trade into Virginia and Maryland, and bring thither and carry thence whatever they please, and to counterpoise the cheapness of their sailing, with dearness of our ships, to pay a set duty and imposition that may countervail the same; and when what they paid formerly will not do it, let it be doubled and trebled, as shall be thought meet, yet still with this caution, that it may not make it as bad as if they were totally prohibited.

In the next place, that all English ships that do go thither to trade, and carry goods to any other country besides England, may be freed of any custom there, more than some certain duty to the use of the colonies. . . .

5. Free Coinage of Bullion at the Mint Proclaimed [*Statutes*, 18 *Chas.* II, 5], 1666.

Whereas it is most obvious that the plenty of current coins of gold and silver of this kingdom is of great advantage to trade and commerce . . . be it enacted . . that whatsoever person or persons, native or foreigner, alien or stranger, shall from and after the twentieth day of December one thousand six hundred sixty and six, bring in any foreign coin, plate or bullion of gold or silver, in mass, molten or alloyed, or any sort of manufacture of gold or silver, into his Majesty's mint or mints within the kingdom of England, to be there melted down and coined into the current coins of this kingdom, shall have the same there assayed, melted down and coined with all convenient speed, without any defalcation, diminution or charge for the assaying, coinage or waste in coinage: so as that for every pound troy of crown or standard gold that shall be brought in and delivered by him or them . . . there shall be delivered . . . a pound troy of the current coins of this kingdom, of crown or standard gold.

6. The East India Company and the Interlopers [*Diary and Consultation Book of Fort St. George, Ed. Pringle, Series I, Vol. III, p.* 49], 1684.

To Sir John Wetwangs, Commander of ship Royal James.

His Majesty the King of England our Sovereign Lord having granted the Honourable East India Company full power and authority to enter into any ship or vessel, and to make seizure of the same, that shall be found in these parts of the East Indies, contrary to his royal will and pleasure,[1] . . . we therefore, the Agent and Council of Fort St. George, for the said Honourable East India Company, do . . . (there being now an Interlopers' ship, the *Constantinople*, merchant, John Smith, master, at Covelon), require you immediately to repair aboard your ship, weigh anchor, and set sail for that port of Covelon, and there seize upon the said Interlopers' ship and bring her into this Road of Madras. . . . Dated in Fort St. George the sixth day of June, 1684.

William Gyfford.
John Bigrig.
Elihu Yale.
John Nicks.
John Littleton.
John Gray.

[1] New Charter granted Aug. 9, 1683.

7. FOUNDATION OF THE BANK OF ENGLAND [*Statutes, 5 & 6, Wm. & Mary, 20*], 1694.

An Act for granting to their Majesties several rates and duties upon tunnage of ships and vessels, and upon beer, ale, and other liquors, for securing certain recompences and advantages in the said act mentioned, to such persons as shall voluntarily advance the sum of fifteen hundred thousand pounds, towards the carrying on the war against France.

XIX. And be it farther enacted by the authority aforesaid, that it shall and may be lawful to and for their Majesties, by commission under the great seal of England, to authorize and appoint any number of persons to take and receive all such voluntary subscriptions as shall be made on or before the first day of August, which shall be in the year of our Lord one thousand six hundred ninety four, by any person or persons, natives or foreigners, bodies politic or corporate.

XX. And be it further enacted, that it shall and may be lawful to and for their Majesties, by letters patents under the great seal of England, to limit, direct, and appoint, how and in what manner and proportions, and under what rules and directions, the said sum of twelve hundred thousand pounds, part of the said sum of fifteen hundred thousand pounds, and the said yearly sum of one hundred thousand pounds, part of the said yearly sum of one hundred and forty thousand pounds, and every or any part or proportion thereof, may be assignable or transferable, assigned or transferred, to such person or persons only as shall freely and voluntarily accept of the same, and not otherwise; and to incorporate all and every such subscribers and contributors, their heirs, successors, or assigns, to be one body corporate and politic, by the name of the governor and company of the bank of England, and, by the same name of the governor and company of the bank of England, to have perpetual succession, and a common seal.

XXVIII. Provided, that nothing herein contained shall any ways be construed to hinder the said corporation from dealing in bills of exchange, or in buying or selling bullion, gold, or silver, or in selling any goods, wares, or merchandize whatsoever, which shall really and *bona fide* be left or deposited with the said corporation for money lent and advanced thereon, and which shall not be redeemed at the time agreed on, or within three months after, or from selling such goods as shall or may be the produce of lands purchased by the said corporation.

8. The Need for the Recoinage of 1696 [*H. Haynes, Brief Memoirs Relating to the Silver and Gold Coins of England* (*in Lansdowne MSS*, 801, *British Museum*), *fs.* 33–48].

The silver money of England as well as the coins of all other countries are liable to abuse by these three following methods :

1st, by alteration of the standard appointed by public authority.

2nd, by melting them down and converting the metal to other uses.

3rd, by exporting them into foreign countries, to carry on a trade.

And by all those methods was the whole stock of the cash of this kingdom excessively impaired before the late grand coinage.

For 1st. the standard of our silver moneys appointed by the Government was notoriously violated. By standard is here meant that particular weight and fineness in the silver moneys which was settled by Queen Elizabeth and continued all her time, and after it, through the reigns of all her several successors down to her present Majesty, and was lately confirmed by Act of Parliament. . .. .

These were the just weights, and the legal fineness of our silver moneys coined with the hammer, of which sort the far greater part of the cash of the whole kingdom did consist; but they were very liable to be clipped and diminished in their weight, because very few of these pieces were of a just assize when they first came out of the Mint. So many pieces, I suppose, were by the Moneyers cut out of a bar of standard silver, as did pretty exactly answer the pound weight Troy ; and the tale of the pieces required in that weight, by the Indenture of the Mint : but though all the pieces together might come near the pound weight or be within remedy ; yet divers of them compared one with the other were very disproportionable, as was too well known to many persons, who picked out the heavy pieces, and threw them into the melting pot, to fit them for exportation, or to supply the silver smiths.

[Pieces of hammered money, "though never clipped, did many of them in their weight and value want or exceed the legal standard." Crowns varied from 5*s.* 3*d.* to 4*s.* 9*d.*, half-crowns from 3*s.* to 2*s.* 4*d.*, etc.]

According to the best observation of Goldsmiths[1] and others the clipping of our coins began to be discoverable in great receipts a little after the Dutch war in 1672, but it made no great progress at first for some years : and the silver moneys of Queen Elizabeth were very little diminished. . . . But the yearly loss by clipping made terrible advances every year from 1686. . . . In the later end of 1695[2] the public loss upon all the clipped money then actually current (if one may judge of the whole by the foregoing table) was at least 45 per cent. by mere clipping and light counterfeit pieces, which upon the whole running silver cash of the kingdom amounts to 2,250,000*l.*[3] . . .

The whole kingdom was in a general distraction by the badness of the silver coin and the rise of guineas, for no one knew what to trust to ; the landlord knew not in what to receive his rents, nor the tenant in what to pay them. Neither of them could foretell the value of his moneys to-morrow. The merchant could not foresee the worth of his wares at two or three days distance, and was at a loss to set a price upon his goods. Everybody was afraid to engage in any new contracts, and as shy in performing old ones, the King subsisted his forces in foreign parts at the disadvantage of seven or eight per cent. interest and five per cent. premio for money borrowed here, besides the loss by the Exchange abroad : and how to provide for the next year's expense, was a mystery.

9. SPEECH BY SIR ROBERT WALPOLE ON THE SALT DUTIES [*Parliamentary History* (*Cobbett*), *Vol. VIII*, *Col.* 943], 1732.

House of Commons. Debate on Sir Robert Walpole's motion for Salt Duties. February 9, 1732.

Sir Robert Walpole stood up and spoke as follows :—

Mr. Speaker,

As there is nothing his Majesty has more at heart than

[1] *Ibid* folio 38. [2] *Ibid* folio 40. [3] *Ibid* folio 48.

the giving all possible ease to his subjects; so, whenever he is necessarily obliged to desire assistance from them for the immediate support of the government, he desires that they would choose those ways and means for raising the annual supplies, which are least burthensome to the people, and which makes the load fall equally upon the subjects in general. When money is to be raised for the public good, for the security of all, he thinks that every one ought to contribute his share, in proportion to the benefit that he is thereby to receive.

As to the manner, sir, of raising taxes upon the people, it is a certain maxim that that tax which is the most equal and the most general, is the most just, and the least burthensome. Where every man contributes a small share, a great sum may be raised for the public service, without any man's being sensible of what he pays; whereas a small sum, raised upon a few, lies heavy upon each particular man, and is the more grievous, in that it is unjust; for where the benefit is mutual, the expense ought to be in common. Of all the taxes I ever could think of, there is not one more general nor one less felt, than that of the duty upon salt. The duty upon salt is a tax that every man in the nation contributes to according to his circumstances and condition in life; every subject contributes something; if he be a poor man, he contributes so small a trifle, it will hardly bear a name; if he be rich, he lives more luxuriously, and consequently contributes more; and if he be a man of a great estate, he keeps a great number of servants, and must therefore contribute a great deal. Upon the other hand, there is no tax that ever was laid upon the people of this nation, that is more unjust and unequal than the Land Tax. The landholders bear but a small proportion to the people of this nation, or of any nation; yet no man contributes any the least share to this tax, but he that is possessed of a land estate; and yet this tax has been continued without intermission for above these 40 years.

10. Pitt's Sinking Fund Act [*Statutes*, 26 *Geo. III*, 31], 1786.

An Act for vesting certain sums in commissioners, at the end of every quarter of a year, to be by them applied to the reduction of the national debt.

[£250,000 is to be set apart quarterly out of the sinking fund.]

IV. Provided always, and be it enacted by the authority aforesaid, that if at any time it should happen, that at the end of the year ending the fifth day of January, one thousand seven hundred and eighty seven, or at the end of any future year, computed as aforesaid, after provision shall have been made for all payments for which monies are previously to be set apart or issued according to the directions of this act, the said surpluses, excesses, and overplus monies, composing the sinking fund, shall not be sufficient to make good as well all such deficiencies as shall have arisen during such year, as the payment of the sum of two hundred and fifty thousand pounds then due, in every such case, the amount of such deficiency or deficiencies, whether the same shall have arisen in any preceding quarter or quarters within such year, or in the quarter ending on the fifth day of January on which such year shall end, shall not be carried forward as a charge on the said sinking fund at the end of the next succeeding quarter, but shall be made good out of any aids or supplies which shall be or shall have been granted by parliament for the service of the then current year; and the amount of such deficiency or deficiencies so to be made good, shall be issued to the governor and company of the bank of England, in the manner hereinafter directed, within ten days after monies sufficient to answer the same shall have been paid into his Majesty's receipt of exchequer, on account of any such aids or supplies.

V. And be it further enacted by the authority aforesaid, that the monies so set apart, at the end of any quarter of a year ending as aforesaid, or of any year computed as aforesaid either for the payment of the sum of two hundred and fifty thousand pounds due at the end of such quarter, or of any part thereof, or for making good such deficiency or deficiencies as aforesaid, shall forthwith be issued and paid to the governor and company of the bank of England, and shall by them be placed to an account to be raised in their books, and to be intituled, 'The account of the commissioners appointed by act of parliament for applying certain sums of money annually to the reduction at the national debt: and that as well all such monies, as any other monies which shall be paid to the governor and company of the bank of England by virtue of this act, to be placed to the said account, shall be applied by the commissioners hereinafter appointed towards the reduction of the national debt, in the manner hereinafter directed, and to no other intent or purpose, and in no other manner whatever.

X. And be it further enacted by the authority aforesaid, that all monies whatever, which shall be placed from time to time to the account of the said commissioners by virtue of this act, shall be applied by them either in payments for the redemption of such redeemable public annuities as shall be at or above par, in such manner and at such periods as shall be directed by any future act or acts of parliament, or to the purchase of any public annuities below par in the manner hereinafter directed.

11. The Suspension of Cash Payments [*Reports of Committees on Bank of England*, 1797 *and* 1826, *in Reports* 1826 (*III*), *pp.* 142 *and* 255–256], 1797.

The alarm of Invasion [in 1796–1797] which, when an immediate attack was first apprehended in Ireland, had occasioned some extraordinary demand for cash on the Bank of England, in the months of December and January last, began in February to produce similar results in the north of England. Your Committee find, that in consequence of this apprehension, the farmers suddenly brought the produce of their lands to sale, and carried the notes of the County Banks, which they had collected by those and other means, into those banks for payment; that this unusual and sudden demand for cash reduced the several banks at Newcastle to the necessity of suspending their payments in specie, and of availing themselves of all the means in their power of procuring a speedy supply of cash from the metropolis; that the effects of this demand on the Newcastle banks and their suspension of payments in cash, soon spread over various parts of the country, from whence similar applications were consequently made to the metropolis for cash; that the alarm thus diffused not only occasioned an increased demand for cash in the country, but probably a disposition in many to hoard what was thus obtained; that this call on the metropolis, through whatever channels, directly affected the Bank of England, as the great repository of cash, and was in the course of still further operation upon it, when stopped by the Minute of Council of the 26th of February.[1]

. . . . . .

Your Committee find, that the Court of Directors of the Bank did, on the 26th October 1797, come to a Resolution, a copy of which is subjoined to this Report.

Your Committee, having further examined the Governor and Deputy Governor, as to what may be meant by the political circumstances mentioned in that resolution, find, that they understand by them, the state of hostility in which the nation is still involved, and particularly such apprehensions as may be entertained of invasion, either in Ireland or in this country, together with the possibility there may be of advances being to be made from this country to Ireland; and that from these circumstances so explained, and from the nature of the war, and the avowed purpose of the enemy to attack this country by means of its public credit, and to distress it in its financial operations, they are led to think that it will be expedient to continue the restriction now subsisting, with the reserve for partial issues of cash, at the discretion of the Bank, of the nature of that contained in the present Acts; and that it may be so continued, without injury to the credit of the Bank, and to the advantage of the nation.

"*Resolved*, that it is the opinion of this Court,[2] that the Governor and Company of the Bank of England are enabled to issue Specie, in any manner that may be deemed necessary for the accommodation of the public; and the Court have no hesitation to declare that the affairs of the Bank are in such a state, that it can with safety resume its accustomed functions, if the political circumstances of the country do not render it inexpedient: but the Directors deeming it foreign to their province to judge of these points, wish to submit to the wisdom of Parliament, whether, as it has been once judged proper to lay a restriction on the payment of the bank in cash, it may, or may not, be prudent to continue the same?"[3]

[1] The Minute of February 26, 1797, suspended the obligation of the Bank of England to pay coin for its notes.

[2] Copy of a Resolution of the Court of Directors of the Bank of England at a meeting on Thursday, October 26, 1797.

[3] The Bank of England resumed cash payments, 1819.

12. PITT'S SPEECH ON THE INCOME TAX [*Speeches of William Pitt, edited W. S. Hathaway*, 1806, *Vol. III*, *pp.* 282–333], 1798.

I shall begin by stating what has been voted as the amount of the supply under the head of the services for the navy, with the exception of what is necessary for the transport services. All these accounts have this day been laid before us; and it appears that the total sum for the ordinaries and extra-ordinaries of the navy and transport services amounts to 13,642,000*l.*, being the same sum, within a very small amount, as was granted in the course of last session, and which I have the satisfaction of assuring the committee is likely to prove sufficient for the whole expenses of the navy, without leaving any necessity for augmentation. The next head of expense is the army, in which the estimates amount to 8,840,000*l.* . . . Under the head of ordnance services, including the expenses which have not been provided for, there has been voted the sum of 1,570,000*l.* The next article is that of the miscellaneous services. The plantation estimates have already been voted, but there are other minuter parts of these services which have not yet undergone a discussion in this house. The amount will be rather less than it was last session. I state it [at] 600,000*l.* To this is to be added the usual sum voted towards the redemption of the national debt, above the annual million, which is 200,000*l.* There are other sums, which are generally voted under the head of deficiency of grants. Among these is a sum due for interest on treasury and exchequer bills paid off, amounting to 565,000*l.*; the discount on prompt payments upon the loan, amounting to 210,000*l.*; the interest on exchequer bills circulated within the year, and charged upon the succeeding year, 300,000*l.*; in addition to this, there is the deficiency of the land and malt in the act passed two years ago, amounting to 300,000*l.* These sums swell the total of the supply to 29,272,000*l.* This total, sir, does not differ in any material degree from the amount of the supply of last session.

[He then estimates prospective sources of revenue:

Land and malt taxes	2,750,000*l.*
Lottery	200,000*l.*
Produce of the consolidated fund	1,500,000*l.*
Import and Export taxes	1,700,000*l.*
	6,150,000*l.*]

The remainder of the sum is that which must be raised either by a tax within the year, in the same manner as the assessed tax bill of last year, or by a loan. It will be to be considered, how the committee will divide that remaining sum between them. The sum to be provided for is upwards of twenty-three millions. Gentlemen will recollect that, in the debates upon the subject of the assessed taxes last session, two fundamental principles were established as the rule by which we should be guided in providing for the supplies for the service of the year. These were, first, to reduce the total amount to be at present raised by a loan ; and next, as far as it was not reducible, to reduce it to such a limit, that no more loan should be raised than a temporary tax should defray within a limited time. In the first place, the tax acceded to by the House last session[1] was for the purpose of providing for the supplies of the year ; and in the next place, for the purpose of extinguishing the loan raised in that year. From the modifications, however, which that measure underwent after its being first proposed, the produce of it was diminished to a considerable extent. Other means indeed were adopted to remedy the deficiency which was thus occasioned. The voluntary and cheerful efforts which, so honourably to individuals and to the country, came in aid of the assessed taxes, and the superior produce of the exports and imports beyond the estimate, brought the amount of the sums raised to that at which they had been calculated. The different articles were estimated at seven millions and a half, and this sum was fully covered by the actual receipts under the distinct heads. It gives me, indeed, the most heartfelt satisfaction to state, that notwithstanding the difficulties which the measure encountered from the shameful evasion, or rather the scandalous frauds by which its effects were counteracted, the total amount which was expected has yet been realized. The meanness which shrunk from fair and equal contribution has been compensated to the public by the voluntary exertions of patriotism. The produce of the assessed taxes, under all the modifications, and all the evasions, is four millions. I had taken it at four and a half after the modifications. The deficiency is supplied by the excess on head of voluntary contributions. . . .

[1] The Triple Assessment, based on the individual's previous payment to the various taxes on expenditure which Pitt had grouped together as the Assessed Taxes.

Satisfactory as it must be to review the circumstances to which we owe those advantages, and the benefits which the mode of raising the supplies to a considerable extent adopted last session has produced, it is unnecessary for me to state that, however the principle may deserve our approbation, it is still much to be desired that its effects should be more extensive, and its application more efficient. . . . Every circumstance in our situation, every event in the retrospect of our affairs, every thing which strikes our view as we look around us, demonstrates the advantages of the system of raising a considerable part of the supplies within the year, and ought to induce us to enforce it more effectually to prevent those frauds, which an imperfect criterion and a loose facility of modification have introduced; to repress those evasions so disgraceful to the country, so injurious to those who honourably discharge their equal contribution, and, above all, so detrimental to the great object of national advantage which it is intended to promote. In these sentiments, our leading principle should be to guard against all evasion, to endeavour by a fair and strict application to realize that full tenth, which it was the original purpose of the measure of the assessed taxes to obtain, and to extend this as far as possible in every direction, till it may be necessary clearly to mark the modification, or to renounce, in certain instances, the application of it altogether. If then, the committee assent to this principle, they must feel the necessity of following it up by a more comprehensive scale and by more efficient provisions. They will perceive the necessity of obtaining a more specific statement of income, than the loose scale of modification, which, under the former measure, permitted such fraud and evasion. If such a provision be requisite to correct the abuses of a collection, to obviate the artifices of dishonesty, to extend the utility of the whole system, it will be found that many of the regulations of the old measure will be adapted to a more comprehensive and efficient application of the principle. If regulations can be devised to prevent an undue abatement, and to proportion the burden to the real ability, means must be employed to reach those resources which, *primâ facie*, it is impossible under the present system of the assessed taxes to touch. While inaccuracy, fraud, inequality, be grievances which it is desirable to remedy, it will be an additional satisfaction, that when compelled to adopt means to prevent the defects of which we complain, we shall be enabled likewise to improve and to extend the benefits we have obtained. The experience which we have had upon the subject, proves that we must correct and remedy, in order to secure the advantages which the measure is calculated to afford. It is in our power to make them our own. I think I can show that whatever benefit the principle upon which we have begun to act, is fitted to bestow, may by a liberal, fair and efficient application, be carried to an extent far greater than has yet been obtained, an extent equal to every object of great and magnanimous effort, to every purpose of national safety and glory, to every advantage of permanent credit and of increased prosperity.

Impressed then with the importance of the subject, convinced that we ought, as far as possible, to prevent all evasion and fraud, it remains for us to consider, by what means these defects may be redressed, by what means a more equal scale of contributions can be applied, and a more extensive effect obtained. For this purpose it is my intention to propose, that the presumption founded upon the assessed taxes shall be laid aside, and that a general tax shall be imposed upon all the leading branches of income. No scale of income indeed which can be devised will be perfectly free from the objection of inequality, or entirely cut ofi the possibility of evasion. All that can be attempted is, to approach as near as circumstances will permit to a fair and equal contribution. . . . The details of a measure which attempts an end so great and important, must necessarily require serious and mature deliberation. At present all that I can pretend to do is, to lay before the committee an outline of the plan which endeavours to combine every thing at which such a measure ought to aim. This outline I shall now proceed to develop to the committee as clearly and distinctly as I am able.

. . . . . .

The next point for consideration then, is the mode of contribution which shall be adopted. On this head it is my intention to propose that no income under 60*l.* a year shall be called upon to contribute, and that the scale of modification up to 200*l.* a year, as in assessed taxes, shall be introduced with restriction. The quota which will then be called for ought to amount to a full tenth of the contributor's income. The mode proposed of obtaining this contribution differs from that pursued in the assessed taxes, as instead of trebling their amount, the statement of income is to proceed from the party himself.

[A detailed estimate of income from different sources follows. One-fifth is deducted to allow for the remission of taxation on incomes under 60*l.* and graduation under 200*l.* from $\frac{1}{120}$ to $\frac{1}{10}$.]

For the sake of greater clearness I will recapitulate the heads in the same order that I have followed :—

The land rental, then, after deducting one-fifth, I estimate at	20,000,000*l.*
The tenant's rental of land, deducting two-thirds of rack rent, I take at	6,000,000*l.*
The amount of tythes, deducting one-fifth ..	4,000,000*l.*
The produce of mines, canal navigation, etc., deducting one-fifth	3,000,000*l.*
The rental of houses, deducting one-fifth.. ..	5,000,000*l.*
The profits of professions	2,000,000*l.*
The rental of Scotland, taking it at one-eighth of that of England	5,000,000*l.*
The income of persons resident in Great Britain drawn from possessions beyond seas ..	5,000,000*l.*
The amount of annuities, from the public funds, after deducting one-fifth for exemptions and modifications	12,000,000*l.*
The profits on the capital employed in our foreign commerce	12,000,000*l.*
The profits on the capital employed in domestic trade, and the profits of skill and industry	28,000,000*l.*
In all ..	102,000,000*l.*

Upon this sum a tax of 10 per cent. is likely to produce 10,000,000*l.* a year, and this is the sum which is likely to result from the measure, and at which I shall assume it.

. . . . . .

I trust that it will not be necessary for me to go into any detail of argument to convince the committee of the advantages of the beneficial mode adopted last session, of raising a considerable part of the supplies within the year. . . . It will be manifest to every gentleman on the slightest consideration of the subject, that, in the end, the measure of raising the supplies within the year is the cheapest and the most salutary course that a wise people can pursue ; and when it is considered that there is a saving of at least one-twelfth upon all that is raised, gentlemen will not suffer a superstitious fear, and jealousy of the danger of exposing the secrecy of income, to combat with a measure that is so pregnant with benefits to the nation. If gentlemen will take into their consideration the probable duration of peace and war, calculated from the experience of past times, they will be convinced of the immeasurable importance of striving to raise the supplies within the year, rather than accumulating a permanent debt. The experience of the last hundred, fifty, or forty years, will show how little confidence we can have in the duration of peace, and it ought to convince us how important it is to establish a system that will prepare us for every emergency, give stability to strength, and perpetual renovations to resource. I think I could make it apparent to gentlemen that in any war, of the duration of six years, the plan of funding all the expenses to be incurred in carrying it on, would leave at the end of it a greater burden permanently upon the nation than would be sustained, than they would have to incur for the six years only of its continuance, and one year beyond it, provided that they made the sacrifice of a tenth of their income. In the old, unwise, and destructive way of raising the supplies by a permanent fund, without any provision for its redemption, a war so carried on entails the burden upon the age and upon their posterity for ever. This has, to be sure, in a great measure, been done away and corrected, by the salutary and valuable system which has been adopted of the redemption fund. But that fund cannot accomplish the end in a shorter period than forty years, and during all that time the expenses of a war so funded must weigh down and press upon the people. If, on the contrary, it had at an earlier period of our history been resolved to adopt the present mode of raising the supplies within the year; if, for instance, after the peace of Aix-la-Chapelle, the scheme of redemption had been adopted and persevered in to this time, we should not now, for the seventh year of the war, have had more to raise from the pockets of the people than what we have now to pay of permanent taxes, together with about a fourth of what it would be necessary to lay on in addition for this year. Fortunately, we have at last established the redemption fund : the benefits of it are already felt ; they will every year be more and more acknowledged ; and in addition to this it is only necessary, that instead of consulting a present advantage, and throwing the burden, as heretofore, upon posterity, we shall fairly meet it ourselves, and lay the foundation of a system that shall make us independent of all the future events of the world.[1]

13. FOREIGN TRADE IN THE EARLY NINETEENTH CENTURY [*Committee on Orders in Council, Reports* 1812 (*III*), *pp.* 38, 40, 41, 132-133, 522-523], *c.* 1812.

[Evidence of Joseph Shaw, Chairman of Birmingham Chamber of Foreign Commerce and exporter of hardwares.]

Have you had occasion to make any estimate, founded upon your own inquiries, of the number of workmen employed in the Birmingham manufactory[2]—and the neighbouring towns? I never particularly estimated for the whole of them, but in the year 1808 I took an estimate of the people employed in the American trade. . . . Those that could be ascertained to be (as nearly as could be) exclusively employed in the American trade were 50,000, exclusive of the nail trade, which employed from twenty to thirty thousand [of whom two-thirds were engaged in the American trade].

. . . .

Can you state to the Committee, from your observation, what proportion the foreign trade generally bears to the trade for home consumption? . . . I should think it was considerably more than one half, including the United States.

Do you think it would amount to two-thirds? I should think not far from it. . . . Do you think the foreign trade is equal to two-thirds of the whole manufacture?—When the

[1] The income tax was recast in 1803, when Schedules of different sources of income, instead of a general return, were introduced. It was again revised in 1806. In 1816 it was repealed. Peel reintroduced it in 1842 for three years, and it then became permanent.

[2] Brassfounding, hardware, plated ware, jewellery, etc.

foreign trade is the same as in the year 1810, not in its present state; it is now very different. . . .

. . . .

To what cause do you ascribe the diminution of your trade to the Continent ?—The risk of sending goods into many ports of the Continent is too great. . . .

. . . .

Then it is the French, Berlin, and other decrees that have produced this diminution of your trade to the Continent ?—To my own particular trade. I cannot say how it is as to others.

[Evidence of John Bailey, exporter and home factor of Sheffield goods.]

What are the principal articles manufactured at Sheffield ?—They are very numerous, I can present a list of them to the House; the principal articles are cutlery, files, edged tools, saws, and a great variety of other heavy articles.

. . . .

Can you speak to the population of Sheffield, and such parts of the neighbouring parishes as are concerned in the Sheffield manufacture ?—The population of the parish of Sheffield, as returned by the overseers in the year 1811, was 53,000 odd; but including those parts of parishes in which Sheffield goods are manufactured, the population amounts to 60,000 at least.

Can you tell what proportion of hands are employed in manufacturing for the American market ?—For the American market, about 4,000 male adults, and 2,000 women and children, making a total of 6,000.

. . . .

How many do you estimate are employed in manufacturing for the home trade ?—Six thousand male adults, and one thousand women and children.

How many do you calculate are employed in the remaining parts of the Sheffield trade, namely, manufactures for the foreign market, exclusive of the American ?—Two thousand male adults, and one thousand women and children.

This last market includes Spain and Portugal ?—Spain, Portugal, the West Indies, South America, and Canada, with some few other parts.

What proportion does the American market bear to the

home market, as far as regards the Sheffield goods ?—The American exports amount, as nearly as I have been able to ascertain, to one-third of the whole manufactures of Sheffield; the home trade to, I think, three-sixths.

[He adds that the American trade had been affected by the Orders in Council and the Non-importation Act of the United States. The home trade with towns in the American trade had been injured also. Goods to the value of £400,000 were waiting in Sheffield and Liverpool warehouses.

[Evidence of Robert MacKerrell, London merchant, dealing in cottons and muslins, and manufacturer of Paisley.]

Can you inform the Committee what the state of the trade was in the years 1808, 1809, 1810, and 1811 ?—In 1807 we felt the whole effect of the Berlin decree, we were entirely excluded from the Continent; I speak with regard to my own transactions and those of a vast number of my friends. We had in 1807, and previous to that, trades to the South of Europe, particularly in Portugal, which were uninterrupted, but which were likewise put an end to by the French invasion in November of that year. In 1808 the trade revived considerably; a great quantity of our goods, and of English merchandise, was introduced into the Continent through Heligoland; considerable exports were made to the Baltic; the trade in the Mediterranean increased very considerably; a very great trade was opened to this country in consequence of the Royal Family of Portugal removing to the Brazils, which likewise made an opening to Spanish South America. In 1809 the trade through Heligoland was most extensive; Bonaparte had his hands full with the Emperor of Germany and with the Spaniards, and had no time to attend to the coast; the trade during that year I may say was uninterrupted. The trade to the Mediterranean increased very much; the quantity of goods taken out that year greatly exceeded any previous year, for reasons that at that time we could not account for. The trade to the Brazils was equally extensive with the year before, vast exportations took place to South America, and in general, trade in the line in which I am engaged was reckoned a fair trade; the markets were never heavy.

[The Orders in Council increased the English export trade to the South of Europe, and Africa and the Levant were supplied with English substitutes for Continental cottons and linens.]

What has been the state of your trade for the last eighteen months, and, as far as you have been informed, of the country in general ?—The state of the trade during the last eighteen months has been depressed ; for the last twelve months it has been recovering, but for the six months previous it was very much depressed indeed.

To what do you attribute that depression ?—We attribute the depression of trade which took place to the effect of the Berlin and Milan decrees. [Northern Europe, the Baltic, etc., were shut against English trade, and English ships were sequestered even in Swedish ports.]

14. DEBATE ON THE CORN LAW [*Parliamentary History*, 1*st Series*, *Vol. XXIX*, *Cols.* 798–818], 1815.

House of Commons. February 17, 1815.

The State of the Corn Laws.

The *Hon. Frederick Robinson* immediately rose. . . . He had never disguised from himself, and he was not ashamed to confess it, the extreme difficulty, as well as the extreme importance, of this question. He could not, however, but feel that the prejudices on this subject had, from further inquiry, been very much removed. But, above all, he was happy to see that the misrepresentations, for so he thought they were, with respect to the motives of those who supported this measure, and with reference to the effects which it was likely to produce, were done away with. There did not now exist in the public mind the feeling by which it was before influenced. It was not now supposed that the object sought to be accomplished by the alteration of the corn law was the mean and base and paltry one of getting, for a particular class of society, a certain profit at the expense of the rest. "For my part," said Mr. Robinson, "I declare to God, if I thought this was the motive which actuated any individual who supported the alteration ; and, above all, if I conceived that such would be the effect of the measure, no consideration on earth could tempt me to bring it forward." . . .

. . . . .

. . . The general result of his reasoning was, in the first

place, that it was quite impossible for us safely to rely on a foreign import. If they so did, a necessary result would be a diminution of our own produce, which would become more and more extensive every year, and consequently call for a greater annual supply from foreign countries—a supply which must progressively increase as the agriculture of the kingdom became less encouraged; and that, when the fatal moment arrived, the system of foreign supply would prove completely illusory.

The next point to be considered was the extent to which protection should be given. That was a point on which, undoubtedly, a difference of opinion was most likely to prevail. Some gentlemen would be for going considerably higher than others. Many thought the prohibition ought to be carried to a price considerably above that, without he obtained which it was conceived the agriculturalist could not cultivate. Others would wish that it should be placed much lower; and contend that because a particular species and degree of burden was likely to be removed, the protecting price ought to be much reduced. Now he would be inclined to agree to the first of these propositions, if the necessary effect of it would not be to bring up the price of corn to the highest possible rate, within the limits of the sum at which importation should commence. This certainly might be the case at the first moment, but he believed the ultimate result would not be so. He thought the final effect of the system would be to give such a powerful support to our own agriculture as would greatly increase the general produce of the country. It would excite a strong competition between the different parts of England, and between England and Ireland; so that the growth of corn, if Providence blessed us with favourable seasons, would be sufficiently large to afford an ample supply for the people of this country, and would enable them to be fed at a much cheaper rate, in the long run, than could be effected by the adoption of any other system.

. . . . . .

Mr. Philips professed himself equally inclined either to proceed with, or defer the discussion, as might be most agreeable to the wishes of the House. Several members calling out "Go on," he began by stating his entire concurrence in the opinion of the right hon. gentleman who had moved the resolutions, that this was not a question on which the interests of the commercial and agricultural classes were at variance, but one in which those interests, when fairly and liberally considered, would be found to accord ; for no resolution upon it calculated to promote the general prosperity of the country could be adopted without materially benefiting both classes. But if this were not the case, if the question were one in which the interests of two or more descriptions of our fellow-subjects were opposed, he should say that it was the duty of parliament not to legislate for the advantage of one class in contradistinction to, or at the expense of another, but to legislate for the benefit of the whole community. Looking at the question under the influence of this principle, he could not help feeling and expressing some surprise at the occasion of their present deliberations. What was the object of their deliberations ? To provide a remedy for the low price of corn. That which all ages and countries had considered as a great national benefit was now discovered to be a great evil, against which we were imperiously called to legislate in self-defence. The real object of the resolutions, however disguised and disavowed, was to raise the price of corn. [Here Mr. Robinson expressed his dissent.] Mr. Philips proceeded to say that this not only was their object, but if that object were not attained, the advocates of the resolutions would regard them as nugatory. The right hon. gentleman must at least allow that their object was to raise the present price of grain ; but he contended that moderation and uniformity of price would be their ultimate effect. It did seem somewhat inconsistent, on the part of the hon. gentleman, to tell the House that the effectual way to lower price was to acquiesce in a measure expressly intended to raise it. But how are this moderation and uniformity of price to be produced ? By contracting the market of supply. Thus, while in all other instances moderation and uniformity of price are found to be in proportion to the extent of the market of supply, in the instance of corn they are to be in proportion to the limitation of it : and in a commodity peculiarly liable to be affected by the variation of seasons, moderation and uniformity of price, and abundance, are to be attained by preventing importations from foreign countries correcting the effect of varieties of climate, and of a scanty harvest in our own. To him it appeared that no measure could be better calculated to produce directly opposite consequences.

. . . . . .

In considering the relation between the price of provisions and of labour, Mr. Philips observed that it was necessary to distinguish the countries and the trades from which examples were taken. In a new country where the value of land is extremely low, and agriculture rapidly progressive, in a new and thriving manufacture, the price of labour may be so high in proportion to that of the necessaries of life as to be little affected by their fluctuations. . . . But this state of things cannot exist in old manufactures, such as those generally established in this country, where competition has reduced profits, and that reduction of profit has brought the wages of the labourer to a level with his subsistence in tolerable comfort. In such manufactures if you raise the price of provisions without proportionately raising that of labour, to what privations and evils must you necessarily expose the labourer! He was ready to admit with the noble lord[1] that, *ceteris paribus*, the immediate effect of a high advance of provisions might probably be a reduction of the price of labour; because labourers being desirous of obtaining the same comforts that they had been used to, might be stimulated to more diligence. They might work sixteen hours a day instead of ten, and thus the competition for employment being increased among the same number of workmen, without any increase of demand, the price of labour might fall. But will any person contend that this state of affairs can long continue? The labourer must go to the parish, or turn to some more profitable employment, if by chance any can be found, or he must emigrate, or work himself out by over-strained exertion. The proportion being then altered between the demand for labour and the supply, its price will rise. This effect sooner or later must happen, but till it has actually taken place how dreadful must be the situation of the labourer!

. . . . . .

Having thus shown both by reasoning and by reference to facts, that the price of provisions must ultimately and on

[1] Lord Lauderdale in evidence before a committee of the House of Lords.

the average regulate that of labour, he proceeded to show the effect that an advance of provisions must have on our manufacturing interests. And here Mr. Philips said that he wishede on such topics, to reduce his reasoning as much as possible to numerical calculation. He would suppose, for the sake of argument, without at all entering into the enquiry, that three-fifths, or 60 per cent. of the labourer's wages were spent in provisions, and that provisions were 80 per cent. dearer here than they were in France, or any manufacturing country on the continent. By multiplying 60 by 80, and dividing by 100, the committee would see that the excess of the price of labour here above that of France would, from these datas, and according to his reasoning, be 48 per cent. He wished the committee to consider what must be the effect of such an excessive price of labour employed in our manufactures, when compared with the low price of labour employed in the manufactures of France, and what an advantage it must give to the French manufacturers in their attempts to rival us on the continent.

. . . . . .

[After quoting Malthus] he observed that there were two ways of equalising subsistence and population, one by increasing food, the other by limiting population, and warned the committee against being led into measures whose tendency might be to produce that effect in the latter way. Why (said Mr. Philips) should a commercial and manufacturing country like this have such a jealousy and dread of the importation of corn ? An importation of corn cannot take place without a corresponding export of commodities on which British industry has been employed. The export will increase your wealth, that wealth will increase your population, and that increased population will produce an increased demand for your agricultural produce. . . . Mr. Philips observed that no country in the world was so interested as this in establishing the principle of free trade, because no other country could profit equally by the general recognition of that principle. Foreign nations, mistaking, like the advocates of the regulation before the committee, the circumstances which have operated against our wealth for the causes of it, are now following our example. They are prohibiting or imposing restraints on the import of our fabrics, in order to encourage their own manufactures, from which they will receive inferior fabrics at a higher price. Let us convince them, by an example, of their mistake. Let us convince them that by leaving industry and enterprise unfettered, and by allowing capital to take its natural and voluntary direction, we are persuaded that the true interests of this country and of every other will be most effectually promoted.

Mr. Philips proceeded to say that Great Britain was geographically a commercial country, that commerce had stimulated her agriculture rather than agriculture had stimulated her commerce. It had given wealth to her people, and diffused fertility over her soil. Take care, said he, that in attempting to change the natural character of your country, you do not stop the progress of national prosperity. . . .

15. The Corn Law of 1815 [*Statutes*, 55 *Geo. III*, 26].

An Act to amend the laws now in force regulating the Importation of Corn.

[Corn may at all times be imported and warehoused free of duty.]

III. And be it further enacted, that such foreign corn, meal or flour, shall and may be permitted to be imported into the said United Kingdom, for home consumption, under and subject to the provisions and regulations now in force, without payment of any duty whatever, whenever the average prices of the several sorts of British corn, made up and published in the manner now by law required, shall be at or above the prices hereafter mentioned; that is to say, whenever wheat shall be at or above the price of eighty shillings per quarter; whenever rye, pease and beans shall be at or above the price of fifty-three shillings per quarter; whenever barley, beer or bigg shall be at or above the price of forty shillings per quarter; and whenever oats shall be at or above the price of twenty-seven shillings per quarter.

IV. And be it further enacted, that whenever the average prices of British corn so made up and published shall respectively be below the prices hereinbefore stated, no foreign corn, or meal, or flour made from any of the respective sorts of foreign corn hereinbefore enumerated, shall be allowed to be imported into the United Kingdom for the purpose of home consumption, or taken out of warehouse for that purpose.

V. And be it further enacted, that the average price of the several sorts of British corn, by which the importation of foreign corn, meal or flour, into the United Kingdom shall be regulated and governed, shall continue to be made up and published in any manner now required by law; but that if it shall hereafter at any time after the importation of foreign corn, meal or flour shall be permitted, under the provisions of this Act, appear that the average prices of the different sorts of British corn respectively in the six weeks immediately succeeding the fifteenth day of February, the fifteenth day of May, the fifteenth day of August and the fifteenth day of November in each year, shall have fallen below the prices at which foreign corn, meal or flour may be, under the provisions of this Act, allowed to be imported for home consumption, no such foreign corn, meal or flour shall be allowed to be imported into the United Kingdom for home consumption from any place between the rivers Eyder and Bidassoa, both inclusive, until a new average shall be made up and published in the London Gazette for regulating the importation into the United Kingdom for the succeeding quarter.

16. FREE TRADE PETITION[1] [*Commons Journals, Vol. LXXV.*], 1820.

The Petition, etc.,
Humbly sheweth

That foreign commerce is eminently conducive to the wealth and prosperity of a country, by enabling it to import the commodities for the production of which the soil, climate, capital, and industry of other countries are best calculated, and to export in payment those articles for which its own situation is better adapted.

That freedom from restraint is calculated to give the utmost extension to foreign trade, and the best direction to the capital and industry of the country.

That the maxim of buying in the cheapest market and selling in the dearest, which regulates every merchant in his individual dealings, is strictly applicable as the best rule for the trade of the whole nation.

[1] Quoted in Hirst, *Free Trade and the Manchester School*, pp. 118-121.

That a policy founded on these principles would render the commerce of the world an interchange of mutual advantages, and diffuse an increase of wealth and enjoyments among the inhabitants of each State.

That, unfortunately, a policy the very reverse of this has been, and is, more or less, adopted and acted upon by the Government of this and of every other country. . . .

That the prevailing prejudices in favour of the protective or restrictive system may be traced to the erroneous supposition that every importation of foreign commodities occasions a diminution or discouragement of our own productions to the same extent, whereas it may be clearly shown that although the particular description of production which could not stand against unrestrained foreign competition would be discouraged, yet, as no importation could be continued for any length of time without a corresponding exportation, direct or indirect, there would be an encouragement, for the purpose of that exportation, of some other production to which our situation might be better suited, thus affording at least an equal, and probably a greater, and certainly a more beneficial employment to our own capital and labour.

. . . . . .

That, among the other evils of the restrictive or protective system, not the least is, that the artificial protection of one branch of industry, or source of production, against foreign competition, is set up as a ground of claim by other branches for similar protection, so that if the reasoning upon which these restrictive or prohibitory regulations are founded were followed out consistently, it would not stop short of excluding us from all foreign commerce whatsoever. And the same train of argument, which, with corresponding prohibitions and protective duties, should exclude us from foreign trade, might be brought forward to justify the re-enactment of restrictions upon the interchange of productions (unconnected with public revenue) among the kingdoms composing the union, or among the counties of the same kingdom.

That an investigation of the effects of the restrictive system at this time is peculiarly called for, as it may, in the opinions of your petitioners, lead to a strong presumption that the distress which now so generally prevails is considerably aggravated by that system, and that some relief may be obtained by the earliest practicable removal of such of the restraints as may be shown to be most injurious to the capital and industry of the community, and to be attended with no compensating benefit to the public revenue.

That a declaration against the anti-commercial principles of our restrictive system is of the more importance at the present juncture inasmuch as, in several instances of recent occurrence, the merchants and manufacturers in foreign States have assailed their respective Governments with applications for further protective or prohibitory duties and regulations, urging the example and authority of this country, against which they are almost exclusively directed, as a sanction for the policy of such measures. And certainly, if the reasoning upon which our restrictions have been defended is worth anything, it will apply in behalf of the regulations of foreign States against us. They insist upon our superiority in capital and machinery, as we do upon their comparative exemption from taxation, and with equal foundation.

That nothing would more tend to counteract the commercial hostility of foreign States than the adoption of a more enlightened and more conciliatory policy on the part of this country.

That, although, as a matter of mere diplomacy, it may sometimes answer to hold out the removal of particular prohibitions, or high duties, as depending upon corresponding concessions by other States in our favour, it does not follow that we should maintain our restrictions in cases where the desired concessions on their part cannot be obtained. Our restrictions would not be the less prejudicial to our capital and industry because other Governments persisted in preserving impolitic regulations.

. . . . .

That in thus declaring, as your petitioners do, their conviction of the impolicy and injustice of the restrictive system, and in desiring every practicable relaxation of it, they have in view only such parts of it as are not connected, or are only subordinately so, with the public revenue. As long as the necessity for the present amount of revenue subsists, your petitioners cannot expect so important a branch of it as the

Customs to be given up, nor to be materially diminished, unless some substitute, less objectionable, be suggested. But it is against every restrictive regulation of trade not essential to the revenue—against all duties merely protective from foreign competition—and against the excess of such duties as are partly for the purpose of revenue and partly for that of protection, that the prayer of the present petition is respectfully submitted to the wisdom of Parliament.

. . . . . .

17. THE FOUNDATION OF THE ANTI-CORN-LAW LEAGUE [*History of the Anti-Corn-Law League by Archibald Prentice, I, pp.* 101–2, 1853], 1839.

Resolutions of meeting of delegates at Manchester, January 23, 1839.

Resolved—1. That this meeting of representatives from all the great sections of our manufacturing and commercial population, solemnly declare it to be their conviction that the prosperity of the great staples upon which their capital and industry are employed, is in imminent danger from the operation of the laws which interdict or interfere with the exchange of their productions for the corn and other produce of foreign nations, and thus check our trade, and artificially enhance the price of food in this country; and believing that the facts upon which this judgment is formed are little known, and of such national importance as to call for their disclosure before the people's representatives, they earnestly recommend that petitions be immediately forwarded from all parts of the Kingdom, praying to be heard by counsel and evidence at the bar of the House of Commons in the approaching session of Parliament.

2. That in order to secure unity and efficiency of action this meeting recommends that delegates be appointed by the several Anti-Corn-Law Associations of the kingdom. Those manufacturing and commercial towns not already possessing such societies are earnestly recommended to form Anti-Corn-Law Associations; and in case they require information or advice, they are invited to put themselves immediately in correspondence with the Manchester Association, whose fundamental rule, prohibiting the discussion of any party or political topics, is especially recommended for the adoption of all similar bodies elsewhere.

3. That the agricultural proprietor, capitalist, and labourer are benefited equally with the trader, by the creation and circulation of the wealth of the country; and this meeting appeals to all those classes to co-operate for the removal of a monopoly which, by restricting the foreign commerce of the country, retards the increase of the population, and restrains the growth of towns; thus depriving them of the manifold resources to be derived from the augmenting numbers and wealth of the country.

4. That this meeting cannot separate without expressing its deep sympathy with the present privations of that great and valuable class of their countrymen who earn their daily bread by the sweat of their brow; many of whom are now suffering from hunger in the midst of boundless fields of employment, rendered unproductive solely by those unjust laws which prevent the exchange of the products of their industry for the food of other countries. So long as a plentiful supply of the first necessaries of life is denied by acts of the British legislation to the great body of the nation, so long will the government and the country be justly exposed to all the evils resulting from the discontent of the people. With a view to avert so great a danger by an act of universal justice, this meeting pledges itself to a united, energetic, and persevering effort for the total and immediate repeal of all laws affecting the free importation of grain.[1]

18. The Bank Charter Act [*Statutes* 7 *and* 8 *Victoria* 32], 1844.

An Act to regulate the Issue of Bank Notes, and for giving to the Governor and Company of the Bank of England certain Privileges for a limited Period.

Be it enacted that from and after the thirty-first day of August, one thousand eight hundred and forty-four, the issue of Promissory Notes of the Governor and Company of the Bank of England, payable on demand, shall be separated and thenceforth kept wholly distinct from the general Banking business of the said Governor and Company; and the business of and relating to such issue shall be thenceforth conducted

[1] The Anti-Corn-Law League was created on the recommendation of a delegate meeting, March 20 following.

and carried on by the said Governor and Company in a separate department, to be called "The Issue Department of the Bank of England," subject to the rules and regulations hereinafter contained; and it shall be lawful for the Court of Directors of the said Governor and Company, if they shall think fit, to appoint a committee or committees of directors for the conduct and management of such Issue Department of the Bank of England, and from time to time remove the members, and define, alter, and regulate the constitution and powers of such committee, as they shall think fit, subject to any bye-laws, rules or regulations which may be made for that purpose: provided nevertheless, that the said Issue Department shall always be kept separate and distinct from the Banking Department of the said Governor and Company.

II. And be it enacted, that upon the thirty-first day of August, one thousand eight hundred and forty-four, there shall be transferred, appropriated, and set apart by the said Governor and Company to the Issue Department of the Bank of England securities to the value of fourteen million pounds, whereof the debt due by the public to the said Governor and Company shall be and be deemed a part; and there shall also at the same time be transferred, appropriated, and set apart by the said Governor and Company to the said Issue Department so much of the gold coin and gold and silver bullion then held by the Bank of England as shall not be required by the Banking Department thereof; and thereupon there shall be delivered out of the said Issue Department into the said Banking Department of the Bank of England such an amount of Bank of England notes as, together with the Bank of England notes then in circulation, shall be equal to the aggregate amount of the securities, coin and bullion so transferred to the said Issue Department of the Bank of England; and the whole amount of Bank of England notes then in circulation, including those delivered to the Banking Department of the Bank of England as aforesaid, shall be deemed to be issued on the credit of such securities, coin, and bullion so appropriated and set apart to the said Issue Department; and from thenceforth it shall not be lawful for the said Governor and Company to increase the amount of securities for the time being in the said Issue Department, save as hereinafter is mentioned, but it shall be lawful for the said Governor and Company to diminish the amount of such securities, and again to increase the same to any sum not exceeding in the whole the sum of fourteen million pounds, and so from time to time as they shall see occasion; and from and after such transfer and appropriation to the said Issue Department as aforesaid it shall not be lawful for the said Governor and Company to issue Bank of England notes, either into the Banking Department of the Bank of England, or to any persons or person whatsoever, save in exchange for other Bank of England notes, or for gold coin or for gold or silver bullion received or purchased for the said Issue Department under the provisions of this Act, or in exchange for securities acquired and taken in the said Issue Department under the provisions herein contained: provided always, that it shall be lawful for the said Governor and Company in their Banking Department to issue all such Bank of England notes as they shall at any time receive from the said Issue Department or otherwise, in the same manner in all respects as such issue would be lawful to any other person or persons.

IV. And be it enacted, that from and after the thirty-first day of August, one thousand eight hundred and forty-four, all persons shall be entitled to demand from the Issue Department of the Bank of England, Bank of England notes in exchange for gold bullion, at the rate of three pounds, seventeen shillings and nine-pence per ounce of standard gold: Provided always, that the said Governor and Company shall in all cases be entitled to require such gold bullion to be melted and assayed by persons approved by the said Governor and Company at the expense of the parties tendering such gold bullion.

V. Provided always, and be it enacted, that if any banker who on the sixth day of May one thousand eight hundred and forty-four was issuing his own bank notes, shall cease to issue his own bank notes, it shall be lawful for Her Majesty in Council at any time after the cessation of such issue, upon the application of the said Governor and Company, to authorize and empower the said Governor and Company to increase the amount of securities in the said Issue Department beyond the total sum or value of fourteen million pounds, and thereupon to issue additional Bank of England notes to an amount not exceeding such increased amount of securities specified in such

Order in Council, and so from time to time: provided always that such increased amount of securities specified in such Order in Council shall in no case exceed the proportion of two thirds the amount of bank notes which the banker so ceasing to issue may have been authorized to issue under the provisions of this Act; and every such order in Council shall be published in the next succeeding *London Gazette.*

XII. And be it enacted, that if any banker in any part of the United Kingdom who after the passing of this act shall be entitled to issue bank notes shall become bankrupt, or shall cease to carry on the business of a banker, or shall discontinue the issue of bank notes, either by agreement with the Governor and Company of the Bank of England or otherwise, it shall not be lawful for such Banker at any time thereafter to issue any such notes.

XIV. Provided always, and be it enacted, That if it shall be made to appear to the Commissioners of stamps and taxes that any two or more banks have, by written contract or agreement (which contract or agreement shall be produced to the said Commissioners), become united within the twelve weeks next preceding such twenty-seventh day of April as aforesaid, it shall be lawful for the said Commissioners to ascertain the average amount of the notes of each such bank in the manner hereinbefore directed, and to certify the average amount of the notes of the two or more banks so united as the amount which the united Bank shall thereafter be authorized to issue, subject to the regulations of this Act.

19. DEBATE ON THE CORN LAWS [*Parliamentary Debates, 3rd Series, Vol.* 73, *Cols.* 68, 69–71, 849–850, 1345–1347], 1846.

Address in Answer to Her Majesty's Speech, January 22nd, 1846.

House of Commons.

Sir Robert Peel.

Sir, the immediate cause which led to the dissolution of the Government in the early part of last December, was that great and mysterious calamity which caused a lamentable failure in an article of food on which great numbers of the people in this part of the United Kingdom, and still larger numbers in the sister kingdom, depended mainly for their subsistence. That was the immediate and proximate cause, which led to the dissolution of the Government. But it would be unfair and uncandid on my part, if I attached undue importance to that particular cause. It certainly appeared to me to preclude further delay, and to require immediate decision—decision not only upon the measures which it was necessary at the time to adopt, but also as to the course to be ultimately taken with regard to the laws which govern the importation of grain. I will not assign to that cause too much weight. I will not withhold the homage which is due to the progress of reason and to truth, by denying that my opinions on the subject of protection have undergone a change.

* * * * * *

Sir, those who contend for the removal of impediments upon the import of a great article of subsistence, such as corn, start with an immense advantage in the argument. The natural presumption is in favour of free and unrestricted importation. It may, indeed, be possible to combat that presumption; it may be possible to meet its advocates in the field of argument, by showing that there are other and greater advantages arising out of the system of prohibition than out of the system of unrestricted intercourse; but even those who so contend will, I think, admit that the natural feelings of mankind are strongly in favour of the absence of all restriction, and that the presumption is so strong, that we must combat it by an avowal of some great public danger to be avoided, or some great public benefit to be obtained by restriction on the importation of food. We all admit that the argument in favour of high protection or prohibition on the ground that it is for the benefit of a particular class, is untenable. The most strenuous advocates for protection have abandoned that argument; they rest, and wisely rest, the defence of protective duties upon higher principles. They have alleged, as I have myself alleged, that there were public reasons for retaining this protection. Sir, circumstances made it absolutely necessary for me, occupying the public station I do, and seeing the duty that must unavoidably devolve on me—it became absolutely necessary for me maturely to consider whether the grounds on which an alteration of the Corn Laws can be resisted are tenable. The arguments in favour of protection must be based either on the principle that protection to domestic industry is in itself sound policy, and that, therefore, agriculture, being a branch of domestic industry, is entitled to share in that protection; or, that in a country like ours, encumbered with an enormous load of debt, and subject to great taxation, it is necessary that domestic industry should be protected from competition with foreigners; or, again—the interests of the great body of the community, the laborious classes, being committed in this question—that the rate of wages varies with the price of provisions, that high prices imply high wages, and that low wages are the concomitants of low prices. Further, it may be said, that the land is entitled to protection on account of some peculiar burdens which it bears. But that is a question of justice rather than of policy; I have always felt and maintained that the land is subject to peculiar burdens; but you have the power of weakening the force of that argument by the removal of the burden, or making compensation. The first three objections to the removal of protection are objections founded on considerations of public policy. The last is a question of justice, which may be determined by giving some counterbalancing advantage. Now, I want not to deprive those who, arguing *a priori*, without the benefit of experience, have come to the conclusion that protection is objectionable in principle—I want not to deprive them of any of the credit which is fairly their due. Reason, unaided by experience, brought conviction to their minds. My opinions have been modified by the experience of the last three years. I have had the means and opportunity of comparing the results of periods of abundance and low prices with periods of scarcity and high prices. I have carefully watched the effects of the one system, and of the other—first, of the policy we have been steadily pursuing for some years, viz., the removal of protection from domestic industry; and next, of the policy which the friends of protection recommend. I have also had an opportunity of marking from day to day the effect upon great social interests of freedom of trade and comparative abundance. I have not failed to note the results of preceding years, and to contrast them with the results of the last three years; and I am led to the conclusion that the main grounds of public policy on which protection has been defended are not tenable ; at least, I cannot maintain them. I do not believe, after the experience of the last three years, that the rate of wages varies with the price of food. I do not believe that with high prices, wages will necessarily rise in the same ratio. I do not believe that a low price of food necessarily implies a low rate of wages. Neither can I maintain that protection to domestic industry is necessarily good.

Adjourned Debate. February 13, 1846.

House of Commons.

SIR DOUGLAS HOWARD said :[1]

* * * *

I have often imagined—and it was for this that I moved for, and obtained the order of this House for, the extensive returns which are now preparing, namely, the various colonial tariffs and commercial relations at present subsisting between all the Colonies of the Empire and the mother country, and between the Colonies themselves—that it might really be possible to treat Colonies like counties of the country, not only in direct trade with the United Kingdom, but in commercial intercourse with each other, by free trade among ourselves, under a reasonable moderate degree of protection from without, and so resolve the United Kingdom, and all her Colonies and possessions, into a commercial union such as might defy all rivalry, and defeat all combinations. Then might colonization proceed on a gigantic scale—then might British capital animate British labour, on British soil, for British objects, throughout the extended dominions of the British Empire. Such an union is the United States of America—a confederation of sovereign States, leagued together for commercial and political purposes, with the most perfect free trade within, and a stringent protection from without ; and signally, surely, has that commercial league succeeded and flourished. Such an union, too, is the German Customs League ; and it has succeeded to an extent that really is, in so short a time, miraculous. But free trade—the extinction of the protective principle—the repeal of the differential duties—would at once convert all our Colonies, in a commercial sense, into as many independent States. The colonial consumer of British produc-

[1] *Ibid.* cols. 849-50

tions would then be released from his part of the compact—that of dealing, in preference, with the British producer; and the British consumer of such articles as the Colonies produce, absolved from his; each party would be free to buy in the cheapest, and sell in the dearest market. I defy any hon. member opposite to say that this would not be a virtual dissolution of the colonial system.

Adjourned Debate. February 20, 1846.

MR. B. DISRAELI:[1]

* * * *

I have now nearly concluded the observations which I shall address to the House. I have omitted a great deal which I wished to urge upon the House; and I sincerely wish that what I have said had been urged with more ability; but I have endeavoured not to make a mere Corn Law speech; I have only taken corn as an illustration; but I don't like my friends here to enter upon that Corn Law debate which I suppose is impending, under a mistaken notion of the position in which they stand. I never did rest my defence of the Corn Laws on the burdens to which the land is subject. I believe that there are burdens, heavy burdens, on the land; but the land has great honours, and he who has great honours must have great burdens. But I wish them to bear in mind that their cause must be sustained by great principles. I venture feebly and slightly to indicate those principles, principles of high policy, on which their system ought to be sustained. First, without reference to England, looking at all countries, I say that it is the first duty of the Minister, and the first interest of the State, to maintain a balance between the two great branches of national industry; that is a principle which has been recognised by all great Ministers for the last two hundred years; and the reasons upon which it rests are so obvious, that it can hardly be necessary to mention them. Why we should maintain that balance between the two great branches of national industry, involves political considerations—social considerations, affecting the happiness, prosperity, and morality of the people, as well as the stability of the State. But I go further; I say that in England we are bound to do more—I repeat what

[1] *Ibid.*, cols. 1345-1347

I have repeated before, that in this country there are special reasons why we should not only maintain the balance between the two branches of our national industry, but why we should give a preponderance—I do not say a predominance, which was the word ascribed by the hon. member for Manchester to the noble lord the member for London, but which he never used—why we should give a preponderance, for that is the proper and constitutional word, to the agricultural branch ; and the reason is, because in England we have a territorial Constitution. We have thrown upon the land the revenues of the Church, the administration of justice, and the estate of the poor ; and this has been done, not to gratify the pride, or pamper the luxury of the proprietors of the land, but because, in a territorial Constitution, you, and those whom you have succeeded, have found the only security for self-government—the only barrier against that centralising system which has taken root in other countries. I have always maintained these opinions ; my constituents are not landlords ; they are not aristocrats ; they are not great capitalists ; they are the children of industry and toil ; and they believe, first, that their material interests are involved in a system which favours native industry, by insuring at the same time real competition ; but they believe also that their social and political interests are involved in a system by which their rights and liberties have been guaranteed ; and I agree with them—I have these old-fashioned notions. I know that we have been told, and by one who on this subject should be the highest authority, that we shall derive from this great struggle, not merely the repeal of the Corn Laws, but the transfer of power from one class to another—to one distinguished for its intelligence and wealth, the manufacturers of England. My conscience assures me that I have not been slow in doing justice to the intelligence of that class ; certain I am, that I am not one of those who envy them their wide and deserved prosperity ; but I must confess my deep mortification, that in an age of political regeneration, when all social evils are ascribed to the operation of class interests, it should be suggested that we are to be rescued from the alleged power of one class only to sink under the avowed dominion of another. I, for one, if this is to be the end of all our struggles—if this is to be the great result of this enlightened age—I, for one, protest against the ignominious catastrophe.

I believe that the monarchy of England, its sovereignty mitigated by the acknowledged authority of the estates of the realm, has its root in the hearts of the people, and is capable of securing the happiness of the nation and the power of the State. But, Sir, if this be a worn-out dream; if, indeed, there is to be a change, I, for one, anxious as I am to maintain the present polity of this country, ready to make as many sacrifices as any man for that object—if there is to be this great change, I, for one, hope that the foundations of it may be deep, the scheme comprehensive, and that instead of falling under such a thraldom, under the thraldom of Capital—under the thraldom of those who, while they boast of their intelligence, are more proud of their wealth—if we must find a new force to maintain the ancient throne and immemorial monarchy of England, I, for one, hope that we may find that novel power in the invigorating energies of an educated and enfranchised people.

INDEX

THE LONDON AND NORWICH PRESS, LIMITED, LONDON AND NORWICH

18.1.33

5